FABLES OF ABUNDANCE

FABLES
OF
ABUNDANCE

A CULTURAL HISTORY OF
ADVERTISING IN AMERICA

Jackson Lears

BasicBooks
A Division of HarperCollins*Publishers*

Designed by Ellen Levine

Library of Congress Cataloging-in-Publication Data
Lears, Jackson, 1947–
    Fables of abundance : a cultural history of advertising in America / by Jackson
Lears.
      p. cm.
    Includes bibliographical references and index.
    ISBN 0-465-09076-1
    1. Advertising—United States—History—19th century. 2. Advertising—
United States—History—20th century I. Title
    HF5813.U6L418 1994
    659.1'0973—dc20   94–12749
                                              CIP

94 95 96 97 ♦/HC 9 8 7 6 5 4 3

For my mother, my father, and my brother Lee
and for my daughters, Rachel and Adin,
in remembrance and hope

"Le superflu, chose très nécessaire."
—Voltaire

"There is no wealth but life."
—John Ruskin

CONTENTS

Acknowledgments   xi

    Introduction   1

PART I
THE RECONFIGURATION OF WEALTH:
FROM FECUND EARTH TO EFFICIENT FACTORY

1.   The Lyric of Plenty   17

2.   The Modernization of Magic   40

3.   The Stabilization of Sorcery   75

4.   The Disembodiment of Abundance   102

PART II
THE CONTAINMENT OF CARNIVAL:
ADVERTISING AND AMERICAN SOCIAL VALUES
FROM THE PATENT MEDICINE ERA TO THE
CONSOLIDATION OF CORPORATE POWER

5.   The Merger of Intimacy and Publicity   137

6.   The Perfectionist Project   162

7.   The New Basis of Civilization   196

8.   Trauma, Denial, Recovery   235

PART III
ART, TRUTH, AND HUMBUG:
THE SEARCH FOR FORM AND MEANING IN A
COMMODITY CIVILIZATION

9.   The Problem of Commercial Art in a Protestant Culture   261

10.   The Courtship of Avant-Garde and Kitsch   299

11.   The Pursuit of the Real   345

12.   The Things Themselves   379

Notes   415

Index   477

ACKNOWLEDGMENTS

I HAVE RECEIVED more help with this book than I can adequately acknowledge here. Nevertheless, I will try, bearing in mind that I will probably leave out some deserving people. I am continually amazed and humbled by the generosity of friends and colleagues, many of whom took valuable time from busy schedules to read and comment on my work, without any reward except the satisfaction of sustaining that most elusive ideal, a community of scholars. Everyone mentioned here helped in some crucial way with the book; I alone am responsible for the flaws that remain.

Research on this book was supported by fellowships from the Guggenheim Foundation, the Rockefeller Foundation, the Woodrow Wilson International Center for Scholars at the Smithsonian Institution, the Center for the Critical Analysis of Contemporary Culture at Rutgers University, and the Shelby Cullom Davis Center for Historical Studies at Princeton University. The last three provided congenial environments where I could develop my ideas. For thoughtful criticism and encouragement, I am especially indebted to Jay Tolson, Michael Lacey, and my research assistant Marguerite Jones at the Wilson Center, to George Levine and Miriam Hansen at CCACC, and to Lawrence Stone and Gyan Prakash at the Davis Center.

I owe much, as well, to archivists and librarians at the Ellis Library (University of Missouri), Alexander Library (Rutgers), Firestone Library (Princeton), the Library of Congress, the Newberry Library, the National Museum of American History, the Wisconsin State Historical Society, Knox

College Library, Dartmouth College Library, the Bridgeport Public Library, and the New-York Historical Society. Cynthia Swank and Anne Marie Sandecki deserve special thanks for guiding me through the archives at the J. Walter Thompson Company in New York City.

In the early going, at the University of Missouri, I benefited from the intellectual camaraderie of Michael and Maurita Ugarte, Ken Plax, Steven Watts, Joel Bleifuss, Teresa Prados, George Hodak, Thomas Quirk, Mark Hirsch, Dina Copelman, and David Thelen, and from the yeoman research assistance of Rod McHugh. During a year at the National Museum of American History I was helped in various important ways by Gary Kulik, Spencer Crew, Susan Myers, Larry Bird, Keith Melder, John Fleckner, Charles McGovern, and Pete Daniel. Students and colleagues at Rutgers have created an atmosphere at once lively, challenging, and supportive. Robert Mensel, Miriam Formanek-Brunell, Mary Blanchard, Grace Hale, and Scott Sandage provided me with leads and bibliographic suggestions. Allen Douglas saved me from computer disaster, and Randy Stearns offered able research assistance. Rudolph Bell, Michael Adas, and Thomas Slaughter read an early version of the argument and commented perceptively on it. John Gillis and Victoria deGrazia brought their transatlantic perspectives to sizable chunks of the manuscript, reducing its parochialism and improving it in a host of other ways. Jim Livingston provided splendid provocation, questioning my fundamental premises at every turn and forcing me to re-examine assumptions I had too easily accepted. Samuel Elworthy and Michael Moffatt gave me anthropologically informed readings of an entire first draft; their suggestions played a major role in reshaping the book into its final form.

Other scholars around the country responded generously to my requests for advice and criticism. Rick Pollay and William Leiss made useful conceptual suggestions. Lynda Roscoe Hartigan at the National Museum of American Art provided last-minute information on Joseph Cornell. Lewis Perry and Leigh Schmidt read and commented helpfully on the entire manuscript. David Brion Davis wisely cautioned me against uncritical use of poststructuralist theory (especially Foucault's). Rodney Olsen, Michael Smith, David Noble, Angela Miller, and Harvey Green supplied encouragement at critical moments. Kenneth Cmiel and Richard Wightman Fox read large portions of the manuscript with exceptional care and critical judgment. Michele Bogart brought her expertise in art history to bear on what became chapter 9. J. Gregory Conti, writing from Perugia, brilliantly illuminated the larger contours of the argument by placing it in a transatlantic framework. And Leo Lionni graciously spent an afternoon with me reminiscing about his years as an artist in advertising.

I am grateful to those university audiences that invited me to try out my ideas. They included Mark Crispin Miller, Gillian Brown, Howard Horwitz, Charles Berger, John and Joy Kasson, Townsend Ludington, Robert Skolnick, Bruce McConachie, Wally Bowen, Bruce Ronda, Cheryl Walker, Daniel Horowitz, Albert Stone, Thomas Lutz, Jonathan Prude, James Harvey Young, Walter Adamson, Steven Tipton, Lary May, Elaine Tyler May, Thomas Haskell, and Patrick Murray. Jun Furuya and his colleagues at Hokkaido University deserve special thanks for inviting me to the Sapporo Cool Seminar at Sapporo, Japan, where I enjoyed an exciting and eye-opening week of conversations with some extraordinarily perceptive students of American culture.

I have been lucky to have two great editors: André Schiffrin, who patiently sponsored this project for years; and Steve Fraser, who saw it through to completion, and whose comments immeasurably improved the final version.

A greater good fortune is acknowledged in my dedication. The memory of my father, Walter Lee Lears; the love and support of my mother, Margaret Baptist Lears, and my brother, R. E. Lee Lears—these have continued to provide me sustenance (more, I am sure, than I have realized) even after years of long-distance separation. My daughters, Rachel and Adin Lears, have been a truly precious gift. Through the often dark and lonely times of work on this project, they have sustained me with their humor, their vitality, and their love. As if this were not enough, Rachel performed valuable photographic services for me; and both she and Adin provided their gifts for crisp imagery and musical language. They have given me the best of all possible reasons to preserve hope for the future.

My greatest debt is to Karen Parker Lears. She has read only a few selected portions of the manuscript; she bears no responsibility for any of my particular arguments. Nevertheless, we have had innumerable conversations about cultural history, and I have benefited immeasurably from her fresh analytic insights, her impatience with formulaic complaint, her assumption that I should try to write something of more than topical value, and her unflagging critical intelligence. She has urged me to make my work both more intellectually rigorous and more philosophically humane.

In pondering alternatives to the culture promoted by advertising, I have been inspired by her artistic work and by her way of being in the world. If this book transcends mere critique, if it promotes even a glimpse at a more satisfying vision of how we might live, I owe that accomplishment primarily to her.

Furman's Corner, New Jersey
February 1994

FABLES OF ABUNDANCE

WHAT do advertisements mean? Many things. They urge people to buy goods, but they also signify a certain vision of the good life; they validate a way of being in the world. They focus private fantasy; they sanction or subvert existing structures of economic and political power. Their significance depends on their cultural setting.

And they can show up almost anywhere. Consider the meaning of advertisements to the Abelam of New Guinea. The Abelam are well known among anthropologists for their tambarans: polychromatic sacred designs embodying the most powerful ancestral spirits of the tribe and covering the outside walls of the houses used for important ceremonies. "Coloured magazines sometimes find their way into the villages, and occasionally pages torn from them are attached to the matting at the base of the ceremonial house facade," the British anthropologist Anthony Forge observed in 1963. "In all such cases I have seen, the pages were brightly coloured, usually food advertisements of the Spam and sweet corn and honey-baked ham type. Inquiries revealed that the Abelam had no idea of what was represented but thought that with their bright colours and incomprehensibility the selected pages were likely to be European tambarans and therefore powerful."[1] In New Guinea as in the industrialized West, advertisements could slip past the narrow, instrumental purpose of selling goods to acquire broader and more elusive cultural meaning.

Without falling into a facile definition of advertising as "the folklore of industrial society," it is possible to admit that the Abelam were on to something.[2] During the last two hundred years, in the capitalist West and increasingly elsewhere as well, advertisements have acquired a powerful iconic significance. Yet they have been more than static symbols: they have coupled words and pictures in commercial fables—stories that have been both fabulous and didactic, that have evoked fantasies and pointed morals, that have reconfigured ancient dreams of abundance to fit the modern world of goods. By the late twentieth century, these fables of abundance—especially the ones sponsored by major multinational corporations—had become perhaps the most dynamic and sensuous representations of cultural values in the world.

Interpretations of those values depend on the observer's angle of vision, and this interpretation is no exception. Rooted like all books in its author's own personal and historical circumstances, *Fables of Abundance* tries to provide evaluation and critique as well as chronicle. It aims to locate the rise of national advertising in the United States within wider transatlantic currents of cultural history: the disenchantment of an animistic worldview with the rise of Western science; the spread of market exchange beyond traditional boundaries of time and place; the growing dominance of an individualistic model of controlled, unified selfhood; the triumph of bureaucratic rationality in the factory system and the modern corporation; and the persistence of irrationalist and animist counter-tendencies in the popular and avant-garde arts of the nineteenth and twentieth centuries. This is the story of how advertising collaborated with other institutions in promoting what became the dominant aspirations, anxieties, even notions of personal identity, in the modern United States. It is an effort to show how advertising helped recast our relationships with material goods and the surrounding environment, and how people on both sides of the Atlantic (some of them involved in the advertising business themselves) sought to sustain or create alternative ways of being in the world.

An obvious retort to such wide-ranging claims is that I am inflating advertising's significance. From this view, the advertising industry is primarily about selling goods, not promoting values, and it is misleading to single out advertising as the source of cultural tendencies that may have originated in other institutions (or in sheer human perversity). There is something to this argument. College professors and other educated professionals were as involved in the disenchantment of the world as advertising people were (perhaps more involved, as even national advertising preserved some attachment to the realm of fantasy). That is why I have

explored the entanglements between advertising people and other occupational groups: ministers, political leaders, physicians, lawyers, social scientists, journalists, writers and artists. Throughout, I have tried to locate the
rise of national advertising within a many-voiced cultural conversation.

I have not tried to write a comprehensive historical survey of American
advertising. Some readers may be disappointed to find that certain agencies, campaigns, or personalities are missing from these pages. Nor have I
asked whether or not a particular advertising campaign has helped to sell a
particular product. This question does not, in my judgment, reveal very
much about the broader cultural significance of advertising. Instead, I
have tried to explore what were, for the most part, the unintended consequences of advertisers' efforts to vend their wares: the creation of a symbolic universe where certain cultural values were sanctioned and others
rendered marginal or invisible.

In a synthesis this broad, even more than in most works of historical
scholarship, the arguments advanced reveal their character as regulative
fictions, metaphors constructed by the historian to make sense of multifarious evidence.[3] The materials he uses for construction will reflect his own
frame of mind at the time of the project. So a brief account of this book's
intellectual genesis is in order.

I

When I began working on this book there were almost no cultural histories
of advertising available. (A number of talented historians, led by Roland
Marchand, have since remedied that lack.)[4] In the United States, efforts to
interpret advertising's cultural significance were embedded in a critical
tradition that included Thorstein Veblen and John Kenneth Galbraith,
Stuart Chase and Vance Packard. Though it was articulated in secular
idioms, their critique derived from Protestant commitments to plain
speech and plain living, as well as from republican fears of conspiracy
against the independence of the individual self. Critics in this tradition
derided advertising for employing deceptive strategies against a passive,
hapless audience, and promoting the cancerous growth of a wasteful consumer culture.

I started research on this book just when that tradition was going out of
style, among both popular and scholarly audiences. Jimmy Carter's calls
for ecologically grounded sacrifice had been drowned out by Ronald Reagan's strategies of systematic denial. America was "back," and weekly

newsmagazines spoke of a "return to elegance"—which mostly meant stretch limousines and suspenders for stockbrokers. In academic circles, scholars re-examined the older critique of advertising and found it wanting. Some discovered the liberating potential in acts of consumption and the creative energies in corporate-sponsored advertising.[5]

Yet more than simply a shift in intellectual fashion was going on. The scholarship of the 1980s raised serious empirical and conceptual questions about the narrowness of the existing critical tradition. The older critics could accurately be criticized for their naive and literalist views of language. They could also sometimes fairly be said to harbor puritanical traits: a distrust of fantasy and sensuous display, a preference for production over consumption, a manipulative model of advertising as social control, and a masculine bias that led them to typecast the mass of consumers as passive and feminine. Implicitly they elevated the rational producer over the irrational consumer, embracing a productivist ethic that devalued leisure and aesthetic experience. Finally, as the social scientists Mary Douglas and Michael Schudson observed, the early critics' Veblenesque attacks on materialism overlooked the nearly universal human tendency to make cultural meaning from material objects. Goods have always served symbolic as well as utilitarian purposes, and advertisers' efforts to associate silverware with status or cars with sex were but a recent and well-organized example of a widespread cultural practice.[6]

In formulating my own perspective on advertising, I tried to take these arguments into account, while acknowledging the power of the plain-speech tradition—especially in political discourse. However naive the plainspoken outrage of an Orwell, it was still a bracing counterpoint to a political culture where constituencies were packaged and presidents were test-marketed. But I hoped to do more than issue another jeremiad against the corruptions created by Madison Avenue. In an era when obsessions with "productivity" had become ecologically dangerous as well as aesthetically repellent, I felt the need for a perspective on advertising that was more open to the symbolic uses of goods, more sympathetically and playfully connected to the material world, than the critiques generally spawned by the existing tradition. Gradually I began to realize that modern advertising could be seen less as an agent of materialism than as one of the cultural forces working to disconnect human beings from the material world.

There were many intellectual resources available for refining this point of view. One was Marxist intellectual tradition, unfashionable but indispensable, which focused on the fetishistic qualities of goods—their capacity to become endowed with "a life of their own." The character of the fetishism changed in accordance with particular economic circumstances. Outside the orbit of industrial capitalism, according to Marxian tradition, products became animated by embodying the beliefs and practices of their particular social milieu; they epitomized a sense of intimate relatedness to the material world. Under industrial capitalism, in contrast, production was severed from consumption, and an atomistic, dualistic worldview prevailed; things were isolated from their origins and seemed to move mysteriously on their own: a different sort of fetishism emerged.[7]

The first version of fetishism envisioned people as the makers of objects, enmeshed with the natural world and each other, exercising a flawed but actual freedom; the second, commodity fetishism, represented humans as the objects of forces, divorced from the material world and one another, caught up in a reified process of development. Technological determinism was the perfect vision of history for a society whose rulers were committed to commodity fetishism: things acted autonomously, creating "cultural lag" between old "myths" and new "realities," requiring people to jettison their cultural baggage if they were to stay on the train of progress. Part of that baggage consisted of goods rendered outmoded by stylistic change and planned obsolescence. Commodity fetishism directed desire toward the acquisition of things but not their leisurely enjoyment; it underwrote a Cartesian vision of an isolated self in an inert world of objects.

This was the dominant attitude toward things enshrined in modern advertising, but (as my own research began to make clear) there were many other attitudes as well: longings for links with an actual or imagined past, or for communal connections in the present; professional aspirations, personal conflicts, idiosyncratic tastes. The rhetoric and iconography of advertising could not be reduced to a mere propaganda of commodities. There were too many variations and ambiguities arising from advertisers' own private needs and confusions.

The Marxist tradition, though it illuminated many issues, did not encourage exploration of idiosyncrasies. Many Marxist thinkers suffered from an attachment to a linear, progressive framework of historical change. Despite their romance with primitive communism, they often embraced the masculine productivist ethos, celebrating "man's" capacity for making more and more things. Promethean optimism, in Marxian as in Veblenian tradition, encouraged a utilitarian, work-obsessed orientation toward the material world.

In my dissatisfaction with the productivist view, I discovered a number of thinkers who had questioned it. American antimodernists from Henry Adams to Lewis Mumford, attacking faith in progress, explored the driven rationality that powered the unending upward spiral of production and consumption. The Frankfurt School theorists Theodor Adorno, Max Horkheimer, and Herbert Marcuse, fresh from their experience with fascism, acknowledged that the sphere of consumption could shelter utopian longings for release from drudgery; but, they charged, advertising and mass culture had colonized leisure, bringing it under the "performance principle" that governed organized capitalism. Unlike critics in the productivist traditions, all of these thinkers realized that the spread of mass consumption had not brought about the promised reign of leisure.[8] The problem, I sensed, was not hedonism but the lack of it—and not materialism, but the spread of indifference toward a material world where things were reduced to disposable commodities.

But what were the alternatives? One possibility was that commodity fetishism was not as universal as critics believed. Anthropological research suggested that most societies sorted things on a continuum stretching from complete commodification (or standardization) to complete singularity.[9] For centuries, powerful institutions—the state, the church, and most recently the art museum—mobilized their resources to sacralize objects and remove them to a "priceless" sphere; ordinary folk did the same with heirlooms, keepsakes, and souvenirs. These projects embodied a desire to create other realms of meaning, based on alternative relationships to objects, alongside the throwaway culture promoted by modern advertising. Efforts to articulate those meanings focused on gift exchange, craftsmanship, and collecting.

Inspired by a rich anthropological literature, a few intellectuals have explored gift culture as an alternative to commodity civilization. Georges Bataille, Jean Baudrillard, and the American poet Lewis Hyde associated gift-giving with an erotic expenditure of energy that paradoxically created a sense of overflowing abundance: "the more I give to thee," says Juliet, "the more I have." This they contrasted with the pinched, prudential outlook allegedly fostered by commodity exchange. Bataille and Baudrillard put a Nietzschean spin on the contrast; Hyde gave it a social-democratic turn. While gift-giving created a sense of abundance even amid poverty, he argued, commodity exchange reinforced feelings of scarcity even amid a cornucopia of goods.[10]

Craftsmanship energized another discourse of objects. Its most distinguished recent articulator was Hannah Arendt. Distinguishing between work and labor, she defined work as the fabrication of durable objects that in their comparative permanence could stabilize human life. Their durability gave them the independence to withstand "the voracious needs and wants of their living makers and users." People could "retrieve their sameness, that is, their identity, by being related to the same chair and the same table." Labor, by contrast, in our "consumers' society," was merely "making a living." As "labor and consumption are but two stages of the same process, imposed on men by the necessity of life, this is only another way of saying that we live in a society of laborers." Arendt rejected that society's utilitarian criteria of worth. "Whatever we do, we are supposed to do for the sake of 'making a living,'" she complained, lodging her hopes in a notion of art as a realm where "the sheer durability of the world of things" appeared with greater "purity and clarity" than anywhere else. But the "consumers' society" made that vision increasingly difficult to apprehend. "The ideals of *homo faber*, the fabricator of the world, which are permanence, stability, and durability, have been sacrificed to abundance, the ideal of the *animal laborans*." Arendt understood that the major flaw in "consumers' society" was not materialism, but an implicit contempt for "the thing-character of the world." Her alternative to consumption was not asceticism but fabrication, maintenance, and care of a durable world of things.[11]

The collector was one ideal type who seemed to answer Arendt's description. Systematic collecting may have been "the most abstract of all forms of consumption," as Baudrillard said, but collecting could occur in many modes. It could be the ordering of rarities by the connoisseur, but also the reclaiming of ephemera by the artist or the devotee of camp, who transforms the kitsch figurine into the sacral artifact, making the impermanent permanent, the outmoded commodity into the "timeless" work of art—still granting its materiality and history, but inverting its place in the cultural hierarchy. Things, like people, could assume different identities at different stages of their lives.[12]

All these ideal types, I discovered, shared a connection to the serious play that Johan Huizinga identified with artistic creation. We refer to the exceptionally talented artist as "gifted," conceive her work as a gift to the world, and focus on the spontaneous self-forgetfulness that is often said to characterize both play and the creative process. Only our reduction of work to labor has led us to stigmatize play as frivolous. "From the standpoint of 'making a living,'" Arendt wrote, "every activity unconnected with labor becomes a 'hobby.'"[13] Play involves the construction of a parallel universe of meaning, with objects that have become charged with symbolic significance.

The child at play and the artist absorbed in her work were, in a sense, engaged in reanimating the world. Both examples of human subjectivity embodied an imaginative connection to the material world that could be found as well in a variety of cultural forms, in animistic or magical worldviews as well as in more contemporary modes of thought. What these cultural forms had in common was an outlook unbound by dualistic conventions of matter and mind, self and world—a point of view that placed the person amid things animated with meaning.

In searching for a critical perspective on advertising, what I found was less a coherent countertradition than a cluster of attitudes that crossed the borders of ethnicity and religion, geographical region and historical epoch, high culture and low. One could locate these attitudes in the popular magic of medieval Catholics and the domestic rituals of nineteenth-century Protestants, in the "local knowledge" of vernacular craftsmanship and the "science of the concrete" practiced by Lévi-Strauss's *bricoleur,* who made do with castoff artifacts and fragments of cultural tradition. And one could find a similar cast of mind in the work of avant-garde artists from James Joyce to Joseph Cornell: blurring familiar boundaries, they engaged in serious play and truthful fantasy.[14]

This animistic sensibility poses fundamental challenges to the subject–object dualism at the heart of Western culture—including the culture promoted by advertising. Enfolding the natural as well as the humanly constructed world, a version of animism has even resurfaced in science, in the growing recognition that a "feeling for the organism" holds the key to sensitive observation of nature. The phrase was coined by Barbara McClintock, the geneticist and Nobel laureate who pioneered research on mutations in maize plants, discovering genetic relationships decades before they were confirmed by molecular geneticists. Some observers claimed this insight bordered on the mystical. McClintock cultivated a sympathetic understanding with the objects of her study until they became "subjects in their own right," as her biographer puts it.[15] This shift away from dualism, with all its ecological implications, captured the philosophical perspective that informs my interpretation of American advertising and its historical significance. That does not mean I pretend to transcend the category of isolated selfhood in my own life, or that I think the notion of separate identity should or could be abandoned; rather, I simply suggest we rethink some implications of human-centered individualism, and some alternatives to it.

II

Throughout this study I have tried to strike a balance between my desire to recognize the contradictory character of advertising's cultural role and my impulse to locate larger patterns of change. So I have ended with contradictory patterns that, I believe, embody some recurring tensions in commercial culture: between the deceptions of the confidence man and the plain speech of the self-made man, between the spontaneous force of consumer desire and the managerial drive for predictability and control. Overall, the balance of tensions has gradually been restructured in accordance with the requirements of organizational rationality, especially during the past century with the rise of national and multinational corporations. But neither confidence men nor consumer longings could ever be entirely integrated into a managerial system. Indeed, it was precisely the variety and unpredictability of the marketplace that had attracted people to it in the first place.

For centuries since the great commercial fairs of early modern Europe, market exchange has been associated with a carnival atmosphere, with fantastic and sensuous experience, perhaps even with the possibility of an almost magical self-transformation through the purchase of exotic artifacts in a fluid, anonymous social setting. Consumer goods, in other words, could still sustain traces of an animistic sensibility, but they began to circulate widely in the West during the early modern period (1500–1800), when the cosmic explanatory power of a magical worldview was becoming problematic for some people. The magic of the marketplace was fragmentary and attenuated; it had less to do with a coherent cosmology than with a developing world of free-floating, shape-shifting selves. But under certain circumstances, it held out a vision of transcendence, however fleeting.

Advertisements preserved that fitful promise down to the twentieth century. Consider a vignette from Henry Roth's autobiographical novel *Call It Sleep* (1934), which re-creates the experience of a sensitive Jewish immigrant boy growing up in Brooklyn before the First World War. Battered by street punks and living in fear of his father's rages, the boy imagines that if he had a tricycle, "he'd ride away," past the telegraph poles on the outskirts of the city, to "a place like a picture in the candy store. That lady who stood on a big box of cigarettes and wore a handkerchief under her eyes and funny fat pants without a dress and carried a round sword. A place where those houses were that she lived in, that all ended in sharp points." His erotically charged ruminations return quickly to his immediate situation; still, for a moment he has been lifted from his chronic anxiety and transported to a fantastic place by remembering a fragment of commercial exotica—perhaps a label from a box of Egyptian Deities cigarettes.[16]

But as rhetorical constructions, advertisements did more than stir up desire; they also sought to manage it—to stabilize the sorcery of the marketplace by containing dreams of personal transformation within a broader rhetoric of control. The urgency of that project was rooted in circumstances peculiar to Anglo-American Protestant culture: extraordinary natural abundance, combined with a proliferation of charlatans and confidence men in a society committed to sincerity and self-command. In the nineteenth century the rhetoric of control often originated outside the advertising business, issuing from ministers and other moralists. Advertisements themselves became a carnival of exotic imagery. But as the marketplace in commercial images became more organized and more dominated by large corporations, the rhetoric of control came from within the advertising business, in the managerial idiom of efficient performance. At about the same time Roth's young narrator was fantasizing about the lady in the fat pants, most national brand-name advertisers and their agencies were sanitizing exoticism and standardizing ideals of beauty. Those newer images tended to show up in the national magazines like the *Saturday Evening Post,* and not in marginal locations like the candy store in Roth's working-class Jewish neighborhood. In the national advertisements, which were designed increasingly in agencies by educated Anglo-Saxon professionals, pleasure was subordinated to a larger agenda of personal efficiency. To be sure, sensuality survived, but it was increasingly clothed in the sterile idiom of clinical frankness. In general—despite a welcome resurgence of irony, humor, and even surrealism during the past decade or so—managerial values have set the agenda for most national advertising down to the present. Even the flagrantly sexual advertisements of recent years have presented erotic appeal as the product of disciplined conditioning.

By emphasizing the centrality of management imperatives, I mean to correct the common assumption (which my own earlier work encouraged) that advertising ushered in a "hedonistic culture of consumption." Consumer culture there was, from the 1910s to the 1970s, but it was less a riot of hedonism than a new way of ordering the existing balance of tensions between control and release. During its heyday, the post–World War II decades, consumer culture was based on an unusual set of institutional circumstances: a system of tradeoffs between labor and management (labor discipline in exchange for steady, high wages), and the temporary global ascendancy of the U.S. economy. As capital became more mobile and management began looking overseas for cheap labor, consumer culture lost its institutional base. Without a well-paid working population, mass consumption could no longer serve as the integrative glue of civil society. Americans could no longer count on a steady increase in their standard of living.

Still, the assumptions and values of consumer culture have lasted down to the present. Presidents and political parties continue to base their claims to power on their capacity to deliver the goods, though the goods are usually defined in abstract statistical terms. Advertisements are more pervasive and brilliant than ever, though their innovative forms mask the conventionality of their content. Despite their sensuous surfaces, most brand-name advertisements remain dominated by the ethos of personal efficiency. They continue to construct a separate striving self in a world of fascinating but forgettable goods.

Without denying the pleasure to be had from participation in that world, it is important to keep in mind the destructive market discipline that supports it. "The market is highly efficient, but it has no goal; its sole purpose is to produce more in order to consume more," the poet Octavio Paz writes. The current conventional wisdom of most managerial elites— the stubborn, unexamined commitment to economic growth despite worldwide depletion of nonrenewable resources; the preoccupation with an empty pursuit of efficiency that impoverishes personal as well as public life—are enough to lead Paz to conclude, "No civilization of the past was ever ruled by such a blind, mechanical, destructive fatality."[17] I am convinced we need to locate alternatives to that deus ex machina, in public policy and in cultural values as well. But I prefer to suggest rather than to prescribe what those alternatives might be.

That may be why words like *magic* and *carnival* acquire an almost talismanic significance in my interpretation, as recurring counterpoints to the managerial values predominant in national advertisements. Beginning (in my narrative) as cultural components with specific historical locations, they become fragmented and attenuated by the time they arrive in the nineteenth-century United States. There are places, in what follows, when

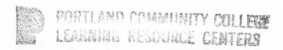

"the magical" or "the carnivalesque" refer to little more than an affirmation of disorder in an overly ordered society, or a preference for the small-scale, idiosyncratic world of retail trade over the standardized compartments of the corporation. (Certainly that is my own preference, as the son of a small business man who was himself an impresario of the carnivalesque.) But the words carry more complex connotations at other points in my narrative. They suggest the unpredictable eruption of inspiration, even among advertising people faced by the demands of modern agency work. And they sometimes signify an escape from epistemological as well as social containment, a reaffirmation of the possibility of mystery in the cosmos, a hint of animistic alternatives to the dualisms of the dominant culture.[18] This is especially apparent in some of the artists and writers I discuss, from Bruno Schulz to Joseph Cornell—people who were drawn to commercial magic but sought to deepen or transcend it.

The book is divided into three parts. Part I concerns mainly the prehistory of modern, corporate-sponsored advertising; ranging from early modern Europe to the United States in the Gilded Age, this section aims to illuminate the impact of the industrial and market revolutions on ideas and symbols of wealth. The overall tendency is toward fragmentation followed by rationalization: commercial adepts promoted a more disembodied imagery of abundance and a more atomistic notion of magical self-transformation than had persisted in animistic modes of thought; emerging elites encouraged new, secular cultural idioms to control the centrifugal impact of market exchange in the developing United States. Yet this first section also suggests that animistic countertendencies survived, even after the rise of a managerial ethos.

Part II charts the triumph of that ethos in American advertising during the first two-thirds of the twentieth century—the period when a consumer culture rose, stabilized for several decades after World War II, and then began to lose its foundation. National corporations employed advertising agencies to represent factory-produced goods to a mass market; the fables they fashioned merged personal and social health, individual and nation, creating narratives of adjustment to a single, efficient system. Throughout this period, advertising people sought professional dignity but could never fully distinguish themselves from their ancestors: the peddlers and pitchmen of the patent medicine era. The survival of their disreputable past presented moral problems to many advertisers, but also preserved certain forms of aesthetic vitality.

Part III explores the borders between advertising and the arts, giving particular attention to the ways that artists and writers struggled to negotiate between advertisers' notion of the artist as technician and the more exalted, romantic–modernist faith in the artist as seer. Here as elsewhere, conflict between authenticity and artifice shaped debate over the cultural significance of advertising. And the most interesting artists and writers (to me) were those who realized that the stark choice between authenticity and artifice might be ultimately circumvented, through the transfiguration of apparently commonplace objects.

My perspective, it may by now be clear, itself depends on a kind of intellectual bricolage. That may be an appropriate strategy for an age that is obsessed with diversity but weary of "making it new." To Lévi-Strauss, the chief drawback to bricolage was its circumscription of innovation through reliance on a limited repertoire of tools and materials.[19] But a "science of the concrete" that seeks reconciliation with the world by making do with "whatever is at hand" is not necessarily an abandonment of inventiveness. To acknowledge limits is not to remain imprisoned in the status quo: indeed much status quo thinking involves denial of limits. For me, at least, intellectual bricolage is based on the belief that creativity can coexist with connectedness to the past, and with a sense of our own finitude in a reanimated universe.

PART I

The Reconfiguration of Wealth:

From Fecund Earth to Efficient Factory

CHAPTER 1

The Lyric of Plenty

FOR CENTURIES the hungry peasant bent to face the earth. *Homo* and humus were twinned. Death and rebirth mingled in the dung heap; filth and fecundity merged in formless, inchoate matter. Intimate acquaintance with dirt shaped dreams of deliverance from want. Ethereal visions of paradise were touched with significant soil.

Many cultural traditions have made no clear distinctions between earthly and heavenly satisfactions, or between human and animal needs. Man and beast alike have faced the implacable pull of hunger. Physical and mental life have been joined in magical worldviews that merged flesh and spirit, thoughts and things. This has been as true in America and Europe as it has been elsewhere throughout the world. Folktales mingle food and fantasy. As the historian Robert Darnton has observed, "Once supplied with magic wands, rings, or supernatural helpers, the first thought of the peasant hero is always for food," and it is always "solid peasant fare." Yet in some forms the fantasies were more elaborate. Amid a cosmology that erected few boundaries between the human self and the material world, man-made as well as natural objects could acquire a life of their own: legends from many European cultures (as well as anthropological accounts of non-European traditions) describe icons that perspire, bleed when struck, and secrete healing oils or breast milk. Spirit was embodied in flesh: symbols of heavenly life were pregnant with earthly meaning. Longings for release from privation resonated with ancient religious hopes. The enduring myth of an earthly paradise melded material abundance with the spiritual abundance of salvation, celebrating eternal ease in a nurturant land of plenty.[1]

Utopian visions of abundance can be traced from classical myth and the Talmud to Elizabethan reports about the New World, on into the early modern era of market fairs and finally into modern, corporate advertising. But the meanings of abundance changed dramatically along the way. For centuries the source of abundance was defined as the fecund earth, whose productive powers were celebrated in pagan feasts that Christians adapted to their liturgical calendar. Catholic and later Protestant devotional traditions introduced a more spiritual dimension to the discourse of abundance, with their emphasis on the overflowing availability of divine grace. Yet many Christians, even among the literate minority, continued to characterize salvation in metaphors of earthly fulfillment.

In agrarian societies haunted by fear of famine, dreams of unbounded plenitude punctuated the rhythms of fat times and lean. The feasting at Carnival time, for example, evoked fabulous visions of excess; it overturned hierarchies of matter and spirit in celebrating physical exuberance and the fulfillment of fleshly desire. Yet the festival derived much of its energy from the ever-present specter of hunger. (Lent made the frequent necessity of fasting into a virtue.)

By the seventeenth and eighteenth centuries, the imagery of abundance began to reflect the expansion of commerce and the opening of trade routes with the Orient. Exotic artifacts—silks, oils, perfumes, and spices—appeared alongside agrarian produce at market fairs. Newer and older icons of abundance coexisted and commingled in the chaotic settings of trade.

In the United States, it was not until the early twentieth century that the rise of corporate advertising brought a disembodiment of abundance imagery, as the carnivalesque celebration of fleshly excess was streamlined into an exaltation of industrial efficiency, and the process of productivity became a model for the organization of everyday life. Even then, older countertendencies survived in the margins of the commercial vernacular. But on the whole, twentieth-century advertising iconography redefined the source of abundance from the fecund earth to the efficient factory.

The few historians who have addressed the cultural significance of American abundance were men who came of age during the mid–twentieth century, when the equation of plenitude with mass production was virtually unchallenged. David Potter and Warren Susman, like their contemporaries, took for granted modern advertising's definition of abundance. Linking the profusion of goods with the rise of mass media, the commercialization of leisure, and the loosening of Victorian mores, they accepted the advertising industry's account of its own historical role in promoting a "culture of abundance" in the twentieth-century United States. This procedure assumes precisely what has to be called into question: the definition of abundance and the discourse we use to characterize its place in our civilization.[2]

Corporate advertisers did not invent the "culture of abundance"; they refashioned its conventions. Their contribution is only one thread in a tapestry of older traditions. One aim of this chapter is to recast the emergent corporate vision against the background of other and older iconographies of abundance. The crucial historical point is that differing definitions of abundance reflect deeper divisions in worldview. What seem like ephemeral changes in visual fashion turn out, on closer inspection, to be struggles over ways of being in the world.

In time, one way tended to become dominant and the others marginal. The disembodiment of abundance imagery involved a movement away from the ancient impulse to symbolize the source of plenitude as female: in the developing corporate iconography, women were reduced to the conduit for corporate-sponsored largesse (purchasing agents and managers of the well-run household) or, more commonly, to mere passive consumers of the stuff generated by the male genius of mass production. The industrial model of abundance provided powerful new support for some old ways of thinking—for the dualistic worldview that Christian theologians and later Cartesian rationalists had been promoting since the early Middle Ages, and for the tendency to see the human self as an isolated, uniquely vital entity amid an inert world of objects. Alternative ways of thinking, which envisioned a relational self participating in an animated universe, persisted in popular culture and in the work of idiosyncratic writers and artists. But by 1900, at least in the industrialized West, animistic modes of thought had lost nearly all intellectual legitimacy.

The meanings of magic became attenuated. Rather than referring to a set of rituals for summoning up supernatural powers within a coherent cosmology, the word *magic* began to imply mere sleight of hand, or a diffuse sense of the marvelous erupting amid the everyday. This latter sense surrounded the exotic artifacts of early market society—the perfumes, silks, and mysterious elixirs that evoked a world elsewhere. Commercial adepts sought to deploy this aura of magic, but by the early twentieth century they realized that the magical atmosphere must be made systematically to dissipate, through doctrines of stylistic progress and policies of planned obsolescence. The process of accumulation had to be kept moving forward, energized by the restless desire for purchase rather than the pleasures of possession. In the modern culture of abundance—which is more precisely labeled a consumer culture—desire was curiously dematerialized. The engines of economic development were powered in part by a dynamic of deprivation which kept fulfillment always just out of reach.

This whole process was neither linear nor one-dimensional. There will be no attempt here to suggest a straightforward shift from a "feminine" to a "masculine" discourse of abundance, or from an animistic to a dualistic attitude toward the material world. To be sure, dualism triumphed in our dominant discourse. But the worldview I am calling animistic (realizing the inadequacy of the term) is not confined to preindustrial cultures. The desire to endow objects with symbolic, perhaps even spiritual, significance persisted in a variety of forms: in the religion of the hearth associated with ideals of domesticity, in the artisan/*bricoleur*'s vernacular "science of the concrete," and in certain idiosyncratic versions of modern science and art.[3]

The reanimation of the world, in other words, does not require a return to a primitive village economy. To be sure, there have been times and places where animism has flourished more fully than it does in the here and now. But the animistic outlook survives nearly everywhere in the modern world, promoting the revaluation of apparently useless objects and the recognition of the connections between matter and spirit, thoughts and things. The magical quality of modern animism is not the magic of brand-name advertising, which reduces objects to empty signifiers of status ascent and stylistic progress, but a magic that grants things their materiality and history. Corporate advertisers' vision of abundance is neither the only nor the final one; it is merely the most pervasive during the past century. To illuminate its historical significance, we need to trace the outlines of older, alternative visions.

The task involves ranging widely and speculatively over several centuries of Western cultural history. The goal is to enlarge the framework for understanding the relationships between American advertising and American culture. It may sometimes be necessary to sacrifice accumulation of detail in order to gain breadth of vision. To begin, we need to try to reconstruct the major features of an animistic outlook on the material world.

AN ANIMATED WORLD

In the Museo del Prado in Madrid is a painting that tells us a great deal about the worldview I am calling "animistic." Alonso Cano's *The Vision of St. Bernard* (c. 1660) shows a statue of the Virgin Mary deftly ejecting a jet of her breast milk into the open mouth of Saint Bernard, while the baby Jesus watches, impressed (or jealous). The image, one of many that depicted this popular legend, suggests the mingling of bodily and spiritual nourishment in traditional notions of grace; it also illuminates the power of images or allegorical representations in a culture that granted them a life of their own.[4]

An animistic culture is one that encourages the growth of what might be called symbolic consciousness. A symbol of persons or beliefs does not, from the viewpoint of symbolic consciousness, merely refer to those persons or beliefs; it embodies them. It contains their real presence—that is, if the symbol is alive. And as the anthropologist Victor Turner writes: "It is alive only insofar as it is 'pregnant with meaning' for men and women, who interact by observing, transgressing, and manipulating for private ends the norms and values that the symbol expresses."[5] Whether it is the milk tree described by Turner as the fountainhead of matriliny among the Ndembu of Zambia, or the statue of the Virgin painted by Cano, the symbol shows the permeability of boundaries between nature and culture, matter and spirit, self and world in an animistic worldview. Symbolic consciousness involves the rejection of dualism, the embodiment of the soul, the ensoulment of the world.

Despite the dualism inherent in much biblical and patristic tradition, for centuries Christians preserved powerful animistic tendencies in popular beliefs and rituals, even in theology. And those tendencies shaped the early discourse of abundance. The doctrine of the Incarnation ("The Word was made flesh, and dwelt among us") and the belief in the resurrection of the body after death brought the earthly and divine realms closer together and sometimes even fused them. Early Christian apologists borrowed from Jewish and classical traditions as well as from popular millenarian fantasies as they imagined a paradise of effortless nurturance. Irenaeus, the second-century church father, wrote:

> The days will come in which vines shall grow, each having ten thousand shoots, and in each of the shoots ten thousand clusters, and on every one of the clusters ten thousand grapes, and every grape when pressed will give five and twenty metretes of wine. And when any one of the saints shall lay hold of a cluster, another shall cry out "I am a better cluster, take me; bless the Lord through me."

Straining for concrete detail, Irenaeus contained superabundant fecundity with numbers; inspired by animistic impulses, he invented fruits that spoke.[6]

Irenaeus's effort to materialize the hereafter was part of his syncretist theological project, the resurrection of the body. He embedded his quantitative and animistic vision of abundance in a polemic against the Gnostics, who rejected the material world as intrinsically evil. The whole point of emphasizing the sensuous delights of paradise was to stress "the salvation of the flesh"—the eventual resurrection of bodies as well as souls, the obliteration of the distinction between earthly and heavenly enjoyments in the life of the world to come.[7]

The vulgar version of paradise was even more immediate and sensual. It emerged as the gastronomic utopia known to the popular imagination of medieval and early modern Europe as the Land of Cockaigne ("little cake"). The Land of Cockaigne was a peasant variation on ancient, elite visions of effortless abundance: its rivers flowed with wine or milk, macaroni fell from heaven (at least in Italy), and pigs ran about with carving knives in their backs crying "Eat me! Eat me!" It was also the world turned upside down: women dominated men, the last runner to cross the finish line won the race. The pattern of reversal could assume grotesque forms. A set of playing cards depicting the Land of Cockaigne, made in Germany about 1535, depicts pigs at play with excrement: rocking a cradle filled with it, roasting it over a spit, devouring it. Here as elsewhere in the Western imagination, a world of overflowing abundance implied the inversion of established hierarchies: the degradation of the pretentious and powerful, the celebration of the most despised earthly creatures and bodily functions.[8]

The upending of conventional forms, along with gastronomic excess, linked Cockaigne with Carnival, the great festival of abundance in early modern Europe. "Cockaigne is a vision of life as one long Carnival," the historian Peter Burke writes, "and Carnival a temporary Cockaigne, with the same emphasis on eating and on reversals." Carnivalesque qualities adhered to festivals throughout the liturgical year, not just to the period between Christmas and Lent, which was, strictly speaking, Carnival time. The whole point of these festivals was leisure and consumption. Poor people stopped work, put on red stockings or any other finery saved for the occasion, then proceeded to eat and drink with abandon, and spend whatever they had on hand. Shrove Tuesday (the day before Ash Wednesday, when Lent began) in England was a time of "such boiling and broiling, such roasting, such stewing and brewing, such baking, frying, mincing, cutting, carving, devouring, and gorbellied gourmandising, that a man would think people did take in two months' provision at once into their paunches," an observer wrote in 1630. Carnival was about food, and about sex. The 440-pound sausage carried by ninety butchers at Königsberg in 1583, and the mock plowing regularly performed by the unmarried women, dramatized the obsessions. *Carne* was flesh, and Carnival celebrated its abundance.[9]

Yet more than simply an outpouring of animal spirits was taking place. The elevation of wives over husbands and servants over masters involved a ritual role reversal through theatrical representation. Comic shows, mummeries, vulgar farces, and open-air amusements of all kinds could turn the whole town into a theater, every actor a spectator, every spectator an actor. Masks conveyed rather than concealed meaning. Surfaces and depths, representation and reality merged in the exuberance of Carnival laughter.

This was the world of Carnival that scholars have come to know through the influential work of the Russian literary critic Mikhail Bakhtin, who identified what he called "grotesque realism" in Carnival laughter. Grotesque realism, in Bakhtin's view, was a subversive discourse of abundance that celebrated a corpulent human body with yawning orifices and protuberant lower regions. "The leading themes of these images of bodily life are fertility, growth, and brimming-over abundance," Bakhtin wrote. "Manifestations of this life refer not to the isolated biological individual, not to the private, egoistic 'economic man,' but to the collective ancestral body of all the people." Leaving aside Bakhtin's cosmic populism, which led him to exaggerate the political significance of Carnival, one can agree that the carnivalesque notion of the self was consistent with an animistic worldview—far more connected to the social and material world than the isolated economic man was.[10]

Nevertheless, it is easy to sentimentalize the vitality and connectedness of the carnivalesque world. The feeding frenzy derived part of its urgency from the fear of famine; the very meaning of carnivalesque abundance depended on its opposition to the self-denial of Lent. Official Church doctrines, though they sought to incorporate the animistic tendencies of popular culture, also aimed at contrary ends: the division of the world into dualistic realms of spirit and matter, body and soul; the promotion of asceticism as a path toward sanctity. (Perhaps the latter stratagem was only making a virtue of necessity.) Upending this spiritual hierarchy, Carnival unleashed demonic energies. Even Bakhtin admitted that the overflowing of animal spirits was not entirely benign: Carnival laughter was not only "gay, triumphant" but "mocking, deriding"—aggression accompanied gluttony and lust. And aggression was often directed against powerless outsiders, especially Jews. Carnival was not simply a sanctioned, temporary challenge to established hierarchies; it was also an occasion to reaffirm popular prejudices.[11]

The complexity deepens further if we consider that Carnival was staged in the marketplace and that Carnival festivities commingled with market fairs. References to fairs and Carnivals in the early modern period (1500–1800) were often virtually coextensive. The market fair, like the marketplace, was not an isolated enclave of rural tradition; it was a crossroads where provincial and cosmopolitan met. During the seventeenth and eighteenth centuries, the emergent bourgeoisie in cities like Lyons and Leipzig, recognizing that their prosperity depended on market fairs, lavishly supported the festival atmosphere surrounding them. The market fair brought locally rooted townsfolk and peasants into contact with the exotic and the bizarre: with magicians and midgets, quacks and alchemists, transient musicians and acrobats; peddlers of soap from Turkey, needles from Spain, and looking-glasses from Venice. The fair linked the individual consumer with major European trade routes as well as with industrial innovators like the ceramics entrepreneur Josiah Wedgwood and the toymaker Matthew Boulton, who by the late eighteenth century were using the fairs to promote new tastes and desires among the populace. "We think it of more consequence to supply the people than the Nobility only," Boulton wrote to a fellow manufacturer in 1794, "and though you speak contemptuously of Hawkers, Pedlars, and those who supply Petty Shops, yet we must own that we think they will do more towards supporting a great manufactory than all the Lords in the Nation." Until permanent shops became a "continuous fair" (as a Russian visitor to eighteenth-century England put it), market fairs were the cutting edge of the commercial revolution, and peddlers were its point men.[12]

Amid carnivalesque confusion, market transactions leavened the imagery of abundance. The dream of a full belly was supplemented by the fantasy of participating in an exotic cosmopolitan world. This addition may have marked a continuation of complex changes in consciousness. Christianity had in principle established a great vertical distance between desire and its spiritual object, salvation. While the growth of Catholic ritual had tended to reduce that distance, creating intimacy through intermediaries, the rise of Protestantism reopened the chasm between human effort and its heavenly reward. The spread of exotic goods through market exchange may have affected consciousness on the horizontal, secular plane. Perhaps there, too, a greater *psychological* distance was opening up between desire and its objects, even as Europeans came into closer *physical* contact with exotic goods. Amid strange and often unattainable artifacts, these early consumers may have sensed a larger possibility for a feeling of deprivation, a more intense experience of separation between the individual self and the material world. Yet available evidence suggests that this change, if it was occurring, was uneven and slow until the end of the eighteenth century—even in England.

Throughout most of the early modern period, the marketplace remained part of an animated world—a mix of the miraculous and the carnivalesque. The events that took place there and the commodities that were sold there continued to provide magical connections between material and spiritual realms. (This was especially, though by no means exclusively, true in Catholic countries, where Church doctrine sometimes sanctioned popular animistic tendencies even as Church authority sought to combat them.) Itinerant peddlers were, literally and figuratively, agents of the marvelous. One who appeared in Florence in 1509 provides a striking example. He was described by a prominent burgher as

> a certain Spaniard who got up on a bench like a quack [*come ciurma-tore*] to sell his prayers [*orazioni*—necklaces containing bits of parchment, on which were written unintelligible or mysteriously indecipherable words]. And he said: "So that you will believe that it is from a saint who makes miracles, and that what I tell you is true, come and take me to an oven which is hot, and I will go inside with this prayer."

The man withstood the heat of the oven, extinguished torches and candles in his mouth, and washed his hands in a boiling pan of oil. "I have never seen a greater miracle than this, if miracle it was," the burgher concluded.

As the historian Richard Trexler has astutely observed, the virtuoso fire-eater stood between two worlds: he was both a miracle-working saint and a Renaissance hero. His heroism depended on his creative capacity to manipulate sacred objects (the prayer necklaces) toward practical ends: the control of fire and, ultimately, his own livelihood as a peddler of prayers. This Spaniard's merging of matter and spirit recalls the shamanistic "science of the concrete" described by Lévi-Strauss. In Trexler's words, "the materials [the fire-eater] used were not yet lifeless objects. That final separation between name and thing, between technician and matter, lay far into the future."[13] The development of dualistic thought patterns, in other words, had not yet disenchanted the material world. The modernization of consciousness was a muddled and erratic process. Commercial expansion introduced new commodities into the discourse of abundance but reinforced traditional habits of mind as well.

This pattern of contradictory impulses emerges clearly in the literature of New World colonization. The European voyages of discovery gave ancient visions of utopia a local habitation and a name. By the sixteenth century the Land of Cockaigne was reputed to be "West of Spain." Voyagers to the West brought back alluring tales that gave new currency to fantasies of material fulfillment. The sensate dimensions of paradise continued to assert themselves. For example, Sir Walter Raleigh's lieutenant Arthur Barlow, writing in 1584 from off the coast of what is now North Carolina, evoked an Edenic atmosphere before he launched an account of his first startling encounter with American plenitude. "The second of July we found shoal water, where we smelt so sweet and so strong a smell, as if we had been in the midst of some delicate garden abounding with all kinds of odoriferous flowers; by which we were assured that the land could not be far distant." Imagine the state the man must have been in: battered by a two-month sea voyage, no doubt hungry, exhausted, and more than a little apprehensive as well as hopeful about the wonders he would witness—with a mind like almost any Elizabethan's, primed for supernatural signs and portents. At this point, to catch an overwhelming aroma of flowers while still at sea would surely have seemed a thrilling prelude to some momentous meeting with an Other, a New World. And truly, in Barlow's account, landfall constitutes an extraordinary moment, something like first contact with a primeval profusion of generative energy. Grapes—that sacramental emblem of abundance—are everywhere, even to the water's edge, where they become part of "the very beating and surge of the sea." Like much of the early literature of colonization, Barlow's account is both an advertisement and a religious document. It promotes the acquisition of a valuable piece of real estate but also preserves a genuine sense of wonder at the pulsating ripeness of the natural landscape. An age so attuned to cosmic symbolism could be pardoned for believing there was something providential, even paradisal, about this New World.[14]

THE BREAST OF PARADISE

Certainly there was theological precedent for belief in Eden as a palpable place. Well into the seventeenth century, many Christian thinkers held that the original paradise still existed as the Garden of Eden—the highest point on earth, from which flowed four sweet-tasting rivers. Sir Thomas More, for one, could barely conceal his impatience with any attempt to spiritualize paradise or turn it into a metaphor. As for those less concerned with theological matters, the contemplation of America prompted them to sift through their common stock of images, mingling sacred and secular in a breathless litany of praise. John Speede, in his *Historie of Great Britain* (1611), celebrated Oriana (the New World) as "the Court of Queen Ceres, the Granary of the Western World, the fortunate Island, the Paradise of Pleasure, and the Garden of God." Despite its materiality and sensuality, New World abundance retained a religious aura as well. The vision of an earthly paradise preserved the venerable tendency to link abundance with divinity as well as natural fecundity and maternal nurturance.[15]

But the commercial and scientific revolutions of the early modern period encouraged more systematic efforts to dominate the natural world, more controlled and masterful models of masculine identity, more disembodied notions of self—defined in opposition to rather than in connection with the universe of matter. This was, in embryo, the bourgeois psychological style that Freud would analyze in its fullest and most extreme development at the end of the nineteenth century. The discourse of New World abundance sometimes echoed an emergent masculine outlook that tended to define the conflict between animistic and dualistic tendencies in gendered terms.[16]

One can see that viewpoint in the letters of Christopher Columbus. On his third voyage, in 1497, as he was sailing off the coast of Venezuela toward the point where the four branches of the Orinoco River empty into the Gulf of Paria, his reckoning indicated that his elevation was rising; the turbulence of the water suggested that the rivers must be flowing from a great height. Their waters tasted sweet. Columbus concluded he was in the neighborhood of paradise. His problem was that the great elevation along the equinoctial line did not fit his notion that the world was a perfect sphere; his need to resolve the conflict sparked a revealing fantasy. He decided that the earth was not round, as Ptolemy and others had argued, but "the form of a pear, which is very round except where the stalk grows, at which part it is most prominent; or like a round ball, upon one part of which is a prominence like a woman's nipple, this protrusion being the highest and nearest the sky." The equation of Eden with maternal nurturance was not an idle conceit or a slip of the pen; Columbus returned to it in the same letter. Yet, having discovered the entrance to paradise, he made no attempt to enter. Instead, he turned and fled to Hispaniola, saying "no one can go [to the earthly paradise] but by God's permission."

Columbus's rhetorical and nautical maneuvers—excited discovery followed by anxious flight—show how the fear of God could shape the gendered language of exploration.[17]

Columbus's pattern of thought was prototypical. In the discourse of New World abundance, the drive for mastery was always threatening to dissolve into chaos, as the male adventurer submitted to the allure of passivity amid plenitude. As in the Land of Cockaigne, where wives rode astride their husbands, American bounty was enticing but also emasculating, perhaps worse. Early icons of America embodied this threat and promise: they were all hefty females, at once nubile and maternal, primitives awaiting awakening by the European male "discoverer" (figure 1.1) but also capable of vengeance and violence (figure 1.2). In the iconography of the four continents that had become standardized by the early 1600s, America was routinely allegorized as an Indian queen who could be a formidable and even menacing figure: she was frequently surrounded by emblems of great wealth—gold ingots, chests of jewels, the occasional cor-

FIGURE 1.1
Theodore Galle, *The Arrival of Vespucci in the New World*, engraving c. 1600. *Library of Congress.*

FIGURE 1.2

Philipp Galle, *America*, engraving c. 1579–1600. *Collection of the New-York Historical Society.*

nucopia—and by jungle fauna such as parrots, armadillos, or alligators; she often carried an ax or a club, and sometimes the severed head of a hapless male victim. The female figure permitted seventeenth-century male artists and writers to express a range of emotions, from courage to fear, as they fashioned images of the New World for European audiences.[18]

One rhetorical solution to the anxiety this representation aroused lay readily at hand: the colonizer could convert childlike passivity into masculine penetration and possession. George Alsop's promotional tract *A Char-*

acter of the Province of Maryland (1666) mixed erotic and nurturant imagery as it suggested the prospect of an earthly paradise. Maryland colonists, he asserted, had a unique opportunity to decipher an Edenic code. "The Trees, Plants, Fruits, Flowers, and Roots that grow here in *Mary-Land,* are the only Emblems or Hieroglyphicks of our Adamitical or Primitive situation . . . their several effects, kinds, and properties . . . still bear the Effigies of Innocency according to their original Grafts." This "Terrestrial Paradice" was explicitly female, with sexual as well as maternal connotations. In Alsop's words, Maryland was

> within her own imbraces extraordinary pleasant and fertile. Pleasant, in respect of the multitude of Navigable Rivers and Creeks that conveniently and most profitably lodge within the armes of her green, spreading, and delightful Woods; as she doth otherwise generously fructifie this piece of Earth with almost all sorts of Vegetables, as well Flowers with their varieties of colours and smells, as Herbes and Rootes with their several effects and operative virtues, that offer their benefits daily to supply the want of the Inhabitant[s] whene're their necessities shall *Sub-poena* them to wait on their commands. So that he, who out of curiosity desires to see the Landskip of the Creation drawn to the life, or to read Nature's universal Herbal without book, may with the Opticks of a discreet discerning, view *Mary-Land* drest in her green and fragrant Mantle of the Spring.

It would be possible to dismiss these metaphors as euphuistic convention, except that they were so pervasive, even obsessive, in the language of New World exploration. The land-as-woman evoked a desire for nurturance— but nurturance threatened to turn into suffocating superabundance and provoked the alternative dream of mastery through possession.[19]

Visions of erotic penetration fit the colonial enterprise more closely than dreams of childlike dependence. The imagery was more extractive than agricultural, and indeed visions of gold and gems could be as gendered as dreams of agricultural plenty—and more likely to suggest genital activism than oral passivity. In male imaginations, nature could be conflated with a nubile woman, and vice versa. John Donne's elegy "On Going to Bed" (1669) expressed the latter pattern perfectly.

> *License my roving hands, and let them go*
> *Before, behind, between, above, below.*
> *O my America! my new-found-land,*
> *My kingdom, safeliest when with one man manned,*
> *My mine of precious stones, my empery,*
> *How blest am I in this discovering thee!*[20]

Unbounded pleasure required the security of absolute possession; Donne's "kingdom" was "safeliest when with one man manned." The dream of technological mastery depended on the success of the masculine effort to contain and productively channel the chaotic energies of a metaphorically female nature. This containment of abundance was a project that was deeply rooted in Western intellectual tradition.

Consider the mythic genesis of the earliest and most durable emblem of plenitude in Western tradition: the cornucopia, or horn of plenty. Cronus, the father of Zeus, had been told that he would be dethroned by his children; he took preventive action by eating them— all but Zeus, whose mother, Rhea, spirited the baby off to a cave in Crete where he was adopted by the nymphs of Ida and suckled by a goat called Amalthea. The nursling grew strong, and one day in play he accidentally broke off the horn of the devoted Amalthea; he gave it to the nymphs, promising them it would be filled with everything they could possibly want.[21]

The creation myth of the cornucopia involved the merging of natural and supernatural, animal and human, human and divine—the nurturance of a divine son by an animal mother. The myth located the origins of cornucopian abundance in the cave of Amalthea, where opposites melded and desires were satisfied. That murky region resonated with persistent mystical aspirations for union with the deity, recalled the enveloping darkness of preconscious life, and foretold the "postconscious" chaos of death; it evoked a world where all carefully constructed categories threatened to dissolve into formlessness. It is at least metaphorically accurate to say that the major traditions of Western rationality have been rooted in an effort to bring light and structure to the cave of Amalthea.

The task has reverberated with gender anxiety. Without falling into psychoanalytical reductionism, one can suggest that the cave of Amalthea—the source of cornucopian abundance—was a realm redolent with female associations, and that the struggle to transcend and control formless matter has been a predominantly masculine philosophical project. Zeus accidentally broke the horn from Amalthea's head, but then deliberately used it as an instrument of his own power and munificence. In Western intellectual tradition, *mater* and matter have been indissolubly linked, and the meanings of matter have been revealingly ambiguous. Matter has been the thing that matters, the essential, original thing, the source—but also the excrementitious, the too, too solid, the gross and weighty as opposed to the spiritual. This latter emphasis was implicit in Aristotelian and scholastic usage and explicit in the Cartesian dualism that structured the scientific revolution of the early modern era.[22]

Cartesian dualism reshaped the traditional imagery of abundance. The Cartesian insistence on the separation of the isolated human subject from the material world of objects reinforced the emergent notion of an autonomous modern self. This was not the only vision of selfhood available in early modern Europe. Apart from popular animism, there were other alternatives as well: one should try to imagine the consequences if Montaigne's sensibility (for example), rather than Descartes', had shaped the modernization of consciousness in the West. Montaigne and other Renaissance humanists encouraged a tolerance for the interplay between body and soul, envisioning an imperfect self in a web of connections between natural and supernatural worlds. But as the philosopher of science Stephen Toulmin observes, "the Cartesian program for philosophy swept aside the 'reasonable' certainties and hesitations of sixteenth-century skeptics, in favor of new, mathematical kinds of 'rational' certainty and proof."[23] The quest for certainty bred a faith in value-free science that elevated universal timeless truths over local, historical knowledge; it depended on an ethos of self-command that encouraged a distrust of immediate, bodily experience. The assumption that individual consciousness had to be willed in opposition to an external objective world was to create a sense of self at once exalted and vulnerable—so tautly crafted that it was subject to the ever-present danger of dissolving into formless matter. And formlessness was the inner tendency of many traditional visions of material abundance, from exaltations of agrarian surfeit to celebrations of carnivalesque corpulence.

Philosophers and scientists working in the developing dualistic framework sought to contain formless matter with categories and other mental structures. The rhetoric of scientific revolution was pervaded by gendered metaphors: nature was female and men controlled it. Of course, the project was not reducible to a battle of the sexes; it was part of a broader struggle to systematize the claims of culture over nature, a struggle that dissolved gender conflict in universalist language. Consider one of the most sweeping and global visions of human supremacy, Francis Bacon's *New Atlantis* (1627). Bacon imagined a utopia governed by a technocratic elite that could accelerate or slow down the growing seasons and create synthetic fruits surpassing the natural ones in taste, smell, and color. It was the modernization of paradise through the dominance of denatured technique.[24]

The fulfillment of Bacon's vision lay far in the future. During the six-teenth and seventeenth centuries, it was much more common for Euro-peans—especially English Protestants—to resort to religious idioms when they sought to structure the unbounded plenitude of a savage unexplored land. In the Puritans' New Israel, the godliness of a religious community, not the expertise of a scientific elite, would prevent the populace from los-ing its righteous identity amid the myriad temptations of fructifying nature.[25]

Yet neither the New Atlantis nor the New Israel exhausted the imagi-native possibilities of New World abundance. Alongside emergent strate-gies for containment, older utopian visions wallowed in abundance rather than keeping it at bay. Perhaps the most durable of these was El Dorado, the mythical kingdom that fired the imaginations of Sir Walter Raleigh and other adventurers, the place (according to Raleigh's account) where men anointed their naked bodies with oil, covered themselves with gold dust, and cavorted in drunken ecstasy for six or seven days at a stretch.[26] This was a far cry from God's New Israel; it was closer to the sensual exuber-ance of Carnival. The tension between dreams of excess and methodical self-control (whether under religious or scientific auspices) embodied a conflict between two overlapping but distinct visions of economic develop-ment: speculative expansion on the one hand, systematic organization on the other. These visions could ultimately be made to coexist, but conflict between them would shape American attitudes toward material abun-dance from the beginnings of a market society to the era of consumer cul-ture.

One can see the opposing positions as early as the 1620s, in the con-frontation between Thomas Morton of Marymount and William Bradford of Plymouth. Morton's satirical account of their struggles, *New English Canaan* (1637), presented its author as an Elizabethan Anglican and pagan, a man unwilling to embrace the sharp dualisms of Puritanism or scientific rationality, and eager to promote the melding of European sub-jects with a New World of arcadian sensuality—a devotee of Dionysus. Morton loved to stage the sorts of theatrical celebrations that Puritans found abhorrent, casting himself as the Lord of Misrule. William Bradford recalled that Morton & Co. "set up a May-pole, drinking and dancing about it many days together, inviting the Indean women, for their consorts, dancing and frisking togither, (like so many fairies, or furies rather,) and worse practises." The Pilgrim Fathers were shocked. As Morton succinctly

put it: "Hee that playd Proteus (with the help of Priapus) put their noses
out of joynte as the Proverbe is." He implied that what outraged the Puritans was not only sexual license, but also the protean fluidity of selfhood
that seemed to characterize the revelry at Marymount. Bradford and his
minions struggled against and ultimately suppressed this cultural subversion in their midst. Morton was arrested (by Captain Miles Standish,
whom Morton ridiculed as "Captain Shrimpe"), tried, and deported to
England.[27]

It would be a mistake to see this as a conflict between Bradford the
Puritan modernizer and Morton the carnivalesque traditionalist. In many
ways Morton was the modernizer. Bradford clung to communitarian constraints on business enterprise, while Morton traded arms and liquor
eagerly with the Indians—indeed, that was one of the primary Puritan
grievances against him. Morton, an ambitious ex-lawyer turned entrepreneur, cherished his own sexually charged vision of enlightenment and
progress. His prologue to *New English Canaan* provided one of the most
explicit metaphorical connections between erotic possession and economic
productivity. Morton's New Canaan was

> *Like a faire Virgin, longing to be sped*
> *And meete her lover in a Nuptiall bed,*
> *Deck'd in rich ornaments t'advaunce her state*
> *And excellence, being most fortunate*
> *When most enjoy'd: so would our Canaan be*
> *If well imploy'd by art and industry;*
> *Whose offspring now, shewes that her fruitfull wombe,*
> *Not being enjoy'd, is like a glorious tombe,*
> *Admired things producing which there dye,*
> *And ly fast bound in darck obscurity;*
> *The worth of which, in each particuler,*
> *Who list to know, this abstract will declare.*[28]

This was an agenda for technological progress. Only "art and industry"
could free "admired things" from the "darck obscurity" of the aboriginal
past, transforming the "glorious tomb" of the pre-contact New World into
a "fruitfull wombe" of marketable commodities.

This version of material progress evoked familiar forms of anxiety
among the Puritan godly. As commercial life expanded, Puritan fears of
corruption focused less on the effects of natural abundance and more on
those of artificial abundance, or luxury; but emasculating ease remained a
female threat. For centuries, Christian iconographers had made luxury a

lustful woman; proponents of early Protestantism translated that tradition into literary figures. Bunyan's allegory of Madam Bubble, in Part II of *Pilgrim's Progress* (1684), captured persistent male fears of surrendering consciousness in exchange for wealth and pleasure. Madam Bubble is a witch who has cast a spell on the Enchanted Ground—one of the most dangerous spots on the pilgrims' road to the Celestial City. "Those that die here die of no violent distemper," says Stand-Fast. "The death which such die is not grievous to them; for he that goeth away in a sleep, begins that journey with desire and pleasure; yea, such acquiesce in the will of that disease." Madam Bubble is a "a tall comely dame," with "something of a swarthy complexion"; she is dressed in "very pleasant attire," and is known to "speak very smoothly, and give you a smile at the end of a sentence." She "loveth banqueting and feasting" and wears "a great purse by her side," with "her hand often in it, fingering her money, as if that were her heart's delight." Connections between money and sexuality (as well as between purses and vulvas) were firmly established in English language and thought ("to spend" colloquially implied the ejaculation of semen). But the figure of Madam Bubble brings those linkages together forcefully, with some new connotations: the hint of New World exoticism suggested by that "swarthy complexion"; the explicit reference to speculative enterprise contained in her name. She was the Protestants' nightmare vision of carnivalesque capitalism. The distrust of graven images, originally focused on Catholic icons, began to turn as well against the proliferating baubles of an emergent consumer society and the women who wore them. By the late eighteenth century, the Fashionable Woman was a stock figure in moralists' polemics against luxury.[29]

But despite the Protestant critique of capitalism, many Protestants did become successful capitalists. If the framework of godliness weakened in their everyday lives, the idea of duty in one's calling continued to prowl about like an uninvited ghost. As Max Weber understood, the Protestant Ethic of self-control persisted even among those too busy to pay much attention to its religious justification.[30] The secular heirs of Bradford and Bunyan piled up wealth but kept its corrupting effects at bay by channeling it into productive investment rather than frivolous consumption. They etherealized moneymaking into a process of self-definition rather than a pursuit of pleasure. The fear of lost control, of a self dissolving into a formless world of overabundance (whether one defined it as natural increase or artificial luxury)—this was the psychic motor that powered the disembodiment of wealth, the separation of it from its origins in the material world.

By the mid-eighteenth century, patterns of Protestant ambivalence pervaded Anglo-American public discourse. Revolutionary American colonists railed against the corrupting effects of imported British luxury and urged patriotic boycotts of frivolous consumer goods from the mother country. As a separate national identity emerged, republican ideologues began to alter the iconography of American abundance. The dominant symbol of America was transformed from a mature Indian queen into a young Indian princess—less tropical, less maternal, less threatening than earlier representations, and more easily placed in the service of didacticism. During the first years of the new nation, the Indian princess was gradually allegorized into a neoclassical goddess of liberty. In what one might call the official vocabulary of national design, the older, earthier icons of abundance were displaced by emblems of freedom, union, progress, or some other abstract concept.[31]

Yet in an agrarian society, the disembodiment of abundance remained problematic. The idea that money, itself an abstract sign of material wealth, could somehow generate more money had seemed the acme of artifice to Christian moralists: hence the many condemnations of usury as *contra natura*. Still, a long tradition of rhetoricians tried to capture the mysterious growth of capital through interest by resorting to generative and germinative metaphors. In "Advice to a Young Tradesman, Written by an Old One" (1748), Benjamin Franklin wrote:

> Remember, that money is of the prolific, generating nature. Money can beget money, and its offspring can beget more, and so on. Five shillings turned is six, turned again it is seven and threepence, and so on, till it becomes a hundred pounds. The more there is of it, the more it produces every turning, so that the profits rise quicker and quicker. He that kills a breeding sow, destroys all her offspring to the thousandth generation.[32]

From the goose that laid the golden egg to the breeding sow of Franklin, emblems of abundance merged the sign of material wealth with its natural (and usually female) origin. However artificial or abstract the processes of capital formation had become, the language of fecundity clung to them like soil to a spade.

The attachment to a traditional language of abundance appeared in *Letters from an American Farmer* (1782) by J. Hector St. John, the pen name of Michel Guillaume Jean de Crèvecoeur. The immigrant, according to Crèvecoeur, "becomes an American by being received in the broad lap of our great *Alma Mater.* Here individuals of all nations are melted into a new race of men, whose labours and posterity will one day cause great changes in the world." The process of regeneration explicitly involved the (male) immigrant's return to childlike dependence on maternal protection, the dissolution of the old subjectivity and the emergence of a new one. Yet, like William Byrd and numerous other colonial celebrants of the American Eden, Crèvecoeur worried about the effects of an overly nurturant landscape on individual character. Despite his attraction to the spontaneous fecundity of the natural world, he was also committed to the republican moralism pervading the colonial elite, a worldview that condemned "effeminate" indolence and celebrated "manly" productive labor. With the characteristic republican concern for preserving virtue from the effects of prosperity, he located what amounted to his ideal moral state on Nantucket Island—the only spot in the colonies where nature was harsh enough to keep men from accumulating temptations to lassitude.[33]

As Crèvecoeur himself knew, this republican synthesis was a precarious one. The presence of unbounded plenitude could not only tempt men to passive self-indulgence or corrosive competition for possessions but also provoke them to orgies of destruction, energized by a mix of glee and rage. By the early nineteenth century, as the countryside was settled beyond the Appalachians, the literature of abundance began to limn these scenes of waste. Descriptions of the sheer multiplicity of codfish or cranes or passenger pigeons concluded with a carnival of carnage. James Fenimore Cooper wrote the classic set pieces of the genre in *The Pioneers* (1823): the seining of mounds of bass, thousands of which were left to rot, by the shores of Lake Otsego (Lake Champlain); the mass murder of pigeons by an ecstatic mob armed with bows and arrows, pistols, muskets, and small cannon.[34]

The crowd scenes in Cooper recalled the unleashing of cruelty at Carnival; the scale of the waste was simply stunning. It is difficult to account for the glee and rage behind the destruction, except by suggesting that nature en masse intensified persistent fears of unbounded plenitude; the wish to dominate became the wish to exterminate. Nature was an implacable foe as well as a source of life. Both husbandman and hunter became weary of the struggle, maddened by its futility. No wonder people sought to circumvent that struggle, to sublimate their fury against nature into an idealist faith in technological development. D. H. Lawrence caught the process in one of his moments of crazed insight, as he commented on Cooper and Crèvecoeur:

> The hunter is a killer. The husbandman, on the other hand, brings about birth and increase. But even the husbandman strains in dark mastery over the unwilling earth and beast; he struggles to win forth substance, he must master the soil and the strong cattle, he must have the heavy blood-knowledge and the slow, but deep, mastery. There is no equality or selfless humility. The toiling blood swamps the idea, inevitably. For this reason the most idealist nations invent most machines. America simply teems with mechanical inventions, because nobody in America ever wants to *do* anything. They are idealists. Let a machine do the thing.[35]

Despite his hyperboles, Lawrence put his finger on a fundamental dynamic in the development of American abundance: the deflection of the human gaze upward, away from direct contact with bodily existence; the industrialization—and rationalization—of consciousness. This was the movement, implicit in both scientific rationality and Puritan self-control, that would ratify separation from the breast of paradise. A reified notion of "the machine" would replace the nurturant earth as the cornucopia. The lyric of plenty would remain profoundly gendered, but the dispensation of sustenance would be reversed. Rather than suggesting an infantilized male suckling at the breast of *Alma Mater*, the developing patterns of rhetoric and iconography would construct a female recipient of factory-generated largesse.

In an industrializing market economy, the severing of production from consumption (and the gendering of both) symbolically divested women of their generative powers. Yet the mythic female consumer was not simply a passive totem of male achievement; in the emerging popular discourse of commodity civilization, she was empowered as an active, desiring subject—the Fashionable Woman—who retained the capacity to devour the male producer through the reckless wasting of his substance.

The rationalization of abundance imagery took place only gradually over the course of many decades, and was not decisively accomplished until the early twentieth century. For much of the nineteenth century, the American commercial vernacular sustained alternative idioms. Beneath official moralism, subcultures of fantasy and sensuality flourished. They constituted a world of seamy promoters and sweaty performers, barflies and prostitutes, mesmerists and magicians. Peddlers promised seductive enchantments to people who purchased their silks and elixirs; department store owners sought to surround their wares with an aura of oriental exoticism; some goods retained the magical charge of the early modern market fair. P. T. Barnum was the impresario of this world, entrepreneurial advertising its lingua franca. In many ways this world resembled the Rabelaisian realm of Carnival described and imagined by Bakhtin; in other ways it was profoundly different.

CHAPTER 2

The Modernization of Magic

IT was the summer of 1872, and James Whitcomb Riley was at loose ends in Greenfield, Indiana. He was twenty-three years old and had earned a reputation as a clever rhymester and sign painter—not to mention a hell of a fellow for a good time. But he never seemed to stick with anything long. People said he drank too much, and slept till noon.

Deliverance for Riley was not far off. It came, he would later recall, in a peddler's wagon, drawn by five horses that "looked as though they were prancing out of an Arabian dream" and driven by a man with "breezy whiskers" who called himself Dr. S. B. McCrillus. His "marvelous brews and decoctions," Riley wrote, "relieved every form of distress, from the pinch of tight shoes / to a dose of the 'blues.' " Riley signed on to work for McCrillus, under an agreement with Riley's father that explicitly echoed Dickens's *Old Curiosity Shop:* it was modeled, in some places word for word, on Mrs. Jarley's agreement to employ Little Nell for "open-air wagrancy" in the promotion of a traveling waxworks.[1]

Riley worked for McCrillus on and off for two years, making himself useful as an advance man and all-round assistant. He suggested that they add bee stings to the list of ailments cured by the doctor's "Oriental Remedy." He imitated an organ grinder and played the Jew's harp while the doctor's other apprentice called attention to their chief attraction: the Wild Girl from the Congo, a "local merry-maker" impersonating a Savage Wonder with strange ancestry, torn garments, and disheveled hair. Riley also told stories and sang while accompanying himself on the guitar, designed trademarks for McCrillus's patent medicines, painted ads for them on farmers' barns (often without the farmers' permission), and wrote doggerel puffing the doctor's Blood Purifier, European Balsam, and Oriental Liniment. Riley remembered his stint in the advertising business as an idyll of cool spring water, fried chicken, and giggling country girls.[2]

Riley returned to Greenfield and spent a miserable year trying to read law, finally fleeing in the summer of 1875 to join a band of itinerant musicians and comedians who performed advertisements for the Wizard Oil Company, one of the more established patent medicine firms, run by a "Dr." C. M. Townsend. One of Riley's jobs was to illustrate the blackboard during Townsend's lecture. The trick was to work in more than one remedy at once. Riley would, for example, begin by printing "Why let pain your pleasures spoil / for want of Townsend's Wizard Oil?" Then he would quickly sketch a bust of Shakespeare, and next to it a bottle of Cholera Balm fighting off the skeletal figure of Death. There were two lectures a day, one in the afternoon and one at night by torchlight, and during the evening performance, Riley recalled, "I was transported to the land of the Arabian nights. It was an Aladdin show." The troupe ranged eastward to Ohio, where Riley became known (he later claimed) as the Hoosier Wizard. As his confidence grew, Riley took to telling fairy tales melodramatically and painting "fantastic illuminations on glass, which set afloat the virtues of Magic Oil." This job, too, proved to be only an interlude for Riley. After a year or so he returned to more respectable pursuits and ultimately to a career as a popular (albeit frequently bibulous) poet of rural virtue.[3]

Riley's fling at "open-air wagrancy" offers a glimpse at the rich and complex carnivalesque tradition in nineteenth-century American advertising.[4] Advertisers have habitually been linked (especially by their critics) to sideshow barkers and other inhabitants of the seamy carnival world. But seldom has anyone explored the broader implications of the theatrical celebrations of carnality, the burlesque subversions of authority, in advertising and American culture generally during the nineteenth century. For most historians, American Victorian culture remains dominated by puritanical devotion to character, an Ice Age of producerist repression before the great thaw induced by a hedonistic culture of consumption. A more capacious approach might acknowledge that the overall pattern of nineteenth-century change was a developing balance of tensions—within the broader society and gradually within advertising itself—between dreams of magical transformation and moralistic or managerial strategies of control. The recurring motif in the cultural history of American advertising could be characterized as the attempt to conjure up the magic of self-transformation through purchase while at the same time containing the subversive implications of a successful trick.

The task of containment was rendered problematic by the extraordinary mobility that characterized early-nineteenth-century American society (extraordinary, at least, by European standards). In the chaotic economy of the emerging United States, carnivalesque subversions were unmoored from traditional ritual, left free to float along the margins of settled society, promoted by picaresque rogues like Riley's employers. In the tradition of hucksters on both sides of the Atlantic, they mingled entertainment and moneymaking, provoking an ambiguous response of titillation, laughter, and suspicion among the populace at large.[5]

Drs. McCrillus and Townsend were part of a subculture of itinerants that included circus performers, puppeteers, and freak show impresarios as well as peddlers. Often the entrepreneurs hired the entertainers as bait, as Townsend and McCrillus did; the word *mountebank*, which by the early nineteenth century had become nearly synonymous with charlatan, two hundred years earlier had meant merely "bench-mounter"—a juggler or other performer who would climb up on a bench in a public space to attract a crowd. As Riley discovered, there were no sharp boundaries between salesmanship and other forms of performance.[6]

To young men of spirit facing a nose-to-the-grindstone adulthood, commercial itinerancy promised escape, adventure, even a transformed identity; to their audience, the itinerants' arts held a similar appeal—more vicarious but still potent. Riley's approach typified much advertising practice throughout the nineteenth century and into the twentieth. Assuming in his audience a knowledge of Shakespeare that today would be largely confined to a cultural elite, he burlesqued the bard by putting his words in the service of painkillers and panaceas. Riley also participated with the rest of the troupe in creating an atmosphere of exotic sensuality and magical metamorphosis. The Wild Girl from the Congo was only the most obvious embodiment of forbidden pleasures; the doctors' almost obsessive preoccupation with "Arabian Nights" and "oriental" remedies resonated with prurient Victorian fantasies about the mysterious East. And the elixirs themselves were invariably described as "magic"; they held out the promise of new life and dramatic self-transformation.

Like the Spanish magus peddling his *orazioni* in Florence, patent medicine vendors made miraculous claims. Yet the magic they invoked was more a rhetorical device than an effort to summon up supernatural powers. It connoted sleight-of-hand showmanship and a diffuse sense of the marvelous, not participation in a coherently animistic cosmos. This was a peculiarly modern version of a magical worldview, reshaped by fluid American social conditions and by Protestant sensibilities. Yet it preserved ancient longings for personal transformation, even as it became a major element in the developing discourse of commerce. By exploring the modernization of magic we can learn a great deal about the emerging pattern of tensions in commercial culture: between control and release, stability and sorcery.

THE DREAM OF METAMORPHOSIS

The desire for a magical transfiguration of the self was a key element in the continuing vitality of the carnivalesque advertising tradition, and an essential part of consumer goods' appeal in nineteenth-century America. The origins of that dream were complex and obscure; certainly it drew strength from ancient folk myths (rings, wands, shoes) as well as Protestant conversion narratives. And certainly it acquired new ambiguity in commercial settings: the faith of the medicine-show audience (for example) in magical change was no doubt bracketed by a healthy skepticism. We have evidence, from Neil Harris and other imaginative historians of American chicanery, that the audience for many such commercial performances expected to be tricked and was often amused by what Bakhtin (see chapter 1) might call the "atmosphere of gay deception." But no matter how skeptical the audiences at medicine shows were, the fact remains that they bought the stuff in enormous quantities. Itinerant peddlers sold everything—from clocks and tinware to silks, perfumes, and essences—but their most profitable item, in the long run, was the magic elixir. Patent medicine companies were the earliest and most successful national advertisers, the biggest spenders, the best clients for the advertising agencies that began to form in the 1860s and 1870s. There are many prosaic ways to account for their success—constant demand, low capital requirements, a largely incompetent and even helpless medical profession—but one can also suggest that the appeal of patent medicines depended on the persistence of magical thinking among the American population.[7]

Historians of early American culture, concentrating on formal religious institutions, have often overlooked the vast unchurched majority. The best recent estimate is that on the eve of the American Revolution only about

15 percent of the colonists belonged to any church.[8] This does not mean that non-churchmembers were unaffected by Protestant moralism, particularly in its more secularized republican forms, but it does suggest that they were susceptible to other, perhaps more obscure, traditions, other ways of making sense of the world.

One of the most resilient was the materialistic magic passed on from medieval European folk thought. A seer's powers of divination were intensely practical: they could be employed to locate lost horses, unfaithful spouses, or hoards of buried treasure. The magician could point the way to dramatic self-transformation through instant betterment of one's material lot in life. In the United States, treasure-seeking through occult means was an obsessive and widespread preoccupation well into the nineteenth century, especially in poorer rural regions where people felt left behind by economic development. American treasure-seekers used seerstones, divining rods, and other occult paraphernalia in a busy "scientific" spirit, assembling empirical evidence and following precise procedures. Caught between their own experience of scarcity and the achievement ethos of a developing entrepreneurial society, they sought economic self-transformation through collaboration with supernatural powers.[9]

Treasure-seeking was one of several ways that early-nineteenth-century Americans used magical thinking to allay anxiety and sustain a dream of instantaneous change in their economic condition. Belief in luck survived Puritan denunciations of pagan superstition and sustained a flourishing subculture of gambling. To be sure, the gambler could display elements of calculation as well as vestiges of magical thinking. Yet in general, gambling represented a popular (sometimes playful) alternative to the diligence supposedly required for economic success. Despite the efforts of ministers and moralists, many ordinary Americans—even those who never went near a crap game or a card table—hoped for a "lucky hit" in one of the myriad lotteries or "policy" games available in most cities. Policy was a nineteenth-century equivalent of the numbers game. Players consulted dream books that claimed to reveal the numerological significance of dreams and coincidences; the player could learn what number to bet on when he dreamed of a policeman, or saw an old lady fall down in the street. This form of magical thinking was not confined to any one class or race. As late as 1879, the Virginia journalist James D. McCabe could observe in *Lights and Shadows of New York Life* that "even men accounted 'shrewd' on Wall Street" were among the purchasers of dream books. (The ironic linkage would not have gone unnnoticed by the economist Henry George and other reformers; by 1879, the resemblance between stock market speculation and gambling had become a major theme in Protestant and republican critiques of capitalism.)[10]

Outside the organized Protestant denominations, a certain kind of magical thinking flourished into the post–Civil War decades: it underwrote longings for luxury goods; it promoted a conception of personal identity more subject to sudden fluctuations of fortune and less under control of the individual will than the ideal of productive citizenship embedded in dominant moral traditions.This version of magic did little to connect the practitioner with a coherent cosmos; it was atomistic, individualized. Nevertheless, it had much in common with more thoroughly animistic beliefs: it often merged esoteric thoughts with everyday things, and it combined a supernatural sense of the cosmos with an intensely practical, even materialistic sense of what magic could accomplish.

Well into the nineteenth century, Americans as well as Europeans consulted astrologers and other custodians of magical lore (known as cunning men or women) for advice on planting and healing as well as relief of trouble in mind. It is possible to see "doctors" like McCrillus and Townsend as a nineteenth-century version of cunning men—appropriating the (comparatively weak) prestige of the medical profession through their use of the ubiquitous honorific, merging that prestige with the older, perhaps more powerful, aura of the sorcerer as well as with popular traditions of herbal healing. But unlike herbal healing, which included many female practitioners, the patent medicine business remained a largely male preserve. Privy to "Oriental" secrets, the medicine man—like ancient cunning men—could claim a special capacity to assist ordinary folk in transcending everyday physical or emotional problems: the pinch of tight shoes, a dose of the blues—not to mention impotence or "that tired feeling." Melding mind and body, patent medicine men joined other heterodox healers in keeping popular animism alive amid the spirit-matter dualism of the dominant culture, as they fed their audience's hopes for self-transformation through magical intervention.[11]

In offering metamorphosis, patent medicine advertisers were making explicit what was implicit and pervasive in many other, more decorous forms of promotion as well, of perfume, jewelry, clothing, household furnishings. By the time Riley hit the road there were still plenty of peddlers about, but more respectable ways of representing goods were available, in smart urban shops or country stores, in department store displays or newspaper advertisements. Nearly all modes of commercial representation involved an ambiguous mix of attractions: the allure of disguise mingled with the threat of deceit, the excitement of sybaritic pleasure with the fear of lost control. By the 1840s and 1850s, a crucial dimension of consumer goods' emotional pull in American culture involved a carnivalization of the psyche—a brief entry into a world brimming with possibilities for self-transformation. This appeal could be overt (as in patent medicine advertising) or discreet (as in promotion of clothing or cutlery as emblems of gentility). Whatever its tone, it suited a mobile, market society: the sense of personal identity was loosening; social distinctions were increasingly based on fungible assets and movable goods rather than land and livestock.

At the same time, the promise of transformed identity posed moral and even epistemological problems for the dominant Anglo-American social code that valued constraint in conduct and clarity in representation. The emerging culture of consumption could hardly be a simple validation of "hedonistic" behavior; it could more accurately be described as a labyrinth of remissions and regulations, centrifugal and centripetal tendencies, attempts to liberate magical powers and stabilize market exchange. This balance of tensions was rooted in the complexity of Protestant tradition, which nurtured an impulse toward release alongside a drive for control.

THE TWO PROTESTANT ETHICS AND THE AMERICAN CARNIVALESQUE

What Weber called the Protestant Ethic was rooted in Calvinist dualism: a solitary soul in a disenchanted universe, yearning for salvation from a sovereign and unanswerable God. There was no point in importuning that temperamental Jehovah. Heaven and earth, spirit and matter, could hardly have been farther apart. The situation was psychologically unsettling. To relieve the pain of relentless self-scrutiny, Weber's Protestant embarked on a frenetic pursuit of his calling, which Luther had redefined to include secular occupations. The consequences were ironic and unintended. The Protestant Ethic provided the psychological justification for the organizational spirit of rational capitalism; a drive toward systematic control of the inner self eventuated in a drive toward systematic mastery of the outer world.

But this was not the only possible reaction to the remoteness of the Calvinist deity. The sociologist Colin Campbell has explored what he calls "the Other Protestant Ethic," which coexisted (and, I would add, interpenetrated) with the Protestant Ethic of self-control. This other ethic flowed from the Augustinian strain of piety, the molten core of emotion often only partly encased by the armor of Puritan theology; it promoted fascination with the ecstatic experience of conversion, the moment when the soul transcended its human limits and fused its identity with God. In other words, this ethic sought to close the gap between earth and heaven through the cultivation of intense inner experience; its emphasis on personal transformation through Christian rebirth exalted a more fluid sense of self than was available under the strict Calvinist dispensation. Emotional excitement was a means of grace. For the many Puritans who veered toward this mystic strain of thought, a state of constant, feverish, spiritual yearning was the sine qua non of salvation. Theologians and moralists, fearing that the rush of heavenly emotion might become an all too human end in itself, sought to contain it in a web of rules; even the account of a conversion experience was required to conform to a precise narrative formula. But as the history of American Puritanism makes clear, narrative structures were unable to contain the drift toward earthly rapture. In various forms, the Other Protestant Ethic has shaped evangelical, romantic, and liberal religious traditions down to the present. It has also seeped into secular cultural forms. And, as Campbell argues, it helped eroticize Anglo-American attitudes toward consumption.[12]

The eroticizing of consumption was a complex and elusive process. In part it arose from a self-defeating pattern of human desire—a pattern that may have been virtually universal and timeless but that resonated especially with the emergent market cultures of the modern West. As early as 1587, Montaigne caught the pattern when he wrote of what he called his "soul-error": "It is that I attach too little value to things I possess, just because I possess them and overvalue anything that is strange, absent, and not mine."[13] This was the dynamic of deprivation at the heart of expanding consumption: purchase brought momentary satisfaction, followed by dissatisfaction and renewed longing.

Protestant emotionalism sometimes came to support a life of longing, whether that support was expressed in evangelical or latitudinarian idioms. As the Anglican divine Isaac Barrow said in 1671, nothing carries "a more pure and savory delight than beneficence. A man may be virtuously voluptuous and a laudable epicure by doing much good." It was only a short step from the the "virtuously voluptuous" man to "the man of feeling," the beau ideal of English and American literary circles during the later eighteenth century. When the man of feeling indulged himself in what his fellow literati called the "the luxury of tears," he participated in an aristocratic cult of sensibility. This was a kind of emotional connoisseurship, a refinement on the "laudable epicure's" arts of taste and consumption.[14]

The Other Protestant Ethic introduced the possibility of a psychological experience of abundance: in the liquid metaphors of conversion, "the outpouring of the spirit" into the more abundant life brought by divine grace. The prayers of the converted came from "the fulness of a heart overflowing with earthly affections, as from a copious fountain," the Reverend Edward Payson wrote in 1830. In time, overflowing fountains came to signify material wealth as well as divine grace. A success manual published in 1854 began with the epigraph "Touch but the Fountain with the Magic Wand of Determination, and the spontaneous flowing will never cease, while you recur to our instructions."[15] Mystic dreams of spontaneously flowing spiritual abundance were translated into the secular language of the marketplace. It may seem a long way from the man of feeling to the modern consumer. But this self-conscious savoring of sentiment—what later generations of cognoscenti would deride as kitsch—would become the heart of many national advertising campaigns in the nineteenth and twentieth centuries.

Both the ecstatic saint and her more genteel relation, the man of feeling, were subversive ideals; they tended to undermine commitments to control, and they seemed to sanctify the quiverings of continuous desire. Like magical thinking, but from within rather than outside the Protestant tradition, antinomian and latitudinarian emotionalism promoted a notion of selfhood more changeable—and more attuned to an experimental attitude, in the realm of goods as elsewhere—than the ethos of mainstream moralism.

Yet the Other Protestant Ethic had this in common with the economic rationality of the Weberian version: it served to direct the human gaze away from the muck of material existence and toward the ethereal realm of the ideal. The savoring of sentiment was consistent with the romantic exaltation of the imagined over the actual—the outlook Keats embodied in "Ode on a Grecian Urn" (1819): "Heard melodies are sweet, but those unheard / are sweeter." Under the aegis of romantic Protestantism, consumption became less a matter of filling one's belly than of looking and longing.[16]

It would not be until the twentieth century that corporate advertisers would routinely combine unfulfilled longings with acts of consumption, seeking to dispel the magic of recently purchased goods through doctrines of stylistic progress and policies of planned obsolescence. But even in the early modern period this dematerializing of desire had begun to shape patterns of purchase. From the early modern consumer's point of view, carnivalesque market fairs specialized in what was "strange, absent, and not mine," and the allure of those exotic goods lay less in the things themselves than in the fantastic possibilities they represented. Peddlers and shopkeepers sought to present sumptuous feasts for the eye, to arrest the shopper's gaze and set up an erotic relationship between consuming subject and desired object. To sustain erotic yearning, fulfillment had to remain fleeting at best.

Religion and commerce combined to redefine abundance in psychic rather than physical terms. Available evidence suggests that early modern consumers may have embraced that dematerialized definition. Apparently they neglected food and shelter in order to purchase fashionable goods. The most careful recent study of preindustrial consumption in England and North America concludes: "Paradoxically, the individual who drank tea in a teacup, wore a printed cotton gown, and put linen on the bed could be the same person who ingested too few calories to work all day and lived in a one-room house." [17]

Undermining elite injunctions about frugality and self-control, the Other Protestant Ethic helped shape the dynamic of deprivation and desire that lay at the heart of the developing commercial culture. Originating in the eighteenth century, the cult of sensibility became romanticized, democratized, and gendered in the nineteenth, as women were assigned sole proprietorship of sentiment. This division of cultural labor reinforced the tendency to link femininity and consumption.

But the romantic exaltation of intense feeling as an end in itself may have had subtler effects as well. It may have combined with Protestant moralism to create an American version of carnivalesque commercial culture. The older European tradition had involved a fluid intermixture of moral and social identities, a celebration of sexuality and violence as inescapable aspects of human experience. The American carnivalesque engaged in similar celebrations but at one remove, vicariously, through furtive glimpses rather than exultant public rituals, and usually with loud insistence on their didactic intent. The printed expression of this attitude was literary sensationalism.

The American reading public was characterized early on by a powerful appetite for sensational fare. By the 1820s and 1830s, American popular literature was rife with scenes of blood-drinking, torture, necrophilia, and child seduction. Sensationalism was a postenlightenment version of the carnivalesque. Calvinist execution sermons had emphasized the universality of evil, the common core of depravity linking the condemned man with the crowd that came to see his hanging; after the spread of romantic and liberal ideologies of human goodness, as the historian Karen Halttunen has perceptively observed, descriptions of violent criminals stressed the abyss of difference separating them from decent ordinary folk. The murderer was no longer a man like any other but a "beast in human form." Even as moralists sought to distance respectable citizens from bestial behavior, purveyors of erotic and violent sensationalism played on their audience's continued fascination with the lower regions of bodily, "animal" existence—or so, at least, their critics charged.[18]

These conflicts were fitfully resolved in the oxymoronic genre the critic David Reynolds has identified as "immoral didacticism." Its didactic intent repeated the strategy that Protestant and bourgeois reformers had brought to bear on European Carnival: they had sought to suppress and contain Carnival where possible and, where not, to isolate a unified, striving self amid the enticements of formlessness and lost control in urban life. To moralists the city was "a horrid recess of filth," as the journalist George Foster attempted to document in New York in Slices (1848)—from the boring, sedentary countinghouse occupations that led lonely and frustrated clerks down the nightmare path of frequent masturbation to the alcohol, drugs, and prostitutes available for cash at any "liquor grocery" or "oyster cellar."[19]

Yet Foster's moralism barely concealed an undercurrent of fascination with opulent sensuality. Consider his description of a particularly elegant cellar:

> This is surely Aladdin's cave that we have stumbled into. On either hand stretches away, mingling and losing themselves in a gorgeous labyrinth of many-colored glass, damask curtains, and shaded lights, a long row of mirrored arcades, festooned with costly blue and crimson silk and wreathed with golden carved work, the interior lined with plate glass, furnished with a luxurious divan of the latest spring pattern, and the walls adorned with exquisite and voluptuous drawings—now a woodcock that might have ruffled the easel of Landseer, and now a half-clad woman who might have glowed beneath the pencil of Brochart.[20]

This exotic vision of abundance brought the cult of sensibility belowstairs, employing the genteel vocabulary of taste—"gorgeous," "exquisite," "voluptuous"—to describe the democratic precincts of an urban saloon.

Foster made the standard rhetorical move, ripping away the veils of luxury to reveal the "libertines, debauchees and gamblers" who used the oyster cellar to initiate unsuspecting young men into the "higher and more seductive mysteries of dissipation." This was the unmasking pattern that typified much didactic sensationalism: the penetration of misleading surfaces to reveal corrupt depths. Amid the shape-shifting of the metropolis, journalists felt an intensified need to expose concealed corruption, but they betrayed an unseemly excitement in the presence of the "filth" they found.

Sensationalism democratized the cult of sensibility and helped reorganize consumption patterns, directing attention from the satisfactions of actual possession to the excitement of anticipated purchase. The exotic goods for sale in the emerging consumer economy carried a carnivalesque charge, as did the peddlers who purveyed them. But the American carnival was involved in the celebration of the flesh more obliquely than its European ancestor had been; its Protestant version of abundance was psychological as well as physical, spectatorial as well as participatory.

The stimulation of fantasy was central to the expansion of the consumer market. By the 1830s and 1840s even the more genteel entrepreneurs began to purvey new sensations along with new goods. Exotica was the stock-in-trade of museum promoters, from Barnum to his backwoods emulators; Barnum's first and most famous estate—itself a gigantic advertisement for his work—was Iranistan, a fabulous "Oriental Villa" built near Bridgeport, Connecticut in 1846 (figure 2.1). The mysterious East had long been associated with luxury goods as well as patent elixirs, and mid-Victorian writers kept that link before the reading public. "India is the Ophir of commerce," a contributor characteristically announced in *Godey's Lady's Book* in 1853. Fashion magazines printed engravings of bare-breasted brown ladies, such as "The Circassian Beauty" in an 1851 issue of *Peterson's*—a kind of pornography made acceptable by geographical and cultural distance. By the 1850s, fashionable clothes themselves were often surrounded by exotic attributes: the Turkish shawl, the Castilian cloak, the écharpe (scarf) Orientale.[21]

The growing popularity of upholstered home furnishings also had exotic implications. Numerous popularizations of the *Arabian Nights* (first translated into English in 1707, but not widely available until the 1830s) made the phrase "magic carpet" a colloquialism and ultimately a cliché. Clichés can reveal embedded patterns of thought: the discourse of commodities was sustaining magical overtones. Even a prudent Scot like the

FIGURE 2.1

P. T. Barnum's estate, Iranistan, engraving, 1846. *Historical collections, Bridge-port (Connecticut) Public Library.*

department store owner A. T. Stewart went with the prevailing fashion in choosing Oriental motifs for the interior of the store he built at Broadway and Tenth Street in New York City in 1863. The store, which replaced an older and dowdier Stewart's a few blocks away, was outfitted (according to *Godey's* observer) with "luxurious hassocks . . . soft persian mats . . . fairy-like frostings of lace draperies." Exoticism had entered the sanctuaries of the proper bourgeoisie.[22]

But this does not mean that Americans were becoming a nation of decadent consumers. Among all classes, anxiety about the accumulation of goods was deep and widespread. The sources of that unease were several and complex. One was simply the elite's fear of upward mobility among the middle and lower classes. But another, more intricate and pervasive, was rooted in the dialectic between the two Protestant Ethics. The Puri-tan–republican moral tradition dominated popular as well as elite consciousness, promoting the common belief that commerce misled men from public good to private gain, setting in motion the slide from civic virtue to social decay. This belief sometimes coexisted uneasily with longings for exotic luxuries, producing mixed feelings about the outward signs of material prosperity.

From the hard-shell republican (and masculine) point of view, exoticism was a symptom of soft "effeminacy." By 1854, Henry David Thoreau was complaining that the railroad car had become no better than the modern drawing room, "with its divans and ottomans, and sunshades, and a hundred other oriental things, which we are taking west with us, invented for the ladies of the harem and the effeminate natives of the celestial empire, which Jonathan [the American] should be ashamed to know the names of."[23] Heated, plush interiors were far more hospitable to the play of erotic fantasy than bare-bones republican simplicity had been.

The conflict between virtue and luxury is well known—at least to the numerous American historians who have studied the Puritan–republican tradition, documenting or debunking its political significance in scores of articles and monographs.[24] What is less well known is how that tradition served as a resource for resolving anxieties about misrepresentation in the marketplace. Ever since the Reformation, the Calvinist and Pietist versions of Protestantism had fostered distrust of theatrical display: salvation depended not on outward observance but on inward experience. Artifice of any kind—in manners, dress, or language—was to be condemned as concealment of the authentic spiritual life within the soul of every believing Christian.

The tension between authenticity and artifice was at the heart of Anglo-American Protestant culture, and the plainspoken "gude-man" was at the center of that culture's moral universe. (A more secular version energized the French Enlightenment.) Prescriptions for communal health involved forthright speech as well as simple living. Ideals of linguistic transparency pervaded republican constitutional debates of the 1770s, prompting demands for "actual" rather than "virtual" representation: legislators, like words, were to be mere vehicles for the intentions of the people who chose them. And calls for plain speech remained a key component of demands for a democratic culture throughout the nineteenth century.[25] Behind the whole plain-speech tradition was a utopian vision of a society where language was unproblematic, where people said what they meant and meant what they said.

AUTHENTICITY VERSUS ARTIFICE

This Protestant discourse of authenticity powerfully reinforced misgivings about consumer goods and the commonest modes of representing them. Indeed, one could argue, following the historian Jean-Christophe Agnew's suggestive analysis, that the Anglo-Protestant tradition of plain speech was an attempt to clarify the ambiguous motives and meanings unleashed when market relations spilled over traditional boundaries and began to pervade English society. In London during the seventeenth and eighteenth centuries, relationships between buyer and seller were increasingly characterized by fluidity, anonymity, and mistrust. Success in the marketplace, for those with something to sell, involved more and more the theatrical manipulation of appearances. As early as 1610, the Jacobean dramatists Thomas Dekker and John Webster could write, "He that would grow damn'd rich, yet live secure / Must keep a case of faces." By 1747, Richard Campbell was writing in *The London Tradesman* that the successful merchant must be "a perfect Proteus, change shapes as often as the Moon, and still find something new" to keep up with the "continual Flux and reflux of Fashion."[26] In anonymous urban environments like that of London and later the American seaboard cities, a variety of observers agreed that the very sense of self could take on a shifting shape.

This destabilizing tendency was reinforced by the emergence of new, more ephemeral modes of representing reality and value. In a developing money economy, paper became a vehicle for fantasy. The proliferation of literary and monetary fictions, novels and banknotes, allowed signifiers to float more easily, to become disembodied from specific objects like flesh or gold. This was the opening for impresarios like P. T. Barnum, who, as his contemporary Aleksandr Herzen said in 1855, "understood the great secret of the age of rhetoric, the age of effects and phrases, exhibitions and advertisements; he comprehended that the most important thing for the contemporary nominalist is the poster!" Herzen was reacting to a swelling trade in images. The middle decades of the nineteenth century saw the transformation of image production into a cottage industry. By the 1850s, chromolithography had become the chief process for mass-producing genre scenes, cartoons, allegorical visions—the various sorts of imagery that were used in trade cards, advertisements, and popular prints of the Currier & Ives variety. Many chromolithographers were German immigrants who set up small shops with a rudimentary division of labor in cities like New York, Baltimore, and Cincinnati; they catered to a diverse audience of farmers, shopkeepers, and middle-class households generally. They drew on a traditional store of images but at the same time sought to be fashionable, up to date, and eye-catching. Among the most successful was Louis Prang (1824–1909), who arrived in New York from Germany in 1850 along with many other liberal exiles in the wake of the failed revolution of 1848. Prang set up shop in Boston in 1856 and was soon doing a brisk trade in prints of American birds and Civil War generals; in the late 1860s he began to mass-produce chromolithographed advertisements for local (and soon national) merchants, hitting on the novel idea of the "stock" trade card: a generic scene that could be stamped with a particular merchant's name and sales message. These were indeed floating signifiers.[27]

Chromolithographers collaborated with popular journalists and novelists in creating the American carnivalesque atmosphere of ever-shifting surface sensations. The impact of proliferating images was intensified by the social conditions of the American metropolis, which a variety of observers believed was having an extraordinarily destabilizing impact on the individual's sense of personal identity. It was not only the anonymity, the sense of being a speck in an amorphous mass of similar specks, but also the mobility, the lack of sustained face-to-face knowledge of one's neighbors and acquaintances, that made for feelings of incoherence. As society became more urban, more anonymous, what Walt Whitman called "the terrible doubt of appearances" became more widespread. In sensationalist novels as well as moral tracts, the metropolis was a place of mystery: characters appeared and disappeared in different guises; nothing was as it seemed; confidence men abounded. The ever-changing plethora of glittering goods and sensations encouraged the suspicion that reality could not be depended on from one moment to the next. The sensationalist American novelist George Lippard captured the connection between psyche and economy in his enormously popular *The Quaker City* (1845), when a character says of urban life: "Every thing is fleeting and nothing stable, every thing shifting and changing, and nothing substantial! A bundle of hopes and fears, deceits and confidences, joys and miseries, strapped to a fellow's back like a Pedlar's wares."[28] The reference to peddlers was revealing: they were bringing the market to the countryside; they embodied and promoted its destabilizing effects.

It made psychological sense, under these circumstances, for moralists in the Puritan tradition to insist on the continuity and transparency of a unified, authentic self—as a norm of ethical conduct if not a description of everyday life. On both sides of the Atlantic, an ideal of linguistic transparency flourished alongside an ethos of self-control; together they constituted a counterpoint to the carnivalesque tendencies that had taken new and more varied forms in the emerging commercial society: the sensuous exoticism associated with proliferating luxury goods, the masque of misrepresentation involved in their sale and use. Distressed by deceit and display, plainspoken moralists aimed to stabilize the centrifugal movement of meanings in cultures unsettled by market exchange. Protestant tradition provided both epistemological and moral ground for unified selves to stand on. But the ground was never really as firm as it seemed; the tradition of antitheatrical asceticism, though powerful, faced external challenges and internal instabilities—particularly in the chaotic cultural setting of the antebellum United States.

THE ANTEBELLUM SETTING:
MAGICAL TRANSFORMATIONS AND
FLUID IDENTITIES

Part of the chaos stemmed from the democratization of Protestant Christianity. By the 1820s, the antinomian and latitudinarian strains of "enthusiastic" religion in the United States had converged in the currents of evangelical revivalism. Charles Grandison Finney and other revivalists were optimistic Arminians: they believed in human beings' capacity to save themselves through choice; the regenerative metamorphosis of conversion was available through human will. But unaided individual effort was often not enough. Finney's "new measures"—particularly the flailing expressiveness of his oratorical style and the looser conversion narrative that became known as the testimonial—were designed to batter sinners' psyches until they cast off the "old self" in disgust and embraced the "more abundant life" promised to the regenerate. Finney and other Arminian revivalists preached a gospel of immanent God and perfectible man. They appropriated the language of the Other Protestant Ethic, describing the experience of conversion (or the later "second blessing" of sanctification) in imagery that implied a liquefaction of the self: the sanctified soul felt "melted . . . in spirit"; the emotional springs of religious faith poured forth "a torrent of pious, humble, and ardently affectionate feelings while our understandings only shape the channel, and teach the gushing streams of devotion where to flow, and when to stop." It was not always easy to distinguish spiritual ecstasy from its more earthly forms; many critics agreed with the Connecticut minister who charged in 1835 that "more souls were begot than saved" at revivals. Even backcountry evangelicals, it appeared, could be "virtuously voluptuous."[29]

By popularizing a pattern of self-transformation that would prove easily adaptable to advertisers' rhetorical strategies, evangelical revivalists like Finney played a powerful if unwitting part in creating a congenial cultural climate for the rise of national advertising. It was not accidental that conservatives like Philip Schaff, writing in 1844, likened revivalists to peddlers: "Every theological vagabond and peddler may drive his bungling trade, without passport or license, and sell his false ware at pleasure. What is to come of such confusion is not now to be seen." Among established elites, fears of cultural "confusion" accompanied the democratization of Christianity as well as the expansion of market exchange.[30]

Revivalists also accommodated magical thinking, not only by promising complete metamorphosis but (as the historian Jon Butler has shown) by appropriating the therapeutic role of the cunning person. When visited by the troubled, the cunning person questioned his clients closely about their personal background before embarking on the occult procedure best suited to the problem at hand; a parallel process characterized the evangelical minister—except he reshaped the problem in a Christian mold, insisting that the anxious seeker's only real concerns were sin and salvation.[31] Even as evangelical religion placed a new set of moral strictures on everyday life, it reinforced hopes of magical self-transformation.

The Arminian revivalists' faith that the individual could effect complete personal change through collaboration with cosmic forces was well suited to the fluid economic conditions of the early nineteenth century. Wealth was increasingly associated with "lucky hits" in real estate or on the stock market rather than with the gradual accumulation of land and livestock. The development alarmed moralists, but seemed inexorable. As early as the 1790s, the Reverend Timothy Dwight was complaining of the speculative tendencies abroad in New York and New England. "In certain stages of society the expectations of enterprising men may with little difficulty, be raised to any imaginable height. Fortunes, they will easily believe, may be amassed at a stroke, without industry or economy, by mere luck, or the energy of superior talents for business."[32] Attempting to circumvent the need for steady work, speculators engaged in a legal form of gambling. A calculating attitude concealed impatient irrationality.

Certainly that was the view of many Protestant critics, who habitually linked speculation with fever, madness, and magic. In 1842, several years after the second major business collapse of the nineteenth century, the novelist Catherine Sedgwick announced:

> The curse of heaven has fallen upon those who make haste to be rich, forsaking toilsome enterprise, patient labour, and the appointed ways of ingenuity and industry for the legerdemain of visionaries and speculators. While the fever lasted, grown up men showed a blind credulity on the one part, and a bold imposture on the other, exceeding the exhibitions of the conjurer's room, where the child believes the flowers have shot up and bloomed instantaneously, without the tedious process of sowing and growing and the slow intervention of earth and water, and where the leaden balls which went into the gun, come out golden guineas. The speculating charlatans slightly varied the trick; they charged with gold and the explosion yielded only sound and smoke. The dupes ought not to be confounded with the conjurers, the deluded with the deluders. The atmosphere was poisoned, and the silly and the wise alike went mad.[33]

While by the 1840s the association of magic with money-getting was commonplace (Marx and Engels would frequently adopt the same rhetorical strategy, beginning in *The Communist Manifesto*), there are also more specific implications in Sedgwick's text. The speculator's magic is represented as an attempt to circumvent natural cycles ("the tedious process of sowing and growing") as well as to avoid hard work; it is in the end merely a failed conjurer's trick, its short-lived persuasive power dependent on the childish credulity of "mad" investors. Sedgwick's was the official view, the one that was enshrined in McGuffey Readers and self-help manuals: only plodding diligence brought lasting success.

But the investors themselves knew better, and occasionally one finds a glimmer of accuracy even in the advice literature. *The Art and Mystery of Making a Fortune* (1854), for example, was an extraordinarily candid (and anonymously authored) antidote to the standard pieties. Ridiculing Poor Richard's maxims, it advocated a sharp eye for the main chance and offered an extended apostrophe to money: "Mighty magician! Does a threadbare reputation or a tarnished character require thy electro-plating influence—blessed existence! thou comest to the aid of the sufferer and coverest him immediately with the garment of injured innocence." The reference to electroplating was a clever allusion to the technical process, only recently devised (in the 1840s), by which cheap pot-metal could be given the appearance of silver or gold. A new alchemy, more flagrantly fraudulent than the old, electroplating captured the plain-speaker's fear that glittering surfaces could be manipulated to conceal corrupt depths (as indeed they were on dinnerware, doorknobs, and other electroplated household goods). The author of *Making a Fortune* went on to prescribe various methods of moneymaking, all of which had a something-for-nothing quality: note-shaving, land speculation, "exhibitions of novel objects," and above all, advertising. The best product—or rather, the best "subject"—to advertise, the author concluded, was patent medicine. It cost virtually nothing to manufacture and multiplied many times over the small initial investment. No one would want to argue that this little pamphlet was typical of antebellum advice literature; what was striking about it was the covert agenda of success it revealed. As the Jacksonian economist Richard Hildreth wrote in 1840, "When speculation proves successful, however wild it may have appeared in the beginning, it is looked upon as an excellent thing, and is commended as *enterprise;* it is only when unsuccessful that it furnishes occasion for ridicule and complaint, and is stigmatized as a *bubble* or a *humbug.*" One can only imagine how many "men of enterprise," who later in life prescribed hard work as the way to wealth, began their careers as the "visionaries and speculators" condemned by Sedgwick. The true prescription for success was articulated succinctly by Captain Simon Suggs, the fictional confidence man created by the humorist Johnson Jones Hooper in the 1840s: "It is good to be shifty in a new country," he said.[34]

It is difficult today to understand just how chaotic economic life was in the early republic, how little impact principles of rationality and order had on market relations. Until 1863, there was no uniform national currency; paper money was issued by commercial banks and even by individual merchants. One could not be sure that any paper money would be accepted as payment for dinner fifty miles from the issuing bank; notes were discounted in accordance with their distance from the bank of issue. Opportunities for counterfeiting were virtually limitless: spurious notes of nonexistent banks, genuine notes with forged signatures, notes of failed banks altered with the names of solvent ones—all these types of commercial paper circulated widely during the first half of the nineteenth century. Moreover, the rapid failure rate of many banks made it possible for the unscrupulous to palm off worthless notes on the uninformed. (A story from the 1850s illustrates the frustration of this potential fraud: Captain Shallcross, a Mississippi boatman, learns of the worthlessness of Atchafalaya bank currency and attempts to unload his supply on an unsuspecting wood-seller. But by the time the Captain has turned the boat around, the wood-seller has learned of the bank's insolvency and will only accept the paper "even up, cord for cord," in exchange for the wood.) Small wonder that there was a brisk trade in periodicals designed to aid in counterfeit detection, or that as late as the 1850s many rural people still preferred barter to cash.[35]

The disordered state of paper currency contributed to a pervasive atmosphere of suspicion, fed by fear of deceptive appearances and shifty identities. The plain-speaker's ideal of social transparency had always devalued external appearances as clues to inner being, but by the 1840s and 1850s, warnings against duplicity had become even shriller. Authors in *Peterson's, Godey's,* and other popular periodicals constantly rang changes on the theme "All is not gold that glitters": the attractive and genteel were constantly exposed as frauds when they were caught unawares, losing a hairpiece in a riding accident or bellowing at a servant behind closed doors. Yet belief in the unreliability of appearances was never complete. The physiognomy, and especially the face, was assumed to contain some clue to the character of the inner man or woman. Phrenology, the "science" of determining character traits from the shape of the subject's head, thrived on that assumption, but so did the equally widespread (if more diffuse) impulse to scrutinize faces for evidence of the sentiments within. (The more exalted form of this belief was Swedenborg's doctrine of correspondences—every natural fact conceals a spiritual fact—which Emerson and the Transcendentalists loosened and popularized.) Increasingly adrift in a world of strangers, the respectable person was advised to look for "the frank and manly countenance" as an alternative to the sinister shifting stare of the confidence man.[36]

Both the virtuosity of the confidence man and the vulnerability of his victim could be explained by reference to a primitive theory of psychological manipulation, the Victorian doctrine of "influence." As this idea played a key role in creating a receptive atmosphere for advertising as well as in shaping advertisers' own assumptions about their audience, it is worth examining in some detail. According to the doctrine of influence, the free-floating urban youth (male or female), disencumbered from family or communal ties, was utterly malleable and susceptible to the wiles of con artists, gamblers, and seducers. The power of influence was exercised through the manipulation of external appearances, particularly the face. The popular novelist George Lippard captured the procedure perfectly in this scene from *The Empire City* (1864):

> As Nameless [his protagonist] felt her gaze upon his pale and wasted features, a strange sensation kindled like liquid fire in his veins. This

sensation was almost inexplicable. It was as though a strange magnetism flashing from the eyes of the unknown woman had possessed his
own being with its power, and for a moment mingled his will in the will
of the beautiful woman.

Lippard's overheated prose typified many such descriptions; influence
often carried an erotic charge.[37]

The origins of the belief in influence are obscure; certainly, as Karen
Halttunen has suggested, it stemmed in part from republican fears of one
person's yielding his autonomy to another, and perhaps as well from the
zymotic theories of disease current in the early and mid–nineteenth century, which held that the mere inhalation of foul vapors could create epidemic sickness. Sinister influence, like cholera, was "in the air" of antebellum cities. But there is no question that these anxieties were exacerbated
by the inchoate sense that unsettled conditions of life had undermined
psychic stability.[38]

The most direct and disturbing manifestation of influence was mesmerism, a practice that came to these shores already bearing overtones of
materialism and libertine sensuality. Franz Anton Mesmer epitomized
American fantasies of the godless Enlightened rogue. His theory of "animal magnetism" claimed to heal bodily and mental ailments by bringing
the patient's "magnetic fluids" to a state of "crisis" and release. Most of his
clients were upper-class women, and he freely admitted employing a corps
of young men to apply "subtle pressures upon the breasts with the fingertips" and to place their hands "in the neighborhood of the most sensitive
parts of the body." American mesmerists were more socially marginal than
the founder but less overtly sexual. Even so, in the anonymous *Confessions
of a Magnetizer* (1845), a Boston man admitted that, having established a
telepathic bond between himself and his (largely female) subjects, he
could not always resist temptation when they "showed themselves willing
to commit indecencies with him." It should come as no surprise that
Nathaniel Hawthorne was horrified when his fiancée proposed visiting a
mesmerist to cure her mysterious (probably psychosomatic) ailments, or
that he defined the "unpardonable sin" as trifling with the affections of the
human heart—in effect, exercising sinister influence. "Magnetism," as the
quotation from Lippard suggests, was often a euphemism for sexual
desire.[39]

Yet there was more to the doctrine of influence than erotic innuendo.
It involved ambiguities that could lead to a variety of interpretations. Particularly in its mesmeric manifestations, it involved surrendering one's will

to another—a loss of conscious control that could only be distressing to apostles of self-reliance. Emerson recoiled at the idea that "an adept should put me asleep by the concentration of his will without my leave" and advised those who wished to avoid manipulation by animal magnetists to "keep away from keyholes." But not everyone was so circumspect: the fluid conception of identity involved in the doctrine of influence could be made to flow in various directions. Evangelical emulators of Finney appropriated the language of influence—often with explicitly mesmeric overtones—to describe their "new measures." One itinerant revivalist, writing from upstate New York in 1837, claimed to be *"recipient and channel of a sensible divine emanation, which he caused to pass from him by a perceptible influence,* as electricity passes from one body to another." The trick for such ministers, as for other moralists, was to catch the errant soul and fix it so firmly in the mold of "character" that more sinister emanations could not shake it loose later.[40]

Despite those hopes, the problem of influence continued to hover over public discourse. After the Civil War, the connotations of influence did become more benign as the sexual dimensions of mesmerism were etherealized into the religious language of mind-cure and the denatured academicism of "suggestion psychology." Under the aegis of the Protestant cure of souls, influence was enlisted as part of a program of holistic regeneration, melding body and mind, transforming mesmerism into a force for good. Indeed, when mesmerism was merged with spiritualism it acquired a redemptive aura as evidence for an afterlife.[41] Yet neither spiritualists nor mesmerists ever shed the taint of charlatanry; as objects of suspicion, they kept fears of sinister influence alive. The popular preoccupation with influence betrayed an anxiety about the fragility of independent selfhood in a society teeming with impostors, any of whom might possess a skillful capacity for masquerade as well as an esoteric store of manipulative psychology. As the century advanced, advertisers fit that profile more and more precisely, no matter how they struggled to escape it by appropriating the newer and more benign connotations of influence.

The concern about influence also pointed to a fundamental problem of representation, one that would continue to affect advertisers and their audiences in the late nineteenth and twentieth centuries: How could one represent value, meaning, or personal identity in a society where all values, meanings, and identities seemed subject to change? The accelerating shift in the basis of wealth, from land to more abstract and fungible assets, made consumer goods more available (and necessary) as vehicles of meaning. Despite the plain-speaker's scorn for the vain fopperies of fashion, by the 1840s and 1850s consumer goods were carrying more and more cultural freight. The new situation provided national advertisers with an unprecedented opportunity.

GOODS AND MEANINGS:
THE DAY OF THE PEDDLER

Most scholars have followed Thorstein Veblen in assuming that the main symbolic meaning embodied in goods—apart from functional use—was a drive for social status. The accumulation of clutter in Victorian homes and the encrustation of objects with ornament have been taken as evidence of a turn away from republican simplicity toward "conspicuous consumption." This view oversimplifies the sellers' representations of the goods and the buyers' motives for acquiring them. Of course fashionable and luxury artifacts constituted an imprimatur of upward mobility, but they had many more complex meanings as well. They signified imaginative participation in a world of exotic, sensuous experience and titillating theatricality, perhaps even a faint and fitful dream of personal transformation. By the 1840s, Orientalism pervaded the exotic visions of abundance put forward by everyone from Barnum to the editors of the ladies' magazines; it was ripe with suggestions of oceanic boundlessness and a return to maternal origins—to a fluid amniotic zone of escape from bourgeois striving.[42] Whether used for social identity or private fantasy, the surplus of meanings embodied in goods pointed toward possibilities for magical metamorphosis in a society where identities were less fixed than official doctrines admitted.

Clothes and other forms of personal adornment, cleverly chosen and worn, had longed possessed the potential both to mask and to flaunt one's flouting of social boundaries. English travelers in Connecticut in the 1790s were impressed that the tavern maids wore earrings and other jewelry, and the historian can only wonder at the significance of this ornament. Whether it was a sign of general affluence or of the triumph of luxuries over necessities, the fashion of wearing earrings also embodied an expression of the female self as a desirable object and desiring subject. By the 1840s and 1850s, the democratization of fashion meant that less affluent as well as wealthy women faced a multiplication of possibilities for reorienting their identities frequently through the use of erotically charged commodities. The world of fashion was pervaded by *glamour*. That word, in its ancient Scottish context, had originally referred to a witch's spell; by the mid-nineteenth century the literal meaning been domesticated, but the magical aura lingered. By assembling the right costume in the right setting, every woman had the chance to acquire her own quasimagical influence—especially over men.[43]

If clothes and furnishings promised transformation of the self's outer layers, patent medicines offered more complete regeneration, in appeals that merged primitivist and exoticist idioms. Almost as soon as they had taken the Indians' land, white settlers began to claim access to their medical lore. During the 1820s, in central New York State, a man who called himself "Professor Popper, the Indian healer" was performing as a fire-eater and magician at a local fair when he decided to reincarnate himself as "Old Doc Hashalew." Hashalew claimed to have distilled the "Secret Arts and Herbal Virtues of the Great Indian Chiefs of the Seneca and Cayuga tribes" into a panacea, which he marketed as Hashalew's Elixir of Life. Dozens of other nostrum manufacturers followed suit, boasting that they had bottled the physical vigor of the Indian or the sexual vitality of the Turk. Orientalism was a particularly useful discourse when impotence was an issue, as Dr. William Raphael demonstrated when he began to market Dr. Raphael's Cordial Invigorant in Cincinnati in 1858. The formula, he insisted, had been secured from Sheik Ben Hadad, a Bedouin king who by the age of 109 had fathered seventy-seven children.[44] The promise of rejuvenation through esoteric knowledge was explicit and pervasive. The cocaine, morphine, heroin, or alcohol in many patent medicines guaranteed at least temporary escape from the Protestant ethos of self-control; the rhetoric and iconography of exoticism fed hopes of self-transformation through magical intervention.

While a broad range of consumer goods began to acquire a strange and alluring aura, a variety of settings fostered the encounter with the exotic. By the mid–nineteenth century, major cities boasted numerous fashionable shops, dry-goods emporia, and even a few department stores. To the extent that a culture of consumption existed in the countryside, it was disseminated by storekeepers and itinerant peddlers.

Among these social types, the peddler was the most revealing forerunner of the national advertiser. He helped set in motion fundamental patterns of purchase, patterns that would intensify and spread in the era of industrial capitalism. To oversimplify a complex process, one could say that the peddler was an early carnivalizer of culture and purveyor of commodity fetishism. Itinerant limners challenged coterie portraiture by making that art form available to a wide audience; book peddlers played a major role in distributing clandestine works deemed morally subversive by the dominant culture: at the beginning of the nineteenth century the biggest underground seller in rural New England, sold almost entirely by itinerant peddlers, was John Cleland's pornographic novel *Fanny Hill; or Memoirs of a Woman of Pleasure.*[45]

The origins of the goods the peddler sold were often mysterious, though this condition applied more to some goods than to others—more to clocks than to tinware, more to perfumes than to fabrics. The most mysterious origins of all were those of patent medicines, whose manufacturers struggled throughout the nineteenth century and into the twentieth to conceal the ingredients of their "secret formulas." (The term *nostrum* derives from "our secret.") But it was not the goods alone that promoted fetishism; it was the combination of the goods and the conditions of their sale.

Unlike the shopkeeper, who sought a place at the center of the village community, the peddler represented the enticements and threats posed by the world beyond local boundaries. He was neither as familiar nor as accountable to his customers as the storekeeper was. (In this he resembled the national advertiser of later years.) The attenuated, unstable relationship between buyer and seller epitomized the most volatile aspects of market exchange.[46]

In the common view, the peddler became a modern trickster, a confidence man who gained his goal through guile rather than strength—particularly through a skillful theatricality. Certainly by the 1830s, the notion of the peddler as entertainer was firmly embedded in the dominant culture. Nathaniel Hawthorne recalled a peddler who came to the Williams College commencement in 1838 and sold his wares by auction: "I could have stood and listened to him all day long," Hawthorne wrote. (There is something almost archetypal about this encounter between a cerebral, silent representative of the emerging print culture and a past master of the ancient arts of oral performance.) Entertainment was a pleasant distraction from the troubling ambiguity of the confidence man's motives.[47]

But in the popular imagination, the peddler was more than an amusing trickster. His mobility and marginality, his rootlessness and strangeness, allowed him to serve as the focus for mythic associations. Nineteenth-century American peddlers occupied the threshold between the village and the cosmopolitan world outside, and also—like the Spanish peddler of *orazioni* on the Florentine square in 1509 (see chapter 1)—between nature and the supernatural. In the tradition of that fire-eating Spaniard, many successful peddlers of lightning rods offered explicitly to serve as mediators between powerful heavenly forces and puny human beings.

More often the peddler's mythic associations were expressed in less direct ways. Like the gypsy crews, strolling actors, and other itinerants who sauntered across the countryside in the antebellum era (and like Riley's medicine show later), the peddler brought spectacles of Oriental splendor to provincial audiences; indeed, the "sauntering" aspect of these itinerants recalled familiar ideas of a spiritual journey or quest—at least to Thoreau, who claimed that the word derived from *saun terre*, holy land, and was used to describe pilgrims en route to the Near East in the Middle Ages. The peddler could seem an emissary of the miraculous in more concrete ways as well. Like the traditional conjurer multiplying rabbits, doves, or scarves, the peddler opened his pack and presented a startling vision of abundance. In Clement Clarke Moore's "A Visit from St. Nicholas" (1823), Santa Claus "looked like a peddler just opening his pack." The peddler's supernatural aura could also have less reassuring aspects. Peddlers were central figures in dozens of the ghost stories that proliferated during the antebellum era; in the winter of 1848, in a remote farmhouse in upstate New York, the ghost of a murdered peddler was the first apparition to contact the Fox sisters, who went on to play a major role in promoting the ferment of Spiritualism, a mass religious movement dedicated to crossing the threshold between this world and the next.[48]

John Bernard, a British traveler who spent the years 1797–1811 in the United States, described the archetypal moment when a peddler arrives in a bucolic Virginia valley. It is sunset and all labor has ceased on the plantation; the cows are wandering home, the children are playing about in the yard, the slaves are laughing aloud in their doorways.

> Look at the group and you would take them for a community of Moravians, with all enemies pardoned and all cares forgotten; when suddenly a pedestrian is seen wandering down the hill, his legs, in the slanting sunbeams, sending their shadows half a mile before him. By his length of staff he might be taken for a pilgrim, but the sprawl of his walk awakens anything but sacred associations. Gradually . . . suspicions are excited; and at length one who may have suffered somewhat more than the rest, perhaps, from the endemic [sic] realizes its symptoms and exclaims, "I'll be shot if it ain't a Yankee!" At these words if there is not a general rout, or springing-up and banging-to of doors, it

must be because their faculties are prostrated by the surprise, and they lie spell-bound, as cattle are said to do on the approach of the anaconda.[49]

It would be foolish to take such a self-consciously literary passage literally. Indeed, its chief interest lies in its literariness, in the ways that Bernard uses literary conventions that framed perceptions of the peddler (and later the advertiser) for decades to come. He begins by invoking a scene of pastoral peace and plenty, with religious overtones; even the peddler might at first be mistaken for a pilgrim. But it quickly becomes apparent that his intentions are anything but pious; his "length of staff" has phallic as well as spiritual connotations. He is, it develops, a deceptive and menacing intruder with a nearly mesmeric capacity to fix the buyer's attention and hold it until he makes a sale, then to be off with mysterious alacrity to the next village or plantation. It is the primal scene in the drama of capitalist "modernization": the rootless representative of cosmopolitan values penetrates the pristine organic community, tempting it with glittering wares, disrupting its rhythms of life, and transfixing its credulous inhabitants with his hypnotic powers of "influence." The point is not that this is precisely the way it happened, but that this story composed a set of images which powerfully influenced conventions of representing commerce for years to come. The drama of modernization could be viewed, of course, in other, more upbeat, ways; national advertisers would systematize them in the latter half of the nineteenth century. But the cultural patterns surrounding that primal scene—the verbal and visual forms available for understanding it—would remain resilient. The conflict between rural and cosmopolitan persisted and often intensified when the Yankee crossed cultural or regional barriers, bringing his calculating "notions" into conflict with the folkways of Pennsylvania Germans or backcountry Virginians.

Peddlers had much in common with ancient cunning men as well as with the evangelical ministry (the cunning men of the Lord). Peddlers flocked to the fringes of revival meetings, relying (as the revivalists did) on "influence," dispensing personal advice and—particularly if they had mysterious elixirs to sell—the promise of magical transformation. Like itinerant revivalists, peddlers kept on the move, offered a special appeal to women, and employed a rhetorical style that combined exhortation with the invocation of testimonials from the saved. From Hooper's Simon Suggs to Mark Twain's Beriah Sellers, humorists presented the confidence man as preacher, and vice versa. To the humorists, the peddler and the preacher both mediated between natural and supernatural, evoking mistrust, excitement, and wonder. Fitz-Greene Halleck caught some of those ambiguities in his poem "Connecticut" (1819), when he referred to

> . . . a few apostates who are meddling
> With merchandise, pounds, shillings, pence, and
>   peddling
> Or wandering through the southern counties, teaching
> The ABC from Webster's spelling book;
> Gallant and godly, making love and preaching,
> And gaining by what they call "hook and crook"
> And what the moralists call "over-reaching,"
> A decent living. The Virginians look
> Upon them with as favorable eyes
> As Gabriel on the devil in Paradise.[50]

Here the peddlers are "apostates," even devils, but also "gallant and godly," all within the space of a few lines. The poem reveals how, like the mythic emblems of Lucifer or Hermes, the image of the peddler could express the deepest contradictions in the wider culture.

Like Bernard's account of the peddler entering the Virginia valley, Halleck's poem suggests how perceptions of the peddler could vary depending on regional or ethnic circumstances. It is "the Virginians" who are particularly prone to demonize the peddler as a meddling Yankee. Folklore tended to label all pre–Civil War peddlers as either Yankees (early on) or Jews (after the 1830s). Both groups were proverbially rootless and conniving avatars of market exchange, aggressively penetrating the countryside, provoking both anxiety and fascination. Through the 1830s, the two groups were interchangeable archetypes.

After that decade, as old-stock Protestants settled into more established businesses, German Jews became a more palpable presence in peddling and its lore. Ancient prejudice made the Jew a natural focus for anxieties about the evanescence and unreliability of commercial exchange. As one author claimed in the *Cyclopedia of Commercial and Business Anecdotes* (1864), the Jews in flight from France to Lombardy during the reign of Philip Augustus (1180–1223) "discovered the means of substituting impalpable riches for palpable ones, the former being transmissible to all parts without leaving behind them any trace of where they had been." The same lack of accountability characterized peddlers; popular assumptions tended increasingly to conflate their mobility and marginality with their

Jewishness. "The Jews are proverbially a restless, roving class," announced Luke Shortfield, the hero of John Beauchamp Jones's *The Western Merchant* (1850). "The Shylocks prefer to be on navigable streams, where it is always convenient for them to take passage for 'parts unknown,' should their necessities or indications render it expedient for them to do so." Antebellum imagery presented the Jew as a liminal figure, shifty as the Yankee and even more exotic. "These wonderful people bear the impress of their Oriental origin even to this day," the novelist Joseph Holt Ingraham wrote in 1860. In physical appearance and social behavior, the Jewish peddler epitomized the commercial arts of the mysterious East. Beginning with Monk Lewis's *The Monk* (1796), as Edgar Rosenberg has observed, the literary Wandering Jew was gradually transformed from an exemplar of Christian doctrine to "a black magician whose sorcery was interesting on secular grounds." The peddler was a Wandering Jew with a pack on his back, promising deliverance from everyday monotonies through the power of purchase; he was also a Shylock who posed the constant threat of fraud. As the carnival moved to the periphery of market society in the Protestant United States, the marginal Jew was transformed from victim to embodiment of carnivalesque impulses.[51]

Whatever his ethnic background, the peddler became a lightning rod for the anxieties of a developing market society. In a world of shifting identities, fraudulent representations, and frequent changes of status, the encounter between the peddler and his prospective customer was both exciting and disturbing. Its implications were explored in a variety of expressive forms.

The most common form was humor. Peddler humor was of a piece with the humbugs and hoaxes that pervaded popular culture during the early nineteenth century; trickery became a staple of jokes in the emerging entrepreneurial society. An example from rural Illinois in the 1850s concerns a Yankee peddling a patent medicine called Balm of Columbia: "good for the hair, and 'assistin' poor human natur,' as the poet says." He sells a one-dollar bottle to the sheriff, who then demands to see his license. The peddler displays an impressive document, which satisfies the sheriff. The sheriff, having no use for the Balm of Columbia, sells it back to the peddler for 25 cents. The Yankee then accuses the sheriff of peddling without a license, files a complaint at the next village, and the sheriff is fined eight dollars. The tale concludes that "you might as well try to hold a greased eel as a live Yankee." There is a familiar pattern here: the peddler as liminal trickster, subverting established authority, mocking its pretensions. In some ways, the pattern may have been reassuring to people caught up in an uncertain and often threatening business environment: one implication of the joke is that the ordinary man can acquire control over apparently superior powers, through judicious application of craft and cunning. If the peddler's victim was an ordinary Jonathan (rather than a local authority figure), then the import of the humor could be more unsettling. In those cases, what the historian Neil Harris has called "the operational aesthetic" might come into play: worries about the humbug's motives could be displaced by preoccupation with his technique. But hostility could never be altogether suppressed. It was no accident that New England folk usage defined a skunk as an "essence peddler," or that many folktales told of peddlers being murdered by their cheated customers, then coming back to haunt the killers. Peddler humor betrayed aggression and fear as well as assurance.[52]

Perceptions of trickery were ambiguous enough; what may have been even more disturbing was the tendency to see selling as seduction. From the late eighteenth century on, many observers agreed that the peddler (like the evangelical preacher) addressed his appeal especially to women. Not that they all responded favorably. Rip Van Winkle's wife "broke a blood vessel in a fit of passion at a New England peddler." But many found the peddler's charms seductive. John Dunton, a roving bookseller in New England, stated in 1811 that a virtuous woman in those parts was generally defined as "one who did not go to fairs in order to meet with chapmen [peddlers]."[53] Even after the rise of *Godey's* and *Peterson's* during the 1830s and 1840s, many women in more remote districts depended on peddlers as fashion advisers.

It was a situation calculated to arouse the ire of the plainspoken husband, who might accuse his wife of mistaking glitter for gold. The triangular relationship of husband, wife, and peddler shaped many depictions of purchase, as in "The Scotch Pedlar," a poem published in *Godey's* in 1841. A peddler arrives in a "secluded Highland glen" with his "tempting wares" on display:

> *Those muslins fine and showy ginghams,*
> *And then that box of gilded thingums.*

So long has he puffed the merits of his goods that "the knavish elf / Has turned believer of himself." Alas, he is a dealer in "bright, but evanescent things."

Those flaunting flowers are born to die
Those colours gay are made—to fly.
When alkalis have spent their power,
You look, and where's the gorgeous flower?
Where all those colours softly blended?
Alas! their short-lived reign is ended;
Those hues, so fair to look upon,
Will, like the Pedlar's self—be gone!

The peddler's own presence is as fleeting as the colors of his goods.

The wife is taken in by the peddler's "wheedling ways," but not the "gude-man" of the house: he is a man of practical knowledge, "gleaned from Nature's open volume . . . Spread wide in market-place and stall / Where chapmen mingle, one and all." (By 1841, even from this critical view, the marketplace has become part of "Nature.") He "stands no fooling."

His hand is on his purse, aware
That danger's nigh; he holds it there.
And from his action it is plain
He means that it shall there remain.

The anthropological and etymological connection between purse and vulva suggests that the rivalry between the husband and the peddler is sexually charged. The poem concludes with the wish that the American educated classes had the gude-man's plain common sense:

In these hard days of banks and bubbles
Of monetary cares and troubles,
When folks, awakening from their dreams,
Of mighty Eldorado schemes,
Blush, when too late, at their confiding
In things that have no sure abiding,
But in the course of one brief day,
Take eagles' wings, and flit away!

From this view, the wife, like the investor, pins her hopes on airy nothings; the peddler's baubles are no more substantial than the speculator's bubbles.[54]

Nevertheless, those glittering goods had an irresistible appeal. The peddler was not only a potential poacher on what the husband conceived to be his private sexual preserve, but also a participant in the mysterious power of influence. Like the evangelical minister and that other itinerant confidence man, the mesmerist, the peddler seemed particularly adept at influencing women. If he sold patent medicine, he also resembled the mesmerist in his access to hidden lore; if he sold clothes, perfume, or jewelry, he dealt in glamour and "fascination"—another word that originally referred to magic spells. While there is no question that by the 1840s, belief in spells was waning, the peddler's brand of influence still possessed powerful connotations; at its worst it could even promote a kind of addiction. That was suggested by "The Banishment of the Peddlers," a poem by Ann Porter published in *Godey's* in 1848—deep enough into the era of German Jewish peddling to contain a harsh note of anti-Semitism. The poem tells the story of a small town where the ladies decide to boycott the shopkeepers until they refuse to sell any more liquor. All but one yield.

> *Ladies, said he, you know full well,*
> *That peddlers haunt this place,*
> *And for their knick-knacks take your cash,*
> *A low and vulgar race.*

> *But if you will refuse to trade*
> *With this same Jewish clan*
> *I'll quit the sale of spirits now*
> *Nor sell a dram again.*

Though "the ladies had some feeling for / These men of heavy packs," they bow to the will of the "brave man": peddlers and liquor alike are banished from the village. The poem dramatizes a developing social conflict between established Protestant retailers and itinerant Jewish peddlers; it is not consumption per se, but consumption from a particularly "influential" source, that is equated with addiction to alcohol. In suggesting that equation, "The Banishment of the Peddlers" evoked the fear that without proper boundaries shopping could undermine self-control; it also identified the act of purchase as an occasion for gender conflict. The proverbial male distrust of female extravagance combined with the sexually charged intervention of the peddler to reinforce the triangular imagery of consumption.[55]

That imagery has persisted down to our own time: selling is still equated with seduction, advertisers with seducers, women with their prey. The resilience of that triangular pattern may account for some scholars' current tendency to count participation in market exchange as a force for women's liberation. From that vantage, the peddler—a particularly fascinating representative of market exchange—might be seen in his trickster guise as an enemy of patriarchal authority; to the isolated rural wife, he points the way out of the confining farmhouse and into a more cosmopolitan world, where women can assert a separate sense of self through personal adornment and display. The problem with this view is not that it is entirely false but that it is culture-bound and schematic. It assumes that female autonomy is possible only in an urban setting, overlooking (for example) the independent cast of mind shown in many Midwestern farm women's diaries. It overlooks the possibility that the female consumer could simply be exchanging one set of male masters for another: rural patriarchs for urban tastemakers. And it ignores women's well-justified distrust of the geographic and financial instabilities induced by the male pursuit of success in a money economy, particularly the fear of separation and loss. Marriage was a traumatic prospect not only because it required submission to the will of a man who might be a dissolute wretch or a demented financial schemer, but also because it often meant permanent departure from family and friends. The liberation promised by participation in market exchange could be exciting but also troubling. So it should not be surprising that women often approached the world of fashion and consumption with profound uncertainty.[56]

And one can find similar confusions among men. As the women's magazines were constantly remarking, men indulged their taste for cigars, wine, and stag outings as often as women fell for clothes and furnishings: profligacy was in the eye of the beholder. More important, the experience of separation, home-leaving, and individuation may have promoted at least as much anxiety among men as among women. In developing patterns of male socialization, the expectation of success and the threat of failure were continuous and demanding. The larger point is that both sexes were attracted by the excitement of market exchange, repelled by its disorienting effects.[57]

The fundamental fear, as "The Banishment of the Peddlers" suggested, was that without proper boundaries consumption could undermine self-control. Participation in market exchange, given its associations with avarice and exotic sensuality, posed powerful temptations. The nightmare vision of Victorian moralists was that the self's moral and intellectual gyroscope would spin out of control as it entered the magnetic field of market relations: the pursuit of personal transformation in a fluid money economy would lead to madness and death. Recall Catherine Sedgwick's charge that during the speculative fever of the 1830s, "the atmosphere was poisoned, and the silly and the wise alike went mad." Popular fiction confirmed the threat, as the mad speculator became a stock figure. An 1858 *Godey's* story, for example, introduced a Mr. Brandon who, "in the reckless spirit of the age, had entered speculation after speculation until success had made him mad; and when failure had met him he still madly persisted until inevitable ruin stared him in the face." Women risked the same fate by entering the realm of fashion. A *Peterson's* editorial of 1866 presented an imaginary conversation between a doctor and another male observer at a fashionable ball; their decorous exchange is frequently interrupted by the screeching "mad laugh" of a lovely and elegant young matron—the most fashionably dressed woman in the room, and also the wittiest (perhaps the most powerful as well, and the most threatening to the men who edited *Peterson's*). The doctor has a hunch he detects insanity in that laugh and, sure enough, after her husband's death in a warehouse accident six months later, the woman has to be packed off to an asylum. The quest for social brilliance could be as perilous as the speculative plunge, sapping one's resources, leaving one vulnerable to psychic as well as financial collapse.[58]

The task, for leaders of the emergent American bourgeoisie in the mid-nineteenth century, was to control the impact of market exchange on culture and psyche. Of course it was not a task they deliberately set themselves, but it was one the importance of which they implicitly understood. Consumer goods carried subversive implications; they promised imaginative transport across the threshold of everyday life to a world of exotic, sensuous abundance. (The magical resonances may have been particularly pronounced when the goods were marketed by figures like the itinerant peddler.) Through a wide variety of means, bourgeois cultural leaders—judges, journalists, ministers and other moralists—sought to contain the centrifugal energies of market exchange.

CHAPTER 3

The Stabilization of Sorcery

How does a group sustain a solid ideal of selfhood in a solvent social setting? By creating an agreed-upon, "commonsense" vision of reality, by certifying certain modes of perception, certain idioms of representation, and discrediting others. The middle and upper classes in the antebellum United States, turning to their own Protestant ethos, elaborated the distrust of artifice and renewed the discourse of authenticity. They created an ideal of unified, controlled, sincere selfhood—a bourgeois self—as a counterweight to the centrifugal tendencies unleashed by market exchange. They articulated that ideal in several idioms that we have come to think of as "bourgeois" or "Victorian"—secular versions of the plain-speech tradition, which served to quiet moral or epistemological doubts and eased the transition to a developed commodity civilization.

IDIOMS OF CONTROL:
SINCERITY, RATIONALITY, MIMESIS

The ideal of sincerity, stemming mainly from Protestant preoccupations, gained new rhetorical force from romantic literary conventions that counterposed the simple private self against the evasions and corruptions of public life. In the mid-nineteenth-century United States, one effective vehicle for popularizing romanticism was the sentimental idiom of domesticity. From the viewpoint of domestic ideologues, the bourgeois home was the place where a man could let his guard down, "be himself" without concern for the pomp of worldly circumstance; it was also the nursery of sincere human relations, sheltered from the corruptions of society, where a woman could (had to) immerse herself in caring for plainspoken children. Domestic sentimentalism was an unstable brew: it blended self-control and plain speech, republican ideals of civic virtue and romantic ideals of conjugal love. It was aimed at men as well as women, and it reflected some of the most powerful emotional needs of an expanding entrepreneurial society.[1]

In the utopian literature of domesticity, home was a stable, secure realm where personal relations were characterized by basic trust. It was everything, in short, that the mobile, shifting world "out there"—the American society that Charles Dickens saw as being pervaded by "universal mistrust"—was not. The great insight of domestic ideologues was that they sensed the psychological imbalance at the heart of the consumer marketplace: the dynamic of deprivation and desire behind the mobility and misrepresentation. Moralizing tales sought to combat widespread discontent by presenting stock cautionary figures: the status-striving matron who was "never contented long" in her pursuit of possessions and social approbation; the "fair and generous-hearted boy" who allowed his vaulting ambition to transform him into a "hard-featured man of the world," as in a *Godey's* story from the 1850s. Attempting to still the restlessness in men as well as women, sentimentalists preached that "contentment is better than wealth," as Timothy Shay Arthur wrote in 1853. (Arthur was a temperance advocate and prolific author of advice literature, notably *Ten Nights in a Barroom and What I Saw There*.) The gospel of contentment was the sentimental alternative to the quest for accumulation; its doctrines were articulated from pulpits, in women's magazines, and (it was hoped) by the hearthside as well. In the sentimental view, mothers, teachers, and other moralists could provide a more humane version of influence than the incitements offered by peddlers and other early advertisers—an inoculation against the epidemic of discontent, rather than an exacerbation of it.[2]

The gospel of contentment, despite its frequent vapidity, suggested a genuine alternative to the individualist striving of the dominant culture. Though men and women alike participated in the sentimental idiom, the attitudes it promoted were those conventionally assigned to the feminine sphere: an acknowledgment of one's own dependence on other people as well as on the natural world; a tendency to cultivate a nurturant relation to the universe. It was not accidental that horticulture was among the household arts recommended by domestic ideologues like Lydia Sigourney.

"The lessons learned among the works of Nature are of particular value in the present age. The restlessness and din of the rail-road principle, which pervades its operations, and the spirit of accumulation which threatens to corrode every generous sensibility, are modified by the sweet friendships of the quiet plants," she wrote in 1840. From this popularized Wordsworthian view, the land was the ground of life, not a commodity to be turned into an abstraction (money). The work of Annette Kolodny has demonstrated that this outlook was not confined to genteel journalists, that it was part of a broader, gendered pattern of perception in nineteenth-century American culture. When they confronted the American landscape, men and women often spoke different languages: if men feared a devouring Mother Nature or desired to possess a "virgin land," women were inclined to peaceful coexistence—they tended to be gardeners, in metaphor and actuality. The uprooted East Coast women described by Kolodny, preserving cuttings from their gardens en route to Missouri or California, embodied a nurturant alternative to the stance of domination. The gospel of contentment sometimes suggested a similar alternative.[3]

Yet a fundamental irony remained. Home was portrayed as a haven from market-driven behavior, a sacred space with nearly sacramental significance, yet it was also increasingly the place one had to leave en route to responsible adulthood. Home-leaving, as the historian Rodney Olsen has argued, became the central psychological fact of many Americans' lives during the early nineteenth century. At various stages in the life cycle, home-leaving was prospect, experience, and memory. It could be exhilarating but also traumatic—or at least painful enough to make the sentimental vision of the vine-covered cottage, the old homeplace, seem appealing. Judging by the available evidence, many of the men and women who created and sustained the domestic ideal led rootless lives, sometimes by choice, more often by economic or marital necessity. One thinks of Harriet Beecher Stowe, following her husband's ministerial career from one makeshift household to another, locked in theological battle with her own father (also a minister), creating the most influential nineteenth-century brief for domestic harmony, *Uncle Tom's Cabin*. Authors like Stowe and innumerable lesser lights idealized a pastoral vision of home from the standpoint of mobile, metropolitan exile. It may be possible that the extraordinary resilience of the domestic ideal owes something to the common psychic experience of both its creators and its audiences: the trauma of home-leaving in a society that increasingly required the severing of family ties as a prerequisite for adulthood. I am not suggesting that "separation anxiety" was peculiar to nineteenth-century America, or to modern market societies; I am suggesting that it acquired a special emotional charge under the chaotic, expansive conditions of the nineteenth-century American economy. And one of the results of that development was the creation of a utopian vision of pre-oedipal wholeness centering on the domestic household.[4]

The idea that the private home could be cordoned off from the corruptions of the public sphere was not entirely fantastic; the bonds of dependence between mother and child resisted reduction to the spurious equivalencies of money. Nevertheless, even domestic ideologues acknowledged that the home could constantly be invaded by the corrosive powers of cash. In popular fiction and advice literature of the mid–nineteenth century, few scenes were more devastating (or more frequently invoked) than the forced auction of household goods—the penalty for extravagant speculation or consumption. As a contributor told *Ladies' National Magazine* readers in 1847, human heartlessness and selfishness were never more apparent than "in a house whose Lares and Penates have been ruthlessly tipped from their pedestals—whose 'broken tea cups wisely kept for show' are turned cracked side out—whose make-shifts are made public, and whose whole nakedness is uncovered, in pursuance of the auctioneers' motive of a sale." Even women push carelessly through, and the person who "stops to think of the bright and happy faces which smiled when . . . the curtains were declared to be match for the carpet" is ridiculed as a "sentimentalist." Everything at an auction was businesslike: "Business is selfishness reduced to rule; and its code . . . is a system of excuses for indifference to the finer feelings of which the hearthstone is, or should be the center and the seat."[5]

The jarring juxtaposition of utilitarian calculation and "finer feelings" was a characteristic and often powerful ploy in sentimentalist rhetoric. Dickens was a master of it. But the writer's other rhetorical move—the representation of the house as a respectable personage "whose make-shifts are made public, and whose whole nakedness is uncovered"—suggested some of the ambiguities in the domestic critique of consumer culture. The house was in effect like a lady of fashion forced to appear in public without corset or cosmetics. The "broken tea cups wisely kept for show" pointed to the role played by the assemblage of domestic artifacts in the display of respectable status. It was not always easy to distinguish between household goods that had sacramental significance and those that were merely props for fashionable performance. So even the home, that alleged sanctuary of sincerity, was at bottom unreliable. The sentimental idiom alone was an insufficient source of stabilization.

But other linguistic and epistemological resources were available, and one of the most important was the developing discourse of legal rationality. If people were forced to honor their agreements by submitting them to a universal, objective standard of legality, then perhaps they would move a step closer toward the ideal of social transparency: the plain-speaker's utopian vision of a sincere society. The effect of antebellum law, whether common or contract, was to create a network of interlocking responsibilities and relationships—particularly in matters of credit and debt. This was the only way one could institute what the historian Thomas Haskell has called an "ethic of promisekeeping" in an economy characterized by multiple and fluctuating mediums of exchange, with transactions occurring over vast geographical areas.[6]

But some transactions were more easily regulated than others. Unlike drummers who called on the same clients year in and year out, most peddlers could slip through the network of legally defined relationships; they bought in cash, sold in cash, and kept moving. So they drew special attention from lawmakers, who sought to ensnare them in the same web of responsibilities that more settled salesmen faced. Laws regulating peddlers were expressions of a broader legal–rational idiom that was designed to make market relations more predictable and accountable.[7]

By the 1820s nearly all the Northeastern states had passed laws requiring peddlers to procure licenses and prohibiting them from trafficking in foreign goods. Connecticut's was frankly named "An Act to Suppress Hawkers, Pedlars, and Petty Chapmen." The success of these statutes was mixed, but court records indicate that they worked at least some of the time. In Plymouth, Connecticut, for example, on May 16, 1832, a peddler named Alvah Merriam made the mistake of answering yes when Jonathan Andrews asked him if he had any Italian silk. Andrews and several other townsfolk filed a complaint against Merriam, and $295 worth of his "goods, wares, and merchandise" was seized by the sheriff. The State Supreme Court upheld the seizure. The following year in Douglas, Massachusetts, Moses Stephens was caught going about on foot selling gold "ear-knobs" to the local women. Massachusetts law prohibited peddlers from selling foreign goods as well as a set list of U.S.-made items, including indigo, feathers, books, tracts, playing cards, lottery tickets, jewelry, and essences. The question before the court was: Did gold ear-knobs count as jewelry? The court decided they did.[8]

To say that these legal actions were efforts to control a chaotic marketplace is merely to begin unpacking their significance. The question is, who was controlling whom and why? Local retailers were among the most obvious sources of hostility to peddlers. During the 1840s and 1850s, *Hunt's Merchants' Magazine* pursued an agenda that looks very much, in retrospect, like an attempt to stabilize the marketplace. *Hunt's* regularly counterposed "the craft and cunning, the shrewd overreaching, and the inordinate grasping of the peddler" against the "the principles of the high-minded merchant." With the peddler, "trade becomes a trick, and mercantile enterprise a game," the magazine warned in 1848. From *Hunt's* view, peddling lacked the gravity and honesty the magazine wanted to associate with business. In 1852 the editors warned their readers against peddlers, offering a cautionary tale about how "one of these wandering Jews," recently arrived from Germany, sold a harried and unsuspecting businessman several yards of silk for far more than it was worth. Upon discovering the deception, the businessman resolved never again "to patronize a peddler, but to extend his patronage to those good tax-paying citizens who have a local habitation and a name."[9] Conflating Jewishness with geographical and moral shiftiness was a time-honored anti-Semitic gambit. Regulation of itinerants was in part a legitimate response of locally rooted merchants who wanted to build up "custom" through service and reliability, but also in part a campaign of established WASP elites to exclude potential rivals by making dubious claims of gentility and morality.

The laws regulating peddlers were efforts to promote business honesty, but they may also have embodied an effort to contain the carnivalesque meanings of goods. Certainly Massachusetts's prohibited list of U.S.-made goods indicated a distrust of potentially subversive frivolity or sensuality. The ban on foreign goods may have been simply a gesture designed to protect home manufactures, but one cannot discount the possibility of a xenophobic reaction against the psychic threat posed by the exotic and strange. When Southern states began to regulate peddlers, the laws were aimed as much against Yankee notions as against European products; a Kentucky law of 1859, for example, forbade the peddling of foreign goods—and defined "foreign" goods as those made out of state. Further, the prevalence of Jewish surnames among peddlers brought to court suggests that ethnic as well as regional antagonisms could sharpen a xenophobic defense of the local community.[10]

The overall effect of these laws is difficult, if not impossible, to gauge. Certainly many itinerant peddlers were stopped in their tracks, either by the laws or by their own desires for respectability (or both). In a sense they followed *Hunt's* prescription. They became complaisant shopkeepers, moving their transactions from the open road to the more confined spaces of the department store, and from the instability of haggling to the comparative predictability of the one-price system. That was the path followed by many peddlers, such as A. T. Stewart and R. H. Macy, who settled into retail trade.[11]

Established local elites, using the legal–rational idiom of the law, created a pattern of constraints on peddlers' transactions. But when one thinks of legal-rationality as a mode of discourse rather than merely a set of institutional controls, the subtler uses of the idiom begin to be more apparent. Legal-rationality promised epistemological as well as institutional control over the marketplace; it seemed to offer a transparent, objective mediation between seller and buyer—a universalist standard to which either could appeal. Yet in practice, legal-rationality was more likely to be turned to account by the seller, who, if he was a skillful enough rhetorician, could use the conventions to create another mystifying form of commercial representation. Objectivity could become opacity; archaic legalese could reassure the rubes.

We will probably never know the full significance of documents like the elaborate contracts drawn up by the Cleveland Lightning Rod Company, which warranted to protect the buyer's property "from damage by Lightning for ten years from this date [September 29, 1869], subjected to the following conditions." In this as in other lightning rod contracts, the conditions included installing and maintaining the lightning rods according to the manufacturer's specifications; the company—or the lightning rod man operating on his own who might call himself a "company"—could easily allege incorrect installation or maintenance to escape responsibility. On the other hand, the contracts may sometimes have been genuine, may sometimes have provided more than psychological security for the buyers.[12]

In lightning rod advertising, the legal–rational idiom could also slide into the scientific; both could be considered variants of Cartesian dualism, examples of the mentality Weber called "instrumental rationality." Some documents merged legalism and scientism. The guarantee offered by the American Lightning Rod Company of Erie County, Pennsylvania, on May 12, 1865, stated "We hereby guarantee the Lightning Rod we have this day put up for Amanda Ingalsbe to be of good material and put up substantially, and upon scientific principles, and to protect the buildings from damage by fire caused by Lightning, or damage by Lightning." Eliza-bethan archaism was yoked to legalistic precision and a vague invocation of "scientific principles." In other ads for the devices, though, a devotion to "scientific principles" could dissolve into a kind of manic empiricism—a flurry of "scientific Facts" and professorial testimonials. Some advertisers understood the need to emphasize the conductive properties of the rod, though they still assumed that what it conducted was "electric fluid." Oth-ers, such as the Lyon Mfg. Co. of New York, were better informed. Lyon sold Otis's patent lightning rods ("The only method of absolute protection against Lightning, as demonstrated by science and experience"), and in a promotional pamphlet of 1858 included a learned, lengthy testimonial from Horace Mann, the education reformer, and a shorter one from Joseph Henry, a founder of the Smithsonian Institution. A dash of scien-tific legitimacy could sometimes prove a potent ingredient in legal–ratio-nal discourse.[13]

But only sometimes. At midcentury, scientific authority was still too widely disputed, the scientist too easily confused with the sorcerer, for a scientifically-flavored discourse to provide more than a weak foundation for cultural stability. If it worked at all it was in the remotely related form of an instrumentalist emphasis on technique and professional expertise. Professionalism emerged as a means of structuring market chaos by weed-ing out charlatans and elevating disinterested knowledge over the cash nexus. But an appeal to technique could be merely a form of mystification.

Itinerant portraitists, for example, sought to appropriate the prestige of technical knowledge without revealing trade secrets. They claimed eso-teric skills and used arcane devices (like the camera obscura), attracting rural business by promising a "correct likeness." James Guild, an artist who began traveling through New England in 1818, admitted that the results of his work were uneven. One of his early portraits "looked more like a stran-gle [sic] cat than it did like [the young girl sitting for him]. However I told her it looked like her and she believed it." It is, of course, impossible to know the basis of this touching belief; one might suggest that the cus-tomer's faith in the painter's professionalism, combined with her desire for artifactual evidence of her own gentility, quieted her fears of fraud.[14]

The preoccupation with acquiring a "correct likeness" (and later, under the spreading influence of the daguerrotype, a "perfect likeness") was part of a broader cultural development: the pervasive rise to dominance of a mimetic conception of art and language. Mimesis, the notion that art must directly mirror reality, had existed for centuries and had produced an endless variety of artistic representations. But in the middle and later nineteenth century, with the triumph of a particular Anglo-Protestant form of bourgeois culture in England and the United States, advocates of mimesis acquired a more unified and authoritative epistemology than had ever served them before—an epistemology that was all the more powerful for remaining implicit. In painting, theater, and literature, devotees of realism assumed that the artist could (and should) provide an unproblematic window on reality, the same sort of clear and unadorned perception embodied in the positivist ideal of scientific observation. The decline of melodramatic gesture in fiction and theater, the shift from an elocutionary to a conversational style of acting, the new premium placed on precise observation in painting and literature—all may be seen as evidence of a new, more insistent literal-mindedness that shaped bourgeois norms throughout the second half of the nineteenth century and into the twentieth.

The literalist version of mimesis was so strenuously articulated—and so broadly influential—that it might justifiably be termed an ideology. Its origins can be traced to the encounter between the plain-speech tradition and the misrepresentations endemic in the modern marketplace. Distrustful of artifice in speech, writing, dress, and other forms of communication, mimetic ideologues longed for perfect transparency in literature and the arts as well as in social intercourse. Unlike legal–rational discourse, the ideology of mimesis did not easily sanction the use of opaque language; "good prose," the plain speaker George Orwell would write, "is like a windowpane." For Orwell and others before him, a naive faith in the transparency of language supplied ethical force if not philosophical depth.[15]

To people who felt engulfed by a flood of deceptive surfaces, the idea that one could fix meaning precisely provided moral reassurance. The new and more literalist version of mimesis seemed to stabilize the language of the marketplace. The peddler's language—like the auctioneer's and later the advertiser's—was notoriously impenetrable; the opaque and pointless quality of "Yankee speech" was a standard source of humor on the antebellum stage, beginning with A. B. Lindsley's *Love and Friendship, or Yankee Notions* (1809). As James Russell Lowell (and later the cultural historian Constance Rourke) would observe, "Yankee speech was not so much a dialect as a lingo: that is, its oddities were consciously assumed. It was another form of masquerade." The ideology of mimesis suggested that the plainspoken "gude-man" could penetrate verbal or visual masquerades and discern true value. Early forms of "consumer education," like the *Report of the Medical Society of New York on Nostrums, or Secret Medicines*

(1827), sought to implement that procedure by demanding that the contents of patent medicines be listed on the labels—that the veil of secrecy be torn aside, and the nostrum exposed in its full vileness. Ever since, an implicit doctrine of mimesis has energized the impulse to unmask commercial chicanery.[16]

Mimetic thinking implied that the plain-speech tradition preserved a transparent discourse, in which language revealed rather than concealed. The Victorian preoccupation with grammatical precision must be seen in this light. Magazine articles warning against the incorrect use of *shall* and *will* or the habit of exaggerated expression were not so trivial as they seem. Decrying the use of exclamations like "I am tired to death!", *Peterson's* observed in 1861: "All such expressions affect, more or less, the habit of veracity, and make us insensibly disregard the exact truth." Prudent management of verbal resources ensured that language would reveal "exact truth," not obscure it. In popular discussions of grammar as elsewhere, a literalist doctrine of mimesis promised to contain the carnivalization of culture.[17]

As a potentially stabilizing idiom in bourgeois culture, mimesis combined the strengths of legal-rationality and sentimentalism: an instrumentalist emphasis on precise techniques of observation and representation merged with the moral authority of the domestic ideal. And, indeed, it was in combination with those other idioms that mimesis acquired its greatest cultural power. When mimetic thinking reinforced domestic sentimentalism, it helped to promote the cult of naturalness and sincerity. Nature, from the sentimental view, never lied; it was a book that could be read without being decoded, just as the "gude-man" in "The Scotch Pedlar" (see chapter 2) had studied "Nature's open volume" to penetrate the peddler's masquerade. With his *Modern Painters* (1849), John Ruskin persuaded a whole generation of Anglo-Americans to use "truth to nature" as their standard for judging a work of art; the same sort of moralized mimesis undergirded a sentimental aesthetic of "sincere" fashion, wherein clothes and cosmetics were valued primarily for the capacity to reveal the inner soul of the wearer. The tendency to endow consumer goods with truth-telling power was counterbalanced by the recognition that things could tell lies—at least in a market society where adulteration was the life of trade. In 1850 Henry Ward Beecher charged that adulterated and fraudulent goods were "incarnated lies": "We that consume are daily in the consumption of lies—we drink *lying* coffee—we eat *lying* food—we patch *lying* clothes with cheating thread—we perfume ourselves with *lying* essence—we wet our feet in *lying* boots—catch cold, however, truly enough—[and] are tormented with adulterated drugs."[18] The obsession with exposing fraud and uncovering "truth to nature" would characterize American criticism of advertising and consumer culture down to the present.

In Victorian times as well as today, it is an open question whether the invocation of "the natural" actually created an alternative to commercial misrepresentation. Ambiguities were arising as early as 1841, when *Godey's* satirized "The Extremely Natural Young Lady." The magazine observed that "there is a class who like so much to have it said of them, 'how very natural!' that they become affected on purpose. The extremely natural young lady is always doing some out of the way thing that she may appear simple and girlish." It was possible for naturalness to become a performance and sincerity a pose.[19]

The same sort of ambiguity characterized the merger of legal-rationality and mimesis. Mimetic doctrines could counteract a tendency toward obfuscation and reinforce faith in the ethic of promise-keeping, but they could have other consequences as well. The literalist devotion to exactitude promoted the equation of word and deed, which formed the basis of contractualism. Far from simply stabilizing social and economic relations, the verbal fetishism of contracts could also fuel unchecked economic growth. A naive faith in the referentiality of language underlay the paper apparatus of economic expansion: from written agreements regarding joint ventures to the maps of half-built speculative settlements, the contract exalted the letter over the spirit, and invested entrepreneurial fantasy with an aura of inevitable accomplishment. As the fictional confidence man Sam Slick said, "Sayin' is doin." The novel was not the only form of "commercial paper" that became a vehicle for fantasy.[20]

Mimetic doctrines were perhaps most effective as a stabilizing force when they were invoked in the service of ethnocentrism—as part of the set of binary oppositions that separated the bourgeois self from the exotic Other. Exoticism was a crucial part of the peddler's sorcery, and of consumer goods' appeal in general; it pervaded Victorian images of the marketplace. A literalist concept of mimesis allowed Anglo-Saxons to assume that they could participate in market transactions without besmirching their principles of plain speech, that they could enjoy the lure of the exotic without descending to the level of the "sensual, degraded" Other.

The Victorian ideology of mimesis was ethnocentric at its core. Plain speech had long been regarded as an Anglo-Saxon property (at least by

Anglo-Saxons). By the mid–nineteenth century, an ethnocentric interpretation of language had begun to coalesce; Anglo-Saxon words and syntax were routinely praised for their clarity, strength, and directness. In 1855, *Godey's* gave thanks that "the body and the sinews of the language remain largely Saxon": only six of the sixty words in the Lord's Prayer, for example, were of Latin origin; the "soul's ambassadors" (that is, words) remained largely undefiled. The ethnocentric view of language promoted a tendency to situate truth among the Anglo-Saxons; other ethnic groups could be characterized as "treacherous." [21]

Depending on the particular social circumstances, the convergence of ethnocentric literalism and institutionalized rationality could have specific consequences for specific groups. In Buffalo during the 1840s and 1850s, for example, the WASP credit investigators employed at Dun & Bradstreet began using anti-Semitic stereotypes to justify denying credit to Jewish businessmen. As the historian David Gerber shows, all the ancient imagery was invoked to separate the Jew from the WASP producer ethic: the Jew was presented as the nonproducer, the predator, "the fraudulent bankrupt; the arsonist cheating his insurers; the shrewd peddler selling trinkets at outrageous prices to the lonely farm wife while her husband labored unknowingly in a distant field." According to credit reports, the Jewish applicants were capable of "no more than Jewish honesty" and their pecuniary affairs were constantly "in the dark." Fears of secrecy and deceit melded with mimetic discourse and promoted its use as an instrument of Anglo-Saxon legitimacy in the commercial world. [22]

Mimetic thinking stigmatized other groups as well: Native Americans (routinely described as treacherous in nineteenth-century history textbooks), Irish, Italians, African-Americans—all the "lesser breeds without the Law" that Kipling later identified as part of the white man's burden. All were labeled untrustworthy, incapable of hewing to Anglo-Saxon standards of honesty. The ironies connected with this enterprise surfaced dramatically at a particular moment in the career of P. T. Barnum. Barnum had arranged to exhibit several Indian war chiefs at his New York museum in 1864; all of the chiefs thought that Barnum was introducing—not exhibiting—them to a huge audience, and praising them at awesome length. In actuality, Barnum gleefully recalled, he was detailing the double-dealings of the Kiowa chief Yellow Bear. "If the bloodthirsty little villain understood what I was saying, he would kill me in a moment; but as he thinks I am complimenting him, I can safely state the truth to you, that he is a lying, thieving, treacherous, murderous monster." The chief smiled

benignly while the audience howled its approval. Barnum never acknowledged any treachery in his own behavior during this episode.[23]

Here as elsewhere, a focus on the untrustworthiness of the subordinate
racial caste reinforced the self-regard of the dominant group. As in the
obsessive references to the sensuality of dark-skinned peoples, this was a
case of self-purgation through allegorical projection. In the ethnocentric
view of language, one can begin to discern a characteristic psychic function performed by the culture of imperialism. All the fears of hypocrisy, all
the suspicions that the successful man was merely a clever manipulator of
appearances, could be projected outside Anglo-Saxon culture onto the
shiftless Sambo, the Indian-giver, the wheedling Semite. The literalist version of mimesis provided the assurance that deceit was not really a feature
of "our" commercial life because "we" were not like "them." While this
sort of assumption reinforced faith in the straight-shooting, clear-eyed
bourgeois self as a counterweight to chaos and corruption, it also underwrote moral arguments for imperial expansion. Advocates of mimesis, like
those who articulated other idioms of control, produced contradictory
effects on bourgeois culture. They developed a rhetorical stance that
allayed anxieties, but also reinforced conditions that had helped to create
the anxieties—accelerating economic development, multiplying desires
and deceptions.

During the decades after the Civil War, the idioms of control would
persist, and national advertising would make good use of all of them. But
what would perhaps prove the most useful to advertisers was an idiom that
was still in its infancy during the midcentury decades, a technocratic language that would merge nicely with the developing corporate domination
of the modern American economy. This mode of expression was rooted in
the assumption that human technical prowess could transform the course
of life into a predictable pursuit of personal well-being. Few visions of
technocratic control surfaced in the antebellum years; among the most
interesting was "The Rain King; or, a Glance at the Next Century" (1842),
one of the rare stories in women's magazines that looked to the future
rather than the present or past. "The Rain King" was a fantasy of the year
1942: the United States has established a strong and independent economy (through the elimination of dependence on imports) as well as a
flourishing consumer culture and physically flawless race (through the perfection of pomades, hair restorers, and corrective surgery). The crowning
achievement has been the capacity to control weather. It is the future as
Disneyland: a steady-state closed system. But the system breaks down due

to conflicting consumer demands on the Rain King, who cannot orchestrate the many requests for fair and foul weather at specific times. The fantasy implied that could we but conquer human perversity, utopia would be a sanitized society in equilibrium, where no desire was aroused that could not be satisfied. But we could not conquer human perversity. It was as if the author had foreseen the rise and fall of consumer culture in the mid-twentieth-century United States, the collapse of a consensus under the weight of conflicting demands. Still, for a time after World War II, at least for those lucky enough to have been inside the consensus, it seemed as if corporate-sponsored technology really had stabilized the sorcery of the marketplace.[24]

The dream of a market culture brought under technocratic control remained undeveloped until the end of the nineteenth century, when writers like Edward Bellamy envisioned more influential hygienic utopias. The technocratic idiom became more useful in the decades after the Civil War, with the rise of modern corporations organized on principles of bureaucratic rationality and geared to systematic pursuit of surplus value. National advertising was a creature of the modern corporation, a key part of a more streamlined commercial culture that sought to stabilize market relations and representations. Yet even for the new breed of advertising "professionals," the process of stabilization was always incomplete: the services they provided were difficult to measure and easy to dismiss as charlatanry. The motives and meanings of their work remained shrouded in the ambiguities of market exchange.

THE FATE OF MAGIC

The earliest advertising agents began to appear during the 1850s and 1860s in Philadelphia, Boston, Chicago, and particularly in lower Manhattan, on Park Row and neighboring streets in what was then the publishing district. This breeding ground of advertising agencies was nestled in the male world of mid-nineteenth-century metropolitan entrepreneurship. It was a world of men in muddy boots, drinking and bantering as they sat around pot-bellied stoves; these men walked the line between bourgeois respectability and the urban subculture of sensuality. For most, there was always the temptation of an afternoon spent over bumpers of rye at the Café Martin, followed by a "leg drama" at Niblo's Gardens. Conviviality was a key to success; few traits were as valued as a clever tongue or a talent for storytelling. (Among the admen in New York in the early days was

David Ross Locke, later known as the humorist Petroleum V. Nasby.) Yet high spirits alone were insufficient; successful ad agents avoided long hours at the saloon and struggled—albeit sometimes ambivalently—to transform their work into a "profession." [25]

In the early years the language of professionalism was mostly moralized mimesis. Ad agents as well as the publishers who stood to gain revenue from advertisements were concerned to distance advertising from carnivalesque frivolity. In 1850 Horace Greeley complained in an early advertising trade journal published by Volney B. Palmer:

> There is a large class who delight to shine in newspapers as wits and poets, and announce their wares in second-hand jokes, or in doggerel fit to set the teeth of a dull saw on edge. If their object is notoriety or a laugh, this is the way to attain it; but if it be business, it would seem better to use the language of business. Leave clowns' jests to the circus, and let sober men speak as they act, with directness and decision. The fewest words that will convey the advertisers' ideas are the right ones.

The gospel of simple and direct separated the circus clowns from the legitimate men of business.[26]

The need for legitimacy was especially acute for advertising agents, who partook of the Barnumesque aura surrounding all publicity enterprises, and whose stock-in-trade epitomized the insubstantiality and elasticity of value in a commodity civilization. At first, they traded in nothing but blank space. The typical pattern: An enterprising young man from the provinces, operating out of a tiny office, persuaded various newspaper publishers to authorize him to sell their space on commission (gradually standardized to 15 percent) to patent medicine manufacturers, dry goods emporiums, and anyone else with a need to advertise. The value of the space depended on the intensity of the advertiser's desire to cry his wares in a particular publication and the urgency of the publisher's need to sell off all his space before press time. The advertising agent served as broker between the two parties.[27]

To the advertising agent, the possibilities for manipulative confidence games were virtually limitless; at the same time, the agents worked to minimize the ambiguities of their transactions so as to maximize their profits. They sought to justify their trade by reasserting familiar moral claims of sincere self-made manhood, but they also began to turn to a newer idiom of efficiency and productivity. They can be seen as part of the "new class" of service-oriented professionals who aimed to manage economic risks and rationalize the pursuit of profits. The advertising agent, in other words, was not only a blend of self-made man and confidence man, he was also a new-model professional.

The complexities of early advertising can be seen in the careers of George P. Rowell and Francis Wayland Ayer. Rowell created *Rowell's American Newspaper Directory* in 1869 and founded the trade journal *Printers' Ink* in 1888. Ayer started N. W. Ayer & Son in 1869, naming the firm for his father. Though the elder Ayer, sometime schoolmaster, had little capital and no business ability to contribute to the operation, he did provide his son with a strong Protestant conscience. The name N. W. Ayer & Son was an act of filial piety as well as an effort to acquire some dignity for a brand-new business. Within two decades F. W. Ayer had turned the firm into one of the most respected in the business. Both Rowell and the younger Ayer sought to transform their ambiguous trade into a respectable profession; neither succeeded completely.

Rowell was one of those young provincials who became a key figure in the rise of national advertising. He was born in a log cabin, in the forest region of northern Vermont near St. Johnsbury, in 1838. He began business as an advertising canvasser for the *Boston Post* in 1858, started his own agency in Boston in 1865, and moved to New York in 1867. In *Forty Years an Advertising Agent* (1906), Rowell used a standard trope of late-nineteenth-century businessmen's autobiographies, presenting his career as an effort to bring order to a chaotic advertising world of carnivalesque tricksters.

But the task was more easily described than accomplished. As Rowell acknowledged, advertising was "one of the easiest sorts of business in which a man may cheat and defraud a client without danger of discovery." Though Rowell quickly added that "no agent who was not superior to this temptation has ever been permanently successful," his autobiography discribed many instances where he profited from a client's ignorance. Rowell wrote:

> Advertisers have very little idea of what an advertisement is worth, and are always well satisfied when they are convinced—not that what they get is worth what they will pay for it, but that they did not pay any more than the smallest sum that would have secured it. Many an advertiser has patted himself on the back in congratulation for a specially low deal forced with much talk, and the canvasser has retired chuckling that he would have been glad of the order at half the price he was to receive.[28]

On one occasion in the late 1860s Rowell was in New York, selling space for the *Boston Post*. His account of a negotiation with a patent medicine firm is worth quoting at length because it effectively captures the improvisational confidence game of early advertising.

> I had in my pocket a large advertisement of a proprietary article, denominated Constitution Water, emanating from a firm—in Liberty Street, I think it was—named Morgan & Allen. To that place I proceeded. It was about noon. On asking for the advertising manager I was directed to Dr. Morgan, who was found in the middle of the floor showing a green porter how to fasten in the head of a barrel that had just been filled with a miscellaneous order for goods, and the admiration his skill evoked from the porter, in connection with the tingling of the blood caused by the unwonted exercise, had put the good man in the best of humor. He was a kindly appearing man anyway—about fifty years of age. "We can't advertise in your paper," said he; "you charge too much." "The trouble is," was my reply, "not that we charge so much, but that you are not willing to pay a fair price." He seemed to pay no particular attention to what I had said, but handed over to the porter the hatchet he had been handling, and I continued—with the advertisement in my hand: "At our full rates that advertisement would cost $800 for insertion for a year." "That's altogether too much," he said. "I don't know about that," I responded, "but if I should ask you half that sum, you would still say the same thing." "No, I wouldn't," said he. "Do you mean that if I will take it at $400 you will pay $400?" was my next inquiry, and to that he said, "Yes," and I said "I'll take it just to meet your views for this once." If the conversation had begun in some other way I do not think I should have ventured to ask more than $300 as a starter.[29]

The whole scene—the patent medicine with the punning name, the huffing proprietor in shirtsleeves, putting up his own product in barrels, as well as the chaffing, conniving conversation between the two men—suggests that the first advertising agents were perfectly at home in the fluid, informal market settings favored by peddlers and assorted other confidence men. The skilled advertising agents could deftly manipulate the appearances necessary for success in the financial service trades that flourished amid the uncertainty of nineteenth-century business relationships. At the same time, though, Rowell and the other founders of advertising agencies sought to make those shifting relationships more systematically predictable—or more systematically profitable, for as Rowell's memoirs indicated, a little vagueness was in the interest of the advertising agent. Rowell's own career focused on stabilizing the relationships between advertisers and publishers on the one hand, and between advertisers and their audience on the other.

One way to minimize ambiguity, Rowell decided, was to establish procedures for setting advertising rates. During the midcentury decades, publishers set their own rates, but in accordance with mysterious and subjective criteria. As M. H. Mallory, publisher of the *New York Churchman*, observed, "Advertising space in a newspaper is somewhat like a lady's favors, which are valued very much as she values them herself." Rates were infinitely variable and more honored in the breach than the observance. Rowell marveled at the arbitrariness of the *New York Herald's* rates: "Evidently it is not the space he occupies that an advertiser pays for, but an indefinite something the exact value of which neither the man who buys nor the man who sells quite understands." Rowell decided to make that "indefinite something" more definite. He set out to discover everything he could about American newspapers, from country weeklies to the *Chicago Tribune:* the number of each printed, the number actually sold, the quality of the paper and typography, the editor's politics and advertising policies, the likely readership. He then packaged this information by region or type of publication (small-town papers in western New York, religious papers, agricultural papers, and so on) and offered it to advertisers for a percentage of the advertising costs. Rowell's focus on circulation figures effectively employed an influential variant of the developing scientific idiom: a popular faith in statistics. Using the belief that "numbers never lie" to ground the airy nothingness of advertising negotiations, Rowell also promoted a fundamental institutional transformation in the business. Even though he was still paid out of the publisher's revenues, he shifted the focus of the advertising agency: rather than selling space for publications, his primary task was to advise the space buyer how and where his money would be most effectively spent—the "media consulting" provided by modern advertising agencies down to our own time.[30]

Besides regularizing the relations between advertisers and publishers, Rowell also aimed to mediate between advertisers and the potential buyers of their products. His magazine *Printers' Ink* was the most influential advertising trade journal for over half a century. In *Printers' Ink*, Rowell and his contributors began to expand their advice to advertisers: outlining the "science" of calculating an advertising budget; promoting new methods of packaging and promoting products that would reach a remote and scattered buying audience; in general, aiming to stabilize market exchange by shortening and standardizing the distance between producer and consumer. Deploying established idioms of plain speech as well as newer ones of scientism, Rowell played a major role in formulating the chief tasks of the modern advertising agency: to serve the interests of its corporate clients by identifying their products with rationality and progress, and to cleanse advertising of its associations with peddlers and other marginal operators.

Francis Wayland Ayer's career was equally central in furthering those developments. When Rowell penned his autobiography in 1905, he identified Ayer as the one man who had always kept an abstemious mien amid the general merriment of the advertising business. According to Rowell, Ayer "thinks of work all the time, eats little, drinks nothing but water; has no vices, small or large, unless overwork is a vice . . . such a man as Oliver Cromwell would have been had Oliver been permitted to become an advertising agent." Named for a prominent academic moral philosopher, Ayer was Protestant productivity incarnate. Brusquely righteous, he was not a salesman but an entrepreneur, organizer, and manager whose manner was cold and reserved. "When he wants a thing he gets it, and he doesn't mince matters about getting it, either," former President William Howard Taft said of Ayer at a testimonial dinner in 1919. Ayer was "a man of simple tastes, and one who took the teachings of Christ seriously, and he disliked ostentation." Precisely the sort of man, one would think, who might bring respectability to the advertising business.[31]

Certainly that was Ayer's own aim. In 1875, after Ayer's father had died and he was trying to decide whether to continue in the family business, a friend told him that an advertising agent was "nothing but a drummer" and offered him a job in a respectable business. Ayer declined. "I have put my hand to this plow and by the help of the Lord I am going to finish the furrow. Before I have finished, if we both live, you are going to come to me some day and say that you respect me for my business as well as myself." The chief obstacle to respect, in Ayer's view, was the commission system. By requiring an advertising agent to serve two masters, the publisher and the advertiser, it created possibilities for corruption. Rowell had redefined the agent's job as one of helping the advertiser buy space, instead of merely selling space. The problem was that the advertiser still expected the agent to get his commission from the publisher, so the agent was still serving two masters. Ayer's solution to this problem was the open contract, which the agency signed with the advertiser rather than the publisher (though the commission was still a percentage of the cost of space). This was the beginning of the end of "ready-made advertising" and the beginning of "made-to-measure advertising." Agencies that followed Ayer's lead had an incentive to keep their clients' sales up and form long-term relationships based on a wide range of services.[32]

N. W. Ayer & Son became one of the first full-service advertising agencies. The firm conducted the first marketing survey in 1879, compiling crop statistics and newspaper circulations for Nichols-Shepard Agricultural Implements. During the 1880s and 1890s, as Ayer & Son dealt increasingly with national corporations rather than local retailers, the main burden of copy preparation shifted from the client to the agency. In 1900 the Copy Department was established. Ayer himself was not entirely comfortable with the new emphasis on copy preparation; it smacked of the clownish entertainment Greeley and others had warned against. But he adjusted to the new developments by restricting their disruptive potential. He forged a tighter relationship with the Curtis publications—models of middle-class propriety like the *Saturday Evening Post* and *Ladies' Home Journal;* he stopped advertising liquor in 1899 and patent medicines in 1906. And he continued to avoid "solicitation by means of revelry" (though not all of his account executives were as circumspect). The firm's slogan— "Keeping Everlastingly at It Brings Success," coined by Ayer in 1886— captured its attempt to embody plodding diligence amid the Barnumesque flash of its competitors.[33]

The significance of Ayer's career was summed up in Taft's testimonial of 1919. "We are honoring a man who has made advertising a science, who has made it useful, and who has robbed it of many of its evil tendencies," the ex-President said, concluding that "we owe a debt of gratitude to Mr. Ayer, for having rendered a form of publicity so useful and elevating, which might have been vicious and deplorable."[34] Though both the moral and scientific claims in that statement are subject to doubt, the mingling of the two modes of discourse was a revealing sign of how national advertising had achieved legitimacy in the half-century after the Civil War.

Of course, the marginal operators continued to flourish even after the turn of the century, but from a contemporary vantage point it is possible to see many of them as increasingly anachronistic, relics of a rural and small-town culture whose success depended primarily on face-to-face performance rather than on long-distance communication of words and pictures. Small-town America was still largely an oral culture throughout much of the nineteenth century; the McGuffey Readers (1836–1920), the most popular texts in rural schoolhouses, were designed to improve declamatory reading, not reading for comprehension. Where the aura of magic persisted most obviously was among the great oral performers of late-nineteenth-century commerce: street fakirs, medicine show impresarios, men of the type epitomized in James Whitcomb Riley's employers (see chapter 2) or Mark Twain's fictional Colonel Beriah Sellers ("The Colonel's tongue was a magician's wand that turned dried apples into figs and water into wine as easily as it could change a hovel into a palace and present poverty into future riches"). Here as elsewhere, one must distinguish between magic as literal belief and as rhetorical device; the Colonel employed the latter approach, as did nearly all his commercial contemporaries. Still, traces of magical properties continued to adhere to products such as patent medicines and lightning rods, and these were among the commonest sold through oral performance.[35]

The cultural conflicts that had plagued peddlers and other oral salesmen remained intractable, as national advertisers succeeded (at least rhetorically) in distinguishing their brands of commerce from allegedly less progressive types. In popular fiction, peddlers continued to play the role of exotic seducers, provokers of rural suspicion; yet they also acquired a patina of nostalgic appeal as representatives of an older, preindustrial version of market exchange. An *American Magazine* story of 1912, "The Peddler," by Lucille Baldwin Van Slyke, summarized some of the ways that the imagery surrounding marginal commerce had changed since the Civil War. The story concerns the plight of Emily Jackson, a young woman who feels chained to her fate in Forbes Corners, New Hampshire, surrounded by piles of her family's coarse underwear and heaps of heavy sheets, until one suffocating summer day her ironing is interrupted by a Syrian peddler in the dooryard.

> He was spreading the things out seductively; fragile silk shawls, a cunningly knit silk scarf, delicately embroidered linens, and fat bundles of lace medallions tied with pretty bits of ribbon. With a swift flash of his tender, bronzed hands he arranged his wares with seemingly lazy grace. Each time, as he spread something before her, he lifted his darkly fringed eyes for her approval and smiled like a child when she nodded. Presently he opened a quaintly carved casket and disclosed rows of shining glass beads, gaudy Oriental bits of color that twinkled in the sunlight through the green shade of the grape arbor above him.
>
> "Oo-ooh!" sighed Emily. "They're real pretty, aren't they? I always did hanker after beads, somehow." She opened the door and came out to sit on the top stair, her fingers rested eagerly on a turquoise-tinted strand. "How lovely!" she whispered.[36]

The peddler is a seducer, arranging "gaudy Oriental bits of color" that embody the sensuous vitality, the possibility of surprise and delight, forbidden in Forbes Corners. ("I get so sick of Forbes Corners," Emily complains. "I get so sick of seeing the same folks and hearing them say the same things.") But the peddler is also "a child"—a familiar enough dismissal, by 1912, of "backward" dark-skinned peoples, but here the designation is not merely dismissive; it carries Wordsworthian connotations of spontaneous innocent pleasure, a "lazy grace" lost in a productivist culture. He even smokes differently from American men, who puff with ridiculous energy and turn pleasure into work. "Thad ees ver' fooleesch," says the peddler, "to make so mooch trouble out of a theeng thad ees so mooch nice fun." [37]

The seduction scene is interrupted when Emily's Aunt Eunice appears. To her, the peddler is nothing but a "tramp." "You'd better pack up that trash and get out of here," she tells him. But Emily and the peddler continue to meet, by chance, when he gives her the necklace she yearns for, and at last deliberately, when she risks the ridicule of the hired men to return his tobacco pouch (with its "Oriental embroidery" and "Oriental fragrance"). The peddler concludes the story with a little lesson, in the heavy and almost self-parodic dialect he is saddled with throughout:

> "Thees ees the theeng you mus' learn, thad weesches [wishes] ees nod leedle theengs, they ees sent by Allah to save the heart. You mus' not let them die, leetle ladee, lest weeth them thy heart—thy soul—die also."
>
> A great longing for something, she knew not what, possessed her but she could not speak.

The peddler tries to describe this unfulfilled longing:

> "Eet ees a flower of the spirit—a theeng within the heart—the heart's beeg weesch. For me it was the weesch to wander—by land, by sea, until my soul could learn the need of my own dear land; for some eet ees lofe, for some eet ees strength, for some eet ees courage; but eet ees the beegest want, leetle ladee—oh, can you nod see?"
>
> "I know," she breathed. "I know—It's going to be whatever I need most!"

The peddler leaves, having been moved by the sight of sheep in the meadow to return to his "own dear land," and Emily goes back to the farmhouse. But she is no longer bothered by the hired men's teasing banter or her aunt's fretting; she frankly acknowledges where and with whom she has been; she has acquired dignity and poise. "Already she had entered her kingdom, the prescient kingdom of desires and wishes, in whose wonderful solitude should blossom the flower of her heart's desire."[38]

From one point of view, this story could be said to vindicate the triumph of "consumerist" values in a developed capitalist society. The encounter between the peddler and the farm family is structured the same way it had been in antebellum fiction and poetry, but the didactic roles have been reversed. The peddler is not a trickster but a teacher. The woman's recognition that desires ("the heart's beeg want") can be the same as needs ("whatever I need most") constitutes a step toward personal autonomy; by allowing the flowering of her heart's desire, she creates a new and more substantial sense of self.

Yet the peddler is hardly an apt representative of "consumer culture"—certainly not the corporate-sponsored version in place by the turn of the century. Rather, he embodies the allure of an earlier preindustrial marketplace. Nor is he a "progressive" carrier of cunning Yankee notions; he is dark-skinned, childlike, androgynous, and consumed with nostalgia for the primitive virtues of his own home. The author's worldview implies romantic antimodernism more than modern consumerism—a rejection of plodding efficiency in favor of some vaguely exotic and sensuous alternative. And the story as a whole suggests that in a rationalizing corporate economy, peddlers and other interstitial agents of commerce were becoming embodiments of a leisurely agrarian past rather than a bustling future. Advertising agencies succeeded at least partially in their effort to distance themselves from the marginal magicians who had earlier epitomized the threat and promise of market exchange.

They could never completely succeed in that effort. The biggest and most respectable advertising agencies (not to mention the smaller and more marginal ones) continued to conjure up destabilizing cultural tendencies, continued to participate in the older carnivalesque discourse even as they sought to limit its effects. Advertising agents were, after all, managers rather than custodians of culture; they had for the most part only an instrumental interest in the allegedly eternal verities represented by the idioms they used. More important, their chief clients—and, indeed, the very basis of many agencies' success—were manufacturers of patent medicine, the product that more than any other still carried a promise of self-transformation. Ayer was virtually the sole exception. And even he gave up patent medicines only after Pure Food and Drug agitation had made the elixirs a major embarrassment. The distinction between legitimate and illegitimate drugs remained murky at best—and Ayer's copy for everything from tea to cigarettes continued to promise magical regeneration through purchase, though the magic was metaphorical rather than literal.

From the beginning, the business of national advertising was saturated in soothing syrup. Rowell's earliest memories (he claimed) were of "a bottle containing a liquid of a golden pomegranate color" (which turned out to be Ayer's Cherry Pectoral—no relation to the ad agency Ayer) and "a certain poster picture of a sort of calico horse of Arabian pattern and vast grace and beauty, all calculated to emphasize the benefits that might be derived from a compound known as Merchants' Gargling Oil." According to Rowell and many other early advertising executives, patent medicines presented the most profitable investment opportunity among all consumer goods: costs of production were low and an efficient distribution system in place; all that was needed was a lavish expenditure on advertising—and therein, of course, lay the agencies' opportunity. The trick was to keep such lucrative clients without being besmirched by their disreputable associations. (A popular late-nineteenth-century anecdote involved two young girls and their mothers making a shipboard acquaintance on a transatlantic cruise. "Emma's papa is the man that makes _____ Bitters," said one girl privately to her mother. "We will be careful not to let her mother know that we know it," was the reply. "It might make her feel badly.") No matter how much wealth they acquired, neither advertising agents nor patent medicine manufacturers ever fully escaped the taint of their carnivalesque origins. In many ways, they preserved the antebellum peddlers' persona but covered it with a patina of sincerity, science, and progress. They continued to promise magical self-transformation through upward mobility or inward regeneration; they continued to provoke the same mix of titillation and mistrust.[39]

Throughout the late nineteenth century and into the twentieth, rural and small-town folk looked askance at the advertiser's seductive influence, even as they celebrated economic growth. In part this suspicion was rooted in the hostility of local shopkeepers toward rivalrous "foreign" (that is, national) advertisers, but the hostility was more than merely economic. National advertising disrupted local "custom" in a cultural as well as a business sense.[40] So advertisers and their agencies persisted in seeking the appearance of stability, yoking the Victorian idioms of control to a new and more encompassing technocratic framework. Gradually their visual and verbal language helped construct an ideal of bourgeois selfhood more standardized than the old Victorian model, more appropriate to the managerial ethos of the turn of the century. But even as early as the antebellum era, a few observers had anticipated and criticized the philosophical assumptions behind this rhetorical appropriation of technology. Perhaps the most prescient was Herman Melville.

MELVILLE AND THE CONFIDENCE MAN

In the early fall of 1853, a number of lightning-rod salesmen began to conduct an aggressive sales campaign around Pittsfield, Massachusetts, where Herman Melville lived with his family. One of the salesmen, according to family tradition, confronted Melville directly. We do not know what was actually said at that meeting, but we do know that Melville transmuted the encounter into "The Lightning-Rod Man" (published the following August in *Putnam's*). The story probed the developing mythology of market society at its most vulnerable point: the promise that people could be released from all fear and anxiety if they would simply trust in the technical expertise of the vendor. This was the sort of confidence game that energized the sale of lightning rods, as well as patent medicines and much of the "progressive" detritus of commodity civilization.[41]

Melville's lightning-rod man is the quintessential liminal figure. Arriving at the narrator's door in the midst of a terrific thunderstorm, he claims to mediate between the heavens and the earth. "A lean, gloomy, figure," he stands quaking in the middle of the narrator's cabin, clutching his wares. He seems an ineffectual mediator, yet he arrogates magical powers: "Say but the word, and of this cottage I can make a Gibraltar by a few waves of this wand," he announces. The narrator presses him, reminding him of the many failures of lightning rods of late in the vicinity; all were installed improperly, the salesman insists, and intensifies his case, in language resembling that of the nostrum-hawker's appeal to fear: "Will you buy? Shall I put down your name? Think of being a heap of charred offal, like a haltered horse burned in his stall; and all in one flash!" Finally the narrator ridicules his pretensions to "avert the supernal bolt" with a mere "pipestem": "Who has empowered you, you Tetzel, to peddle round your indulgences from divine ordinations? The hairs of our head are numbered, and the days of our lives. In thunder as in sunshine, I stand at ease in the hands of my God. False negotiator, away!" From this essentially Calvinist perspective, the fundamental deception of the lightning-rod man was the deification of human technical prowess—the assumption of godlike control over an unpredictable natural world.[42]

Melville had not finished brooding on the philosophical implications of systematic deceit. Four years later he published *The Confidence-Man.* The novel is a poststructuralist's dream. Its dense and circling prose, its self-canceling sentences, ultimately deconstruct language as a medium of communication, ridiculing all claims of social transparency and calling all fixed meanings into question. Melville locates this bleak vision within a setting on the exotic borders of market society: the steamer *Fidele,* meandering down the Mississippi. Its "long, wide covered deck, hereabouts built up on both sides with shop-like windowed spaces," seemed like "some Constantinople arcade or bazaar, where more than one trade is plied."[43]

But the only trade that is plied is the unceasing manipulation of deceptive surfaces by a succession of confidence men, all or none of whom may be the same person. *The Confidence-Man* is, among other things, a devastating assault on nearly all the cultural idioms that mid-nineteenth-century Americans hoped might stabilize the sorcery of market relations: sentimentality, rationality, mimesis—above all, the belief in a transparently communicative language and a plainspoken autonomous self who utters it. At the same time, the book echoes "The Lightning-Rod Man" in offering a prescient critique of the technocratic idiom that would become a major rhetorical resource of twentieth-century advertisers.

The very notion of character was part of the bourgeois ideal of unified selfhood that Melville sought to undermine. Nevertheless, even in this disembodied novel, Melville creates recognizable and memorable characters. Perhaps the most important for my purposes is the "yarb-doctor," or patent medicine man, who speaks an opaque language compounded of orphic Emersonian religiosity and advertising rhetoric. (Entire pages of his conversation could have been lifted directly from mid-nineteenth-century advertising copy.) Despite his verbal pirouettes on behalf of "true Indian doctors" and the healing powers of nature, he is less a nostalgic primitivist than a harbinger of things to come. As patent medicine firms were among the most heavily capitalized and bureaucratically organized vendors of consumer goods, many men who sold elixirs like the herb doctor's Omni-Balsamic Reinvigorator were corporate employees. The "Missouri bachelor," an embodiment of the older entrepreneurial society, suspects as much of the herb doctor: "Is not that air of yours, so spiritlessly enduring and yielding, the very air of a slave?" he demands. "Who is your master, pray, or are you owned by a company?"[44]

The herb doctor's ideological stance prefigures the secular faith in progress preached by the modern corporation. Dilating on the merits of his Samaritan Pain Dissuader, he is accosted by a brooding "dusk giant" who seems to be the guardian of a nervous and puny half-breed girl. The giant, with a "voice deep and lonesome enough to have come from the bottom of an abandoned coal-shaft," asks:

"Does [the medicine] produce insensibility?"
"By no means. Not the least of its merits is that it is not an opiate. It kills pain without killing feeling."
"You lie! Some pains cannot be eased but by producing insensibility, and cannot be cured but by producing death."[45]

As in "The Lightning-Rod Man," the object of Melville's ire is not only the confidence man's deception, but also the self-deception behind it—the belief that one can escape inescapable pain through the ministrations of spurious science. "Confidence," in this broader context, is another name for hubris: to have confidence is to believe that the experts know best. The confidence man asks his dupe to accept specific product claims as well as the myths of human centrality and power supporting those claims. Here again, Melville unmasks the flimsiness of that humanist ideological apparatus.

Yet unlike the earlier story, *The Confidence-Man* contains no affirmation, however oblique, of any trust in a providential order behind the veil of deceptive appearances. In Melville's deconstructed version of commodity civilization, there is no idiom of authenticity to counteract the proliferations of artifice. Probably he was too quick to dismiss any possibility of communication, however flawed, between people in market society; without question, his literary achievement showed that one might construct an authentic voice, however precariously, amid the claims of confidence men. Yet Melville's own conclusion was pessimistic. Long before Roland Barthes announced that "to write" is "an intransitive verb" and made delight in the pointless play of surfaces a centerpiece of his aesthetic, Melville recognized that language could be fundamentally incommunicative and self-referential. The difference is that Melville was not delighted but appalled by the discovery.

CHAPTER 4

The Disembodiment of Abundance

By the late nineteenth century, as peddlers were being relegated to the backwaters of commercial culture, proponents of technocratic idioms were recasting the traditional symbols of abundance. In the developing commercial imagery, female figures were rendered less formidable; industrial icons replaced agricultural; the source of sustenance became the efficient factory rather than the fecund earth. Yet this was not a simple linear process. The makers of the new iconography, as well as the population generally, were caught up in strong currents of cultural conflict. If Americans felt any anxiety about the redefinition of material plenitude, it was not only because they clung to the frayed remnants of republican tradition, but—more important—because they preserved some attachment to the land-as-mother, some memory or fantasy of wholeness, however fleeting, in a pastoral world of warmth and plenty. These conflicts surfaced most dramatically in the emergent "media culture" of chromolithography, which turned increasingly toward advertising after the Civil War.

THE MOTHER GODDESS AND THE MACHINE

The chromolithographers' iconography of abundance veered toward titillating exoticism on one hand, sentimental agrarianism on the other. To metropolitan consumers only recently removed from the land, chromolithographers offered reassuring genre scenes, nestling visions of abundance in settings of self-sufficient agriculture and extended kinship ties. They reconstructed a personal past redolent with fantasies of childhood bliss and pre-oedipal harmony (figure 4.1) The late-nineteenth-century ideal of gemeinschaft—the self-sufficient, organic community—achieved its embodiment in commercial imagery long before it was codified in sociological texts. Like academic theorists, urban chromolithographers re-created a vision of preindustrial life that may have resonated with their own nostalgic memories; the etymological root of *nostalgia* is "homesickness." The same incipient media culture that popularized the rhetoric of domesticity in ladies' magazines also represented the visual embodiments of the domestic ideal: the old homeplace, the vine-covered cottage, the still point of the turning world. Rootless urban publicists promoted a pastoral ideal of rootedness, containing commercial life's impact on personal identity by locating abundance in a domesticated rural landscape, awash in associations with maternal nurturance.[1]

Similar memories or fantasies affected even the exoticism and primitivism of patent medicine chromos. Orientalist idioms preserved the ancient link between fecund sexuality and material abundance; the connotations of the imagery were maternal as well as erotic. The critic Edward Said has observed that "one always *returned* to the Orient," to what

FIGURE 4.1
The Four Seasons of Life: Middle Age, Currier & Ives, 1867. *Library of Congress.*

Goethe had called "the profound origins of the human race." As the New World landscape became more settled and less available as a focus for fantasy, Orientalist exoticism may have provided an alternative way to express longings for renewal through a return to origins—a particularly apt project in a culture that demanded home-leaving as a prerequisite for manhood.[2]

At the same time, the changing iconography of abundance recycled mother-goddesses in other visual idioms as well. In 1890, Mellin's Food ("for infants and invalids") distributed chromolithographs titled *Maternity* as merchandising aids: they pictured a marble statue of a naked Rubenesque mother holding two naked babies on her lap.[3] The image recalled the "broad lap of *Alma Mater*" in Crèvecoeur's vision of American abundance, and linked eroticized maternal images to more domesticated icons of plenty. This sort of imagery sanitized the psychodrama of the bourgeois madonna and the separate (male) self, the struggle between fantasies of pre-oedipal wholeness and a need to be up and doing, dominating the world of *mater* and matter.

Given this mix of conflicting desires and the changing conditions of image production, it is not surprising that the images generated by chromolithographers sometimes bore the marks of that allegedly "postmodern" form, pastiche. The Indian princess, for example, survived in this vernacular tradition of commercial iconography, sometimes surfacing in new and revealing guises. A Currier & Ives print labeled simply *America* (figure 4.2) presented the Indian princess as a seductive odalisque. The stars on

FIGURE 4.2
America, Currier & Ives, 1870. *Library of Congress.*

her headband are the only concession to patriotic symbolism; despite her necklace of bear claws and her quiver of arrows, she is decked in the rich ornaments traditionally employed in representations of luxury. Her plump chin rests lightly on her fat, bejeweled fingers; her skin and features are decidedly Caucasian. She is remarkably soft and sensual, an inappropriate candidate (one would think) to carry the allegorical baggage of "America."

About ten years later, an even more problematic pastiche appeared. The 'Swheat Girl (c. 1880, figure 4.3) became a recurrent figure on stock trade cards for agricultural supplies, flour, and baked goods. She wears the sort of skirt traditionally designed for Indian icons of abundance, though it

FIGURE 4.3

A 'Swheat Girl (c. 1880), trade card for Quinnipiac Fertilizer Company. *Warshaw Collection of Business Americana, National Museum of American History, Smithsonian Institution.*

is made of wheat rather than corn. But she also wears high-button soubrette's shoes and daintily tests the tip of her sickle with her finger. An urban vision of rural plenty (and sweetness), she is also a blade-wielding menace to manhood. The 'Swheat Girl was at least remotely related to the earliest female icons of American abundance, those passive earth goddesses carrying severed heads (see figure 1.2), as well as to fin-de-siècle representations of Salome, the favorite castrating female of the decadent imagination.[4]

The cultural significance of this commercial iconography is open to many speculative and interpretative possibilities. Certainly the pastiche form possessed a carnivalesque quality, as it mingled disparate elements from high and low aesthetic traditions. Advertisers routinely raided high culture for sales slogans, melded human and animal forms (figure 4.4),

FIGURE 4.4
Trade card for Lord and Taylor, c. 1895. *Warshaw Collection.*

and arrayed fantastic glyphs in rebuslike formations (figure 5.6). Yet the bizarre imagery could also serve as a veneer for rational appeals to health, efficiency, and economy. The mix of fantasy and rationality took different forms, depending on the commodity advertised and its intended audience.

Consider the advertising for agricultural implements and other farm supplies, the area where female icons of fecundity flourished most dramatically. During the last quarter of the nineteenth century, catalogs for reapers, threshing machines, and fertilizers displayed a remarkable profusion of sexually charged mythic figures—buxom goddesses beneficently befriending tumescent vegetables. Inside each catalog were technical specifications and product descriptions, unadorned prose addressed to the farmer looking for the best investment, but the cover offered food for fantasy: dispensers of largesse who were formidable, sexual, and female (figure 4.5). Yet even the cover sometimes self-consciously consigned the maternal figure to the preindustrial past (figure 4.6).[5]

The cultural significance of this imagery is difficult to assess, but it is possible to suggest that mythic female figures embodied audience values as well as advertising strategies. Of necessity, farmers remained more attuned than city folk to the unpredictable furies and favors of the natural world; small wonder that some farmers, even the most "progressive," might still feel some fitful need to propitiate the goddesses of increase. The available evidence suggests that as late as the post–Civil War decades, more than a few farmers were still attracted to a worldview entangled with myth and magic. Preoccupation with providential portents, belief that certain individuals had supernatural powers of prophecy or divination, faith that one might locate the never-failing nostrum to cure all diseases of man or beast—all these habits of mind lingered in rural areas long after they had been discredited elsewhere by the conventions of rationality. Perhaps the most durable feature of the magical worldview was the conviction that celestial bodies influenced earthly events, a belief that helped preserve the practice of "moon farming" (planting, pruning, grafting, and even cutting timber by the phases of the moon) throughout much of the nineteenth century.

None of this is meant to suggest that late-nineteenth-century farmers were not calculating and commercial, still less to imply that they lived in harmony with the natural world. Indeed, recent research suggests that during the decades after the Civil War, many Midwestern farmers, at least among the wealthier classes, eagerly embraced participation in the international market, invested heavily in mechanization, and sought to master the "science" of economic forecasting. Yet by the 1890s even the most eager

FIGURE 4.5
Catalog cover, Walter Wood Implement Company, 1889. *Warshaw Collection.*

FIGURE 4.6
Catalog cover, McCormick Harvesting Machine Company, 1894. *Warshaw Collection.*

capitalists found themselves baffled and defeated by forces in the futures markets they could neither understand nor control. The feeling that the world was not entirely susceptible to rational management sustained superstitious habits of mind—the shreds and patches of magical tradition if not the tradition itself. That could help explain why advertisers might have felt that mythic emblems of abundance would resonate with the farmer's experience even as he strove to be modern.[6]

Whether those emblems drew on a primitivist or Orientalist promise of regeneration or a more traditional iconography of plenitude, they tended to identify the source of abundance as female. When men appeared in patent medicine advertising they often embodied prudent self-maintenance. If they were associated with agriculture, it was as the virtuous husbandmen of republican mythology. Rarely, if at all, did men represent the sources of psychic or physical abundance.

Nevertheless, by the post–Civil War decades powerful countertendencies were reshaping the commercial iconography of abundance. Perhaps the subtlest and most pervasive was an ideology of national progress that merged technological, intellectual, and spiritual development. That merger was dramatized in John Gast's 1872 painting *Westward Ho!* which was lithographed by George Crofutt and widely distributed as *American Progress*. It accurately reflected a century-long process: the denaturing and disembodiment of female icons of abundance (figure 4.7). Apart from the enormous floating female, the iconography of the picture closely resembles that in Currier & Ives's popular print *Westward the Course of Empire Takes Its Way* (1868). The course of enlightenment proceeds inexorably, led by white men in wagons, stagecoaches, or railroads, carrying tools or pushing plows, also pushing Indians, bear, and bison into the darkness on the left edge of the canvas, and ultimately off the canvas altogether. The female exists in a different order altogether, hovering above the action in her chastely revealing allegorical garb, carrying a volume plainly labeled "school book" and connected to the rest of the painting only by the telegraph wire she is carrying. Woman was here etherealized into the guiding spirit of male-sponsored technological progress.

The print captured some broad cultural tendencies that accompanied the rise of an urban market economy: the displacement of middle- and upper-class women from economic to moral functions; the rise of the notion of "woman as civilizer"; and the erosion of the older identification of women with nature and men with culture. The source of material wealth became more abstract, moving from dirt to gold to currency to

FIGURE 4.7

George A. Crofutt, *American Progress*, 1873, chromolithograph of John Gast, *Westward Ho!*, oil on canvas painting, 1872. *Library of Congress.*

"prime commercial paper"; the economic landscape became populated by "artificial persons" called "corporations"—the word itself suggested not only a reification of the organization as an extension of the person, but also a rationalization of the body, or *corpus,* into an economic abstraction. In such circumstances, it was easier (especially for people in urban commercial centers) to forget the actual, biological sources of material abundance and to attribute generative powers to male-dominated institutions. The culmination of this tendency came during the late nineteenth century with the rise of industrial production and the emergence of a powerful new icon of abundance: the factory (figure 4.8).[7]

With the rise of advertising agencies toward the end of the nineteenth century, as national corporations claimed a major share of the mass circulation of images, the symbolism of abundance began to be more systematically rationalized. The new corps of admakers were more educated and affluent than the chromolithographers had been; they were also more uniformly white Anglo-Saxon Protestant. They were corporate employees rather than artisan–entrepreneurs. The images they designed reflected the marginalizing of female generativity in the managerial worldview. (For a fuller account of the social origins of advertising agency personnel, see chapter 7.)

Of course, the process was never that clear-cut. Images of voluptuous womanhood still had many uses in the streamlined commercial iconography that flourished under corporate auspices. Regressive motifs could be counterbalanced by modernizing paeans to personal efficiency. In 1903, for example, a Shredded Wheat campaign modernized a madonna image, presenting a photograph of a dark and vaguely Hebraic woman draped in biblical robes, head tilted protectively over the child in her lap; the copy accompanying it was composed in the rhetoric of secular perfectionism: "Perfect Food Means Perfect Health. Shredded Wheat Biscuit is the perfect food because it is complete in itself for the perfect nourishment of the

FIGURE 4.8
Trade card, Babbitt's Best Soap, 1889. *Warshaw Collection.*

whole body. Its daily use means bright, sparkling eyes, a clear complexion, a sweet breath, sound, white teeth, an active brain and a symmetrical body." Advertisers yoked traditional maternal imagery with an emergent effort to systematize bodily processes and sanctify physical symmetry. The strategy made for an awkward combination of visual and verbal idioms.[8]

Employing an iconography of imperial primitivism, the developing discourse of abundance contained atavistic urges in a rhetoric of rationality. In 1906, for example, the United Fruit Company orchestrated yearnings for psychic abundance in a pamphlet called *A Short History of the Banana and a Few Recipes for Its Use*. The frontispiece was a bit of phallic exoticism (figure 4.9). A blond woman in flowing robes leans against the banana while she writes with a quill pen in a huge folio volume; despite her (somewhat vague) erotic potential, she is entrusted with the tools of literacy—and alleged West-

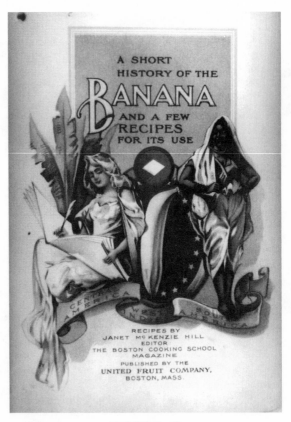

FIGURE 4.9
Pamphlet, United Fruit Company, 1906. *Warshaw Collection.*

ern supremacy. On the other side of the banana stands a barefoot black woman. The white woman smiles slyly; the black woman grins salaciously. Inside, before getting down to the bland business of banana recipes (provided by the prim Boston Cooking School), the text invokes a revealing "fancy": "Until within the last 25 years the fruit of the so-called banana *tree* had been looked upon by people of northern climes with something akin to reverence and awe. The feeling arose, perhaps, from the almost universal fancy that this was the forbidden fruit of the Garden of Eden. The specific name *M. paradisaca,* and the habitat of the fruit in tropical countries, helped foster this idea." Having conjured up mythic associations, the text explained them away by resorting to the idiom of expertise. The Edenic aura, dismissed as the fiction of a more credulous generation, nevertheless was allowed to linger and add luster to rejuvenative fantasies. The mingling of primitivist exoticism and scientific rationality revealed the growing influence of managerial over vernacular styles of commercial discourse.[9]

Corporate advertising was part of a broader surge of managerial ideologies and institutions—a pervasive "incorporation of America," as the cultural historian Alan Trachtenberg has called it, that permanently reshaped the verbal and visual idioms of abundance.[10] To the extent agency executives were able to appear "professional," they won a certain legitimacy among more established professional groups—above all, among those social theorists who accepted the hegemony of the modern corporation as inevitable and beneficent, and who sought new cultural values that would assimilate ordinary folk into the new corporate society. In a sense, this agenda continued the projects of bourgeois moralists, but while the moralists had tried to contain the impact of proliferating goods by preaching a gospel of self-control, the managerial theorists began to develop a new approach, more suited to absorbing the output of the engines of mass production. The economist Simon Nelson Patten (1852–1922) was perhaps the most prescient of these thinkers. He created the disembodied vision of abundance that has pervaded corporate advertising, and American thought generally, throughout most of the twentieth century.

MANAGERIAL ABUNDANCE: DISEMBODIMENT, DISENCHANTMENT, DOMESTICATION

Patten argued that the United States had passed from an "era of scarcity" to an "era of abundance" characterized by a never-ending stream of mass-produced goods and amusements. Yet the consumption of industrial abundance did not have to divert the people from their devotion to disciplined labor, as Protestant moralists had always feared. The desire for cultural and material betterment would keep people striving for more things as they struggled to maintain an ever-rising standard of living.

An unlikely prophet of abundance, Patten was raised as a strongly Calvinist Presbyterian on an Illinois farm. He sustained a lifelong distaste, as he admitted, for "bright colors, curved lines, fancy dress, and pretty faces"; after graduate study at the University of Halle in Germany, he returned a superficially secular and sophisticated young man, entered the University of Chicago Law School and quit after six weeks when his eyesight failed for no organic cause. This apparently psychosomatic ailment sent him back to the farm for three years until it was corrected by a "specialist," according to his biographer, who adds somewhat vaguely that the eye problem was "perhaps a product of guilt about rejecting organized religion and perhaps related to his lifelong distaste for sexuality." Whatever the source of his pain, Patten was clearly a deeply troubled man. He finally found a niche in the economics department at the University of Pennsylvania, where he became an influential and well-loved teacher as well as a widely read commentator on public policy issues. His wife left him for a younger man in 1903, instigating divorce proceedings on grounds of "mental cruelty" and publicly humiliating Patten. But by 1907 the demoralized economist had pulled himself together enough to write *The New Basis of Civilization,* which summarized his ideas in popular form.[11]

Patten's vision of abundance depended on a faith in technological control of nature that rivaled Bacon's *New Atlantis.* "The Secretary of Agriculture recently declared that serious crop failures will occur no more," he announced. "Stable, progressive farming controls the terror, disorder, and devastation of earlier times. A new agriculture means a new civilization." But while we had achieved control over our natural resources, we had yet to utilize all our human resources. What Patten wanted was a dynamic equilibrium: "Leisure and work may supplement each other so fully that every family may have the culture that is the product of the one, and the efficiency that is acquired by the other." Like other "progressive" social theorists from Jane Addams to Walter Lippmann, Patten assumed that modern industrial routine numbed workers' minds and drove them to waste their energies in "sedative pleasures" that were "irrational and extravagant"; the question, for Patten as for the others, was "how shall activity be made pleasurable again, and how shall society utilize the workingman's latent vitality in order to increase his industrial efficiency and give to him the rewards of energies, now ineffective, within his body and mind?" Despite this humane intention, Patten did not challenge the hierarchical organization and division of labor; instead, he assumed that workers would seek satisfaction off the job, and urged that they be taught how to enjoy themselves, how to be consistent consumers of entertainment and goods.[12]

The trade-off between routinized labor and zestful consumption would become the basis for a successful consumer culture throughout much of the twentieth century. But Patten believed the multiplication of wants would do more than merely keep the machines in motion; he insisted it would lead to workers' broadening their horizons and taking pride in their lives, becoming (almost) middle-class.

> During a phase of many young workers' lives they regularly attend the theatre, engaging "season seats" in cheap houses for thirty or fifty cents a performance. Their zest for amusement urges them to submit to the discipline of work, and the habits formed for the sake of gratifying their tastes make the regular life necessary in industry easier and more pleasant. . . . as time passes, the habits formed for purely selfish, economic needs become new motives in the improving type of man. . . . Industrial efficiency, fortified by the sense of enlarging relationships, brings the class to a plane where family life is desired and possible. The horizon of wants and consumption widens. . . . The woman who in girlhood learned to be punctual at her factory bench impresses her acquired quality upon her family and is proud to be named by her tenement neighbors the most particular woman in the house. . . . Her desire is to add to the number of her things, and because of the rapid cheapening of commodities this primary aesthetic longing is among the first to be gratified. The working-man's home is crowded with tawdry, unmeaning, and useless objects; each pointless ornament is loved, however, as the mark of superiority and success, and its enjoyment energizes the possessor.[13]

For Patten, mass-produced abundance was an agent of the civilizing process. To gratify their zest for amusement, young men became habituated to the demands of industrial routine and eventually sought the pleasures of "enlarging relationships"; they married, and their wives reinforced the family's commitment to ever-increasing consumption. Proliferating things, no matter how "tawdry, unmeaning, and useless," were markers of economic and cultural ascent. These assumptions became characteristic features of managerial social science throughout the first half of the twentieth century.[14]

Patten's originality lay in his observation that increased consumption was compatible with the persistence of older puritanical norms.

In the course of consumption expanding by orderly processes the new wants become complex, oppose each other, project themselves into the future, and demand forethought in their balances. The worker steadily and cheerfully chooses the deprivations of this week in order to secure the gratifications of a coming holiday. From this motive the virtue, abstinence, at length emerges and is established as a motive for activity. Men idealize the future and depreciate the present; they advance into a period of restraint and morality, puritan in essence but various in form.[15]

Guided by professional advice in everything from nutrition to artistic taste, the working class would learn to sublimate its grosser pleasures into the pursuit of higher things. Chaotic energies would not be suppressed but would be channeled into a dynamic new form of labor discipline: an incessant cycle of production and consumption. Assuming the bureaucratic and hierarchical organization of labor as a given, Patten focused exclusively on consumption and devised an agenda for the dematerialization of desire.

The political advantage of this strategy was that it allowed Patten to ignore the imperial structures of power that shaped the mass distribution of goods. Two of his examples of luxuries that had become necessities in the new "era of abundance" were sugar and bananas. Workers' developing taste for products like these, he predicted, could be met by the plentiful supplies "latent in Porto Rico and Cuba, and beyond them by the teeming lands of South America, and beyond them by the virgin tropics of another hemisphere." The managerial vision of abundance was rooted in imperial expansion, as the World's Fairs of the early twentieth century made clear. Like the World's Fair promoters and other prophets of corporate-sponsored abundance, Patten subordinated any sense of imperial power relations to a technologically determinist vision of progress. "Rapid distribution of food carries civilization with it," he wrote, "and the prosperity that gives us a Panama Canal with which to reach untouched tropic riches is a distinctive laborer's resource, ranking with refrigerated express and quick freight carriage."[16] By endowing "prosperity" and technology with autonomous force, Patten sanitized the spoils of empire. This became a characteristic strategy not only in managerial thought, but also in twentieth-century corporate advertising. The inhabitants of the "virgin tropics," who had been endowed with a measure of independent existence by the primitivist commercial vernacular of the nineteenth century, were reduced rhetorically to little more than ciphers in this newer discourse.

But it would be ahistorical to point to Patten's blindnesses while ignoring his insights. Unlike most of his predecessors in the economics profession, he sought to bend capitalist productivity to humane purposes; he courageously championed the abolition of poverty. Rather than resurrecting a rural version of republican ideology, he sought to adapt civic virtue to an urban milieu. Insisting on an egalitarian basis for the emergent consumer culture, Patten correctly saw the need to maintain some equilibrium between production and consumption through the maintenance of a well-paid working population. He wanted not only to channel uninformed consumer spending through professional expertise, but also to stabilize the business cycle through the equitable distribution of goods. When that equilibrium was lost through maldistributed prosperity, as in the 1920s and 1980s, the basis for a consumer culture was badly eroded. Patten would not have been surprised.

Still, Patten's greatest importance in the present context is the illustrative value of his thought, its capacity to summarize and illuminate the broad redefinition of abundance that was occurring during the early twentieth century under the auspices of managerial thought. Patten revealed clearly (if unwittingly) what others sensed vaguely. Popular notions of abundance were moving away from their origins in the rhythms of agrarian life and bodily existence. It was not simply that farmers were displaced from the land but that, in the scientifically managed workplace, factory and office employees were increasingly cut off from the vernacular artisanal traditions that linked brain and hand in "local knowledge."[17] What was obscured was any sense that abundance could be the result of patient cooperation between the human mind and the material world. In a disembodied discourse of abundance, enjoyment of the fruits of one's labors became less important than the pursuit of disposable goods.

Disembodiment directly affected the carnivalesque dimensions of abundance imagery: they were more sanitized in twentieth-century corporate advertising than in the nineteenth-century commercial vernacular. After 1900 the sheer amount of flesh on display decreased; the grotesque body of Carnival virtually disappeared, except as a warning of what might happen if one failed to heed the morning exercise instructions from Metropolitan Life or refused to reach for a Lucky instead of a sweet. Protuberant bellies, breasts, and buttocks gave way to firmer, tighter, more youthful figures; men became more boyish, women more girlish. Eroticism was deprived of its exotic and primitive qualities; rather than "introducing sex into advertising" (as so many admen's memoirs claim), corporate advertising preserved the older prurience in a newer idiom of health and clinical frankness (figure 4.10). (Exotic prurience survived in working-class entertainments like burlesque shows and nickelodeons, in pornography, and in general on the margins of the man-

FIGURE 4.10
Woodbury's Facial Soap advertisement, *Good Housekeeping*, 1936.

agerial culture.) Changes in visual and verbal conventions also reflected the marginalizing of the carnivalesque. Surreal merging of humans and animals, punning and word play, the ironic raiding of high culture for sales slogans—all these gambits became less available to the advertiser under managerial auspices. Ad agencies turned increasingly toward realism.[18]

Along with the containment of Carnival, the disembodiment of abundance also involved the devaluation of female authority. The imagery surrounding advertised commodities showed a definite movement away from formidable mother figures to giggling teenagers. The American Ceres (figure 4.11) became the girl next door, as when Kellogg's introduced the Sweetheart of the Corn in 1907 (figure 4.12); the image was widely repro-

FIGURE 4.11
American Cereal Company, pamphlet, 1900. *Warshaw Collection.*

FIGURE 4.12
Kellogg Cereal Company, advertisement, 1907. *Warshaw Collection.*

duced and circulated. The invocation of the mythic was replaced by an apotheosis of the everyday. And even where mythic females survived, they were disempowered, as in the feminine icons of electricity that American Telephone & Telegraph and other corporations produced during the early 1900s. As the literary critic Martha Banta has observed, there was "something trivial in the scale of these Electricity Girls, something hand-me-down about the aesthetic traditions that lie behind their unsexy bodies and smooth faces." They were messengers from the gods, but not the gods themselves—just as, in the developing imagery of abundance, women were mostly bearers of good news from the deus ex machina of the factory system.[19]

By the 1910s, most commonly, women in advertisements were merely beneficiaries of the largesse generated by the male genius of mass production—new emblematic expressions of old masculine anxieties. Women had been associated with suffocating superabundance and "effeminate luxury" for centuries. The Fashionable Woman was the focus of many republican and Protestant polemics against luxury, but in the twentieth century, men (and a few managerial-minded women) developed a less moralistic, more secular idiom. In modern advertising, the Fashionable Woman became "Mrs. Consumer." The passions of the Fashionable Woman were constrained by internalized moral strictures; the passions of Mrs. Consumer were constrained by her own commitment to managerial rationality. This iconic representation of the modern woman was girlish rather than authoritative, and reassuringly dependent on corporate expertise. To be sure, Mrs. Consumer remained potentially dangerous in her new guise: her ravenous appetite for goods would still be a stock gag in comic strips and vaudeville humor. But corporate advertising sublimated women's imagined voracity into efficient household management (figure 4.13), and rationalized the link between femininity and luxury.[20]

Similar patterns could be discerned in the iconography of psychic abundance, as patent medicines came increasingly from well-lighted laboratories rather than dark forests. By the 1920s, science was reified and venerated as an autonomous force. While the imagery of science was superficially neutered, the scientist himself was universally male, a modern magus penetrating surfaces to reveal untold mysteries in hidden depths. Of course there was nothing genuinely scientific in advertising's evocation of technological miracles and white-coated wizards, but the fictive realm represented in these advertisements was thoroughly disenchanted—a universe of inert objects, manipulable by a separate human subject.

The disembodiment of abundance imagery was clearest in agricultural

FIGURE 4.13
Advertisement, N. W. Ayer & Son, *Saturday Evening Post*, 24 March 1928.

advertising. After 1900, with startling abruptness, machine replaced *mater;* mythic emblems of fecundity yielded to unadorned photographs of male-operated threshers and harvesters, sometimes juxtaposed against drawings of primitive peasant methods. The slogan "Every farm a factory" implied a depoliticization as well as a disenchantment of familiar agrarian imagery. At about the same time that republican pastoralism breathed its last, as representatives of Eastern capital defeated the Populist movement for a democratically managed currency, images of virtuous yeomen became as scarce as those of mythic maternal females. Advertisements directed to farmers caught the new and more frankly commercial orientation. In a *Farmers Journal* for 1897, the Quinnipiac Fertilizer Company claimed to be "Nature's Assistant"; its advertisement showed a man hoeing gold coins and advised farmers that they could "Sow Quinnipiac and Harvest Dollars." A pamphlet addressed to wheat farmers by the Provident Investment Bureau in 1903 presented a standard cornucopia scene, with many traditional icons of abundance in the background—shocks of wheat, pink-cheeked babies, hollyhocks in profusion, and apples ripe to bursting—except that out of the cornucopia poured a stream of gold coins. By 1924 the dairy farmers' trade association pamphlet *The Home Cow Care Doctor* was making the farmer's role more explicit: "One of the biggest leaks in dairy profits is in maintaining cows that do not pay," the association warned; systematic record keeping was necessary to spot the unproductive milkers and treat them with Dubl-K brand Kow Kare and other food supplements. In agricultural advertising, the sturdy yeoman was being stripped of his symbolic garments, reduced to an efficient manager.[21]

The point is not that commercial agriculture was new in the early twentieth century but that it was entering a more rationalized phase. The changes in iconography reflected familiar shifts in political economy and ideology, as well as less familiar changes in gender mythology. Throughout the latter decades of the nineteenth century, the ancient idea of the maternal origins of abundance preserved a powerful but oblique appeal even as it was gradually consigned to realms of idle fancy and decorative frivolity. After the turn of the century, it was abandoned almost altogether—at least by the makers of mass-produced images.

The devaluation of maternal authority was accelerated by aesthetic as well as sociological programs for rationalization. In *Concerning the Spiritual in Art* (1914), Wassily Kandinsky announced a key item on many modernist agendas when he proclaimed his intention to "free art from its bonds to material reality." For an artist, that goal seems self-contradictory, but it does suggest the strain of masculine protest that runs through so many modernist polemics—particularly the functionalist critique of ornament and clutter in interior design. In the United States the flight from *mater* more commonly ended in the aesthetic compromises of the Arts and Crafts movement and the ideological compromise of "masculine domesticity," wherein men were encouraged to spend more time in familial pleasures. Female hegemony over domestic space could never be overturned completely without a challenge to the sexual division of labor—a challenge no male modernizer (artist or advertiser) was willing to mount. Nevertheless, in the domain of objects—the domestic interior—as in the rhetoric and iconography of commodities, one can see parallel devaluations of female authority.[22]

Still, the nurturant dimensions of abundance imagery could not be suppressed altogether. Beneficent providers survived, often as desexualized members of subordinate castes (figure 4.14). In this 1907 advertisement, Rastus, the grinning, obsequious provider of Cream of Wheat who had been introduced in 1893, made one of his rare appearances without an apron. The form recalls the 'Swheat Girl (figure 4.3), the urban-rural pas-

FIGURE 4.14
Cream of Wheat advertisement, 1907. *Warshaw Collection.*

tiche—the chef's hat combined with the bib overalls of an agricultural laborer (or slave) and the consciously archaic scythe. Yet unlike the blade of the 'Swheat Girl's sickle, Rastus's scythe blade is concealed; his aggressive/erotic potential is masked and immobilized. Like Aunt Jemima, created in 1890, Rastus is rooted in a static, folkish vision of preindustrial abundance.

The significance of these figures cannot be written off as "racial stereotyping." The question is, Why did these particular stereotypes survive and flourish anomalously amid the disenchantment of abundance imagery? Part of the answer may be that the creators as well as the consumers of these images were recalling the nurturant world of warmth and plenty embodied in an older iconography of abundance. Those sorts of desires remained largely subterranean in corporate advertising until the 1930s, when the shock of the Depression intensified the white middle class's yearnings for psychic as well as economic security. The reassuring vision of an organic, cohesive American Way of Life pervaded WPA murals and Popular Front posters as well as popular cultural artifacts from *Porgy and Bess* to the film version of *The Grapes of Wrath*, from *Oklahoma!* to *It's a Wonderful Life;* in most of its mainstream versions, this folkish ideology presented the American family as the center of that Way of Life. Desires for the restoration of abundance focused on idealized and often preindustrial domestic settings: witness Norman Rockwell's *Saturday Evening Post* covers celebrating material and psychic abundance: "Freedom from Want" and "Freedom from Fear."[23]

This sensibility also seeped into corporate advertising, where it coexisted uneasily with the celebration of mass-produced abundance. Currier & Ives visions, embodying an imagined world of preindustrial domestic harmony, were enlisted in the service of canned goods and other processed foods (figure 4.15). Domesticity and disenchantment were twinned in the emerging corporate version of the American Way of Life. During and after World War II, as American business set out to recapture much of the prestige it had lost during the Depression, corporations reclaimed their role as benevolent mediator between science and the suburban family. Du Pont's promotional photographs from the 1950s (figure 4.16) explicitly merged domestication and disenchantment, placing the family amid a surfeit of standardized things.

Patten had wanted consumers to turn their attention to higher things, but by the 1950s it had become apparent (at least to Patten's descendants in the social sciences) that the progress he had predicted had not in fact

FIGURE 4.15
Hurff's Soups advertisement, *Life* magazine, 1936.

FIGURE 4.16
Promotional photograph by Alex Henderson, Du Pont Chemicals, from *Better Living* magazine, November 1951. *Courtesy of Hagley Museum and Library, Wilmington, Delaware.*

occurred. Consumption had indeed proved to be a goad to labor discipline; more people had steadier jobs, and more things, than at any other period in modern American history. But the tenor of cultural life had not improved, at least from the vantage of critics like William H. Whyte and David Riesman. They argued that Americans had settled down into a postheroic age of suburban affluence, with no higher aspiration than the multiplication of their creature comforts. Was this to be the fulfillment of all those utopian dreams of abundance? Backyard barbecues and Simonized Buicks? Suburban security, tedious routine, rampant anxiety? Riesman and his contemporaries were distressed. No wonder Riesman titled his 1963 collection of essays *Abundance for What?* The dreams of liberal improvement, as well as those of socialist utopia, had come to nothing on the shoals of roast beef and apple pie.[24]

Or so it seemed to post–World War II cultural critics, who had a tendency to view the United States—and, indeed, the modern world—through the standardizing lens of "mass society" theory. But if one removes that lens, one can glimpse alternative visions of abundance surviving amid the emergent consumer culture, vestiges of the carnivalesque, glimmers of magical transformation to a state of ease and plenty. Under the right circumstances, certain kinds of commodities could still carry a charge of animation, could still connect the self to the material world. Maybe the promise of modernity was not entirely false.

A REANIMATED WORLD

The ancient paradisal promise survived in the idiom of imperial consumption, but that promise was framed in new forms of gender, class, and cultural differentiation. Two scenes from American social history illustrate the pattern. In Arrow Rock, Missouri, in 1914, a local male journalist described a recurrent ritual of the developing consumer culture:

> I have often seen a hard-worked country lady come into a store and inquire for all the handsomest goods in the stock, and admire them, comment on them, take out great strips of pretty patterns, and with her knotted fingers fold them into pleats and drape them over her plain skirt, her face illumined with pleasure at the splendor of such material could she wear it. It was really pathetic and deserving of sympathy. The love of what is beautiful was as intense in her soul as that of her more fortunate sister who could afford to wear it. Bright, harmonious colors, and fine fabrics, over which she would draw her tired hands caressingly, soothed and gratified her. Who could grudge her such a privilege?[25]

From this condescending but sympathetic male perspective, several salient themes emerge. Consumer goods were artifacts of an aesthetic dimension, a realm of compensation for the work and worry of everyday life, a mental and emotional space where one could express "the love of what is beautiful" and luxuriate in the sensuous experience of material abundance. The providers of abundance were mostly male, and women were usually the recipients of their largesse. For the less affluent, like this "hard-worked country lady," the possibility of purchase lay forever out of reach, but the pleasures of sensuous contact were at least fleetingly available.

Ten years later, in 1924, a similar scene was witnessed by Gerald W. Johnson, a reporter for the *Baltimore Sun,* in Greensboro, North Carolina. It was Saturday, the day the mill villagers filled the streets downtown, and one young couple with three children had pushed their way through the throng to a store window where a luminescent display of silks cascaded to the floor. They stared and stood. "Languidly chewing gum and inspecting rich brocades woven for mistresses of empire and broad seas," the wife was "perhaps justly an object of derision," Johnson wrote. "But I pray you pardon me if I do not join in your mirth, for I am somehow not in the mood for laughter. I have seen the gleam in her eyes."[26]

More thoroughly than the scene in Arrow Rock, the Greensboro moment enacted a dematerialization of desire. Even had the mill woman been able to purchase the rich brocades, doctrines of stylistic progress might have decreed a disenchantment sooner rather than later. But she was not able. She was part of a proletariat reduced to unfulfilled longing for the goods in the glittering shop windows of consumer culture.

Despite Johnson's urgings, though, one cannot dismiss the gleam in the mill woman's eye as merely the sad signature of her victimization. Both for her and for the farm wife, visions of plenty had potentially political implications. In Greensboro as in Arrow Rock, the longing for luxury, for a life of ease in a land beyond toil, posed an alternative to the work-obsessed visions of modern capitalism and socialism. Among the earliest to recognize this were the theorists associated with the Frankfurt School, who sought to free Marxist cultural criticism from its productivist past. "We cannot blame people that they are more interested in the sphere of privacy and consumption rather than [in] production," Max Horkheimer wrote Leo Lowenthal in 1942. "This trait contains a Utopian element; in Utopia production does not play a decisive part. It is the land of milk and honey. I think it is of deep significance that art and poetry have always shown an affinity to consumption." Theodor Adorno had already criticized Thorstein

Veblen's attempt to reduce all consumption to status display. In Frankfurt, as in Arrow Rock, Missouri, social observers were beginning to recognize the connections between "the sphere of privacy and consumption" and what Herbert Marcuse would later call the aesthetic dimension.[27]

Utopian fantasies of abundance appeared only fitfully in the discourse of political radicalism, flickering through the hobo and labor songs of the early twentieth century, notably "The Big Rock Candy Mountains." This song, written around 1910 by the Industrial Workers of the World organizer Mac McClintock, was full of reworked images from the Land of Cockaigne.

> In the Big Rock Candy Mountains
> You never change your socks,
> And little streams of alcohol
> Come a-tricklin' down the rocks. . . .

> There's a lake of stew and whisky, too
> You can paddle around 'em in a big canoe
> In the Big Rock Candy Mountains.

> O—the buzzing of the bees in the cigarette trees
> Round the soda-water fountain,
> Where the lemonade springs and the blue bird sings
> In the Big Rock Candy Mountains.

> The farmer's trees are full of fruit,
> The barns are full of hay,
> I'm going to stay where you sleep all day,
> Where they boiled in oil the inventor of toil
> In the Big Rock Candy Mountains.

Here, as in the Land of Cockaigne, the pleasures are primarily food and rest rather than sex—to say nothing of more ethereal delights. It may not be the most edifying utopian vision, but it may, from time to time, have been an empowering one. From the proletarian point of view, the hope of effortless abundance may have been a more inspiring ideal than the commitment to relentless productivity ensconced in both the Marxist and liberal traditions.[28]

At their most optimistic, some Frankfurt School thinkers spun out the theoretical implications of this antiproductivist impulse. For Erich Fromm as well as (at times) for Walter Benjamin and Herbert Marcuse, the argument ran something like this: The psychic foundations of capitalism were patriarchal, but its triumph opened the way for the possibility of a return to a matriarchal culture—that is, by providing access to an abundance of goods and services, capitalist institutions allowed the development of a less achievement-oriented reality principle. Socialism, to maintain any popular appeal, had to preserve this promise of a return to a more nurturant, matriarchal culture.[29]

This was a powerful and important critique of orthodox Marxist thought. Looking back to Patten's hopes for a wider working-class horizon, the Frankfurt School argument looked forward to the experience of young people born after World War II in the more affluent sectors of Western society. Temporarily freed from the grip of necessity, by the 1960s they were able to move beyond narrow economic concerns to pose fundamental questions about the quality of life in an overorganized social system.

Yet the Frankfurt School view, advanced most forthrightly in Marcuse's *Eros and Civilization* (1955), failed to acknowledge that the utopian promise of consumer culture foundered on a fundamental contradiction. Whatever the abundance of things that could be efficiently produced and distributed, the machinery of production and distribution still required the habits of mind that had marginalized matriarchal values in the first place: the commitment to technical rationality and systematic productivity, the disdain for genuine leisure and idle curiosity. Patten had correctly foreseen the trade-off that would have to be made to sustain an "era of abundance" under the auspices of corporate capitalism: routinized labor discipline for high-level consumption. The utopian elements that survived in the iconography of corporate advertising were vitiated by the images' instrumentalist purpose; they were designed to sell particular products and sanctify a particular economic system. Neither aim had much to do with hedonism.

That may be why the most memorable utopian visions of abundance in the modern world were sometimes created not by advertisers or social theorists on the cutting edge of change, but by writers, thinkers, and artists—popular as well as avant-garde—who remained rooted in places where the disenchanting movements of modernity had not thoroughly penetrated, provincial backwaters where the carnivalesque commercial vernacular as well as older iconographic traditions had been partially preserved. These people were not "ascetics," as critics of consumer culture are so often alleged to be. Indeed, their visions of material abundance were charged with far more enduring life than those of their contemporaries in corporate advertising. They were engaged, among other things, in reanimating the world.

One of the strangest (and most revealing) lyrics of plenty in this alternative tradition came from the pen of the visionary novelist Bruno Schulz, a Polish Jew who lived during the early twentieth century in an obscure Galician town. He taught art to high school students, wrote and drew in his leisure hours, and died in 1942, casually shot by the SS in the street when he had ventured into the "Aryan" section of his town. His prose fiction constituted "an attempt at eliciting the history of a certain family, a certain house in a provincial city." Part of the history of that family involved the impact of mass-produced American abundance—more in fantasy than in actuality—on the local population, the people living out their lives in "mournful villages under skies as white as paper, hardened by the prose of daily drudgery. . . . creatures chained forever to their tiny destinies." Into their lives intruded the imagery of advertising and American mass culture. They hurried aimlessly through everyday business to the tune of barrel organs playing "Daisy, Daisy, give me your answer do."[30]

Advertising imagery had a special significance for Schulz. His father was a textile merchant, forced by mysterious ailments to take to his bed, where he did nothing but paste exotic colored decals into a huge ledger. Bruno was fascinated by his father's new "work" and indeed by all the detritus of old-fashioned commercial life. He became a devotee of the esoteric "cinnamon shops":

> [Their] dark and solemn interiors were redolent of the smell of paint, varnish, and incense; of the aroma of distant countries and rare commodities. You could find in them bengal lights, magic boxes, the stamps of long-forgotten countries, Chinese decals, indigo, calaphony from Malabar, the eggs of exotic insects, parrots, toucans, live salamanders and basilisks, mandrake roots, mechanical toys from Nuremberg, homunculi in jars, microscopes, binoculars, and, most especially, strange and rare books, old folio volumes full of astonishing engravings and amazing stories."[31]

This realm was threatened (in Schulz's view) by the tawdry American-style commodities that were beginning to appear on what Schulz called *The Street of Crocodiles* (1934). In *Sanatorium Under the Sign of the Hourglass* (1937), Schulz tried to capture some of his own childlike confusion in the face of such developments.

He began in an attempt to invoke the chaos of preconscious life, "the vastness of the transcendental," by describing what he called The Book. This extraordinary artifact was more sensuous than cerebral, more important for the visual imagery it unleashed than for any ideas it contained. A mass-produced commodity, The Book was also a central, magical embodiment of Schulz's connectedness to the material world. He associated it with his father and located both in a penumbra of generative imagery.

> The Book . . . Somewhere in the dawn of childhood, at the first day-break of life, the horizon had brightened with its gentle glow. The Book lay in all its glory on my father's desk, and he, quietly engrossed in it, patiently rubbed a wet fingertip on the top of decals, until the blank pages grew opaque and ghostly with a delightful foreboding and, suddenly flaking off in bits of tissue, disclosed a peacock-eyed frag-ment; blurred with emotion, one's eyes turned toward a virgin dawn of divine colors, toward a miraculous moistness of purest azure.[32]

The vision of a "virgin dawn," the feeling of a "miraculous moistness," stem not from mother but from father. Yet The Book itself possesses extra-ordinary power to generate images of natural abundance. Left alone with The Book, the boy watches the wind rustle through its pages, lifting the pictures, "merging the colors and shapes . . . freeing from among the let-ters flocks of swallows and larks." The birds recall the flocks of pigeons that James Fenimore Cooper saw at the source of the Susquehanna, and the flurry of doves produced by the circus conjurer's trick. The wind opened the book "softly like a huge cabbage rose; the petals . . . slowly dis-closed a blue pupil, a scattered peacock's heart, or a chattering nest of hummingbirds." It is a moment of pre-oedipal bliss, but with the parental sexes reversed:

> That was a very long time ago. My mother had not appeared yet. I spent my days alone with my father in our room, which at that time was as large as the world.
> Then my mother materialized and that bright early idyl came to an end. Seduced by my mother's caresses, I forgot my father, and my life began to run along a new and different track with no holidays and no miracles.[33]

Then one day, peering lasciviously over the shoulder of the serving maid, he reads the story of Anna Csillag, a Moravian woman who had been "struck with a poor growth of hair" but who had "received signs and por-tents and concocted . . . a miraculous nostrum that restored fertility to her scalp." She began to "grow an enormous stole of hair"—and so did her brothers, brothers-in-law, and nephews. She became the benefactress of the village, and now wished, by promoting her nostrum, to become the apostle of hairiness to all humanity. As he reads, the boy is stunned. He realizes "this was The Book, its last pages, the unofficial supplement, the tradesman's entrance full of refuse and trash!" The maid and the mother have been tearing a few pages from it every day to wrap the father's lunch. Not many pages remained—"Not a single page of the real text," the boy laments. "Nothing but advertisements."[34]

The advertisements offer a mere simulacrum of the visions of abundance released by the "real text." Page after page of nostrum advertisements are followed by an offer of "real German canaries from the Hartz mountains, cageloads of goldfinches and starlings, basketfuls of winged talkers and singers . . . destined to sweeten the life of the lonely, to give bachelors a substitute for family life, to squeeze from the hardest of hearts the semblance of maternal warmth brought forth by their touching helplessness." Even the semblance of warmth soon disappears in "a display of boring quackery"—a gaggle of confidence men raising their voices to a "maniacal babble." Among the most prominent is "a gentleman [who] offered an infallible method of achieving decisiveness and determination and spoke of high principles and character." But the last page of the book presents a transvaluation of those values, a destruction of male "character" by a female consumer–dominatrix.

> A certain Mme. Magda Wang who specialized in the "dressage" of men—the last word underlined by an ironical flash of her eyes. And strangely enough she seemed to be sure of the approval of those about whom she spoke so cynically, and in the peculiar confusion of her words one felt that their meaning had mysteriously shifted and that we had moved to a totally different sphere, where the compass worked from back to front.[35]

This last page, Schulz admitted, "left me peculiarly dizzy, filled with a mixture of longing and excitement."

What are we to make of this fantastic encounter in a provincial town between a writer and the commercial paean to plenty? Schulz unwittingly replicated what by the 1930s had become a characteristic modernist move among male writers: the resort to a discourse of authenticity as a basis for criticizing mass culture. Juxtaposing the authenticity of The Book against the artificiality of the advertisements, Schulz linked the latter with domineering women. But he did not pretend to divorce himself entirely from the magic of the commodity realm. Though he dismissed the advertised version of abundance as little more than a "maniacal babble," he admitted it filled him with "a mixture of longing and excitement." The advertisements, moreover, were bound up under the same cover with The Book, which was itself a magical commodity. Indeed, one could argue that The

Book embodied the fundamental premises of symbolic consciousness: it was the union of thoughts and things; it was the word made flesh. And rather than isolating its possessor on a progressive path of status ascent, it reconnected him with other people and the past.

The Book lay far outside the universe of discourse constructed by corporate advertising. Yet its powerful significance for Schulz, along with its connections to the carnivalesque commerce of the cinnamon shops, suggest its capacity to illuminate some fundamental relationships between advertising and the wider culture. Throughout the twentieth century, people have imagined alternatives to the disembodied corporate vision of abundance; many have fastened on the detritus of commodity civilization itself as they seek another way of being in the world. Bricolage, verbal or artifactual, has been a strategy for reanimating matter. What the reanimators were up against is explored in the following section, which traces the rise of national advertising as a force in the shaping of American social values.

PART II

The Containment
of Carnival:

Advertising and
American Social Values from the
Patent Medicine Era to the
Consolidation of Corporate Power

CHAPTER 5

The Merger of Intimacy and Publicity

DISTINCTIONS between public and private have always been artificial. All intimate human experiences come freighted with some sort of cultural baggage—some burden of expectations, aspirations, and inhibitions that reflect the dominant values of a particular moment and milieu. Yet in the bourgeois cultures of the modern West, the relationship between public and private became a problematic issue. The two spheres were both more carefully separated and more subtly meshed than they had been in earlier times.

The apotheosis of private selfhood coincided with the emergence of new ways to invade privacy—and new justifications for the invasion. Intimate matters, once thought beneath the attention of the governing classes, became topics of urgent public debate. The quality of one's family life, even of one's sexuality, became increasingly linked to citizenship and success. A tightening connection between individual and national health emerged in the rhetoric of Victorian reformers: they opposed masturbation and meat-eating as menaces to public good; they advocated rehabilitative prisons, schools for social order, and asylums that redefined "insanity" as "mental illness."[1] By the early twentieth century, body and soul had merged in new, more diffuse and sweeping definitions of normality. The developing managerial idiom sanctioned systematic intrusion into the "private sphere."

The work of Michel Foucault, in particular, has drawn scholars' attention to these connections between intimate experience and public discourse. Studies of "the rhetoric of the body" have become virtually a cottage industry. This body of thought (at its best) illuminates the dispersed forms of power exercised by managerial elites in modern societies; it shows how, during the early twentieth century, new notions of personal health and well-being could come to constitute a new model of human subjectivity, one that sanctioned the authority of the sorting and categorizing institutions which were emerging to dominate the managerial order: prisons, schools, corporations, government agencies.[2]

Corporate advertising played a crucial role in promoting the ethos of management. Through market research, advertisers pioneered the statistical surveillance of private life, a practice that would become central to the maintenance of managerial cultural hegemony. Perhaps more important, advertisers created powerful images of human subjectivity that embodied the values of the emergent social system. If any one value dominated all others, it was a new and more demanding notion of individual well-being that could be summarized as "personal efficiency." The phrase signified a tighter fit between the supposedly private realm of physical or emotional health and the public world of organized competition for success.

In promoting this link, advertisers revealed their connections to other managerial professionals: social scientists, business executives, physicians, psychotherapists, even some liberal Protestant ministers. Despite their many differences, all these groups unwittingly shared some common concerns. They wanted to create and put to use a new "science of man" that reflected their own experience and aspirations more accurately than the evangelical ethos had done, a worldview that seemed more appropriate for the emerging twentieth century.

The managerial professionals' project was not merely a power grab. It assuaged popular anxieties with new therapies and explanatory models. It clarified the confusion of the late-nineteenth-century "knowledge marketplace" by substituting universal (often quantifiable) standards for the rule-of-thumb "local knowledge" that had generally governed vernacular usage. It was often rooted in an understandable yearning for clear and stable meaning in a market society where transcendent standards were losing legitimacy, and in a laudable desire to combat ignorance and raise material standards of living.[3]

But managerial values were, in a fundamental sense, imperialistic: they sanctioned a dualistic pseudoscientism and systematized an anxious, driven mode of personal conduct—a self made transparent through ideals of clinical frankness and coherent through the relentless expenditure of energy. The managed self was not a departure from but a continuation of the Protestant effort to stabilize the epistemological sorcery of the marketplace. Like earlier, more overtly moralistic idioms of self-control, the managerial idiom marginalized other ways of knowing, other ways of being in the world.

Yet the success of the managerial drive for domination remains an open question. A growing number of historians and anthropologists have begun exploring the variety of means that ordinary Americans have used to preserve vernacular ways of knowing, refusing to conform to the standardized models held out to them by national advertisers.[4] Regional, religious, ethnic, and occupational traditions survived and nurtured alternative modes of conduct and consciousness. Despite advertisers' assumptions, not everyone has wanted to look or be like the people pictured in advertisements. Advertisers' reconstitution of personal well-being probably worked most effectively among would-be professionals like themselves.

Even among professionals, there was social and personal conflict. Advertising executives and copywriters felt it acutely. On the one hand, they were the point men of modernization, promoting managerial ideals of human subjectivity in a variety of cultural sites: visual and verbal texts in magazines, newspapers, and other mass media. They were well positioned to serve as the agents of the new and diffuse kinds of cultural power that characterized the governing institutions of the modern world. As products of a common Protestant culture, they embraced both older and newer versions of linguistic transparency. Yet for many, the claim to provide a window on a particular commodity was a superficial gloss; admakers continued to behave as if they were involved in a rhetorical performance intended to mesmerize an anxious audience. Despite their disdain for the patent medicine era, national advertisers remained wedded to its principal strategy: the promise of magical self-transformation through the ritual of purchase. Seeking to appropriate newer idioms, they remained attached to older traditions. The self constructed by managerial thought was still filled with boundless desires that could not be entirely harnessed to corporate purposes, that kept spilling over the boundaries of personal efficiency. It was as if advertising people sensed that the management of desire could never be complete, in their own lives or any others, and that behind the search for total control lay the specter of absolute panic.

These anxieties grew out of Puritan tradition. Preoccupation with bodily purification and control linked advertising executives with the Protestant past as well as the professional present. For centuries, the saint's struggle for purity had been spiritual but not by any means ethereal. Poets and preachers described sin in excremental terms and conversion as a form of purgation. By the later nineteenth century, the program of purification was shifting from soul to body: concerns about "self-pollution" took increasingly physical form. Old anxieties survived on a secular basis.[5]

The secularization of self-distrust was a leitmotif of Victorian cultural change. Increasingly in advertising appeals as well as other forms of popular literature, it was not the soul that was making the body feel bad but the body that was behind the soul's distemper. Cartesian dualism persisted, but materialists gained the upper hand. This provided an opening for mainstream allopathic physicians. For decades, the practice of medicine had been a dark and bloody ground of conflict between allopaths (who sought to cure specific disease entities) and homeopaths (who aimed to treat the entire organism), along with assorted naturopaths, water-cure therapists, and herbal healers. Materialism provided allopaths with a bedrock of scientific legitimacy.[6]

In the emerging somatic style of professional medical thought, Protestant habits of mind mingled with materialist metaphysics. The influence of the First Law of Thermodynamics, formulated by Hermann von Helmholtz in 1847, encouraged the literate public to think of the body as a crude input/output system: food in; energy, including thought, out. Among many educated Americans in the waning decades of the nineteenth century, mind was increasingly held to be a direct expression of body. Scientific racism helped to promote such practices as anthropometry, which explored the link between facial angle and mental capacity. Mechanistic metaphors proliferated. By 1900, a contributor to *Popular Science Monthly* summarized decades of conventional wisdom when he described the body as an engine.[7]

Yet the dogmatism of the materialist metaphysic reinforced a vitalist countercurrent, flowing from the Protestant hope for personal transformation as well as the romantic and evangelical emphasis on the fluidity of the self. From the vitalist view, religious beliefs could be evaluated with respect to their impact on psychic and physical well-being. Liberals and evangelicals alike—Arminians all—were preoccupied with sustaining beliefs that made people feel better. Beliefs could do more than "calm the mind" (as *Godey's* said of guardian angels); they could sustain or revitalize the body.

This was the faith associated with the traditional Protestant "cure of souls"; it was also the claim of many mesmerists, animal magnetists, and a host of other healers on the margins of professional respectability. Among them was Phineas Parkhurst Quimby, mentor to Mary Baker Eddy, who insisted that certain beliefs could open the floodgates of the mind's unconscious depths, allowing the "magnetic fluid" to energize the entire organism. By the 1870s, other, more scholarly observers were commenting on the mind's mysterious influence on muscle sensations, especially pain, but Quimby's idiom was the more popular. References to magnetism and electricity—benign, invisible powers—began to appeal to devotees of vital force. Using physiological language, the vitalist tradition preserved the faith in transfiguration—the hope that the self-distrustful soul might be released from the endless process of purification into a harmonious realm of abundant psychic energy.[8]

Conflicts among materialists and vitalists, doctors, ministers, and irregular health reformers made the debate over personal well-being a muddle of conflicting theories and impulses. Patent medicine advertisers eagerly entered the fray. The melding of mental and physical health in popular discourse, combined with the lack of any clear standard of medical expertise, created opportunities for vendors of packaged nostrums to make extraordinary claims for their products' regenerative powers. Nostrum advertisers often stayed close to Christian sensibility: without attacking belief in Providence directly, they emphasized the individual's responsibility for choosing health over disease. Merging an Arminian stress on choice with a humoral conception of illness, many advertisers offered a materialist version of Protestant purification.

Materialist assumptions became more overt during the latter half of the nineteenth century, but so did a vitalist countercurrent that energized the growth of primitivist and exoticist commercial iconography. Icons of lush sensuality constituted a common pool of imagery which melded magic elixirs with breakfast foods, cosmetics, perfumes, clothing, corsets, and other products that promised bodily regeneration. In this era when corporate advertisers and their agencies had not yet consolidated control over commercial image production, the symbolic universe of advertising preserved idiosyncrasies rooted in the diversity of local, entrepreneurial enterprise. The golden age of patent medicines, from 1880 to 1906, when the Pure Food and Drug Law was passed, was also a golden age of commercial rhetoric, iconography, and performance.

The theatrical dimensions of the business were most apparent in the medicine show, which grew more spectacular even as its impresarios were being relegated to the margins of commerce. A leading participant, Nevada Ned (N. T. Oliver), observed:

> Full evenings of drama, vaudeville, musical comedy, Wild West shows, minstrels, magic, burlesque, dog and pony circuses, not to mention Punch and Judy, pantomime, movies, menagerie, bands, parades, and pie-eating contests, have been thrown in with Ho Ang-Nan, the great Chinese herb remedy, gratis or for a nominal admission, and med shows have played in opera houses, halls, storerooms, ball parks, show boats, and tents, as well as doorways, street corners, and fairs.

The circus atmosphere fostered attachments to exoticism. One of Nevada Ned's ventures in the 1880s was a tonic he called Hindoo Patalka; he "hired two Syrians out of a rug store and a Hindoo who was doing a magic act in variety, and decked them out in Oriental costume." An elephant, borrowed from a Philadelphia circus man, completed the ensemble. The troupe endured a series of misadventures until the elephant went "through a bridge in Jersey and through the ice in the stream below." Nevada Ned returned the elephant to its owner, dismissed his assistants, and went back to marketing liver pads to the black community of Wilmington, North Carolina, who embraced the pads (Ned thought) as "a new and potent conjure."[9]

But more respectable advertisers also employed theatrical exoticism, in print and pictorial advertising as well as sidewalk spectacles. Patent medicine appeals merged with other health-related advertising in contributing to a carnivalesque commercial vernacular.[10] Together they constituted a fantastic counterpoint to the official idioms of repression in late Victorian culture. Vernacular advertising promoted the persistent dream of bodily revitalization, and preserved the popular notion that life could be lived on multiple planes of meaning.

MULTIPLE WORLDS: BODY AND SOUL IN THE PATENT MEDICINE ERA

The basic pattern in most patent medicine advertisements was a materialist version of Protestant regeneration. Early on, they depended on the ancient Galenic theory of the four humors, and traded in the rhetoric of nature. Copy promoting Wright's Indian Vegetable Pills, marketed in Philadelphia in 1844, announced: "The Red Man of the Wilderness . . . guided only by the light which nature furnishes" had discovered a mixture of blood-purifying roots and herbs; the pills made from them were "founded on the principle that the human frame is in reality subject to only one disease—

namely, corrupt humors." The remedy was massive expulsion: "the natural, or Indian theory of purgation [consists] not in simply cleansing the stomach and bowels, but in opening all the natural drains—a general Jail Delivery, as it were, by which all impurity is driven from every part of the body." The "theory" brooked no opposition: "IT IS TAUGHT BY NATURE, AND THEREFORE MUST BE TRUE."[11]

But appeals to nature often sounded suspiciously secular to evangelical audiences. Other strategies could be more effective. By the mid–nineteenth century, the narrative pattern of many patent medicine advertisements closely resembled the standard accounts of conversion experience. The use of testimonials drew directly on patterns of evangelical culture: the cries of the converted testified to the soul's deliverance from suffering. In the patent medicine literature, soul-sickness took bodily form and required physical intervention. Suffering was caused not by sin but by constipation, catarrh, bilious liver, seminal losses, or the ubiquitous "tired feeling."

Whatever their symptoms, the conditions from which the sufferer was saved often sounded like the boredom, lassitude, apathy, and overwhelming depression that preceded the sinner's admission of sin and discovery of the path to salvation. In 1875, a Mr. Karl Barton of Buffalo, New York, recalled his life before he ingested his first bottle of Dr. Chase's nerve pills: "It was a pretty hard matter for me to call attention to anything in particular. It was a general, debilitated, languid, played-out feeling, and while not painful, depressing." And here were the effects of catarrh as told by copy promoting Childs catarrh remedy in 1877: "The patient becomes nervous, his voice is harsh and unnatural; he feels disheartened; memory loses her power; judgment her seat, and gloomy forbodings hang overhead,—Hundreds, yea, thousands in such circumstances feel that to die would be a relief—and many do even cut the thread of life to end their sorrows." Despair had physical origins, and physical remedies.[12]

The mingling of spiritual and bodily health appeared in advertisements for cosmetics as well as for patent medicine. "The first duty of religion is to secure perfect health—so much the usefulness and purity of the spirit depend on it," a women's wear trade journal asserted in 1897. Indeed, "all the rites of religion link personal and spiritual purity in baths and baptisms, and putting on of clean linen, which are the essentials of health." The merging of religious and secular language reached nearly self-parodic form in the testimonials the Reverend Henry Ward Beecher gave for Pear's Soap. "If Cleanliness is next to Godliness," Beecher observed, "then surely SOAP is a means of GRACE." What might have been scandalous to an old-time Calvinist had become merely mildly amusing to advertisers' emerging audience.[13]

Transfiguration, as well as purification, could become a matter of earthly experience. Like vitalist health reformers, advertisers sought to capture the process of regeneration with metaphors of electricity. Dr. Franklin Miles (who founded the company that would later be known as Miles Laboratories, makers of Alka-Seltzer) claimed in *The Family Doctor* (1892), "The brain is the 'battery' which generates the nerve fluid, and endows the body with vitality—with life." Nerve fluid was the key to thinking, breathing, and seeing; hence Dr. Miles's nerve fluid restorative was a true panacea. The makers of Mosko silver pills (c. 1900) promised, "Electricity is in every pill and as Mosko comes into contact with the gastric fluids of the stomach the latent electrical properties are at once active, producing improved nerve force. To feel young again, to realize the joyous sparkle of nerve life as it infuses the body with its growing vitality; to feel the magnetic enthusiasm of youthful ambition"—all these experiences were available to the purchaser of Mosko pills, which probably contained a hefty dose of cocaine.[14]

Longings for physical and emotional vitality preserved fantasies of self-transformation in sensual guises. Despite the efforts of Anthony Comstock and other purity crusaders to set up rigid boundaries between high and low, body and soul, the upper and nether realms of the culture continued to meet and mingle. The focus on spasmodic purgation of "impurities" offered a way of distancing the self from its infernal lower regions, but also revealed an obsessive fascination with those regions (a fascination epitomized in costume by the bustle). The desire for jolts of rejuvenation had even more direct connections to sensual (and sexual) experience. (Many impotence remedies depended on the mystique of electrical stimulation applied to "the afflicted parts themselves.") During the last two decades of the nineteenth century, this complex set of attitudes helped generate an exuberant outpouring of primitivist, exotic, and erotic imagery in the commercial vernacular of advertising.

Late-nineteenth-century advertising dramatized the contrarieties of Victorian culture. During this era when image production was still relatively local and entrepreneurial, the commercial discourse of the body sought both to tame the beast within and tap its vital powers; advertising celebrated the triumph of a "civilized morality" of self-control even as it revealed a powerful fascination with the exotic and the primitive.

The carnivalesque dimensions of this advertising were perhaps most apparent in its treatment of animals. As in the circus, animals in commercial imagery were dressed in human clothes and made to do human things. The posters for Adam Forepaugh's circus in the 1890s described him as "the most gifted teacher of the Brute Creation that ever lived [, whose] control over the whole animal kingdom is something really marvellous, probably unexampled in the entire history of Brute Culture. . . . His latest achievement is the training of the fighting elephant, John L. Sullivan, to engage in a pugilistic encounter with hand gloves." Nearly any circus worth the name made use of waltzing dogs, roller-skating bears, or at least "industrious fleas." Advertising was equally full of humanized animals (figure 4.4): cows in spectacles, shawls, and caps, slicing cheese (Brock's Cash Grocery, Philadelphia); a bespectacled pig in waistcoat and crown reading a newspaper with the headline "Corn As Food" (James Wright's Potted Meat, Brooklyn); frogs sitting around the swamp talking about all the awards Mayo Beans have received; grasshoppers performing feats of skill on a high wire after a hearty bowl of Quaker Oats. The aim was no doubt to elicit amusement (and attention) through incongruity, but as always, humor could conceal nervous aggressiveness. Popularized Darwinism may well have made many Americans anxious about the line that separated man from beast, and eager to remind themselves of just how different "they" were from "us." (A parallel function was performed by the use of animals to display ethnic stereotypes, as when monkeys and black people were dressed up in the same vaudeville finery, or a bulldog was cast as an Irish washerwoman.) By the 1880s, ads for baking soda and gargling oil were humorously presenting monkeys as "man's progenitor" and "Darwin's grandpapa," but the mere fact that such jokes could be made indicated how strained the humor might have been.[15]

At the same time, some patent medicine advertisements implied that humans and animals could not be separated so easily. It was not simply that St. Jacob's oil and many other liniments were prescribed for horses and men alike, without irony or apology, though that practice was surely significant. From the naturopathic side of the spectrum came the insistence that humans might actually have something to learn from animals. "The Brute Creation is more enlightened to-day in medicine than the allopathic profession," a pamphlet for Northrop's Botanic Compound and Medicated Appliance asserted in 1880. The boundaries between humans and animals were porous. Between them was a dialectic of similarity and difference.[16]

The mingling of humans and animals was of a piece with the primitivist appeal to nature that pervaded nostrum vending. By the late nineteenth century, patent medicine advertising was steeped in herbalist lore and incantatory references to the product's magical effects. An overwhelming number of patent medicines claimed a primitive tribal origin: kola from the heart of Africa, coca from the mountains of Peru, "sagwa" from the North American Indian herb doctors—elixirs that cured everything from impure blood to sexual debility to indigestion. In 1893, for example, the Kickapoo Medicine Company promised its customers "a stomach like an Indian—he never worried about dieting. Why can't we live like the Indian, in a healthy, hearty, natural way?" The Church Kidney Cure Company made common assumptions explicit in an 1896 pamphlet for Church's Kava-Kava Compound ("Nature's Cure for Diseases of the Kidneys, Blood and Urinary Organs"): "There is no doubt whatever but that many of the best botanical remedies used in medical science, have first become known through their use by savage or semi-barbarous people."[17]

The construction of an ideal of naturalness followed a pattern one might call imperial primitivism: the white man enters the dark interior of a tropical land, extracts mysterious remedies, and puts them to the service of Anglo-Saxon civilization. One clear example of this formula was a pamphlet describing the discovery of Peruvian Catarrh Cure (1890). The story was allegedly told to the narrator by Dr. Edward Turner, "an adventurous and daring Englishman," on the eve of his death by ambush at the hands of "black devils" in Zululand, Africa. Troubled with catarrh since boyhood, Turner endures the failures of "medical men, with whom I got disgusted" until he learns of Mosca, a red root that could be ingested in powdered form. Having acquired some Mosca from a Catholic missionary in Indian Territory (now Oklahoma), Turner is thrilled by its effects and heads for the source: the Cotahuasi Indians of Peru. The chief of the Cotahuasi likes Turner's pluck and even more his apparent desire to help others. Turner, he believes, is not like the other "palefaces," who care only for money. The irony is that Turner wants to make a business of the cure but conceals his aim because he fears the chief might want too many presents in exchange for the secret ingredient. "I therefore left him with the idea that I was one of the few palefaces who don't care for money. That, you know, may work among the Indians, but not with us." The narrator rescues the secret from the dying Turner and it brings relief to millions. The convoluted path of discovery, the aura of mystery and secrecy, the key moment when the shrewd Caucasian outwits the natives—the narrative pattern was repeated often. It was captured visually in an 1888 advertisement for Warner's Safe Remedies, which shows a white gentleman's head on a muscular brown body, paddling a canoe toward the heart of primitive darkness (figure 5.1).[18]

Imperial primitivism implied a dialectical rather than a dualistic relationship between white Christendom and the "lower beings." The vaguely subversive part of this interchange was the idea that knowledge was not all on one side—that "inferior" races, even animals, possessed some fundamental sort of knowledge, especially of physical nature and its needs. But this acknowledgment, when it became explicit, was always hedged about with qualifications. Beneath the trademark of an Indian woman with a papoose, an 1888 pamphlet for Dr. Wrightsman's Sovereign Balm of Life announced: "It is not our belief that woman was doomed to suffer in [childbirth] as so many thousands are compelled to do at the present day. It is contrary to all natural laws, and, since the advent of this valuable

FIGURE 5.1
Detail from pamphlet, Warner's Safe Remedies, 1888. *Warshaw Collection.*

preparation, all doubts are dispelled." The Indian trademark was chosen, the copywriter claimed, because "Indians experience little or no pangs of childbirth," due to their simple life in the open air. "Of course no enlightened woman envies their way of life, except insofar as it promotes ease of parturition." Despite disclaimers, the anxiety was there, the suspicion that ascent into "civilization" had brought loss of physical vitality. Primitivist yearnings revealed the doubleness of Victorian respectability: the division between public morality and private yearning may have promoted hypocrisy but also allowed room for fantasy.[19]

Some of the most pervasive fantasies were voyeuristic. The dream of glimpsing half-dressed women unawares was a staple of popular lithography as early as the 1840s (figure 5.2). As the century advanced, the ideology of separate spheres made headway too: gender segregation reinforced homosocial patterns of leisure and placed a premium on keyholes. Many Victorian trade cards were designed to produce a peep-show effect. A trade card for Bortree corsets from the 1870s titled "The Secret Out At Last—Why Mrs. Brown Has Such a PERFECT Figure" showed two

FIGURE 5.2

A Bed-Room Bombardment, lithograph, c. 1840. *Peters Collection, National Museum of American History, Smithsonian Institution.*

women peeking through a keyhole and whispering to each other; the card opened to expose lovely Mrs. Brown seated before her mirror, clad only in Bortree's adjustable duplex corset. The following decade, the Holmes Union Suit Company showed an attractive lady dressed for a ball, with the caption "She has nothing on but Holmes and a gown." The card folded out to reveal the lady standing in her union suit. Another trade card, one that chromolithographers supplied to a variety of businesses in the 1880s, showed a beach scene with a cabana cut away to reveal two women in dishabille. One can only speculate about the significance of such images to their audiences, but in an era when men's hearts pounded at the sight of a well-turned ankle, the erotic appeal may have been considerable.[20]

During the latter decades of the nineteenth century, commercial eroticism was increasingly placed in exotic settings, the sort of places that might still be labeled "unexplored" in the parlor atlas. Each such place was marked, Conrad's Marlowe recalled in *Heart of Darkness* (1899), with "a blank space of delightful mystery—a white patch for a boy to dream gloriously over."[21] For North Americans as for Northern Europeans, the culture of empire spawned the stuff of dreams.

Advertisements for cosmetics as well as for food and even laxatives wallowed in exoticism during the last three decades of the nineteenth century. Breath and body perfumes, talcum powder and toilet water, all were placed in settings redolent of luxuriant sensuality. There was a strikingly overt eroticism about many of these images, in specific icons (figure 5.3) and more generally in the air of languorous ease displayed by the mature and voluptuous woman, whom historians of fashion have identified as the beau ideal of the late nineteenth century (figure 5.4). She was hardly a sexless Victorian, and her origins lay in the carnivalesque subculture that continued to flourish in urban burlesque halls and hotel bars.[22] Fleshy nudes like Bouguereau's *Nymph and Satyr*, a celebration of sensuality which hung over the Hoffman House Bar in New York City during the 1880s, typified the merging of high and low in the commercial vernacular.

In her sexual power, the voluptuous woman bore some resemblance to the devouring females of the fin-de-siècle imagination. Exoticism may have helped to distance her threat, but there is no question that formidable and fecund women in whatever guise evoked a tense ambivalence among Victorian men. The literature of patent medicines offered a telling counterpoint to official doctrines that emphasized women's lack of passion. Kawa, the "Great Peruvian Remedy" advertised in the 1890s, presented itself as "a Speedy and Permanent Home Cure for all forms of nervous and

FIGURE 5.3

Trade card, Love's Incense Perfume, c. 1880. *Warshaw Collection.*

FIGURE 5.4

Trade card, Dr. Petzold's Genuine German Bitters, c. 1885. *Warshaw Collection.*

sexual debility, failing memory, sleeplessness, fading sight, despondency (the blues), atrophy, involuntary losses, loss of appetite, varicocele, etc., etc." It was "guaranteed identical in physiological effects as that used by the natives of Peru." Then came the punch line: "If you are about to marry, do not think lightly of the future. As you expect to have a woman for a wife, be sure that she has a man for a husband." This was only one of innumerable cures for "weak men" that made similar appeals.[23]

Perhaps the commodity that best embodied the complex Victorian fascination with sexuality was the corset. Long dismissed as an emblem of patriarchal domination, the corset could be associated with explosive fecundity and female sexual energy, as well as with voyeuristic fantasy (figures 5.5, 5.6). The process of removing the corset offered possibilities

FIGURE 5.5
Trade card, Dr. Warner's Coraline Corset, c. 1890. *Warshaw Collection.*

FIGURE 5.6

Trade card, Warner Brothers' Coraline Corset, c. 1890. *Warshaw Collection.*

for protracted foreplay, amatory skills, the erotic buildup of tension. Even before the Civil War, a print called *The Wedding Night* caught the parodic potential of those possibilities by showing a bride looking demurely behind her at her husband who is pop-eyed, flushed, and on his knees unfastening her corset; clearly, despite the parody, the process is intended to look exciting for both of them (figure 5.7). Opponents of the corset recognized this, attacking its capacity to stimulate sexual excitement. Tightlacing could be as much an emblem of exotic decadence and rebellion against female quiescence as a sign of submission to prudery.[24]

How does one infer any particular set of cultural meanings from the imagery surrounding the body in entrepreneurial advertising? It is often difficult, if not impossible. The voyeuristic trade card for Warner corsets (figure 5.6), for example, demonstrates how chromolithographers could assemble a bizarre amalgam of hieroglyphs. One of the Cupids photographing the corset is holding St. Joseph's staff, with lily attached—a traditional emblem of male virginity. The corset is an object of prurient fascination, yet it is set in a hard, dry desert landscape. It is giving birth to vegetation (as in the corset ad shown in figure 5.5), but the growth is cactuslike, not luxuriant or inviting. The stone wall suggests the parallel function of the corset: a barrier to be overcome, a fetishistic aid to excitement. The whole picture seems animated by a muddle of male fears and anxieties. In its surrealist yoking of dissimilar images as well as in its voyeurism, this trade card typified the vernacular tradition of commercial iconography.

Maybe the most coherent conclusion one can draw about the ferment of fantastic advertising during the late nineteenth century is that it played counterpoint to the dominant culture's celebration of mind over body. Its emphasis on personal revitalization preserved the Protestant counterculture of soul-cure; its fantastic elements kept alive the tradition of living life on multiple planes of meaning, a tradition that included popular theater, carnivals, sports, and ritual. The popular philosophy of multiple worlds involved the metaphorical or actual construction of special spaces where cultural meanings were explored through playful performance, and self and world were melded. Calvinist and Cartesian countertraditions had sought to separate self and world, and make the "outside" world all of a piece, a single sphere of transparent meaning. Positivistic science had taken up the task in the later nineteenth century, seeking universal, objective truth through laws of nature. The commercial vernacular of advertising preserved vestiges of the carnivalesque amid the tightening idioms of control. But by the 1890s, the world of advertising was changing.

FIGURE 5.7
The Wedding Night, lithograph, c. 1840. *Peters Collection.*

THE EARLY IMPACT OF PROFESSIONALIZATION

Amid the profusion of rival claims and exotic imagery, men like George P. Rowell and Francis Wayland Ayer developed advertising agencies (see chapter 3). Increasingly they sought national markets for corporate clients. And the way to win big clients was by establishing professional legitimacy, by exuding an aura of efficiency and rationality. In 1902, *Printers' Ink* was applauding "The Passing of the 'Expert.'" The quotation marks defined the "expert" as a freelance charlatan. "To-day, after a decade of development in the advertising field, the 'expert' is as extinct as the Buffalo," the editors announced. "In his place are the business man who has learned to manage his own publicity and the legitimate agent who has a scientific, definite, and above-board knowledge of advertising." The passing of the "expert" meant the triumph of the expert, at least according to *Printers' Ink.* Like advocates of professionalization in other fields, advertising trade journals claimed they had created and were adhering to a single, universal, and objective standard of knowledge.[25]

While they embraced the secular ideology of managerial professionalism, agency executives also preserved some ties to Protestant tradition. All available evidence indicates that by the early 1910s, the most influential agencies with the biggest accounts were staffed by a remarkably similar group of Anglo-Saxon males: college-educated, usually at prestigious Northeastern schools; Protestant, many the sons of Presbyterian or Congregationalist ministers; commonly from small towns or suburbs in the Midwest and Northeast. They were the sons (only 3 percent were women) of the late-nineteenth-century liberal Protestant elite, and they clung to a secularized version of their parents' worldview: a faith in inevitable progress, unfolding as if in accordance with some divine plan. They also had a tendency to cast themselves in a key redemptive role. This was a secular doctrine of postmillennialism—the belief that Christ would return after human beings had created the Kingdom of God on earth.[26]

This merger of professionalism and postmillennial Protestantism marked a major change in the social conditions of commercial image production. Advertising agency staffs were more affluent and ethnically homogenous than the chromolithographers, and their work was more systematically organized. The autonomy of the chromolithographic artisan, always problematic at best, disappeared in the interdependent, bureaucratically organized operations of the advertising agency; illustrations and copy were subject to revisions at the hands of art directors, copy chiefs, account executives, and clients. In the new regime, advertising copy tended toward blandness and standardized predictability. But it was, without question, more polished and professional.

Nevertheless, the ad agencies' quest for legitimacy ran into problems early on. Despite efforts to raise themselves to unprecedented professional heights, admakers kept a foot in the commercial vernacular. Much, and in many cases all, of their business remained in the realm of magic elixirs and universal restoratives. They faced the difficulty of reconciling their aspirations toward respectability with their disreputable clientele.[27]

The difficulty was intensified by the growing prestige of the allopathic medical establishment. In the two decades around the turn of the century, mainstream medical practitioners acquired unprecedented legitimacy, largely due to the growing popular awareness of such therapeutic breakthroughs as the rabies vaccine (1885) and diphtheria antitoxin (1891). Doctors' efforts to weed out charlatans and standardize credentials suddenly began to bear fruit. The allopaths' atomized, disease-specific model of treatment meshed with the emergence of an increasingly impersonal, bureaucratic, and technologically oriented medical system. Nostrum advertisers had long lacked legitimacy by comparison to physicians, but at the turn of the century, just when the advertising industry had begun to deny its disreputable past, the medical profession began to ascend into the realm of genuine expertise. The gulf between doctor and adman seemed to be growing wider than ever before.[28]

Patent medicine advertisers struggled to maintain a foothold in the medical community. They successfully sought endorsements from physicians and continued to run many advertisements in medical journals. They aimed to insinuate a cozy relationship between the manufacturer and the medical practitioner. "Suppose we find the patient a little giddy upon rising in the morning," a pamphlet for Celerina Nerve Tonic proposed to doctors in 1895. "This means that the nerves do not have perfect control over the muscular system." Have the patient stand with his feet close together, eyes closed—does he reel? Or ask him three simple questions in rapid succession: if he hesitates, dose him with Celerina four times a day, "to increase the nerve capital of your patient." (The monetary metaphor was common to products that promised "universal restoration" of lost energies and strengths.) Both "ethical" medicines, which revealed their ingredients, and patent nostrums, which did not, advertised in medical journals. By the 1890s there were so many patent medicines falsely claiming to be ethical preparations that it was difficult to tell the two categories apart. Nevertheless, the mainstream medical profession began to grow restive, demanding that products like Ayer's Cherry Pectoral disclose their contents in the advertisement itself. In 1898, the makers of Ayer's refused, though they agreed to reveal the secret formula to the medical journals' editors. Many journals turned down the advertisement.[29]

Apologists for nostrum advertising, squirming under the scrutiny of doctors and health reformers, went on the defensive. A favorite rhetorical tactic in the trade press, one that has been used every few years since the 1890s, was to claim that once, not so very long ago, patent medicine was awful, but that was then, this is now; calm and reasonable arguments have replaced the bogus and extravagant rhetoric of olden times. The inaccuracy of this statement would have been apparent to anyone who read the trade press during the late 1890s, when critics began to assault the shrillness and silliness of "agony" testimonials with scare headlines like "SNATCHED FROM THE GRAVE!" But other contributors rushed to defend these practices. Why not sock people in the guts with talk of "the knife and the grave" as the Wine of Cardui people do? Edith Gerry, a *Printers' Ink* contributor, asked in 1900. It works! Patent medicines like "Wine of Cardui" were a palatable alternative to the specter of surgery. Even those who advocated reform did so halfheartedly. Away with mystery in advertising proprietary remedies, another contributor told *Printers' Ink* readers in 1902. "Tell the people *some* of the chief ingredients used in compounding them." Nobody—except the fastidious Francis Ayer—was willing to give up the secrets at the heart of the nostrum business.[30]

But it was not long before events dictated fuller disclosure. During the 1890s, the publisher Cyrus H. K. Curtis forbade proprietary ads in all his magazines. (Ayer's decision to drop nostrums was partly a shrewd effort to keep the huge Curtis account.) Then Curtis's son-in-law, Edward Bok, who edited *Ladies' Home Journal*, began to investigate patent medicines. The *Journal's* crusade was part of the resurgent temperance movement, whose leaders were now sophisticated enough to realize that Bumstead's Worm Syrup or Dr. Pierce's Favorite Prescription might contain "an unwitting or secret tipple," as the historian James Harvey Young observed. In 1904, *Collier's* picked up the scent. The magazine's editor, Norman Hapgood, commissioned the successful muckraker Samuel Hopkins Adams to write a series of articles exposing the evil of patent medicines, which were later published in book form as *The Great American Fraud* (1906). In it Adams was careful to distinguish the vile nostrum appeals from legitimate advertisements, which he celebrated; like other progressive reformers, he tended to let the larger corporate advertisers off the hook and to focus on marginal entrepreneurs. Detailing at length the alcohol and addictive drugs that made up the active ingredients in many patent medicines, Adams can be seen as part of the swelling chorus of progressive reformers demanding a wholesale purification of the body politic. He was a product of the burned-over district of western New York, the region swept by waves of revivalism in the early nineteenth century, and he was still full of evangelical fire. "A character inherited from a line of insurgent theologians gave him firm conviction in his beliefs," his colleague Will Irwin wrote; Adams "gloried in combat." In the end, his efforts provided the chief inspiration for the Pure Food and Drug Act of 1906. It required patent medicine makers to disclose the presence of certain drugs—alcohol, the opiates, chloral hydrate, and a few others—and it prohibited them from claiming any ingredients that were not actually present in the amount specified. As with most regulatory legislation, the regulated industry soon found many loopholes in the law. Nevertheless, the Pure Food and Drug Act ended the patent medicine era; never again would national advertising present such a carnival of claims for magical transformation.[31]

Sensing the drift of power, advertising agencies sought a modus vivendi with the managerial professionals in mainstream medicine, people like Dr. Harvey Wiley, the chemist in the Agriculture Department who drafted the Pure Food and Drug Act. "Is it imagination, or has Old Reliable Dr. Blank, with his cures for 'weak men,' really disappeared from the reputable newspapers?" *Printers' Ink* asked in 1907. We hope so, the editors said, because the publication's advertising is only as strong as its weakest link. Advertisers like Dr. Blank became a cartoonish Other, a shadowy buffoon against which the managerial professionals in the business could measure How Far We Have Come. Even Scott's Emulsion, among the most hysterical nostrum vendors, began to tone down its copy and abandon scare headlines; the trade press applauded such moves. Other patent medicine manufacturers openly sought a truce, advising customers to "Ask Your Doctor" about indications and dosage.[32]

Patterns of regeneration persisted, but they were attached less often to medicines, more often to food products ranging from cereal to candy and gum. Rather than deriving restored vigor from nerve foods, blood purifiers, tonics, and exhilarants, target audiences were urged to turn toward

Coca-Cola, Quaker Oats, or Welch's Grape Juice. Advertising for breakfast cereals sometimes seemed part of the broad agenda for revitalizing bourgeois masculinity that was being enacted under the auspices of Theodore Roosevelt and other strenuous-lifers. The Quaker Oats campaign of 1903 identified the cereal as "the Work Food" and promised, "It puts its whole strength straight into your system [providing] Will to Do—Power to Do It—Spirit and Energy, parents of Success." The campaign (the appropriately martial term for advertising strategies emerged in the trade press at about this time) also included this poem:

Men who Achieve,—
with hands or brain—
Who rise, who lead, who Win, who Act
They fight their fight on simple Grain—
on Quaker Oats, to be exact
The Will and Brain that Conquer fate
The Rugged Health, the Bone and Thew
There's every trait that makes men Great
in Quaker Oats, the food—for you.[33]

This poem recalled the late-Victorian rhetoric of manliness, but other cereal advertisements presented their products as harbingers of twentieth-century modernity. A bowl of cereal for breakfast was a departure from the heavy meal of corn mush and ham (or variations) that characterized most morning menus in nineteenth-century America. Rather than a stolid march toward Greatness, an ad for Shredded Wheat in 1902 promised "BOUNCE!": "If you want to be rid of that stomach heaviness after eating breakfast and in its place have that 'feeling of bounce'—an elastic step—a bright eye—an alert mind and the spirit to dare and do—try this simple yet satisfying dish for breakfast." By 1916, the copywriter for Quaker Oats had picked up the emphasis on dynamism, pronouncing the product "The Foe of the Easy Chair."

> Folks who love the chimney corner don't love Quaker Oats. Mark the lovers of Quaker Oats. They are the wide-awakes, active and ambitious, whether they are seven or seventy. They believe in keeping young. For oats create vitality. They feed the fires of youth. They are vim-producing, spirit-giving. Light and laughter seem to bubble from them. They make folks "feel their oats." Quaker Oats are luscious, fragrant, flavory—But it's their tonic effect—the life-force that's in them—that makes them the staple of millions. Lovers of life eat them liberally. Lovers of languor don't.[34]

Patent medicines had promised rejuvenation, but had usually defined it in more sensual terms: the restoration of the capacity for intense taste, smell, or sexual arousal, as well as the revitalization of energy. The newer advertising more explicitly linked regenerative products with "wide-awake" consciousness, dynamic movement, and urban modernity; it dismissed the chimney corner as a relic of sleepy rural life. Corporate advertising was less hedonistic and more hectic than the earlier advertisements, heralding a world where "languor" was deemed the opposite of "life." This newer form of advertising was nearly devoid of primitive sensuality and exotic decadence; it was set amid the everyday lives of the striving middle and upper classes.

These tendencies were apparent in the advertising for Coca-Cola, a product that enjoyed an extraordinarily advantageous market position during the early twentieth century. It was first billed as a temperance beverage, but it increasingly emphasized the tonic properties of the drink—a boon to the tired businessman or the woman weary of shopping. The revitalizing effects of the drink came from the caffeine and (in the early years) the cocaine it contained. "Coca from Peru, Cola from Africa," a 1907 advertisement candidly announced "comes [sic] to the Modern Business Man [in] Coca-Cola [.] To the Invigorating properties of the Coca Leaf are added the sustaining properties of the Cola Nut. . . . Relieves fatigue that comes from over-working or over-thinking. Puts vim and 'go' into tired brains and weary bodies"—including, one assumes, the dapper and confident executive in the advertisement.[35] This ad placed the process of regeneration in a specific context: the white-collar workplace. The emergent office civilization, of which advertising executives were a part, had begun to put new demands on workers, more nebulous but also more constant. Instead of the periodic jolt of a "brace-up," regenerative products began to promise a steady supply of "vim."

This merger of dynamism and efficiency was consistent with the emerging ideology of professional advertising, which sought to distance current practitioners from the long-haired literati and bunco artists who had dominated the business during the patent medicine era. Agency executives, attempting to duplicate the success of allopathic physicians, struggled to sanctify their trade as "a living science." By 1909, the N. W. Ayer agency was solemnly advising its clients to "choose your [advertising] agent as you would your lawyer or your doctor"—then leave the rest of the work to him.[36]

Like postmillennial Protestants, advertising professionals believed they were playing a key role in lubricating the mechanisms of economic growth and moral progress. In a typical statement, the *J. Walter Thompson Book* (designed for use in new business presentations) asserted in 1909 that

> advertising is *revolutionary*. Its tendency is to overturn preconceived notions, to set new ideas spinning through the reader's brain, to induce something that they [sic] never did before. It is a form of progress, and it *interests only progressive people*. That's why it thrives in America as in no land under the sun. Stupid people are not much impressed by advertising. They move in a rut of tradition.

Later in the same pamphlet, the authors defined progress more specifically: "The chief work of civilization *is to eliminate chance,* and that can only be done by foreseeing and planning." The effort to stabilize the random movements of market exchange was being intensified. The equation between civilization and the elimination of chance typified the managerial worldview, joining advertising executives with social scientists and other professionals in a search for systematic control of their environment.[37]

Another link between advertising and the broader managerial ethos was the tendency to conflate cultural standardization with moral advance. Advertising executives identified their national outlook (and the national brands they promoted) with a cosmopolitan "new American tempo"; they dismissed local custom as sluggish provincial reaction. The definition of publicity as education was a common "Progressive" reflex during the early twentieth century; advertisers stressed not the exposure of corruption bred in filthy places (as muckrakers and other reformers had done) but the dissemination of a modernized standard of physical well-being. The nature of advertisers' "power for good" was nowhere more visible, they claimed, than in the sanitation of Americans' daily lives and personal appearance: the plumbing of bathrooms from Maine to California, the elimination of the American carnivore's traditional greasy breakfast; the disappearance of beards and expansive stomachs among men, of body hair and facial blemishes among women. Historically contingent fashion, as at other points in modern cultural history, was endowed by advertisers with universal moral significance. As early as 1910, a contributor to *Printers' Ink* noted "the spick-and-spanness of American people as compared with people abroad" and concluded that "without any doubt the advertising artist is responsible for it." Implicitly rejecting the ancient Protestant distrust of appearances, national advertisers equated the smooth face with the regenerate heart.[38]

Yet ad executives sometimes dropped their salesman's baggage and embraced a secular missionary role consistent with their Protestant past (especially when addressing an audience other than potential clients). During the 1910s, national advertising increasingly won legitimacy by staging truth-in-advertising campaigns and participating in the ideological mobilization for World War I. By the 1920s, many advertising people had come to take themselves extraordinarily seriously, anointing their trade "Arch Enemy of Poverty and Disease."[39] Helen Rosen Woodward, a copywriter and executive for many years (but still an outsider in her gender and her Jewishness), succinctly summarized twenty years of professionalization in 1926:

> The heads of most advertising agencies before 1905 were not business men as they are to-day; they were literary men, whose pens turned out advertising instead of essays. Since the business was new and the trails had to be blazed, they were also gamblers, men who liked the new and extraordinary, the dramatic.
>
> Nobody knew twenty years ago what it cost to write an advertisement, to handle an account. To-day this is all accurately figured out. Advertising has the solid mentality usual in a large, established business with heavy investments. It no longer attracts the lovers of chance, but rather those who look for safety. It has a pontifical dignity which robs it of much of its earlier fire.[40]

Pontifical dignity suppressed the old carnivalesque traditions. Patent medicine advertisements were consigned to the margins of economic life. By the late 1930s, the progressive journalist William Allen White found them only in the religious press, "particularly that section of the press which appealed and still appeals to the larger denominations and to the little churches of St. Moron in the lower strata of our economic life;" the ads' inanity, in White's view, revealed "the dull, unsocial minds of certain candidates for salvation."[41] Alert and social minds presumably paid more attention to national advertising.

But while the church of St. Moron continued to foster superstitious adherence to nostrums (at least according to progressives like White), more liberal forms of Protestant thought survived in national advertising. A postmillennial faith in progress combined with a perfectionist quest for transfigured selfhood to shape new images of health and beauty. Advertising icons of personal well-being began to embody the anxieties and aspirations of the professional managerial class.

CHAPTER 6

The Perfectionist Project

B<small>Y</small> the early twentieth century, among the metropolitan middle and upper classes the evangelical drive for what revivalists called "entire and perfect sanctification" was becoming a largely secular project, the creation of human subjects whose bowel movements were as effectively regulated as their performance in office or kitchen, and who looked as fresh and youthful as the generic "young marrieds" in the national magazine advertisements. The symbolic universe of advertising merged distinctions between intimate and social experience in the perfectionist ideal of personal efficiency.

But that did not mean the triumph of a uniform vision of human subjectivity, even within the idiom of national advertising. Perfectionist agendas could be inflected in different accents: a mechanistic emphasis on steady-state functioning; a vitalist stress on dynamism and growth; a preoccupation with physical well-being; a fascination with psychic energy. If the materialist attitude promoted a physiological perfectionism, the vitalist outlook came to constitute a kind of psychological perfectionism. In many ways the two traditions overlapped and complemented each other, but they also led in different directions.

PHYSIOLOGICAL PERFECTIONISM

The coming of national advertising brought bureaucratic rationality to the iconography of the body. Carnivalesque sensuality survived in the street theater of the medicine shows, but these were increasingly confined to the rural districts or the poorer, blacker neigborhoods of cities. ("Harlem is overrun with them," Nevada Ned said in 1929.) Exotic and primitive icons persisted in more respectable quarters of entrepreneurial life as well; they were inscribed on the walls of fashionable restaurants and cosmopolitan movie houses. But in national advertising those images were sanitized and transmuted.[1]

The sanitation process took a variety of forms. The advertisers who promoted the early-twentieth-century vogue of tanning, for example, distanced dark skin from its overtones of lush tropicality and linked it instead with bracing outdoor vigor (figure 6.1). Imperial primitivism gave way to imperialism, a dualistic rather than a dialectical relation with the nonhuman world and with the humans supposedly "closer to nature" than the Anglo-Saxons were. This attempt to draw sharper boundaries between the civilized world and the rest of brute creation was in part a response to the popularization of Darwinian biology and paleontology as well as to the increased knowledge of the nonwhite world gained through colonial adventures. Even if one had to accept apes for ancestors and Hottentots for cousins, one did not have to acknowledge that there was anything of value to be learned from them. The resulting cultural pattern, at least as expressed in advertising iconography, was less an attempt to extract regenerative secrets from mysterious interiors than an effort to impose civilized values on "inferior" native populations.[2]

And those values were invariably defined in terms of cleanliness and good grooming. In an Ivory Soap series from 1900, for example, an assembly of Plains Indians recalled their old ways of dirt and disorder:

> Our blankets smeared with grease and stains,
> From buffalo meat and settlers' veins . . .

Then:

> Ivory soap came like a ray
> Of light across our darkened way
> And now we're civil, kind, and good
> And keep the laws as people should
> We wear our linen, lawn, and lace
> As well as folks with paler face.

This newer imperial rhetoric was nothing if not universal in its ambitions, as B. T. Babbitt's announced that "Soap is the Scale of Civilization" and Gillette proclaimed its razors' predominance "from Boston to Bombay."[3]

In one sense this was nothing new. A preoccupation with cleanliness, often carrying racial overtones, had been a central theme in bourgeois culture for at least half a century. It intensified as technological advances made soap and water more widely available. Personal hygiene became a crucial piece in the puzzle that upwardly mobile strivers were constantly trying to assemble. As early as the 1850s, clean hands joined white skin, white bread, and white sugar as emblems of refinement.[4]

By 1900, though, soap had begun to imply not cleanliness per se but a certain kind of cleanliness, purged of any decadent, hedonistic associations, oriented toward productive activism and a broader agenda of control. In 1899 the *Yale Review* noted that the "philosophy of modern adver-

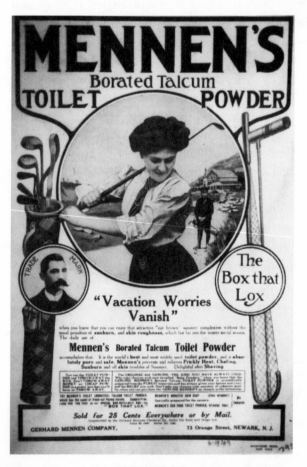

FIGURE 6.1
Mennen's Borated Talcum Powder advertisement, *Town and Country* magazine, 1909. *Warshaw Collection.*

tising" was beginning to elevate soap and water over "perfumery and enervating pleasures." What the *Review* failed to note was that earlier advertising had celebrated "enervating pleasures" for most of the nineteenth century—it was only with the growing dominance of corporate advertising
that the iconography of the body began to be sterilized and submitted to
the ethos of rationalization.[5]

The rationalization of bodily imagery in advertising reflected broader
movements in American society. Perhaps the most apparent was the transformation of the workplace under the aegis of scientific management. The
movement began with the experiments in time-and-motion study inaugu-
rated by Frederick Winslow Taylor and popularized by disciples of efficiency like Frank Gilbreth and Ellen Richards, both of whom sought to
extend the principles of scientific management beyond the factory and
office, into the realms of housekeeping and self-maintenance. It is all too
easy to dismiss these people as obsessive-compulsive neurotics (which is a
plausible description) and fail to recognize the long-term influence of their
ideas. The "efficiency craze" was not merely a zany cult born of the reform
mania in the Progressive Era; it marked a key moment in the managerial
ideal of personal efficiency.[6]

In many ways national advertising embodied the most influential representations of that ideal. It reinforced a host of fundamental changes in
the ways people construed their own physical experience. By the end of
the century, for example, nostrum vendors' shopworn pitch for occasional,
heroic purgation was being streamlined into an emphasis on "regularity"—
a more methodical regime better suited to the emerging rhythms of modern life. Even as Americans' diets improved, the rhetorical assault on constipation grew shriller. "Be a real man—a live man," a laxative advertisement
(disguised as a medical pamphlet) admonished readers in 1900. "Don't be
satisfied to be a lump of inert, half-dead, rapidly decaying flesh"—which is
what you are, the copywriter implied, when you are constipated. In 1916
the syndicated columnist "Dr." Frank Crane identified "The Colonic"—the
constipated person—as a worse menace to decent society than the alcoholic. "The first requisite to sanctity is to keep the intestines open," Crane
concluded. The materialist appropriation of Protestant purification seemed
complete.[7]

Sanctity, for Crane and his contemporaries, turned out to be little more
than peak performance. According to the evolving conventional wisdom,
in advertising as well as advice literature, the sedentary conditions of modern urban life led to the buildup of proteins and other undigested nutri-

ents in the bowels. The result was "autointoxication," and the term became a catchphrase diagnosis for virtually every human ailment throughout the 1920s. (A variant, nearly as alarming, was "intestinal fatigue.") Thomas Edison, when asked in 1928 "what was the most hostile feature of the average human being's environment," replied without hesitation: "His lower bowel. The average human being is a traveling poison factory. . . . I believe that auto-intoxication causes most of our diseases."

The chief menace of autointoxication was its diffuse impact; it poisoned the mind and will as well as the intestinal tract. "When there seems no end to work, no fun in playing, no thrill to life—GUARD AGAINST INTESTINAL TOXICITY," a 1929 ad for Eno effervescent saline warned, beneath a picture of two college joes looking suspiciously at a third who, unlike them, is dressed formally, looks gloomy, and isn't carrying golf clubs. "Doctors pretty well agree," a strapping swimmer told *Saturday Evening Post* readers of a Nujol advertisement in 1930, "that (barring germ diseases) most illness and headache, most lack of pep and ambition, most cases of seeing the world through blue glasses generally, are due to failure or inability to keep 'clean inside.'" National advertising translated longings for self-transformation into a secular rhetoric with political as well as personal significance. The obsession with expelling "alien filth" caught the connection between bodily and national purification: the eugenic dream of perfecting Anglo-Saxon racial dominance in the United States through immigration restriction.[8]

The drive for efficiency also involved a growing intolerance of pain. This was a developing strain in bourgeois culture throughout the nineteenth century. As John Stuart Mill observed, "One of the effects of civilization (not to say one of the ingredients in it) is, that the spectacle, and even the very idea of pain, is more and more kept out of the sight of those who enjoy in their fullness the benefits of civilization." Still, most patent medicine advertising assumed that pain was part of life, an occasional nuisance to be dealt with. But the rise of allopathic medicine encouraged a systematic effort to exclude pain from areas of life where it had been previously taken for granted.[9]

One example of this effort was the use of anesthesia in childbirth. Without question, this was a boon for many women, one that the male historian dismisses at his peril; but it was part of a broader consolidation of medical authority with complex cultural implications. Edith Wharton captured some of them in her novel *Twilight Sleep* (1927). The title was the popular phrase for the state induced by the hallucinogen scopolamine; a

character called Mrs. Manford rhapsodizes over childbirth under its influence: "'Of course there ought to be no Pain, nothing but Beauty. It ought
to be one of the loveliest, most poetic things in the world to have a Baby,'
Mrs. Manford declared, in that bright, efficient voice which made loveli-
ness and poetry sound like the attributes of an advanced industrialism, and
babies something to be turned out like Fords."[10] Wharton implied that the
conquest of pain was part of a broader pattern in managerial thought: the
attempt to subject unpredictable biological processes to factorylike standards of efficiency, and to suffuse the whole procedure with an aura of
sanctity.

One can see that agenda clearly in a manifesto called *The Efficient Life*
(1920). Its author was Luther Gulick, Jr., a leading spokesman for the
emergent subculture of professionals involved in youth work. Gulick dismissed pain as sand in the gears of the human machine. "A man has no
right to be wasting his energy or cutting down his supply when he could
just as well have an abundance of it," Gulick wrote. "Pain is costly. It unfits
us for giving attention to other things. It keeps us on a constant strain. It
destroys efficiency." Gulick's determination to meld mental and physical
life into a single systematic process—the purpose of which was never
clear—marked a major preoccupation in managerial culture. The new performance ethic comported comfortably with the mechanistic metaphors of
the body that had become popular among domestic scientists, nutrition-
ists, and medical professionals.[11]

The most immediate and obvious impact of this mechanistic style of
thought was a slimming down of ideal body types. Fat became unfashionable. Throughout much of the nineteenth century, doctors acknowledged
the dangers of obesity but claimed that a moderate corpulence constituted
a "reserve fund" against debility in times of illness. The characteristic nineteenth-century concern with conserving physical resources to withstand
periods of impoverishment paralleled the idea of prudential accumulation
in the economic realm. But around the turn of the century, as mechanistic
metaphors proliferated, the conventional wisdom shifted. In 1903, for
example, a *Popular Science Monthly* contributor argued that "unnecessary
consumption of food is physiologically uneconomical. In our efforts to
maintain a high degree of efficiency we are in reality putting upon the
machinery of the body a heavy and entirely uncalled for strain which is
bound to prove more or less detrimental." The plain fact of the matter, he
concluded, is that fat interferes with "the free running of the machinery."
Once the chief task of bodily existence was defined as the effort "to main-

tain a high degree of efficiency," the war on fat soon followed. Corpulence no longer signified an appreciation of abundance but an attachment to backward and uncontrolled eating habits. Though many psychotherapists (amateur and professional) still counseled the preservation of psychic resources for the maintenance of mental equilibrium, the laying-in of flesh "in reserve" was now seen as little more than a bungling intervention in that "self-regulating apparatus of extraordinary efficiency," as a *Century* contributor called the human body in 1904.[12]

Insurance companies reinforced the popularization of slimness among the educated and affluent by creating statistical definitions of normality and linking overweight with shortened life expectancy. In 1897 the Association of Life Insurance Medical Directors commissioned Dr. George R. Shepherd to compile a table of standard height and weight by five-year intervals based on data from 74,162 male applicants for life insurance in the United States and Canada. Though this was not the first such table (they had been in use since the 1840s), it was by far the most extensively researched and the most influential. In 1909 Dr. Brandreth Symonds, chief medical director for Metropolitan Life in New York, popularized Shepherd's findings in *McClure's* magazine, analyzing the data in terms of insurance risk. He concluded that even a moderate condition of overweight reduced the average life span; fat was not a bank account but a burden. What was to be stored was not embodied in flesh but was a more evanescent quality: sheer energy, the capacity for intense, sustained activity.[13]

That emphasis heightened a preoccupation with youth. As large organizations increasingly sorted the population into age categories, older people in particular were isolated and their experiences devalued. The spread of compulsory retirement policies during the first three decades of the twentieth century was only the most programmatic manifestation of a tendency that was rooted, as well, in changing medical definitions of aging. As early as 1890, Dr. Charles Mercier joined the corps of authorities who were redefining senile dementia as a normal byproduct of aging rather than an occasional aberration. The psychological process of aging, he wrote, "is a continuous, gradually progressive loss. Conduct, intelligence, feeling, and self-consciousness gradually diminish and at last cease to exist. The decadence of old age is, in fact, a dementia, a deprivation." When these kinds of sentiments seeped into popular consciousness during the next several decades, they reinforced the invidious distinction that was being institutionalized in the modern corporation: above all, the premium on mental quickness and verbal agility rather than the accumulated wisdom of experience. And nowhere was that premium higher than in advertising, marketing, and sales. A veneration for youth was embedded in the habits of speech, the verbal tics and humorous asides of the advertising business. When Grace Crawley Oakley reported on her New York advertising club's trip to Indianapolis in 1920, she described the 147 club members as "male and female, tall and short, fat and thin, young and—well, you know, advertising people never get that way." By 1925, when the sales manager of Borden Food Products asked *Printers' Ink* readers: "Is the Salesman Over Forty a 'Has Been'?" he indicated the pervasiveness of the conventional wisdom even though he aimed to challenge it. Personal efficiency was primarily a possession of youth.[14]

National advertising reinforced these developments through some dramatic shifts in its representations of health and beauty. The most striking change was the growing emphasis on standard images of physical perfection on the Anglo-Saxon model. Ethnocentric notions of normality defined immigrants' subversive potential in physical terms: in 1919, Attorney General A. Mitchell Palmer identified the radical threat as "alien filth," with "sly and crafty eyes . . . lopsided faces, sloping brows, and misshapen features." But the new paragons were as different from their predecessors as they were from the immigrant hordes. Within Anglo-Saxon tradition, the voluptuous woman and the portly, bearded man yielded to smoother, cleaner, more athletic, and more obviously youthful models of beauty (figure 6.2). Exotic settings faded in favor of the more immediate and familiar: the soda fountain and the suburban neighborhood.[15]

The form of these images changed as well: surrealist pastiche yielded to literalist realism, often assisted by photography and linked to didactic narrative. In general, pictures were more thoroughly meshed with words, more commonly illustrating a particular text, than they had been in the days of freelance chromolithography (figure 6.3). This "editorial-style" advertising, which Stanley Resor of J. Walter Thompson claimed to have introduced in the early 1920s, came to resemble closely the fiction and advice literature in the national magazines. In its visual and literary forms, corporate-sponsored culture was becoming all of a piece, in keeping with the universalist assumptions of managerial–professional thought.[16]

Despite the public's durable faith that national advertising was liberating them from Victorian norms (a faith often fostered by admen themselves), a fundamental continuity remained between nineteenth- and twentieth-century preoccupations. Like the moralists of earlier generations, advertising executives and other professionals wanted to contain the

FIGURE 6.2

J. C. Leyendecker (illustrator), Ivory Soap advertisement, 1901. *Warshaw Collection.*

FIGURE 6.3

Ipana toothpaste advertisement, *Saturday Evening Post,* 1936.

impact of market exchange on personal behavior and structures of meaning—to create new principles for validating truth even as they sought to maximize their profits. And managerial values, in their systematic universality, were in many ways more constraining than the Victorian ethos had been.[17]

By the 1920s and 1930s, advertisements for food, clothing, housekeeping supplies, and cosmetics displayed an almost panicky reassertion of culture over nature—an anxious impulse to extirpate all signs of biological life from one's immediate personal environment. That impulse had been spreading widely for decades, as methods of mass production were brought to food processing and distribution. The industrialization of eating was not merely an economic development; it was also an important expression of the nervous desire to control biology. "I do not fancy paws and perspiration in my bread; the idea is unpleasant even to speak of," said Edward Atkinson, a leading promoter of a mechanical bread kneader, in 1896. Technological triumph over "paws and perspiration" became a chief preoccupation of corporate food processors. At country stores and corner groceries, open bins of unbranded staples gave way to Uneeda Biscuits, Quaker Oats, and other packaged national brand-name goods. National advertisers strove successfully to surround their products with a halo of uniformity and purity. "Look out for trouble if you buy exposed butter," a Parksdale Butter advertisement warned in 1909, beneath a drawing of an unsuspecting mouth about to close on a piece of bread bearing a cartoon devil, an emblem of disease rather than immorality.[18]

But biology also posed more diffuse threats. Physical processes that had previously been taken for granted began to acquire ominous qualities, as one can see (or smell) in the changing attitude toward odor. The coming of an urban society and the increase in person-to-person contact engendered a growing anxiety about offensive breath, perspiration odors, and other bodily exhalations. One can find scattered advertisements for breath and body perfumes from the 1830s on, but in general, genteel folk worried a lot less about odor in the nineteenth century than in the twentieth. Dress and suit shields, marketed in the 1880s, were designed to stop perspiration stain but not odor.

Yet by the 1930s, odor was virtually an obsession. Popular magazines were full of faces (male and female) contorted with disgust over everything from "sneaker smell" to "smelly hands." And more and more people had shown themselves willing to submit to the difficult practice of applying deodorant to their underarms. John B. Watson, the behaviorist psychologist who had left Johns Hopkins University for J. Walter Thompson in 1920, told a JWT staff meeting in 1928 just how cumbersome that procedure was. The best-selling product, Odorono, was "pretty hard on sensitive skins," not to mention clothing, Watson reported; the user had to hold his or her arms aloft for ten minutes after applying the ruby red paste, taking care not to let it touch any article of clothing, as it would eat into the fabric.[19]

Within national advertising's symbolic universe, the recoil from odor was part of a general revulsion against biological processes that seemed to permeate the middle and upper classes throughout the first half of the twentieth century. In part this may have involved an intensified distaste for bodily fluids—a change of sensibility that may have been tied up with the desire to draw sharper boundaries between human culture and animal nature, as the vision of a uniquely human soul grew dimmer among educated professionals. (Certainly Watson and the behaviorists denied the soul altogether.)

The new version of the ascent of man required distinction from the beasts on cultural rather than spiritual grounds: release from bent-backed toil; deflection of the gaze upward, away from the muck of biological existence—protection from the "paws and perspiration" that had so horrified Atkinson. A Kleenex advertisement of 1934, for example, spoke for an entire genre when it presented a nearly nauseated housewife who allowed as how washing dirty handkerchiefs was "the worst job on earth!" But it was no longer necessary, due to throwaway tissues. Defining well-being by one's distance from demeaning toil was not a new development in cultural history, but in the early twentieth century the advertised definition of "demeaning" acquired a particularly biological resonance.[20]

The revulsion against biology was encouraged by broader developments, including the popularization of germ theory and the allopathic medical establishment's assumption that treatment of disease involved war against nature rather than cooperation with it. Popular accounts of bacteria had long reverberated with the sounds of battle. In 1908, Hood's Sarsaparilla evoked a vision of "swarming myriads of tiny, but powerful enemies of life, those soldiers of death's dark legions" that "always and everywhere surround us, and incessantly make war upon us. The wonder is not that we are ever ill, but that we are ever well." The notion that health required a constant defense against ubiquitous, invisible adversaries was unsettling, even terrifying; no wonder it intensified the desire to repel the soldiers of death's dark legions even after they had breached the citadel. By 1930, advertising people were beginning to glimpse the possibility of total victory. Watson excitedly told the J. Walter Thompson staff about S.T. 37 mouthwash: "If one could be taught to rinse the mouth in the morning after breakfast, after lunch, and at night, one would have, ALMOST ALWAYS, a sterile mouth!" The medicalization of the discourse of the body meant that hospital standards of cleanliness were being applied to previously unregulated areas.[21]

Much advertising copy seemed animated by an itch to eliminate all signs of organic life from a pristine home environment, and an assumption that the audience felt a similar urge. As a copywriter for Zonite antiseptic (also peddled as a contraceptive douche) claimed in 1931, "The feminine world now demands an absolute cleanliness of person, a real surgical cleanliness." That demand extended to death's door and beyond: in 1926, Guardian Memorials claimed of their mausoleum, "The thought of its clean, dry, airy above ground crypt is a constant consolation to those still living." What had once been a set of pious maxims about cleanliness and godliness had become an almost obsessive desire for a sanitary environment.[22]

Managerial standards transformed the home from moral refuge to sterile laboratory. The burden of keeping it sterile fell on women, who were encouraged to conflate their own and their families' bodies with their domestic surroundings. "Do you wash 'most of the sand' out of the spinach?" an advertisement for Hoover vacuum cleaners asked *Saturday Evening Post* readers in 1930: "of course you don't; and you don't want merely to clean most of the dirt from your carpets." Variations on that theme constituted a lengthy campaign. A long-running Lysol ad in the early 1930s underscored the microbial menace of the world outside the home by presenting a cellophane-wrapped guest at the front door: "If callers also arrived in sanitary packages, we wouldn't need Lysol." But they don't, so we do.[23]

Many advertisements sought to demonstrate the superiority of human technology by metaphorically cooking the raw energies of nature. As early as 1910, advertisements for processed foods began claiming that "we can the balminess of Summer for ready use during the dreariness of Winter." In advertising's symbolic universe, cod began leaping into cans of Burnham's fish flakes, tomatoes into Campbell's Soup. Paint was "barrelled sunlight" and cod liver oil "bottled sunshine." "Choosing fruit and vegetables from fresh smelling bins" was "like picking them from your own garden!" said a visitor to the Piggly Wiggly grocery store on Hollywood Boulevard in a 1930 ad. The more advanced technological products, rather than merely seeking to contain nature, actively asserted their superiority over it. "The

Banana skin signals what's inside," Du Pont told *Good Housekeeping* readers in 1931, "but transparent CELLOPHANE beats Nature! . . . signals aren't necessary [when] you know at a glance what you're getting. Thus cellophane beats nature." Human beings themselves were judged inadequate when measured against the impersonal standards of "science," by which the advertisers usually meant technology. A *Saturday Evening* Post advertisement announced in 1928:

> See the Fidelity Curve which shows the naturalness of Eveready Radio Reproduction. It isn't fair to ask your ear to do the work of science. Unaided ears can make mistakes, but instruments cannot, and so we show you the Eveready Fidelity Curve. This impersonal, scientific record reveals the results of laboratory tests of Eveready Radio Sets, tests that show how each sound and musical note is reproduced.

Perfect "naturalness" required the subordination of nature to technology.[24]

The triumph of a positivistic version of Cartesian dualism required the sanctification of a particular vision of science. Nineteenth-century patent medicine advertising had played on ancient notions of the scientist as magus, mixing mysterious remedies from secret formulas. But national advertising was different. The coming of corporate control coincided with the consolidation of allopathic medical authority; science became an idiom for stabilizing the sorcery of the market, rather than for intensifying it. The relabeling of Scott's Emulsion illustrates the point. In the 1890s it had been a successful patent medicine, its ingredients as mysterious as those of most patent medicines; by the 1930s it was Scott's Emulsion of Norwegian Cod Liver Oil. Apparently some movement had occurred from science-as-concealment to science-as-revelation.

More systematically than older literalist doctrines, the new idiom promised a clear window on reality—an unproblematic communication of advertisers' motives. The invocation of reified Science, floating neutrally above the self-interested scufflings of the marketplace, became a characteristic ploy of national advertisers: "Science looks at whiskers"; "Science discovers the perfect antifreeze." The trick, as an art director named W. Livingston Larned wrote in *Printers' Ink* in 1930, was to shift responsibility for claims, "with science talking, rather than the advertiser." The reification of science was rooted in advertising people's need for some solid standard of meaning, but it also served as a useful rhetorical strategy, one of several they used to appropriate the rapidly growing authority of professional medicine.[25]

Pharmaceutical companies occasionally tried to humanize their operations by identifying themselves with the friendly family doctor or druggist. Ads for toothpaste, laxatives, and even toilet paper were often populated by grave professional faces warning of the need to patrol the "danger line" where gum disease could start, to flush out clogged intestines (figure 6.4), and to avoid the mortal danger posed by harsh toilet paper (figure 10.3). The pervasiveness of these images by the late 1920s and early 1930s suggests how automatically advertisers sought to borrow the legitimacy of mainstream practitioners. Two decades after the passage of the Pure Food and Drug Act, it appeared, national advertising and the medical profession

FIGURE 6.4

Fleischmann's Yeast advertisement, *American Magazine*, 1930.

had achieved a rapprochement under the umbrella of physiological perfectionism.[26]

But there was a problem. The advertised version of physiological perfection was rooted in a mechanistic worldview that, despite its continuity with Cartesian tradition, tended to undermine familiar assertions of human centrality. By the early twentieth century, the allopathic medical establishment had begun to redefine the patient as little more than a configuration of organs and potential symptoms. The emerging outlook was caricatured, but only slightly, by the young clinic assistant in a New York hospital who told his supervisor one morning in 1909 that there awaited "a pretty good lot of material. There's a couple of pretty good hearts, a big liver with jaundice, a floating kidney, three pernicious anemias, and a flatfoot."

This dismemberment was partly class-related; upper-class people tried to assert more control over their own bodies. An advocate of twilight sleep, Charlotte Tell, announced in 1915 that "we are all, men and women alike, inclined to think of our bodies, not as instruments of cosmic forces, but as personal possessions of ourselves, tools of our own desires—very exalted desires, in many cases, but still merely personal." The "we" referred to educated, affluent people like herself. Yet even though the twilight sleep movement was based on assumptions about the primacy of personal desire, it helped reinforce the hegemony of the mainstream medical profession. "Ironically, by encouraging women to go to sleep during their deliveries and to deliver their babies in hospitals," the historian Judith Walzer Leavitt has written, "the twilight sleep movement helped to distance women from their bodies."[27]

This distancing reinforced the objectification of the body. Human physiology became part of the spectacle at international expositions. A J. Walter Thompson staffer returning from the Chicago World's Fair in 1934 reported: "It is very evident, even without the testimony of the nudists, that the human body and all it entails has come into its own and that prudery and blushes are publicly outmoded." Fairgoers flocked in greatest numbers to the embryology exhibit, the Transparent Man, and the thyroid glands in the Mayo Clinic booth: "They want to understand, and they welcome the voice of disinterested, trustworthy authority."[28] This seemed a magna carta for the reification of science, but not everyone was certain that was a good thing.

By the middle and later 1930s, the advertising trade press and major middle-class magazines were full of complaints about the incessant references to bodily functions in advertising. Perhaps the advertisers were merely following the "cult of dirt" fomented by Hemingway, Faulkner, and Wolfe, a *Printers' Ink* contributor mused in 1937: "Hundreds and thousands of literate men and women now read dutifully of the inconsequence of the intellect and the supreme importance of the nether parts of the body." In any case, another complained, "Thinly dramatized physiology cascades unchecked from clattering typewriters." The copywriter Ervin M. Shafrin of Paul Block and Associates took up the cudgels on behalf of clinical frankness. "There is no such thing as a cult of dirt," he wrote. "The natural functions and desires of people cannot really be criticized, because they are, ipso facto, natural functions." The real cult of dirt, he charged, was the Victorian mix of prudery and prurience that national advertising had displaced.[29]

It is possible, though, that critics of the physiological obsessions in advertising had more complex motives than simply a censorious desire to maintain Victorian standards of delicacy. Mechanistic habits of mind threatened to reduce humankind to a sack of guts. A single advertisement for Squibb Petrolatum in 1932 revealed the implications of much medical advertising. It juxtaposed the heads of an attractive young woman and a handsome German shepherd: "He is an animal—So Are You," the caption read. No one wanted to hear this; the ad was never repeated. But more than gentility was needed to salvage the myth of human separateness and superiority from the corrosive impact of mechanistic thought. Vitalist impulses toward regeneration leavened the managerial discourse of the body, reinstating human centrality in forms more vigorous and defensible than the purely physiological. The vitalist apotheosis of energy promoted a tendency to equate American advertising with the ferment of urban modernity—a tendency that was particularly strong among certain Futurist sectors of the European avant-garde. But, here again, what seemed to many to be a radical departure from tradition was actually rooted in the Protestant past.

PSYCHOLOGICAL PERFECTIONISM

Mechanistic thought was not the only discourse of the self available to advertisers. The antinomian side of the Protestant heritage sustained more fluid notions of personal identity. Mesmerists, mind-curists, and Christian Scientists groped toward a more dynamic conception of mind–body relations than the static dualisms enshrined in rationalist and orthodox Christian tradition. Pastors and doctors sought to bridge the gap between body and soul with new theologies and therapies. Therapies became more theological, theologies more therapeutic.[30]

By the 1920s, religion and psychotherapy had merged to meet the needs of the educated middle and upper classes. The convergence was promoted by secular preachers like Bruce Barton, cofounder of the Batten, Barton, Durstine and Osborn agency, whose *The Man Nobody Knows* (1925) presented Jesus as model businessman, and whose magazine parables appropriated the language of popular psychology. "The devils which Jesus expelled from . . . sick folk were the devils of shattered nerves and divided minds, and what we term 'complexes,'" Barton explained to *Good Housekeeping* readers in 1928. When the prodigal son "came to himself" in Jesus's parable, Barton wrote, he illustrated the truth that "every man is a combination of many different personalities, a battlefield in which the fighters are his different selves. Jesus recognized that the best self is the real self." This insight appealed to the nervous audience described (and addressed) by the liberal minister Harry Emerson Fosdick: the "multitudes of people [who] are living not bad but frittered lives—split, scattered, uncoordinated."[31]

The promise of wholeness lay at the heart of the resurgent effort to cure souls. At its best, this movement promised to heal the Cartesian division between body and soul, to restore red blood to anemic sprituality and a religious lift to rampant somaticism. Barton railed against "the milk-and-water, lap-dog type of preacher" so often shown in the movies, and wished "the theatrical magnates would visit Dr. Fosdick, take a good look at him, feel the muscles in his forearms," and recast their ministers accordingly. Health and religion were not at odds. On the contrary, "health means wholeness or holiness," the psychologist G. Stanley Hall wrote in 1920, succinctly eliding the sacred and the secular.[32]

The emphasis on wholeness also implied an appealing alternative to the relentless busyness behind the pursuit of personal efficiency. Mind-cure writers like Annie Payson Call decried the frenzied pace of managerial life and insisted that "in the use of time, as in everything else, we need a quiet, steady equilibrium." She longed to recapture "the age of unconsciousness," infancy: "In each new experience we find it the same,—the healthy baby yields, lets himself go, with an ease which must double his chances for comfort." Could we but learn to do so, "our lives would lengthen, and our joys and usefulness strengthen in exact proportion." Call's emphasis on strengthening usefulness as well as joys revealed underlying utilitarian aims. Her relaxation techniques were intended to increase her readers' capacity for truly productive labor. Even those who adopted her program sometimes broke down, she acknowledged, but they got a lot more done *before* their collapse than those who had not followed nature's laws. Mind-cure thus merged with the utilitarian prescriptions of "mental hygiene." Instead of an unrelenting emphasis on disciplined effort, mental hygienists urged an alternating rhythm of busyness and regenerative relaxation.[33]

Call, Hall, and other advocates of mental hygiene celebrated play but in a restricted context. After declaring play a "fundamental instinct," Hall announced: "Everyone, especially those who lead the drab life of the modern toiler, needs and craves an occasional 'good time.' Indeed we all need to glow, tingle, and feel life intensely now and then." The assumption that modern work (whether in office or factory) was bound to be dull linked Hall with other advocates of "the efficient life" such as Luther Gulick, who argued: "Everyman ought to have a hobby of some kind or other, one which demands a certain amount of physical work, so that when he gets through his business there will be something interesting for him to do— something he can talk and think about with pleasure." In *The Philosophy of Play* (1920), Gulick urged that modern play be organized, as industry and education had been. Even brief moments of spontaneous pleasure could be fit into an overarching system of labor.[34]

Many mental hygienists assimilated vitalist impulses and rhetoric into an ethic of psychological perfectionism. The "chief end of man," Hall announced, is "to keep ourselves, body and soul, always at the very tip-top of condition." Failure to stay in shape could have sad consequences. "Children inevitably grow away from mothers who do not keep themselves growing and their lives vivid," Gulick warned. "Full living, high-level living, is one of the conditions of continuous growth." The emphasis on continuous growth paralleled the movement from evangelical to liberal models of Protestant self-development; it also raised the stakes in the effort to construct a coherent identity.[35]

National advertising intensified these cultural tendencies. As early as 1901, the J. Walter Thompson Company was using the key words that characterized "the new American tempo": "Besides being new, the advertisement must be virile, snappy, magnetic," a JWT circular advised. By the late 1920s the quest for "aliveness" as an end in itself pervaded the culture of corporate advertising: Elizabeth Arden advised *Good Housekeeping* readers how to be "Wholly Alive" through skin care, and the account executive Hugh Baillie told a JWT representatives meeting, "One of the real reasons for being in the advertising business is that you have to be alive, if you are any good at it; that is true of the individual and the organization." The celebration of "aliveness" drew the fascination of the European avant-garde; it made advertising seem a key feature of urban modernism (see chapter 10). But the ad industry itself linked vitalist rebelliousness to utilitarian purposes.[36]

Advertisers presented many of their products as the keys to sustaining the vitality of a busy, energetic people. "AT THIS NEW PACE," began the copy for the Eno Effervescent Saline laxative, beneath a drawing of a fashionably dressed woman emerging from a taxicab, attended by a fawning young man in a top hat. "Alertness is more necessary than ever at our new tempo. Life speeds up—grows rich and variegated and exciting. Yet this new pace *is* a strain. And now that keenness is more than ever desirable, it becomes all the harder to keep always keen. Thousands are finding ENO helpful in solving that problem." Hills Bros. Coffee contained "the secret of injecting new life into any gathering"; it "put new snap into mind and body." Rather than transfiguration of body and soul, "new life" came to mean merely the capacity to adjust to continuous social or personal demands—to avoid what copy for Sunkist Orange Juice called "the increasingly common human habit of 'slipping,' mentally and physically."[37]

The new performance ethic helped reshape common metaphors of the body. Electricity was redefined from a periodic jolt to a continuous system of force, one that was consistent with mechanistic models of bodily processes as well as with the vitalist language of mind-cure. "To recognize our own divinity and our intimate relation to the Universal," the mind-curist Ralph Waldo Trine wrote, "is to attach the belt of our machinery to the power-house of the Universe."[38] The dream of tapping into a vast reservoir of energy quickened the plodding piston strokes of nineteenth-century mechanism, casting a supernatural aura over what had been a grimy industrial landscape. It was not only Henry Adams who felt the urge to bend a knee before the dynamo. Yet what seemed like divinity to Trine (or Adams) seemed like success to more secular souls.

Infinite power could be harnessed to finite purposes: electricity provided idioms for the celebration of energetic ambition. "Every American is potentially a live wire," *The J. Walter Thompson Book* proclaimed in 1909. "He lives in an atmosphere of action. He is always looking for new ideas; he appreciates improvements and inventions; he understands the value of time, and of taking short-cuts to get what he wants." This conventional wisdom entered the advertisements themselves. A Shredded Wheat ad in 1908 announced that the standard American greeting should be not "How ya doin'?" but "What's yer horsepower?" or better, "What's yer man-power?" This would be "more in keeping with the spirit of our modern progress; for isn't it a fact that the human machine nowadays is expected to develop a certain amount of Power?" A man like Governor William Barnes of New York, profiled by the *Saturday Evening Post* in 1910, was an example of successful adjustment to the new tempo. Barnes "has the vital spark and is sparking regularly," the *Post* reported. Electricity provided the power for the human machine; vitalist and mechanical metaphors were wed.[39]

The marriage of periodic revitalization and continuous achievement flourished during the early decades of the twentieth century, as crusades against alcohol and narcotics made those means of "letting go" less available. By the 1920s, patent medicines constituted a much smaller proportion of a typical agency's billings than during the period before the Pure Food and Drug Act. National advertisers promoted new therapeutic vehicles for temporary escape, vehicles more consistent with the "new American tempo" of continuous growth and regular sparks. Among the most common were tobacco products. The transformation of tobacco advertising epitomized the triumph of psychological perfectionism.

Cigars had long been linked with relaxation. A typical campaign of 1903 for Cremo cigars showed a businessman puffing away in a wicker easy chair, with the caption "Cremo lullaby—The smoker's reverie of luxurious pleasure—his rendezvous from care and worry." But the pace of cigar smoking soon began to seem too leisurely for the pattern of life promoted by national advertisers. New methods of mechanically rolling cigarettes allowed manufacturers to flood the market with a smoke that could be integrated into a more hectic everyday routine. (Whether daily schedules actually were more crowded than before is an open question; certainly advertisers seemed to think so, and assumed their audience would agree.) Well into the 1900s, however, advertisements associated cigarette smoking with ample-bosomed sultanas in exotic settings, as in American Tobacco's Sporting Girls series.[40]

Not until 1913, when the R. J. Reynolds Tobacco Company began advertising Camels in earnest, did cigarettes begin to be integrated into the managerial world picture. Agencies like N. W. Ayer (which handled the Camel account) spent a decade describing the unique flavors of particular brands; then in the 1920s they began to locate cigarette smoking in leisure settings (figure 6.5). Beneath a drawing of the smart set in a convertible at a golf course, the copy in a 1927 Camel advertisement explained: "The people of this modern age are the busiest workers of all time. But they are wise enough to seek relaxation, and they place Camel first among cigarettes." Camels, a 1929 campaign proclaimed, were "a boon for a breathless age . . . sometimes even Youth likes to sit down for a golden moment . . . at which times a really *good* cigarette is like the Dawn of a New Day." When things got really tense, you could "Build yourself a CAMEL SMOKE-SCREEN. We claim, with good evidence to back

FIGURE 6.5

Camel cigarettes advertisement, 1926. *N. W. Ayer Collection, National Museum of American History, Smithsonian Institution.*

us, that a cool cloud of Camel smoke is a practically perfect protective smoke-screen. Outside the charmed circle of its mellow fragrance, troubles and worries and sundry pothers hover baffled. Within, all is peace, pleasure, content." What lay behind all the celebrations of new opportunities for leisure, in cigarette ads as elsewhere, was the omnipresence of a demanding and often monotonous work environment. "Now, if ever, we must escape the commonplace," an ad for Jordan Motor Cars insisted in 1919, "—must have more life and less drabness—more snap, less sameness." The implied monotony of everyday life gave the snatched moments of leisure their special meaning.[41]

Advertisements and advice literature alike revealed that the emergent managerial culture offered not a critique but a continuation of Protestant patterns of thought. Religious longings for purification and regeneration were reincarnated in an ethos of personal efficiency. The "soft" side of that ethos was represented by Annie Payson Call and the mind-curists—the temporary withdrawal of affect from frenzied finance, the ingestion of leisure in momentary doses. The "hard" side was epitomized in Frederick Winslow Taylor's scientific management. Taylor and his many followers helped make "the elimination of waste in industry" the chief preoccupation of employers, providing them with a new legitimating language for labor discipline. Advertising played a major role in accelerating this pursuit of efficiency, extending it into the most intimate areas of life. The managerial reconstruction of gender relations offered a revealing illustration.

THE LITTLE WOMAN

Since the mid–nineteenth century, if not earlier, the home had been an arena for gender-based conflict over consumption. Women's magazines like *Godey's* and *Peterson's* habitually assailed the Fashionable Woman as a frivolous consumer, the ruin of her hardworking spouse; the same magazines often turned the argument around, attacking self-indulgent male expenditures on cigars, wine, and stag outings. Yet the attempt to promote prudential habits often ran counter to celebrations of elegant home furnishings and personal adornment. However inconsistent this discourse of domesticity, it was based on clear-cut boundaries between men's and women's spheres. The transition to a post-Victorian culture marked a blurring of those boundaries, with the spread of masculine domesticity and the movement from homosocial to heterosocial styles of leisure—men and women, boys and girls together. National advertising ratified (and thus encouraged) this development, but the liberating qualities of this more companionate pattern (at least in its advertised version) were open to question.[42]

The Gibson girls and Yale men, later the flappers and frat boys who populated the national advertisements of the early twentieth century, seemed emblems of youthful exuberance. Their age was a clue to their social significance; in their thoughtless activity and dependence on corporate expertise they embodied an infantilized version of male and female adulthood. The voluptuous woman and the bearded man had been far more formidable figures than the perpetually boyish husband and his giggling girl-bride—two icons who came to dominate the fiction as well as the advertising pages of the national magazines during the 1910s and 1920s.[43]

The devaluation of authority was particularly marked with respect to women. The positioning of men's bodies vs. women's (figure 6.6) reaffirmed masculine authority, a pattern the sociologist Erving Goffman has noticed in contemporary advertisements. More important, advertisements broadly reflected the introduction of managerial professionalism into previously feminine domains, notably the kitchen. The application of industrial methods to agriculture affected the preparation of food as well as the production, processing, and distribution of it. Domestic scientists and processed-food advertisers, addressing middle-class women who were increasingly isolated from kin and communal foodways, sought to reassure their audience by providing them with a sense of control, a new set of rules bearing the imprimatur of "scientific cookery." As Laura Shapiro writes in *Perfection Salad,* "By scientific they meant rational, objective, and methodical—traits that gave the term a definite air of maleness." Eager to haul sentimental ignorance into the light of clinical objectivity, food advertisers and their female allies sought to re-create man's world in woman's sphere. No longer, in their ideology, would the home be a refuge from the calculating world outside; instead, it would mimic the steady productivity of the modern factory. Despite its aura of clinical neutrality, the rationalization of the kitchen expressed the ethnocentrism of Northeastern WASP elites. The advocates of scientific cookery, Shapiro observes, "hoped to regulate the messy sprawl of American society and to filter out the most unsettling aspects of its diversity." A Bostonian visiting the Georgia Exposition of 1903, for example, was horrified by all the meals she was served except the chicken salad and gelatin lunch.[44]

This prim regional and ethnic imperialism may have amused the

FIGURE 6.6

Advertisement, G. Mennen Company, *Town and Country*, 1908. *Warshaw Collection.*

worldly souls who worked in national advertising, but its orientation was fundamentally congenial to their cultural style. Like advertising executives, domestic scientists treated standardization as moral advance; they praised processed cheese over farm cheese because the factory version possessed "greater uniformity." This was in accordance with the food processors' advertisements as well as with a recurring chant in corporate culture: "the best surprise is no surprise." What was even more appealing than this habit of mind, to both admakers and their clients, was the domestic scientists' attitude toward the widespread adulteration of mass-produced foods: they treated it as a problem of consumer education rather than of industrialists' malfeasance.[45]

Similar patterns surfaced in other areas of women's lives. It was not simply that men dominated women but that middle- and upper-class men and women alike conflated the ascendant ethos of professionalism with a masculine—and superior—frame of mind. A case parallel to that of food processing evolved from the institutionalization of the allopathic medical establishment in hospitals, universities, and professional organizations: male doctors asserted their authority over childbirth, shunting midwives aside with the eager cooperation of many educated and affluent women. Like the rise of scientific cookery, the spread of medical intervention in childbirth reaffirmed the professional authority of Anglo-Saxon males and marginalized female folkways that had been preserved in regional and ethnic traditions. By the 1920s, women's magazines were cheering the process on. "Slowly but surely," *Good Housekeeping* editorialized, "childbirth is being lifted out of the realm of darkness into the spotlight of new science."[46] Ironically, "the realm of darkness" had been characterized by women's control of the birth process.

Here, too, national advertisements endorsed and furthered the process of masculine-sponsored enlightenment. A Lysol advertisement in 1934 showed a roadster racing along a two-lane blacktop on a dark and stormy night; overhead flew a stork carrying a baby, and just behind the stork was a huge hooded figure marked INFECTION. "The stork, the doctor, and infection are running a three-cornered race. All three speeding for the same destination. Which will arrive first? Three human beings, a mother, a baby, and a doctor [where's Poppa?] are vitally concerned with that question. If the doctor wins . . . all's well. But if either of his two rivals keeps the lead, there's trouble ahead." By the mid-1930s, the centrality of the doctor's role in childbirth was unquestioned, at least among the educated middle-class audience reached by the national magazines.[47]

No one would deny that women had reason to welcome the medicalization of childbirth, particularly if it meant a triumph over pain and death, as the professional ideology promised. But the meanings of medicalization were complex. The triumph over pain through anesthesiology was often genuine and immediate, but the risk of death from infection was reduced only gradually. In fact, historians of childbirth have convincingly argued that the doctor's intervention often increased the risk of death from puerperal fever, as late as the 1920s. But by then the enlightened way to have babies was in a hospital, under anesthesia and a doctor's authority. The idea that babies could be "turned out like Fords" by doctors marked a major shift in cultural symbolism. As in the industrialization of cooking, an ideology of mass production enveloped a matriarchal ritual. Even more systematically than men, woman were reduced (at least rhetorically) to dependence on managerial expertise.

These changes helped reshape the imagery of advertising. The older entrepreneurial ads, besides celebrating voluptuous womanhood, had also indulged in vaudeville versions of ancient misogynist imagery. In its very hostility to women, that imagery had acknowledged their potential power: mother-in-law jokes; little kids downing Yuengling beers behind a fence while a female authority figure peeked over it; the "Old Virgin" who would never let a tobacco-chewing man kiss her, counterposed to the sweet young thing who didn't object, provided you chewed the fragrant Virgin Leaf. The newer corporate advertising contained almost nothing but sweet young things. In 1909 a *Printers' Ink* contributor joined others in the trade press in complaining about the prevalence of "pretty girl advertising," yet he acknowledged its relevance to products like candy: "Woman is in her realm here and her smiling countenance will at once give the impression of a sweet, delicate, pure, dainty, luscious and winning bonbon." Helen Rosen Woodward, remembering her years as a copywriter at Frank Presbrey and other agencies, perceived the male anxieties behind the notion of woman as bonbon. "In Europe it is not so disgraceful to be forty," she wrote in 1926. "There experience, individuality, character, showing in the face, are considered seductive; here we put a higher value on youth and sweetness. In the United States men look on sophistication with fear." That fear may have intensified as the birth rate dropped and women's sphere became less clearly defined; in the iconography of advertising, at least, women shed their voluptuous and maternal connotations and began to look (as well as behave) more like girls.[48]

Still, even bonbons had domestic responsibilities, albeit different ones from those of their grandmothers. Earlier ideology had emphasized women's duties to their children and community; husbands were secondary and peripheral. The newer, corporate-sponsored version of domesticity, in national advertisements and the magazines they supported, recast women's role. It placed comparatively less emphasis on women's responsibility to the wider culture, through the nurturance of civic virtue in the next generation, and more on their duties to the boy-men who were their husbands. ("Are You Responsible for Some Man's Health?" a typical advertisement of the 1920s asked.) Advice literature and advertising alike dwelled on the comparative helplessness of husbands, their need to be pleased but also managed. "Indeed it will not be long," as a contributor told brides-to-be reading *Good Housekeeping* in 1931, "before you have learned that your job is to be a manager of men as well as menus." In the emergent conventional wisdom, wives were not only "purchasing agents for their families" (see figure 4.13) and efficient managers of their households, but also persuasive group leaders who maintained family harmony by subtly commanding the allegiance of husband and children alike. Margaret Sangster's story "Other Woman," in a 1935 issue of *Good Housekeeping*, showed one way the process was supposed to operate. A good housewife outpoints a déclassé slob who has temporarily aroused her husband's pity (and/or sexual desire). The housewife invites the d.s. to dinner after the d.s. has lost her job. This gives the wife a chance to shine, and the husband a chance to get bored with the d.s. The wife manages to locate the estranged husband of the d.s. ("Mister Van Nest"), who drags the d.s. home, hoping that this time she'll feed him a decent dinner for a change. Effective care of husbands was a means of exercising influence.[49]

By the 1920s and 1930s, doctrines of influence had been reformulated in the new idiom of "democratic social engineering." This was the "group process" method of manipulating consensus: a persuasive group leader, often possessing scientific expertise, would foster a sense of spontaneity, experimentation, and participation while leading the group toward an "appropriate" goal. The method was hailed (or used) by authorities as various as John Dewey, Dale Carnegie, Walter Lippmann, and Edward Bernays. It was employed in settling labor disputes, promoting effective salesmanship, and devising schemes for personnel management and progressive education. It could also be used within the family, by managerial wives and mothers.[50]

Not that husbands lacked their own capacity to manipulate obedience to dominant norms. By the early 1930s, *Good Housekeeping*'s ad pages were full of husbands scolding their wives for looking cheap in their ruby red lipstick or ruining the family finances by getting runs in their stockings. Perhaps the worst critics were the silent, brooding types. "I could feel his eyes accusing me!" a woman exclaimed in a 1932 Drano ad. "He's a man who doesn't talk very much . . . but I could feel his eyes accusing me every time the bathroom drains slowed up. He'd look at me as much as to say, 'Your fault!' " The non-nurturant female was no longer the devouring woman but the "Husband-Wrecker" who didn't give her man Grape-Nuts for breakfast. The fiction and advice literature of the period were never quite so melodramatically male-centered; in fact, there were many articles advocating at least the option of career choice for women. But the interpretation of companionate marriage in the ads was mutual manipulation, with the man in the end on top: a woman was to please her boy-man by catering to his whims.[51]

The most relentless pressure on women, though, came not from husbands but from the (often invisible) corporate authority that claimed to be "making the modern woman possible."[52] The managerial worldview of the 1930s not only demanded that housewives turn the home into a sterile laboratory, it also updated Victorian ideals of domesticity by assuming that women were responsible less for instilling the voice of conscience than for promoting their family members' smooth integration into the larger society: Dad at work, kids at school and play.

According to the emerging doctrines of "adjustment" in popular psychology, psychic and political health were functionally interrelated. In the burgeoning child guidance clinics, as in other therapeutic settings, the objectives of treatment became "the betterment of the patient's total adjustment to life rather than the removal of a particular symptom," as two therapists wrote in 1934. According to the historian Warren Susman, the presiding therapeutic genius of the 1930s was Alfred Adler. The Adlerian prescription that one should overcome one's "inferiority complex" and "adjust" to collective norms was well suited to middle-class Americans during the 1930s. Pervasive economic and emotional insecurity brought not only feelings of inferiority but also the desire to transcend them through a sense of belonging to a larger whole. Many popularized versions of Adlerian psychology appeared alongside the advertisements in the national magazines. The advice from *Good Housekeeping* and similar magazines was "Don't be afraid to conform," or to encourage your children to. The family became the factory turning out "well-adjusted" adults.[53]

Or at least that was the hope of many helping professionals. But as the Depression intensified worries of all sorts, the family constructed in the managerial image became a snake pit of strained harmony. Child-rearing advice in articles as well as advertisements upped the emotional ante of parental responsibility, holding parents (especially mothers) accountable for their children's present and future happiness as well as their health. "Sulking through her playtime . . . one moment fretful—the next, screaming in a childish tantrum . . . a difficult girl at home, a problem at school . . . What is the future of this child? Her parents ask themselves—'why is Mary so contrary?'" The answer? Vitamin A and D deficiency, remedied by Scott's Emulsion of Norwegian Cod Liver Oil! There was nothing wrong, as any parent knows, with the idea that cranky children might be crying for nutritious food. But ads for so many different products (cereals, eyeglasses, correspondence schools) repeated this sort of scene so often that one begins to see it as a vast projection of the admakers' own familial anxieties—the tense preoccupation with proper "parenting" (though the awful word had not been coined yet) that was common among the professional–managerial groups. Magazine advice literature on the one hand asked in anguish "WHAT is WRONG between us and our children?" (we are too permissive) and on the other hand ordered *"Do not be overanxious about your children"* (lighten up, for God's sake).[54]

For the journalist William McDermott, writing in *Good Housekeeping* in 1934, the solution to child-rearing problems seemed to be a modified form of democratic social engineering. McDermott, without actually using the phrase, applied the method to child-rearing. "I Want My Daughters to Marry," he declared, and told of his efforts to promote that goal. His account was the same muddle of contradictions that bedeviled most attempts to describe democratic social engineering. "I am as much interested in my daughters' having a happy girlhood, cultivating the right kind of boy friends, as in maintaining high averages in the classroom." The young man in law or medical school needed a wife to cook for him, guard his health, encourage his ambition—"she can become the next thing to a doctor." And so his girls were in training for that role. "They are acquiring *of their own volition and by their own initiative* a good taste which will be at once their chief charm and their chief defense all their lives . . . *By subtle suggestion and wise strategy* we seek to convey to them that the major sin is the violation of good taste," and if they slip into slovenliness in housework or personal care they know "they will be all but disowned as far as their mother and father are concerned." The same combination of iron fist in velvet glove that characterized personnel management and other forms of democratic social engineering could also be brought to bear in the family circle.[55]

McDermott's familial social engineering was an updated version of the "influence" advocated by Horace Bushnell and other liberal child-rearing advisers since the mid–nineteenth century. But the whole idea of submerging one's opinion and deferring to a reassuring consensus acquired an intensified appeal amid the insecurities of the Depression era. It could even provide a basis for expansion of state power. What the evidence suggests is that the therapeutic corporate state was not simply an imposition (as Foucault and his followers have sometimes implied) but a *collaboration* between the populace and their rulers.[56]

The link between popular longings for connectedness and a paternalistic managerial state surfaced with particular clarity in a 1935 article in *Good Housekeeping* called "Uncle Sam Wants Your Mark." The author, Vera Connolly, urged voluntary compliance with J. Edgar Hoover's plan to fingerprint all Americans. The benefit of this program, she believed, was that it would end "a travesty on our modern civilization"—the anonymous burial of decent citizens in potters' fields. "Almost every 'unknown' is known to and loved by someone. Behind almost every commitment to that soil is family heartbreak somewhere. For it is chiefly the decent who are buried here. The criminal seldom is. His fingerprints are on file." The longing to belong could legitimize new forms of hierarchy and surveillance.[57]

So it is possible, using advertisements and other symbols of managerial ideology, to form a bleak vision of the kind of society emerging in the United States during the 1930s: a society where intimate needs and desires had been successfully integrated into the larger purposes of private and public governing bodies, a society that needed only the mass mobilization of war to complete the integration process. This was the vision that lay behind the functionalist sociology of Talcott Parsons, whose text *The Social System* (1951) implicitly enshrined the hegemony of managerial professionals in the impersonal jargon of social science. Foucault's work was in many ways a critical mirror-image of Parsons's.

But powerful countertendencies were at work, even within the dominant world picture. Alongside the minatory judgments of much advice literature and the hectoring of the advertisements, both the fiction and nonfiction in women's magazines contained many confident and accomplished heroines—professional women who were not forced to choose between marriage and a career. If corporate advertising was monolithic, the broader mass culture was not—it expressed a diverse range of options for women throughout the midcentury decades.

There were subtler tensions at work as well. Consider the private life of John B. Watson, the psychologist and J. Walter Thompson executive whose behaviorist views epitomized the managerial agenda of control. The man who believed that a malleable self could be harnessed to a regime of unceasing productive efficiency was himself an emotional wreck. He was estranged from his children, who resented a childhood that had been treated as "a business proposition." He could not sit through a play; he fled serious conversation or even momentary stillness into a whirlwind of compulsive activity, building barns, repairing fences, and devouring huge mounds of detective novels and Westerns. Especially after his second wife died in 1935, Watson withdrew more and more to the solitude of his Connecticut estate, where he raced his speedboats at top speed and drank a quart of bourbon a day. As his biographer, Kerry Buckley, perceptively notes, "Watson's preoccupation with being busy suggests something other than a search for pleasure; his constant mechanical motion more resembles a flight into the oblivion of activity. One gets the sense of sheer panic, barely suppressed." It may be that many other acolytes of personal efficiency were energized by "sheer panic" in their desires for systematic control of their inner and outer environments.[58]

There were alternatives to panic, particularly for advertising people who did not take themselves or their mission too seriously. Watson was a social scientist who believed he had discovered the key to directing human destiny. Not all managerial thinkers were so filled with hubris, and advertising copywriters in particular had an alternative tradition that elevated entertainment over earnestness. In their quest for legitimacy, agency executives did their best to suppress memories of their ancestors in the commercial vernacular. But the carnivalesque heritage survived—troubling at some times, liberating at others.

THE MAN IN THE GABARDINE SUIT

Corporate advertising aimed to clarify confusing claims by presenting a transparent window on the product for sale. Yet the appearance of transparency was often merely a surface effect designed to win the confidence of the consumer—mystification in the guise of demystification. There were awkward moments when professional aspirations collided with commercial necessities, albeit behind the closed doors of agency staff meetings. At a meeting in 1928, William Esty, a senior copywriter at J. Walter Thompson, presented his plan for a new approach to selling Herbert Tareyton Cigarettes. Taste and throat appeals had already been tried; now the nerves were the key: get ordinary folks to say that they smoke all they want and Tareyton doesn't upset their nerves. As Esty observed, "A great deal of what we think is in a sense reaction, is purely imaginary. That is more true of cigarettes, perhaps, than of any other commodity. . . . If [consumers] think—here's a cigarette which is more of a sedative, won't it be a sedative?" Chairman Stanley Resor asked for comments from the group. Another copywriter, William Mims, burst out: "I think it's _____. [sic]. I just feel, as a member of this company, resentful of our being willing to invent out of whole cloth the theme copy and then manufacture the evidence. It depresses me to see us apparently adopt the criterion of success as the only criterion. I say that the storm is going by and I seem to be out of tune with what is accepted as the philosophy here." Resor, a group process leader par excellence, agreed that Mims had raised a real point: "On this particular presentation we have come as close to the line as we want to come." Let's keep it fresh and within the facts, he concluded vaguely to Esty.[59]

Such disagreements were rarely recorded, but there were times when new recruits had to be told what the agency was really up to. At a JWT staff meeting in 1930, for example, a naive new copywriter named Wengler questioned an old hand about the scientific basis of intestinal fatigue:

MR. WENGLER: At what age do people become liable to this intestinal fatigue? Do very young people have it?

MR. DAY: People have it all ages.

MR. WENGLER: Do people in their early 20s suffer from this condition at all?

MR. DAY: Fatigue is universal; we simply have to credit it to the intestines, that's all.[60]

At such moments the carnivalesque qualities of national advertising remained concealed behind closed doors; the advertisement itself preserved the objectivist facade, the lab coated doctor telling his bleary-eyed patient the bad news about his sluggish jejunem. But in many advertisements the older equation of science with magic was overt and insistent. Since the 1880s, Edison and his assistants had used theatrical displays of lighting to dazzle potential consumers of electricity. Edison himself was "the wizard of Menlo Park," who had created a "fairyland" there and at a wide variety of expositions. General Electric preserved this language in an impersonal corporate setting. An advertising campaign of 1930 referred to GE products coming "out of the house of magic"—a phrase the folksy commentator Floyd Gibbons coined to describe the GE Research Laboratory. Gibbons appeared prominently in the campaign, apologizing for using "twenty-nine-dollar words" (like *electron*) and consistently characterizing the GE scientists as "wizards." The GE magic show climaxed at the 1939 World's Fair, when a master of ceremonies presented electrical experiments in a darkened auditorium ("Defying the law of gravity, this heavy metal dish floats freely in the air"), much to the disappointment of scientists who had held out hope that the fair would perform an educational service.[61]

They should have known better. For several decades before the fair, national advertising had played a major role in making science mysterious and promoting a superstitious reverence for technology. Beneath a drawing of a dad fiddling with the radio dial while the kids watch raptly, an Eveready batteries ad warned: "Don't tamper with tone. Beware of interfering with illusion. Power that reveals its presence by its noise is like a magician's assistant who gives the trick away." The magic was not only in the illusion of reality that electronic instruments could maintain, but also in the sense of personal autonomy that automobiles, telephones, and radios could provide to the people (most of them men, it was assumed) who used them. A 1923 advertisement for Tuska Radio caught the connection between the invocation of technological magic and the construction of a weary mass man in search of a sense, however fleeting, of freedom. "Let the day's troubles sink with the sun. Then turn to your Tuska Radio, and be whisked around the world. In those precious hours between work and sleep, you live in Radio Fairyland, where you are master of distance and ruler of a host of entertainers." The promise of magical transformation preserved the carnivalesque tradition for a technological age.[62]

The evocation of magic and fantasy, along with the self-conscious artifice of "Radio Fairyland," should remind us that advertisers were still engaged in theatrical performance in the 1920s and 1930s. Both inside and outside the agencies, many people found it difficult to take national advertising as seriously as its spokesmen demanded. The magazine *Ballyhoo*, which first appeared in 1929, had as its stock-in-trade satire of corporate advertisements. Soon there was more than ever to satirize. Radio advertising brought a return of oral performance and snake-oil style; the impact of the Depression intensified the hysteria of product claims and encouraged the resort to nude women as attention-grabbers. Despite the rhetoric of clinical frankness, nudity maintained an undeniably prurient fascination that recalled earlier celebrations of the flesh. And sometimes the whole business seemed like a big joke, even to its practitioners. By the mid-1930s the trade press was running satirical lists of the mythical maladies copywriters had invented. It was hard to be absolutely earnest about sneaker smell and smelly hands.[63]

Despite all they had in common with the emergent professional–managerial class, advertising executives could never quite shake the feeling that they were charlatans and fakers, could never fully convince even themselves that they were trading in truths as objective as those produced by other plumbings of the public mind. Most probably didn't want to. Despite strivings for "sincerity," even the most earnest advertising people may have at least ambivalently enjoyed the playful and performative aspects of visual or verbal language, the delights of commercial discourse as well as the anxiety, the secret self-contempt. It was as if there were a carnival barker in a shiny gabardine suit, ready to step out from inside the gray flannel.

CHAPTER 7

The New Basis of Civilization

By the early twentieth century, national advertising had become part of the iconography of everyday life. But the very success of the agencies began to distance them from common experience. Nothing illustrated this relationship more vividly than the huge electric signs that began to light up Broadway in 1905 and 1906, celebrating products like Gold Seal Champagne and Heatherbloom Skirts. "Flowers in natural colors stand out against the night sky. Garlands and drapery are traced in many-tinted fires," *Printers' Ink* observed in 1908. "Delicate jewels of ruby, gold, and turquoise, are suspended over dingy buildings in the sight of thousands of the hurrying ants called men." The effectiveness of this advertising depended on its capacity to create a brilliant realm above and beyond the gray bustle of the "hurrying ants" enmeshed in metropolitan routine. Having fashioned that realm, agency people began to believe they inhabited it.[1]

In a literal sense they did. As the national advertising business became "solid with money," in Helen Rosen Woodward's phrase, its practitioners came to constitute an extraordinarily privileged elite, increasingly elevated above and isolated from the concerns of ordinary Americans. After 1927, when Stanley Resor moved the J. Walter Thompson Company to the new Graybar Building, next to Grand Central Station, the firm's copywriters and executives could ride the train in from Connecticut or Westchester, break for lunch in the colonial-style executive dining room, and return home in the evening, all without ever mingling with the crowds on the sidewalks of New York. No wonder their outlook on their audience seemed to reflect the view from the thirty-sixth floor.[2]

The distance between corporate advertisers and consumers was confirmed in 1936 by an in-house survey of New York copywriters conducted for J. Walter Thompson. It found that not one copywriter belonged to a lodge or civic club; only one in five went to church except on rare occasions; half never went to Coney Island or any other popular public resort, and the others only once or twice a year; more than half had never lived within the national average income of $1,580 per family a year, and half did not know anyone who ever had. While 5 percent of American homes had servants, 66 percent of J. Walter Thompson homes did. The profile was affluent, metropolitan, secular, and (superficially) sophisticated, and this was typical of the most prominent agencies with the largest accounts.[3]

Given their exceptionally privileged position, how did advertising people understand their relationship to the milling crowds on the street below, as well as to other powerful groups? How did they define their role in American political culture? This chapter and the next trace some answers to those questions, from the beginnings of professional advertising to the post–World War II era.

Although they were part of the emergent managerial–professional class, advertising people were never fully at ease with doctors, lawyers, and college professors. The carnivalesque past of the advertising business kept resurfacing in the workaday life of the agencies, rendering ridiculous any claims to scientific objectivity. The solidarity between advertisers and other professional elites was strongest during the two world wars, when American society came most closely to resemble the "industrial army" envisioned by the utopian Edward Bellamy in *Looking Backward: 2000 to 1887* (1888), and advertisers were enlisted in the task of ideological mobilization. But a common front was more difficult to maintain during peacetime. Throughout the twentieth century, tensions between the ideology of professionalism and the experience of everyday life persisted inside the agency.

Corporate advertisers felt constantly called to the task of self-justification. Like public relations counselors, they claimed the ability to perform managerial wonders: to conquer the problem of overproduction by stimulating demand, to flatten the curves of the business cycle by persuading manufacturers to advertise in good times as well as bad; to maintain a smooth-running "distribution system"; to legitimate policies of planned obsolescence by promoting doctrines of technical and stylistic progress; to promote labor discipline by dangling the carrot of consumer goods in front of the worker's nose. In short, corporate advertisers aimed to contain the carnivalization of meaning in commercial society by realizing Simon Nelson Patten's vision of perpetual progress: reinforcing rhythms of repetition and variety in a well-paid working population; creating a consumer culture characterized by equilibrium between labor and leisure, supply and demand.

The containment of the carnivalesque was a difficult project. Consumer culture was always threatened in hard times with the loss of its economic base, in good times with the sheer boredom induced by standardized affluence. And it was never easy for advertisers to draw a clear bead on those crowds of consumers. The construction of "the consumer" required various rhetorical strategies, depending on the audience addressed. To their clients and often to members of other managerial elites, advertisers increasingly presented the consumer as "mass man," alone or in the aggregate a manipulable mound of putty; the alleged doltishness of the masses justified the persistence of Barnumesque tactics that might otherwise seem inappropriate to a serious profession. To critics and to consumers themselves, on the other hand, advertisers described the consumer as the sovereign of all he or she surveyed. Even though the sinister implications of mass man kept overshadowing the sunny vision of consumer omnipotence, advertisers during World War I and throughout the 1920s were able to balance the rhetorical constructions of mass man and sovereign consumer. It was not until the Great Depression that the balancing act became more difficult.

PROFESSIONALISM AND PROGRESS, 1890–1917

Patten's *New Basis of Civilization* had envisioned the coming together of popular entertainments and popular edification in a corporate-sponsored pattern of progress. The development of World's Fairs during the late nineteenth and early twentieth centuries dramatized that hope. Potentially subversive amusements were at first eliminated (as in the clearing of whole neighborhoods around the Philadelphia Centennial Exposition in 1876), then segregated (as at Chicago in 1893, when the fair promoters separated the seamy Midway from the uplifting White City), and finally integrated as exhibits in an imperial vision of progress (as half-naked "savages" were at Omaha in 1898 and Buffalo in 1901.)[4]

During the years before World War I, corporate advertisers believed they too might participate in this integration process. By the 1890s, even, many trade press writers were convinced they had transcended the dark old days when the advertising business was dominated by bunco artists. "Ten years ago the majority of people looked upon all advertising as dishonest," the copywriter Charles Austin Bates announced in 1895. "Now the majority of people look upon the majority of advertising as strictly honest business news." A swelling chorus insisted that advertisements be factual and product-oriented. "Truth may be less brilliant, but the statement of fact must convince," wrote the copywriter Helen Mar Shaw in *Judicious Advertising* magazine. Factual advertising was devoid of so-called "advertising ideas"—cute puns and pretty girls that glittered and flashed and told nothing about the product. The popularity of irrelevant but catchy "advertising ideas," *Printers' Ink* claimed in 1906, "passed with the notion that advertising is literature or art."[5]

The factual basis of copy was the cornerstone of "reason-why" advertising. Reason-why was the brainchild of John E. Kennedy, a former officer in the Royal Canadian Mounted Police who (according to agency lore) checked into the Palmer House in Chicago one spring day in 1904, headed for the bar, scribbled a note on his business card, and gave it to the bellboy to take up to the rooms of Albert Lasker, an executive with the Lord & Thomas agency. The note said that if Lasker wanted to know what advertising really was, there was a man in the bar who could tell him. Lasker took the bait, and over tumblers of Canadian Club, Kennedy informed him that advertising was simply "salesmanship-in-print." He insisted that the advertiser needed to make detailed arguments on behalf of his products, shunning all irrelevancies.[6]

An emphasis on the informative powers of ads encouraged the belief that national advertising was a key part of "the great distributing machinery brought into existence by the era of combines," as a contributor wrote in the advertising trade journal *Fame*.

> Under the new system the producer will talk to thousands at a time instead of employing a drummer to talk to each person individually. How is he going to do it? Through the printed catalog, the artistic booklet, the attractive poster, the pages of the magazines and weekly periodicals, the columns of the daily press, and the thousands of ingenious and unique devices for catching the public eye, designed by the brightest and cleverest minds in the country.

A "young man with nothing but brains" would do well to consider employment in "this new and vast system of publicity." John O. Powers, a legendary copywriter for Wanamaker's department store in Philadelphia, summarized the significance of national advertising to readers of the *Annals of the American Academy of Political and Social Science* in 1903: "Advertising is to the field of distribution what the railroad is to transportation." The centrifugal effects of advertising were contained in a neutral language of technique; from this view, advertising was a value-free instrument in an emerging, impersonal system.[7]

Interdependence and specialization were key features of that system. "The specialist will be the dominant force in the business world of the twentieth century," a *Saturday Evening Post* contributor predicted in a 1901 article that was excerpted in the advertising trade press. "The day of the all-round man is over." Teamwork was nowhere more necessary than in the modern advertising agency, where the preparation of a campaign (or even an individual advertisement) was increasingly subjected to a minute subdivision of labor. "The final advertising plan is more a cooperative result than it is the work of any one man," the agency head Earnest Elmo Calkins wrote in 1915. "It is the perfection of mental team work just as the baseball nine is the perfection of physical team work." What became the clichés of corporate culture in the late twentieth century were still newly minted in the pre–World War I era.[8]

References to interdependence and teamwork were efforts to come to terms with a vast transformation of the social and economic landscape. National advertising agencies were part of the burgeoning "service sector" of an emerging oligopolistic economy in the United States. Between the Civil War and World War I, the making and distribution of consumer goods, as well as more "basic" forms of production and processing, came under the unprecedented direction of national corporations. To take an example that reflects the values as well as the economic structures of the new corporate system, wristwatch manufacturers, who had done $2.8 million worth of business in 1869, quadrupled that amount to over $14 million by 1914; yet the number of firms making watches decreased from thirty-seven to fifteen—eleven of which were brand-name advertisers in the national magazines. By World War I, it was possible to see national advertising within the developing outlines of a huge, self-perpetuating cultural–economic circuit.[9]

Though small businesses survived and flourished more widely than many historians have acknowledged, the economic power of large corporations had far-reaching consequences for cultural as well as entrepreneurial life. National magazines, for example (such as *Saturday Evening Post* and

Ladies' Home Journal), were expressions of the managerial order: they were cheaper than the great maiden aunts of quality journalism—magazines like the *Atlantic Monthly* or *Harper's*—largely because they were supported by advertising revenues rather than subscriptions. And their advertisers were nearly all large corporations aiming their goods at a national market. The advertising executive James Collins told a congressional committee in 1907:

> There is still an illusion to the effect that a magazine is a periodical in which advertising is incidental. But we don't look at it that way. A magazine is simply a device to induce people to read advertising. It is a large booklet with two departments—entertainment and business. The entertainment department finds stories, pictures, verses, etc. to interest the public. The business department makes the money.

Small wonder that the fiction in many of the magazines sometimes came to resemble the advertising copy—in narrative strategies and iconography if not always in ideology. National brand-name advertisements were a key cultural expression of the hegemonic professional–managerial bloc that was hesitantly emerging out of the wreckage of the war between labor and capital.[10]

During the first decade of the twentieth century, tensions sharpened between the advertising industry and other managerial–professional groups. Critics of corrupt business practices began to demand government regulation. As the debate over the Pure Food and Drug Act made clear, advertising was often implicated in the sins of its clients. But publishers' growing dependence on advertising revenue raised problems more complex than fraud; it posed a serious threat to the emergent ideal of objective journalism. With the decline of the openly partisan press of the late nineteenth century, reporters and editors who aimed for professional stature embraced the standard of objectivity as an updated version of plain speech and linguistic transparency. Yet the publishers' need to placate powerful advertisers threatened to transform objective journalism into a veil for the protection of established interests. Muckraking "media critics" sensed the danger by the early twentieth century. *Collier's* dramatized it in a 1911 cartoon that showed brutish "industrial interests" holding the club of advertising over a cowering editor at a rolltop desk, while a tiny female statue of "Truth" looked on from the desk top (figure 7.1).[11]

The muckrakers' critique tended to take the part for the whole, focusing on specific instances of corrupt influence, overlooking the broader, systemic formation of a hegemonic culture. The easiest target was the "red

The Presence in the Sanctum

FIGURE 7.1

Boardman Robinson, cartoon, "The Presence in the Sanctum," *Collier's* magazine, 27 May 1911.

clause" in patent medicine advertising contracts, which informed publishers that the contract would be void "if any law is enacted by your State restricting or prohibiting the manufacture or sale of proprietary medicines." After the federal Pure Food and Drug Act had rendered this kind of intimidation less effective, other more covert practices remained. The muckraking journalist Will Irwin, whose article accompanied the *Collier's* cartoon, for example, mentioned in a follow-up piece the Boston newspapers' refusal to report that Red Fox Ale and Harvard Beer, both heavily advertised, had been judged adulterated and their manufacturers indicted. Like other muckrakers, Irwin concentrated on local events and personal relationships, highlighting advertisers' determination to buy space only from "our kind of people"—that is, from publishers who were responsive to the "tacit offer of friendship" embodied in an advertisement. True to the plain-speech tradition, muckraking critics sought to yank aside the cloak of deceit and expose corrupt influence. Like other Anglo-American reformers before and since, they were animated by the plain-speaker's faith that all would be well if communication could be rendered transparent.[12]

The problem with this approach was that its literal-minded definition of influence led critics to search for a smoking gun, while they overlooked subtler hegemonic structures that were beginning to take shape. Without specific evidence of a publisher yielding to an advertiser's pressure, it was easy to assume that objectivity reigned. Meanwhile, the broader pattern of publishers' dependence on advertising revenues continued to spread, encouraging inoffensive blandness and a general climate of support for the advertisers' worldview. The rise of corporate cultural hegemony was not summarized in specific changes of position on specific issues; it involved a more diffuse process, as editors and publishers came to assume that certain points of view, certain areas of discussion, were simply unfit for inclusion within the boundaries of permissible debate.[13]

The muckrakers' critique of advertising slid into a typical pattern of regulatory reform. They focused on flagrant abuses by marginal operators—rubber stock schemes, phony correspondence courses, patent medicine panaceas—while they dismissed national advertisers with a tolerant smile. National advertisers, Samuel Hopkins Adams believed, were guilty only of pardonable exaggeration, which was an endearing national trait. "We are enthusiasts, 'boomers' by nature and by the impulsion of our overstrained nerve centers. We speak and think in capital letters, and subconsciously we allow for that not unamiable trait in our estimation of our fellows." Adams's resort to *we* revealed his own ambiguous position; like other crusading journalists, he was writing for a publication (in this case *Collier's*) whose bills were increasingly paid by national advertising. By the 1910s, ten-cent magazines and penny newspapers began to acknowledge openly that they owed their existence to the largesse of advertisers.[14]

The interests of journalism and advertising converged in the emerging idiom of "publicity." Under the umbrella of publicity, advertisers, journalists, and the proliferating hybrids who called themselves "public relations experts" could all claim that they were engaged in informing the public, educating the mass of people to higher and better things. As recently as the 1890s, the advertising trade press had straightforwardly advised advertisers: "Don't attempt to make the public believe you are in business for anything other than profit—legitimate profit." But the attempt to distance themselves from Barnumesque entrepreneurship led many advertising people to define their public role in more exalted ways. "There is a wide difference between publicity and notoriety," *Art in Advertising* magazine warned in 1893, making a distinction that might have baffled Barnum. By 1915, Earnest Elmo Calkins had caught the full significance of the new idiom. Advertising, he wrote,

> deals with a powerful force called "public opinion." This force it creates, controls, and focuses on certain desired ends. These ends are frequently idealistic, requiring a far-reaching vision to grasp and faith to attain. The effect of such endeavors is beneficial to all—to the public, to the advertiser, to his employee, to the shopkeepers who distribute his goods, and to the conduct of all business.[15]

The ideal of public opinion was rooted in managerial professionals' need to locate a transcendent source of meaning, a secure basis for values in a society whose religious and moral foundations were increasingly problematic.

But it was also a strategic breakthrough for advertising spokesmen. The creation of public opinion as a central category of common discourse allowed them to dissolve discussion of profits in a universalist rhetoric of progressive reform. Faced with reformers' critiques, advertisers declared themselves reformed, deflecting assaults onto the patent medicine era of the recent past. Consumers Leagues and other organized expressions of disbelief in advertising were simply the sign that "we are paying in Biblical measure for 'the sins of the fathers,' " Harry Tipper, advertising manager of The Texas Company, told the League of Advertising Women in 1915.[16]

By then, professional advertising people had already begun a successful counterattack against the early stirrings of a reformist consumer movement. They established the Associated Advertising Clubs of America and at their first meeting in 1911 they launched the truth-in-advertising movement. Their immediate aim was to promote the passage by state legislatures of the *Printers' Ink* model statute. Under the proposed law, the advertiser responsible for "any assertion, representation, or statement of fact which is untrue, deceptive, or misleading shall be guilty of a misdemeanor." Prosecutions focused on loan sharks, real-estate speculators, and mail-order frauds—confidence men on the margins of business respectability. Corporate offenders went virtually unscathed. Spokesmen for the movement preached a program of efficiency and public service. They attacked the "waste" and "unfair competition" promoted by deceptive advertisers; they sought to separate professional advertising from sordid salesmanship. As Joseph Appel, advertising manager for Wanamaker's department store in Philadelphia, told the 1911 convention: "*Advertising is not to sell, but to help people to buy.* . . . We stand in the shoes of the customer. We are *outside,* not behind the counter. We are counselors for the public." Like other aspiring professionals, spokesmen for truth-in-advertising aimed to reassure themselves as much as their audience, declaring their disinterested involvement in the new public space defined by the corporations.[17]

The truth-in-advertising movement offered national advertisers a chance to reaffirm their ethnic solidarity as well as their commitment to ideals of public opinion. Movement leaders rearticulated the widespread association between Protestant plain speech and professional probity. Many of the men identified as offenders by state vigilance committees had Jewish surnames, and anti-Semitic stereotypes sometimes surfaced at committee meetings. In 1916 one New York organizer explained his group's approach to the false advertiser: "We appeal to his selfishness if not his morals—you can't get by with that on the average 'kike'—you can't do it." Patterns of prosecution comported well with the durable belief that Anglo-Saxons had a unique claim on sincerity and plain speech (see chapter 2). Ethnocentrism reinforced professionalism.[18]

But the ethnocentric cast of mind was concealed by the universalist rhetoric of modernity. Mail-order catalogs helped rural folk submerge local and regional idiosyncrasies in standardized commercial style; national advertisements showed recent immigrants how to assimilate to "American" ways, as defined by corporate sponsors. The growing uniformity of taste was simply evidence of progress, from the vantage point of advertisers and other professionals.[19]

Advertisers' faith in their own progressive influence led to extravagant claims. Some spokesmen for the industry, assuming that advertising was the solution to the problem of distribution, moved from that assumption to equate advertising with civilization itself. Advertising was realizing the socialist millennium by eliminating the middleman, James Collins asserted in *Printers' Ink* in 1902; a "space annihilator" like the trolley, the train, and the telephone, national advertising removed consumers' personality from the mere business of survival, freeing them for higher things as it filled a larger and larger role in distribution. Four years later another trade press contributor played a variation on this theme. According to George Sherman, "socialists and single-taxers" had demonstrated the possibility of completing all necessary labor in four hours a day, but to concentrate on essential tasks alone would produce "a world of nothing but actual necessities—unadorned, matter-of-necessity dwellings, built like grain elevators; colorless furniture and a uniform style of apparel; one grade and one style in each article of manufacture; no advertising and no competition. In all righteousness we should be a race of deaf, dumb, and blind."

By widening the sphere of necessity to include ever-higher levels of consumption, national advertising kept the population hard at work, improving themselves and their surroundings. This was one of the beneficial "By-Products of Advertising" enumerated by the copywriter Waldo Warren in Collier's in 1909: the cultivation of a competitive spirit in the American population "through constant repetition of the idea that this is an age of enterprise, and that one must be enterprising even to hold one's own." For Warren and other promoters of national advertising, Patten's formulation seemed to fit the facts: far from undermining commitments to labor discipline, advertising reinforced them.[20]

Advertisers' claim to be key agents of progress was part of a broader reworking of postmillennial thought. For many progressive reformers, the exercise provided them with moral legitimacy in a culture still largely wedded to Protestant habits of mind; for advertisers it served the added purpose of distancing them further from their disreputable origins. "One of the very definite phases of our work is to be educators," the J. Walter Thompson Newsletter announced in 1916, with a solemnity that might have provoked gales of laughter in an earlier generation of admakers.[21] Far from contributing to the centrifugal confusions of the marketplace, as their entrepreneurial predecessors had done, spokesmen for corporate advertising claimed to be stabilizing a steady movement toward a secular millennium.

The intellectual assumptions behind this sort of hubris pervaded managerial–professional groups during the early twentieth century. Like other aspiring professionals of the era, advertising executives participated in the regnant fantasy that "we" (the managerial elite in question) had acquired the capacity to predict and control "them" (the consumers) through "social science." The epistemological basis for this worldview was a positivistic dualism. Social scientists' claims that they were actually scientists depended on their maintaining a clear disjunction between observer and observed—an assumption that the observer could analyze the object of study without his or her own attitudes and prejudices intruding.[22]

Though they carried this positivist and dualist baggage from the nineteenth century, many American social scientists also participated in a wide-ranging "revolt against formalism" that discarded certain positivistic and dualistic modes of thought.[23] Social scientists' (and advertisers') notions of mind–body relations, and of individual selfhood generally, were becoming more fluid, spilling over the boundaries of traditional Cartesian categories. Along with many other middle- and upper-class Americans during the first decade of the twentieth century, advertisers and social scientists alike began to employ the catchwords of "the new psychology" (see chapter 6). This involved a general tendency to view the mind as an instrument engaged in helping human beings adapt to their environment, rather than as a static collection of faculties. The new psychology encouraged a more flexible and pragmatic outlook on everything from sexual conduct to government policy; it promised liberation from rigid categories and endless dualisms. Yet its Darwinian emphasis on adaptation carried conformist implications. For the pragmatist psychologist John Dewey, adaptation meant creative innovation in problem-solving rather than acceptance of the status quo. But popularizers of the new psychology, in publications like *Good Housekeeping* and *The American Magazine,* distorted Dewey's definition beyond recognition. They naturalized existing social structures and processes, promoting normative psychologies that preached the virtues of "adjustment."[24]

The new psychology's link between psyche and society led to a social scientific critique of classical economics, a critique that merged in some forms with the managerial worldview. In *Social Process* (1902), the sociologist Charles Horton Cooley charged that the "economic man" model "is false even as economics, and we shall never have an efficient system until we have one that appeals to the imagination, the loyalty, and the self-expression of the men who serve it." (The word *system* no longer referred to static classification schemes but to a fluid "social process" that at peak efficiency remained in dynamic equilibrium.) The new conditions of interdependence—always a talismanic word for professionals—led to a symbiotic emotional relationship between society and the individual.[25] Reform-minded social scientists believed that relationship could be used to promote valuable social goals, through the practice of democratic social engineering (see chapter 6). As Cooley implied, the leaders could play on "the imagination, the loyalty, and the self-expression" of the group in working toward the goal of consensus. Neither Cooley nor Dewey imagined this method to be a tool for maintaining existing hierarchies, but that is what it became. By the 1920s, managerial thinkers like Walter Lippmann were increasingly recommending the group-process method as a sleight of hand to solve labor disputes and other forms of social conflict.[26]

Advertising spokesmen never (to my knowledge) used the term "democratic social engineering," but they embraced a parallel agenda, with similar sources in the new psychology. In 1903, Walter Dill Scott, a professor of advertising at the Northwestern University School of Business, began publishing the articles that became his influential book *The Psychology of Advertising* (1908). Dozens of similar works appeared during the first two decades of the twentieth century. Nearly all contained lists of "instincts" ("the home instinct," "the herd instinct") and depended on an associationist notion of causality that was compatible either with behaviorism (as John B. Watson, the "father" of that wretched child, later demonstrated during his career at J. Walter Thompson), or, more commonly, with "suggestion psychology."[27]

The popularity of suggestion psychology revealed the continuities between national advertisers and nineteenth-century peddlers, mesmerists, and other practitioners of "influence." In 1892, a contributor to the trade journal *Fame* compared advertising to hypnotism, observing that "the public is obeying a 'suggestion,' not acting upon reason." As late as 1905, one of the early agency heads, Joel Benton, was still suggesting that the advertising writer had to cultivate an occult capacity for mind reading: "He must know how to fathom human traits and premises of thought." But by that time the popularization of psychoanalysis was beginning to provide suggestion psychology with a new vocabulary. John Lee Mahin, an agency head from Chicago, summarized much of the conventional wisdom in 1910 when he wrote that the "consumer nearly always purchases in unconscious obedience to what he or she believes to be the dictates of an authority which is anxiously consulted and respected." The growing preoccupation with plumbing the unconscious mind and the determination to *be* that "anxiously consulted and respected" authority gradually but profoundly influenced advertisers' vision of their audience before World War I.[28]

The growing sense of distance between advertisers and their audience resulted from gender as well as class distinctions. Like their "influential" predecessors, admakers often assumed that their primary audience was female. "From the philosopher's standpoint," James Collins wrote in 1901, "woman is an incidental helpmeet to man; from the standpoint of the wise advertiser she is queen of the nether world, mistress of the privy purse, keeper of the rolls, the hounds, and the exchequer." By the early twentieth century, the notion that 85 percent of consumer purchases are made by women was embedded in the conventional wisdom (though no one ever seemed able to cite a source for that figure), as was the tacit assumption that women's minds were vats of frothy pink irrationality.[29]

This condescension toward women was the dominant attitude among female as well as male apologists for the industry. Only a few women rose to prominence in national advertising, despite frequent observations in the trade press about how well suited they were for the work. Perhaps the best known in the early years was Jane J. Martin, advertising manager for Sperry & Hutchinson (the purveyors of Green Stamps). Martin came from the same sort of New York society that produced Edith Wharton; like most privileged men, she believed that her achievements were the reward solely for her personal merits. In an interview with the *New York Tribune* in 1915, Martin announced that "only the exceptional woman is big-minded and of moment"; most women, she said, would never succeed in business because "they don't know how and they won't learn how to really work." Women who rose to positions like Martin's could become as pontifical as any male business ideologue.[30]

Still, in general, advertisers' sense of superiority to their audience cut across lines of gender solidarity, stigmatizing men as well as women. "Few men wish to know from a pure love of knowledge—that implies too much time, too much trouble for the average mind," *Fame* editorialized in 1892. "The many are content to wonder." By 1911 a *Printers' Ink* contributor was evoking Eliotic visions of mass society as he listed "some reasons why 'reason why' copy often fails." Convincing arguments don't always convince because "the average mind either cannot or will not follow [the advertiser's] arguments to their logical conclusion." Let the reason-whyer study the census reports and see how many people work at jobs a monkey could do; let him stand on a street corner before dawn any morning—he'll see plenty of people who won't respond to reason-why!

Without actually using the language of mass-society theory, advertising people were beginning to construct the consumer as a member of a mass society.[31]

THE INCORPORATION OF THE BARNUMESQUE: TOWARD AN IDEOLOGY OF MASS SOCIETY

The audience was constantly being invented and reinvented in the pages of the trade press, but by the early twentieth century a subtle shift was under way. In 1895, Charles Austin Bates had warned potential admakers: "It is not well to expend too much effort or space in 'catching' the eye. The magazine reader is a leisurely person. He gets into a comfortable chair with his feet up and a cigar in his mouth after dinner. . . . No need to yell at him with black type." By 1910, James Collins was formulating a differ-ent image of the potential consumer. Collins told the story of "a retail hardware dealer in a certain Eastern city" who had some hunter's axes that he couldn't move, so he put them in his front window:

> While he was at lunch, those baby axes were all sold, being carried away by the noonday crowd in the business district. Men stopped to look at a miscellaneous display of tools, most of which were strange to an office population. But they understood the hunters' axes at once. They were bright, touched with red paint, and sharp. They made office men feel as though they wanted to chop something, and they bought them.

This movement away from the leisurely magazine reader and toward the frenetic "noonday crowd" was a significant one.[32]

After 1900, advertisers became more concerned with reaching milling mobs on the run. In *Printers' Ink* and similar journals, this preoccupation led to articles with titles like "Interesting the Slapdash Hasty Newspaper Reader." It implied a nascent perception of a mass society enmeshed in hurried routine and eager for novelty. Trade press writers placed products in the emerging rhythm of life, arguing that advertisers should combine the constant repetition of trademarks with a variety of changing imagery. The assumption that the routinization of everyday life required frequent doses of novelty began to shape discussions of product design; a few ven-turesome advertisers developed a rationale for planned obsolescence dur-ing the early twentieth century. Despite skepticism among the old guard, *Printers' Ink* asserted in 1911, the strategy of launching a "new model" worked as "advertising bait"—not only in clothes but in typewriters, automobiles, and other apparently prosaic items where the actual changes might be small (a new coat of paint, a slightly different tilt of the front seat) but the appeal to the consumer was great. The magnetic power of novelty was rooted in the consumer's anxiety and boredom, and the attraction to it was underwritten by the spread of installment plans. With planned obsolescence and installment buying, two cornerstones of consumer culture were beginning to fall into place.[33]

The most subtle change in advertisers' outlook involved their views of consumer sensibility: the "office men" who "wanted to chop something" seemed animated by a level of frustration and longing that was absent from earlier depictions of the advertising audience. The bright red axes were toys for grown-up, desk-bound boys. How pervasive their frustration and longing actually were is impossible to determine. What matters is that advertisers increasingly believed in the existence of a childlike mass audience, and treated it as an opportunity for creative salesmanship. "We could all, with profit, turn our thoughts oftener to more childish things, for the building block age is the time when mental images have full sway, and we see how largely the impulses they arouse govern one's actions," a trade press writer observed in 1910, asserting the importance of "mental images as sales factors."[34]

To be sure, the creation of mental images could be grounded in hard facts. After the turn of the century the most venturesome agencies followed N. W. Ayer's lead in developing the practice of market research. To know consumers, one had to do more than speculate about their psyches or observe them in hardware stores: one had to count them, categorize them by income, neighborhood, ethnicity, and religion, correlate these data with their brand preferences, and test their reactions to specific ads. This last was first done systematically by the J. Walter Thompson Company in 1903. The bureau of design in their Chicago office solicited reader reactions to full-page advertisements that had been inserted in twenty-five national magazines: they received over 30,000 responses, discovering that "the [middle- and upper-class WASP] public" did not like ads without illustrations, or for beer. This survey suggested that market research involved not only the measurement of objectifiable data such as income and place of residence, but also the slippery task of investigating cultural and psychological attitudes.[35]

And that returned the advertiser to the problem of plumbing the consumer mind. All the statistical surveys and claims of professionalism could not, in the end, get advertising past the old confidence game of guessing what would resonate with the wants of the consumer. The more childlike or irrational the consumer's image became, the more justifiable seemed the resort to carnivalesque sensationalism or emotional appeals.

Despite their drive toward professionalism, advertising executives could never cast aside their Barnumesque inheritance, could never make common cause with the clinicians of society whose ideology they emulated. Part of the problem was the limited nature of their authority: unlike doctors and lawyers, they claimed professional expertise but always bowed to the opinions of the client, however inexpert he might be. Yet a deeper difficulty was embedded in the very nature of the advertising business: it had always involved the clever orchestration of surface effects, in a fashion that undermined all pretensions to sincerity and claims to objective truth. Straining to stabilize meanings with resort to a managerial idiom of expertise, advertisers remained surrounded by the ambiguities of their trade.

Advertising executives and copywriters were confronted with a fundamental conflict. The professional–managerial worldview put a scientific gloss on Protestant plain speech: in epistemological matters it created a vast apparatus for disproving and verifying universalist truth-claims; on ethical questions it encouraged the welding of private and public personas into a single systematic life. Yet the admakers themselves came out of a carnivalesque tradition that subverted unified meaning and promoted the pursuit of success through persuasion, theatricality, and outright trickery.

The persistence of that tradition put the devotee of facts at a disadvantage—especially as the standardization of technological advances made product differentiation more difficult. Automobile advertising was a case in point. The advertising manager of the Winton Motor Car Company stated in 1909:

> When a man buys an automobile he purchases a specific entity, made of so much iron, steel, brass, copper, leather, wood, and horsehair, put together in a specific form and manner—an entity possible of producing certain results. Why attract his attention to the entity by something foreign thereto? Has the car itself not sufficient merit to attain that attention? Why suggest "atmosphere," which is something he cannot buy?

But this plainspoken view was soon passé, except among the manufacturers themselves. Among advertising people, the Chalmers and Pierce-Arrow automobile companies were soon being celebrated for "word painting the auto's seductive joys" and soft-pedaling any emphasis on "mechanical excellence" (as in figure 7.2). The triumph of "atmosphere" in automobile

FIGURE 7.2

Franklin Automobile Company advertisement, 1913. *Ayer Collection.*

advertising involved the incorporation of fantasy into the emerging distribution system (figure 7.3).[36]

Yet few spokesmen for professional advertising would admit the carnivalesque connection. Seeking to deny their origins, most protested too much. On the hundredth anniversary of Barnum's birth, in 1910, *Printers' Ink* disavowed the prophet. To celebrate his "advertising ability," the magazine charged, would be like doctors celebrating a quack as their godfather. Barnum "played upon a streak of American character which is rapidly

FIGURE 7.3

Jordan Automobile Company advertisement, 1920. *Ayer Collection.*

declining—the streak of bizarre appetite for the abnormal, the admiration for trickery and the fascination of the horrible." Relegating that cultural style to the benighted backward past and the backwaters of the present, the editors were willing to acknowledge that Barnum had progressed in ethics and taste: he had become the serious impresario who, in bringing the Swedish soprano Jenny Lind before the American public, "began to exhibit and advertise something substantial and real, rather than what was little short of fraud." Reality remained a rhetorical benchmark against which advertisers could measure their achievements.[37]

In the producerist atmosphere of early-twentieth-century American business culture, the results were not always reassuring. "A very well-known manufacturer said recently, after a trying session with his advertising agents," *Printers' Ink* reported in 1908, " 'Good Lord, let me get back to the factory where I can touch and handle things and see them in front of me with my eyes! Every time I get mixed up with my advertising problems I feel the ground sink away from me, and I am floated away into the imponderable ether, where I can't clutch at even a straw for support!' " On the one hand, this outburst expressed the discomfort of the producer in the presence of the middleman who manipulated floating signifiers for financial gain; on the other, it dramatized the unease of the materialist amid the dematerialized desire that animated consumer culture. The manufacturer correctly sensed that advertising was not about the things themselves, but about the representation of wishes for things.[38]

The strain of trying to establish their own solidity sometimes drove even the editors of *Printers' Ink* into a tone of pleading defensiveness. "Doubtless the advertising business would be better off if all of us—publishers, agents, and advertisers—would take advertising a little more seriously," they wrote in 1915. "Each of us has something to sell, and just because it is invisible and intangible is no reason why it is not real." That was the nub of the problem: the realization that advertising, like other service sector jobs, dealt in airy nothings by comparison to farming or manufacturing.[39]

An ephemeral quality had long characterized salesmanship, at least since the days of itinerant peddlers. The process of persuasion was as important as the product in question—sometimes more so. Advertising writers acknowledged this in attempting to define the elusive nature of their craft. In 1912, one contributor to the magazine *Judicious Advertising* described advertising as "the spark to the selling engine," through which "it is possible to create mental attitudes toward anything and invest it with a value over and above its intrinsic worth." The notion of a thing's "intrinsic worth" was rooted in producerist definitions of the real; advertising copywriters (like peddlers and other salesmen before them) refashioned commercial reality by recognizing the open-ended role of imagination in manipulating appearances, winning confidence, and creating value.[40]

An acknowledgment of the imagination sometimes led to surprising admissions. Joel Benton, writing in 1902, observed that adept practitioners of "the persuasive art" could make people believe preposterous propositions, as street-corner fakirs did: "If an advertiser would only steal the fakir's warmth and seductive accent, his present old dead advertisements might possibly attain a new life." The search for "new life" in advertisements could lead advertisers to look backward rather than forward, toward antecedents like the street-corner fakir. Too much professionalism led to standardization and boredom. "Magazines and newspapers are filled with ads which show plainly on their face that they are the product of the 'layout' man, of the typographic artist, and of the advertising 'expert.' We seem to hear the creaking of the machine and hear the wheels go round," *Printers' Ink* complained in 1908. Fear that professionalism might extinguish "the spark to the selling engine" led many in the advertising business to resist rationalization and insist on the importance of "being human in writing advertising," as the self-help ideologue Elbert Hubbard put it in 1910. Despite the efforts of agency executives to turn their organizations into smoothly functioning arms of business productivity, everyday life inside the agency remained chaotic and unpredictable, "colored by the fury of creation," as Helen Woodward recalled. Advice to copywriters constantly emphasized the importance of creativity as an antidote to smooth professionalism and an alternative to bureaucratic notions of expertise.[41]

But what was creativity? Partly it was a euphemism for ethical flexibility in dealing with clients. The furious competition for accounts made the advertising world a Hobbesian jungle as early as the 1890s: "There is altogether too much copying of ideas," a writer in the trade journal *Fame* complained in 1894, "as though the world of thought were fast becoming a howling wilderness." The trade press early on realized the importance of flattery and complaisance—the seductive arts of "influence"—in selling to clients as well as to consumers. "There is a method of ordering twenty-five-cent cigars, as if in honor of your guest, without making him feel outclassed because he doesn't always smoke them," an advertising solicitor confessed in 1896. "There is a time to order just one more bottle of wine than is necessary, just to show that it flows freely. There is an art in making a man feel satisfied with himself, and convincing him that he is greater than he knew." Yet in talking to clients, admen could at least point to the bottom line as a quantitative index of success; in talking to consumers, their authority was even more precariously based—not on precise knowledge but on the mere appearance of it.[42]

So the preparation of copy inspired the most fulsome paeans to creativity. Throughout most of the early twentieth century, despite the growing emphasis on "eye appeal," admakers' main concern was with literary rather than visual artistry. When an anonymous contributor to *Profitable Advertising* magazine in 1893 defined an advertising expert as "one who knows the value of words," he spoke more prophetically than he knew: despite the effort to embrace an objectivist cognitive style, "mere word-slingers" remained essential to the success of every advertising agency. The copywriter was compared variously with the actor, the stage director, the filmmaker. The point in every case was that he or she was using words and images to entice the audience into the agreeable scenes being created.[43]

If the idea of the admaker as dramatic artist was hardly congenial to managerial ideology, neither were the terms sometimes used to characterize the creative processes of the successful copywriter. For some it was akin to romantic frenzy: "To create good selling copy advertisement writers must be bubbling over with enthusiasm," a *Judicious Advertising* contributor insisted in 1912. "A day's work with the glow of magic fire is worth a week of galley slave plugging. Real copy 'artists' are self-hypnotists." This trancelike state comported ill with managerial conceptions of the advertising business, and with objectivist truth-claims generally. Despite the myriad invocations of "sincerity" as the sine qua non of all effective advertising, admakers continued to realize that the crucial task was "the *creation of a feeling of confidence on the part of the purchasing public.*" And public credulity gave them a wonderful opportunity. "This is an age of faith," the *J. Walter Thompson Blue Book* announced in 1906. "All ages have been ages of faith. . . . Disbelief requires an effort of the will, while belief requires only acquiescence. *Advertising turns human faith into an asset.*" Given "an age of faith," and a lot of money to be made from acquiescent belief, the temptation to lie was overwhelming. It provoked advertising executives to muddled but revealing rumination.[44]

The JWT executive Cyrus Eaton's *Sermons on Advertising* (1908) was exemplary—the title evoked the persistence of the missionary mode, albeit perhaps ironically.

> A lie is an abomination to the Lord and a very present help in time of trouble. A lie well told is believed almost as readily as a truth. The teller must believe in himself; that is, in his ability to lie successfully. His animation and enthusiasm and self-confidence must be the genuine article. A strong personality can add a heavenly halo to a very ordinary hobo lie.
>
> The average advertiser doesn't mean to lie; that is in a deliberate

sense; but he is knowingly reckless in the use of truth which amounts to the same thing.

All conventional life is more or less sham; as spotted with hypocrisy as a child with measles. Everyday speech is saturated with exaggeration. The honest advertiser must square himself with conditions. If he uses the plain blunt kind of truth that-mother-used-to-make he fails to draw the trade. . . .

But apart from the question of ethics does it pay to lie?

I say no; positively no. Truth can be made far more entertaining than falsehood. But the advertising must be intelligible to the people; written in terms which they can understand.[45]

The statement was a farrago of self-revelation. Eaton's description of the convincing liar might easily have applied to the advertising copywriter: someone who was tremendously enthusiastic and eager to persuade, but to no particular purpose and on behalf of no particular product. The process was all; sincerity itself could become a performance. (As a *Harper's* commentator on advertising put in 1917: "Sincerity is nearly always taken at its *face value.*")[46] The rest of Eaton's "sermon" was equally revelatory. After noting the hypocrisies of "conventional life" and the exaggerations of everyday speech, Eaton asserted that the advertiser had to adjust to these "conditions" or else fail to "draw the trade." He turned quickly to a hollow and unconvincing defense of truth as "more entertaining than falsehood," concluding with a reminder that advertising had to be tailored to suit "the people"—whom he had already described as hypocritical and prone to exaggeration.

Eaton revealed the conflict at the heart of the advertising business, between the objectivist pretensions of managerial professionalism and the epistemological subversions of the carnivalesque; but he also pointed to a way out. By reaffirming their sense of superiority to their audience, disparaging popular mentalities, and developing a rhetoric of "mass man," advertising spokesmen could relax the tension between managerial and carnivalesque discourses: rationality for the few, irrationality for the many. World War I and its aftermath provided new opportunities for this ideological project.

WORLD WAR I AND AFTER: CHEERLEADERS FOR THE NATION

In wartime, when the state's demands for conformity were at their height, managerial elites cooperated among themselves most effectively. A controversial war, fought far from home, required unifying emblems to mobilize a disparate and contentious population. Providing those emblems, mobilizing that population, national advertisers acquired unprecedented legitimacy. Even Barnum could have a place as the chief morale booster of Bellamy's "industrial army." The coming of World War I gave agency people a superb chance to demonstrate their respectability and reaffirm their ties to other aspiring professionals. Admen played a major role in George Creel's Committee on Public Information; the Anglo-Saxon Protestant composition of the national advertising industry made it a fertile breeding ground for interventionist and prowar sentiment.[47]

The war marked the high tide of progressive faith in the beneficent powers of "publicity." In November 1917, a *New Republic* contributor urged advertisers to strive for standards higher than the puerility embodied in their recent war advertising. "Such sailors as appeared were the same blond youths who had demonstrated the neat fit of Arrow brand collars in the street cars." War advertisements should imaginatively touch the public soul, as a number of artists had done with their Liberty Loan posters: "A nation is forced to advertise its needs in order to win recruits, just as a manufacturer is forced to advertise his promises in order to gain purchasers." On this point, advertisers and the *New Republic* were in full agreement.[48]

During World War I, spokesmen for national advertising began to formulate what has since become a reflexive analysis of government policy: they began to trace political success or failure to the success or failure of particular marketing strategies. To be sure, political candidates had been advertising since at least the 1890s, and political parties had been hiring advertising agencies since Theodore Roosevelt's administration. But the world war was the first time that government policy itself had been systematically promoted through commercial techniques of mass persuasion.[49]

For some advertising people, the government's chief problem was that its marketing strategies were too limited and inflexible to counter German propaganda. In the summer of 1917, according to a senior staff member at J. Walter Thompson, men drove about "one of the Virginia cities, not over one hundred miles from Washington, telling the farmers' wives not to can their fruit as the government intended to confiscate it"; the government was helpless to respond to this "species of German propaganda," while any commercial firm would have simply advertised the truth in a local newspaper.[50]

But as the war dragged on and national advertisers became more directly involved in the government publicity effort, their evaluations became more sanguine—and self-serving. "The war has been won by advertising, as well as by soldiers and munitions," *Printers' Ink* announced three days after the Armistice. "It has been a four years strife between the powers of repression and concealment and the powers of expression and enlightenment." Organized publicity was crucial to Americans' most astonishing achievement: the "voluntary personal mobilization" of over 100 million people. The Versailles treaty, on the other hand, was "the world's greatest advertising failure," according to the advertising manager for Wells, Fargo & Co. Express, Edward Hungerford, in *Advertising and Selling* magazine. President Woodrow Wilson should have replaced George Creel with a top-notch advertising solicitor. Creel had no tact; he herded journalists onto the second-class *Orizaba* while he and the president traveled first class on the *George Washington;* nor did he look after the members of the press after they arrived in Paris. The press should have been wined, dined, and set up in a sort of gentlemen's club; but opportunities, and the treaty, were lost. Or so it seemed from the professional advertisers' viewpoint.[51]

The war did more for national advertisers than popularize the value of media management; it also integrated the culture of corporate advertising into the sorting and categorizing institutions that were being developed by other managerial elites. Chief among these were the Army intelligence tests, which accelerated the displacement of vernacular, local knowledge by spuriously universal, professional knowledge. An awareness of corporate advertising slogans was officially included as part of the norm of "intelligence." Fully 10 percent of the questions on the Alpha Test (the one designed for those literate in English) depended on information gleaned from national advertisements. Recruits and draftees were required to puzzle out problems like these:

Revolvers are made by
   Swift & Co.   Smith & Wesson   W. L. Douglas   B. T. Babbitt

"There's a reason" is an "ad" for a
   drink   revolver   flour   cleanser

The Pierce-Arrow car is made in
   Buffalo   Detroit   Toledo   Flint[52]

Rarely has the category of "knowledge" been so obviously constructed by particular social groups with particular ideological agendas. The Army intelligence tests revealed the merger of corporate advertising with social science, in the continuation of the project begun by Theodore Roosevelt and his Progressive allies at the turn of the century: the revitalization of elite Anglo-Saxon authority through the assimilation of new cultural idioms and modes of thought.[53]

The key idiom promoted by the war was summarized in a newly fashionable word, *system.* In the war atmosphere its social connotation was disciplined, coordinated effort by the entire nation. In March 1918, Guy Emerson, a vice president of the National Bank of Commerce in New York, professed to be inspired by "the spectacle of a great nation acquiescing in a law which ran contrary to the established traditions of the nation"—the military draft. "Without publicity this would have been inconceivable." We had only to look at "the lack of coordination of thought and effort in Russia" to realize the enormity of the alternative, Emerson wrote. The success of advertising in mobilizing prowar sentiment "has proved that the American people is sound at the core, is more truly a unit than we would have dared believe could be moulded from the heterogenous jumble of races that makes up the nation. Through nation-wide publicity, the American people has discovered itself."[54] A crucial dimension of the national awakening was the appearance of consent, the creation of consensus. Advertising the war effort was an exercise in democratic social engineering, not Prussian regimentation. To be sure, there was plenty of regimentation involved in the firing of pacifist college professors or the intimidation of "slackers" who had failed to buy war bonds. But despite advertising's inclusion in the rigidly hierarchical procedures of intelligence testing, in general it represented the "soft" side of ideological mobilization—not the imposition of Kultur but the promotion of morale.

During and after the war, the notion of morale acquired unprecedented power in the work of the psychologist G. Stanley Hall and other reform-minded therapeutic professionals. If morality involved obeying precepts outside the self, morale meant unlocking the self's inner resources in a noble cause. For ministers like Harry Emerson Fosdick, the Christian's morale depended on his ability to harmonize his ideals with his "necessities of action"; rather than harness his noblest powers to the thrill of combat alone, he should attach them to higher purposes: "spirit of adventure, loyalty, self-sacrifice, scorn of danger." However vague those values sound, they represented a serious effort by Fosdick to promote individual moral integrity in the face of overwhelming pressure for social conformity.[55]

But from the social scientist's view, morale merged the psychic health of the individual with the social vitality of the nation. For G. Stanley Hall, Annie Payson Call, Luther Gulick, and other advocates of this doctrine, morale was a corporatist version of influence in the guise of democratic social engineering—a model for social control through the simulation of self-actualization. It depended on the idea that through some alchemy of desire, each individual could most efficiently serve the public needs of a reified society by pursuing her or his private emotional fulfillment. This was a psychological version of Bernard Mandeville or Adam Smith, and indeed, advocates of morale, like other democratic social engineers, sometimes presented their arguments as correctives to classical economics. People yearned to serve some higher goal for the sheer emotional thrill of it; the state needed willing soldiers and loyal civilians. What better solution than to marry desire and duty in obedience to what Gulick called "the corporate conscience that is rendered necessary by the complex interdependence of modern life"? An aggregate of fluid, manipulable selves constituted a fluid, manipulable society. Rooted in progressive faith in the power of public opinion, the doctrine of morale was one of the early American efforts to formulate a method for making the masses want to do what they had to do.[56]

Advertising's version of morale took a variety of forms. Sometimes it was merely patriotic sentiment and the simulation of sacrifice. In the July 1918 issue of *Cosmopolitan,* an ad showed a hand holding a glass of Coke, casting a shadow in the shape of the Statue of Liberty's torch, with the caption: "Your glass of Coca-Cola represents materials allotted by Mr. Hoover and your Government after conservation has taken its heavy toll. The Coca-Cola Company accepts its war duty as a privilege and, although reduced in output, is endeavouring to maintain its usefulness as industry." But sometimes the agenda was more ambitious. By arrogating the authority of educators, admakers could claim to be among the keepers of that "corporate conscience" identified by Gulick. By "speaking humanly" to the multitudes, advertisers could truly become "the cheerleaders of the nation," as the president of Eastman Kodak claimed they had become in 1918.[57]

The advertiser as cheerleader, rousing inert masses into disciplined enthusiasm for the exploits of the demigods on the field: it was a striking illustration of the way advertisers were beginning to integrate the emerging discourse of celebrity into their constructions. "Great Actors, as Other Great Men, Are More Alive Than the Herd," *Vogue* announced in 1917;

the great actor communicated "unconsciously a sense of life to many other people who seemed dead before he walked among them." Redemptive celebrity figures became standard features in the testimonial advertising that blossomed after the war. No longer a recital of the travails of the suffering, the testimonial became a celebration of the larger-than-life vitality of the singers, actors, and society matrons who smoked Lucky Strikes, washed with Lux Soap, and took Fleischmann's Yeast Foam Tablets. The "cheerleaders of the nation" defined the new importance of spectacular celebrity as a metaphorical mode of crowd management in the emerging social system.[58]

Elite perceptions of the crowd, meanwhile, were undergoing a gradual transformation. A historiographical cliché has it that progressive faith in the common man was dashed by the failure of Wilson's crusade to make the world safe for democracy. Like most clichés, it contains a core of truth. "Publicity, the hope of the Progressive Era, became propaganda, the scourge of the twenties," the historian Richard Tedlow writes. The war had produced the disturbing spectacle of whole populations mobilized to hate an enemy they never saw. On both sides of the Atlantic, a wide variety of intellectuals, from poets (T. S. Eliot) to social engineers (Walter Lippmann), were haunted by a growing fear that the thinking individual had been subsumed in the irrational mass. The film director King Vidor dramatized that fear in The Crowd (1928), which recounted the descent of a modern Everyman from small-town dreams of independence to submersion in a sea of desks by day and gaping vaudeville crowds by night. The inanity of the rural yahoos and the suburban "booboisie" became an article of faith among cultural critics like H. L. Mencken and Sinclair Lewis. Even John Dewey worried about the susceptibility of crowds to mass persuasion. By 1929, a Nation contributor could compare the audience addressed by national advertisers to the audience addressed by the champion hogcaller in Kansas who said: "The words don't matter, friend. It's feeling that counts. The great thing is feeling. You got to put passion into it. You got to make that hog believe you got something that hog wants."[59]

The idea of the swinish multitudes drew strength from several quarters. Some were foreign: the crowds flocking around Mussolini, the working classes of Europe trooping off to slaughter in World War I. But others were closer to home. Popular journalistic accounts of the Army intelligence tests, promoting the notion that the "typical American" had a "fourteen-year-old mind," encouraged belief in the childlike credulity of the mass audience. So did the emergent "profession" of public relations.

Edward Bernays, in seeking to transform the public relations counsel from "a lineal descendant of the circus advance man" to a modern professional, emphasized the limits of human malleability, the importance of playing on existing beliefs and prejudices. Yet Bernays's sweeping claims could also contribute to the construction of a manipulable mass man. "Human nature is readily subject to modification," he wrote, asserting that "in the sphere of politics or business, in our social conduct or our ethical thinking, we are dominated by the relatively small number of persons who . . . understand the mental processes of the masses." Amid the pervasiveness of sentiments like these, liberal and Protestant ideas of independent selfhood became increasingly difficult to sustain.[60]

Advertising executives and copywriters stood in a problematic relationship to the emerging discourse of mass society. They claimed to be among "the relatively small number of persons" who understood "the mental processes of the masses," but they were not always clear about whether they were serving the sovereign consumer or channeling her desires. They wavered between a postmillennial rhetoric of uplift through professionalism and a sweeping contempt for their audience. Embracing a shifting notion of selfhood, they shackled it to a dualistic distinction between autonomous advertising subjects and manipulated consumer objects: an apparently emancipatory psychology was harnessed to hierarchical purposes. Incorporating carnivalesque tactics into a managerial mold, they recast commercial traditions to fit the developing distribution system.

The wartime prominence of national advertising had sent its spokesmen's pretensions soaring to unprecedented heights. "Before the war there was a certain demand for uplift in business," a contributor to the *New Republic* noted in 1924, "but it was not until 1917–1918 that we began to demand it as part of our daily rations." As always, the key question was, who were "we"? Advertising people themselves sometimes spurned uplift in favor of the language of neutral technique. A J. Walter Thompson new business presentation of 1925 claimed that "advertising is a non-moral force, like electricity, which not only illuminates but electrocutes. Its worth to civilization depends upon how it is used." Agency heads like Stanley Resor and Bruce Barton announced that advertising had banished the specter of overproduction and was about to solve the problem of distribution. Such achievements led beyond the technical realm; they promoted undeniable progress: "Life is richer and richer as we live along," Barton announced in 1925. College presidents and even Calvin Coolidge himself (in a speech ghostwritten by Barton) sang the praises of advertising for educating the people in the uses of prosperity. Systematic national advertising, executives claimed, had reduced the risks involved in both buying and selling, creating a smooth-running "distribution system." It remained for some to put a moral gloss on this achievement. "We advertising writers are privileged to compose a new chapter of civilization," the copywriter James Wallen wrote in 1925. "It is a great responsibility to mold the daily lives of millions of our fellow men, and I am persuaded that we are second only to statesmen and editors in power for good." The post-millennial vision could not have been put more strongly.[61]

As the advertising business became more professional, its effort to mold the daily lives of millions was increasingly based on statistics. By the 1920s, market research was being hailed as a major achievement of the national advertising agencies. The most recent leap forward in advertising, according to J. George Frederick's whiggish account of "The Story of Advertising Writing" (1925), occurred when " 'arm-chair' copy-writing gave way to market-survey built copy. Intuitive insight into the public mind began to be supplemented by research-backed judgments of consumer-reactions." In 1930 a *Printers' Ink* contributor summarized three decades of development toward a marketing orientation: "I prefer knowing my consumer to knowing my product," he announced. As Frederick saw it, advertising copy was the "the apex of a solid merchandising plan," which included data questions for the manufacturer as well as research into consumer types, preferences, and influences; finally, the copy analyst would use proofs of varied copy to "conduct a carefully graded test on consumers (so planned that their unconscious judgment and not their conscious judgment be obtained)." Despite the reassuring impersonality of numbers, market surveys were still energized by the researcher's eagerness to catch the consumer unawares and penetrate the inner sanctum of his or her motivation.[62]

Success in advertising continued to require a mix of precise management and intuitive speculation. The growing prestige of the industry after World War I prompted recurrent questions like "Has Advertising Reached the Dignity of Finance?" and "A Professional Status for Advertising?" Yet the movement toward stability ran aground on the chaotic conditions that characterized agency life. The new subspecialty of "personnel management" that emerged during the 1920s seemed to offer a scientific method for regulating the notoriously nomadic habits of admakers, whose high turnover rate had given them what a *Printers' Ink* contributor called "an odious reputation among business men." "Do You Select Employees by a

Bertillon System?" asked this personnel executive in 1927; he recommended the late-nineteenth-century French positivist's system of categorizing character types as a way of picking employees who would stay with the firm. But this emphasis on organizational efficiency inevitably provoked protest from those who insisted that "the creative mind is the basis of everything that we call advertising." They argued that the high incidence of "job jumping" stemmed from copywriters' inability to tolerate the hyperorganized atmosphere at many agencies. Creative souls, from this view, changed jobs frequently because they were too often expected "to operate an adding machine with one hand and a typewriter with the other"; burden the copywriter with facts and figures and you bury "the life and fire and vitality of advertising copy."[63]

Despite the panoply of statistics, charts, and graphs that accompanied nearly every new business presentation by the 1920s, advertising remained less science than art. In 1924, though industry spokesmen were claiming that business types had triumphed over literary types, an *American Mercury* profile of "The Advertising Agent" described the copy department as "the temporary camping ground of free lance writers out of inspiration, and of reporters out of jobs," as well as "bobhaired graduates of the female academies"; "the typical copy writer" was "a college graduate two or three years removed from the elms, with no notion with what to do with himself in life, a hazy taste for English composition, and unlimited enthusiasm." Judging by the people who were drawn to writing it, successful promotional literature required more (or less) than objectivist cognition and clinical frankness.[64]

What it did require was a little more difficult for copywriters to specify. Whenever they tried, they unwittingly revealed their Barnumesque ancestry. "To be a really good copywriter requires a passion for converting the other fellow, even if it is to something you don't believe in yourself," Helen Woodward admitted in 1926. "This is an emotion in itself and has little to do with its object"—that is, with the product in question. For most copywriters, their job was less a matter of factual reporting on products than of "magical effects with pen and ink." As the senior copywriter James Wallen wrote in 1925, "You do not sell a man the tea, but the magical spell which is brewed nowhere else but in a tea-pot." Rather than carnivalesque subversion, this magic was a form of corporate mystification—as Wallen made clear when he advised visual artists to rise above the gritty details of literalist realism. "When it is necessary to show in an advertisement the interior of a foundry, an artist like Everett Shinn puts the wonderful miracle of

industry into the picture, rather than the hardships of labor as George Bel-
low might do," he observed. Platitudes like "the wonderful miracle of
industry" revealed the limitations of the miraculous in national brand-
name advertising.[65]

Invocations of magic often boiled down to little more than a constant
imperative to "be human" through the effective use of sentiment—a prescription that paralleled the developing practice of "human interest" journalism. Joseph Appel predicted the defeat of "brazen, big-type, blatant,
extravagant advertising" by "red-blooded, truthful, plain, simple, dignified,
cultured, courteous, common-sense 'human' advertising—because people
with those attributes rule the world and make it progress." In just a few
decades, J. George Frederick claimed in 1925, advertising had "changed
from a museum of inert waxworks into a wonderful stage of living players,
who gave the public thrills and real values." Copywriters remained dramatists, as in the days of Barnum, but now they dealt in "real values" as well
as providing "thrills." The bottom line was the deft conjuring of vital feeling from inert commodity. "Soup can produce emotion," Edith Lewis
announced in a J. Walter Thompson new business presentation of 1923;
"you can write as emotionally about ham as about Christianity." With that
call to action, advertising people revealed their kinship with the manufacturers of morale. Though copywriters' immediate aim was merely to please
a particular client, the larger consequence of their work was to merge sentiment and system, mobilizing popular support in the service of a developing consumer culture.[66]

As Patten had done twenty years before, advertising spokesmen in the
1920s discovered the link between mass consumption and labor discipline.
From their view, the spread of installment buying and the systematic use
of stylistic novelty as a marketing tactic, far from undermining the work
ethic, actually reinforced it. Advertising played a central role in accelerating progress toward the utopian reign of "obsolescence, free spending, and
creative waste" glimpsed by J. George Frederick at the end of the 1920s.
"The American conception of advertising is to arouse desires and stimulate
wants, to make people dissatisfied with the old and out-of-date and by constant iteration to send them out to work harder to get the latest model—
whether that model be an icebox or a rug, or a new home," the agency
head Bruce Barton told a radio audience in 1929. He was, in effect,
describing "Andy Consumer," the cartoon embodiment of the consumer
used throughout the 1920s by *Life* magazine to promote the publication as
an advertising vehicle (figure 7.4). Andy was just a regular guy, working

FIGURE 7.4

Detail from advertisement for *Life* magazine, *Printers' Ink,* 1926.

harder and harder so he could spend more and more to make life better and better for himself and his family.[67]

However much he might resemble a squirrel in a cage, Andy Consumer was meant by his creators to represent an active, progressive individual. Certainly Barton and other advertising apologists believed they were endowing the consumer with power, choice, and purposeful direction. Still, there were always ambiguities in the discourse of consumer sovereignty. Some became apparent in a *Collier's* editorial in 1930.

The old kings and aristocrats have departed. In the new order the masses are master. Not a few, but millions and hundreds of millions of people must be persuaded. In peace and in war, for all kinds of purposes, advertising carries the message to this new King—the people.

Advertising is the king's messenger in this day of economic democracy. All unknowing a new force has been let loose in the world. Those who understand it will have one of the keys to the future.[68]

It was still too soon after the stock market crash for the tone to be defensive, but there were revealing strains in the argument. Who the message is from is never clear: by 1930 the shift from highly visible robber barons to faceless executives had already occurred; the invisibility of corporate leadership became one of the keys to its hegemony. In this particular text, after the old forms of oppression have made their ritual departure, the masses are molded into a single master. Then the voice shifts to passive: the master does not act, though he has to "be persuaded." Advertising, meanwhile, metamorphoses from a mere messenger to "a new force . . . let loose in the world," and finally to "one of the keys to the future." The empowerment of the consumer was overshadowed by the hubris of the advertiser.

The dialectic between the autonomy of the consumer and the majesty of the corporation was played out in the ads for the high-technology products of the 1920s. Automobiles, radios, batteries, and electric ranges all claimed to provide their purchasers with an extraordinary mastery over their environment. The dream of total control over one's destiny has been a long-running feature of high-technology advertising—computer advertising offers the most striking recent example. But in the 1920s the promise was not merely personal control but magical power. None of these promises were meant to be taken literally, but they appeared so often one begins to suspect they were partly projections of copywriters' own longings for power in a business where creative fires were often banked by managerial demands. In any case, the power they promised consumers was purely fanciful. "Two fingers and one lever—that is all you need to tune the Thompson Minuet," a radio advertisement of 1925 announced. "Swing the single lever of this new, radically different receiver and, as you would play a giant searchlight over the city, picking out its famous buildings and parks and bridges, so do you reveal to the charmed listeners in your home the beauties of radio." Tuning the radio dial offered the illusions of centrality and choice; there is a striking similarity between the chuckleheaded beneficiary of technology imagined by this advertisement and and the *Natur-*

mensch imagined by José Ortega y Gasset in *The Revolt of the Masses* (1930)—the modern mass man who understands nothing of automobile mechanics but "accepts his motor car as the fruit of an Edenic tree." The *Naturmensch* was hardly a model of consumer sovereignty.[69]

For most agency executives, the notion of consumer sovereignty was a veneer over a deeper structure of belief that equated the consumer audience with a mass of doltish dupes. By the 1920s, the idea of audience manipulability had well-established academic justification. The doctrine of influence had been professionalized into the psychology of suggestion, which cast the consumer as an easy mark for the informed marketing strategist. Arthur Holmes, a marketing professor at Northwestern University, summarized (and up to a point inflated) the conventional wisdom in 1925:

> People unacquainted with psychology assume that men have the power to say "Yes" or "No" to an advertisement. The assumption is only partly correct. A man has the power to decide in the first stage of the game, not the last. . . . If the printed word can seize his attention, hold him chained, drive from his mind all other thoughts except the one "Buy this!" standing at the head of an organized sentiment from which every opposing idea, perception, feeling, instinct, and disposition have been driven out or smothered to death, then HE CANNOT SAY "NO"! His will is dead.[70]

This extraordinarily violent statement suggests some of the imperial impulses behind the positivistic "science of human nature." An "organized sentiment" holds the consumer's attention chained, then drives out or smothers to death everything else in his mind including finally "his will" itself. The drive to predict and control human behavior could lead to intoxicating fantasies. What is interesting about this one is that it shows how a fluid conception of selfhood could be placed in the service of authoritarian purposes; an apparently liberating psychology could be be merged with a vision of totalitarian domination. The key to this merger lay in Holmes's radically dualistic epistemology—his capacity to separate subject and object, the analytical gaze of the psychologist from the befuddled stare of the consumer. While even Holmes's fantasy was prefaced by the acknowledgment that "in the first stage of the game" consumers were free to choose whether or not they would attend to the advertisement, suggestion psychology in general underwrote belief in a malleable mass man.

Despite all their pretensions to statistical precision, advertising people then as now were imprisoned by the pop-sociological clichés of their time—the sneers of Sinclair Lewis, the hootings of H. L. Mencken. By the 1920s, advertising spokesmen had developed their own version of a world-view expressed in more elegant form by Ortega, T. S. Eliot, and other fastidious observers of the emergent urban societies in the early twentieth century. This outlook required that admakers emphasize the social and intellectual chasm separating themselves from their audience.

Advertising's version of the typical consumer, if not quite Eliot's "young man carbuncular," was just as much a vacant-eyed straphanger, stupefied by monotonous work, craving instinctual release and a sense (however fleeting) of personal autonomy. The copywriter John Starr Hewitt wrote in 1925:

> In spite of his seeming sophistication, the American citizen is naive, fresh, essentially childlike, full of generous enthusiasms and the capacity for wonderment. His everyday life is pretty dull. Get up—eat—go to work—eat—go to bed. But his mind is constantly reaching out beyond this routine. This is one of the reasons why the American is such a great fiction reader—movie goer—talking machine and radio fan. He compensates for the routine of to-day by the expectation of what his life is to be to-morrow.

And if that expectation was not at odds with his current situation, the admakers object was to make it so, to "make each reader dissatisfied with himself until he follows your suggestion," as a *Harper's* commentator of 1917 wrote.[71]

The idea of consumption as compensation is familiar enough, as are its connections with the bread-and-circuses notion of mass culture; what was overlooked by defenders of advertising and mass culture was that the liberation they offered depended on the assumption that people were mired in "the rut of everyday existence," as a Paramount Pictures advertisement called it in 1930.[72] Like the pleasures promoted by cigarette advertising, the fun in the ideology of mass consumption was a matter of moments snatched from a life depicted as relentlessly hectic or dreary. There was a symbiosis between managerial demands for personal efficiency and the temporary relief from them offered in advertisements.

Corporate-sponsored hedonism legitimated the idea that everyday living must inevitably be gray—an idea that in turn gave much advertising its raison d'être, particularly in the realm of fashion. Helen Woodward summarized the prevailing view in 1926:

> The restless desire for change in fashion is a healthy outlet. It is normal to want something different, even if many women spend too much

time and too much money that way. Change is the most beneficent medicine in the world to most people. . . . The woman who is tired of her husband or her home or her job feels some lifting of the weight of her life from seeing a straight line pass into a bouffant, or gray pass into beige. Most people have not the courage or the understanding to make deeper changes.[73]

Advertising had helped to transform dominant views of fashion among the respectable bourgeoisie from frivolous, vain self-display to justifiable relief from boredom. No doubt there was plenty of boredom in the nineteenth century, but it did not become a social issue as it did in the twentieth-century discourse of "masses." By conceiving "most people" as mired in monotony but too timid or befuddled to make deeper changes, advertising executives developed a functional justification for their own existence—one that reinforced the closed distribution system of consumer culture. Offering superficial novelty, they would temporarily satisfy "the restless desire for change" without risking anything more profound.

From time to time more thoughtful efforts were made to grapple with the boredom that seemed so pervasive in modern life. Some resembled the darker visions of Eliot or Ortega. Paul H. Nystrom, a professor of marketing at Columbia University, traced fascination with fashion to the prevalence of what he called a "philosophy of futility":

At the present time, not a few people in western nations have departed from old-time standards of religion and philosophy, and having failed to develop forceful views to take their places, hold to something that may be called, for want of a better name, a *philosophy of futility*. This view of life (or lack of a view of life) involves a question as to the value of motives and purposes of the main human activities. There is even a tendency to challenge the purpose of life itself. This lack of purpose in life has an effect on consumption . . . concentrating human attention on the more superficial things in which fashion reigns.

Nystrom was groping toward some recognition of the purposelessness behind the instrumentalist standards his own profession epitomized. But his objectivist assumption that a radical disjunction existed between observer and observed prevented him from including himself in the diagnosis. More rarely one heard an actual cri de coeur from the managerial ranks. "Is it not fairly plain that the chill of fear and misgiving called forth by the great production monster we are attending is principally one of ends, and of *meaning*?" J. George Frederick asked in 1930, as the monster was beginning to clank to a halt. "We do not know where the monster is heading; we do not know why he is heading anywhere at all."[74]

More commonly, though, advertising executives refused to consider that they themselves might be part of the anomic modern masses. They preferred to focus on the distance separating their own intelligent, purposeful lives from those of the vast majority of the population, "sunk in invincible ignorance." The same publicists who celebrated "the people, our masters" were privately dismissing the common man as an intellectual cipher. Let us not mince words, William Esty told his colleagues at J. Walter Thompson in 1930: "We say the Hollywood people are stupid, the pictures are stupid; what we are really saying is that the great bulk of people are stupid."[75] Emphasis on the stupidity of the audience comported well with the rhetoric of mass man, allowing advertising spokesmen to preserve their own pretensions to rationality and objectivity while engaging in deception of the multitudes.

Yet in the end, Ortega, Eliot, and other intellectual critics of mass society were far more pessimistic than advertising copywriters, who despite their contempt for the consumer's intelligence sustained a belief in the redemptive powers of corporate-sponsored technology. One suspects that some celebrations of technology were rooted in ad writers' own gee-whiz attitudes rather than merely a desire to deceive. And perhaps even more important than their technophilia was their faith in their own capacity as social engineers—a faith that linked them, despite all their differences, with other managerial professionals. All shared a belief that ordinary folk could not negotiate the complexity of modern life without the aid of experts like themselves.[76]

The Great Depression changed everything and nothing. At first there was a lot of brave talk, reasserting managerial ideals or claiming that older producer values had acquired new luster in the harsher economic climate. But within two years of the Crash, one can discern the growth of anxiety and despair inside the agencies as clients cut back appropriations or canceled orders, sending a wave of firings through the ranks of copywriters and account executives. Advertisements themselves became shrill, sometimes even hysterical, as they clamored for scarce consumer and client dollars; the rise of radio accelerated the resurgence of a carnival barker's style. Pretensions to dignity and professionalism became more difficult to maintain as an increasingly organized consumer movement attacked national advertising first for its bad manners, later for fraud and waste. Various New Deal policies aimed to recognize consumer interests and regulate the abuses of advertising. But by the mid-1930s, spokesmen for national advertising, along with other representatives of "American Business," had begun a serious counterattack. Repudiating carnivalesque clamor, they sought more reassuring rhetorical strategies: the impersonality of the statistical survey, the neutrality of the "public service" announcement, the resurgent authority of corporate-sponsored expertise. Management began to find its contemporary voice.

CHAPTER 8

Trauma, Denial, Recovery

DECADES of complacence had left admakers vulnerable to adversity. The stock market crash of October 1929 interrupted their aria of self-congratulation. The epidemic of joblessness deflated their pretensions and encouraged assaults on their extravagance. In industry apologetics, the rhetorical balance between mass man and sovereign consumer became more difficult to maintain.

As businesses failed and magazines' advertising sections grew thinner, advertising executives were attacked for their failure to live up to their claims, usually by other managerial professionals in the government or the emerging "consumer movement." Critics stayed within the framework of plain speech, social transparency, and the imperative need to contain the carnivalesque qualities of commerce—which seemed in resurgence as radio revived traditions of oral performance and agencies strained for sensational effects in a desperate drive to keep clients.

By the late 1930s, though, corporate advertisers had begun a successful counterattack against their critics. They rehabilitated and politicized the fiction of consumer sovereignty by broadening the practice of market research to include opinion polling; they democratized the imagery of the masses in promoting the ideological mobilization for World War II; they redefined the essence of the American Way of Life from a vague populism to an equally murky notion of free enterprise. Advertisers played a crucial hegemonic role in creating the consumer culture that dominated post–World War II American society. Changes in the industrial workplace underwrote the spread of mass consumption. After the open class strife of the late 1930s, labor and capital struck a tense and temporary bargain. Most unions gradually curbed their militance, accepting longer hours and labor discipline in exchange for steady work at a family wage. Consumer culture acquired a firmer social base than ever before: a well-paid (white, male) working class. Once again Patten's vision seemed about to be realized.

Nevertheless, there was anxiety. The rise of totalitarian social movements in the 1930s had persuaded many observers to erase the progressive aura surrounding "publicity" and redefine the shaping of public opinion as "propaganda." The sinister side of mass man reappeared, not with a bang but a whimper, in the postwar American suburbs—or at least in the critique of suburban conformity fostered by sociologists and bohemian poets. American social practices and values may have been as diverse as ever, but the dominant discourses of consumer culture required the systematic denial of diversity. Advertisers collaborated unwittingly with their critics in creating rhetorical constructions that construed the vast majority of the population as passive, manipulable objects.

The reappearance of a carnivalesque counterculture during the late 1960s was in many ways a protest against that objectification, a cri de coeur against the bland equilibrium of a successful distribution system. Though by 1970, managerial elites had constructed a new and allegedly benign version of mass man in the "Silent Majority," the economic base of consumer culture soon began to erode, as multinational corporations eliminated many high-paying jobs and exported others overseas. The jobs that remained were subjected to a speedup, as employers aimed to produce more with fewer employees; the result was hardly the reign of leisure predicted by Patten and Riesman.[1] Hopes for a progressive consumer culture had foundered on the shoals of mobile capital's search for low labor costs and high productivity. Yet many "free market" ideologues continued to assume that the growth of American consumption could be identified with the progress of civilization itself. Belief in the beneficence of consumer-driven economic growth outlasted the bargain between labor and capital— the bargain that had fostered that faith in the first place, as management struggled to regain legitimacy amid Depression devastation.

THE GREAT DEPRESSION

In the advertising trade press and national magazines of the early 1930s, the presence of the Depression was often signified by its absence. " 'You would never think we were in a depression to look at *Good Housekeeping*'s advertising's pages,' one of our friends said the other day," the magazine claimed in June 1933. " 'There seem to be as many ads and they are more enticing than ever.' "[2] The business strategy for dealing with hard times was systematic denial.

Nevertheless, within months after the Crash, there were signs of distress. Women's magazines began to advise families on how to make do "with benefit of budget"; they encouraged a general scaling down of expectations. "We are now realizing that the vital thing is not that the individual shall manage to do creditably the thing he undertakes, but that he shall undertake the thing that will bring balance and equilibrium into his own personal life," a *Good Housekeeping* contributor wrote in October 1931. As white-collar unemployment mounted, advertisers and publicists rediscovered the virtues of the old producer economy. "Are You Happy in Your Work?" Bruce Barton asked in 1930. "If not, stop and start again." In a thinly veiled exhortation to the downwardly mobile, Barton wrote: "White collar jobs, that require only a pleasant personality, lead nowhere; the future leaders of industry start in the shops, among the section gangs, in the stock-rooms." This sort of talk made a virtue of necessity.[3]

The rhetorical revival of producer values remained coupled to an ethic of controlled consumption. Walt Disney's Silly Symphony version of "The Grasshopper and the Ants," featured in comic-strip format in a 1934 issue of *Good Housekeeping*, dramatized the trade-off between work and play. The grasshopper, who has had fun all summer, is in danger of freezing; the ants find him despairing and nearly dead on their doorstep, take him in and minister to him; in the end, he plays the fiddle for their winter banquet: "He's learned his lesson: you must work and save, and never shirk, / And then, when you have earned the chance, there's lots of time to sing and dance!"[4]

But bromides about work could not keep economic disaster at bay. Advertising agencies and national magazines both had to confront the dwindling of orders for advertising space. Both groups insisted on the crucial importance of continuous advertising in good times and bad; indeed, they argued, advertising appropriations should actually *increase* in times of economic depression. Advertising alone could create that "willingness to buy" which precedes "actual demand," could even "make spending fashionable again." In the 1920s, agencies had been able to make all kinds of extravagant claims to their potential clients. "In the field of advertising to advertisers," the consumer advocate Frederick Schlink observed in 1929, "these experts plainly hold their colleagues almost as gullible as the general public upon whom they work their chief medicine show marvels." By the early 1930s the sales pitches began to sound a little strained. Advertising could even out the peaks and valleys in the employment cycle and mitigate seasonal downturns, allowing a garden tool manufacturer to add snow sleds in winter, a date packer to add grapefruit, the agency executive Roy Dickinson claimed as he articulated the ultimate managerial fantasy. Advertising, in short, could pry "the skinny fingers of that gaunt specter of unemployment" from "the throat of our economic life."[5]

This personification of unemployment revealed some of the tensions in agency life. It was not only factory workers but managerial professionals whose salaries were being slashed and jobs were being eliminated. By 1931, *Printers' Ink* was pleading with executives to stop the "whipcracking" over their harassed salesmen; morale was the key to recovery, the editors insisted, as they published upbeat articles like "You Can't Keep a Good Advertising Man Out of Work." By mid-decade, at the middle and upper creative levels in the big New York agencies, the carnage was fearful.[6]

Those who remained in the agencies were beset by increasing pressures to get and please clients. Account executives who held key personal contacts with important clients were able to hang on to their jobs despite their high salaries. "They gotta die or lose all their clients before they get the gate," the *Printers' Ink* columnist Groucho observed. This staying power generated resentment among the younger or less fortunate agency people, who dismissed the account executive's job as "bootlegging and bootlicking." But more than theater tickets, pedigreed dogs, and expensive scotch were required to keep clients during the depths of the Depression. As clients grew more careful, ad campaigns themselves became more strained and provocative.[7]

The Depression forced a revival of carnivalesque tactics. Unemployed models in New York's garment district took part-time jobs as sandwichboard advertisers for beauty parlors. Magazine advertising came to be dominated by thick black type, scare headlines, and discussions of the body's lower regions (figure 8.1). And radio advertising brought a return of oral performance and snake-oil sales tactics. "Radio gave birth to impertinent advertising," complained William J. Cameron, director of public relations for the Ford Motor Company, in 1938. "Never before the advent of radio did advertising have such a golden opportunity to make an ass out of itself. Never before could advertising be so insistent and so unmannerly

FIGURE 8.1
Advertisement for Lysol disinfectant, *Good Housekeeping*, 1935.

and so affront its audience." Yet for many unemployed advertising people, radio was the only game in town. By mid-decade, thousands of copywriters were among the jobless: déclassé college men with nothing to sell but clever ideas, sitting hour after hour by the radio, listening for contests with cash prizes to keep the wolf from the door. The fate of the unemployed copywriter epitomized advertising's descent from dignity.[8]

Not everyone was sympathetic. Since the war, a consumer movement had gradually been building strength, focusing on the continuing fraud and waste in the allegedly efficient distribution system. In 1927, Frederick

J. Schlink and Stuart Chase published *Your Money's Worth,* which became the springboard for the Consumers Union and *Consumer Reports;* the next year, Chase offered a broader indictment, *The Tragedy of Waste.* Magazines like *Ballyhoo* began to lampoon the earnestness and excess of national ads, even at the height of what business publicists called the New Era. After the stock market crash, popular distrust of advertising intensified. People with shrinking pocketbooks were more sensitive to fraud and waste; advertising, meanwhile, was becoming an easier target. The middle- and upper-class subscribers to national magazines encountered a spreading swamp of bogus and irrelevant science, non sequiturs, poor taste, misinformation, and scare tactics in their ad pages. Even top executives like H. A. Batten admitted that by 1932, much advertising had become "a stench in the nostrils of the civilized world." No wonder many managerial professionals began calling themselves "consumers" and declaring themselves offended.[9]

Despite advertisers' claims that the stench had been produced by a mere handful of bad apples in the industry, the burgeoning consumer movement was more than a matter of outraged taste (or smell). Its intellectual origins stretched back to John Ruskin's justly famous assaults on classical economics, particularly his distinction between socially necessary "wealth" and socially harmful "illth." But the movement's more immediate antecedent was Thorstein Veblen; Chase was especially indebted to him. More generally, consumer advocates' preoccupation with correcting fraud through accurate labeling was rooted in the plain-speech tradition, and their concern with eliminating waste stemmed from the republican producer's hatred of (allegedly "parasitical") middlemen. But the idiom they used was technocratic and managerial. Sharing this discourse with other professional groups, consumer advocates used the ideal of systematic efficiency to measure national advertisers' shortcomings and discredit their claims to professionalism.[10]

Ultimately, the consumer movement's emphasis on efficiency proved both empowering and imprisoning. Polemicists like Chase and T. Swann Harding (*The Popular Practice of Fraud,* 1935) skewered the double standard that deplored "wasteful government spending" while assuming "that anything private enterprise does is necessary and laudatory." Business was full of boondoggles, many quite costly to the consumer, and consumer advocates rightfully exposed them. The emphasis on transparent communication made sense as well; precise labeling was not only the most efficient but also the fairest way to continue the stabilization of sorcery in the food and drug trade. And, at least for Chase and some of the more theoretically inclined among the consumer advocates, the preoccupation with waste could lead in more interesting directions, toward a thoroughgoing critique of capitalism.[11]

Up to a point, Chase's analysis of the Depression paralleled that of many corporate managers. The American economy, they would have agreed, had reached the stage of "disaccumulation" (to use Marx's term): the capacity, through advanced technology, to make more and more goods with fewer and fewer workers; they coupled this with the common recognition that the problem of "overproduction" was also a problem of "underconsumption." Consumers were not adequately absorbing the proliferating produce of the industrial system. So far, Chase and many national advertisers were in tandem. But Chase gave the argument a further turn when he emphasized the ill effects of maldistributed income: a huge portion of the American population did not make enough money even to cover basic necessities, let alone absorb their fair share of industrial output; a tiny percentage of the population, meanwhile, had so much loose capital that it was constantly looking for investment opportunities with an eye toward quick returns rather than social needs. The result was more useless factories, more useless goods, more natural resources wasted, more human needs unmet. Chase's consumerism had both an egalitarian and an environmentalist dimension. But his managerial proclivities took over when he sought an alternative to the capitalist "tragedy of waste." In 1931 he concluded: "The only final way out lies through planned production. We have to scrap a large fraction of *laissez-faire,* and deliberately orient productive capacity to consumption needs. In Russia they build no more shoe factories than are necessary to supply Russians with shoes."[12]

It would be a cheap (and ahistorical) shot to discredit Chase's ideas by associating him with sentimentality toward the Soviet experiment. During the early 1930s a serious economic thinker might be pardoned a longing glance at the latest five-year plan, and in any case Chase acknowledged the vast gulf in cultural traditions separating the United States from the Soviet Union. Still, the Soviet reference revealed the managerial cast of Chase's mind, an outlook that also characterized the consumer movement as a whole. Like Veblen, Chase was truly a "tribune of the technostructure," in the historian Robert Westbrook's phrase. Both Veblen and Chase wanted to free the engineers from the dominion of the businessmen, assuming that rationality would then reign. Neither had much feeling for the aesthetic, imaginative uses of consumption; both preached technocratic versions of the plain-speech gospel—Chase's *Tyranny of Words* (1938) turned this positivist approach toward language, demanding transparent relationships between words and their referents. Theodor Adorno had accurately labeled Veblen's critique of consumption an "attack on culture"; Chase's preoccupations reveal that the same puritanical producerism bedeviled later generations of critics.[13]

Indeed, throughout the consumer movement of the 1930s, one senses the predominance of a gray managerial worldview. To be sure, not all consumer advocates succumbed: Ralph Borsodi, for one, developed a convincing decentralist critique of corporate advertising, calling for a revival of retailing and face-to-face exchange in small communities.[14] But by and large, the consumer movement's preoccupation with labeling and grading products was linked to a larger vision of life in a fully rationalized "functional society," where the unpredictability and variety of the market were controlled through central planning. Despite their ideological distance from advertisers, consumer advocates shared with them a common faith in the benevolent direction of society by professional expertise.

The question was, what sort of expertise? Undoubtedly there were differences between planning for the profit of the producers and planning for the needs of the consumer. Those differences were fought out in the legislative battles of the New Deal era. During that period, consumers came into their own as a political entity, achieving official representation alongside business and labor in the National Recovery Administration—despite the baffled question of the NRA head, General Hugh Johnson: "Who is the consumer? Show me a consumer." Still, the policy results remained meager. During the early 1930s, efforts by the assistant secretary of agriculture Rexford Guy Tugwell to promote a stiffer Pure Food and Drug Act were emasculated by the concerted efforts of advertisers and publishers; later in the decade, Assistant Attorney General Thurman Arnold's threats to prosecute advertising under the antitrust laws came to naught as well. Even the passage of an undistributed-profits tax in 1936, a move consumer advocates had championed, underwrote larger advertising expenditures as industries preferred paying ad agencies to paying the IRS. Consumer protest in the 1930s led to little beyond a mild strengthening of the Federal Trade Commission in 1938.[15]

The more lasting impact of the tussles between advertising and the New Deal was the creation of a common managerial political culture that has survived down to our own time—a culture increasingly dependent on systematic advertising. Governor Franklin Roosevelt spoke more prophetically than he knew in a 1931 address to the New York chapter of the Advertising Federation of America. National advertising had been educating us for prosperity, he said; now its great and necessary powers should be applied to government. "Help us," Roosevelt said, "to interest people in the machinery and the production of government, and to show them what is good and what is bad in the completed result." Within a few years, Roosevelt would become a master advertiser of government, using Blue Eagles to symbolize the National Recovery Administration and Fireside Chats to win support for all his programs. (The Blue Eagle was designed by Charles Coiner, art director at N. W. Ayer.) Roosevelt and his bitterest critics would come to share a common assumption: that the electorate constituted a huge mass audience, waiting to be persuaded to vote for the agendas packaged by various organized elites, both inside and outside the government.[16]

Advertising agencies and their clients gradually began to realize that the mass audience was the prize in the struggle between American Business and Big Government. Privately, agency people remained contemptuous of the masses. In an early-1930s lecture to J. Walter Thompson copywriters on the difficulties of reaching radio listeners, William Colwell recalled the typical bright adman's experience among the lumpish crowd at a neighborhood movie theater. "You'd find that you had finished laughing—if you did at all—before the others [the masses] started. There is as much of a difference in the audience as that. We think that something similar is true in a radio program. You can't hop from one idea to another so fast that only the keenest minds [like ours] can follow you." But as the Depression dragged on, advertising spokesmen increasingly de-emphasized the distinctions between the keen minds of advertising copywriters and the sluggish ones of the multitude. "Meet your masters," announced the new monthly magazine, *People*, that J. Walter Thompson began publishing in 1937. "It is only by acknowledging their control that the means of influencing the direction of their leadership can be conceived." Tortuous locutions like this denied popular power even as they sought to celebrate it.[17] The actual limitations on popular autonomy were revealed in another *People* advertisement which presented an old man at a diamond-grille pay window and a young housewife being shown a wringer washer.

> Whether they line up at a pay window or clip coupons, few people want money for any purpose but to spend it. There may not be as much romance in earning the dollars—someone else is usually the boss on that job—but in parting from them, the buyer is boss.

Selecting a necktie gives him a gratifying sense of power. Buying a
fur jacket is a great adventure for a woman—she in the seat of authority, with salespeople eager to do her bidding.

Yes, spending is fun. No wonder all the increase in national income
will not be spent "sensibly"—for the rarer the purchase, the greater the
adventure.[18]

This was the great advantage national advertisers had over government
spokesmen and consumer advocates: spending was more fun than performing civic duties. On the other hand, if citizenship could be likened to
consumption, gray government could appropriate some of the glitter of
advertising. That was what gradually began to happen: boundaries became
blurred between the discourses of the public and private sectors. Methods
for measuring consumer demand migrated from corporate boardrooms to
government offices; market research became opinion polling, and public
opinion was depoliticized. Managerial elites increasingly defined public
opinion in the spuriously neutral jargon of statistical science: the central
ritual of American politics shifted away from "the people out of doors" (as
republican tradition had referred to the electorate) overtly expressing their
beliefs to the pollster quietly measuring "the pulse of democracy"—the
revealingly medical phrase George Gallup used to title his book of 1940.[19]

Just as private corporate welfare schemes predated and set the pattern
for government programs like workmen's compensation insurance and
Social Security, market research pioneered the efforts to manage public
opinion later practiced more openly by political pollsters. Gallup, to take
just one example, cut his teeth at the Young & Rubicam agency during the
early 1930s. *Fortune* magazine caught the broader applications of market
research in 1935: "No one—and least of all the journalists—seems to have
remarked that what the advertisers had developed was a mechanism
adapted not only to the selling of toothpaste but to the plumbing of the
public mind." No one, that is, until *Fortune* pointed the way with its first
public opinion survey, conducted that same year.[20]

This was a key moment in the fine-tuning of managerial thought about
mass society. Statistical sampling, whether sponsored by business or government elites, soon became an instrument for rendering public debate
more manageable and predictable. The survey became another threatening force against which people had to struggle to maintain alternative
visions of reality. And yet survey research advanced under the banner of
popular sovereignty. Through opinion polling and market research, government and business were supposed to become more responsive to their

masters, the people. But what actually happened, as Tocqueville had predicted, was that the more responsive huge organizations seemed to be, the more they were able to set the boundaries of public discourse. Advertising executives and other practitioners of the "human sciences" promoted this convergence of corporate and government interests, as they shared not only an objectivist cognitive style but a preoccupation with the management of public opinion.[21]

The rise of opinion polling coincided with a broad counterattack by business interests against the New Deal, the consumer movement, and organized labor. Sometimes the counterattack was conducted in soft conversational tones, as, for example, when the public relations firm Howard Downey Associates sent unemployed actors disguised as Fuller Brush salesmen into the homes of striking autoworkers in Flint, Michigan, to tell the workers' wives that union leaders were driving around in Cadillacs and smoking twenty-five-cent cigars. But more commonly, when business found its voice during the late 1930s the note its spokesmen struck was louder, blander, and more reassuring. Seeking to rise above salesmanship, advertising agencies turned toward wider ideological ventures, such as J. Walter Thompson's pamphlet *A Primer of Capitalism* (1937). Trade journals showed greater awareness that national advertising was part of a broad coalition—"American business"—locked in struggle with Washington. Confronted with consumerist critiques, industry spokesmen repeated the slogan that advertising was merely a neutral technique for promoting efficient distribution and material progress. They aimed to appropriate the legitimacy of other professional identities, not only through the language of expertise but through more direct means as well. For example, James Webb Young, a senior executive at J. Walter Thompson, took a leave of absence from the agency in 1935 to teach at the Northwestern University Business School and began publishing articles like "The Professor Looks at Advertising" in *Good Housekeeping*. Masquerading as professorial experts, admakers sought to huddle with other managerial elites under the umbrella of professionalism. Through institutional advertising, they tried to bring their clients under that umbrella as well, allying major corporations with noble causes from public health to highway safety. Increasingly, the bigger agencies rejected raucous carnival barking for the denatured dignity of the public service announcement.[22]

But in the anxious atmosphere of the late 1930s, denatured dignity was not enough. As Warren Susman has suggested, the persistence of economic depression at home and the rise of dictatorships abroad intensified middle-class Americans' yearnings to belong to a reassuring collective whole. By 1940, everyone from the Communist Party leader William Z. Foster to the liberal poet and ideologue Archibald MacLeish had been celebrating the American Way of Life as a transcendent communal identity; national advertising helped corporate industry appropriate that identity and redirect its chief connotation from populism to "free enterprise." [23]

The coming of war provided the key opening. "Business Rushes to Government's Aid in Preparedness Crisis," *Printers' Ink* announced in August 1940, hailing "a new relationship between business and government." Well before Pearl Harbor, executives from advertising agencies and other businesses flocked to Washington to race around town in cheap taxicabs and make the case for deregulated industry. At last the bureaucrats were willing to listen: some had begun to understand Keynes's argument that aggregate demand could be stimulated as effectively through private as through public investment; more probably shared *Printers' Ink*'s opinion that "in this day of mechanical warfare, national defense and industrial mobilization are nearer than ever before to being synonymous." And even the mobilization brought by the Lend-Lease Act of 1941 was enough to send a flurry of increased profits through many ad agencies. War, if not the health of the state, proved again to be the health of the advertising business. [24]

Wars have characteristically offered bourgeois society a mixed bag of opportunities: new possibilities for commercial plunder but also the chance to rise above self-seeking by making a commitment to the larger whole. Individualism and Civism have often been at odds. But since the American age of empire began in 1898, the cunning of the dominant culture in the United States has been to relax old republican tensions between market values and martial virtues; American business has done well by doing good—or what government leaders declared was good. National advertisers, having helped to arrange this merger of commerce and civic virtue during World War I, performed the feat with even more dramatic success during World War II. Rather than a Wilsonian world "safe for democracy," they offered Americans a more immediate vision to fight for: a revitalized vision of "home" colored by pastoral memories and fantasies but surrounded by modern creature comforts.

After the war, American corporations emerged reborn from the distrust of the Depression years, senior partners in the coalition of elites—business, labor, agriculture, government—that emerged to set the policy agenda for the peacetime consumer culture. The term "consumer culture" had unprecedented validity as a description of the sprawling suburban society developing in the wake of war-built prosperity. Production and consumption began to accelerate in tandem; organized labor, having abandoned its fight for the thirty-hour week in the late 1930s, saw working hours begin to climb upward during and after the war. Labor and management struck a tacit bargain: in exchange for escalating pay, labor would no longer demand increased leisure.[25]

As in the 1920s, people had some cash in their pockets, but the institutional and social bases of affluence were broader. The Full Employment Act of 1946 signaled the government's commitment to playing some role, however ambiguous, in sustaining prosperity. By the late 1940s, government and business had begun to collaborate in constructing a permanent war economy; the multiplier effect of military Keynesianism sent waves of stimulation through whole sectors of the economy and regions of the country. The postwar depression, so widely feared, never happened. Once more, production and consumption seemed to relate in dynamic equilibrium; the managerial model of a mixed economy seemed vindicated.

WORLD WAR II AND AFTER:
CRUSADE FOR COMFORT

In November 1941, as a Japanese task force began steaming east by southeast from the Kuril Islands toward Pearl Harbor, national advertisers were meeting in Hot Springs, Arkansas. It was a time of guarded optimism, a sentiment reinforced by Leon Henderson, the consumer advocate and New Dealer who addressed the convention in his new role as administrator of the Emergency Price Control Act. Advertising executives viewed Henderson as a minion of Satan. He reassured them that they faced "no special or extraordinary peril" from the Roosevelt administration. "I have always assumed and I now assume that advertising performs a useful economic function," he added. Coming from Henderson, whom industry leaders ritually denounced as advertising's Enemy No. 1, this was an astounding statement. The admakers leaped to their feet and gave the New Dealer a prolonged standing ovation. His calming words signaled the spread of a new, more sympathetic attitude toward business in Washington, as "Dr. New Deal" gave way to "Dr. Win-the-War."[26]

Even before Pearl Harbor, the wartime emergency provided advertising spokesmen with opportunities to redeploy the managerial idiom as a solvent of serious differences between commerce and commonwealth.

Writing in mid-November 1941, the agency head H. A. Batten insisted that advertising could not be equated with selling. "No, advertising has one specific thing to do; and that is to inform, and often—but not necessarily always—to persuade," he announced. "*Advertising is a specialized technique for mass communication.* . . . Because advertising is a technique, it has no existence in itself. It has no existence at all in the absolute." The invocation of technique neutralized familiar conflicts of power. To be sure, Batten admitted, advertising was most often used by management, but just about every worthwhile activity in the modern world was a form of management: "Government is Management. . . . Organized Charity is Management. . . . Education is Management. Public Health is Management. The Nutrition Movement is Management. . . . Every religious sect and creed is Management. Every league, club, society, federation or association is Management." All wanted to inform and persuade. The much-derided "propaganda" could be serviceable as well as sinister.[27]

Batten's attempt to uproot managerial values from a particular class and cultural position was a characteristically universalizing rhetorical strategy—advertising apologists had long taken the "everything is advertising" line in attempting to disengage their work from specific social associations. But the strategy involved the creation of institutions as well as the redeployment of rhetoric. The Hot Springs convention gave birth to the Advertising Council, the group that did more than any other to rehabilitate national advertising during the war, and to sponsor a corporate idiom of public service after 1945 (popularizing highway safety, inventing Smokey the Bear).

The Advertising Council (which became the War Advertising Council from Pearl Harbor to V-J Day) ultimately included representatives from ad agencies, their clients, and the media, but from the beginning the executives from the large agencies dominated. The first president was Chester J. LaRoche of Young & Rubicam, who led the group's fight to provide free advertising space to the government and in general to demonstrate that advertising agencies and their corporate clients could be viewed as patriotic citizens. This they accomplished by cooperating with the government's Office of War Information in placing public service announcements, promoting scrap salvage campaigns, selling the importance of women's war work, and chastising advertisers who refused to go all out for the war effort. The OWI itself was increasingly dominated by corporate advertising people like Price Gilbert of Coca-Cola, who headed the Bureau of Graphics and Printing. His presence provoked the liberals in the office to produce a mock poster of a Coca-Cola bottle wrapped in an American flag with the caption "Step right up and get your four delicious freedoms. It's a refreshing war." Critics could rage and even resign in protest, as many did in 1943, but the death of the OWI that same year, due to lack of congressional support, only underscored what everyone already knew about wartime publicity: the "private sector" was in the saddle. A *New Republic* columnist recognized the importance of corporate control in "silencing other positive points of view" as he observed: "Shouldering the OWI out of the picture paved the way for selling America all over again on an all-important idea that industry is not only winning the war with production but is much more devoted to the public interest than is government, now prohibited from telling the story, or than labor, which is without the funds or the technique to enter the field." The displacement of the OWI by the War Advertising Council was a major victory in the business counteroffensive against the New Deal.[28]

In 1942, the historian Curtis Nettels worried that "the great opportunity for constructing a better world which now confronts the United States may soon be lost in a Babel of advertisers' voices, urging us to buy, to get, to have, to enjoy this or that trivial product or minor pleasure." That was not exactly how things turned out. The War Advertising Council, its peacetime successor, and their industry supporters did manage to conceal much of the crassness with a patriotic haze. But national advertisers nevertheless reduced Nettels's vision of "a better world" to a proliferation of creature comforts nestled in nurturant settings of domesticity and small-town community (figure 8.2). Advertisers appropriated the folkish ideology of the 1930s—the ideology of the WPA and the Popular Front—to further an agenda of economic development that was anything but friendly to the folk and their traditions.[29]

After the war, national advertisers, led by the Ad Council, became increasingly adept at submerging institutional advertising in a warm bath of information and uplift. In 1948 an article in the *Saturday Review of Literature* noted the increasingly common tendency for corporations to sponsor documentary films about their industry. The key to success, the author argued, was "More Seeing, Less Selling." An Eastern Airlines documentary, narrated by the company's president, the World War I flying ace Eddie Rickenbacker, contained too much upfront salesmanship; but the brilliant *Louisiana Story*, which was directed by Robert Flaherty, father of documentary filmmaking, and sponsored by Standard Oil of New Jersey, set the standard for excellence. It detailed "the impact of a vital modern

FIGURE 8.2
Advertisement for Imperial whiskey, *American Magazine,* January, 1945.

industry on a simple and even backward people. . . . A small boy, whose only previous contact with technology has been his rusty rifle and an occasional glimpse of a motor boat passing his father's shack, learns that there is another kind of life beyond his bayou which is a wonderland in itself." The translation of corporate interests into neutral "technology," the association of technology with progress but also with a magical "wonderland"—these rhetorical tics, common in advertising since the 1920s if not earlier, continued with greater force into the postwar era.[30]

Often government got into the act as well, as in the 1956 overseas campaign of the United States Information Agency. The keynote was "People's

Capitalism." President Dwight Eisenhower had picked up the idea from Theodore S. Repplier, president of the Ad Council. The campaign presented the American economic system as a deus ex machina which erased class lines, transformed workers into capitalists, and eliminated all forms of drudgery. This message was sent at taxpayers' expense, underscoring the renewed alliance between corporate advertisers and the federal government.[31]

The effort to ally advertising with the American Way of Life, begun in the dark days of the Great Depression, came to full fruition in the ideologically charged atmosphere of the Cold War. Advertising apologists mixed all the old rhetorical strategies with renewed fervor and added a few new ones as well. Advertising was not only necessary commercial information, they claimed, it was the basis of free speech, as it provided the economic foundation for mass-circulation newspapers and magazines. And advertising was fun, the ebullient expression of a triumphant, spirited people. This last point allowed the apologists to characterize their critics as humorless old maids—a strategy that did not come fully into its own until the 1980s.[32]

At the pinnacle of their prestige in the 1950s, though, national advertisers began to come under renewed critical fire. Even Neil Borden of the Harvard Business School, whose *Economics of Advertising* (1942) had lent the industry much legitimacy, admitted that there was no way to test whether particular advertisements "paid" or not. When recession hit, as in 1957–58, corporate advertisers made Madison Avenue the whipping boy as they cut back appropriations; agencies put many copywriters out on the street. Yet even at the height of prosperity, public mistrust of the industry was increasing. This was more than a matter of complaints about hard-sell tactics and other abuses: the consumer culture's fundamental synthesis of private needs and corporate interests was beginning to show some strains. In spite of the imprecision and unreliability of market research, agencies stepped up their statistical snooping, sometimes coupling survey information with the latest variation on suggestion psychology, "motivation research." This was the term for the vaguely manipulative brew cooked up by the psychoanalyst Ernest Dichter in the late 1930s and popularized in the agency world after the war. The melding of intimacy and publicity, mass psychology and market research, sealed the systematic containment of the carnivalesque in a new and "scientific" package.[33]

The intrusiveness of this strategy inevitably provoked uneasiness. Humor revealed anxiety. A *New Yorker* cartoon from 1945 showed a man in business attire addressing a housewife in bathrobe and curlers on an affluent suburban doorstep: "Good morning, madam, the J. Walter Thompson Company would like to know if you are happily married." [34] JWT characteristically used the free publicity as part of a new business presentation, but other observers of advertising were probably not so amused. Anxieties were particularly acute among cultural critics who accepted the notion of a manipulable mass society, which had acquired unprecedented force during the midcentury decades. "All the social nightmares of our day seem to focus on some unending and inescapable form of mob rule," the literary critic Northrop Frye observed, invoking the specter of "the self-policing state, the society incapable of formulating an articulate critique of itself and of developing a will to act in its light." The rise of fascism had yielded the spectacle of masses at monster rallies, spellbound in hate; Soviet and later Chinese Communism provided other frightening images of the mass mobilization of consciousness. From totalitarian hordes to Americans in golf shirts was a bit of a stretch, but the suburbs of the postwar United States, underwritten by federal policy through the FHA and VA loan programs, did give a local habitation to a more benign vision of mass society. In their very inoffensiveness and desire to fit in, suburban Americans seemed to critics to embody our own national version of the "self-policing state"—the society that had sailed into a calm, dead-level ocean of conformity.[35]

Few observers followed Theodor Adorno and his colleagues in ascribing authoritarian tendencies to large sectors of the population, but many fretted about that population's lamentable lack of taste, addiction to creature comforts, and political quietism. The preoccupation with matters of taste among critics of postwar society was epitomized in John Kenneth Galbraith's famous description of the Eisenhower years as a period when "the bland lead the bland"—a comment that, however witty and accurate, demonstrated how completely political discourse had been consumed by questions of style. The assumption that issues of material inequality had been solved pervaded the popular sociology of the period. "The fruits of social revolution are always more desirable in anticipation than fact, and the pink lamp shade in the picture window can be a sore disappointment to those who dreamed that the emancipation of the worker might take a more spiritual turn," William F. Whyte wrote in The Organization Man (1956). (One thinks of Patten's hopes, as well as those of the young Karl Marx.) "It is a sight, however, that we can well endure," he concluded. Other, more acerbic critics rejected Whyte's stance of stoical resignation. Thinkers as serious and diverse as Dwight Macdonald, David Riesman, and Irving Howe contributed to a mounting chorus of complaint about "this age of conformity." But even those avowedly on the Left, like Howe and Macdonald, paid little systematic attention to the power relations underlying the emergent consumer culture. So their work sometimes took on the cast of a critique of manners.[36]

Defenders of consumer culture could dismiss such critiques as the work of snobs, and could cite their own academic authority: Talcott Parsons, the Harvard sociologist who in *The Social System* (1951) and other works provided an updated version of Patten's vision. In Parsons's systematically organized society, as in Patten's, production and consumption existed in dynamic equilibrium, though they occupied differentiated realms. The Parsonian concept of differentiation put a scientific gloss on the revival of domesticity that was taking place in the suburbs. Family and work were functionally related. In *Beyond Conformity* (1961), a Parsonian critique of consumer culture criticism, the sociologist Winston White argued that much domestic mass consumption was for durable goods (washing machines, for example) that fueled basic industries: "The appliances have been bought with funds that could have been spent on beer and skittles, but instead were plowed back into 'plant equipment.' "[37] As in Patten's *New Basis of Civilization,* consumption was described as serving the cause of production. Domestic-based consumption, White argued, might also help the family perform its function of "personality-management" in a society where home experience was increasingly isolated from work experience and extended kinship ties were stretched or absent. In a differentiated "social system," all the disparate parts fit into an integrated whole. What critics like Macdonald bewailed as "adjustment" or "conformity" was, from the Parsonian view, functional efficiency.

The fly in the functionalists' ointment was the possibility that the consensus they applauded was not a consequence of spontaneous popular consent but of manipulation by managerial elites. Concerns about advertisers' abuse of motivation research converged with images of "brainwashed" GIs chanting Communist slogans in North Korean prisons. The overall effect of these perceptions was to reaffirm the assumption that the human mind was a pathetic lump of clay. Far more charming than the Communists, the admaker was nevertheless the American version of a devious master manipulator, orchestrator of a corporate system that to some nervous critics was beginning to work too well.[38]

The growth of motivation research was rooted in advertisers' need to sell off backed-up inventories of consumer goods—to keep the circulation going. Eager to find a new selling formula, agencies and their clients turned to psychological consultants like Dichter, head of his own Institute for Research in Mass Motivation. According to the copywriter Joseph Seldin, Dichter told them they had "entered a 'psycho-economic' age in which emotional rather than technical factors determine the consumer's purchases"—a period when national advertisers "must either sell emotional security or go under." Longings for emotional security, spawned by the anxieties of the Depression decade, now formed the basis for the psychological clichés of the "age of conformity." As always in advertising and market research, what passed for innovative theory was curiously congruent with the formulas of popular sociology. Motivation research was the ultimate expression of dualistic social science: the dispassionate observer pretending to a complete separation from the helpless objects under examination. Dichter and his colleagues tried to penetrate the verbal responses of their interviewees to reveal hidden fears and aspirations. Through motivation research, the Book-of-the-Month Club learned how a quantitative emphasis could backfire, as subscribers developed "a sense of inferiority" amid piles of unread books; the Tea Council learned that appeals to the tired and nervous merely reinforced the stereotype of tea as a drink for invalids, so they turned to the slogan "Make It Hefty, Hot, and Hearty." In short, corporate advertisers bought "common sense dressed in the trappings of science," as Seldin observed. The consumer population was once again reduced to inert illustrations of managerial conventional wisdom. The reduction was rhetorical rather than behavioral; the vast majority of Americans went about their business indifferent or skeptical toward advertising. But advertisers' assumptions had important consequences, both for their own strategies and those of their critics.[39]

The rise of television reinforced fears of advertisers' manipulative powers. Here was an instrument even more seductive and intrusive than the radio, especially when it was directed toward children. If they named one of Lassie's puppies, they won a year's supply of Fab for Mom; if they brought their parents into a Sylvania television store, they received a Sylvania Space Ranger kit. Difficult as it was (and is) to take such strategies seriously, many observers viewed them with alarm. As Seldin rightly pointed out, a double standard was at work. "Manipulation of children's minds in the fields of religion or politics would touch off a parental storm of protest and a rash of congressional investigations. But in the world of commerce children are fair game and legitimate prey."[40]

By 1957, alarm about manipulative advertising was coming to a head. Perhaps the most sensational revelations concerned the latest manifestations of the doctrine of influence, the practice of subliminal advertising, which involved embedding verbal or visual messages below the level of the buyers' conscious awareness, keeping them ignorant of being influenced. The search for death's heads in cigarette packages and naked women in ice cubes began in earnest. More thoughtful observers pointed out how limited in effectiveness such strategies were likely to be; many alleged instances of "subliminal seduction" were merely the result of bored copywriters or layout artists trying to slip a trick past the copy chief and the client. Nevertheless, the furor over subliminal advertising was a symptom of the mounting belief that hapless consumers were puppets in the hands of invisible wire-pullers. Vance Packard's best-seller *The Hidden Persuaders* (1958) captured and catalyzed popular anxieties. The book was a blend of plainspoken outrage at fraud and republican concern about mysterious conspiracies, updated to dramatize postwar preoccupations about mass manipulation. Elsewhere, Packard resurrected the early-twentieth-century muckrakers' critique of the threat to free speech posed by publishers' dependence on advertising revenues. Advertising apologists could dismiss Packard's assault on manipulative strategies as paranoia, but they had a harder time responding to his analysis of publishing. Fairfax Cone (of Foote, Cone & Belding in Chicago) offered a typical example. "There have been many disputes by advertisers and their agencies about articles published in magazines to which they took exception, and scheduled advertising has been cancelled," he admitted in an *Atlantic Monthly* reply to Packard. "But I can see no difference between this and the action of an irate individual who cancels his subscription because of an article or story that he doesn't like." Did this businessman, so sensitive to questions of economic power when they impinged on agency policy, really believe that the price of a subscription could be equated with the price of a page of advertising? As in earlier debates over advertising's influence on publishing, a focus on individual "abuses" obscured the implicit, systemic legitimation of corporate advertisers' interests throughout the major media.[41]

Other critics of advertising drew on different discourses. Some, like John Kenneth Galbraith, aimed to update the Veblen–Chase tradition to fit the "unseemly economics of opulence" that characterized postwar society. Galbraith and other managerial liberals censured advertisers' stimulation of demand for "tobacco, liquor, chocolates, automobiles, and soap in a land which is already suffering from nicotine poisoning and alcoholism, which is nutritionally gorged with sugar, which is filling its hospitals, and cemeteries with those who have been maimed or murdered on highways, and which is dangerously neurotic about normal body odors." In their hor-ror of excess and display, as well as their attraction to rational planning, Galbraith and similar critics preserved some of the puritanical qualities of the Veblen–Chase critique. But they also kept its egalitarian edge. Assault-ing a consumer culture that countenanced private affluence amid public squalor, they observed that 60 percent of the American public lacked the discretionary income to participate in the "galloping consumption" pro-moted by national advertisers as the new American Way of Life. But like their mentors before them, critics in the Veblen–Chase tradition were remembered less for their egalitarian critique of the limits of consumer culture than for their assault on the bloated excess induced by reckless prosperity.[42]

The alleged author of that excess, national advertising, lumbered into the 1960s beset by criticism and self-doubt. Much of the creative fire had gone out of the business in the 1950s; the dominant mode of television commercial was dependent on the clanking, formulaic invocation of the Unique Selling Proposition. The quest for the USP, identified by the influ-ential executive Rosser Reeves as the key to all successful advertising, led to a return invasion of pseudoscientists in lab coats, preaching the merits of Gardol, Dynalube, or some other secret formula that supposedly distin-guished the product in question from all its competitors.[43] For many Americans, the corporate advertising business was becoming the chief symptom (if not the major cause) of a sick consumer culture which had contained chaotic impulses and spread middle-class prosperity, but at the price of chronic nervousness.

Yet even in the 1950s, in the margins of the dominant culture, stirrings of a carnivalesque revival could be detected. The children who were nam-ing Lassie's puppies and dragging their parents to the TV store so they could get a Sylvania Space Ranger kit were also reading *Mad* magazine, founded in 1952. *Mad* was (and is) a satirical publication dedicated to sub-verting pomposity and fraud wherever it could be found. Much could be found in the advertising of the 1950s. *Mad*'s founders were mostly prod-ucts of the New York Jewish subculture; they preserved its edge of manic comedy while they skewered the (still largely WASP) world of advertising at every opportunity. *Mad* spoke directly to the generation coming of age in the postwar suburbs. It fixed in many minds (especially young male minds) a feeling for the rage and aggression behind the bland surfaces of suburban normality. It linked the world of advertising not with fun but with anxiety. *Mad*'s "Madison Avenue Primer" (1957) began:

See the man.
He does advertising work.
He is called an "ad-man."
See his funny tight suit.
See his funny haircut.
Hear his funny stomach turn.
Churn, churn, churn.
The ad-man has a funny ulcer.
Most ad-men have funny ulcers.
But then, some ad-men are lucky.
They do not have funny ulcers.
They have funny high blood pressure.[44]

More influential than this satire of the business were *Mad*'s parodies of the advertisements themselves: Melvin Furd, whose teeth have all been knocked out in a fight, endorsing Crust Gumpaste, which coats the gums with "a hard, white enamel finish"; Betty Furness being crushed beneath a Westinghouse refrigerator door that opens from both sides at once (figure 8.3).[45] In the end, the most effective response to the relentless crusade for comfort was scabrous humor, which exposed the foolish pretensions of

THERE IS A GREAT DEAL OF CONFUSION about what is progress. I think one of the fine examples of the difference between "Night People" and "Day People" can be observed when they both watch Betty Furness do a commercial for Westinghouse. You know the one where she says "Another new miracle has been wrought! Mankind once again progresses! The new Westinghouse refrigerator for 1957 opens from *both sides!*" Well, a "Day People" sitting there says,

"By George, we really *are* getting ahead!" And he feels great. He can see Mankind taking another significant step up that great pyramid of civilization. But a "Night People" watching this thing can't quite figure out what's the advantage of a refrigerator which opens from both sides. All he wants to know is, "Does it keep the stuff cold?"

He's not quite sure there's been any great mark of progress, while there's still wars and stuff going on!

FIGURE 8.3

"The Night People vs. 'Creeping Meatballism'": writer, Jean Shepherd; artist, Wally Wood. *Mad* magazine, No. 32, April 1957. © *E. C. Publications, Inc., 1957, 1985. Used with permission of* Mad *magazine.*

established authority and buried its representatives beneath the weight of their own technology. The stage was being set for the return of repressed impulses.

During the 1960s, in response to the Vietnam War, subversive theatricality resurfaced as political protest and cultural critique. It is possible to see both the antiwar movement and the broader ferment of the counterculture as (in part) reorchestrations of Carnival themes: the overturning of conventional hierarchies of authority and standards of physical attractiveness, the flagrant celebration of the body's lower regions, the revolt against dualism embedded in the turn toward mystical experience, the revival of spontaneous outdoor performance and ritual pageantry—what critics like Robert Brustein called "revolution as theater."[46] As in all carnivalesque performances, there was much mindless excess. But there was also a challenge to managerial values, a rejection of "the system" that recognized how easily conventional critiques could participate in the common professional ethos of efficient productivity, losing ethical force in the process.

Managerial elites met the countercultural challenge with a familiar strategy. By 1970, opinion pollsters had begun to construct a statistical model of belief that seemed to counteract countercultural protest: a "Silent Majority" of respectable Americans, unrepentant beneficiaries of consumer culture whose "silence" was now construed as civic virtue. Whether these Americans actually constituted a majority was open to question.[47]

In any case, the matter was soon moot. Within a few years, as American corporations went multinational and began to export more and more jobs overseas, the economic basis of consumer culture began to erode. Prosperity had never been equally distributed, but it had been real for a sizable portion of the population; indeed, by the 1960s even "the Negro market" was being courted by corporate advertisers. But by the mid-1970s, the dynamic equilibrium between production and consumption began to look like the product of a particular historical moment, when the United States economy could exist in isolation from and domination over other world markets. Now the rest of the world population was beginning to stir. There were problems more pressing to worry about than the specter of mind manipulation.

PART III

Art, Truth, and Humbug:

The Search for Form and
Meaning in a
Commodity Civilization

CHAPTER 9

The Problem of Commercial Art in a Protestant Culture

DURING recent years, in certain circles, the surest way to silence a would-be critic of advertising has been to cite its artistic achievements. Whatever we may think of the products or the sponsors, this argument runs, we have to admit that those creative types in the agencies are deucedly clever, sometimes even brilliant. The only influence—far from sinister—they have exercised has been to enliven our cultural atmosphere with the staccato visual and verbal rhythms of the commercial vernacular.

This is true and false. The more systematically advertising was assimilated to managerial purposes, the more thoroughly integrated into carefully organized marketing campaigns designed to offend as few people as possible, the less it resembled vernacular idioms and the more it took on the qualities of a predictable, "official" art form. Yet to lose touch with the carnivalesque traditions of the commercial vernacular was to risk ascent into dignified, irrelevant monotony. The rise of art in advertising was in part an effort to keep the specter of boredom at bay.

That effort has been at least fitfully successful. Since the late nineteenth century, advertising has given people who like to write, draw, or shoot film the opportunity to get paid regularly (maybe even well) for it. The industry has attracted many extraordinarily talented people. These artists and writers have served, in a sense, as emissaries between social universes: the agency–client world and the wider population; art and big business; museum and commercial culture. They have worked various boundaries, sometimes creatively reconnecting aesthetics and everyday life, more often conforming out of necessity to the constraints of agency organization. Whatever their accomplishments, they deserve more than a passing glance: their experiences illuminate enduring conflicts and dilemmas in the history of advertising and American culture.

The story of the artist in advertising is part of the larger story of the artist in American society. Debates over literary and visual technique in advertising were more than a matter of merchandising strategy; they involved issues that had been debated for centuries: fundamental moral commitments, assumptions about the nature of reality. Questions of taste, apparently superficial, were charged with ontological significance—at least for those educated Americans who publicly discussed the relations of art and society. The intensity of their concern reflected ingrained habits of mind in a culture still dominated by Protestant distrust of graven images.[1]

Most Western traditions of art, classical or Christian, have connected surfaces and depths in a common core of meaning; indeed, the use of objects to bear symbolic meaning has been a virtually universal practice throughout human culture. Yet certain Christian beliefs have fostered periodical puritanical critiques of materialism as moral corruption; the Calvinist and Pietist movements of early modern Protestantism gave those beliefs particular theological and emotional force. Iconoclastic reformers distanced spirit from matter by desanctifying material objects, seeking meaning in depths of inward spiritual experience, distrusting all "mere forms" of outward observance. In few places was this iconoclasm fiercer than in the English settlements along the Atlantic coast of North America; it accounted for the supreme anomaly of early American cultural development, succinctly summarized by Neil Harris: "Before Americans made pictures, they used words."[2]

Even after they began to make pictures, many among the Protestant majority of Americans continued to distrust visual display. The puritanical tendency to prefer depths to surfaces survived in secular idioms and shaped Americans' perception of a novel situation: the emergence of art into the marketplace, the development of graven images as mass-produced commodities. Two forms of potential duplicity, art and commerce, were merged; both were arenas where sinister motives could be concealed and misleading appearances created, through artifice.[3]

But both realms also offered new opportunities for goods to be used to create meanings. Indeed, the multiplication of commercial goods and images in the mid–nineteenth century posed the possibility that surfaces and depths might be reconnected in reanimated commodities, that the humblest household objects might acquire a symbolic significance. No doubt objects were sometimes transfigured in that way, particularly the proliferating icons of the domestic sphere—the photograph albums, chromolithographs, and ceramic figurines that sometimes might acquire an almost sacramental quality in the Victorian religion of the hearth. The possibility of reanimating everyday life suggested an escape from stale contradictions.[4]

Still, within much of the dominant discourse of the educated classes the centrifugal spread of commercial objets d'art provoked a reassertion of familiar dualisms—deep meanings vs. superficial appearances, art vs. advertising—whether in a moralistic, aesthetic, or scientific idiom. The contrast between authenticity and artifice has persisted down to the present. It shapes the conflict between the modernist fascination with depths and the postmodern celebration of surfaces, as well as the constant media chatter counterposing "image and reality"; it has had an unfortunate impact on cultural debate. Dualism has inhibited the free play of ideas by implying the existence of only two alternatives: to relax our critical sensibilities in a warm bath of floating signifiers, embracing the emancipatory potential of commodity civilization; or to base our critique in an attitude of renunciation, devaluing the here and now of immediate sensuous experience.

The spread of advertising created an arena where artists and writers could probe beyond this conventional divide. A few moved in new directions, combining truth-telling and aesthetic playfulness in commercial designs. But their explorations were constrained by the utilitarian imperatives of agency work. Their struggles raised fundamental questions about the artistic enterprise in American society, questions still debated in our own time. To begin examining the tangled relations between art and commerce, we must return to the days of P. T. Barnum.

AESTHETICS AND EVERYDAY LIFE: FROM BARNUM TO WILDE

By the 1840s and 1850s, romantic notions of the artist had spread among the literate population. Emersonian sentiments had liberated artists from European foppery, only to ensnare them in a contradictory American mission. The artist was to engage the palpable actualities of everyday life—"the meal in the firkin; the milk in the pan; the ballad in the street; the news of the boat; the glance of the eye; the form and gait of the body," in

Emerson's litany—yet these were merely appearances to be penetrated en route to a profounder Reality. Emerson's idealist metaphysics, derived from Coleridge, dictated that common things were valuable only as entryways into the universal truth of Reason; on the everyday level, they represented merely the local knowledge of Understanding.[5]

The difficulty of securing democratic patronage reinforced disdain for common existence. Under the Emersonian aegis, the historian Joseph Ellis observes, "artists and writers began to conceive of themselves as refugees from the American mainstream, the specially endowed inhabitants of a transcendent region sealed off from the hurly-burly of the marketplace, the banality of popular opinion, and the grime of industrialized society."[6] Part of a broader pattern of compartmentalization that accompanied the rise of an urban market society, the notion of culture as a "transcendent region" developed symbiotically with Victorian gender ideology. Under the new, more rigidly formulated doctrine of separate spheres, the appreciation (though not the "serious" production) of aesthetic form was assigned to the feminine round of life. The aesthetic realm, like the domestic sphere, was implicitly cut off from the world of masculine strife.

The need to create a discrete world called "fine art" was aroused and reinforced by moralists' fears that art and commerce were becoming indistinguishable. As art was transformed from a luxury into an ordinary marketable commodity, it acquired all the commodity's capacity to excite desire and embody deceit. The chaotic expansion of trade during the 1840s and 1850s, when peddlers brought the market to the countryside, intensified the tendency to define art as deception. The artist could be not only an Emersonian visionary, but also a confidence man.

There was some historical warrant for this assumption. Limners and portraitists were, like peddlers, among the commercial itinerants who scurried across the Alleghenies to the great interior. Popular literature linked peddlers and artists, conflating or contrasting them depending on the author's didactic intent. In a *Godey's Lady's Book* sketch of 1840, "the travelling artist" is a buffoon posing as a portraitist, who takes in the protagonist Cecelia Johnstone because her head is filled with platitudes about the exalted life of art—until she sees the awful product of his labors. Both peddlers and portraitists, it was implied, preyed on isolated women who were eager for emblems of cultural refinement.[7]

Yet few would deny that such refinement might actually be attained. The trick was to authenticate it. Amid popular entertainments and poetical merchandising, aesthetes were increasingly concerned with distinguishing true art from ephemeral trash. In 1853, *Godey's* published "The Peddler": the poem compared a neglected poetic genius to a peddler whose superior wares were forced to compete with "tinsel goods," whose gold was called a "copper cheat," and who finally gave his things away when he found he could not sell them. Dependence on the market meant the poet was as vulnerable to popular caprice as was the luckless peddler. Moreover, in the atmosphere of "Universal Distrust" (Dickens' phrase in *American Notes*) generated by market exchange, fears of misrepresentation bedeviled artistic as well as monetary transactions. Authentic expression could be mistaken for counterfeit goods.[8]

The tensions between art and humbug formed revealing patterns in the life of Phineas Taylor Barnum (1810–1891), whose name became a synonym for charlatanry but who also won respect as an impresario of culture. Barnum was born in Bethel, Connecticut, amid the rural and small-town culture that constituted the peddler's major market. Confidence games were a daily fact of life, conniving contests between shopkeepers and customers or between peddlers and townsfolk. Barnum's arrival in New York in 1834 altered the scale and intensity but not the rules of the game. Recalling his early search for business opportunities, Barnum wrote: "When I had wended my way up flights of dark, rickety, greasy stairs, and through sombre, narrow passages, I would find that my fortune depended firstly upon my advancing a certain sum of money, from three dollars to five hundred as the case might be; and secondly, uopn my success in peddling a newly-discovered patent life pill, an ingenious mouse-trap, or something of the sort." Finding nothing in the mercantile line, Barnum embarked on his career as an itinerant showman, exhibiting the likes of Joice Heth, an ancient black woman who claimed to be the 161-year-old nurse of George Washington ("I raised 'im, I raised 'im"), and gathering a touring troupe of musicians, magicians, and dancers. After seven years on the road, Barnum had been threatened with loaded pistols half a dozen times and was nearly destitute; deciding the life of a traveling entertainer was not for him, he determined to purchase Scudder's Museum of "relics and rare curiosities" at Tenth and Broadway in Manhattan. He succeeded by winning the confidence of the museum building's owner, who extended him credit, and by publicly discrediting the rival buyers for issuing worthless stock. At thirty-one, he became owner of the American Museum, the institution that would acquaint its customers with the Fejee Mermaid and the Wooly Horse, and would for decades be associated with the name of Barnum.[9]

During the antebellum era, museums mixed entertainment and edifi-cation; the line was not easy to draw. Collections were such, according to the British traveler Frederick Marryat,

> as would be made by schoolboys and schoolgirls, not those of erudite professors and scientific men. Side by side with the most interesting and valuable specimens, such as the fossil mammoth &c., you have the greatest puerilities and absurdities in the world—such as a cherrystone formed into a basket, a fragment of the boiler of the *Moselle* steamer [which exploded in 1835], and Heaven knows what else besides.

Barnum was one of those schoolboys, an especially shrewd one. He and other showmen merged art and humbug, encouraging the notion that museums were places where one went to be entertained by clever decep-tions. In his autobiography, Barnum told how the superintendent of the Hague museum, unaware of Barnum's identity when the showman visited there in 1855, had disapprovingly mentioned the Fejee Mermaid hoax. Then he took Barnum aside and, sotto voce, tried to sell him some "pre-cious specimens of art" from a recently deceased gentleman's estate at a very low price. When the superintendent then turned to his memorandum book to reveal an obviously fabricated list of "distinguished Americans" who had bought some of the paintings, Barnum gave his card to the man, who stammered an apology for his earlier criticism of Barnum's duplicity. Barnum was bemused by this combination of gentility and hypocrisy. "And how many very worthy persons there are, like the superintendent of the Hague Museum, who have been terribly shocked at the story of the Fejee Mermaid and the Wooly Horse!" The moral of the story, for Barnum, was that the world is full of humbug respectable folk practice unawares.[10]

Yet Barnum also yearned increasingly for respectability. By the 1860s, he systematically sought rare species, donated specimens to Harvard and the Smithsonian, and in general approximated the scholarly, pedagogical ideals embodied by early museum builders like Charles Willson Peale of Philadelphia. Humbug could be redeemed by scientific truth, and by strict personal morality. In his autobiography, Barnum made much of his capaci-ties for self-control, not only his teetotalism (a practice he embraced in middle age) but also his absolute calm, even on receiving the news of the museum's burning in 1865. Despite his puckish poses, he wanted no one to think of him as a mere carnival trickster, tossing offal to the groundlings. His successful promotion of the Swedish soprano Jenny Lind won him enormous approbation among the Victorian middle classes, who felt he had helped to claim opera for Northern European Protestants.[11]

Still, Barnum felt he had to justify his puffery to suspicious plain-speakers. Recalling the museum's heyday in his autobiography, he wrote:

> It was the world's way then, as it is now, to excite the community with flaming posters, promising almost everything for next to nothing. I confess that I took no pains to set my enterprising citizens a better example. I fell in with the world's way; and if my "puffing" was more persistent, my advertising more audacious, my posters more glaring, my pictures more exaggerated . . . than they would have been under the management of my neighbors, it was not because I had less scruple than they, but more energy, far more ingenuity, and a better foundation for such promises. In all this, if I cannot be justified, I at least find palliation in the fact that I presented a wilderness of wonderful, instructive, and amusing realities of such evident and marked merit that I have yet to learn of a single instance where a visitor went away from the museum complaining that he had been defrauded of his money.

This was written in 1869, as Barnum was beginning to move toward the outlook that colored his final decades as circus impresario: he sought self-vindication as a purveyor of benign entertainment to a childlike audience. This strategy relaxed the tension between authenticity and artifice, justifying exaggerated claims as a sop to popular taste. As Barnum said, "The public appears disposed to be amused, even when they are conscious of being deceived."[12] Impatient with literalist demands for plain speech, Barnum nevertheless claimed to be dealing in "wonderful, instructive, and amusing realities." Conflict between appearances and realities dissolved in the mix of titillation and uplift that came to constitute Barnum's mature entertainment style—a mix that would also characterize much of twentieth-century advertising and mass culture.

Barnum's fellow New Yorker Walt Whitman posed a more overt challenge to antimaterialist dualism. In many ways, he was the laureate of commodity civilization, the poet of proliferating things. He took Emerson's democratic admonitions more seriously than any of his contemporaries; as the critic Miles Orvell observes, Whitman's never-ending, infinitely expandable poem *Leaves of Grass*, stuffed with multifarious detail, was modeled on the most popular cultural forms of the age: the daguerrotype gallery, the panorama, and the exhibit hall. Why should ordinary industrial or household objects be denied their poetic possibilities? he asked. Insisting on the poetry of the mundane, Whitman developed an aesthetic of everyday life that embraced the kitchen as well as the machine-shop floor. In feminine as well as masculine spheres, commonplace things could be endowed with enduring cultural worth. Indeed, the symbolic possibilities of the ordinary were nowhere more apparent than in the domestic interior. Bibelots were mass-produced into bric-a-brac, the Japanese fans, ceramic collies, and other useful or ornamental gimcracks we seldom seem able to see except through the eyes of their modernist detractors. Bric-a-brac filled urban interiors; it even found its way into remote little houses on the prairie. Laura Ingalls Wilder recalled that on the mantel of every homestead the family started during the 1860s and 1870s, her mother placed the same ceramic figurine, a lady clad in the finery of the ancien régime; it seemed an emblem of familial continuity amid incessant mobility. Whitman celebrated the material world in a fraternal rather than a familial idiom, materializing the male camaraderie of the machine shop in lists of industrial artifacts, exalting vulgar stuff as the connective tissue of democracy. Yet unlike William Morris, another egalitarian aesthete of everyday life, Whitman neglected to consider the constraints on the artist in an increasingly organized market society.[13]

Whitman's invocation of the Muse "installed amid the kitchen ware" coincided with the emergence of poetical merchandising techniques on both sides of the Atlantic. When George Packwood, the British razor-strop manufacturer, was asked who put the lilt in his advertisements, he replied, "La, sir, we keeps a poet!" If everyday life was to be made aesthetic, and commerce pervaded everyday life, then art would have to become commercial and razor strops (or at least the advertisements for them) artistic. Yet Whitman could never have been Packwood's kept poet. He was never an uncritical celebrant of commercial culture, and in *Democratic Vistas* became its bitter critic. He remained troubled by "the terrible doubt of appearances," the solipsistic anxiety that seemed to lie at the core of market society, as well as by the recurrent hypocrisies of social and economic life. But he periodically put those doubts to rest with catalogs of commodities and dreams of cosmic fraternity.[14]

For many of Whitman's contemporaries among the Protestant middle and upper classes, those dreams were less appealing. Confronted with a mélange of objets d'art and commodities, they hesitated, torn between enthusiasm for the apparent democratization of taste, and faith in fine art as a refuge from confusion. The increasing importance of a separatist notion of fine art became clear in the debate over the cultural significance of chromolithography. Amid multiplying commercial images, the boundaries between art and commerce remained difficult to draw. By the post–Civil War decades, chromolithographic reproductions of conventionally defined masterpieces were proliferating, produced by the same firms that cranked out merchandising brochures for patent medicines. In many homes, advertisements became the chief means of brightening a dreary visual environment. The late-nineteenth-century illustrator Joseph Pennell recalled "the gorgeous, or rather gaudy Barnum and [Adam] Forepaugh [circus] posters, in which for a period Americans found most of their art." Devotees of the arts were having difficulty distinguishing between the gorgeous and the merely gaudy. Mark Twain's Connecticut Yankee celebrated the chromos in his Hartford parlor as a democratic alternative to medieval hierarchies of taste, but the Yankee became a deeply problematic figure— a violent, bragging fool—and elsewhere Twain himself defended the chromo primarily for its capacity to uplift the taste of the masses. From this view, the chromo could cross the border between commodity and objet d'art, serve pedagogical purposes, and still fall short of fine art. Yet Twain's attachment to a separatist notion of high culture could not conceal the fundamental drift in the wider culture: standards of artistic authenticity—and of artistic excellence—were growing vaguer amid the emergence of mass media and the broadening of an audience for commercially reproduced images.[15]

This was disturbing to many middle- and upper-class Americans, especially given their tendency to invest art with profound emotional significance. Protestant traditions encouraged Americans to exclude sensuous delight from the category of fine art, to define it as a blend of realistic representation and noble sentiments. This version of bourgeois realism was rooted in the epistemological and ethical needs of an anxious art audience. Throughout the second half of the nineteenth century, John Ruskin's formula of "truth to nature" remained the chief criterion of artistic value. The rendering of a familiar "landscape of fact" in painting and literature embodied the assumption that art was transparent rather than performative; the occasional tincture of didacticism reminded everyone of art's agency in moral elevation. For many devotees of the real, the mingling of art and commerce revived old impulses to connect aestheticism and deceit. In a commodity civilization, moralists feared, the man of artistic genius might be merely an especially acute manipulator of dazzling surfaces. Under such circumstances, the Nation's editor E. L. Godkin warned in 1874, the very notion of culture could be trivialized into "chromo-civilization," reduced to a superficial gloss that one "picked up" by assembling the appropriate status markers.[16]

The idea that an aesthetic life could be lived as a masquerade mocked the stabilizing faith behind the doctrines of bourgeois realism: the belief in social transparency and unproblematic communication. The bipolarity of surfaces and depths continued to frame late-nineteenth-century aesthetic thought. The aesthetic poseur presented a fundamental (but unacknowledged) challenge to the bourgeois worldview by playing out the corrosive impact of market exchange on cultural meaning.

The most prominent poseur was Oscar Wilde (1854–1900). Wilde was a haunting presence. He upset familiar boundaries and epistemological conventions; he dramatized publicly what people sensed privately about the chaotic circulation of meanings in market society. He was a Barnum who disdained Victorian idioms of control, a Barnum set free.

The mass production of artifacts and images allowed Everyman to be his own "Wilde aesthete," without questioning the utilitarian organization of society or probing the philosophical issues raised by Wilde's critique of mimetic pieties. Like Nietzsche, Wilde struggled to articulate a worldview that broke down conventional antitheses by acknowledging the truth of masks, the seriousness of play, the reality of fantasy. But most Wildean poseurs overlooked these questions. In aestheticism, they found opportunities for constructing and reconstructing a self through purchase and display, as they sought to satisfy the imperious need for ever-new sensations.[17]

The rise of national advertising enhanced those opportunities. As technological advance bred standardization, and makers of fundamentally similar products competed for a burgeoning consumer market, the orchestration of surface effects became a major industry. Corporations hired ad agencies to surround mass-produced goods with an aura of uniqueness, to show a herd of consumers how they could create a sense of individuality by buying things that were essentially the same.

An army of writers and artists was needed for the task. There were unprecedented opportunities for creative people to make a comfortable living by plying their craft. At last, it seemed, writers and artists might escape the withered hand of want—if they were willing to abandon romantic pretensions to autonomy and adjust their aspirations to the needs of the organization.

Yet neither artists nor business executives acknowledged the affinities between market exchange and aesthetic display. Artists clung to the notion that they occupied a distinct, higher sphere. Thomas Anshutz's *The Ironworkers' Noontime* (1881) epitomized the mix of realism and ennoblement that late-nineteenth-century Americans sought in art. When Harley Procter, the Cincinnati soap magnate, saw the painting reproduced in *Harper's*, he recognized its commercial possibilities. *The Ironworkers' Noontime* departed from older mythic images; it represented the ironworker as human being rather than Vulcan-at-the-forge—as an embodiment of that healthy manliness that advertisers like Procter were trying to capture in commercial images. When Procter modeled an advertisement on it, Anshutz was outraged; what made the Procter & Gamble advertisement objectionable to him was not only the unacknowledged debt to his work but also the subordination of his noble aims to commercial purposes. Yet most late-nineteenth-century Americans would know *The Ironworkers' Noontime* only in its Procter & Gamble version. Anshutz retreated to portraiture, a safer bastion of fine-art tradition.[18]

While artists maintained a separatist notion of artistic autonomy, entrepreneurs clung to plain speech. What the historian Thomas Haskell has called an "ethic of promisekeeping" had long been needed to stabilize the epistemological sorceries of the marketplace. The developing web of credit, whatever its actual consequences in furthering chaotic development, was rooted in the fiction of universal trust. The official aspirations of American business, whatever its actual practice, were oriented toward plain dealing. Wilde traced business philistinism in America to the national mythology of truth-telling. "The crude commercialism of America, its materialising spirit, its indifference to the poetical side of things, and its lack of imagination . . . are entirely due to that country having adopted for its national hero a man who, according to his own confession, was incapable of telling a lie," he wrote. Early advertising agents genuflected at this shrine of truth as they struggled to regularize relations between advertisers and publishers. George Rowell, for example, who founded the trade journal *Printers' Ink* (see chapter 2), sought to impose the ethic of promisekeeping on publishers by providing an accurate account of newspapers' circulation figures to suspicious advertisers in search of effective media. Only gradually and reluctantly did advertising spokesmen embrace their role in marketing surface effects; for decades they clung to a rhetoric of sincerity. Artists and businessmen alike sustained an ethos of authenticity amid artifice.[19]

After the turn of the century, advertising artists tended increasingly to eschew the exotic and the flagrantly fantastic. Instead, they duplicated scenes from everyday life and bathed the presentation in sentiment, following the lead of popular academic realists like Edwin Landseer and Rosa Bonheur. Northrop Frye has given this scrubbed social vision the label "stupid realism." It is, he writes, "a kind of sentimental idealism, an attempt to present a conventionally attractive or impressive appearance as an actual or attainable reality." This strategy, the sociologist Michael Schudson observes, has characterized much official art of the past century—not only the socialist realism created by Soviet party functionaries but also the "capitalist realism" embodied in American advertising.[20]

Yet even as the compromise of capitalist realism seemed successfully to evade the conflict between authenticity and artifice, tension between the two poles was building. On the one hand, the fin de siècle saw a new and more rigorous search for dark truth beneath the veil of appearances—the search pioneered by Freud and Frazer, Conrad and Lawrence. On the other hand, the play of glittering surfaces seemed to accelerate beyond control, with the multiplication of commercial images, the emergence of a celebrity culture, the spread of retail pageantry, and the arrival of strange new immigrants from carnivalesque cultural traditions. Notions of artistic genius reflected this sharpening conflict between surfaces and depths. The artist could be a brooding seeker of authenticity or a dapper devotee of artifice.

REAL LIFE AND SENSUOUS SPECTACLE:
THE REFASHIONING OF GENIUS

By the end of the nineteenth century, dissatisfaction with both Victorian sentimentality and romantic exoticism led many writers and artists toward a conviction that realist writing and painting were not realistic enough, not sufficiently alive to the palpitating actualities of wilderness and urban slum. This was the rationale for the novels of Frank Norris and Jack London and for the paintings of the Ashcan School; despite their apparent novelty, they were rooted in a long tradition of demands that art be "true to nature." But the seekers of dark truth redefined nature as something raw and disturbing.

In spite of their delight in physical sensation, devotees of this vitalist cult of experience were at odds with the modern corporation's need for the systematic manipulation of surface effects. What was particularly distressing, for a writer or artist fired with vitalist longings, was the air of inauthenticity that hung about the finished advertisement. Pushed and pulled by the conflicting needs of the agency staff and the client, "real life" in copy could become simply stupid realism.

Yet even as vitalists urged a probing of the depths, the traffic in surfaces soared. The rise of the factory system meant that not only more goods but more images of goods were available to greater numbers of people. On both sides of the Atlantic, perceptive observers from Hippolyte Taine (1855) to Henry James (1907) noted the centrality of spectacle in modern urban society. The amusement parks at Coney Island, or the three rings of Barnum & Bailey's circus, were only the most visible examples of novel, sensational entertainments attracting hordes of people. The new commercialized forms of leisure tended to be brief bouts of relief from industrial routine, reinforcing rather than undermining the hierarchies of the developing managerial order.[21]

Yet the new cultural forms raised issues more complex than the breakdown of social control or the vulgarization of taste. The transformation of selling into poetical merchandising eroded the boundaries that had been carefully erected by Victorian moralists: between culture and commerce, truth and illusion, the simple private self and the public world of artifice. Cheap magazines and newspapers, dependent on advertisements rather than subscriptions for their main source of revenue, intensified "the itch for publicity," multiplying words and images, transforming modern society into a "servants' hall" filled with "idle chatter"—or so a *Nation* editor named Rollo Ogden claimed in 1893.

> Privacy is rapidly becoming one of the lost arts. A man who professes to wish to be by himself, to refuse to take the public into his confidence as to all his thoughts and plans, social, political, literary, and religious, is set down as an obstinate curmudgeon, or a semi-lunatic, or else as a peculiarly crafty fellow who makes a show of reserve only to provoke greater interest in the clean breast of all his affairs which he proposes to make.[22]

The triumph of pseudo-intimacy and self-promotion had direct implications for culture. "It is actually no longer considered indecent for a writer to puff his own works in advance of publication," Ogden complained, or even to indulge in "shocking indiscretions and immodesty" in pursuit of "the jingle of the guinea."[23] The manufacture of literary celebrity signaled a new notion of art and artists, a new willingness to treat the artistic or literary enterprise as a performance rather than a search for truth. Apart from Wilde and Nietzsche, few writers suggested that the artist should not necessarily have to choose between those two options. In the hall of mirrors that was the developing celebrity culture, even the most apparently spontaneous gesture could be bracketed with irony; a desire for privacy could be merely a crafty career move designed to whet the public appetite for confessional performance. Amid evanescent images, all that mattered was the frisson of the fleeting sensation.

In some ways, national advertising was the quintessential institution of the developing image empire. Through the mass circulation of visual aids to fantasy, it promoted perpetual, unfulfillable longings, and focused those longings on commodities. Yet national advertisers needed to do more than stimulate excitement; they needed to sell goods. Salesmanship counted more than art; utilitarian purposefulness crowded out the spirit of play. Ultimately neither sort of artist—neither the detached connoisseur of spectacle nor the vitalist devotee of "real life"—was at home in the modern advertising agency.

Few writers captured that discomfort more forcefully than Theodore Dreiser (1871–1945); few were as honest about the exhilaration as well as the suffocation possible in agency life. Unlike wealthy commentators on consumer culture such as Henry James and Edith Wharton (see chapter 12), Dreiser had to search constantly for a source of income. His lifelong obsession with money and material comfort was rooted in the wretched poverty of his boyhood in Terre Haute, Indiana, and other Midwestern towns. Like many other young artists and writers, tired of hunger and insecurity, he was willing to endure a loss of autonomy in exchange for a regular paycheck—willing even to enter the belly of the commercial beast, the advertising agency.

When he assumed the chief editorship at Butterick Publications in 1907, Dreiser had been gaping at the goods in the shop windows of consumer culture for some time. His older brother Paul had left home to join the medicine show troupe of the Lightning Liniment Company when Theodore was only seven, and went on to a brief but successful career in New York as a popular songwriter and Broadway dude. Periodically Paul would return to the Dreisers' bleak household, resplendent in silk hat and fur collar, bearing food and gifts and seeming, to Theodore, "like the sun, or a warm cheering fire." In Theodore's youthful imaginings, Paul became a powerful embodiment of a glimmering world elsewhere, a sexually charged cityscape of promenading swells, fashionable women, and lush interiors smelling faintly of perfume and perspiration. For years Theodore sought to penetrate that world, with only fitful satisfaction.[24]

The failure of *Sister Carrie* (1900) led Dreiser into poverty and suicidal depression, but with the timely intervention of Paul he stopped his skid. He managed to secure an editorial job on *Smith's* magazine and later *Broadway*, transforming moribund tabloids into lively examples of the new celebrity media. His reputation as a "magazine doctor" led to his position with Butterick. He was dismissed after less than three years for refusing to break off his pursuit of Thelma Cudlipp (Dreiser called her "Honeypot"), the eighteen-year-old daughter of an assistant editor. Even Dreiser (never a titan of self-awareness) appreciated the anomaly of a self-styled cultural radical supporting himself by managing the fortunes of some women's sewing magazines. He was moved to ponder the relations between art and commerce in *The "Genius"* (1915).[25]

This lumbering autobiographical novel was Dreiser's account of how a young artist, carrying nineteenth-century cultural baggage, fared in the corporate world of advertising and publishing that was emerging around the turn of the century.[26] Its protagonist, a painter called Eugene Witla, is among the most symptomatic characters in all of American literature. In some ways he is the very archetype of fin-de-siècle aestheticism, from his quivering lower lip to his soft cap and flowing collar; in others he is the quintessential vitalist visionary, the Ashcan painter exposing the palpitating raw nerves of the metropolis. Longing for intense emotional and sexual experience, he conducts a ponderous quest for authenticity; but he is also a bit of a confidence man, delighting in social performance and the play of appearances, obsessed by clothes, sensuous luxury, the delights that money can bring. In other words, he is very much like Dreiser himself.

As Eugene moves from studio to ad agency, the genius becomes a "genius." Ironic detachment, alienation from one's inner impulses, points the path to success. In the end, Eugene cannot become a man of mere hard, shining surfaces; he remains susceptible to titanic emotions that seem to signify "real life." He cannot abide either of the sites in Protestant culture—the workshop or the hearth—where surfaces and depths could be made to cohere, and commodities could signify connectedness. *The "Genius"* prefigured the dilemmas of creativity that would be aired in the advertising trade press in subsequent decades. The conflict between authenticity and artifice remained a live issue for artists in and out of advertising throughout the twentieth century.

Eugene Witla comes of age in Alexandria, Illinois, in the 1890s. His father is a sewing machine salesman who peddles a little insurance on the side. By the time Eugene is sixteen he senses "the smallness of his father's business, the ridiculousness of any such profession having any claim on him" (16). As Eugene works on the local paper, "the theory of advertising began to dawn on him." He is struck by the dullness of the local merchants' newspaper ads and wonders why the language can't be livelier and why the advertisers can't put some "little drawings" in them. "Eugene had seen and in a way studied the ads in the magazines. They seemed so much more fascinating to him" (29). He is the stereotypical teenager of Dreiser's fiction, yearning to escape from his hick hometown, envying the lords and ladies of the local social elite when they flounce by, "dressed in a luxury of clothing which was beyond his wildest dreams" (31). Like his creator, the lad lies brooding in his bunk, wondering "what was this thing, life?" Then he picks up a Saturday afternoon Chicago paper, the one with all the "human interest" features, and he is swept away. "The thought of car lines, crowds, trains, came to him with an almost yearning appeal," Dreiser wrote with characteristic woodenness. "All at once the magnet got him. It gripped his very soul, this wonder, this beauty, this life." He is off to Chicago on the four o'clock train (34).

The city awakens Eugene sexually and artistically. Instead of mooning over high school girls, he becomes an obsessive erotic conquistador. Struck by the poetry of factory sites and railroad yards, he begins to imagine the kinds of pictures he would like to draw: "only pen and ink, and that in great, rude splotches of black and white. That was the way. That was the way force was had." At length he has saved enough from two menial jobs to enroll in classes at the Art Institute; like the other students, he longs "to assume the character and habiliments of the artistic temperament as they were then supposed to be; to have a refined, semi-languourous, semi-indifferent manner; to live in a studio, to have a certain freedom in morals and temperament not accorded to the ordinary person—these were the great things to do and be" (48–49). This fin-de-siècle idyll is only briefly interrupted when Eugene returns home. "It was smaller, narrower than he had ever thought" (57), but at a party he meets the intriguing Miss Angela Blue, from Wisconsin—a flagrant re-creation of Dreiser's first wife, Sara White, from Missouri. Returning to Chicago, Eugene discovers his instructor "took art as a business man takes business"; the art teacher has no patience with pretenders, so his praise (when it comes) is all the more thrilling to Eugene (67). Before long, Eugene has developed a double aim: to go to New York to make a career for himself in art, selling his drawings to the magazines or getting a job on some newspaper; and to marry Angela. Despite this apparent firmness, "he was always at the breaking point over any romantic situation" (87). At the same time, he can only care for one of his conquests "as one cares for a girl in a play or a book" (130). He remains a compound of overwrought sentimentalist and detached aesthete.

In New York Eugene is overwhelmed by the glitter of wealth and his longings for it: "he came to the conclusion he was not living at all, but existing" (142). He falls in with a bohemian crowd in Waverly Place and dreams of having his own studio. His fantasy, a parody of fin-de-siècle fashion, "would cost in the neighborhood of two thousand dollars" (180). Unlike James or Wharton, Dreiser never forgets that it can cost a lot of money to surround oneself with an aesthetic atmosphere. Lacking trust funds or a country estate, Eugene must enter the corporate world of work to satisfy his aesthete's longings.

But first, having married Angela and brought her to New York, he tries to make his way in the galleries. The public is not ready for raw reality in its parlor. Critics applaud his work, but no one buys it. After a summer in Paris, he breaks down, exhausted and unable to work. For a time, he lounges about his apartment, sighing and trying to convince Angela that he still loves her after she discovers one of his infidelities. Finally he takes a job in upstate New York, as a day laborer for a railroad. "Day laborer! How fine, how original, how interesting," he thinks. The work is brutal, but Eugene is unbowed: "He did not look like a working man and could not be made to do so. His spirit was too high, his eye too flashing and incisive" (312). After some months he tires of the monotony and determines to "behave himself" in order to return to the world of white-collar respectability. Resurrecting some of his old contacts in the New York art world, he quickly moves from a newspaper job to a position as art director at the Summerfield advertising agency.

Eugene is drawn easily into advertising. He has always been fascinated by it. He is verbally as well as visually facile: years earlier, he had done some feature writing for a Chicago newspaper. "The charm of Eugene's writing was that while his mind was full of color and poetry he had logic and a desire for facts which gave what he wrote stability" (85). This was precisely the combination of qualities that the ad trade press claimed was needed in copy—just as it claimed a need for Eugene's capacity to combine quick surface effects with a vitalist version of realism. (*Printers' Ink* might have said a realism with "ginger.") Drawing on his own experiences in celebrity journalism, Dreiser gathered in Eugene the same talents the advertising world would have noticed.

In the career of the man who hires Eugene, Daniel C. Summerfield, Dreiser epitomized admen's view (and his own view) of recent American cultural history. The son of a lackadaisical, half-starved cotton farmer in Alabama, Summerfield had risen from rural backwardness to urban slickness by recognizing the aesthetic needs of the emergent corporate system. "He foresaw the drift toward artistic representation of saleable products, and decided to go into that side of it. He would start an agency which would render a service so complete and dramatic that anyone who could afford to use his service would make money." He implemented this ambition with ruthless efficiency. "The great office floor which he managed was a model of cleanliness, order—one might almost say beauty of a commercial sort, but it was the cleanliness, order, and beauty of a hard, polished, and well-oiled machine."

The trick was to find a place in this mechanism for art. Summerfield had nothing but scorn for artists. "Why, God damn it, they're like a lot of children." He bullied his art directors (Eugene's predecessors) shamelessly: "Jesus Christ; I could hire an ashman and get better results. Why God damn it, look at the drawing of the arm of that woman. Look at her ear. Whose [sic] going to take a thing like that? It's tame! It's punk! It's a joke! . . . You ought to know our advertisers won't stand for anything like that. Wake up! I'm paying you five thousand a year." The art director "was usually humble and tractable under the most galling circumstances. Where could he go and get five thousand a year for his services? How could he live at the rate he was living if he lost this place?" (392–96).

Those were the key questions faced by artists in advertising, at least by those who had risen to high positions. For the meagerly paid underlings, the carrots were less abundant but the sticks were just as evident. Their artistic productivity was absolutely subjected to the standards of bureaucratic rationality. "Their output was regulated by a tabulated record system which kept account of just how much they succeeded in accomplishing in a week, and how much it was worth to the concern." Summerfield's relentless drive, his "nagging and irritating insistence," had infected all the employees at the agency. "The result was a bear-garden, a den of prize-fighters, liars, cut-throats, and thieves in which every man was for himself openly and avowedly and the devil take the hindmost" (407, 409). Into this den walked Eugene.

But he was harder and tougher than his predecessors. He had "changed his style from the semi-artistic to the practical." And style was critical at the Summerfield Company. Summerfield disliked Eugene's silly soft hat but took to his self-assured banter, thinking the artist just might be the "genius" he needs to run his art department. "I like your looks," he says, and decides on the spot to hire the reformed *précieuse*. On being shown the office that would be his if he took the job, Eugene "could not help stiffening with pride a little as he looked at the room . . . where a large, highly polished oak desk was placed and where some of the Summerfield Advertising Company's art products were hung on the walls. There was a nice rug on the floor and some leather-backed chairs." It was not quite an aesthete's salon, but it was artifactual evidence of power. "Oh, what a splendid vision of empire was here before him." Eugene is put off by the "crassness" of the stenographers and canvassers—particularly one canvasser with a bright red tie and yellow shoes. "These people seemed to him somewhat raw and voracious, like fish. They had no refinement." The artists were more appealing: "men very much like himself, in poor health probably, or down on their luck and compelled to do this." The line between philistine business people and refined artists is easily drawn; it is a matter of taste, style, appearances. Eugene overcomes his aversion and decides to join the firm (403–406).

Within a few months he finds himself changing in appearance and attitude. "The soft hat had long since been discarded for a stiff derby. He looked more like a young merchant than an artist." He becomes hardened and embittered by the Hobbesian atmosphere in the office. Outside the art department the other employees view him as "a man who could not last long." They dislike him because he seems to be Summerfield's current favorite, and because of his distant air: "In spite of himself he could not take them all as seriously as he should" (413, 415). Amid the conflicting office factions, the idea of artistic autonomy becomes a joke.

> Departmental chiefs stormed his room daily, demanding this, that, and the other work immediately. Artists complained that they were not getting enough pay, the business manager railed because expenses were not kept low. . . . Eugene was soon accused of delaying work generally, of having incompetent men (which was true), of being slow, of being an artistic snob. He stood it all calmly because of his recent experience with poverty, but he was determined to fight ultimately. He was no longer, or at least not going to be, he thought, the ambling, cowardly, dreaming Witla he had been. He was going to stand up, and he did begin to (416).

There is a way out. Once Eugene takes artistic control, the ads of the Summerfield organization begin to command attention. The Kalvin Publishing Company of Philadelphia (modeled on Curtis, which published the *Saturday Evening Post* and *Ladies' Home Journal*) gets wind of Eugene's achievements, and hires him as the advertising manager of a new weekly. After only a couple of years in Philadelphia he returns to New York to assume charge of the editorial, art, and advertising departments of Hiram Colfax's United Magazines Corporation. At this point Eugene's assimilation into the corporate world seems complete. He has become an expert at the orchestration of surface effects, recommending to Colfax that he redecorate his offices so as to achieve "a look of prosperity," and seeking the same look in his own home but with a patina of aestheticism (452). Indeed, he is finally able to afford the aesthetic accoutrements he dreamed of as a young artist: the bleeding Christ, the heavy bronze candlesticks, the green-brown tapestries, even a leering bust of Nero. But he has given up all dreams of rendering his own idiosyncratic vision of "real life." As he tells an art dealer who begs him to start painting again: "Art is very lovely. I am satisfied to believe I am a great painter. Nevertheless, I made little out of it and since then I have learned how to live" (502). He has embraced the notion that "real life" is not a matter of gritty, intense experience but rather of accumulation and display; Angela believes him "a genius in every respect," but Dreiser seems to think he is little more than a professional beauty. Colfax looks him over "much as one might a blood horse or a pedigree dog" (467, 469). Eugene himself has mastered the art of social performance so well that (unlike the plainspoken Angela) he can assume a stance of witty self-assurance "whether he felt it or not" (470). He glories in the harmony of luxury and beauty that he has witnessed in the lives of the very, very rich. "Here was no sickness, no weariness apparently, no ill health or untoward circumstances. All the troubles, disorders, and imperfections of existence were here carefully swept aside and one saw only the niceness, the health and strength of being" (472). It is as if he has walked into one of his own advertisements.

The dream of harmony is shattered when Eugene yields to his longings for the eighteen-year-old Suzanne Dale. Telling himself that he is drawn to her because she has "the soul of an artist," he is reduced to an adoring blob of jelly in her presence. It is a last, self-destructive surge of romantic vitalism. In the end, her mother exposes the affair to Colfax and Eugene is fired—stripped of the things that have become the very basis of his identity. "He had lost this truly magnificent position, $25000 a year. Where would he get another like it? Who else—what other company could pay any such salary? How could he maintain the Riverside Drive apartment now, unless he married Suzanne? How could he have his automobile—his valet?" (647). It is a consumer tragedy.

The novel ends in melodrama. Eugene drifts into Christian Science, though he recoils from the tastelessness of its practitioners' parlors. "Didn't Divine Mind know any better than to present its representatives in such a guise as this?" he wonders (684). He ends contrite at the dying Angela's bedside, as she gives birth to their daughter. Assuming paternal responsibilities, Eugene returns to success as a studio artist, expressing "some of his feeling for life" in great panels that are displayed in banks and government offices. The marriage between art and commerce is at last successfully consummated, but the harmonious conclusion rings hollow (perhaps deliberately).

Eugene's rise in the corporate hierarchy requires him to abandon his romantic dreams of autonomous creativity, to embrace a new career in impression management. It is only when his business career is over that he returns to the notion that painting should be a form of authentic self-expression. The idea would be ludicrous in the scientifically managed corporate settings of advertising agencies and magazine publishers. Dreiser's novel suggests not that the new world of national advertising stifled art, but that it encouraged some forms of art and suppressed others. Certainly it reveals that the success of a young romantic aesthete depended on his ability to orchestrate artifice rather than pursue authenticity. Yet the advertisers' fascination with "human interest" and "real life" as emotional appeals meant that they would be reluctant to adopt a stance of ironic detachment. They would always preserve a large reservoir of sentimentality. The catch was that, for the copywriter as well for the artist, the capacity to simulate feeling became more important than the feeling itself.

The "Genius" unwittingly showed the winning combination of attributes that could lead the aspiring young writer or artist to success in advertising. Eugene Witla, like Theodore Dreiser, combined sentimental longings for "real life" with a fascination for clever and luxurious display. Early advertising agencies gradually came to similar formulations. By the 1890s there was a growing but inchoate impatience with the polarity between authenticity and artifice. Sensitive outsiders like William Dean Howells as well as writers in the advertising trade press began to realize that appearances—even fantastic appearances—were part of reality, and that part of their task was not merely telling the truth about a product but "making the truth sound true." This was not simply an intellectual exercise. The imperatives of pleasing the client and attracting the consumer also shaped rhetorical and iconographic conventions. Admakers faced the problem that contemporary advertisers call "clutter"—too many ads competing for a distracted public's attention. So they turned increasingly to humor, fantasy, and entertainment in order to stand out. But utilitarian literalists in the business still held the upper hand. Sniffing the degeneracy of Wilde and Aubrey Beardsley, they distrusted the "professional beauties" created by overly aesthetic copywriters and designers. The result was a compromise: the melding of product description with conventionally attractive imagery and "human interest" narrative—entertainment, yes, but of a scrubbed and sentimental kind. The compromise papered over fundamental issues, such as just where artists or writers fit into the agency, or whether they fit at all.[27]

TOWARD CAPITALIST REALISM:
ART IN ADVERTISING, 1890–1915

When advertising agencies began to form in the 1860s and 1870s, they had at their disposal the vast fund of images that were being generated by commercial chromolithographers. But there were obstacles to tapping it. The initial raison d'être of advertising agencies was their capacity to provide a liaison between manufacturers and newspapers or magazines; those publications were technically limited (especially with respect to color reproduction) and aesthetically conservative. Patent medicine firms, circus companies, and other businesses that contracted directly with lithographers could continue to turn out extravagant posters, pamphlets, almanacs, and calendars, but the agencies were necessarily copy-oriented. It was not coincidental that the longest-lived (1888–1967) and most influential trade journal was called *Printers' Ink*. During its early decades the agency field attracted many young men with experience in journalism, whose aspirations were literary as well as entrepreneurial.

By the 1890s their impact was apparent. Contributors in the trade press agreed that copywriters had adopted "that familiar style of expression which had already become fixed with reporters and even editorial writers on newspapers." Many were convinced that reporting was ideal training for copywriting. "The young adwriter should start out in journalism," an agency head advised in 1899, "not only because it will teach him to write but because it will teach him human nature." Journalism had appealing resonances for literary young admen who wished to demonstrate their engagement with the rough male world of work and avoid accusations of effeteness.[28]

Yet the parallel with journalism could not be pushed too far. In an advertisement, many trade press pundits claimed, facts alone were not enough: they must be presented "brightly, attractively, magnetically." And there must not be too many of them. "Don't tell too much," a contributor to *Fame* magazine warned in 1892. "Excite the imagination and pay due

attention to its humble and vulgar sister, curiosity." Embryonic notions
about the pace of modern life and the incapacity of "the many" to absorb
much information gave carte blanche to writers eager for sport with words.
Puns proliferated. So did jingles. "Within the past few years 'poetry' has
become a very substantial factor in the advertising world," the magazine
Art in Advertising announced in 1895.[29] While the quotation marks suggested a certain discomfort with claims to high art, in the late nineteenth
century the boundaries between elite and popular culture were still per-
meable enough for copywriters to quote Shakespeare or raid the rhythms
of acknowledged masterpieces. A classic of the genre was "Here, I Want
It!", a parody of Longfellow's *Hiawatha* published in a pamphlet for Montgomery Ward & Co. in 1895.

> *In the city of Chicago*
> *By Lake Michigan, the windy—*
> *Near the shore, where leap the wavelets,*
> *Stands a large, imposing structure.*
> *Stories nine and numbers seven—*
> *Seven buildings, altogether,*
> *And from roof down into basement,*
> *Merchandise to please the people.*[30]

Some copywriters were willing to claim that advertising was not merely
journalism but literature. As the copywriter Wolstan Dixey wrote in *Printers' Ink* in 1898, "Good advertising is based on the same principles as good
literature"; both were "personal, human, forceful, and honest"—composed
not merely of fine phrases but of eloquence. The latter distinction was difficult to maintain, as *Printers' Ink*'s chief obeisance to writing style in its
first decade was to publish the "bright sayings" of adsmiths—the "terse
and epigrammatic expressions" which became models of advertising language. The relationship between advertising and literature remained problematic for several reasons.[31]

Occasionally a writer in the trade press sought to explore the problem.
Will B. Wilder, writing in *Fame* in 1892, felt it necessary to tamp down his
fellow copywriters' poetic aspirations. "Is Advertising an Art?" he asked.
Not in any exalted sense, Wilder concluded, for

> these three reasons—that advertising is mercenary in aim and in
> means, that it is not above suspicion, and that it is somewhat opposed
> to the traditions of good breeding—. . . all reasons that will to some
> extent justify the refusal of the public to give it rank among the fine
> arts. . . . Let [the copywriter] then be content with his hire, and not

claim in addition that the world should cherish his name as that of a poet whose work it took without pay.[32]

The tension between fine-art aspirations and the actual conditions of agency work would remain a feature of life in advertising throughout the twentieth century.

Wilder's dismissal of artistic aspirations among copywriters rested on the assumption that fine art resided in a sphere beyond economics. But novelists who wrote for pay knew better. William Dean Howells was one, and he sensitively explored the parallels between literary art and advertising in 1896, when he reviewed Charles Austin Bates's book *Good Advertising* in *Harper's Weekly*. Howells imagined a conversation between himself and a "friend of mine who professes all the intimacy of a bad conscience with many of my thoughts and convictions," in which Howells himself says:

> "There are some kinds of advertisements that I read all the same without the slightest interest in the subject matter. Simply the beauty of the style attracts me."
>
> "I know. But does it ever move you to get what you don't want?"
>
> "Never; and I should be glad to know what Mr. Bates thinks of that sort of advertising—the literary, or dramatic, or humorous, or quaint?"
>
> "He doesn't contemn it quite. But I think he feels that it may have had its day."

Passing over the question of literary advertising's impracticality, Howells observes that

> the ad-smith seems to have caught the American business tone as perfectly as any of our novelists have caught the American social tone."
>
> "Yes," said my friend, "and he seems to have prospered as richly by it. You know some of those chaps make $15000 or $20000 by ad-smithing. They have put their art quite on a level with fiction pecuniarily."
>
> "Perhaps it *is* a branch of fiction."
>
> "No; they claim that it is pure fact. Mr. Bates discourages the slightest admixture of fable. The truth, clearly and simply expressed, is the best in an ad."
>
> "It is best in a wof, too. I am always saying that."
>
> "Wof?"
>
> "Well, work of fiction. It's another new word, like lunch or ad."[33]

Howells's imaginary conversation, by exploring the similarities and differences between advertising and fiction, captured many of the dilemmas facing copywriters. Their art, like the realistic novelist's, required a mix of imagination and accurate observation. But the aim of ad copy was strictly instrumental; it was meant to sell goods. If it failed to accomplish that task, its beauty was irrelevant. That was why, even while the "literary fellers" were having their say in the trade journals, many more businesslike contributors were complaining about the tendency of "longhairs" toward "oversmartness" in copy.[34] *Printers' Ink* presented an archetypal confrontation between a young copywriter and his boss, "a solid man of business," who rejects the copywriter's ad because "it's too pretty."

> "My son," said the Old Man, "you have made what I call a 'professional beauty' advertisement. You want your wife, when you get money enough to support one, to be an attractive, handsome woman, but at the same time you would hardly like to marry a professional beauty. You will want your son to grow up into a fine, handsome young fellow, but you don't want him to pose as a king of the dudes. Advertising is not a beauty show. Advertising is not always for the purpose of pleasing your critical friends and the 'experts'; it's the great public you are after and they don't give a continental whether you have been to college or not, what they want is facts; if they are reading your ad for amusement in all probability you don't want their trade."[35]

This was a constant refrain in the trade press, and it embodied the persistent distrust of aestheticism in bourgeois culture—the tendency to link aesthetic preoccupations with effeminate dudes and fashionable women of questionable virtue. The antidote to the "professional beauty" advertisement, for Bates as well as for this anonymous author, was the pursuit of "facts." As Oscar Wilde understood, American business culture was always ready to counteract the aesthetic ideal of useless play with the utilitarian value of mimesis.

But the issue was not settled so simply. As the advocates of imagination argued, it was not at all clear that "the great public" wanted merely "facts." And even if the advertisers were devoted to "the truth, simply and clearly expressed," they were not separating themselves from writers of fiction: Howells wryly observed that he and Bates were as one in their devotion to "pure fact"; the adsmith, if he followed Bates's advice, was in the camp of Howells's own version of realism. The question, for copywriters as well as novelists, was how prosaic reality had to be.

And here the advocates of imagination had an edge, on instrumentalist grounds. By the 1890s, even the trade press published complaints about the sheer number of advertisements littering the print landscape. "A paper full of display advertisements," Howells observed, "is like a crowd of people trying to make themselves heard by shouting, each at the top of his voice." And the din was growing louder every year. If advertising kept on increasing at its present rate, Howells said, "there will presently be no room in the world for things; it will be filled up with the advertisements of things." For Howells the proliferation of ads was "an image of our congested and delirious state of competition"; but for the advertiser it posed a more immediate problem: how to attract attention amid so much confusion.[36]

The preoccupation with appearances and the need to stand out amid commercial clutter combined to preserve a hospitable atmosphere for art in advertising. Factual accuracy was less important than making the truth sound true. Amid a cacophony of competing claims, the most convincing were often the quietest. Not truth but sincerity became the touchstone of copy merit. As early as 1901, trade press contributors were applauding "the sincere trend" in advertising—the attempt "to be earnest without being heavy." This turned the copywriter once more toward the staccato rhythms (short declarative sentences, one-sentence paragraphs) and (allegedly) conversational tone of popular journalism and away from the "vacuous verbosity" of the self-consciously literary style. "The chief reason why literary writers are poor ad writers," George Powell declared in *Advertising Writing Taught* (1903), "is because they have not learned to condense a long story and boil it down into crisp sentences." For decades after the turn of the century, the trade press preached the gospel of simple and direct.[37]

The aim of condensation was to achieve "such modest force that the modesty attracts irresistibly, while the force impels unconsciously." Subtlety of persuasion was the desideratum of style; sincerity was not a moral stance but a sales technique. As *Judicious Advertising* magazine observed in 1917, "Judicious understatement has at least three useful functions which may profitably be borne in mind. First, that it is a time-tried and effective literary device for securing emphasis; second, that it may be an excellent antidote to exaggeration and superlatives; and last, that it is readily adaptable to the uses of humor." Despite its veneer of sincerity, the movement toward understatement was little more than a codification of the laconic speech of the Yankee peddler—a tactic for employing indirect language to exercise subtler influence.[38]

Yet even before the turn of the century, it was becoming apparent, at least to some advertisers, that literary techniques were not enough to create effective copy. According to a *Printers' Ink* contributor in 1898, not words but pictures constituted "the quickest-acting medium for the transmission of one man's thought to another man's mind." Despite their orientation toward copy, by the 1890s agency heads were awakening to the importance of what they called "the picture habit" among the American people. Yet when they looked for examples of advertising art, they were satisfied with neither the existing stock of trade card imagery nor the "poster craze" inspired by Aubrey Beardsley and other European aesthetes. Neither vernacular exoticism nor avant-garde experimentalism would do.[39]

Beardsley came in for particular abuse. "Nothing but Nordau's degeneration theory will explain why a man who can draw well deliberately chooses to draw ill—nay, why he draws worse than anybody could ever draw before, and then calls upon the world to see that he has made a discovery in art, and founded a new school," complained one critic, who decried Beardsley's habit of merging the picture of a woman, say, with that of a serpent, a flamingo, and a fish. When American ads for certain upscale products began to display some of the same characteristics (figure 9.1), advertising theorists dismissed them as "irrelevant" at best. But toward the end of the 1890s, the trade press began to note a shift in the tide of taste. "There seems to be quite a let-up in the demand for the Beardsley style of weird and multicolored barbarities in the way of 'art,' " *Printers' Ink* reported in 1897. "Advertising posters that make the best and most lasting impression are generally those that are most true to nature and the furthest remove from the illustrated nightmare style of art." The need to locate an acceptable American advertising art led commentators to reaffirm the Ruskinian idea of "truth to nature," but with a new emphasis on technical facility and instrumentalist applications.[40]

At first grudgingly, then enthusiastically, most big agencies integrated illustrations into their copy plans—nearly always hedging them about with arguments for their utility. One such claim involved the influential cliché that pictures constituted a universal language. People "want to see with their own eyes," the trade journal *Profitable Advertising* insisted in 1906. "Illustration has forced the advertiser to be honest with the people." The idea that pictures could be an unproblematic window on reality was reassuring; the trick for the agency, one commentator noted, was to hire newspaper artists with some experience of the real world, not effete studio artists, to do the work. The disdain for studio artists also fed into the trade press preoccupation with practicality and expertise. The real need, one commentator argued in *Judicious Advertising* in 1906, was for "cooperation between copy and picture. The advertising manager must see to it that the picture helps familiarize the appearance of the goods to the pub-

FIGURE 9.1

An example of an irrelevant illustration from Harry Hollingsworth's book *Advertising and Selling*, 1913.

lic. . . . Here is where the very great need of *sound and able* cooperation between copywriter and illustrator comes in. If copy must be expert, then picture must be no less expert." Here as elsewhere in the culture of advertising, industry spokesmen invoked professional expertise within a cooperative web of interdependence, to stabilize the vagaries of the artistic imagination.[41]

Yet a strictly utilitarian approach was inadequate. The most intractable problem was not only the predominance of artistic preciosity but also the tendency for the reader's eyes to glaze over when confronting a mass of competing appeals for increasingly standardized products. As technological developments were incorporated into the manufacturer's merchandising plan, it became more and more difficult for him to differentiate his product from those of his competitors. In 1890, soda crackers in sealed packages were a novelty; ten years later dozens of such brands were available. The trick to setting one's product apart was to learn how to participate in what the advertising executive James Collins called "the economy of symbolism"—to surround the product with condensed clusters of words and images that gave it symbolic as well as utilitarian value. In a sense, the task involved reversing the process described by the critic Walter Benjamin in "The Work of Art in the Age of Mechanical Reproduction" (1935): restoring an aura of uniqueness to products that had become standardized into banality.[42]

For Benjamin, the aura had been religious, traceable to art's origins in the effort to express the inexpressible; for admakers, it was reducible to an attention-getting instrument. But particular tactics varied dramatically. Some of the earliest experiments in the economy of symbolism were surreal juxtapositions of dissimilar images, intended simply to stop the reader in her tracks. As early as the turn of the century, trade journals were praising surreal compositions. The McCormick Company's 1899 advertisement picturing a huge hand holding a map of most of North America, labeled "The Continent in Hand," was "ingenious and attractive" (figure 9.2). The Frank Presbrey agency's 1901 campaign for the North German Lloyd Steamship Company, showing "a colossal new twin-screw steamship . . . on keel, in front of the Equitable Life Building, in Broadway, her smokestacks far overtowering the buildings on either side," was acclaimed as one of "the best advertising ideas that have been used in the past five years."[43] But this sort of imagery was limited in its appeal. It dramatized the size and power of the company in question, but it was too similar to European poster work in striving for the striking image at the expense of the "human touch." And in an increasingly impersonal marketplace, advertisers were more and more preoccupied with casting a haze of pseudo-intimacy over the relations between producer and consumer.

That preoccupation shaped the dominant conventions of advertising art in the early twentieth century, pulling them toward capitalist realism. A writer in *Fame* pointed out the path as early as 1892. "Many advertisers seem to be satisfied with anything which is artistic or striking in its effect, without regard to the sentiment it expresses," he complained. "Better far a

FIGURE 9.2
Advertisement for McCormick Implement Company, *Printers' Ink,* 1899.

homely, everyday incident, which appeals to our better feelings and arouses our sympathy, than the stateliest and grandest figure an artist can produce." Calls for liveliness in copy began to boil down to a single panacea: the need for the copywriter and illustrator "to introduce 'life' " into the advertisement. The quotation marks suggested the admakers' sense of the ambiguities involved in fabricating authenticity and manufacturing spontaneity. Still, amid acres of stereotyped claims for mass-produced commodities, there was no question in many minds that the way to stand out was by incorporating "the vital spark" of "red-blooded human-ity" in copy.[44]

In search of language to characterize the aura they sought, trade press writers resorted to the idiom of "vitality" or "personality." As W. R. Emery, an advertising manager for *Everybody's Magazine,* wrote in 1910: "Every machine, every enterprise, every product has its personality which may contribute to the advancement of the salesman, the distributor, and the manufacturer himself. It is a tangible asset when capitalized and applies equally and as strongly to your line as it has come to be with a patent med-icine or the Edison phonograph." The idea that an evanescent quality could be transformed into a "tangible asset" was not new to retail business people, who had historically traded on reputation and "good will." What was new was the idea that a manufacturer could hire an expert to perform this sleight of hand systematically.[45]

Emery's main examples illustrating "the personality of a product" were conventional tales of the manufacturer's rise from penniless to powerful. By melding personality with narrative, he caught a fundamental drift in the logic of copy, a convergence with the conventions of commercial fic-tion. In subsequent decades more and more ads would tell stories about actual or imagined characters. By 1915, Newton Fuessle, a former adver-tising manager for Chalmers Motor Company and a frequent contributor of fiction to popular magazines, was explaining "what copy-writers can learn from story-writers" such as Maupassant, Kipling, and O. Henry. "The use of atmosphere, character delineation, and the narrative form are being adopted more and more widely by the best copywriters of to-day," he observed. Others agreed that "the necromancy of narrative" could combine with "character interest" to weave a spell around even the most prosaic of commodities. But when should one wave the wand? "My sug-gestion," another copywriter said, "is that you follow the lead of inter-est."[46]

> If your fifty-dollar watches are cut to twenty dollars that is interesting and needs no human interest story. But if you have a rather highpriced alarm clock to sell you had better look for some thing humanly inter-esting. Naming the clock Big Bill endows it with personality, makes it a sentient being, takes it out of the class of alarm clocks—it is not an alarm clock, it is Big Bill. And people will actually pay the big new price because you tell them that *he,* not "it," is a big, fine, jolly fellow with a brave, cheerful voice. The idea that you should hate your alarm clock vanishes when you are told to love Big Bill.[47]

This author characteristically exaggerated advertisers' power to mold minds, but captured a key development by describing the transformation of an alarm clock into a "sentient being." Emery had discussed the chief reason for capitalizing personality in similar language: "It is that personality that vitalizes an inanimate object, that makes it mean more than a mere expression of power, that kindles enthusiasm, that brings about the intimacy of acquaintanceship."[48] This strategy epitomized a fundamental pattern in the emerging commodity civilization: the reanimation of the inanimate world under the aegis of major corporations.

In the case of "Big Bill," the object in question was an alarm clock, the very emblem of routinized labor discipline in the emerging bureaucratic order. The copywriter was being paid to fetishize the commodity (in Marxian terms), to obscure its "mere expression of power," to render it a focus of fantasy and an intimate friend. One may question how many consumers would develop a cozy relationship with their alarm clocks: the point is not to claim that the audience dumbly accepted the premises of the trade press, or even that advertisers believed they would, but to suggest that the effort to endow the commodity with life reinforced broader agendas of personalization in advertising art. One can see those agendas at work in advertisers' discovery of "the smile that sells goods." By 1911, an agency art director named William Livingston Larned was telling advertisers that there was an "actual cash value in having your illustrations 'look pleasant.' " The number of smiling faces in advertisements was decidedly on the increase. This development reinforced national advertisers' faith that they had led Americans out of the puritanical dark ages when everyone was in a perpetual funk, or too embarrassed by his rotten teeth to show them. But the smile was also an emblem of the "vitality" and "personality" that advertisers were straining to impart to their products. The smiling face became an icon in the official art of corporate capitalism.[49]

By the early 1900s, the program "to introduce 'life' " was already bearing fruit. National advertising images were being assimilated to broader currents of popular art and entertainment, as commercial chromolithography had been in previous decades. The poster craze had inspired denunciations reminiscent of the *Nation* editor E. L. Godkin's assault on "chromocivilization": "A vulgar taste becomes very soon a depraved taste by feeding on suggestion, and quickly breeds lewdness," the *Bookman* had railed in 1895. But the same article also acknowledged that well-designed posters had the potential to introduce beauty into everyday life. Seven years later, that seemed to be happening, as John Brisbane Walker of *Cos-*

mopolitan magazine applauded the rise of good taste in advertising art; advertisers, he observed, had apparently abandoned experiments with "indelicate drapery." While that observation may have been premature, the consensus both within and outside the industry seemed to be that the quality of advertising art was on the rise. Within a few years, national advertisers had succeeded in domesticating commercial poster art, sanitizing the exoticism and reviving the sentimental genre traditions of nineteenth-century chromolithography, and claiming major advances in professionalism. There were, to be sure, still some complaints that advertising pictures were "too pretty," some demands that advertising portray, as a *Printers' Ink* article put it, "real people and real work." The application of photography promised more realistic representation, but as late as the 1910s its use was still limited. Besides, if one defined advertising as lighthearted entertainment, then the need for reality was not so pressing.[50]

And that definition was becoming more popular as national advertising became more pervasive. Even muckrakers who claimed to be exposing the evils of advertising acknowledged its entertainment value. In 1909, Samuel Hopkins Adams noted

> a distinct entertainment value in the best of advertising. Think how much duller your ride to business would be if the car hoardings were blank, instead of being filled with color and print. They are decent and companionable myths, these folk of Ad-land; the smiling chef of Cream-of-Wheat, the frolicky Gold-Dust Twins, the gaily youthful, toothful Sozodont girl, the round-eyed chubs who fatten to bursting on Campbell's Soups, and the hale old friend of Quaker Oats.

For this one viewer, at least, the effort to associate products with "personality" had succeeded. With critics like Adams, who in the advertising world needed friends? Only the marginal bunco men, the sellers of fraudulent real estate schemes and correspondence courses. Those were the targets of Adams's muckraking. For the national brand-name advertiser, he had little but praise, concluding that "in a sense, the ad-man is a public entertainer, only too eager to do his share toward the world's entertainment, gratis." The idea that advertising entertainment was free can most charitably be written off as a touching bit of naïveté.[51]

In a few years, the convergence of advertising and entertainment was nearly complete. Copywriters strained to emulate the formulas of mass-produced fiction, and popular authors like Edna Ferber celebrated the dynamism and "personality plus" of advertising people in her novels. Advertising illustrators increasingly sought to replicate the pictorial styles

of the slick magazines. This produced some confusion. W. L. Larned wrote
of the art of the advertising illustrator Fanny Munsell: "It really isn't commercial at all. The design could be lifted from the advertising pages and
dropped into a magazine story." The lines between art and commerce,
blurred by Barnum and his contemporaries, now seemed to be disappearing altogether. The idiom of entertainment was the eraser.[52]

In the city, the ploys of the outdoor advertiser could easily be viewed as
a source of amusement. A German visitor to Seattle in 1892, for example,
noticed seven sandwich-card men in fantastic costumes, advertising a
seven-letter hygiene product; by mid-afternoon the men had visited several watering holes and the orthography was hopelessly garbled. This sort
of unwitting vaudeville contributed to the carnival atmosphere of urban
commerce that persisted even after the rise of corporate advertising; Joyce
and other writers would turn that atmosphere into the poetry of the modern city. Even Charles Mulford Robinson, a landscape architect from
Rochester, New York, who led a crusade against billboards, acknowledged
in 1904 that colorful posters, window displays, and electric signs all put
urban passersby "unconsciously into a holiday mood."[53]

Still, the nineteenth-century aesthetic heritage remained tenacious.
Older commitments survived, as did older suspicions about advertising's
artistic value. Not everyone was amused by advertising's efforts at entertainment, especially as billboards began to corrupt the pastoral purity of
the countryside. The problem was not advertising, Robinson charged, but
its ubiquity: "Shall we hold nothing sacred, sky or ocean, rock or tree, public building, church, or monument?" Robinson asked. The idea that the
propaganda of commodities should swallow up all available public space
seemed a kind of desecration.[54]

At times the crusade against billboards articulated an important legal
principle: that the right of private property did not always override the
interest of the public in preserving the aesthetic value of the landscape.
But except for a few guerrilla bands, reformers were always quick to
explain that the regulation of billposting did not pose a challenge to the
right to advertise outdoors. Outdoor advertising was an inevitable part of
modern business methods. "To lose sight of this fact," Frederick Law Olmsted Jr. (son of the park designer and himself an urban planner) remarked
in 1900, "would lead us to overshoot the mark and defeat our ends by
putting ourselves in opposition to common sense." Since no one wanted to
oppose "common sense," what ultimately emerged was a typically pragmatic compromise that suited the class interests of the combatants: the

development of zoning restrictions that effectively consigned "the menace of the bill sticker" to the neighborhoods least able to challenge it.[55]

The potential for this rapprochement was embedded in the progressive faith of most antibillboard agitators, who applauded the mechanical advances introduced by modern commerce but wondered why aesthetic progress had not kept pace with them. This was the kind of "cultural lag" inanity that proved enormously influential among progressive reformers; resting on the assumption that changes in material life were linear and irresistible, it allowed critics to focus on the need for cultural values to "catch up" with economic and technological realities. The critique of advertising, from this view, simply boiled down to a demand that advertisers mind their manners and polish their cultural style.[56]

Some advertising spokesmen were eager to comply. A small minority had long striven not only to improve the technical quality and instrumental value of illustration, but also to appropriate the prestige of high culture. In 1886, Pear's Soap Company, a British concern, had pointed the way by using John Everett Millais's unimpeachably sweet painting *Bubbles* in an advertisement. During the 1890s, Hires Root Beer had offered a free chromolithograph of *The Parting of Ruth and Naomi* with every six-pack. This sort of work had the cachet of fine art but none of the decadent air of Beardsley posters and much of the popular appeal of sentimental genre painting. Within a few years, some in the trade press were claiming a major aesthetic advance. "The magazine page and advertising calendar intended for free distribution to-day puts [sic] to shame the picture that only a few years ago would have been welcomed on the wall of the average moderately well-situated family," *Fame* asserted in 1904. The idea that advertising art, if it was technically proficient, might adorn the homes of the people, just as chromos had done in the nineteenth century, seemed natural to industry spokesmen.[57]

Even outside the business world there was talk that national advertising might become a source of fine art for the people. Away with "aristocratic" artists' snobbish disdain for their commercial brethren, the copywriter Waldo Warren wrote in *Collier's* in 1909. Of course, many illustrations used in advertisements did not conform to the "accepted definition" of art—"the adequate expression of a typical emotion"—but "commercial art might easily be made to express a far greater degree of the real art spirit than it usually does." It was not true that artists in advertising were too constrained by organizational imperatives to produce creative work, Warren claimed. "In a great majority of cases the commercial artist is given sufficient room to conceive his picture with true artistic intent, and at the same time serve the purpose of the advertiser." The commercial artist could reach a far larger audience than the studio artist; quantitative circulation made up for qualitative compromises. "If the question were raised as to which had the greater opportunity to serve humanity—the artist whose exhibited picture may use up 80 per cent of its real art possibilities, or the commercial artist who may be able to inject 10 per cent of typical emotion or real art into a picture that is to be multiplied by the press ten million times," then Warren was inclined to choose the latter.[58]

Not everyone was so sure. Certainly most advertising artists or copywriters would have dissolved in derisive laughter at Warren's quantitative estimates of their autonomy. Only if they were financially secure and had already established a reputation were they sometimes able to chart their own course; even then, they often found commercial work unsatisfying.

The career of Maxfield Parrish (1870–1966) was a case in point. Parrish came from a family of wealthy and cultivated Philadelphia Quakers. His great-grandfather Joseph Parrish was a distinguished surgeon and abolitionist; his father, Stephen Parrish, was an aspiring artist whose ambitions were thwarted by his family's conviction that art was sinful. Finally, in middle age, he sold his stationery store and devoted himself to painting full time, achieving some repute as a landscape artist. Stephen Parrish was determined that his son should not repeat his own experience, which included hiding in the attic to draw and paint in secret. He gave the two-year-old Frederick (who later took the name Maxfield) an embossed leather sketchbook and filled fifty pages of it with cartoons of monkeys and other animals; the boy was intrigued and delighted, and his parents did everything they could to encourage his flourishing fascination with art.[59]

Given their education and affluence, they were able to do a lot. Maxfield Parrish was surrounded by the best music, art, and literature that late-Victorian taste could provide. In 1884 he and his parents began a two-year tour of Europe that included attendance at Victor Hugo's funeral. "I was fifteen," Parrish remembered, "and climbed a tree on the Champs-Elysées. The avenue was jammed, but I scattered the crowd when a branch of my tree broke with a noise like a pistol shot. They thought it was the beginning of a nihilist demonstration." That was about as close as Maxfield Parrish came to the swirling social unrest of the late nineteenth century. His career path was smooth: college at Haverford; art training at the Pennsylvania Academy, an extended return trip to Europe; marriage to a young painting instructor from the Drexel Institute; and a country home next to his father's near Cornish, New Hampshire, a retreat for well-connected artists and intellectuals.[60]

Despite his exceptional privilege, Parrish was never idle. He worked constantly, making the most of his family contacts. Wilson Eyre, the architect who was designing Stephen Parrish's New Hampshire house, was also renovating the Mask and Wig Club at the University of Pennsylvania; Eyre commissioned Maxfield to paint the *Old King Cole* mural at the club while the young artist was still in school. Parrish's first commission provided the sort of visibility that gave him an early start in magazine illustration and advertising design. He developed a distinctive style that merged with the dominant mode of light entertainment in commercial art, but that preserved a playful note of fantasy, a genteel exoticism. And he executed all his work with an extraordinary technical proficiency. Advertising art, like other forms of art, presented a series of problems to be solved through color and composition. Parrish was well enough established from the outset of his career to be able to choose which problems he wanted to bother with. A letter to Rusling Wood, owner of a New York advertising lithography firm, in 1915 typified Parrish's attitude to advertising work.

> [S]uggesting the use of Lowney chocolates by 'Highbrows' . . . it just occurs to me that could we carry it up to royalty we could get something very good in the way of design. . . . a king and queen upon their respective thrones being presented with a box of the subject in question. As a design and a vehicle for holding color I think it would work out quite effectively. Also there is a good chance for the human interest: the action of the three people can be made to express their appreciation of the confection. The king and major domo could be made mildly humorous and the queen as pretty as possible. . . . I do have a faint idea that it would be a contrast to the usual run of realism and prettiness. I do know I could make good with this idea, as it seems to be in my own line.[61]

Six years later, this proposal finally appeared, as an advertisement for Jell-O. Like Parrish's other work, it was indeed "a contrast to the usual run of realism and prettiness." His reputation allowed him to sustain his individual vision. When advertisers hired an established artist, they used his distinction to add luster to their product. For Parrish, as for other successful commercial artists, no-nonsense professionalism relaxed romantic tensions between art and mammon; questions of form and technique—such as how to arrange rectangles to achieve "dynamic symmetry"—subsumed the old opposition between surfaces and depths.

Still, Parrish ultimately felt oppressed by the repetitive demands of advertising clients. After years of producing enormously successful calendars for General Electric, Parrish finally announced: "It's an awful thing to be a rubber stamp. I'm quitting my rut now while I'm still able." He decided to to turn to landscapes. "There are always pretty girls on every city street, but a man can't step out of the subway and watch the clouds playing with the top of Mount Ascutney. It's the unattainable that appeals."[62] These sentiments recalled Oscar Wilde's critique of quotidian realism. In effect, Parrish feared being dragged toward standardization—Waldo Warren's "adequate expression of a typical emotion." Parrish's alternative was a romantic, idealist realm of fine art. Posing the unattainable against the overly familiar, he reinstated the opposition between surfaces and depths, though the depths he had in mind were the heights of Mount Ascutney.

The compromise of capitalist realism was unsatisfactory to artists for a variety of reasons, including its affinity with "stupid realism." Formulaic blandness offended artists and writers reared with a romantic faith in their own special vision, their capacity to depict a more intense reality than the one manufactured by advertising agencies. Even Parrish, for all his professionalism, shared this faith. But by the early twentieth century, the romantic quest was being reformulated in modernist idioms: the pursuit of pure form beneath the encrustations of ornament, the search for throbbing vitality behind the civilized lies of society. In either its formalist or vitalist modes, modernism promised to penetrate the evasions of capitalist realism. Many modernists, in their contempt for the superficial things of this world, remained inside the dualisms of surface and depth, matter and spirit. A few eccentric souls sought a more encompassing vision.

CHAPTER 10

The Courtship of Avant-Garde and Kitsch

THE EMERGENCE of modernism recast the relationship between art and advertising during the early twentieth century. Any attempt to illuminate that change has to grapple with the muddled meanings of the word *modern* itself. An incident recalled by the poet Stephen Spender illustrates some of the semantic ambiguities. During the 1920s, Harrod's, the London department store, asked three literary luminaries—George Bernard Shaw, Arnold Bennett, and H. G. Wells—to write testimonials for the store. They declined for a variety of reasons but took the proposal seriously, sympathetically, and at such length that their refusals were ultimately printed as advertisements. These writers all approved of modernizing tendencies: the hegemony of technical expertise and bureaucratic organization, the mass production of goods. The Fabian socialists Shaw and Wells might have complained about private ownership or unequal distribution, but all would have felt responsibility to a constituency of modern consumers: the same constituency as Harrod's.[1]

But this progressive version of modernity was profoundly different from the one embodied by Joyce, Eliot, Lawrence, or Woolf. One should try to imagine, Spender suggests, their response to Harrod's request for a testimonial. Each would have treated it as a joke; they felt "an entirely different kind of responsibility" from the one assumed by Shaw, Wells, and Bennett. It was, according to Spender, "a responsibility to a past which had been degraded by commerce, a past of realer values betrayed by advertising. They [felt] . . . that their responsibility was as artists, and not as

money-makers producing a consumers' product." The contrast is com-
pelling: on the one hand the enthusiasts for technical artifice and economic development, devotees of democratic immersion in the everyday
life of commerce; on the other the acolytes of authenticity, inhabitants of
an autonomous artistic realm where they sought to preserve the "realer
values" of the past.[2]

But the division is a little too neat. Technocratic modernists were not
always uncritical celebrants of commerce: they could develop their own
discourse of authenticity, a plainspoken critique of commercial chicanery,
even as industry apologists tried to appropriate the prestige of scientific
expertise and identify advertising with technological progress. Nor were
aesthetic modernists always devoted to the past—the very term *avant-
garde,* which they sometimes appropriated , implied a notion of cultural
development as forward movement. Aesthetes could look not only to the
past for "realer values" but also to the future—and to the allegedly timeless and objective realm of pure form.[3]

All the idioms of modernism contained contradictory elements of
protest and affirmation, longings for transcendence as well as desires to
merge with the commonplace. The formalist idiom, which this chapter
explores, was no exception. In theory, it offered the opportunity to get
beyond dualisms: to find content in form; to celebrate surface as depth; to
locate significance in structural relations rather than mimetic correspondences; to return to the things themselves, rejecting endless interpretation
and revaluing play.[4] Yet these theoretical possibilities, shaped by romantic
traditions and commercial circumstances, remained only fitfully realized.
In many minds, art and life continued to occupy separate spheres.

Hermes, the god of trade, seemed to provoke a hermetic art. A resurgence of formalist concerns supplied new strategies for artists to preserve
faith in their autonomy. To protect their product from commercial debase-
ment, they could make paintings about painting and poems about poetry.
As the critic Clement Greenberg wrote in 1939, "In turning his attention
away from the subject matter of common experience, the poet or artist
turns it upon the medium of his own craft." From this view, what Ortega
called "the dehumanization of art" shut out ordinary citizens from the
precincts of the avant-garde, leaving them vulnerable to the allure of
kitsch, the salable, sentimental art that remained engaged with "the subject matter of common experience." The "difficulty" of much avant-garde
art—which was often construed as a form of masculine heroism—became

another means of insulating it from the allegedly corrupting effects of the consumer audience—which was often construed to be passive, feminine, and unheroic.[5]

The failure of those aspirations toward autonomy has by now become proverbial. The capacity of commercial society to absorb avant-garde protest has become one of the leitmotifs of recent cultural history; a cottage industry has arisen to show how flimsy were the modernists' claims of artistic autonomy, how tied they were to capital by "an umbilical cord of gold."[6] Yet metaphors of infantile dependency do not quite catch the complexity of the relationship between bohemian and bourgeois, the mingling of fitful tension and longings for union. Courtship seems a more appropriate metaphor for the tortuous engagement between experimental form and familiar content, particularly as it unfolded in advertising.

In some ways, the formalist idiom appeared tailor-made for artists and writers in advertising. An emphasis on stylistic innovation resonated with the rage for novelty at the heart of consumer culture; advertisers' preoccupation with staying a half-step ahead of the pack allowed them to embrace a modified version of Ezra Pound's dictum: Make it new, but not too new. Perhaps more important, the tendency to exalt technique promised new dignity for troubled souls. Concentrating on the deftness of one's brushstrokes allowed one to forget that one was painting a pack of Parliaments; the artist could preserve some self-esteem as he or she submitted to the subdivision of labor in the broader bureaucratic scheme. (As early as 1910, one agency was employing a "smile specialist" whose only job was to touch up the "smiles that go wrong.") At the end of a long production process, the question of individual responsibility was moot. "And whose piece of copy is it when it is finished—who wrote it?" John B. Watson asked in 1928. "The group wrote it. The whole agency wrote it. The most anyone can say is that he worked on the account." The advertisement could not be traced to any particular creator, but the artists and writers could at least take pride in the stylish techniques they used to please the client.[7]

Yet along with exalting technique, a formalist aesthetic also undermined referentiality, and this was problematic for agency executives. The preoccupation with form and style led to a neglect of prosaic issues like communicability and content. In subtle but unmistakable ways, the advertisement became detached from the product to which it referred. "Advertising design" became a value in and of itself, without reference to the sales that design was intended to generate. People remembered the cleverness of an ad but forgot what it was "for." The gap between signifier and signified opened the same epistemological issues explored by René Magritte, who titled his painting of a pipe *This Is Not a Pipe*. The representation of a thing could not be equated with the thing itself.[8] The recognition that advertisements could be floating signifiers evoked William Dean Howells's vision of a world where things had been shunted aside by advertisements for things. It was not a world where many clients felt at home.

At bottom, of course, the idea that an ad—or a painting—could be "only about itself" was a delusion. The purpose of advertising was persuading people to buy goods. That required some reference to the "real world" of getting and spending. Advertising, like political propaganda, needed "human interest" and "real life." At its most effective, advertising might even mimic popular idioms convincingly enough to achieve the quality of "ventriloquism" that the critic Stuart Hall has identified as a key feature of mass-produced commercial culture.[9]

Groping unwittingly toward that goal, some agency people gradually learned what Greenberg and other academic formalists never fully understood: it was possible to yoke formal innovation to thematic predictability and experimental techniques to familiar scenes—in short, to marry avant-garde with kitsch. The search for "objective" form could be reduced to the mastery of tricky surface effects. The contemporary soft-drink commercial—the rapid-fire montage of scrubbed adolescents in transports of youthful energy—marks both the consummation and routinization of that marriage. So does the repetitive celebration of mercantile banality in the work of Andy Warhol and his imitators. The marriage has become a merger of art and the corporation, a cliché of postmodern criticism. Only occasionally—as in the Coca-Cola Classic campaigns of 1993, where reggae music animates the flotsam and jetsam of everyday life, and polar bears perform Olympic feats of luge—does formal innovation break the boundaries of sentimental convention.

Today it is difficult to recapture the intoxicating feeling of aesthetic possibility that once surrounded national advertising. But for a while, especially during the early years of the courtship, it seemed to many artists as if advertising embodied exhilarating energy, rather than merely impoverishment of spirit. During the 1920s, within certain avant-garde circles and among the more venturesome advertising people, a rhetoric of "machine civilization" dissolved the Veblenian divisions between technical rationality and commercial culture. The modern corporation seemed to some to be sponsoring artistic as well as technological innovation. For artists and writers, this perception marked a departure from earlier suspicions.

MACHINE CIVILIZATION:
THE MUFFLED RAPTURE OF THE MODERN

The American avant-garde of the early twentieth century recovered Whitman's feel for the kaleidoscopic and kinetic delights of the city. For most artists, even Chicagophiles like Dreiser, the ultimate city was New York, emblem of American modernity. Urchins copping fruit, pianists sweating ragtime, advertisements flashing slogans and brand names—all worked together to immerse the artist or writer in a sea of urban sensations. Ashcan painters and naturalistic novelists agreed that the task of the moment was to make art of modern metropolitan life. Yet their search for pulsating reality led them toward the Negro bars in Hoboken rather than the towers of lower and midtown Manhattan. It was not the corporate cutting edge of urban modernity that appealed to the restless rising generation, but the carnival atmosphere that flourished in the margins and the interstices of the spreading metropolitan grid.

During the 1910s, the cutting edge began to slice more swiftly. Tendencies toward systematic rationalization of the workplace, which had been building for decades, began to reshape office work as well as factory labor. The labor discipline at the Summerfield Agency described by Dreiser was characteristic. The rhetoric of system valued speed and energy, but only when harnessed to efficient productivity; the assembly-line slang term *speedup* captured the process perfectly. The American experience of World War I increased the value of managerial currency, as the victorious (and comparatively unscathed) United States came to embody a dynamic "machine civilization," and national advertising its characteristic cultural expression.

The melding of posters and jazz with machines and buildings, all in one standardizing system, marked the discourse of machine civilization, whether it was articulated in advertising agencies or literary magazines. Celebrants and doubters shared similar deterministic assumptions. The French poet Blaise Cendrars arrived in New York with a kopek and a quarter, took a job in a slaughterhouse, and retreated to a basement apartment in the Village where he grew a beard "in reaction against all the clean collars and shaved faces." For four months he wanted to die, "when suddenly he understood and stopped fighting. The barber in the Brevort [sic] extracted his whiskers, he bought an Arrow collar, became like an American, and has never been the same since," the young expatriate Harold Loeb reported in the avant-garde journal *Broom* in 1921. What Cendrars understood, Loeb implied, was the inevitable triumph of "the machine." Given that inevitability, why not embrace rather than revile our modern master?[10]

Some American artists and writers had already come to this conclusion. Consider the early career of Stuart Davis (1892–1964). The son of a successful commercial artist for the Newark *Evening News,* Davis began as a devotee of the real under the tutelage of Robert Henri, mentor to the Ashcan School. Davis and his friend Glenn Coleman "were particularly hep to the jive," Davis recalled, and they frequented the Negro dives in New Jersey where ragtime pianists played "for the love of art alone." What appealed to Davis about ragtime was the same energetic, objective, and precise sense of form he found in the European modernist painting at the Armory Show of 1913, where he exhibited some of his own work.[11]

Quitting his job as an art director at the radical journal *The Masses* in 1913, he embarked on a quest for the "objective order" he had glimpsed in the Armory Show. It was a Whitmanesque project for the modern age, defiantly nationalistic and optimistic. "I too feel the thing Whitman felt— and I too will express it in pictures—America the wonderful place we live in," Davis wrote in his notebook in 1921. He decided to make pictures from "an alphabet of letters, numbers, canned goods labels, tobacco labels, in a word let these well-known, purely objective things be used to indicate location and size." An aesthetic of "purely objective things" would refute romantic illusions of depth. "A picture should be as romantic as a streetcar conductor and nothing more. It should be strictly utilitarian, nothing more, 'made to look at.'" This objectivist manifesto was realized in Davis's paintings and collages of the early 1920s, which incorporated advertising labels and other fragments of commercial culture.[12]

The aesthetics of packaging required an impersonal stance that would have felt foreign to Whitman. In his notebooks Davis began referring to himself in the third person: "the artist expressed the opinion that the change from barreling in bulk to individual packaging symbolized the achievement in modern life of a very high civilization." Besides repeating major themes in advertising apologetics, Davis also slipped into orphic self-objectification. "I am not a member of the human race," he announced to his notebook, "but am a product made by the American Can Co. and the New York *Evening Journal.*" Though the statement prefigured Andy Warhol's refrain "I want to be a machine," Davis was too much the Whitmanesque "urban democrat," too enamored of the variety and unpredictability in the carnivalesque commercial vernacular, to foster a cult of monotonously replicable gestures. Apparently indifferent to the economic power behind the advertising he admired, Davis nevertheless clung to democratic sentiments which led him to head the American Artists Congress, a Popular Frontish organization, in the 1930s. His political views were never fully compatible with his celebration of the commodified object and his denial of the human subject.[13]

No such ambiguity characterized the thought of the young editor and writer Matthew Josephson, who repeatedly invoked a reified, anthropomorphic notion of "the machine" to celebrate the advance of American civilization. "The machine is our magnificent slave, our fraternal genius. We [Americans] are a new and hardier race, friend to the skyscraper and the subterranean railway as well," he announced in 1922, predicting that "we may yet amass a new folklore out of the domesticated miracles of our time": the rhythms of jazz bands and jackhammers, "the incandescent messages shooting fitfully over the dark waters [of New York harbor]: COLGATE'S . . . HECKER'S FLOUR . . . AMERICAN SUGAR REFINERY."[14]

There was no question, for Josephson, that the new folklore of machine civilization was being amassed in the advertising agencies.

> The particular restrictions of the medium make for extraordinary ingenuity in the "copy writer;" the call for vigor of style, conviction, and interest, are probably more stimulating by far toward creating beautiful conceptions than an intensive course in Victorian poetry at Harvard University. The terse vivid slang of the people has been swiftly transmitted to this class of writers, along with a willingness to depart from syntax, to venture sentence forms and word constructions which are at times breath-taking, if anything, and far more arresting and provocative than 99 per cent of the stuff that passes for poetry in our national magazines. They [copywriters] are a most amiable band of poets, without the piffle of the teacup type, their hair closely trimmed, their shoes thought-inspiring. All design on immortality, on seats in the Academy, all schemes for hoodwinking posterity, have been renounced by them in favor of ample salaries and smoothrunning motor cars.[15]

This was a mix of healthy impulses and inane thinking. Josephson displayed an understandable preference for the "terse vivid slang" of vernacular speech over the "piffle of the teacup type" of poetic diction. But in equating advertising slogans with the rough and virile language of the people, Josephson was uncritically buying the national advertisers' view of their own historical role as agents of democracy. Josephson, like many subsequent apologists for mass culture, overlooked the elite origins of national advertising as well as its capacity to legitimate existing hierarchies. His head was turned, as Dreiser's had been, by the executives with "ample salaries and smoothrunning motor cars." And Josephson's claim that advertisements embodied "terse vivid slang" was simply not borne out, even by the evidence he supplied. "'The pliant but positive gears engage silently . . .' is a profound utterance, reverberant with meanings and shadows," he wrote, in all apparent seriousness. Josephson's attitude toward modern advertising, unlike that of the mordant European Dadaists whose work he praised, was not playful but earnest. "It is a thrilling business, a fascinating genre," he wrote, "and it is easy to see *why our literature is so impoverished and where all the creative genius has gone.*"[16]

Josephson was not an isolated crank. Other artists and writers felt stirred by the sheer energy embodied in advertising. As early as 1914, Edna Ferber's novels *Emma McChesney & Co.* and *Personality Plus* celebrated the same vision of success found in J. C. Leyendecker's Arrow Collar advertisements. Ferber's heroic admen, like those in magazine fiction generally, were clean-favored and imperially slim; they radiated contempt for the fat, old-fashioned salesmen sweating in hotel lobbies. In Ferber's view, the admen represented a higher stage in the evolution of American commerce. What fueled their ascent was "personality plus," a force "like electricity" that often seemed indistinguishable from mindless enthusiasm, but was frequently equated with creativity. Thus in middlebrow as well as avant-garde circles was energy worshiped for its own sake, without regard to any larger purpose.[17]

During the 1920s, cultural commentators from Professor Brander Matthews of the Columbia University English department to H. L. Mencken, the mortal enemy of all professors, agreed that advertising agencies might well be the nurseries of new creativity.[18] The question remained: Whatever intellectuals may have thought about the aesthetic possibilities of advertising, what did artists and writers themselves actually experience inside the agencies? For them the rapture of the modern was muffled by the need to fit into a smoothly functioning organization.

There was a world of difference between the people out of doors, composing Whitmanesque paeans to the cityscape, and the people inside the agencies, composing slogans for Sunkist. Stuart Davis could play at being "a product made by the American Can Co.," but the advertising artist or copywriter might actually feel like one for weeks at a time. The objectivist epistemology articulated by Davis and endorsed by other advocates of machine civilization was compatible with the behaviorist psychology that John Watson installed at J. Walter Thompson: both outlooks collapsed depths into surfaces, denying any inner dimension to life and underwriting the idea that art was an expression of "forces" rather than individual human beings. This last was a popular notion, much favored by advertising apologists themselves; it embodied a technologically determinist view of history that reduced form to technique and the artist to a technician. The determination to paint or write or draw the reality of one's own time turned out, for the devotees of machine civilization, to mean the loss of the capacity to imagine alternative realities. The fate of montage was symptomatic: it began (in John Heartfield's anticapitalist political satire during the Weimar republic) as an effort to rearrange existing social and cultural hierarchies and ended (in American soft-drink advertising) as a means of reaffirming them. The organizational imperatives of agency life were far more powerful than Josephson & Co. realized.[19]

So the fit was rarely perfect between artists and writers and agency work. The novelist John P. Marquand's experience was illustrative. Hired by JWT in 1920, when he was twenty-seven, Marquand sat brooding one day during a Creative Staff meeting while another copywriter repeated the slogan he had crafted for Lifebuoy soap: "Every day an oily coating lightly forms upon your skin." Marquand abruptly sat up and began chanting along with the copywriter: "Lives of great men all remind us / We can make our lives sublime," and then cried "It scans! It scans! Don't you hear it? It's trochaic tetrameter. Who says there isn't poetry in advertising?" In the shocked silence only Stanley Resor managed a thin smile. "John, I don't think you really have the business instinct," Resor said. Marquand was politely fired soon after the episode.[20]

Still, many others stayed, not only for the "ample salaries and smoothrunning motor cars" (which in any case were available only to an elite handful of employees), but also for the opportunity, however problematic, to get paid for doing what they wanted to do. The situation was improving. During the 1920s, the agency atmosphere became distinctly more hospitable to advertising that had aesthetic aspirations—what the product-oriented client might call "high-hat stuff." By the end of the decade, E. B. White expressed alarm that a copywriter "should pluck from the realm of pure creation a name like Post Toasties or Seald Sweet and think of it as a poet's dream"; it made White wonder how much advertising was inspired by sound business principles and "how much by the simple desire of people who write and draw to write and draw." White grasped some of the appeal (as well as the absurdity) of high-hat stuff for artists and writers in ad agencies. Naturally they wanted to forget about the trivial realities of their actual task and forge an imaginary relationship with the Muses. By the end of the 1920s, that task was accomplished more easily than ever before. The aesthetic aspirations and prestige of national advertising had never been higher.[21]

A large part of the credit for advertising's new artistic respectability belonged to Earnest Elmo Calkins (1868–1964), the cofounder of the Calkins & Holden agency, who spent half a century urging the industry to adopt higher aesthetic standards and more innovative styles. His career typified the national advertising man's characteristic journey from prairie Protestantism to urban sophistication. And his apologetics for modernism became, for a time, the conventional wisdom of the industry.

EARNEST ELMO CALKINS AND THE INCORPORATION OF MODERNISM

Calkins was born in 1868, in the small Illinois town of Galesburg. His father was a lawyer, his uncle a prosperous farmer. His Baptist upbringing was sufficiently harsh to fit the adman's formula for rural barbarism. By the time he was six, the family's scrubwoman had filled him with fears of God's arbitrariness and omnipotence. He saw the flames of hell in the heat lightning that flickered across the Illinois plains. His mother's evangelical asperities were softened by her own sanity and his father's skepticism; nevertheless, she forbade fiction ("even Arabian Nights and Jules Verne were taboo") and demanded that her son attend the First Baptist Church. Young Earnest endured the periodic mental agonies induced by revivals and dutifully sang the Moody and Sankey hymns with the rest of the congregation, led by Elder Haigh, who "looked like a skull."[22]

Those hymns were the only music Calkins would ever know. By the time he was fourteen he was almost completely deaf, the result of a case of measles when he was six. But he pressed on, attending the local Knox College, where he came to believe that "the only thing that matters in conduct is character"; supernatural beliefs were pleasant and congenial to his optimistic temperament but irrelevant to the moral life. Looking back from the 1920s, Calkins admitted he had not been in church in twenty-five years except for weddings, funerals, and "aesthetic visits" to European cathedrals.[23] As he reached maturity, Calkins turned from the terrors of the evangelical inner life to a more detached contemplation of beautiful surfaces—a fin-de-siècle version of aestheticism, but refashioned to fit the business ethos of a small Midwestern town.

While Calkins was editing a newsmagazine at Knox, he received a letter from George Rowell offering him a free subscription to *Printers' Ink* if he would promote it in an editorial. He would. As Calkins recalled, "that little magazine was the first influence that turned my thoughts toward advertising as a career." While he was working summers as a columnist for the Galesburg *Mail,* he organized an advertising office and attempted to put the ideas of *Printers' Ink* into practice. Galesburg was too small for an ambitious young advertising man. Calkins headed for New York after graduation in 1891, and soon took a job with Charles Austin Bates's agency, then joined with Ralph Holden, a fellow employee at Bates, to form their own firm in 1902.[24]

Calkins and Holden claimed to be "the first full-service agency," offering copywriting and design as well as space brokerage and media selection. "It would no longer be possible," Calkins wrote to a journalist in 1926, "for a deaf man to do in advertising what I did then." By the 1920s, copy had become a composite creation; social interaction was an inescapable part of the ad-making process. But the turn of the century was different. "Advertising was so poor in those days that anything done to it was an improvement, and it was possible for me to sit at my desk and evolve from my own inner consciousness copy that was an improvement on what was then being used." The firm specialized in bright jingles and cute characters, such as Phoebe Snow, who vouched for the cleanliness of the Buffalo & Lackawanna Railroad: her "dress stayed white / along its road of anthracite." Their most famous creation was Sunny Jim, trademark of the unappetizingly titled Force Food, a breakfast cereal made by Edward Ellsworth's H-O Company. Sunny Jim was Jim Dumps before being revitalized by eating Force; he became a household figure in a matter of months. But the H-O Company failed and Ellsworth disappeared. So did Sunny Jim. In the trade press Sunny Jim became a cautionary figure, a reminder of what could happen when creativity displaced sound business sense. The memory of Sunny Jim dogged Calkins for years, marking him in some executives' eyes as one of those imaginative types who was not to be fully trusted.[25]

Despite the occasional failures, Calkins built a successful career as he gradually turned his attention from slogans and jingles to design reform. In 1908 Rowell gave him a column in *Printers' Ink;* Calkins used it to assault "the hard-faced, mechanical, lifeless dummies that appear in magazine pages and upon posters," and to urge more animation in the portrayal of people and things. Ad agencies should hire the same illustrators that the magazines hired for their editorial space—men like James Montgomery Flagg (designer of the Uncle Sam "I Want You" poster) and Edward Penfield. "Surely all of the magazine goes to the same person." This proposal provoked the grumbling response from another *PI* contributor that selling, not art, was the sine qua non of advertising. But as advertising and entertainment converged and corporate-sponsored art became all of a piece, Calkins's view began to prevail.[26]

Meanwhile, he moved on to higher ground. European travel proved a crucial catalyst in Calkins's aesthetic education. Like legions of American travelers before him, Calkins experienced Europe as a series of theatrical scenes; like them, too, he lamented the standardizing impact of industrialization on the quality of the show, complaining that "the picturesque and the progressive seem to have nothing in common." He spent the rest of his career trying to prove that beauty and modernity had something in common after all.[27]

In fashioning his role as apostle of taste, Calkins emulated "the modish Parisiennes." He sported spats and a beard and styled himself as something of a dandy. He became a respectable executive version of the Wildean aesthete, a corporate connoisseur of artifice. As he traveled in Europe in the early 1920s, his preoccupation with artistic precedent framed nearly all his perceptions. The garden at Bagnone, Italy, was "as artificial as one of Maxfield Parrish's pictures, and it has the same charm." At Fountains Abbey in England, "the picture framed by the great empty arch of the east end, a picture of blue sky and fleecy heaps of clouds, the finest thing I have seen on this tour—a sort of superior Maxfield Parrish." In Palermo the goatherds descending the hillsides were "like a passage from Theocritus. I am constantly entertained by the primitiveness of it all." At Tunbridge Wells he encountered "a marvelous dream garden such as M. Parrish might draw." (Somehow he could not get away from Parrish.) This apparent incapacity for unmediated perception was the aesthetic malady most feared by devotees of reality in and out of advertising. Calkins's case was chronic, exhibiting the characteristic symptom of amoral detachment. For him, almshouses were "the most charming things in England," and even Lourdes, which moved him to pity and denunciation, could be dismissed in the end as "a dramatic *mise-en-scène*." Judged by his letters from Europe, Calkins sometimes seemed nearly a caricature of the detached aesthete for whom every human experience could be reduced to a picture.[28]

True to the aesthete stereotype, he also was a bit of a snob. He wrote to his office from on board the *S.S. Minnewaska* en route to Europe in 1924 that he was accompanied by "a most interesting group of passengers, nice people, no Jews, no vulgar rich—for J.P. [Morgan, who happened to be on board] is rich without being vulgar—and no foreign buyers or Babbitts." His social prejudices mirrored those of the WASP elite that dominated the advertising business.[29]

But in his public pronouncements, Calkins suppressed his ethnocentrism and sought to temper his aestheticism with a sense of social responsibility. Part of his rhetorical project was simply a rehash of the familiar claim that national advertising people were professionals on the cutting edge of progress, but Calkins recast this apologia in his own terms. The old craftsmen produced things of beauty; machine production replaced them with ugly things; then the "profession" of national advertising intervened and began to promote mass-produced beauty. By 1927, Calkins saw evidence of beauty's new business role in sculpted perfume bottles, variegated motor cars, smart new shops, and landscaped factories. Even industrialists were beginning to discover the importance of orchestrating surface effects. "I have spent much of my life," Calkins wrote privately in 1925, "trying to teach the business man that beauty has a dollars and cents value, because I feel that only thus will it be produced in any quantity in this commercial age." Only by providing utilitarian service as "the new business tool" could art justify its existence in "our modern industrial civilization." By the late 1920s, in Calkins's view, that task had been accomplished.[30]

Calkins's instrumentalist defense of art in commerce led not to realism (as it did for so many of his colleagues) but to modernism. Here again the influence of Europe was decisive. In 1925, like other advertising executives and industrial designers, Calkins visited the Exposition Nationale des Arts Décoratifs Ancien et Moderne in Paris. He described it to his stay-at-home staff at Calkins & Holden:

> It is extremely "new art," and some of it too bizarre, but it achieves a certain exciting harmony, and in detail is entertaining to a degree. [Everything is] arranged with an eye to display, a vast piece of consummate window dressing. I spent a whole afternoon in the printing and bookmaking sections, wishing I could buy up a truckload and dump it down in the art department. Believe me, it is stimulating. It is not always beautiful, but it is diabolically clever.[31]

This son of the American prairie felt a fierce attraction to the "diabolically clever" strangeness of modern French art. He became a tireless advocate of a formalist version of modernity in commercial art and industrial design. The quest for the "lifelike" had ascended to "the dead line [of] excellence," he wrote; it had become predictable and boring by virtue of its very success. The new art was "imaginative rather than realistic," concerned with suggesting rather than showing. René Clarke and other advertising illustrators began creating patterns of uncommon beauty out of "such common homely units as tin cans of vegetable oil, fried eggs, vegetables, rolling pins, and skillets." But what seemed to be a new method for transfiguring commonplace objects became for Calkins a means of disconnecting form and content, thoughts and things. "Modernism offered the opportunity of expressing the inexpressible, of suggesting not so much a motor car as speed, not so much a gown as style, not so much a compact as beauty." It offered, in other words, a new aesthetic idiom for dematerializing desire.[32]

Like Stuart Davis, Matthew Josephson, and others among the avant-garde, Calkins justified modernist forms by insisting that there had to be an organic relation between design and cultural values. Instead of the old romantic motifs drawn from nature, modern commercial art could create designs more relevant to "our life and our needs" by incorporating "some bit of our modern life, a map of New York City, a couple dancing the Charleston, 'Gentlemen Prefer Blondes,' a graph or statistical chart, or a group of steam cranes." This was the version of modernity that animated the Italian Futurists as well as American devotees of machine civilization: the fascination with metropolitan life, the worship of energy and dynamism as ends in themselves.[33]

Yet Calkins's apparently straightforward prescription deserves closer examination. Like other advocates of machine civilization, he mixed utilitarian rationality with sensuous irrationality, a graph or statistical chart with a couple dancing the Charleston. And he ignored the possibility that any of these images might express or conceal class inequalities. His first-person plural ("our modern life") pretended to universality but actually referred to people like himself and his colleagues, metropolitan elites who were bored by traditional religious art, who were sufficiently detached from industrial production to see steam cranes as aesthetic objects, and who could afford tickets to *Gentlemen Prefer Blondes*. Like other advertising people before and since, he conflated his own class's values with those of the whole society.

The idea that art must embody the values of the surrounding society was deeply problematic: it involved a rejection of the nineteenth-century belief that art could constitute a realm apart from and perhaps even opposed to the drift of everyday social practice; it also rested on a technologically determinist view of history that was as congenial to Calkins as it was to Davis and Josephson. "The forces that are making our fast-paced, bright-colored, sharply-defined civilization are producing our modern art," Calkins wrote.[34] In a world that was increasingly subjected to bureaucratic regimentation and the rhythms of rationalization, it was easy to imagine that art was created by "forces" rather than artists.

By the late 1920s, Calkins claimed that advertising created "a humble picture gallery for millions who never see the inside of an art museum."[35] Yet the choices available to the individual artist providing this civilizing process were not always clear. Calkins admitted privately that the advertising artist was a mere instrument in the hands of the agency art director, but publicly he insisted throughout his life that the advertising artist was as free and as generously supported as any Renaissance master had been.

> The specifications with which [the advertising artist] approaches his work do not differ greatly from those given Michelangelo when he painted *The Last Judgment* for the Sistine Chapel. The quality which makes art Art does not depend on the fact that Michelangelo painted religion instead of motor cars, but in the fact that Michelangelo was a great artist. His work was applied art, and advertising art is in the same category. Its quality depends on the artists who practice it, not on the conditions under which they work.[36]

Calkins's belief in universal standards dovetailed with his need to fit the artist into the functional rationality of a large bureaucratic organization. The crucial assumption underlying his project was the formalist faith that meaning and subject matter were irrelevant to the quality of the artist's work. Motor cars and biblical scenes were interchangeable; superior technique was the main criterion of achievement. Modernist formalism elevated advertising art to an ethereal realm of composition and style, by submerging substantive questions in a bureaucratic ethos of "problem-solving."

The impact of formal experiment on agency practice is difficult to determine with any precision, partly because advertisers' notions of modernism were no more definite than anyone else's. Sometimes it simply meant a greater attention to composition and form, as in a Cammeyer Shoe campaign that *Printers' Ink* praised for successfully incorporating "foreign art ideas." In other cases the incorporation of modernism involved a conscious embrace of "technique which deals in two planes only." W. L. Larned applauded this approach in celebrating the "postery treatment" of an advertisement for New Jersey Zinc; the artist achieved "tricky effects" by massing solid black and white, and "romance was thrown about a rather commonplace industry" (figure 10.1). Larned's emphasis was typical; for him, as for other art directors, modernism was merely a bag of tricks the artist could use to set an ordinary product apart.[37]

The notion that the artist in advertising was an impresario of stage effects dated from the day of the peddler; modernism revived it in a new idiom. "Futuristic Monstrosities Are All the Rage," a *Printers' Ink* contributor proclaimed in 1925, observing that in Futuristic ads "the most extravagant ideas are employed; ideas which do not mean anything but which attract the reader's eye beyond the shadow of a doubt." Mystification, not clarity, was the keynote of the newer work. "Things that people can't quite understand seem to interest and hold them. It [Futurism] keeps them guessing." Photography was perhaps even more proficient than illustration at producing Futuristic effects: "Figures are posed against meaningless backgrounds: draped allegories seem to belong to another world. Lights flash from unexpected places and shadows crop up from nowhere." All of this made the advertisement sound like nothing so much as a nineteenth-century cabinet of curiosities, and indeed modernistic experiments could sometimes be used to reanimate traditions of "magic" in advertising strategies. Larned celebrated the attainment of "magical effects with pen and ink" in ads for Squibb Pharmaceuticals. "The homely and rather unattractive containers are transformed. One would never have suspected that a bottle of cod liver oil could be idealized to this astonishing extent, or a small box of soda given genuine artistic glamour." In skilled hands, Larned claimed, pen and ink could be "a magic wand which transforms the ugly duckling and makes a princess of the most humble Cinderella." The search for "glamour" in everyday objects revealed the resurgence of an older idiom of commodity fetishism; the notion that the advertiser could endow objects with magical properties had survived since the day of the peddler. Whatever techniques could produce "magical effects" could still be stowed in the artist's portmanteau.[38]

But modernism was not reducible to "magical effects"; it carried a double aura of cosmopolitan culture and avant-garde style (figure 10.2). In many publicists' statements (as in Calkins's polemics), the spread of modernist forms indicated the aesthetic coming-of-age of American advertising. "Men of vision are at the helm in big business today and are not blind

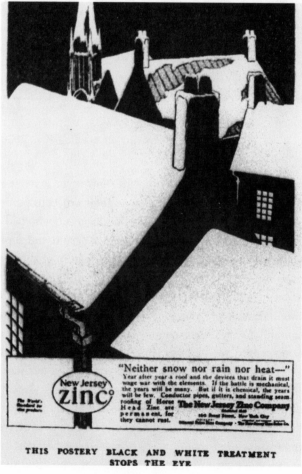

FIGURE 10.1
Advertisement for New Jersey Zinc, *Printers' Ink*, 1925.

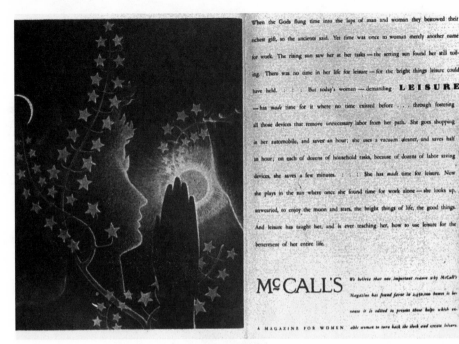

FIGURE 10.2
Ad for *McCall's* magazine, *Saturday Evening Post,* 1930.

to the appeal of beauty," wrote Manuel Rosenberg in *The Art of Advertising* (1930). Visionary ad executives allowed their artists to participate in an international community of graphic designers, a group who had maintained the vibrancy of the high-fashion poster tradition despite the depredations of the utilitarian calculus. The business appropriation of modernist forms, from this view, signaled the marriage of prestige and power; it transformed ruling-class culture from an eclectic assemblage of outmoded artifacts into a streamlined emblem of industrial might. "Modernistic art has sloughed away sentiment, stodgy detail, overslickness of painting and conventional forms of composition and design," Rosenberg wrote. "It has succeeded in taking the wheels and angles which are the symbols of our mechanical age and using them as a basis of design. It has taken the broken rhythms and atonality of our present-day music and translated them into line and tone." Like Calkins, Rosenberg and other industry spokesmen preferred to assert that corporate-sponsored modernism expressed the zeitgeist of a techno-logical society, rather than to acknowledge that it embodied the needs and aspirations of particular groups within that society.[39]

The tendency to deny the hegemonic significance of advertising art was not confined to corporate boardrooms. It affected everyone from academic art critics to folksy popularizers like Carl Sandburg. In an effort to praise Edward Steichen's modernist experiments in advertising photography, Sandburg referred to them as "justifications of the machine age."[40] This sort of oracular pronouncement was typical of the era. The idea that formalist compositions could "justify" anything, let alone anything so murky as "the machine age," went unchallenged amid the enthusiasm for corporate-sponsored versions of modernity.

American advertising agencies had at last caught up with "the machine age." The emphasis on technique over subject matter linked formalist modernism with bureaucratic rationality. By transforming a recognizable object into an abstract design, the advertising artist elevated the commodity into a denatured realm of pure form. The language of aesthetics reflected the changes since the fin de siècle. Theorists claimed to be looking for design principles rather than decorative ornament; they spurned frivolity and celebrated functionality. Elwood Whitney, an art director at J. Walter Thompson, summarized the shift toward a more overtly formalist idiom:

> It is common opinion that art is primarily spiritual, intellectual, or aesthetic feeling expressed through the medium of paintings and sculpture. This is not true. Art is very fundamental, very *vital*, very *objective*. Perhaps it would be simpler to understand it if, instead of using the term *art*, I spoke of *FORM* because form immediately conveys to the mind a physical shape. And that is exactly what I mean.[41]

This objectivist emphasis, recalling Stuart Davis, characterized the vocabulary of many modernist manifestos as well as managerial memoranda. Seeking to rescue the physicality of art from the vapors of Victorian abstraction, objectivist assertions sometimes implicitly devalued or even denied an inner life of intellect and feeling. Only a few idiosyncratic poets and artists—William Carlos Williams and Joseph Cornell, for example— could meld a passion for the object with the subtleties of subjective experience.

But in advertising apologetics, cold objectivity could be concealed by reassuring visions of progress. A deterministic optimism was consistent with certain versions of modernist dogma. The idea that outmoded art forms should be jettisoned to keep pace with technological advance was congenial to executives who thought they were the avant-garde of international business. "Art is no longer concerned with the antique or the traditional or rather sentimental subject matter of so many masterpieces of the past," a *Printers' Ink* contributor asserted in 1930. "It is concerned with relations of form and color and rhythm which may be found in a vista of shack roofs or cafeteria tables as well as in the Alps or the Himalayas." Again, this was an apt apotheosis of the ordinary, but note the aestheticizing distance of that "vista of shack roofs"—the view is still from the thirtysixth floor. In any case, *Printers' Ink's* concerns were primarily intramural: "The future of the hard-bargainer and the go-getter and the reason-why thumper looks far from rosy," the piece concluded.[42]

Similar predictions were issued at about the same time. From the perspective of Thomas Masson, a former *Saturday Evening Post* editor writing in 1931, the eclipse of realism in advertising vindicated the assertion of Oscar Wilde: "Art begins with abstract decoration, with purely imaginative and pleasurable work dealing with what is unreal and nonexistent." Masson attached Wilde's defense of imagination to a progressive framework: "What the [advertising] artist visualizes as a wild dream will be the commonplace of another generation, and will then be replaced by something 'better' "—that is, by something more aesthetically satisfying. In the bathroom fixtures trade, for example, what had once been fantastic visions of luxury were being mass-produced for the millions. So the modern use of imagination was not to be confused with the crude misrepresentations of the circus barker. Admakers "are beginning to create a fairyland, and . . . are on legitimate ground," because they were creating the dreams that sustain modern society, Masson claimed. The aesthetic imagination could be merged with progressive technophilia in a joint rhetorical venture that would reappear (among other places) in the slogan of Walt Disney's Epcot Center: "If we can dream it, we can do it." Given the legitimacy and power of the advertising vision, Masson concluded, "the conflict between the old realism and the new romanticism (known better by the term 'modernistic')" was bound to be settled in favor of the latter. Other apologists followed Masson's strategy, echoing Simon Nelson Patten in their tendency to equate consumption and civilization.[43]

The desire to see advertising as an agent of aesthetic progress affected verbal as well as visual design. Despite the growing prestige of illustration and the bemusement of novelists like Marquand, the 1920s were the high tide of literary aspiration in advertising. Copywriters, encouraged by the praise of professors and avant-garde polemicists, began to think of themselves as agents of progressive cultural forces. "The same [commercial] forces that resulted in a renaissance of English speech in the golden age of

Elizabeth are again operating to enliven the language of this century in America," the copywriter Amos Bradbury wrote in *Printers' Ink* in 1925. "What the great wits and poets of Shakespeare's and Marlowe's time did for the current speech of Merrie England, the advertising men of our day are doing for the popular vocabulary of the United States." He and his colleagues, Bradbury believed, were "forcing speech into new channels of expression," breaking down "the barriers that artificially dam the progress of our Anglo-Saxon speech."[44]

As in discussions of advertising art, a new attention to form crept into trade press debates over ad writing in the 1920s. The gospel of simple and direct came under attack for the first time since the passing of the patent medicine era; the critique involved a plea for the restoration of sorcery to commercial rhetoric. Arguments for "common speech" in copy overlooked "the magical power of words to move human feelings," the copywriter Richard Surrey wrote in 1925. The power of emotional language "*is* magical—in the sense that no scientific explanation of it has been satisfactorily advanced." Like commercial artists, copywriters possessed the mysterious capacity to move millions through the strategic employment of aesthetic forms—or so Surrey and many of his colleagues claimed.[45]

The new validation of literary copy produced a plethora of unwitting self-parodies: exercises in biblical eloquence applied to correspondence schools (Bruce Barton's "Years the Locusts Have Eaten" for the Alexander Hamilton Institute); personified products who spoke in super-simplified sentences, such as this radio speaker in 1925:

I AM THE VOICE

I am the violin. I am tom toms. I am grand opera and vaudeville. I enchant the youth like the Pied Piper. I am a teacher. I am town crier.
Verily I shrink the world . . . But never am I my own master.[46]

High aesthetic aspirations played a complex counterpoint to the everyday demands of agency work. There was a crucial tension between the desire for unique forms of expression and the need to merge them into a coherent merchandising plan that satisfied the varied tastes of copy chiefs, art directors, account executives, and, above all, clients. Writers and artists in advertising liked to think that they were free spirits, "a little bit crazy," or at least possessed of an idiosyncratic personal vision. The vestiges of the romantic cult of genius survived even in the corporate setting. "We cannot achieve individuality in advertising until a man first achieves it for himself, that is, assuming that he has any to begin with," F. Irving Fletcher wrote in *Masters of Advertising Copy* (1925). But the effort to "achieve individuality in advertising" required the submergence of the admaker's own individuality in a broad cooperative process.[47]

The problem was a little less severe for visual artists than for copywriters. Through the 1920s (and after), most agencies contracted their artwork out to artists who were not employees of the organization. As a free agent, the artist could command better pay than the copywriter, especially if he or she had established a reputation. And if the artist's signature carried some cachet, it was sometimes allowed to appear on the advertisement. Most art directors had been trained in art schools and maintained second careers as exhibiting artists. Their artistic aspirations sometimes broke down the barriers of business rivalry: Charles Coiner of N. W. Ayer and Ross Shattuck of J. Walter Thompson held a joint exhibit of their paintings in 1927. In general, the directors were sensitive to the need to preserve artistic freedom for their freelance artists.[48]

Even so, most visual artists had to sacrifice autonomy to the larger organizational agenda. It was agency policy whenever possible to eliminate the artist's signature, so as to focus attention on the advertisement itself and to hold costs down by keeping the artist anonymous longer, maintaining him or her in a merely instrumental role. Even Earnest Elmo Calkins acknowledged that "the art director uses the visible supply of artists in making up his plans exactly as the rate man uses the visible supply of mediums." The art director kept artists' names and samples of their work on file, selecting one who seemed especially able to execute the image required for a particular advertisement: a shimmering shoe, a shining face, a cozy Christmas scene. The assignments were routine, and made more nettlesome by meddlesome clients—"detail hounds" who didn't know art but knew shoes, cars, or whatever, and who insisted on tampering not only with the depiction of the product but also with the little touches that made up an advertisement's mood or spirit.[49]

To copywriters this sort of intervention was even more familiar. Copy chiefs and other executives performed major surgery on the writer's work, leaving truncated images, fractured metaphors, missed connections, and mystified readers. Harried copywriters began by trying to harmonize the conflicting views of their superiors and ended by producing self-parody. "When the kettle is a-simmerin' over cracklin' logs and the aroma of harvest's choicest viands strains one's appetite to the breaking point" began an ad for Lea & Perrins Worcestershire Sauce in 1917; it was produced by an

N. W. Ayer copywriter who no doubt was also at the breaking point. "Given an advertising executive who has difficulty making his concepts clear to a writer, and a writer who has not learned to interpret those expressions correctly and you have the situation of the writer trying frantically to 'get something up that will please him,'" an agency vice-president wrote in 1927. The result was strained mush in copy and a frustrated copywriter—the model for the stock character in later fictional treatments of advertising, the thwarted genius with the manuscript in his desk drawer.[50]

The rising discontent of copywriters surfaced at the end of the decade, in a debate that revealed two major conflicts surrounding art in advertising: between the dream of artistic autonomy and the demands of the organization, and between the delight in self-conscious artifice and the desire to preserve an air of authenticity. The debate opened when the copywriter Mac Artzt argued in *Printers' Ink* that copywriters should sign their copy; it would give the ad a personal appeal and the writer the notice he desired. He was becoming a "recognized craftsman," like the artists who signed advertising illustrations. The day was not far off, Artzt claimed, "when the copywriter will be recognized as an individual—when he will find deeper inspiration and greater glory in his work—when he will be building a reputation on a par with an established writer or artist!" At that halcyon moment, Artzt predicted, "the copywriter will be given a personality." It would be bestowed on the writer from outside, as audiences came to expect a particular style from a particular author. From this view, the hallmark of individuality was not a unique inner self but a distinctive external manner. What Artzt failed to realize was that, from the agency point of view, the artisan endangered the entire enterprise when he called attention to his own artifice.[51]

That became clear as Artzt's plea provoked a furious response from agency executives. In their view, the copy was part of a larger whole—the advertisement—which represented the views of the advertiser. Not even the artist's individuality should be acknowledged, let alone the copywriter's; if anyone should sign the advertisement it should be the company president. Further, warned G. W. Freeman of the Conklin-Mann agency, the copywriter's signature would make the advertisement less believable. It would seem less like an advertisement than an artistic performance. Artzt had cited film credits as a precedent for copy credits, but Freeman said: "God forbid that we should turn to the stage and screen for our precedents. The egoism of the actor has no place in sincere advertising. Let us not forget that the Greek word for actor was 'hypocrite.'" Reminding his readers of "the self-preserving need of truth and sincerity in advertising," Freeman charged Artzt with threatening to undermine the consumer's faith in advertising. "A large number of people believe what they read in the advertisements. Let's keep them in that happy frame of mind." Copywriters had to remain anonymous for the ad to seem all of a piece.[52]

Like other advertising spokesmen, Freeman confused truth with what a later age would call credibility: the manufactured appearance of truth that would keep consumers in "a happy frame of mind." Freeman knew, as Artzt did, that the actor, the confidence man, and the copywriter were all brothers under the skin. But Freeman wanted to conceal that kinship to produce a more convincing facade of reality in advertising. He used the rhetoric of "truth and sincerity" to rationalize the effacement of personal responsibility and the transformation of the ad into a seamless web of illusion.

Advertising executives justified the lack of authorial presence by citing a realist aesthetic. Despite the cachet of modernism, most advertising people remained discomfited by its tendency to undermine referentiality and dehumanize art. Modernist techniques could impart a magical aura to a product, but that was often insufficient. By the 1920s, the rise of market research and the growing prestige of the field of psychology had shifted agency executives' attention from the product to the purchaser. Freeman's emphasis on the need for clever illusions that would command belief and keep the consumer in "a happy frame of mind" was consistent with the emergent marketing orientation.[53]

The marketing orientation undermined formalism, redirecting the application of "magical effects" from the representation of the object to the mind and soul of the consumer. The chief goal of much advertising became not merely to endow the object with an aura of uniqueness but to associate it with human subjectivity. The project provided a prescription for preserving "human interest"—narrative, sentiment, recognizable scenes—all the baggage of nineteenth-century bourgeois culture that formalist modernism had sought to cast aside.

THE PERSISTENCE AND RESURGENCE OF "REAL LIFE"

The effort to enfold product and purchaser in a warm atmosphere of relatedness became more insistent as business rivalry increasingly involved "a healthy competition of near-duplicates," in one executive's phrase. As Richard Surrey said: "Machine-made products, turned out by the millions, must be assimilated to the destiny of things not machine-like; must be translated . . . into human terms." That often required the orchestration of human emotions. Even at the height of modernist enthusiasm in the 1920s, human-interest illustration preserved the solid bourgeois tradition of sentimental realism. While some designers experimented with pure form, others were still advising illustrators to "look through the walls of a home and transcribe what you see there." Clinging to the realist conventions of artistic transparency, many art directors continued to claim that the advertisement, like the realist painting, could provide an unproblematic window on reality. The more easily recognizable the scene, the better the ad. "The picture that does not go far afield from real people, doing real things, seen in everyday life, is the one of widest appeal," announced a *Printers' Ink* contributor in 1922. Authenticity, not artifice, was the benchmark of achievement.[54]

This was not simply a matter of factual accuracy; "real life" in advertising referred to the ad's capacity to resonate with the reader's subjective experience. Despite the rhetoric of realism surrounding it, the human-interest approach did not require the abandonment of imagination in advertisements. On the contrary. "No one ever in his life bought a mere piece of merchandise—*per se,*" the copywriter John Starr Hewitt argued in 1925. "What he buys is the satisfaction of a physical need or appetite, or the gratification of some dream about his life." The most usable genre for this purpose was sentimental, didactic narrative realism. Advertising preserved some fundamental affinities with mass culture even in the heyday of the high-hat stuff. When the agency head W. H. Heath argued for "giving the consumer booklet a real literary flavor," the example he gave was Colgate's booklet on Cashmere Bouquet talcum: it told "the Story of Fragrance" rather than the story of the Colgate factory, and it was "just the sort of beautifully written and sentimental literature that women will read." The key moves in the rhetoric of national advertising remained the tropes of bourgeois realism: not only the endlessly repeated pattern of upward mobility, perhaps even magical self-transformation, but the technique of eavesdropping—the letter referring to bad breath or soiled underwear that the inamorato "decided to print as an ad." In this genre, writers were reduced to abbreviated imitators of pulp fiction and artists to transcribers of everyday life.[55]

The pursuit of realism put a high premium on photography. The idea that photographs constituted a "universal language" could be traced to the time of Daguerre. In the early-twentieth-century United States, the notion spread, popularized by prophets like the poet Vachel Lindsay who lumped photographs with cartoons and movies and predicted the onset of a "hieroglyphic civilization." As advertisers searched for forms of communication that were quickly and easily understood, more and more turned to the camera. Between 1922 and 1927, the percentage of full or half-page advertisements in *Ladies' Home Journal* using photographs rose gradually from 14 percent to 25 percent. Literal-minded manufacturers were persuaded that photos could "prove" beyond argument the purity or high quality of a product. Not all advertising executives were enchanted with this aspect of the medium. Paul Cherington of J. Walter Thompson preferred line or wash drawings, which "convey something besides a vulgar, half-witted literalness."[56]

Yet literalism was not the main appeal of photography. As early as 1922, W. L. Larned was celebrating the influence of photography on advertising illustration in general. "Natural people are doing natural things. Affectation is taboo. . . . Style appeal is vastly more than an exact reproduction of the garment. . . . There is far more action in the illustration of today—go, zip, animation. Copywriters have assisted in this, by seeking farther than the commercially obvious for opening leads for advertising stories." If (as Larned implied) the pulse of life quickened when it was felt by a photographer, then the camera was an appropriate instrument to stimulate consumer desire.[57]

What especially attracted the advertiser to photography was the medium's promise of combining "sincerity in displaying his product and drama in portraying its virtues," to quote the catalog for a 1930 exhibition of advertising photographs at the N. W. Ayer gallery. When the occasion required it, the photograph could be coolly objective or energized with emotion. The secret of the photograph's success, resolutely ignored by the general public and much of the advertising press as well, was its manipulability. "In fact, every photograph is a fake from start to finish, a purely impersonal unmanipulated photograph being practically impossible," the young Edward Steichen wrote with pardonable hyperbole in *Camera Work* (1903). Of course, there were technical limitations in the early days; there are some today. (Tuna fish never has photographed well.) In 1917 a J. Walter Thompson crew tried to photograph the Shoshone Canyon for the Burlington railroad but discovered that the camera could not capture the canyon's size and grandeur; "the new illustration was made from a sketch we submitted in which the canyon was exaggerated so as to give a true and realistic impression of the vastness which one actually sees and feels when driving through." A "true and realistic impression" of a subjective feeling required the intervention of an interpreter more subtle than the photographer.[58]

But by the late 1920s this was no longer the case. JWT account executives were routinely discussing how the photographer Hiller White had "faked some very interesting interiors" in several campaigns. What is remarkable, given such practices, is the durable utility of the belief that photography provided a transparent window on life itself: Sloan's Liniment, for example, appropriated the documentary authority of Lewis Hines's work when its agency hired him to depict the working-class beneficiaries of the product. The illusion of reality was assisted by the practice, increasingly prevalent in the 1920s, of omitting the photographer's signature and simply including the words "actual photograph." In that illusion of actuality lay advertising's opportunity, as Manuel Rosenberg observed in 1930: the public still believed in the "truth-telling" power of photography, no matter how thoroughly it was manipulated. So "the cameraman, too, is an artist," Rosenberg announced, and his work had a great selling value.[59]

Probably the person who did the most to raise advertising photography to the status of an art form was Steichen (1879–1973). Beginning his photography career around the turn of the century as a pictorialist who later helped Alfred Stieglitz start the Photo-Secession Group, Steichen shared the fin-de-siècle passion for maidens under moons and misty symbolism. But he differed from many of his experimentalist contemporaries in his exceptional capacity to attract elite patronage. After a stint in aerial photography during World War I, he was converted from pictorialism to "straight" photography—hard-edged and apparently objective. He resurfaced after the war in New York as a fashion portraitist for Condé Nast Publications and quickly established a reputation for crystallizing the public persona of a celebrity. Like many other young and ambitious Americans emerging from the crucible of war, he was habituated to teamwork and hungry for creature comforts. In 1923 he signed an exclusive contract with J. Walter Thompson and remained on their payroll for twelve years, until he was hired by Charles Coiner at N. W. Ayer.[60]

It is easy to dismiss Steichen as a sycophantic servant of corporate capitalism, as many of his contemporaries did. Walker Evans wrote: "[Steichen's] general note is money, understanding of advertising values, special feeling for parvenu elegance, slick technique, over all of which is thrown a hardness and superficiality of America's latter day, and has nothing to do with any person." Steichen echoed other advertising apologists in claiming that "the great art of any period was produced in collaboration with the particular commercialism of that period," but he added, "or by revolutionaries who stood clear and clean outside of that commercialism and fought it tooth and nail and worked for its destruction. In the twilight zone of the 'art for art's sake' school all things are still born." To these false antitheses and superannuated straw men, Steichen added a dash of pseudopopulism, the sort favored by Calkins and other industry spokesmen. "When I was putting my soul onto canvas, and wrapping it up in a gold frame, and selling it to a few snob millionaires who could afford it—after I got to thinking about it, I did not feel quite clean," Steichen told a JWT staff meeting in 1928. "But now I have an exhibition every month [in the magazines] that reaches hundreds of thousands of people through editorial and advertising pages." Steichen may have really believed this, but he also had reason to flatter the assembled executives. During his early career at JWT he was not only paid well but was given unprecedented autonomy, and unlike any other photographer in the business, he was allowed to sign his advertising work, at least for a while.[61]

Despite Steichen's atypicality, in many ways his advertising work reflected broader developments in commercial photography. Like other photographers in the 1920s, he played along with the prevailing belief that the camera's reality was unmediated. His move from pictorialism to straight photography was an attempt to offer an objective rendering of "things as they are"—especially the things advertised by JWT clients. Yet it was also a modernist move in the formal sense that straight photography did not pretend to be painting or drawing or anything but photography; it relied only on the unique capabilities of the camera as a medium. While many of Steichen's commercial photographs assisted in the modernist fetishizing of the commodity, what especially excited advertising executives about his work was his capacity to evoke a subjective response in the observer. Despite his obeisance to objective form and hard-edged reality, Steichen remained true to the pictorialist tradition in his theatrical manipulation of effects designed to create particular emotions in the audience.[62]

In an address to the JWT staff in 1928, Steichen showed how skillfully he could orchestrate human-interest themes. "The value of the camera is its objectivity," he began. "But you can have objectivity in many ways. I believe it is impossible to get the whole truth and nothing but the truth in any photograph." What was possible to get was the truth of a particular human emotion at a precise moment. Speaking of a newspaper photograph of an accused murderer stepping off a train after a night of interrogation, Steichen said:

> That thing has something of Michelangelo in it. Its tremendous power is simple—a person, nerve-wracked and shattered, eyes closed and mouth open. If ever I saw a handsome man under a great strain, as in one of the Greek tragedies, it is that fuzzy gray snapshot in the newspaper.
>
> That is the greatest kind of objectivity photography is capable of. That is the kind of thing I'm trying to put into photographs all the time; to bring it down to more simple things—aliveness. To show the difference between a young lady coming home from work, says she has a headache, is bored, mother wants her to help wash dishes, so tired—telephone rings and it's Bill, wants to go to the movies—And it's all gone. That's the quality of aliveness.[63]

Perhaps Steichen's paean to "aliveness" was a response to executives' preoccupation with human interest. Agency needs pressed Steichen and other photographers to move away from the modernist fetishism of commodities and toward the conventions of bourgeois realism: recognizable scenes, didactic narrative, relentless sentimentality. Though Steichen paid lip service to the fetishizing of objects by recalling his own experiments with a matchbox, his vignette of the tired girl represented the real future of advertising photography. Photography began to seem the perfect vehicle for middlebrow alternatives to high-hat stuff.

The onset of the Depression sharpened that perception. As the economic news worsened, many in the trade press professed to hope that hard times would mean an end to "the artificial 'sophistication' which many of us have been pleased to regard as modern," and a turn toward the humble actualities of ordinary people's lives. This change was never fully accomplished: many people at the big agencies clung to the notion that a patina of ruling-class elegance could be painted over everything. In 1933, Helen Resor introduced Margaret Bourke-White to the creative staff at JWT with the hope that Bourke-White could "remove some of the artificiality in our photos: our workers look like capitalists." (Several people in the audience grumbled, "They want to look like capitalists.") But despite the persistence of the class-bound belief that the clean-cut executive constituted a universal ideal, there was no question that in advertising, the Depression at first undermined and then virtually eliminated high-art aspirations. Photography was a key instrument in the process, especially appealing because it was less expensive to hire photographers (apart from big names like Steichen or Bourke-White) than freelance illustrators.[64]

Still, the move toward photography was not simply a case of the survival of the cheapest. It was part of a broader attempt to restore an emotionally charged vision of "real life" to national advertising—an effort that led agencies increasingly to borrow motifs and formats from the world of mass entertainment. Steichen's work, as the art historian Patricia Johnston suggests, moved from the stiff, posed quality of the 1920s campaigns to the melodramatic vignettes he devised for Scott Tissues, in which the photographer achieved a "voyeuristic motion picture sense" by backlighting faces against a dark background; they appeared crisp at first glance but on inspection grainy (figure 10.3). The overall effect was to reinforce a clear

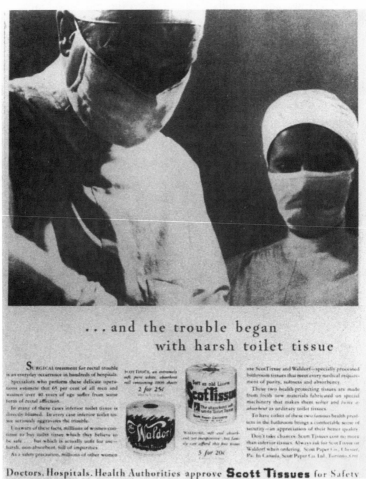

FIGURE 10.3
Scott Tissues advertisement, *Saturday Evening Post*, 1931.

sense of dramatization, though the dramatic model was the emergent Hollywood cinema rather than silent film. This meant a further move away from any vestigial "staged" effect and toward a more thoroughgoing illusionism.[65]

During the early thirties, the advertising trade press regularly discussed the prospect of "injecting motion picture drama into the photographic picture" and recommended the use of photography that "elevates your sales message to the heights of a stirring drama in real life." As early as 1931, an art director named James Yates told a JWT staff meeting to take a lesson from Hollywood: Mrs. Jones doesn't want reality; that's a wolf at the door. She wants *romance*. Many advertisements came to resemble the more lurid versions of Hollywood melodrama.[66]

There was not much movement in the opposite direction, toward advertising in films. The longest-lived relationship was what is now called the tie-in. In 1930, the JWT executive Dan Danker reported from Hollywood that Lever Brothers, Swift & Company, Jergens, Libby McNeill & Libby, Standard Brands, and Shell Oil had all managed to get their products in grocery store and drugstore windows in the Hal Roach comedy *Our Gang*. "Our clients should know this service is available," Danker told his colleagues. "They might be willing to pay a fee for it." While tie-ins became commonplace by the later 1930s, beyond that there was continuing tension between Hollywood and Madison Avenue. Advertising people were alternately bemused and annoyed by the sensationalizing of agency life in films like *The Easiest Way* (1931) and *Turnabout* (1940). But a good part of the conflict was ethnocultural. The young WASP executives at JWT, for example, returned from the West Coast smirking about their sojourn among "the semitic tribes." It was as if Jewish moviemakers reminded admakers of their common peddler past; anti-Semitic reflexes were intertwined with the desire to distance national advertising from its disreputable origins. As the account executive George Faulkner acknowledged to a JWT group meeting in 1930, the big agencies had become shy of showmanship: "The word showman carries an undignified, cheap connotation. It has a vaguely Semitic, Barnumish, Broadway air to it. One thinks of ornate movie cathedrals, blatant advertising, overpolite ushers." Given those attitudes, small wonder that national advertising kept its distance from the movies.[67]

The Protestant past of the advertising business continued to assert itself, even at the height of Depression-induced competition for clients. The influence of formalist modernism was short-lived; during the early and mid-1930s it passed out of advertising and into industrial design. The sobering impact of the Depression only made the representation of "real life" a more urgent task. Plain speech lived, tricked out in tawdry clothes. Overwrought faces were linked to literalist, didactic narrative with themes familiar from bourgeois literature: status anxiety, upward mobility. Advertising incorporated exotic or surreal elements from mass culture and drained them of vitality by channeling them to its instrumental purposes.

Nowhere was this clearer than in the appropriation of comic strips by advertising. The "funny papers" had been part of American popular consciousness since the 1890s. Their strip format was a concession to linear narrative, but their bizarre characters, pervasive violence, contempt for authority, and dreamlike atmosphere constituted a definite departure from the conventions of bourgeois realism—a vision of a reanimated world. It is possible to overstate the "subversive" potential of early-twentieth-century comic strips, but there is no question that some, such as Winsor McCay's *Little Nemo,* could be characterized as genuine contributions to a popular surrealist tradition (figure 10.4). Within a few decades, William Randolph Hearst and other newspaper owners had syndicated comic strips and subjected them to corporate market discipline. McCay himself was the first casualty: he allowed himself to be lured away from Little Nemo by Hearst and spent the rest of his career cranking out boring editorial cartoons, some of them in praise of national advertising. By the early 1930s, most strips had become comparatively respectable embodiments of petit-bourgeois norms. In George McManus's *Bringing Up Father,* for example, Jiggs could lie to Maggie, but not vice versa. Still, as the persistence of George Herriman's surreal *Krazy Kat* until the artist's death in 1944 suggested, the comic strip form preserved some vestiges of vernacular antiauthoritarianism.[68]

National advertisers had used cartoon characters for years, but not until 1931 did they discover the comic strip, when a full-page comic-strip ad for Grape-Nuts, titled "Suburban Joe," appeared in Hearst's *Comic Weekly.* Other advertisers quickly followed suit, and soon the funny pages were among the most desirable advertising space in newspapers. By the summer of 1932, comic-strip advertisements were appearing in *Good Housekeeping* and similar national magazines. As *Fortune* magazine noted in 1933, these "thriving but uncultured children of the depression" would have been unthinkable in 1928; they were a sign that advertising agencies had deliberately sacrificed their "airs and graces" in a frantic scramble for sales. The pioneers in "continuity copy" (as comic-strip advertising was

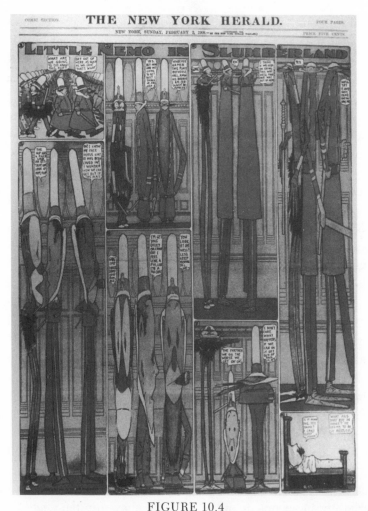

FIGURE 10.4

"Little Nemo in Slumberland," from *New York Herald*, February 2, 1908.

called) were advertisers of low-priced goods: Lever Brothers (Lifebuoy, Rinso, Lux) and General Foods (Grape-Nuts, Postum, Post Toasties, Jell-O, Minute Tapioca). But the format soon spread to more expensive commodities. To critics, the use of continuity copy, with its crude "before and after" themes and its general abandonment of "restraint and reason," was a return to the bad old days of the patent medicine show.[69]

There was something to this. Comic strips' reliance on narrative allowed for heavy emphasis on rhetorical strategies rooted in nineteenth-century evangelical culture and perfected by patent medicine peddlers: the use of testimonials, the promise of self-transformation. Continuity copy (like "editorial style" ads) also recalled novelistic conventions—not only the themes of personal development and status ascent but also the technique of eavesdropping. Through conversation balloons the comic-strip artist created a vigorous vernacular version of the effect that had been sought by novelists from Charles Brockden Brown to Henry James and Edith Wharton.[70]

Admakers saw the comic strip as another popular art form they could use to enliven their overly dignified craft. But while their hopes may have been borne out in sales, the artistic vitality of the advertisements did not improve. National advertisers linked the comic-strip form to the most leaden and literal commercial conventions available. The results were nearly self-parodic. To take one of innumerable examples, in a Quaker Oats ad of 1934, figures made with Quaker Puffed Wheat enacted a standard breakfast table scene: Father scolds, Mother frets, Junior won't eat; Mother's friend advises puffed grains; Junior is transformed into a heroic cereal eater. More commonly the characters were recognizably human: they struck wooden poses and wore the bland expressions common to illustrations in didactic, sentimental magazine fiction (figure 10.5) This was a far cry from Krazy Kat.[71]

After a few years, the comic-strip formula began to pall. One March day in 1933 an editor of Hearst's *Comic Weekly* told the J. Walter Thompson creative staff that continuity copy had failed to come up with characters comparable to those in the comics. "You can't say they're *like* anybody," he said of the "young marrieds" and other generic figures in the ad strips. By 1937, W. J. Weir, a copywriter at Fletcher & Ellis, was speculating on the reasons for the rise and (incipient) decline of the format. In his view, advertising people found in "the continuity strip the *tangible* thing that they had been looking for for years." By providing a simple, almost syllogistic formula, it seemed to offer a sense of solidity to business executives who did not realize that advertising was "as tangible as spider webs"; they did not know, Weir said, that it doesn't matter whether you make a logical argument if "your message isn't *vital*." Continuity copy was a wooden, didactic reinterpretation of popular forms that were potentially surrealist and subversive.[72]

Despite attempts to borrow the emotional resonance of mass culture, national advertising still too often lacked the pulsating throb of sincerity. Perhaps this was inevitable, given advertising's utilitarian aims and reliance on repetitive formulas. Like the movie studios and publishing houses, the biggest New York advertising agencies were lumbering oligopolistic giants

FIGURE 10.5
Advertisement for Lever Brothers Company, *Good Housekeeping*, 1936.

who sought to minimize economic risk and maximize control over large sectors of a national market. Even as corporations aimed to endow their goods with an aura of uniqueness, concentration of economic power promoted standardization of sales imagery as well of the products it was designed to promote. The same logic that encouraged formulaic movies and magazine fiction reinforced the sameness of advertising art.

Neither in advertising nor in other forms of mass culture was the predominance of formula a result of industry executives' "giving the people what they want." Despite market research, nobody really knew what the people wanted, except that they wanted to be entertained; the trick, for advertisers as well as publishers and movie producers, was to keep profits predictable by entertaining as many as possible. As the historian David Paul Nord has written, "Formulas are, if anything, more likely to reflect producers' rather than audiences' values. . . . *The greater the market power a producer has (the greater the opportunity to control risk), the tighter and more standardized will be the formulas.*"[73] The convergence of formulas in advertising and mass entertainment during the Depression embodied the common interests of corporate image producers in an era when competition was declining and oligopolies were consolidating their market power.

The meshing of advertising and entertainment became clearest in the rise of radio. There was a brief period during the early 1920s when the future of radio as a commercial medium remained in doubt, but after 1925, national advertising invaded the airwaves with stunning speed. By 1928 the notion of buying radio time was as firmly established at the big agencies as the notion of buying newspaper or magazine space. The difference was that in radio the advertiser (through the agency) controlled the entertainment as well as the messages about the product. The result was a complete subordination of art to commerce. "What is the test of a radio program's merits?" Robert Simon of J. Walter Thompson asked in 1932. "It comes to you in one word: sales." A boring, unintelligent program "is still a 'good' program if it induces people to buy the stuff it advertises."[74]

Successful writers for radio tailored their scripts to sell specific products. Irna Phillips, for more than three decades an author of well-known soap operas, revealed the process at work in a proposal she submitted to General Foods Corporation, manufacturers of La France and Satina laundry products. During the early thirties, La France and Satina, through the Young & Rubicam agency, sponsored Phillips's *Today's Children*. The serial dramatized the conflicts between Mother Moran and the Young Moderns of the next generation, especially her daughter Fran (an artist with Lane Advertising), her son Terry, and Fran's sometime fiancé Bob Crane (an aspiring lawyer and local reform politico). Phillips imagined a situation where "Mother Moran takes it on herself to help Terry" keep his job selling laundry accessories. "She comes to the mike at the end of one episode and starts to appeal to her radio friends to help Terry. The announcer interrupts her to give her the good news that 'La France' has just contracted to buy many thousands."[75]

This approach typified network radio programming from the 1930s through the 1940s. It seemed to solve the advertiser's perennial problem of introducing the product in a "natural," uncommercial atmosphere, weaving it into a seamless web of illusory "real life." As a JWT staff member noted in 1930: "The story always marches down the copy slant straight to a commercial which does not seem like an intrusion." Whether this affected the artistic vitality of radio drama was a difficult question.[76]

Part of the difficulty stemmed from the impossibility of comparing radio directly to print media. Many people in and outside advertising recognized that radio in some ways represented a return from literacy to orality—the world of the public lecturer but also of the carnival barker and the patent medicine impresario. E. P. H. James, the promotional director for NBC radio, summarized the upbeat version of the conventional wisdom in 1940 when he said that radio was a return to "the oldest advertising medium—the spoken word. Undoubtedly, the first commercial attempts to 'win friends and influence people' were oral." But this did not, for James, represent a reversion to preliterate primitivism: "It is easier to sell a product by sound than by type. The voice is infinitely more capable of giving emphasis to certain points than is type, even with such artificial aids as bold face, italics, underscore, etc." James and other advocates of radio recognized that the medium offered unprecedented possibilities for generating an atmosphere of personal intimacy between advertiser and audience—the goal that print advertisers had been trying to reach for many years.[77]

Yet many in the big agencies, even those whose clients sponsored numerous radio programs, remained skeptical. Print-oriented copywriters and account executives doubted that radio could convey any idea more complicated than those that could be found on a billboard. For them, the radio announcer embodied not intimacy but pseudo-intimacy, a return to the repressed past of advertising. Indeed, by the mid-1930s the idea that radio represented a recovery of "the carnival spirit" had become a commonplace in the discourse of advertising. For some, this development was a disastrous decline in dignity, for others a pragmatic adjustment to parlous times. Radio advertising offered a revised version of the patent medicine appeal—smoother, more technically sophisticated, more wedded to emergent mass culture formulas, but still dependent on narratives of transformation and "sophisticated hokum."[78]

The notion of the advertiser as snake-oil salesman and smirking seducer resurfaced, prompted by the hysteria and prurience of copy appeals. Advertisers began to conclude, as they had in the 1910s, that if they were going to avoid government regulation thay would have to give at least the appearance of regulating themselves. Limits were put on the search for ever-more-melodramatic presentations of "real life" in advertising. The recoil from kitsch reopened the door, at least a crack, for the return of the avant-garde.

TOWARD MARRIAGE:
AVANT-GARDE AND KITSCH, 1937–1970

Advertisers began to rediscover modernist forms in the late 1930s as alternatives to mainstream narrative and sentimentality. When the Franklin Mint held an international exhibit of modernist advertising and propaganda posters in 1937, the art critic Christian Brinton celebrated their "rigorously considered design patterns" and "euclidean explicitness," but also counseled viewers to "capitulate . . . to the daring enchantment of their spells." Merging ordered geometry and phantasmagoria of movement, the modern posters melded rationality and magic, but in no sense did they evoke common experience. "The essential point to grasp," Brinton wrote, "is that modern poster [art], despite its specific objective, is not realism, not reality. It is super-reality—reality stripped of irrelevant, disturbing detail." The antirealist foundation of modernist poster design assured that it would have a more direct influence on lettering, packaging, and corporate logos than on advertising art. Even after the resurgence of war-built prosperity in the early 1940s, when advertisers again had surplus cash available to purchase the cachet of fine art, they often turned to representational painters of the American Scene—"the corn-belt gothic, or sage-brush baroque tradition," as Brinton had scornfully called it. For many advertisers, highbrow kitsch remained preferable to formalist modernism.[79]

Yet the early 1940s became something of a golden age for avant-garde commercial artists as well as for their more conventional competitors. Brinton was not far off when he predicted that the Franklin Mint exhibit would have an impact on "publicity design" comparable to that of the Armory Show of 1913 on studio art. The 1937 exhibit coincided with the emergence of a large émigré community of European artists and intellectuals, refugees from fascism, in New York. A few visionary corporate leaders, led by Walter Paepcke of the Container Corporation of America

(CCA), began to hire modernist designers. Paepcke signed up László Moholy-Nagy of the Bauhaus to redesign his trademarks and trucks, and the prominent poster artist Cassandre to supervise an advertising campaign. For Paepcke this was only the beginning. He became a leading patron of modernism in commercial art, and the advertising agency that handled his account, N. W. Ayer, became a haven for an extraordinarily free-spirited group of artists.[80]

Ayer had long been in the lead of agency efforts to suffuse national advertising with an atmosphere of high art. The company ran its own art galleries in Philadelphia, where Charles Coiner and the other art directors showed the canvases they had painted on evenings and weekends. Ayer commissioned Georgia O'Keeffe for a Dole Pineapple campaign and Rockwell Kent for Steinway pianos. Coiner recalled, "We were trying to use [art] to get readership, attention, and character to the advertising of our clients." As the art historian Michele Bogart has observed, this practice made the distinction between fine and commercial art into a marketing strategy. Among the beneficiaries of this effort were artists as well as advertisers. Ayer was the only big agency that was truly open to modern graphic design in the late thirties and early forties. Ironically, given the mythic stature of this period in the history of the New York art world, Ayer's location in Philadelphia was a distinct advantage for the artists who worked there: separated from the regimented corporate world of midtown Manhattan, they cultivated a more relaxed rhythm of work and life.[81]

The experience of Leo Lionni at Ayer typified the best an artist might hope for in advertising during this period.[82] Lionni was born in 1910 in Amsterdam to a Dutch mother and an Italian executive with the Atlantic Richfield Oil Company. When Leo was twelve the company transferred his father to the United States; four years later Leo joined his parents there for a year. It was 1926, and American advertising was expressing the furious energies of modernity—or so it seemed to an alert sixteen-year old. In just a year, Lionni recalls, he became "very American." He returned to Genoa and immediately set about cartooning an ad campaign for Campari. Traveling to Milan alone, he presented the cartoons to the president of the company, who applauded the young man's ambition without adopting his work.

Like many of his European contemporaries, Lionni tried to meld modernist art and proletarian politics. A self-taught artist, he exhibited some of his paintings in a major Futurist show in 1932, moved to Milan, started a graphic design business out of his home, and celebrated Bauhaus architecture in occasional essays. Fascism and war ended this interlude. In April 1939, Lionni came to America with seventy dollars in his pocket. Landing in New York, he went to all the employment agencies and found nothing. Then he went to Philadelphia, where he had attended school in 1926. Atlantic Richfield was a client of N. W. Ayer, and Lionni's father knew some people at the agency. So Lionni was able to secure an interview with Coiner. Ayer eventually hired Lionni at fifty dollars a week as an assistant to one of the art directors, Leon Karp, whom Lionni described as a "post-impressionist." By the fall Lionni had saved enough to send for his wife and children.

At Ayer in the 1940s, Lionni learned the trade of advertising art. He took over Coiner's night school class in layout, staying just a step ahead of his students but confident that he "knew typography and layout instinctively." He had done cartooning, collage, and abstract design but never any "real painting." But like the others in the Ayer art department, he began painting in his off-hours. He also joined a left-wing Italian organization which sought vainly to bring socialism to the city's Italian workers. Lionni protected his socialist commitments in a sealed compartment while he worked for major capitalist organizations. "I don't mind doing anything, as long as it's morally not offensive," he said. When AT & T ran an ad campaign against socialism in the early 1940s, part of the post–New Deal resurgence of business ideology, Lionni refused to participate. No one at Ayer complained, partly because Lionni had forged a special relationship with Coiner.

Within a few years, Lionni had proved his value to the company. He began in the trenches, knocking out 4 × 6 sketches of Florsheim shoes in ten minutes, until the arrival of a young man named Andy Warhol, who lived with his mother and ten cats, had "clammy hands" (Lionni remembered)—and perfected "the five-minute shoe." Lionni moved on to more responsibility, using several springboards. One was a campaign for *Ladies' Home Journal* in which he introduced the slogan "Never underestimate the power of a woman." Another opportunity presented itself when a crisis developed in the Ford account, the largest at the agency. Coiner asked everyone in the art department to submit proposals; Edsel Ford picked Lionni's "European-looking" campaign. Lionni was beginning to establish a reputation as a man who could bring modernist flair to mass-produced goods. He consolidated that reputation by helping Coiner to assemble avant-garde artists (mostly émigrés) for the CCA account as well by contributing his own designs to Paepcke's wartime campaigns.

Though Lionni was offered double his Ayer salary by J. Walter Thompson, he preferred the "bohemian atmosphere" in Philadelphia. But within a few years, Ayer too seemed constraining. In 1948, Lionni recalls, "I became very nostalgic for both painting and Italy. By painting I mean being freer." At Ayer he was bumping his head on the organizational ceiling. "I couldn't go any further because Charlie [Coiner] was in the way. I loved him." He proposed to the president that a new job be designed for him—a position as liaison between sales, copy, and art that would later be called creative director. "You want to star, don't you?" the president asked. Lionni admitted he did. "Well, I want my company to star," the president said. The exchange summed up the obstacles to artistic autonomy that even the most fortunate artists faced in the corporation—even during this period of resurgent high-art aspirations.

Formalist modernism took some of the sting out of corporate constraints. As Lionni said, it was possible "to teach the creative pleasures of craftsmanship" to commercial designers; it was even possible to believe that by refashioning billboards, packages, and corporate trademarks they were creating "a more civilized visual environment." That was a necessary and honorable goal.

Nevertheless, within two years after his exchange with the president of Ayer, Lionni had left the agency. He took a year's leave of absence to paint in Italy, returned to Ayer, and in the midst of laying out a toilet paper campaign decided he had had enough. Determined to create more design leeway for himself, he started his own firm but was soon lured back into corporate work as art director for *Fortune.* The magazine gave him at least as much freedom as Ayer had; Henry Luce even defended Lionni when the witch-hunting group Red Channels attacked the artist for joining with his friend Ben Shahn to organize the National Emergency Civil Liberties Committee. As at Ayer, Lionni's leftist politics were his own affair, provided he produced the designs his employers wanted.

At the age of fifty Lionni decided he wanted to stop working for other people. When he told his supervisor at *Fortune,* Del Paine, of his intention to quit, Paine asked: "Aren't you happy here?" Lionni said, "I'm very happy." "Then why quit?" Paine asked. "I don't want to be that happy," Lionni told him. He could not spend the rest of his life simulating the perpetual bonhomie required of middle and upper management in the American corporation. He was not sure what the alternatives were, but on the commuter train home to Connecticut one day when his grandchildren happened to be with him, he tore little splotches of blue and yellow out of a stray *New Yorker* magazine and made up the story of Little Blue and Little Yellow. It became a successful children's book and Lionni began another career as an author and illustrator—a career that allowed him both to develop his gift for collage and to express more openly his pacifist and socialist sympathies.

Lionni's career suggests that even in the best of times, under the most privileged circumstances, the artist who had an individual vision of the world, who wanted to be more than a skilled technician, faced frustration in the modern ad agency. Corporate advertising was radically different from past forms of patronage. The analogy between modern commercial artists and Michelangelo, so dear to Calkins, Carl Sandburg, and other apologists, collapsed on close inspection. As Rockwell Kent observed in 1947, had the Sistine Chapel been decorated according to modern advertising methods, the agency would first have shown a series of color sketches to the cardinals, then tried to incorporate their criticisms. Finally the agency would have "sent for Michelangelo and, spreading the sketches before his astounded eyes, have told him what he was supposed to do. Michelangelo, like every self-respecting artist before his time or since, would have declined."[83]

Even if the artist was not on an agency payroll (and Kent was not), the problem of autonomy was present. Art by committee, like writing by committee, was a recipe for mush; marketing considerations dictated systematic inoffensiveness, or the formulaic sweetness of kitsch. The only risks the artist could hope to take were in the area of formal innovation. Modernist designers had to check their political and cultural convictions (if they had any) at the agency door. (Lionni's refusal to work on the AT&T campaign was the exception that proved the rule.) All that was wanted from modernists was their technical virtuosity.

Still, there were a few attempts by advertisers to allow artists substantive as well as formal autonomy. Paepcke took the lead, inaugurating a CCA campaign that was designed to restore artists' interpretive power by having them illustrate "Great Ideas of Western Man." He hired Mortimer Adler to select quotations from his Syntopicon (or index) of the ideas in the fifty-four Great Books of the Western World. The Ayer agency then distributed several quotations to each of the artists it commissioned. The artists each chose a quotation and interpreted it in any medium or style they wanted. The range of artists commissioned was wide, and some of the resulting work embodied a powerful idiosyncratic vision (figure 10.6).[84]

Nevertheless, the project had built-in limitations. Paepcke admitted in

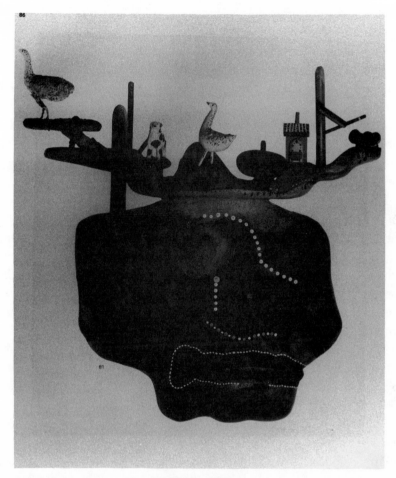

FIGURE 10.6

"What Can I Do?... Become What You Have Always Been," 1967, Roy Dean De Forest, painted fiberglass and wood. *National Museum of American Art, Smithsonian Institution.*

1955 that he had omitted controversial authors whose names would reduce or distort the effect of their statements. "Karl Marx, for example, could hardly have made a statement of moral principle, no matter how true or sincere it might have been, which could have been universally accepted at face value by the American people." The focus on truths that would be "universally accepted at face value" led to broader difficulties than the predictable blacklisting of Marx; it ruled out the exploration of disturbing (or even mildly controversial) truths; it ended by promoting a pervasive blandness. The Great Ideas began to look like an indiscriminate bunch of humanist bromides; Nietzsche emerged from it as a burgermeister spouting aphorisms after a heavy meal.[85]

The yoking of formal innovation to humanist sentimentality portended the shape of things to come: avant-garde technique could be wedded to familiar subject matter. Throughout the 1950s, the more venturesome agencies like Ogilvy & Mather and Doyle Dane Bernbach continued to incorporate modernist designs, resisting the influential Rosser Reeves, who maintained that the chief task facing advertising people was to adapt the clunking logic of the Unique Selling Proposition to the new medium of television.[86]

But in the early 1960s that medium was invaded by filmmakers with hand-held cameras. Their impact was most apparent when the Pepsi Generation burst onto America's TV screens in 1964, nubile bodies cavorting in transports of joy so intense the kids might have required hospitalization had the ecstasy lasted more than sixty seconds. In many ways, this was California kitsch: all the scenes that have become the visual clichés of soft-drink advertising were beginning to fall into place, as were the modernist forms for representing them.

The sanitizing process that has always been so important to capitalist realism became especially apparent in 1969, when Batten, Barton, Durstine, and Osborn (BBDO, the agency handling the Pepsi account) hired a filmmaker named Ed Vorkapich to drive across the country, shooting film that could be used with Pepsi's new slogan: "You've got a lot to live, and Pepsi's got a lot to give." Vorkapich knew, first of all, the scenes had to be uniformly upbeat. Conventional wisdom at BBDO and Pepsi mirrored that of the media at large: "the country was depressed" by protest against the war in Vietnam (though not, for some reason, by the war itself). "It was the sociological nadir of the American spirit," a Pepsi executive recalled. "Protests. Woodstock. Drugs. A surly and sullen generation occupying the dean's office, burning it down—whatever it was. It was all that sixties stuff." The determination to airbrush "all that sixties stuff" out of the picture melded with the longstanding desire to appropriate some of Coca-Cola's All-American iconography. The result was an impulse to create "an adult voice" lecturing rebellious youth (as a Pepsi staffer put it): "Hey, for Godsakes, it ain't too terribly bad what we've got going for us in the good old U.S. of A. OK, we do have a wonderful country." This was all fine with Vorkapich; he was "feeling positive" about America too, and he was perfectly willing to follow the agency's explicit instructions: no jeans, no long hair, no "hippie types."[87]

Despite this systematic conventionality, the Pepsi campaign displayed some venturesome techniques. The rapid-fire clustering of images recalled early-twentieth-century modernist antecedents; the Imagist return to "the things themselves," the Vorticist attempt to capture dynamic movement in precise forms, and most directly, the technique of visual montage developed in the photographs of John Heartfeld and the films of Sergei Eisenstein. What had originated as forms of protest found widest circulation as expressions of power.

Aesthetic innovation also marked Vorkapich's lighting techniques. He imagined himself a "gunfighter" in a roomful of "organization men." The image retailored the artist's role to meet familiar male anxieties: still a romantic outsider, he was nevertheless tough and effective among the eunuchs of Madison Avenue. When Vorkapich shot his first commercial for Pepsi, Hollywood convention held that you couldn't shoot after four in the afternoon because the light would look yellow. "But that's the prettiest time!" Vorkapich protested. He proceeded to shoot in the late afternoon, with the sun behind his subjects. "What the hell is going on here? . . . We're not making art films! We're making commercials!" a Pepsi executive complained when he saw the film. But the new style prevailed; backlighting and sun flares became staples of commercial filmmaking.[88]

In a sense this was appropriate. The filmmaker who had pioneered the use of backlighting was Leni Riefenstahl, an adept at the art of merging avant-garde and kitsch. In the section on the 1936 Olympics in her Nazi propaganda film *The Triumph of the Will,* the German divers, unlike any others, were backlit; their bodies were transformed into shimmering icons. Vorkapich, like other filmmakers, revered Riefenstahl's virtuosity and deliberately quoted her technique.[89] The connection was most apparent in the "rope swing" commercial he did for Pepsi in 1967, where the imagery of Currier & Ives met the propaganda techniques of the Third Reich. If one defined one's modernism solely as formal innovation, then modernist experiments could be used to promote just about any sentiment at all. In the world of advertising, as in that of mass politics, the courtship of avant-garde and kitsch could finally be consummated in marriage. The growing prestige of pop art signified the legitimacy of the marriage, its acceptance by critics and curators as well as by agency clients.[90]

The convergence of formal experiment and predictable sentiment suggested that the relationship between art and advertising could never be understood through purely aesthetic categories. For Clement Greenberg and other critics in the formalist tradition, the distinction between avant-garde and kitsch recalled earlier antinomies between high and low culture; the difference between the two could be discerned only by the cultivated individual able to decode the difficulties of self-reflexive art. For at least a century, critical discourse was characterized by this assumption. Under the aegis of aestheticism, the Marxian concept of alienation was transformed. For Marx it had implied an unjust set of power relations that separated the worker from the fruits of his work; for twentieth-century art critics it became a synonym for the emotional disaffection of the aesthete in a philistine world. From this view, the artist turned admaker had betrayed a sacred trust by pandering to the oafish sentiments of the mob.

This critique, by isolating the objet d'art from the broader material conditions of its production and distribution, left itself vulnerable from two directions. On the one hand, defenders of mass culture who shared the aesthetes' indifference to power relations could dismiss Greenberg et al. as a pack of snobs, unable to hear the pulsating heart of "the people" amid advertising jingles and soap operas. On the other hand, once advertising did begin to incorporate avant-garde techniques, formalists were forced to acknowledge that many advertisements were technically superb; the basis of their critique began to melt away. We are left with the current situation: would-be critics feel a visceral sense of unease when confronted by advertising but are silenced by the general celebration of its technical brilliance.

But there are fuller criteria for criticism than the question of aesthetic excellence. The tension between art and advertising involves more than a matter of taste. Modernist art and literature, like so much art and literature before it, has been in part an effort to grasp some fundamental truth about human experience. Despite their obsessive search for "real life," ad agencies generated imagery that seemed fundamentally inauthentic—at least to many artists and writers whose talents matured during the rise of national advertising. With no individual presence behind it, the art of advertising seemed merely an exercise in manipulating meaningless surfaces—an "official" account of reality, more dynamic and sensuous than the bureaucratic memorandum or the college catalog but no more expressive of human experience. Recoiling from factitiousness, many artists and writers refused to fly to the illusion of pure form; they remained preoccupied with telling some difficult truth about human experience. The question was, Why should it be so difficult?

CHAPTER 11

The Pursuit of the Real

ONE fine April evening in 1927, Josephine Herbst and John Hermann (her beau at the time) joined Ezra Pound, William Carlos Williams, and a host of other avant-garde literary figures in a ritual celebration of modern industrial life at Carnegie Hall. It was the American premiere of the New Jersey–born Parisian composer George Antheil's *Ballet mécanique*. Herbst waited eagerly with the others for the performance to begin, but when it did, it seemed only a "din of saxophones, xylophones, trombones, drums evoking a maddened collision of braying steamboats, screeching factory whistles, with a yelp of human joy wriggling through a murderous clash of cymbals." Herbst was troubled:

> What did the music mean? I longed to be moved as all our friends seemed to be, including John, but it seemed to me I had heard no more than a hallelujah to the very forces I feared. My longing for a still small voice, for a spokesman not for the crash of breakers on a rock but for the currents, down under, that no eye could see, made me feel alone, but not an alien, and I looked at John, too, coldly, as one who had joined forces with some mysterious enemy. Was Antheil to be the symbol of an opposition to the Philistine? In a corner of my heart, a slow movement of the pulse began to turn my attention elsewhere.[1]

Herbst articulated the countercurrents of resistance that survived within the swirling avant-garde celebration of machine civilization. Much of modernism was rooted in hostility toward the modernizing ideological moves embodied in national advertising and embedded in the culture of advanced capitalism: the equation of material and moral progress, the celebration of noise and hustle, the contempt for the past. It should not be surprising, then, that one finds modernist and antimodernist sympathies coexisting, often within the same individual: a thirst for artistic novelty and experimentation, combined with longings to express the intense, unmediated realities that seemed absent amid the everyday business of modern life.

Ideals of authentic expression surfaced in a bewildering variety of forms. But all began in yearnings for a more intense and palpable experience of the world than was available in commodity civilization, for a solid sense of truth beneath a tissue of misleading appearances. Those sentiments, though often inchoate, resonated with the unmasking tendency at the heart of much modernist thought.[2] Conrad, Freud, and Nietzsche were all coming to the conclusion that bourgeois civilization (perhaps all civilization) was founded on denial of instinctual actualities. The biggest lie was the utilitarian chant (to be heard most insistently among the advertising fraternity) that civilization could be organized to satisfy human desire. The question was, once one had discovered this dirty little secret, what was to be done? Accept the hypocrisies of civilized life with stoical resignation, as Freud or Conrad might have advised, or howl with rage and pain, like Nietzsche? To speak with an authentic voice, did the artist have to live outside civilization, become an outlaw? It was an appealing convention—and that was the problem. Late-romantic palates craved rebellion à la mode. The pursuit of authentic expression became more arduous, as even authenticity became a pose.

For avant-garde artists and writers who exalted life in extremis, the situation could be maddening. It was becoming more difficult to distinguish themselves from an ever more knowing bourgeoisie; they felt a mounting disgust at the evasions and compromises that seemed to pervade everyday life. An aura of violence sometimes clung to the quest for authenticity. In 1962, when the critic Lionel Trilling wanted to identify "the modern element in modern literature," he settled on "the idea of losing oneself up to the point of destruction, of surrendering oneself to experience without regard for self-interest or conventional bonds, of escaping wholly from social bonds."[3] The eagerness to move beyond formal experimentation, to immerse oneself in the flood of "experience," led many an avant-garde writer and artist to frenzied self-destruction. Herbst's reference to "the currents, down under, that no eye could see" contained a hint of the modernist longing for oceanic depths.

To critics, the discourse of authenticity was all that was left for the middle classes after the dissolution of Christian belief. "If nothing else can be bindingly required of man," Theodor Adorno wrote in 1951, "then at the least he should be wholly and entirely what he is." The notion that this stance promoted an antimodern critique of commodity civilization was, to Adorno, based on self-deception. "The more tightly the world is enclosed by the net of man-made things, the more stridently those who are responsible for this condition proclaim their natural primitiveness," he wrote. In Adorno's view, the ideal of genuineness was at worst (as in Heidegger) "a means of usurping religious-authoritarian pathos without the least religious content," and at best (as in Kierkegaard) an "obstinate insistence on the monadological form which social oppression imposes on man."[4]

For half a century, critics on the Left have echoed Adorno's critique, emphasizing the ease with which the discourse of authenticity has melded with an individualist consumer culture. The pursuit of the genuine could be reduced to the cultivation of a richly variegated inner life, of the capacity for penetrating insight and fine discrimination—and these qualities could be attributes of the intelligent consumer. To take a trivial but telling example: In 1919, the same year the advertising copywriter Sherwood Anderson declared his determination "to see beneath the surface of lives" in his short-story collection *Winesburg, Ohio*, an advertisement for Camel cigarettes presented a thoughtful, mustachioed middle-aged man in a three-piece suit, gazing at a lit cigarette between his thumb and forefinger. "Camels are made for men who think for themselves," the caption read. "They're the men who demand real quality in everything they buy. They look deeper than the surface." The idea that "men who think for themselves" expressed their individuality through mass-produced goods became a staple of advertising campaigns throughout much of the twentieth century. The quest for personal authenticity, as many critics have observed, became the project of assembling the right brand-name goods.[5]

Recent critiques of modernism have exposed additional flaws in the discourse of authenticity: the epistemological naïveté involved in the assumption that reality always resides beneath the layers of appearances; the suspicion of visual pleasure that cohabited with the primitivist fascination for unmediated experience. And sometimes more challenging questions have arisen. The identification of the authentic with the primitive, some critics observe, was an instance of rhetorical imperialism—a profoundly gendered effort to exorcise the generative energies of nature even as one sought to evoke them. The quest for the real was nearly always a male quest; Herbst was a rare exception. Stemming from the masculine need to preserve a precarious sense of unified personhood, the pursuit of authentic self-expression reflected male anxieties that pervaded both bourgeois culture and the modernist attempts to transcend it.[6]

Similar anxieties structured critiques of advertising and mass culture. According to the cultural critic Andreas Huyssen, the discourse of authenticity was at the core of the modernist attempt to disengage the autonomous work of high art from the corrupting effects of mass culture. That project rested on "the notion which gained ground during the nineteenth century that mass culture is somehow associated with woman while real, authentic culture remains the prerogative of men." The links between women and mass culture were forged in the overheated atmosphere of fin-de-siècle social thought: "The fear of the masses in this age of declining liberalism [was] always also a fear of woman, a fear of nature out of control, a fear of the unconscious, of sexuality, of the loss of identity and stable ego boundaries in the mass." These fears affected the bohemian as well as the bourgeois. "Thus the nightmare of being devoured by mass culture through co-option, commodification, and the 'wrong' kind of success is the constant fear of the modernist artist, who tries to stake out his territory by fortifying the boundaries between genuine art and inauthentic mass culture."[7]

These are powerful and important arguments, but they do not capture the full complexity of the modernist discourse of authenticity, at least in the American setting. To cast a wider net, we need to recall what Adorno emphasized in much of his writing on art: the utopian possibilities of the aesthetic dimension. As Adorno's Frankfurt School colleague Herbert Marcuse wrote, in the modern West "the truth of art lies in its power to break the monopoly of established reality (i.e. of those who established it) to define what is real." The work of art appears "in the 'beautiful moment' which arrests the incessant dynamic and disorder, the constant need to do all that which has to be done in order in order to keep on living." This is not a formula for romantic escapism; on the contrary, Marcuse said, art "bears witness to the inherent limits of freedom and fulfillment, to human embeddedness in nature." At its strongest, the modernist discourse of authenticity, like its romantic predecessor, sought not to retreat into pure subjectivism but rather to find the eternal in the ephemeral, the cosmos of hope amid the kingdom of necessity. Often this meant a recovery of cultural or personal memories: to Marcuse, "the authentic utopia is grounded in recollection." For devotees of the authentic, remembrance of things past could mean the metaphorical return to an artisanal realm, where brain and hand were joined in a "science of the concrete"; or the imaginative return to a childhood play-sphere where self and world were connected through "transitional objects." In either way of being in the world, the aesthetic dimension pervaded everyday life. Utopian realities, recollected or imagined, could provide challenging alternatives to the version of reality promoted by national advertising.[8]

But modernists posed those challenges in various idioms. The dominant one, in some ways closest to the managerial worldview, was a cognitivist version of plain speech. The historian David Hollinger has coined the word *cognitivism* to identify the branch of modernist thought that placed the knower at the center of cultural advance—particularly if his or her knowledge had the sanction of organized professional expertise. This point of view resembled what I have been calling positivism, except that the cognitivist was more open to the possibility of continued uncertainty, less preoccupied with formulating ironclad laws.[9] In Anglo-American circles, at least, the cognitivist stance derived some ethical force from the republican tradition; the virtuous knower melded with the virtuous producer.

A cognitivist outlook has shaped the mainstream American critique of advertising, from *The Theory of the Leisure Class* to *The Affluent Society*, and has animated the consumer movement since the 1930s. Longings for linguistic transparency linger in the literature of comparison shopping. The ancestors of *Consumer Reports* were the manuals advising their readers how to recognize counterfeit notes, and how to tell false self-representation from true. By the early twentieth century, the rise of national advertising supplied critics of fraudulence with an obvious target; from the plain-speaker's view, here was a single institution that bore the bulk of the blame for the atmosphere of inauthenticity that pervaded American life.[10] The problem with this critique of advertising was that (in its less thoughtful forms) it implicitly absolved other powerful economic institutions (investment banking, for example, or steel manufacturing), provided they gave the appearance of solidity, responsibility, and productivity.

The plainspoken critique of advertising could also serve as a focus for more personal concerns. Advertising agencies were not only the masters of misrepresentation but also the heralds of the ever-increasing material comfort that mass production brought. For many advocates of plain living and plain speaking, who overlooked the driven rationality behind much advertising ideology, advertisers could be blamed for slackness and self-indulgence as well as for systematic deceit. As Trilling said, universalizing the experience of the comfortable classes in the modern West, the "relative ease of material life leaves us confronting areas of choice which require us to look for a hardness somewhere, for a kernel of actuality and experience which perhaps we have to find for ourselves."[11] For most seekers of authenticity in the plain-speech tradition, the world of advertising was soft; reality was hard, precise, and measurable. But some moved beyond cognitivist definitions of the real in more interesting psychological directions.

A KERNEL OF ACTUALITY

A good place to begin examining this discourse is with H. G. Wells's *Tono-Bungay* (1908). Like Veblen's *Theory of the Leisure Class,* Wells's novel addressed the concerns of a professional–managerial class that felt itself to be surrounded by a factitious civilization. *Tono-Bungay* charts the rise and fall of a patent medicine empire run by Teddy Ponderevo, an endearing swindler whose nephew George serves as narrator.[12] Through George, a budding aeronaut, Wells exalts the ascetic pursuit of science and the craftsmanship of the technician against "the philosophy of the loose lip and the lax paunch" embodied in confidence men like Teddy. To Wells, all social relations in a commodity civilization seem shot through with fraudulence. "It's a bluff. It's all a bluff," says Teddy of French pronunciation, a skill he considers necessary to rise in polite society. "Life's a Bluff—practically. That's why it's so important," he tells his wife Susan, "for us to attend to Style. Le Steel say Lum. The Style it's the man. Whad you laughing at, Susan?" (282). This fakery was not merely an aristocatic excrescence; the apparatus of commercial credit, the security of bank deposits, indeed the vast network of interdependent relationships underlying the whole society were founded on bluff. So George came to believe after several years trying to manage his uncle's enterprises.

Yet, as Wells recognized, the hollowness at the heart of commodity civilization was paradoxically a source of its strength. Advertising intensified feelings of factitiousness but also promised release from them by satisfying what the artist Ewart calls "the hunger to be—for once—really alive to our fingertips!" (181). Patent medicine advertisements intensified this hunger even as they claimed to satisfy it. The only way to escape from the cycle of deprivation and desire, in *Tono-Bungay,* is to find a reality more genuine than the advertised version. George yearns for "real work," rather than merely "laborious cheating"; this is what leads him to "science."

She is reality, the one reality I have found in this strange disorder of existence.... You cannot change her by advertisement or clamor, nor stifle her in vulgarities.... I've never been in love with self-indulgence. That philosophy of the loose lip and the lax paunch is one for which I've always had an instinctive distrust. I like bare things, stripped things, plain austere and continent things, fine lines and cold colours.... You can go through contemporary life fudging and evading, indulging and slacking, never really hungry nor frightened nor passionately stirred, your highest moment a mere sentimental orgasm, and your first contact with primary and elemental necessities the sweat of your death bed. So I think it was with my uncle; so, very nearly, it was with me (324–26).

This passage expressed a pervasive response, on both sides of the Atlantic, to the civilization sustained by advertising. The longing for a kernel of hardness amid the stew of slogans and sentiments could lead in any number of directions, including a cult of martial valor and an attachment to primitive religious faith.[13] But Wells's idiom was applied science, in this case aeronautical engineering—George was aloft in a glider while he reflected on the inauthenticity of modern life. The equation of science and reality linked Wells, on the one hand, with modernist design reformers who (like George) were drawn to "bare things, stripped things, plain austere and continent things"; on the other hand it placed Wells amid a camp of social engineers, people like Veblen and Lippmann, who were fashioning a technocratic version of American liberalism, one that seemed to them more suited to twentieth-century conditions. Indeed, Lippmann quoted George's peroration in his *Preface to Politics* (1913), assimilating it to his own model of mass society and using Wells's critique of modern aimlessness to justify social control by educated professionals like himself, people whose expertise allowed them to penetrate the misrepresentations of the marketplace and discover the core reality beneath appearances.[14]

Yet by the 1920s, similar discontents were leading American critics of advertising in different directions. Some of them (mostly novelists, many former advertising copywriters) questioned confident cognitivist notions of reality; they explored murkier regions, notions of personal authenticity that incorporated a vitalist fascination with intense physical or sensuous experience. Consistent with plain-speech tradition, the vitalist outlook still presupposed a self to be true to, a persistent core of identity at the center of one's being. With the popularization of psychoanalysis, the question remained open as to whether the self would be defined in terms of ego ideals or id processes; the more cognitivist of the plain-speakers gravitated toward the former, the more vitalist toward the latter. But for all, the

coherence of that self had to be sustained against the civilization embodied in advertising. Their alternative to inauthenticity veered closer to Wells
than to Lippmann; it involved a vision of personal moral responsibility
rather than a prescription for social engineering.

Among the best known plain-speakers of the 1920s was the novelist
Sinclair Lewis, like many admen a product of the small-town Protestant
Midwest, shipped East to attend one of the "better colleges" (Yale, 1907).
The closest Lewis came to working in the advertising business was in 1913,
when he was hired to edit a syndicated book page, which contained publishers' advertisements as well as book reviews. He stayed on until the syndicate disbanded a year later. Lewis survived on the fringes of the publishing world until *Main Street* (1920) made him a literary celebrity.[15]

In *Babbitt* (1922), Lewis turned his scalpel toward the jocular emptiness promoted by advertisers, boosters, and other poets of pep.[16] The middle-class realtor George F. Babbitt epitomizes the inauthentic self. "These
standard advertised wares—toothpastes, socks, tires, cameras, instanteous
hot-water heaters—were his symbols and proofs of excellence; at first the
signs, then the substitutes, for joy and passion and wisdom" (81). But Babbitt longs to recover the "joy and passion and wisdom" for which he has
substituted advertised commodities. His effort to do so energizes the
novel's episodic plot. Nearly every scene illustrates his search for the lost
springs of authentic being: his trip to the Maine woods with Paul Riesling,
roofing manufacturer and violinist manqué; his infatuation with Tanis
Judique and her bohemian set.

In the end, Babbitt's quest for authenticity comes to nothing, except
that he recognizes the legitimacy of his son Ted's refusal to follow the path
of pep. Ted elopes with his flapper girlfriend and takes a factory job at
twenty dollars a week. To Ted's amazement his father approves, saying:
"Don't be scared of the family. No, nor all of Zenith [his hometown]. Nor
of yourself, the way I've been. Go ahead, old man! The world is
yours!"(319). As "the Babbitt men marched into the living-room and faced
the swooping family," they vindicated the masculine producer ethos
against the feminine claims of domestic respectability and the parasitical
world of promotion and salesmanship.

Seeking alternatives to a packaged sense of self, Lewis clung to a faith
in the redemptive powers of craftsmanlike devotion to a calling. This
became equally apparent in *Arrowsmith* (1925), which detailed Dr. Martin
Arrowsmith's struggles to pursue pure scientific research amid commercial
and political pressures that had turned public health into public relations.

As in *Tono-Bungay,* an ascetic devotion to science seemed the only authentic alternative to professions tainted by status-striving and false luxury. Like Wells, Lewis remained true to an updated version of plainspoken producer ideology, though he expressed it in his own idiosyncratic idiom.

A few years into the 1920s, advertising had become a popular target for literary satire. The satirists, like Lewis, were educated Anglo-Saxon Protestants already well acquainted with the world of publishing. Roger Burlingame, for example, was the son of an editor at Scribners and a 1913 graduate of Harvard. Upon graduation he wrote one-inch squibs for the *Independent,* then took a job as publicity manager for his father's employer. He became such a facile copywriter that he began to think his talents were wasted in the book trade, so he told his father that he had decided to seek a job with an advertising agency. The older man told him: "In the past few years I have come to know you have a real talent for creative writing. And I promise you as solemnly as I have ever promised anything that if you go into advertising you will never write another word. Never. Remember what I say while you think it over." The son was elated. "You can write, you can write, you can write," he told himself as he went to bed that night. He stayed at Scribners, where after he returned from the war he became "a bona fide editor" who included John P. Marquand among his authors. Soon after his father died, Burlingame began *You Too* (1924) during his off-hours. The book "was meant to be a scathing satire on advertising," a debt of gratitude to his father for steering him away from agency life.[17]

You Too tells of the rise and fall of Gail Winbourne, son of the famous painter Daniel Winbourne and himself a budding novelist trapped in the sales end of Hartwell Publishing.[18] When Gail's father dies and the insurance money comes, Gail heads for the hills in the middle of New York State, determined to take up writing in earnest in the hamlet of Glenvil. But he falls for an upscale summer visitor named Muriel Gay. Her mother insists that if the boy is to marry his daughter he must have real work with a real income, and leave the art for after hours. Ultimately Muriel agrees, and Gail finds himself on the train back to New York City. Here as elsewhere in American fiction by men, the women are made to be the agents of bourgeois responsibility.

On the train Gail confronts the ubiquity of national advertising. A billboard advertising a kidney remedy sets him and the other passengers to grimacing with discomfort. A picture of steaming griddle cakes with "That Tang of Fresh Molasses" turns out to be a magazine advertisement for

tobacco; this sets Gail to brooding about the decline of direct communication in "our refined civilization" (86). The rest of the novel reinforces the
relation between advertising and unreality. Gail lands a job as a copywriter
with B. Minturn Outwater, Adviser in Advertising, Publicity Engineer; he
marries Muriel and they move to a suburb for sensible strivers in New Jersey. At that point the inauthenticity of their lives is banged home on almost
every page.

Gail's growing hubris, as he climbs to the top of "the ad game," recalls
the cruder celebrations of machine civilization among the avant-garde.
After a while he begins to believe the progressive platitudes he had satirized in his days at Hartwell Publishing. As Gail and Muriel stand on the
roof of atop the Bella Vista Apartments, high over Broadway, "midway
betwixt the blissful yawn of the Fisk-tire boy and the incredible peacock
pageant of the Wrigleys," Gail exults that the building's "good vistas are all
tributes to man's doing."[19] Muriel is unmoved. When Gail crows "How big
it is!" she answers "Too big. . . . And why does it keep you so much away?"
(240–41). Here she is not merely the neglected wife, or the spokeswoman
for bourgeois values, but the representative of the human-scale household
against the "big, delirious, powerful things" created by the machine civilization.

A fired coworker warns Gail that "sensitive people like you and me,
who were intended to think real thoughts" eventually come to laugh at the
whole inflated business (152–53). But Gail never thinks those "real
thoughts" he is allegedly destined to think. After Muriel leaves him, he no
longer feels moved by the splendors of advertising's symbolic universe, or
by much of anything else. He goes mechanically to the office: "He had
learned the habit of knowing from the face of the raconteur when the
point was coming, and laughing convulsively just ahead of it" (292). This
was the nightmare vision of Victorian hypocrisy, updated for a managerial
setting: a man so thoroughly alienated from his "true self" that he had severed all ties between outer appearance and inner being. Indeed, there was
some question whether he could even be said to possess an inner being.

This "other-directed character" did not supplant the older "inner-
directed character" celebrated in nineteenth-century success tracts; on the
contrary, the two sets of norms had coexisted uneasily for centuries, rooted
in the moral compromises between market society and Protestant culture.[20] But from the viewpoint of critics like Burlingame, the advertising
business systematized what would come to be called "other-direction,"
placing an unprecedented premium on the ability to fabricate a facade of

sensitivity. It eviscerated any sense of personal authenticity by requiring copywriters to curry favor with obtuse clients and bosses—by committing "people who were intended to think real thoughts" to trivial sloganeering.

This attitude typified the literary critique of advertising as it developed in the 1920s. It appeared in the work of William E. Woodward (1874–1950), a copy chief at J. Walter Thompson who quit to write fiction and biography. Married to Helen Rosen Woodward, who wrote copy for the Frank Presbrey agency and later two critical books on the advertising business, he developed an equally skeptical attitude toward advertising. Neither he nor his wife could take the business seriously enough to stay with it for life.

Woodward was born to a poor farming family in South Carolina, won a state-sponsored scholarship to the Citadel, and after an academic career dominated by gentleman's C's, embarked on a series of low-level newspaper jobs, the most distinguished of which was proofreader on the *Atlanta Constitution*. Fearing that he had hit a dead end and would never get a chance to write, Woodward decided to head for New York. It was 1898, the year Theodore Dreiser took his first stroll down Broadway, and the city was as exciting to the Southern boy as it was to the Midwesterner. Like Dreiser, Woodward lived in a series of cheap boardinghouses, and held a series of jobs with hole-in-the-wall publishers. Woodward finally signed on with a firm called the University Society and began to write advertising copy for a four-volume edition of the World's Best Music. "It was devoid of life or humor," he recalled, "but it sold in a big way." As he warmed to his task, Woodward "became an advertising fanatic," poring over his weekly issue of *Printers' Ink,* occasionally writing articles for the magazine, and sending them examples of ads he had written. In 1907, his work caught the attention of Clarence Hope at J. Walter Thompson, who hired him as copy chief (though Woodward admitted he was "not chief of copy nor of anything else").[21]

These were the declining years of the founder at JWT; Stanley Resor had not yet taken over and rationalized the operations. The agency atmosphere recalled the chaotic conditions of the 1880s. Woodward managed to introduce a few improvements—he promoted regular conferences between clients and copywriters, for example—but in the end, agency life began to seem farcically self-important. Woodward sometimes could not muster sufficient earnestness to please the client. One day he was having lunch at the Astor Hotel with Jacob Ruppert, who made a popular cheap beer. Ruppert was a man of elephantine whimsy, so Woodward thought he could risk a joke about the product. When Ruppert praised the slogan "Carnation Milk from Contented Cows" in the *New York World,* Woodward suggested they adapt it for the Ruppert campaign: a picture of horses at pasture with the caption "Ruppert's Beer from Contented Horses." Ruppert's good humor vanished, and the next day he requested another copywriter be assigned to the account.[22]

Woodward was ready to leave by 1913, when he developed the syndicated book page that Sinclair Lewis edited. After the syndicate failed, Woodward worked as publicity manager for the New York Hearst papers and, for four years, as a banking executive. By 1920, he was bored with his lot and had enough money to quit and write the novel he had long been plotting. It became *Bunk* (1923), a satire of advertising and celebrity culture that introduced the word *debunk* into the American language.

The novel's protagonist was Michael Webb, inventor of a device for detecting bunk. Woodward's account of Webb's career revealed that literalism still lay at the heart of the plain-speech tradition, reinforcing an unproblematic conception of reality. "Reality is to bunk like a lighted match to powder," says Webb. "That's why I move so slowly in my debunking business. We must handle reality carefully." Like Veblen, Woodward counterposed the engineer and the businessman, the producer and the profiteer.[23]

But in *Bread and Circuses* (1925), Woodward briefly exposed a weakness in the rhetorical pursuit of the real, though he quickly returned to the standard critique of inauthenticity. His foreword tells the story of "a man who lived in expectation of the time when he would see and hear Great Things. He felt that there was something thrilling and vivid which all men experience." So he went about his daily affairs, loved women, made money, fell into vices, reformed, raised a family, traveled a little, read a little. When the Angel of Death came, the old man complained: "I've never seen Life." What did you do all those years? Death asks, and the man tells him he worked, talked, loved, hated, laughed, built some houses, raised some children, thought a little. "'That was Life,' said the Angel of Death, as he led the old man away."[24]

Maybe the problem was not simply the aura of inauthenticity promoted by advertising but the heightened expectations of authenticity that seemed to characterize so much of psychic life in modern society—the conviction that everyone would experience "something thrilling and vivid" in the normal course of events, that a failure to do so meant that one had not "really lived." Wells and others in the plain-speech tradition had traced this belief to a reaction against the comfortable but aimless life promoted in part by national advertising; they suggested that advertising, having helped to create this unease, also promised to cure it through the purchase of packaged intensity. Woodward raised another possibility: that the fault lay not in our corporate masters, but in ourselves—in our own romantic disdain of everyday life.

That theme would be picked up in subsequent decades by George Orwell and other defenders of the commonplace; Woodward did little more than allude to it. Nevertheless, he glimpsed the wave of life-worship as it surged across the coasts of bohemia and into suburban living rooms. Babbitt was one victim of it. The feeling that one had somehow been cut off from intense emotional or physical experience spread among the comfortable classes as well as their avant-garde critics, acquiring intellectual respectability from the recovery of the unconscious under way in novels and psychiatric offices as well as some advertising agencies. Like the celebration of "energy" in the discourse of machine civilization, the exaltation of "life" without a larger purpose could lead to circularity and self-absorption.

Yet some writers sought social rather than spiritual or psychological diagnoses for the sense of sameness in everyday life. Turning to the idioms of mass-society criticism, they focused on the cultural standardization promoted by national advertising. Malcolm Cowley, writing in *Broom,* responded to Matthew Josephson's paeans to publicity with his parodic "Portrait by Leyendecker" (1923). The entire verbal collage was little more than earnest slogans stitched together. Cowley's account of a day in the life of C. Wesley Brown (Brownie) epitomized the brisk but empty self one could construct from advertised commodities, including the commodity of advice.

> A Daily Dozen before the open window, after which he dresses with the energetic but unhurried efficiency which characterizes the smallest acts of his daily life. He owns a razor which shaves the right side of his face in 33 seconds and the left in 45, making a total of 78 seconds. The time he spends on dressing (his Dressing Appropriation, he calls it, since Time is Money) shows a reduction of 33 1/3% since he has been wearing a Goobbye Old Flannel Lining the Tie that Goes on in a Jiffy. He dons his Press-together Cuff Links and appears before the breakfast table at 7:39.
>
> Only Seven Minutes to Exercise and Dress!
>
> You can equal or better this record if you tear off and fill in the coupon at the lower right-hand corner.[25]

Despite the heavyhanded brushstrokes of this portrait, Cowley caught something that devotees of machine civilization often missed: he knew that advertising was not of a piece with jazz as parts of a vibrant popular culture. The vitality embodied in national advertising was rationalized and bent toward productivity and profits. Writers who feared an overorganized society fastened on advertising as its symptom and emotional intensity as its cure. After reading Josephson's praise of advertising in *Broom,* the poet Hart Crane wrote to a friend:

> Some things he says must be true,—but how damned vulgar his rhapsodies become! I would rather be on the side of "sacred art" . . . than admit that great art is inherent in the tinsel of billboards. Technique there is of course, but such gross materialism has nothing to do with art. Artistry and fancy will be Matty's limit as long he is not willing to admit the power and beauty of emotional intensity—which he has proved he hasn't got.[26]

Crane's preference for emotional intensity over artistry typified the romantic vitalist quest for authenticity, which led him toward his own self-destructive rendezvous with oceanic depths, suicide by drowning.

Sherwood Anderson was luckier and more ambivalent. For more than twenty years he supported himself writing advertising copy. Railing against the slick pseudoculture created by the corporations, he was proud of his ability to survive in it. Longing for the innocent vitality of the American village, he was nonetheless relieved to be rid of its prim respectability. Anderson presented advertising copywriters as people like himself, tormented by self-loathing as they subordinated their literary talents to commercial necessity. "There would have been two or three of us who dreamed of someday becoming real writers," he recalled. "This fellow was, in secret, working on a play, that fellow on a novel." Some became drunks, others committed suicide. One fat man among them claimed they had all been sinners in another life who were being punished: "We are in the advertising department of hell," he said.[27]

It may be that the hellishness of this picture was partly a result of cultural fashion. Anderson recounted these anecdotes in the version of his memoirs he published in 1933, when many of his literary contemporaries had embraced a Communist variant of the producer ethos. But Anderson's producerist outlook was never simply tied to prevailing political doctrine. He had always cultivated a notion of writing as a preindustrial craft and ad writing as a betrayal of craftsmanship. Words were tools for expressing "the Real," and to use them deceptively was to defile them. "I am soiling my tools," Anderson complained of his copywriting. On many other occasions he described advertising as a "universal whoredom," revealing the persistent basis of producerism in masculine anxieties.[28]

Anderson leavened the producerist critique of advertising with primitivist sentiments: not merely a pastoral fondness for vanishing preindustrial life, but a positive fascination with the people who had been left behind by the engine of progress, the people who had somehow not managed to secure tickets on the Twentieth Century Limited. Anderson's loving preoccupation with these "grotesques" in *Winesburg, Ohio* (1919)— "The Book of the Grotesque"—was not an isolated trait. Some of the canonical modernist works of twentieth-century literature have been concerned precisely with people who have been disdained (or even exterminated) by modernizing elites. Faulkner's Yoknapatawpha County and Garciá Marquez's Macondo, like Anderson's Winesburg, are populated in part by "twisted apples" trampled underfoot in the rush to development. Yet in all cases the authors stressed the toughness and resilience of these despised preindustrial folk. Their resistance came not from morality but from idiosyncrasy. They were "queer," and in queerness there was strength.

This outlook was a revitalized, bohemian version of producerist mythology. Anderson's views remained grounded in the same epistemology of "the real"—the same mistrust of smooth talk, the same assumptions that language could be transparent—yet his angle of vision also depended on a deification of authentic experience as an end in itself. The circularity of Anderson's quest ended during the 1930s, when he linked his reality-worship to a formulaic version of radical politics: "the people" became the avatars of the real. "I wish I could be something real," says Red Oliver, a college student turned labor organizer in Anderson's novel *Beyond Desire* (1932); Anderson juxtaposed the dirty-faced kindness of the working poor against the "bright shining hatred" in the adman Fred Wells, whose "faultlessly correct" clothes made him look like one of his own advertisements.[29]

In Anderson as in other writers, Popular Front culture promoted a rebirth of producerist mythology, with "the workers" as the new avatars of authentic experience. Matthew Josephson, who had celebrated advertising during the 1920s, was by 1935 attacking "the gentlemen who spend their days and nights counterfeiting and misrepresenting, the copy-writers, the knights of press-agentry, the Junior Leaguers and the tennis champions who give lying testimonials," posing their hypocrisy against the "true, simple human dignity" that could be found in "the most threadbare Soviet student or the grimiest of coal miners."[30]

This epistemology crossed political boundaries; socialist realism shared a common sense of reality with American Scene regionalism. Consider Thomas Hart Benton, who counterposed the truth of his art against the lies of advertising in an account of his dispute with the American Tobacco Company in 1943. The company, pioneering what has become a standard business practice, sought to counteract its federal conviction for price-fixing by hiring N. W. Ayer to surround it with "jes' folks" imagery. Benton was a natural choice for the assignment: his work was accessible but carried connotations of high-art legitimacy. Yet when Benton was sent to the hills of south Georgia, and painted what he saw—black people harvesting tobacco—the agency executives complained. "The Negro institutions would boycott our products and cost us thousands of dollars if we showed pictures of this sort. They want Negroes presented as well-dressed and respectable members of society. If we did this, of course, then the whole of the white south would boycott us. So the only thing to do is avoid the representation of Negroes entirely in advertising." So Benton went to North Carolina "where the hillbillies handle tobacco" and produced a picture of an old man and his granddaughter; the agency thought it was fine but that the girl was too skinny. "'Everything about tobacco must look healthy,' the advertising people declared." Ultimately Benton cut out the girl and came up with a picture of a golden codger fondling tobacco leaves—but the leaves were not golden enough, according to the advertising executives, so Benton bypassed the agency and made a successful personal appeal to George Washington Hill, the paterfamilias of the company. True to the producer ethos, Benton's account of his interview with Hill the manufacturer was far more sympathetic than his account of his encounters with the middlemen of the agency, who manufactured nothing, not even cigarettes.[31]

But with respect to the episode as a whole, Benton was bitter. "Advertising is a lying art," he told an interviewer from the New York newspaper *PM* in 1945. "Write that down. It depends on suggestions that aren't wholly true. And you can't expect art to deal in half-truths. Business can't expect art to tell its lies for it. If we do, then we're pure prostitutes and should be paid high. I'm not a prostitute and I'm sick of advertising." Benton's association of deception with prostitution recalled Anderson's rhetorical tics, as did the painter's conviction that the authentic American culture lay in the countryside. In the same interview, Benton declared that art was not propaganda but the expression of culture; American culture was rural, and was expressed by Currier & Ives before the Civil War and not much after because the American artists had picked up the French bacillus, producing imitations of European decadence that culminated in "precious, pansy arts above the public comprehension." Benton became obsessed by homosexuality; in 1940, the painter was dismissed from a teaching post at the Kansas City Art Institute for complaining publicly that art was being ruined by museums and by "the third sex." Benton was repelled by the crossing of gender boundaries, which seemed to him to cloud the clarity essential to sexual identity as well as to plain speech.[32]

Like a nineteenth-century republican ideologue, Benton was consumed by the notion that European art (academic or avant-garde) was encrusted with artifice and aristocratic preciosity. Authentic expression was peculiar to Americans of "pioneer stock." It did not trouble Benton that most advertising executives were from that same stock. But by the 1940s, Benton was becoming increasingly outrageous from the vantage point of the intelligentsia—a redneck ranting in the wilderness. This was not mere snobbery. There were epistemological as well as ethical questions to be raised about the producerist critique of advertising, particularly in the simplified form Benton expressed it. The notion that art could unproblematically represent reality, which lay at the heart of Benton's worldview, had begun to provoke skepticism among the American avant-garde. The quest for authentic expression—the attempt to define art against advertising—would be taken up in idioms other than plain speech.

Victorian ideals of sincerity were based on the tacit assumption that language was either true or false to the simple soul within; modernist notions of authenticity tended to assume that language was not a transparent representation of an unproblematic reality, but rather a somewhat arbitrary code fitted to prevailing social and cultural conventions. The severing of any immutable tie between words and their referents lay behind the puns and language games played by many modernist writers and linked them with postmodern celebrations of surface display. But to sever the tie between word and referent was not necessarily to deny the relationships between the two; nor did it require ignoring the existence of a world to which language referred, however imperfectly or obliquely.

Implicit in *The Psychopathology of Everyday Life, The Ambassadors,* and other canonical modernist texts was the assumption that language was a garment to be unbuttoned to reveal a secret life. Whether or not they used the language of psychoanalysis, many modernists sought to move beyond plain speech toward a more rigorously introspective pursuit of artistic truth.

The modernists of the *Partisan Review* circle in the 1930s were energized by a desire to complicate the discourse of authenticity—part of their larger effort to distance themselves from progressive orthodoxy, liberal or Stalinist. Rejection of the Popular Front required a broader repudiation of simpleminded notions of reality. A key manifesto in the campaign was Lionel Trilling's review of Vernon Parrington's *Beginnings of Critical Realism in America.* "Reality in America," published in *Partisan Review* in 1940, dismissively summarized the major assumptions of Parrington's epistemology. "There exists," Trilling wrote, "a thing called reality; it is one and immutable, it is wholly external, it is irreducible. Men's minds may waver, but reality is always reliable, always the same, always easily to be known."[33] This allegedly "critical" realism represented an affirmation of Victorian notions of transparency; for Trilling and for other writers or artists interested in the truths of the unconscious, this would never do. They turned, with renewed intensity, to an introspective ideal of authenticity, an ideal that reflected the catastrophic events of the 1930s and 1940s as well as the persistence of masculine anxiety.

THE REAPPEARANCE OF THE STOIC ISOLATO

During the 1940s, *Partisan Review* modernists, Abstract Expressionist painters, along with numerous film noir directors and other creators of popular culture, all participated in the construction of an updated version of "modern man"—more complex and riven by inner conflict than his producerist predecessor, but just as tough an individualist as ever. The project renovated powerful motifs in the classical literature of American manhood: the Deerslayer became the gangster as tragic hero. "A man who keeps his moral integrity hard and intact," D. H. Lawrence called this character type in his *Studies in Classic American Literature* (1923). "An isolate, almost stoic, enduring man, who lives by death, by killing, but who is pure white."[34] This figure reappeared and flourished in an era of chastened social hopes and "tough-minded realism."

To be sure, not all these men were killers, even metaphorically. Some were drawn to the brooding personal style of the stoic isolato (to borrow Melville's term) as an alternative to the manufactured bonhomie of the white-collar workplace and the willed optimism of the culture promoted by advertising. It was a culture, as the critic Robert Warshow observed in 1948, where cheerfulness was virtually an official duty. Pessimism was un-American; it implied doubts that we had reached the pinnacle of world history.[35] Masculine toughness was a defensive pose certain modernists adopted while they tended to more serious matters. This was true of the first generation of Abstract Expressionists. Seeking authentic self-expression that would resist incorporation into the world of advertising and commodity culture, they developed a critique of formalist modernism.

By the time the Abstract Expressionists came of age, in the early 1940s, the agencies were showing a yen for a representational, illusionistic strain of surrealism that had surfaced most clearly in the work of Salvador Dali and René Magritte. The key to these artists' appeal, at least for advertisers, was their capacity to attract attention by defamiliarizing the familiar. Magritte's own artistic aims were hardly reducible to visual stunts (as Dali's increasingly were); his early work especially was a struggle to express and exorcise overwhelming feelings of psychic devastation and loss. Yet the philosophical dimension of his work led him, albeit circuitously, toward advertising. As Magritte said, he wanted to "put the real world on trial" by subverting the mimetic assumption at the heart of realism: the identity of image and object. Attacking illusionism with illusionistic methods, Magritte used bizarre metamorphoses, incongruous juxtapositions, and well-placed captions, all to emphasize the arbitrariness of representation. The basis of representation, Magritte insisted, was not mimesis or resemblance but merely knowledge of the linguistic and visual conventions that constitute the rules of the game. The project reversed established advertising strategies, which depended on an uncritical acceptance of those conventions (a rural scene connotes pastoral harmony; a volleyball game at the beach, athletic sexuality). Yet by the 1940s the problem of clutter had induced some of the more venturesome advertisers to shop for new attention-getting devices. Despite his intellectual aims and his disdain for advertising, much of Magritte's later work was commissioned as part of corporate publicity campaigns.[36]

Part of Magritte's appeal to advertisers was that he continued to use an illusionist style even as he mocked its philosophical basis. His work could be incorporated into a brand of advertising that aimed at stylistic daring, rejected literal representation, and called attention to its own artifice—that sought to supersede capitalist realism but persisted in exalting smooth surface-illusionism. From the advertisers' view, the surrealist fantasies of Dali and Magritte were little more than "deceptive journalistic tricks" designed to stop viewers in their tracks—precursors to the high-tech high jinks of "special effects."

The phrase "deceptive journalistic tricks" was used by the Abstract Expressionist painter Barnett Newman in 1946, contrasting the academic surrealism of Dali with the work of primitive oceanic artists, then on display at the Metropolitan Museum of Art. Newman revealed that imperial primitivism, which had pervaded the commercial vernacular in the patent medicine era, was now being appropriated by the modernist avant-garde. Oceanic artists were made to supply the "complete and naive" vision that was unavailable in commodity civilization. From the primitivist view, surrealist illusionism was, like advertising, the work of a con artist, a magician who did not seek to "feel the magic" but to manipulate the audience through "theatricality" and "journalistic tricks." Newman presented himself as a modernist magus, resistant to the false values of consumer culture, isolated and heroic.[37]

Yet there was more going on here than masculine posturing. Newman caught the distinction between a magic that was embedded in a coherent animistic worldview and the modern magic of the market that was often little more than sleight of hand. The Abstract Expressionists were involved in an effort to return enchantment to the world of art—though not, unfortunately, the world of everyday life—through a re-engagement with mythic subject matter (see figure 11.1). Their resistance to commodity civilization contained a critique of formalism. Nearly all the Abstract Expressionists insisted that their problem was not how to paint, but what to paint. As the painter Adolph Gottlieb put it in 1943: "There is no such thing as good painting about nothing. We assert that the subject is crucial." The critic Robert Goldwater summarized the project succinctly. The Abstract Expressionists, he said, "were engaged in 'telling the truth' and they talked a good deal about it. The truth was an emotional truth which would emerge from themselves if they knew how to allow it."[38]

This was not simply a retreat from social to individual concerns, or from the messy actuality of history to the timeless realm of myth, though it has often been characterized as such by engagé observers. Stuart Davis's reaction to the Abstract Expressionists typified an outlook that has since resurfaced in Left historiography. Dismissing Abstract Expressionism as

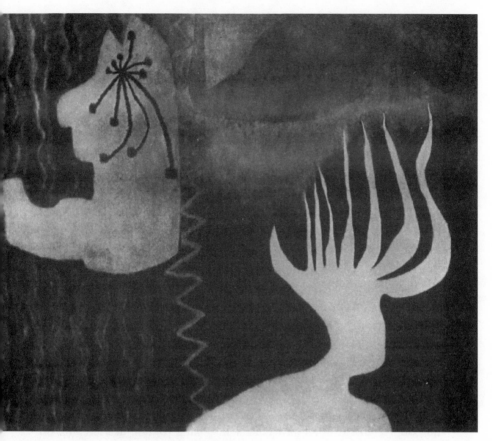

FIGURE 11.1

William Baziotes, *The Flesh Eaters*, 1952. *Courtesy of BlumHelman Gallery, Estate of Ethel Baziotes, New York.*

"a belch from the unconscious," Davis compared his own attitude to that of Arshile Gorky. Davis was an organizer of the Artists' Congress and other political protest groups during the 1930s. "I was in these things from the beginning and so was Gorky. I took the business as seriously as the serious situation demanded and devoted much time to the organizational work. Gorky was less intense about it and still wanted to play." As the art historian Irving Sandler observes, "By 'play,' Davis meant 'paint.'" The hostility to art as play, the determination to turn it to instrumentalist purposes, was not confined to national advertisers; it affected Left ideologues as well.[39]

What they failed to see was that the Abstract Expressionists were involved in an effort to recover some truths that were inadmissible to any progressive version of reality, from the socialist realism of the Popular Front to the capitalist realism of advertising. By the late 1930s, to many artists and intellectuals who stood in the shadows of total war, some darker vision seemed the only honest alternative to managerial schemes of rationality and progress. Gottlieb, for example, insisted on the need for the artist to nurture the "constant awareness of powerful forces, the immediate presence of terror and fear, a recognition of the brutalities of the natural world as well as the eternal insecurities of life." As the art historian Michael Leja has observed, this awestruck rhetoric was the staple of perorations on "modern man" in the 1940s; still, one must recall how palpable "the immediate presence of terror and fear" must have been in 1943, when Gottlieb wrote those words.[40]

Like the literature of the grotesque, Abstract Expressionist painting sought to grasp experiences that would never appear even in the most outré corporate imagery: from insoluble sexual conflicts (Arshile Gorky) to impossible spiritual yearnings (Mark Rothko). The attempt to assimilate unassimilable subjects led to a quest for more "authentic" methods: a preoccupation with energy and spontaneity, with rough "unfinished" canvases; with encrustations and chaotic drips of paint. Surveying the results of this frenzy in 1957, the critic Meyer Schapiro captured much of its cultural significance. In a culture dominated by mass production and the division of labor, he observed, paintings were among the few remaining artifacts that still bore the marks of an individual self seeking communication with others; the Abstract Expressionists wanted to create emblems of personal identity in a world where private selfhood seemed precarious and perhaps even obsolete. Their work testified to a persistent tension between advertising art and an art that aspired to truth.[41]

Ultimately, Abstract Expressionism met an ironic fate. The painterly exploration of the unconscious, like the concept of the unconscious itself, was co-opted by marketing tactics. Strategists in the cultural Cold War appropriated Abstract Expressionist paintings as emblems of freedom for export abroad.[42] Despite the painters' determination to resist incorporation, by the early 1950s much of their work had become a lucrative investment opportunity. The subject matter, which had been essential to the first generation of Abstract Expressionists, was obscure enough that it could be overlooked; style alone became the chief attraction for investors and even advertisers. By 1960 the work of Abstract Expressionist epigones had entered the referent system of commodity culture, signifying sophistication. One could find imitations of Pollock or Rothko serving as backdrops for corporate images of the good life set in minimalist urban apartments. Abstract Expressionist art became another cultural prop, available for manipulation by the ever-alert "creatives" at the big agencies.

There was a further irony as well. The Abstract Expressionists wanted to capture an emotional truth that could be verified through personal experience. But their vision was so private, so rooted in the ideal of stoic isolation, that their truth sometimes risked an absolute subjectivity. In that case it could be judged only with reference to its "seriousness" or "sincerity." The desperate search for artistic truth may have been accelerated by the fear that there was no truth. The specter of nihilism may have haunted both the artist and the adman, whose key to success (the trade press agreed) was his "sincerity." Without some firmer ontological ground, the quest for authenticity could slide from sincerity to self-destruction. Certainly that was true for Jackson Pollock, who finally drove his car into a tree after years of flailing in puddles of alcohol and machismo, as well as for Rothko, who began by sharing Newman's commitment to make "cathedrals . . . of ourselves" and ended by commiting suicide because, Rothko said, "there are no more temples to paint."[43] Subjective temples were not enough.

Writers and artists who sought to resist commodity culture found the task increasingly difficult. The problem was more complex than the capacity of advertising to turn everything, even "a belch from the unconscious," into a form of status display; it was also the ambiguity of alternative, believable frameworks of meaning. With the collapse of progressive orthodoxies, there was much talk about a return to the stoical pessimism embedded in the Jewish and Christian traditions—as well as in the later writings of Freud, which became a kind of summa for Trilling and some of his contemporaries. But what this often translated into was a tacit acceptance of Cold War politics in the name of "tough-minded realism" and a withdrawal into mass-culture criticism. Questions of power were translated into matters of taste. Intellectuals who were self-consciously alienated from Madison Avenue began unwittingly to embody its assumptions in their categories of analysis.[44] The pursuit of authentic self-expression began to seem a question of choosing the appropriate personal style: tough, reticent, renunciatory.

The stoic isolato reappeared in a variety of cultural settings, including the literary critique of advertising. Victor Norman, the hero of Frederic Wakeman's best-selling novel *The Hucksters* (1946), was the Madison

Avenue equivalent of Humphrey Bogart in *Casablanca*.[45] Wakeman, a former ad writer, presented Norman as a hard-boiled veteran of the Office of
War Information. Home from the propaganda war, Norman lands a job as
an account executive handling the Beautee Soap account for the Kimberly
and Maag agency. The owner of Beautee Soap is Evan Evans, a caricature
of the patriarchal old-school manufacturer and client-as-martinet. The Old
Man has everyone at the agency (as well as on his own staff) hysterical with
the fear of displeasing him. Norman won't buy into this; his "personal
creed" is "screw 'em all but six and save them for pallbearers" (291). He is
frankly in it for the money, but he is sickened by the fawning, by the
hypocrisy—he engages in the familiar litany of complaint to business associates, bed partners, and himself. "I don't like peddling and I don't like
cringing," he says.

On the Twentieth Century Limited, Norman meets and falls in love
with Kay Dorrance, whose husband is a foreign service officer still on
assignment in China. She spots Norman for a bitter, disillusioned type:
"Your face, it's like a mask. Nothing impresses it very much. Your eyes,
they're totally lacking in expression, they don't light up. And when you
laugh, it's a muscular laugh, and it leaves your face in an instant and there
is no feeling of gaiety at all. You seem to be remote, a man who sits with
people but is not ever a part of them in anything" (130–31). Norman
admits he doesn't fit in anywhere. "You see, Kay, a real honest-to-good-
ness artist has an easy out—his ivory tower. It's we characters who haven't
any ivory tower to run to that are really trapped. And we find out later
that a thousand dollars a week won't help us much either." Norman dis-
dains writers (except "the few good ones") as "a bunch of not very convincing poseurs," and he considers "the American intellectual' " to be "the
world's most outrageous example of sterility" (132–33). The exaltation of
the aloof (male) individual, skeptical and detached, alienated from prevailing ideologies and repelled by the compromises necessary to success
in a corrupt consumer culture, linked *The Hucksters* with postwar documents as various as Ayn Rand's *The Fountainhead* and F. A. Hayek's *The
Road to Serfdom*.

In the end, Norman devises the strategies necessary to hold on to the
Beautee account, but the taste of victory is sour and Norman quits his
agency job. In the final scene he telephones Kay to end their affair; he
wants her to stay with her husband. "If we did this thing," he says, "I don't
think I'd like myself" (306). It is the climax of *Casablanca*, the moment
when authenticity is realized as stoical renunciation.

Given the emptiness of this alternative, its lack of any purpose save a sense of integral selfhood, one should not be surprised to see that a countergenre developed. In novels like George Orwell's *Keep the Aspidistra Flying* (1936) and Eric Hodgins's *Blandings' Way* (1950), sensitive refugees from commerce flee to bohemia (or to the Connecticut countryside), only to discover that the aesthetes are the real poseurs (or that the pastoral idyll is a bill of goods). From this view, the way to live authentically was to pay the bills, show up at one's job every morning, acknowledge that there was a kind of heroism in meeting the responsibilities of everyday life—even if the results were sometimes tedious or tasteless. In short, keep the aspidistra (the ubiquitous potted plant of the British lower middle class) flying.

This approach targeted the chief chink in the armor of the isolato. The demon that haunted the search for authenticity was not the Miltonic Lucifer but *l'homme moyen sensuel*. The same horror of ordinariness linked Hemingway and the Abstract Expressionists with popular novelists like Frederic Wakeman. All assumed at least tacitly that the pursuit of artistic truth required the disavowal of any connection with everyday domestic or economic life. Authors like Orwell and Hodgins, fed up with the jargon of authenticity, emphasized the arrogant self-delusion so often embedded in that longing for transcendence.

Nevertheless, there were subtle and challenging versions of transcendence available within the literary critique of advertising. Two of the most remarkable appeared in the work of William Gaddis (b. 1922) and Frederick Exley (1930–1992). Both Gaddis's *The Recognitions* (1955) and Exley's *A Fan's Notes* (1968) bore the marks of the discourse of authenticity: its distrust of surface deception, its masculine rage at mass culture. But both departed significantly from dominant conventions. Ultimately, Gaddis and Exley abandoned anxious questing and sought a sense of stillness amid the manic haste of modernity, a more enduring connection with the material world.

A LONGING FOR STILLNESS: GADDIS AND EXLEY

The Recognitions is an enormous compendium of contemporary ephemera and ancient arcana that explores the relations between authenticity and artifice, high art and advertising, in the setting that spawned the Abstract Expressionists: New York City, below Fourteenth Street.[46] Gaddis knew that setting well. After being asked to leave Harvard following a scuffle with the Cambridge police, he spent several years among the Village bohemians while he worked as a fact checker for the *New Yorker*, fleeing in late 1947 with a vow to his literary rivals: "I'll be the first to publish!" He traveled in Central America, Spain, and North Africa for five years, supporting himself as a machinist's assistant and radio scriptwriter for UNESCO, finally returning to a farmhouse in rural New York State to finish the novel.[47]

The Recognitions defies summary, but its main thread concerns the struggle of the painter Wyatt Gwyon to find an authentic form of self-expression amid a carnival of promoters and poseurs. Wyatt is the son of a Congregationalist minister in rural New England; when the boy was small his mother had died at sea while she and the reverend were en route to Spain, her childhood home. Her death sends the bereaved widower on a spiritual quest through Catholic Europe. He returns home with a Barbary ape, a roomful of Catholic artifacts, and a fascination for pagan lore. He is finally sent packing by his congregation after attempting to sacrifice a neighbor's bull. Long before his father's disgrace, young Wyatt has left home, first to study for the Episcopal priesthood, then to a career as a brilliant forger of fifteenth-century Flemish masterpieces, in the employment of Recktal Brown, the cloacal capitalist, and Basil Valentine, the Jesuitical mephisto. The main narrative line concerns Wyatt's growing recognition that authentic expression cannot be found in imitation, even the preternaturally perfect form found in his own work; it also follows his effort gradually to disentangle himself from Brown and Valentine in search of a more integrated sense of selfhood through a symbolic reconciliation with his dead mother—though he is only slowly aware of what he is about. That quest leads him back across the Atlantic. For Gaddis, as for many earlier American writers, the Old World is the abode of maternal Muses; it offers a kind of redemption through a return to the (artistic) mother. Wyatt ends having achieved a sort of salvation but still performing a penance, restoring medieval frescoes at a monastery in Spain, absorbed in the (re)creation of durable things that Hannah Arendt, writing around the same time, described as meaningful work.[48]

In *The Recognitions*, secular modernity and American consumer culture are twinned; it is only the backward Spanish who are unaware of the New World of goods and mistake tampons for incendiary bombs. Advertising is the background noise accompanying the aimless confusion of nearly all the characters' lives. Its influence counterfeits science, corrupts art, commodifies the sacred. A radio program, *The Lives of the Saints,* is sponsored by Necrostyle, the wafer-shaped sleeping pill. Ellery, the most prominent adman in the book, is a Yale man, Skull and Bones, who looks like all his predecessors in the literary critique of advertising: "Ellery was lithely, easily, built. . . . Clothes looked well on him: he was what tailors had in mind when they designed loose-fitting jackets and pleatless narrow-leg trousers" (366). In a variation on an established theme, Ellery and his fellow Bones man Morgie Darling happily admit that "this [advertising] is the whoring of the arts and we're the pimps, see?" (736). Art and commerce seem hopelessly entangled in a common net of duplicity.

By the end of the book, aesthetes and admen are celebrating a festival of forgery in Rome, where the pope shaves with an electric razor and account executives wonder whether he can be induced to provide a testimonial. "Lovers of beautiful things" are thronging, "thick as thieves" (946). Inauthenticity is universal, as in Melville's *Confidence-Man,* only the setting is not a steamboat but an outdoor café. "At the next table a girl said,—Plagiary? What's that. Handel did it. They all did it. Even Mozart did it, he even plagiarized from himself" (941).

The effort to locate an authentic sense of self is more problematic for Gaddis than it was for Anderson or the Abstract Expressionists. The stance of authenticity has become a fashionable pose. Max, an American poseur/painter, becomes the beneficiary of the "unfinished" vogue: his mistress slips him her husband's discarded unfinished canvases and he touches them up, selling them as his originals. Another successful painter "climbs up a ladder with a piece of string soaked in ink, and he drops it from the ceiling onto a canvas on the floor" (941). The reference to Pollock's drip paintings is unmistakable.

Gaddis's attachment to artisanal values made him recoil from an art that lacked craft. In 1950, in a *Harper's* piece about player pianos, he dismissed that instrument as "an answer to some of America's most persistent wants: the opportunity to participate in something which asked little understanding; the pleasure of creating without work, practice, or the taking of time; and the manifestation of talent where there was none."[49] One of Max's earlier successes is a workshirt that he has framed; *The Recognitions* is full of artists who disdain careful workmanship for self-promoting performance. That may be part of Gaddis's rationale for Wyatt's forgeries. Each is a perfectly executed and absolutely anonymous work of craftsmanship, the antithesis of the work done by modernist epigones. To craft these works, Wyatt has to "co-operate with reality"—not the heroic proletarian version, but the shit-smeared reality of business, embodied by Recktal Brown, for, as Basil Valentine tells Wyatt, "Brown is reality" (244).

Yet from the beginning, Wyatt is uncomfortable with this capitulation. Brown is not merely a capitalist but a pioneer in the scientific marketing of the arts. Already he has "started this business of submitting novels to a public opinion board, a cross-section of readers who give their opinions, and the author makes changes accordingly. Best sellers, of course." It is a vision of the copywriter's life in the agency, and Wyatt imagines artists in a similar fix: "submitting paintings to them, to a cross-section? You'd better take out . . . This color . . . Those lines, and . . . He drew his hand down over his face." This recalls many articles in the trade press as well as the critique of advertising by artists like Rockwell Kent. It is the nightmare of lost autonomy.

But Wyatt's difficulty runs deeper. He complains to Valentine that Brown places orders for particular forgeries "as though it was like making patent medicine."

> —He heard a Fra Angelico had sold somewhere for a high price once, and he thought I should do a Fra Angelico, toss off a Fra Angelico . . .
> —All right now . . .
> —Like making patent medicine. He turned to Brown.—Do you know why I could never paint one, paint a Fra Angelico? Do you know why? Do you know how he painted? Fra Angelico painted down on his knees, and his eyes were full of tears when he painted Christ on the Cross. And do you think I . . . do you think I . . . (242)

What is missing, for Wyatt, in the modern art world of cleverly manipulated surfaces is some sense of gravity, some deeper purpose. His father had complained that there was "no mystery, no weight to anything at all" (57) in the modern world, and his son believes that the reason Flemish painters gave every object a special density was "because they found God everywhere. There was nothing God did not watch over, nothing"; indeed, Wyatt insists that "that's the only way anything can have its own form and its own character and . . . shape and smell, being looked at by God." By contrast, "everything today is conscious of being looked at, looked at by something else but not by God" (251); like his father, he feels "there is often now the sensation of weightlessness, or weighing very little" (359). Spiritual gravity was disappearing in a disenchanted world; that for Wyatt (and Gaddis) was the key to the pervasive sense of inauthenticity in modern art and culture.

Wyatt is not the only character in search of spiritual depth amid misleading appearances. Esme, a young poet, is another artist in search of a still center, where there is perfect harmony between meaning and representation, intent and artifact. Like Gwyon, she struggles to strip away the "million inanities" that a mass-mediated culture has imposed on words and images, seeking a realm where "work and thought in causal and stumbling sequence did not exist, but only transcription: where the poem she knew but could not write existed, ready-formed, awaiting recovery in that moment when the writing down of it was impossible because she was the poem" (299–300). This longing for "origin," for a preverbal union between the self and its language, embodied a desire to escape the dualisms of the dominant culture. It was the dream of wholeness that lay behind the animistic worldview, the dream of a universe suffused with supernatural meaning.

For some, like the ascetic young musician Stanley, the quest for origin could lead to Catholic orthodoxy. Wyatt toys with traditionalism, too, for a while, fancying himself "a master painter in the Guild, in Flanders," who has vowed to use pure materials in the sight of God. But he cannot sustain this fantasy. Stanley's fate signifies the self-destruction that awaits a quixotic antimodernism. He has composed a piece of sacred organ music that he is determined to play in an old Italian church. When he pulls out all the stops, the vibrations from the bass notes cause the church to shudder and fall to the ground. Wyatt, in contrast, ends at the Real Monasterio in Spain "restoring" paintings by scraping the paint off them: undoing his forgeries, "living it through," a vaguer and more psychological redemption than the one sought by the hapless Stanley.

Still, there is something self-destructive about Wyatt as well: his heavy drinking, his contempt for creature comforts. He is always cold; he needs a winter coat but won't buy one. He is very much the artist as tough-guy tragic hero, reticent, even inarticulate: for Gaddis, as for Anderson and others, inarticulacy and authenticity were twinned. He is also a confirmed isolato, incapable of forming lasting relationships with other people. His wife Esther complains:

> You haven't . . . ever shared anything with me . . . you won't help me do things, you do them for me but you won't help me. That set of Dante you had, *we* couldn't have it, it was as though it couldn't exist without being yours or mine so you gave it to me, but it couldn't be ours. You . . . even when you make love to me you don't share it, you do it as though . . . so you can do something sinful (116).

Wyatt's responses to Esther are characterized by long silences, and unfinished sentences. He is the brooding man alone.

Wyatt's character was rooted, no doubt, in the repugnance Gaddis felt for the therapeutic standards of normality that had come to dominate the managerial–professional culture of the 1950s, the cant of "healthy sexuality," of cooperation and togetherness. And Wyatt's decision to "work through" the suffering he had experienced by determining "to simplify . . . to live deliberately" (894) had a long and honorable lineage, not only in Christian literature but in more heterodox pilgrimages like that of Thoreau. Yet in Gaddis, as in Thoreau, the horror of everyday routine and ordinary domestic life gave their critique of bourgeois banality a misogynist, maybe even a nihilist tinge. It is no accident that Wyatt looks stricken when Esther mentions having children. In the lonely quest of the stoical hero, there is no room for nurturing the next generation.

The nihilist implications of the search for authentic expression are even more apparent in Frederick Exley's *A Fan's Notes*, a fictionalized memoir that details his postcommencement gropings for a writerly vocation, as he lurches drunkenly from advertising agencies to mental institutions through the 1950s and 1960s.[50] In the postwar "affluent society," many of Sherwood Anderson's grotesques have been officially stigmatized as deviant, and shut up in asylums. The repeaters at the Avalon Valley asylum develop their symbolic power in opposition to the standardization of the dominant social world, "a world to which the passionate and singular aspiration have been forbidden" (199).

> These repeaters were the ugly, the broken, the carrion. They had crossed eyes and bug eyes and cavernous eyes. They had club feet and twisted limbs or—sometimes—no limbs. These people were grotesques. On noticing this, I thought I understood; there was in mid-twentieth century no place for them. America was drunk on physical comeliness. America was on a diet. America did its exercises. . . . I saw the comfort America could purchase by getting rid of them (77).

The grotesques are a collective Other for a society set on narrowing the boundaries of normality. The agent of that process is not mass culture in toto, since mass culture can at least produce grotesque alternative visions. (Exley's narrator imagines the hunchback Quasimodo displacing the Marlboro Man on a billboard, leering at Julie London in "an advertisement to delineate the Male Ideal" [77].) Rather, boundaries are standardized in advertising, through the embodiment of demographic types: the "carmine-hued, ever-sober 'young marrieds'" (77) in the Schlitz beer ads, the "Technicolored and felicitous goons" in the Kodak ad at Grand Central (240). Contemplating that Chartres west front of corporate capitalism, Exley's narrator muses: "Surely this was the coveted America, those perennially rosy cheeks and untroubled azure eyes, those toothy smiles without warmth, eyes without gravity, eyes incapable of even the censorious scowl, eyes, for that matter, incapable of mustering even a look of perplexity. Well, it was *not* the America I coveted" (240). *A Fan's Notes* was filled with loathing for the physical ideal as constructed by national advertising, for the flaxen hair and vacant eye of today's young guy or gal on the go. If it is true, as Exley at one point claims, that "hate can redeem as well as love" (335), then his fictional persona is among the blessed.

The novel concludes with "a dream of sanguinary ends," a commitment to continue the fight against the fair-haired airheads epitomized in the Kodak ad. Exley has returned to his mother and stepfather's home and taken to walking the roads of upstate New York. Station wagons and sedans swoop by, filled with contemptuously hooting geezers and adolescents extending their middle fingers. Exley cannot understand their hostility until he realizes that he has been mistaken for one of the "ban the bomb" demonstrators who have been "walking for peace" near the local Air Force base.

Then he begins to have a recurring dream, that a carload of jeering, cashmere-clad college boys is forced to pull over a mere hundred yards from the spot where they passed him. Imagining "they will all live to be a hundred and fifty, watching reruns of Ed Sullivan on a colored screen twenty feet high," Exley runs to them, beseeching them to remember that "of itself longevity is utterly without redeeming qualities, that one has to live the contributive, the passionate, life"; "John Keats was dead at twenty-six!" he shouts. When one boy stares at him blankly, Exley strikes him in the face. Exley fights well but is finally "beaten bloody and senseless by a phalanx of cashmere clubs . . . engulfed by this new, this incomprehensible America." Every night before going to bed he imagines that he will have the restraint not to run to them, to walk on about his business. "But when again that vision comes, I find that, ready to battle, I am running: obsessively *running*" (384–85). So the book ended with two characteristic romantic/modernist conceits: that authentic expression requires contempt for security and safety, maybe even an impulse toward self-destruction, and that embittered marginality (if not madness) constitutes the basis of insight.

Yet Exley repeatedly undercuts his own oppositional stance. Self-deprecating humor pervades the book, preventing it from dissolving in a broth of alcoholic rage and self-pity. In a burlesque of his own literary pretensions, Exley compares himself, a supercilious Poet seeking a "mephistolean pact" with Madison Avenue, with Clark Gable, who played Victor Norman in the film version of *The Hucksters*. It is hardly a portrait of a stoic isolato.

> Where . . . Gable had been resplendent in pin stripes, charcoal grays, and midnight blues, I had only one shiny suit, which now became perfect for my purposes—just hideous enough to keep me hopelessly removed from the world of my interviewer. Where for character Gable had his famous mustache, I bought a Yello-bole which, stuck in my teeth, gave me, I thought, a strikingly ruminative air. Finally, for the *coup de grace*, I substituted for Gable's striking Homburg a coiffure modeled after an idol of the moment, Truman Capote (45).

Exley's unsparing examination of his narrator's tendency toward idol worship was a key to the strength of the book. His deepest and strangest attachment is to the New York Giants' halfback Frank Gifford—on the surface as complete an embodiment of standardized physical perfection as might be imagined. Gifford, like Exley's father, is a superb athlete whose performances constitute "something truly fine, something that only comes with years of toil, something very like art." Exley shares with Gifford only a diploma from the University of Southern California and "a desire to escape life's bleak anonymity" (134), but that is enough to make the football star an alter ego for the writer manqué. The night after Gifford's crumpled body is carried from Yankee Stadium, his career apparently at an end, Exley comes to the painful realization "that it was my destiny . . . to sit in the stands with most men and acclaim others. It was my fate, my destiny, my end, to be a fan" (357). That recognition is an antidote to self-important posturing; it involves Exley's realization that he is one of "them," at least in some sense a part of the mass audience he despises.

The question remains: If the America of perfect teeth and deodorized bodies was "*not* the America he coveted," what was? It was a particular part of America, "the cold, cow country up yonder," the St. Lawrence and Hudson river valleys in upstate New York where he had spent his boyhood. When he evoked that country, Exley dropped his habitual tone of raillery and slid into a pastoral idiom, revealing some of his own deepest longings for a sense of connectedness to people and place—longings tied to childhood memories of a time "when neither success or failure mattered nearly so much as popcorn and fudge on a Sunday evening" (225).

Exley's elegiac tributes to the Valley folk—"rooted people with a sense of the past" living in "old limestone houses" with "cavernous hearths"—are more than mere sentimental effusions; they illuminate his assault on advertising's version of American modernity. Exley is constantly on the move, as mobile as any hard-bodied hero in Mailer or Kerouac. The difference is Exley hates it, and seeks a sense of stillness amid the manic activism of his culture. The problem, as he recognizes, is that his alternative to frenzied dynamism is too often the davenport in his mother's living room. Still, he muses, "in a land where movement is a virtue, where the echo of heels clacking rapidly on pavement is inordinately blest, it is a grand, defiant, and edifying gesture to lie down for six months" (185). For Exley, as for William James, indeed for generations of writers and artists before him, invalidism was an alternative to the oppressive achievement ethos of the dominant culture.

Exley's longings for stillness lead him off the davenport, to seek a more enduring connection with place and purpose, a more solid foundation in the material world. Exley realizes that for all its alleged materialism, the culture of advertising has created an oddly dematerialized vision of satisfaction in life: the rising generation of "this new, this incomprehensible America" finds the prospect of landing on the moon more attractive than the exploration of the "heart-stoppingly beautiful" St. Lawrence River, right under their noses (384).

The worship of dynamism, Exley believes, has disconnected modern Americans from place. Whenever he returns home, he fears his departure, because "on leaving I would be once more 'on the move,' be a part of the bewildering and stultifying movement that America has become; and the curse of movement is that during it one is never doing one's own work but that of the world." The yearning to do his own work, to discover a calling, makes him feel "antiquated and musty" (372–73), but leads him to make a sustained effort to come to terms with his hometown. He takes a job teaching English in the local high school, rents an apartment overlooking the St. Lawrence, and furnishes it with "a clear-finished pine bookcase I had made from an old china cabinet; and my cynosure and source of pride: a much-knotted pine coffee table made from an ancient ironing board" (375). Here, as in Thoreau and other American writers, the search for stability amid the activism of advertised America required a reconnection with the physical world, a feeling of craftsmanship, an unmediated experience of things.

Exley was too much the restless malcontent, too much the modern artist, to leave it at that. His dream of reconciliation with home quickly turns sour. The high school principal is an incompetent who picks his nose and cravenly curries favor with irate parents complaining about their children's grades; the superpatriots in station wagons hoot at Exley on the highway. The world intrudes quickly on his pastoral idyll. Yet in the end, one has to imagine that if there is any salvation for Exley's alcohol-saturated soul, it will be at a pine desk in the cold cow country—a fan and no fan, seeking self-transcendence through the redemptive word.

Exley's odyssey was both typical and idiosyncratic. His recoil from the inauthenticity of advertised America led him to adopt a series of rebellious stances: literary poseur, deviant, madman, drunk. Amid the discourse of authenticity in post–World War II American culture, any of those stances could easily have succumbed to self-caricature. Yet by distancing himself from those various selves, through humor, and by embedding them in an extraordinary confessional narrative, Exley performed a major feat of memory and imagination. The alchemical force was Exley's voice: personable, eloquent, and (for a madman) astonishingly sane. It was the voice of a man you wouldn't mind having on the barstool next to yours.

Was he delivering a jeremiad against the vices of commerce, in the Protestant tradition? Yes and no. Certainly it was a lament for a lost America of honest workmanship and neat clapboard villages, and certainly Exley did not hesitate to link himself with major Anglo-Protestant thinkers: there was, he admitted, "something Miltonian or Emersonian" about his desire for a calling (373). Yet there were many ways that Exley escaped the limits of the jeremiad and the Protestant tradition. The jeremiad was characterized neither by humor nor by a desire for stillness amid relentless busyness.

In some ways, that desire suggests Exley's most important contribution to the literary critique of advertising. It links his work with some of the most profound moments in the quest for authentic expression: William Butler Yeats, lying down "where all the ladders start, / In the foul rag-and-bone shop of the heart"; Mark Rothko, painting somber monochromes for nonexistent temples.[51] The longing for stillness led out of the labyrinth of authenticity into other cultural idioms. It could be said to characterize a misunderstood and largely ignored strain in modernist culture—a body of work whose creators were as enchanted by surfaces as by depths, as engaged with commercial artifacts as with high art, and yet as concerned as any seeker of authenticity to distinguish between their art and advertising. Revaluing the things of this world, they sought to create a sensuous place of grace.

CHAPTER 12

The Things Themselves

THE figure of the stoic isolato overshadowed the pursuit of the real. The discourse of authenticity could rarely be disentangled from a masculine stance of renunciation. If what is renounced is reprehensible, renunciation may be a good idea; much of the discourse of authenticity has retained its power for that reason. Yet the modernist quest to make art an emblem of spiritual heroism devalued some of art's other, perhaps older, aims: the reaffirming of social bonds, the giving of pleasure.[1] Distrusting the play of surface display, the seeker of genuineness preserved the puritanical cast of mind that has afflicted many advertising critics (along with many advertisers themselves). Nurturing a half-conscious disdain for the things of this world, many participants in the discourse of authenticity unwittingly collaborated in the philosophical project embedded in consumer culture: the construction of a separate, striving subject in a world of alienated objects.

There was, though, another modernist critique of capitalist modernity that did not fall into these difficulties. This critique can be pieced together from hints and suggestions in the work of a handful of writers and artists: Henry James, Edith Wharton, Rainer Maria Rilke, Marcel Proust, James Joyce, Kurt Schwitters, Joseph Cornell. Their outlook could be characterized as aesthetic rather than ascetic; they delighted in surfaces as well as depths; they saw material artifacts as a mode of making meaning rather than merely concealing it. These idiosyncratic figures rejected the view of material goods as emblems of an individual's status or modernity, building blocks in the construction of a commodified self; instead, they saw material things as portals of connectedness to the past, or to other beings in the present, and to the natural or man-made landscape. Much of their work implied a reanimation of playful relationships between people and things, against the disenchanting power of productivist rationality.

What may be most interesting about these writers and artists, in the end, is that their projects—for all their esoteric aspects—were versions of a broader cultural enterprise. An emerging interdisciplinary literature has begun to examine the persistence of what one might loosely call an animistic worldview (for lack of a better term) in Woods Hole, Massachusetts, tidewater North Carolina, and upstate New York, as well as in Zambia and New Guinea, in twentieth-century African-American folk artists as well as quattrocento masters. Whether they are anthropologists using Lévi-Strauss's idiom of bricolage ("the science of the concrete"), Victor Turner's of "symbolic consciousness," or Clifford Geertz's of "local knowledge," whether they are feminists engaged in the critique of positivistic science, or art historians involved in an assault on formalistic criticism, a variety of scholars have discerned a widespread but implicit challenge to the Cartesian ethos of consumer culture. Without denying multiplicity and separateness, they have refashioned dualism to admit more intimate connections between the thinking self and the material world.[2]

The figures in this chapter implicitly formulated similar challenges, first in the precincts of high-art aestheticism, later in the interstices of the industrial landscape. Seeking transcendent meaning through the materials at hand, a few turned toward the lowliest of objects, redeeming them from the contempt of a throwaway society. To cast their achievement in relief, we need first to recall the relation between things and the self in the dominant discourse of commodities.

With the coming of mass production and planned obsolescence during the early twentieth century, many manufacturers still sought systematically to surround their products with a magical aura, to overcome the growing distance between the manufacturer and the buyer by personalizing the impersonal commodity. But they also faced the need to forge new bonds with new commodities, to render the old magic obsolete when next year's model appeared. The agenda of national advertising was to subordinate the magic of product to the magic of process: the constant creation and re-creation of new fetishes, in accordance with the imperatives of technological determinism. But those imperatives were never uncontested, even in advertisers' own minds; marketing needs combined with their own internal conflicts to ensure that the discourse of commodity fetishism would continue to meld personality and impersonality, magic and rationality, a yearning for the past and a celebration of the future.

THE MEANING OF THINGS:
MEMORY AND AMNESIA
IN COMMERCIAL DISCOURSE

Domestic life provided the major focus for discussions about the meaning of things. By the end of the nineteenth century, contradictory impulses shaped the artifactual imagery of home. Advertisers repeated the modernist critique of Victorian clutter, demanding new commodity-based standards of cleanliness and efficiency. Yet their own fantasies of nurturant warmth and plenty combined with a persistent ideology of domesticity to ensure that their vision of the American home would not become a functionalist "machine for living," that it would retain its status as a "feminine divinity" to whom tasteful tributes must be made.[3]

Beginning in the 1890s, mainstream decorating magazines like *House Beautiful* took up the growing outcry against "the tyranny of things" and "the bric-a-brac habit." Often their arguments were hygienic and psychotherapeutic: overstuffed rooms and furnishings not only sheltered dust and microbes, they also embodied the sickness of the self who resided within. Voluminous draperies, fussy ornamental patterns, and nervous, discordant colors were the outward and visible signs of psychic disorder; the search for harmonious design was a search for spiritual health—or if the idiom turned managerial, a search for personal efficiency. Psychic and social rationalization met in the doctrines of euthenics, "the science of the controlled home environment" promoted by the home economist Ellen Richards. Her work was the reductio ad absurdum of managerial interior design; it exalted a robotlike self in a sterilized shell.[4]

More commonly, when decorating magazines and advertisements used managerial language, they transformed the home into a corporation rather than a laboratory. *House Beautiful* dubbed the housewife "purchasing agent and manager" in 1920 (see figure 4.13), about the same time that dozens of advertisers were appointing her to the same position. In this discourse, the housewife was in charge of assembling the goods that enabled her to run the home efficiently—and also to express the modernity of the family within. A National Home Furnishings (the furniture trade association) advertisement of 1930 worried that visitors at one's home "cannot fail to notice out-of-date or inadequate furnishings. And nothing else so surely detracts from your rightful social standing." This idiom put a new, progressive spin (the fear of looking "out-of-date") on an old appeal to status anxiety; it domesticated technological determinism. The consumer was expected to keep pace with the (apparently autonomous) development of new materials (linoleum rather than wood, say), using goods to demonstrate that she (and her husband) could afford to maintain modern standards.[5]

But the relationship between things and the self could never be fully shackled to the managerial mode. The ideology of home decorating contained countervailing tendencies. Despite paeans to simplicity, the magazines' primary criteria for evaluating interior design were "sincerity," "individuality," and "personality." Generally speaking, a *House Beautiful* contributor noted in 1920, most homes were too monotonously alike; they needed "originality, difference, or 'punch,' as we may choose to term it," he concluded.[6]

The language sounded surprisingly like that of the advertising trade press during these same years, when admakers were beginning to worry about the problem of enabling mass-produced products to seem unique. The trick was not only to stand out in the crowd but also to sustain the belief that each consumer chose goods freely to express his or her sense of self: this was far more appealing than admen's privately held notion of consumers assembling standardized packages of modernity under the direction of a technocratic elite. The modern was only one of many choices available amid the wide range enjoyed by the sovereign consumer, as Emily Post suggested in *The Personality of a House* (1930). "Its personality should express your personality, just as every gesture you make—or fail to make, expresses your gay animation or your restraint, your old-fashioned conventions, your perplexing mystery, or your emancipated modernism— whichever characteristics are typically yours."[7] The choice of the "old-fashioned" was legitimized, even after decades of disdain for old things amid the makers of managerial opinion.

Of course, there had always been exceptions to the progressive trend. The conflict between progress and nostalgia had intermittently shaped commercial imagery since the era of chromolithography. The chromolithographer Louis Prang and his contemporaries had mass-produced pastoral scenes; advertisers of luxury goods had sought to associate their products with vanished eras of elegance and craftsmanship; patent medicine vendors had located a primitivist paradise lost.

But about the time Emily Post was issuing her pronouncements on personality, advertisers began an unprecedented effort to associate their products with the past, particularly with the recent but fading folk community embedded in notions of traditional society. This reinvention of tradition had a variety of cultural meanings, but one of its most significant was an implicit, half-conscious recognition that the vision of a consuming self was psychologically unsatisfying without a sense of connectedness to the past. At the same time, that recognition was undercut by the rhetorical strategy governing the ads, which dissolved the tension between past and present in the soothing syrup of pseudotraditionalism.[8]

Advertisers' rediscovery of the past in the 1930s was part of a broader recovery of reassuring folkish imagery in the face of economic crisis—a project that linked commercial iconography with WPA murals, Frank Capra films, even the music of Aaron Copland and the choreography of Martha Graham. "Perhaps the campaign demands an 'old-fashioned' atmosphere," a *Printers' Ink* contributor wondered in 1931, as he noted advertisers' growing need to represent their "soundness" amid the collapse of confidence in business. By mid-decade, "emancipated modernism" was out according to the conventional wisdom, and "old-fashioned convention" in; trade journals advised advertisers to address "Grandma Jones, Buyer," who was more concerned with "comfortable living" than with fashion. Corporate food processors shifted their emphasis from purity to "home-cooked flavor"; Hurff's Soup, for example, took consumers into the enveloping warmth of the rural hearthside rather than the sterility of the scientifically managed kitchen (see figure 4.15). Other advertisers linked mass-produced goods with preindustrial craftsmanship and family solidarity. By 1936, *Fortune* magazine was marveling at the tendency of national advertising to "bury its alert head in the sands of the past." Advertisers, like other symbol-makers in the 1930s, had turned to a mythic version of the American past to validate their present identity.[9]

This surge of folkish sentiment stemmed from Depression-bred longings for security, but it had deeper roots as well. Despite their faith in economic development, the good burghers among the advertising fraternity had always been suspicious of fashionable snobs and had often linked them with urban modernity. Given advertisers' tendency to identify the path of progress with their own upper-class habits, it was only a short step (for skeptics) from suspicion of snobbery to suspicion of modernity.

The tendency to sentimentalize a vanishing rural past also reflected the growing fear that new waves of immigrants had overwhelmed what the popular novelist Clarence Budington Kelland called "the honest old New England strain." Among the Anglo-Protestant managerial class, ethnocentric anxieties helped fuel the fascination with an imagined colonial era, an Anglo-folk utopia where black people knew their place and immigrants were absent. Advertising executives participated with others of their class in this Anglophilia: they designed "colonial" or mock-Tudor residences, searched for antiques in New England villages, supported the restoration of Colonial Williamsburg. The ethnocentrism in these ventures was perhaps more powerful for remaining implicit. At J. Walter Thompson, chairman Stanley Resor commissioned a colonial-style executive dining room in 1922; when the company moved to the Graybar Building (near Grand Central Station) in 1927, the dining room was moved piece by piece and reassembled in the new quarters—where it remained, incongruously surrounded by art deco splendor. Even at the height of the "prosperity decade," the pilots in the cockpits of modernity were eager to preserve some connection with their imagined preindustrial past. Pseudocolonial artifacts cemented a sense of continuous, coherent group identity.[10]

There was more to this sentiment than yearnings for Anglo-Saxon purity. The most famous folk icons in advertising were black: Rastus, the Cream of Wheat man (figure 4.14), and Aunt Jemima. It is easy to dismiss these figures as emblems of white disdain, but their meanings were multivalent. Without question, they epitomized a whole constellation of nurturant values associated with preindustrial household and community life. They provided sustenance; they took care of (white) people. In this they resembled Betty Crocker, the embodiment of old-fashioned neighborliness, created in 1921 by General Mills, or the Mennen Company's Aunt Belle (1920): "Belle is a real person and that is her real name. She really understands babies. She would like to correspond with you about your baby."[11] These figures were created by and for an uprooted suburban bourgeoisie; they may well have helped focus one of the deepest psychic needs of both admakers and their audience: a longing to overcome the sense of separation and loss endemic in a mobile market society, to recreate in fantasy what could not be achieved in everyday life—a renewed connection with the *Gemeinschaftliche* worlds of extended family, local neighborhood, and organic community. The motives of their makers were too numerous to name, but perhaps the basic impulse was an effort to fabricate a stable point of origin for the ever-developing self—though the only materials available might be snippets of memory, half-formed wishes, and clichés from *Life* magazine. As blacks or females (or both), the folk icons fit a familiar role projected for the Other in the white male imagination: like the ideal Victorian woman, they could remain static, sheltering timeless values so that "progressive" men could ignore them in the forward rush to the future. They helped transform certain consumer goods into ballast for the free-floating self.

Still, it would be foolish to treat these motifs as direct expressions of their makers' emotional needs: they were calculated moves in carefully orchestrated campaigns. They were also instances of a rhetorical strategy that has often been employed by American ideologues of progress. No matter how fervently they chanted the gospel of newness, advertisers knew they had to establish some common ground, some sense of old-shoe familiarity between the purchaser and the product. Folk icons served that purpose. They allowed the adepts of progress to have it both ways: to assert that the best of traditional values survived even as modernization whirled ahead at full tilt.[12]

That was the key move in advertising's rhetorical appropriation of the preindustrial past: the innovator presented himself as a traditionalist at heart; the mortal enemy of folklife declared he was its chief defender. This had long been a successful gambit of modernizers, from the federalist orator Tench Coxe to the New South ideologue Henry Grady. But the people who brought this strategy to full fruition were the rhetoricians employed by the modern corporation. In selling home-cooked canned goods, promoting mass-produced craftsmanship, or linking fast-food meals with "family values," twentieth-century advertisers have turned the trick on a scale that Coxe and Grady could hardly have imagined.[13]

By surrounding modern products with a pseudotraditionalist aura, advertisers scrambled past and present, stripped material goods of their actual historical associations, and allowed them to enter a sphere where the object itself was less important than the desires that could be projected onto it. Here as elsewhere, the materialism promoted by advertisers was antimaterial; the success of the corporate economy depended less on the esteem accorded material things than on the constant restimulation of the desire for more of them. The "cult of the transitory," characterized by Henri Lefebvre as "the essence of [capitalist] modernity," promoted a profoundly ambivalent attitude toward material goods: they were something to be longed for, acquired, then superseded and discarded. Planned obsolescence promoted disdain for as well as desire for material goods.[14]

Though the pseudotraditionalist strategy was less direct than the celebration of commodities as status markers for an ever-developing self, the result was the same: goods became floating signifiers, assimilable to the utilitarian purposes of self-salesmanship and the pursuit of success, just as an art that has been reduced to technique becomes assimilable to the needs of advertising. Whether the goods in question signified "old-fashioned convention" or "emancipated modernism," their enlistment in an instrumentalist program transformed a Wildean performance from play to work (or labor, in Hannah Arendt's definition of "making a living").

Yet the appropriation of the past could only succeed as a rhetorical strategy if some traditionalist assumptions (however vague) lingered in the minds of the audience. Something really has been lost in transit to industrial modernity, the ads seem to suggest, some direct, sincere or "folk" quality, and *we* have miraculously preserved it—authenticity in the midst of artifice, all the charms of yesterday amid the comforts of tomorrow. This effort to supply some psychological ballast for free-floating signifiers suggested that even many advertisers themselves recognized the inadequacy of their progressive program.

One question behind this vague unease was how to disentangle an aesthetic view of life from commodity fetishism—how to distinguish the love of things from an atomistic, manipulative worldview emphasizing self-aggrandizement through clever representation. Advertisers never posed this question, let alone sought to answer it. But the writers and artists explored in this chapter did. They rejected commodity fetishism, but they could hardly have recaptured a "precapitalist" worldview even if they had wanted too. (The image of the fastidious Henry James gone primitive is the stuff of burlesque.) All of these figures were deeply immersed in the modern urban, commercial world. They were products of it, they were engaged with it—and they were engaged with exploring the shadowy terrain between art objects and commodities, negotiating "values" with all the ambiguities that term implies.

If an objet d'art could become a commodity, why not the other way around? If so, how? Through intervention, resituation by the artist. The collective result of many disparate efforts (though not necessarily their motive) was the creation of an alternative language of objects. It emphasized continuity rather than severance between past and present, connoisseurship rather than consumption; a reanimated symbolic universe. These figures' appraisal of objects involved a move beyond both use value and exchange value; instead, they estimated an artifact's worth with reference to its capacity for exciting memory or imagination. By approaching material things in the spirit of play, they transfigured those things into art. As Johan Huizinga observed in *Homo Ludens* (1938), the "innate tendency of the mind, which invests the objects of ordinary life with personality, is in fact rooted in play"; it is also one of the key "elements of mythopoesis."[15]

Henry James (1843–1916), Edith Wharton (1862–1937), and Marcel Proust (1871–1922) were all concerned with the processes of artistic creation amid the crowd of commodities and objets d'art that had come to signify so many social meanings in fin-de-siècle culture. All were intrigued by the convergence of aesthetic and commercial worldviews in an objectified social universe where people could be treated as marketable goods. All suggested a critique of aestheticism as a way of life, without rejecting the sensuous enjoyment of things in themselves. James and Wharton were too caught up in the *rentier* world of their origins, the world of afternoon teas and tableaux vivants, to provide an alternative that might be available to people who did not live on their investments; Proust's approach opened a slightly broader access. The fulfillment of that prospect would have to await the twentieth century, when artists began to fashion a more democratic discourse of objects, not from aristocratic objets d'art but from the detritus of commercial civilization. Still, the work of James and Wharton represented a key intervention in Anglo-American thought about things: a break from the endless opposition of authenticity and artifice, and toward a subtler understanding of how material goods connect people with the world and each other. Proust deepened the psychological dimension of that understanding, redirecting the language of objects toward new and fruitful forms of expression.

A NEW LANGUAGE OF OBJECTS: JAMES, WHARTON, PROUST

James was engaged with the issues surrounding aestheticism throughout his career, but two texts in particular elaborate his concerns: *The Portrait of a Lady* (1881) and *The Ambassadors* (1903). The first is a little more schematic in its account of a plainspoken young American woman caught in the coils of European deception; it relentlessly juxtaposes American moralism against European connoisseurship, depths against surfaces, authenticity against artifice. But by the time James wrote *The Ambassadors,* these categories had become scrambled: the United States had emerged as a leading manufacturer of deceptive surfaces, and European aestheticism had come to seem (to James at least) a life-enhancing alternative to Yankee utilitarianism. The two novels mark James's growing awareness of the United States's emergence as the world's leading commodity civilization.

Portrait tells the story of Isabel Archer, an intelligent and innocent young woman from Albany.[16] After her father dies, Isabel is rescued from a life of provincial obscurity by an aunt, Mrs. Touchett, who swoops in from England with the intention of taking her off to Florence and giving her "a chance to develop" (38). Within a matter of weeks, Isabel has so turned the head of her uncle, Mr. Touchett, that when the old invalid dies he leaves her seventy thousand pounds. Financially as well temperamentally independent, Isabel gradually slips away from her republican convictions and enters a world of rootless cosmopolites. She marries the most aesthetically sensitive of them, Gilbert Osmond, only to discover that he is little more than "a sterile dilettante" (269) and to reach the final damning conclusion that "the man in the world whom she had supposed to be the least sordid had married her, like a vulgar adventurer, for her money" (425).

Eager to ensure an absolute identity between exterior and interior, surface and depth, "Isabel was stoutly determined not to be hollow" (54–55). She begins, in short, as a fine representative of post-Calvinist moralism, turning from theological to medical standards of normality. When such a woman comes in contact with European aesthetes, there are bound to be conflicts. She looks at life "as a doctor's prescription" (189); they look at it as a theatrical performance. She sees objects as barriers to self; the Europeans see them as expressions of self.

Metaphors of theatricality and consumption pervade the novel. From the beginning, James presents social relations as matters of taste: characters are constantly perceiving each other as luxury objects to be consumed (at least visually), as performers in a play, or as some combination of the two. Isabel's cousin "Ralph Touchett had learned more or less inscrutably to attend, and there could have been nothing so 'sustained' to attend to as the general performance of Madame Merle [Osmond's former mistress]. He tasted her in sips, he let her stand, with an opportuneness she herself could not have supposed" (212). But Isabel carries enough American cultural baggage to see a sadness in Madame Merle's role: "She had remained after all something of a public performer, condemned to emerge only in character and costume." To Isabel there was "a sense in [Madame Merle] of values gone wrong or, as they said at the shops, marked down" (269). When people were reduced to commodities, what was to be done with damaged goods?

The chief agent of objectification in the novel is Osmond. When he is among his "things," Osmond's manner is "an odd mixture of the detached and the involved. He seemed to hint that nothing but the right 'values' was of any consequence" (215). It soon becomes clear that Osmond wants to make Isabel the most precious bibelot in his collection, and that she is at least half-willing to allow it. While she is waiting for Caspar Goodwood (an American suitor) in Rome, planning to tell him of her decision to marry Osmond, Isabel "felt older—ever so much. And as if she were 'worth more' for it. Like some curious piece in an antiquary's collection" (270). As for Osmond, Isabel's intelligence "was to be a silver plate, not an earthen one—a plate that he might heap up with ripe fruits, to which it would give a decorative value, so that talk might become for him a sort of served dessert" (290).

After the marriage, Ralph Touchett surveys the extent of the damage: like a Victorian physiognomist, he focuses on her face. "There was something fixed and mechanical painted on it; this was not an expression, Ralph said—it was a representation, it was even an advertisement." The significance of this change was clear: "The free, keen girl had become quite another person . . . the fine lady who was supposed to represent something" (323–24). And that something was Osmond's exquisite taste.

Yet there is in *Portrait* at least a suspicion that the aesthetic outlook might be made to mean more than simply a delight in arranging floating signifiers. Compare, for example, Osgood's elegant house, with its "incommunicative character," to Mrs. Touchett's

> high, cool rooms where the carven rafters and pompous frescoes of the sixteenth century looked down on the familiar commodities of the age of advertisement. Mrs Touchett inhabited an historic building in a narrow street whose very name recalled the strife of medieval factions; and found compensation for the darkness of her frontage in the modicity of her rent and brightness of a garden where nature itself looked as archaic as the rugged architecture of the place and which cleared and scented the rooms in regular use. To live in such a place was, for Isabel, to hold up to her ear all day a shell of the sea of the past. This vague eternal rumor kept her imagination awake (208).

Mrs. Touchett's house does communicate something: an unpretentious moderate cost; an immediate relation to the natural world; and above all, a powerful sense of the past, but with an eclectic rather than an archaelogical sensibility—"pompous frescoes" are mixed with "familiar commodities," and none is denied its historicity. In Mrs. Touchett, James presents us with an aesthete who has a palpable sense of self; Osmond identifies her as "a sort of old-fashioned character that's passing away—a vivid identity" (205). She is a benign, eccentric, maternal figure who uses material artifacts to cement her relatedness with other people and the past. Nor is she simply a nurturant mother; she is an incitation to imagination. The "vague eternal rumor" of the past in her house kept Isabel's imagination awake.

That broader, richer meaning of aestheticism, only briefly suggested in *Portrait,* animates *The Ambassadors.*[17] The old binary oppositions seem at first glance to be in place. The protagonist, Lambert Strether, has been sent to Paris by Mrs. Newsome, the rich widow of a manufacturer in Woollett, Massachusetts. Strether's mission is to bring her son home from Paris (where he has been sent for seasoning) to run the family business. Strether's reward will be the widow's hand in marriage. When he arrives, Strether discovers that Chad really has come into his manhood—everyone remarks on what an Adonis he has become—and that he has been keeping company with a certain Madame de Vionnet, Mrs. Newsome's opposite number, the maternal Muse of Europe. For most of the book, though, Strether is led to believe that Chad's attachment is to Madame de Vionnet's daughter; it is only toward the close that he learns the older woman and the younger man are lovers. Strether falls under the spell of the Old World, feels his senses reawakening in the regenerative aesthetic atmosphere, but in the end remains too much the Woollett moralist to allow himself to "get anything" out of the episode. So Strether, having alienated Mrs. Newsome by falling in with the aesthetic crowd, spurns the seductive proposals of the charming Maria Gostrey and leaves Europe with only his "impressions." Chad, meanwhile, tires of Madame de Vionnet and determines to return to Woollett, where he will apply "the science of advertising" to the family business.

In Paris the relationship between surfaces and depths is more complicated than in Woollett. As in *Portrait,* the same multiplying motifs of theatricality and consumption are deployed: Strether watches Chad "as from the pit" (304), characters taste people as well as experiences, people (especially Madame de Vionnet and her daughter) are described as objets d'art. But the biggest difficulty facing Strether is one he resolves by turning it to his own advantage. It has to do with the Paris light. Paris "hung before him this morning [his first in the city], the vast bright Babylon, like some huge iridescent object, a jewel brilliant and hard. . . . It twinkled and trembled and melted together; and what seemed all surface one moment seemed all depth the next" (57). The difficulty of distinguishing surfaces and depths in Paris suggested that the Victorian categories might be misplaced, maybe too insistently dualistic—what if the sensuous surface of things carried meanings as significant as those buried in the hidden depths?

That, in fact, is what James suggests. He persistently associates aestheticism not with deception (as in *Portrait*) but with regeneration. The seeds of Strether's suppressed imagination respond quickly to the Old World atmosphere.

> Buried for years in dark corners, these few germs had sprouted again under forty-eight hours of Paris. The process of yesterday had really been the process of feeling the general stirred life of connections long since individually dropped. Strether had become acquainted even on this ground with short gusts of speculation—sudden flights of fancy in Louvre galleries, hungry gazes through clear plates behind which lemon coloured volumes were as fresh as fruit on the tree (55).

In a crucial scene where Strether visits Maria Gostrey amid her things for the first time: "Wide as his glimpse had lately become of the 'empire of things,' what was before him now still enlarged it; the lust of the eyes and the pride of life had indeed thus their temple. It was the innermost nook of the shrine—as brown as a pirate's cave." The womblike, sensuous warmth of Maria's "cave," enhanced by the presence of her things, make it not only an emblem of erotic attachment and maternal nurturance but also of human companionship: "The circle in which they stood together was warm with life, and every question between them would live there as nowhere else." In such an atmosphere, no wonder Strether concludes: "Well, they've got me now!"(75–76).

One of the key signs of Strether's seduction by Old Europe is his changing sense of time. Walking lazily along the Boulevard Malesherbes, "Strether had not had for years so rich a consciousness of time—a bag of gold into which he constantly dipped for a handful" (71). One of the crucial distinctions between American utilitarianism and European aestheticism in the novel is the difference in time sense: Americans hoard time, save it, spend it; Europeans pass it. Strether is haunted by the passage of time, by the fear that he will not get Chad back to Woollett "on time," but gradually he lays this anxiety aside. This is appropriate, as the mysterious articles manufactured at Woollett are almost certainly clocks. Disengaging from clock time, Strether comes to see his own devotion to bourgeois notions of productivity and respectability as a colossal waste. "Live all you can; it's a mistake not to," he tells Chad's friend Little Bilham. "It doesn't matter what you do in particular, so long as you have your life. . . . Do what you like so long as you don't make *my* mistake. For it was a mistake. Live!"

(134). As Madame de Vionnet recognizes, Strether quickly learns that "the great thing . . . is just to let one's self go" (234).

He also learns to cultivate a profounder sense of history, which comes to him in "gusts" as he waits to see Madame de Vionnet for the last time in her rooms. She and Strether are about to have an awkward conversation concerning her relationship with Chad, which the lovers had concealed for so long and which she now fears is about to end. Strether begins to realize that the array of glass and gilt objects, gleaming faintly in the subdued evening light, "would help him, would really help them both." This collection was not the result of a contemporary curiosity (like Maria Gostrey's "little museum of bargains"); it was an assemblage of relics—"medallions, mouldings, mirrors"—accumulated over generations. He would never see their like again, for he was going back to Woollett, "where such things were not, and it would be a small mercy for memory, for fancy, to have, in that stress, a loaf on the shelf." The objects in the room are precious not because of their rarity or cost but because of their capacity to evoke the "memory and fancy" surrounding Madame de Vionnet. And that lady's outlook, at this stage, is not acquisitive but generous. "What it comes to is that it's not, that it's never, a happiness, any happiness at all, to *take*. The only safe thing is to give. It's what plays you least false" (346–49). Here, as in Maria Gostrey's "cave," the European aesthete's "empire of things" provides the setting for declarations of connectedness and renunciations of restless desire.

But Chad is restless. Strether makes one last appeal to him to stay with Madame de Vionnet. The conversation reverts to market motifs, then Chad suddenly announces that he has "been getting some news of the art of advertising"—probably on a recent trip to London. "Advertising scientifically worked presented itself as the great new force. 'It really does the thing, you know.' " Strether looks blank: " 'Affects, you mean, the sale of the object advertised?' " " 'Yes—but affects it extraordinarily; really beyond what one had supposed,' " Chad says. " 'It's an art like any other and infinite like all the arts.' He went on as if for the joke of it—almost as if his friend's face amused him. 'In the hands, naturally, of a master. The right man must take hold. With *him* to work it—*c'est un monde!*' " The idea that advertising is an art like any other seems a joke to Strether (and probably to James as well), but Chad is dead serious. He means to go back to Woollett and "make the whole place hum" by applying "the secret of trade," advertising, to the faltering family business. In James's formulation, Chad chooses to leave a sensuous paradise for a world that is (as Strether says) "all cold thought"—governed by utilitarian standards, clock time, and "ubiquitous advertisement" (367–69).

The Ambassadors provided a powerful counterpoint to the facile assumption that advertising promoted sensuous enjoyment and personal liberation. Far from echoing the long lament about "materialism" that has characterized the major American critique of consumer culture, James's novel was rooted in a passionate attachment to the material world. It was also a defense of hedonism. According to many historians, hedonism was the most important cultural product marketed by national advertising; James recognized early on the falseness of this claim: the advertised version of hedonism was meant to fit brief bouts of enjoyment into the regular rhythms of industrial society. Celebrating the unbought, unhurried grace of life in European sanctuaries, James underscored the connection between American corporate advertising and the post-Calvinist positivism that was ravaging the natural landscape and routinizing the everyday life of the early-twentieth-century United States.

The Ambassadors in effect accuses advertising of dematerializing material life by disconnecting objects from their moment and milieu; goods circulating in the service of "economic rationality" have lost the mysterious aura of memory that adheres to artifacts taken out of circulation and collected for the connections they provide to other times and beings. This is not as rigid and dualistic as it sounds; the boundary between collected goods and consumer goods, while not exactly flexible, can be crossed and recrossed. Even some of the most cherished relics have been bought and sold at times. James did not deal harshly with contemporary commercial goods; in Mrs. Touchett's house, he suggested, they might be part of an appealing tableau. But for the most part, ordinary commodities were simply beneath his notice. It would remain for Joseph Cornell to expose what he called "the pathos of the commonplace" by collecting and transfiguring "the familiar objects of the age of advertisement."

Of course, there were problems with James's juxtaposition of aestheticism against advertising. In *The Golden Bowl* (1904), he would return once again to the darker, more acquisitive dimensions of collecting and explore its affinities with commodity exchange.[18] The grace of life in Europe was not really unbought; in *The Ambassadors*, as in nearly all his other work, James evoked an atmosphere of extraordinary privilege. He had done so in *The Portrait of a Lady* as well, but in that novel, money is an issue—characters refer to its necessity, scheme to get it, and sometimes have it fall into their laps. By the time he wrote *The Ambassadors*, James seems to have imbibed the prescription attributed to Edith Wharton's mother: "Never talk about money, and think about it as little as possible."[19] The philistine argument could be made that James's critique of American utilitarianism is the dilettantish parlor game of a *rentier* class, the parasitical beneficiaries of business people whose exertions they deride. That would reduce the substance of his writings to a mere reflection of their economic origin. It would also be to ignore his sensitivity to the shortcomings of the aesthetic view of life, and to deny the very real possibility that, whatever the limitations of his demographic range, about the utilitarianism of advertising he may well have been dead right.

Edith Wharton's critique of commodity civilization filled in some of the sociological spaces left blank by James. She refused to take her mother's advice to heart. She wrote, at least some of the time, about American women who lacked Florentine palaces and assured inheritances, who felt compelled, for reasons of ambition or survival, to compete in the marriage market of late-nineteenth-century bourgeois culture. If they were lucky they became collectible objets d'art; if not, they were damaged goods. This was the social scene that Veblen had satirized, the mingling of old and new money among the upper classes during the American belle epoque. But Wharton was smarter, wittier, and more observant than Veblen.

She also had a keener sense of pathos. In *The House of Mirth* (1905), she chronicles the decline and fall of Lily Bart, a lovely and intelligent woman with every prospect of becoming a priceless artifact—the most prized possession of a coupon-clipping mediocrity. But she lacks sufficient resources to keep herself afloat en route to that destination. She becomes indebted to Rosedale, a Semitic caricature who (like nearly all the gentiles in the book as well) is given to "appraising people as if they were bric a brac." Resolving to be "the one possession in which he took sufficient pride to spend money on it," she nevertheless continues to face "a mounting tide of indebtedness." She descends from her status as art object in a fashionable drawing room to poverty, isolation, and (probable) suicide in a bare rented room.[20]

In *The Custom of the Country* (1913), Wharton created a very different version of the American woman in the market for a husband.[21] Undine Spragg, the archetypal bitch-goddess of consumerism, is bewitchingly successful at acquiring rich husbands. After divorcing Elmer Moffatt, a local boy from her home town of Apex, Indiana, she moves from Ralph Marvell, a stolid scion of Knickerbocker New York, by whom she has a son; to Raymond de Chelles, a French nobleman; and back to Moffatt, who has become an extraordinarily successful Wall Street speculator. The social trajectory is circular: Undine ends with her own kind; the economic trajectory is from a modicum of old money to bucketfuls of new. But in all cases, the men tend to be collectors, while Undine is the consummate consumer. David Riesman could not have found a better example of other-direction: as Ralph observes, "Undine's faculty of self-defense was weakened by the instinct of adapting herself to whatever company she was in, of copying 'the others' in speech and gesture as closely as she reflected them in dress; and he was disturbed by the thought of what her ignorance might expose her to" (159–60). (He needn't have worried.) Her passions are not merely accumulationist; they are specifically consumerist; that is, she feels an erotic charge in the act of spending itself, rather than in the possession of things. She haggles with dressmakers, not to save money but to "prolong and intensify the pleasure of spending" (181). In a sense, her consumerism is romantic and antimaterialist; once the object is purchased, the thrill is gone—so it has to be renewed by another act of purchase. Undine is the embodiment of Montaigne's soul-error, despising what is near, wanting what is distant, absent, and not hers.

Even as she disposes of two husbands, Undine continues to meet Moffatt, who has fascinated her ever since they met in Indiana. At first glance he seems a common enough variety of arriviste. When Undine asks him whether he'll ever remarry, he says, "Why, I shouldn't wonder—one of these days. Millionaires always collect something; but I'll have to collect my millions first" (419). Yet as they gradually resume a relationship, Moffatt reveals to her his secret zeal for collecting. Not long after he has seen her second husband Raymond's family tapestries, Moffatt "began to talk of his growing passion for pictures and furniture, and of his desire to form a collection which should be a great representative assemblage of unmatched specimens. As he spoke she saw his expression change, and his eyes grow younger, almost boyish, with a concentrated look in them that reminded her of long-forgotten things" (538). Here, as in James, we have an instance of Walter Benjamin's maxim "The collector's passion borders on the chaos of memories."[22] But in this passage Wharton associates collecting not only with memory but with a kind of rejuvenation through recollection of childhood—and with the self-forgetful concentration that could be located in the sphere of "deep play."

In the ambiguous character of Moffatt, Wharton took a major step toward elaborating an alternative language of objects. If the consumer looked toward the future, the collector aimed to arrest or even reverse the flow of time through contemplation of the thing itself. If collecting bordered on "the chaos of memories," that may have been because the collecting impulse was rooted in the recesses of early childhood. As any parent knows, children can be among the most passionate of collectors. And when collecting becomes child's play, it can transfigure even the most banal detritus of everyday life into the numinous stuff of art. The wealth to acquire rare artifacts was not a prerequisite for the collector's attitude toward things.

Ironically, one writer whose work suggested this conclusion was Marcel Proust, quintessential chronicler of the bondholding class in France before the First World War. In its swelling, ornate style and precise dissections of snobbery, *Remembrance of Things Past* (1913) documents the triumph and decline of a commodity civilization; in its memory method, the novel resists that civilization's soul-destroying march into the future. The recurring pattern of that method: the narrator awakens from sleep, feeling a sense of disorientation; the fragments of selfhood are gradually recombined through the memory of interior spaces and the things within them.

> . . . when I awoke in the middle of the night, not knowing where I was, I could not even be sure at first who I was; I had only the most rudimentary sense of my existence, such as may lurk and flicker in the depths of an animal's consciousness; I was more destitute than the cave-dweller; but then the memory—not yet of the place in which I was, but of various other places where I had lived and might now very possibly be—would come like a rope let down from heaven to draw me up out the abyss of not-being, from which I could never have escaped by myself: in a flash I would traverse centuries of civilization, and out of a blurred glimpse of oil-lamps, then of shirts with turned-down collars, would gradually piece together the component parts of my ego.[23]

In this passage from the Overture, the narrator describes his artistic method: the conscious channeling of the flood of memory through the elaborate architecture of his novel. But he is also describing the process by which he arrived at his adult commitment to write fiction. The blurred recollection of objects—oil lamps, shirts with turned-down collars—transforms a preconscious, almost vegetative existence into a coherent sense of self and (ultimately) of artistic vocation. Before the narrator fully awakens to adult and artistic consciousnesss, all perceptions are in fluid motion. "Shifting and confused gusts of memory" lead him toward "first one and then another of the rooms in which I had slept during my life and in the end I would revisit them all during the course of my waking dreams." Walls adapt themselves to the shape of each successive room, furniture appears and disappears, the narrator feels his own body shifting shape amid the whirl. It is only when "the good angel of certainty had made all the surrounding objects stand still" that he begins "remembering again all the places and people I had known, what I had actually seen of them, and what others had told me." Selfhood and art surface together, linked through memory amid the stillness of familiar household objects.[24]

The course of Proust's narrative confirms the wisdom of the philosopher Gaston Bachelard's observation that "memories are motionless, and the more securely they are fixed in space, the sounder they are." Through the recollection of particular spaces the narrator reconstructs his decision to become a novelist. He begins in the womblike "fixed space" at Combray, where desire and its objects are one. "The congruence of his faith in desired things with the real presence of those things close to him produces a wholeness of experience that stays in his memory," the critic Roger Shattuck observes.[25]

The path of the narrator proceeds out from this Eden into a social world driven by a restless desire for status, sexual partners, and precious furnishings. It is the same *haut-bourgeois* world dissected by Wharton and James: characters are constantly described as "collector's pieces" or objets d'art. The quintessential inhabitant of this world is Swann, protagonist of the first of the novel's seven parts, whose story prefigures dominant patterns in the work as a whole. Swann lives on his (mysterious) investments; he collects beautiful objects, but he is fatally drawn toward those he cannot satisfactorily possess, above all Odette, the commonplace ninny who leaves him in a state of panting, unfulfilled desire.

Swann yearns to be a true collector, in Benjamin's sense, but he ends by succumbing to soul-error. The narrator must suffer in the same driven world for years before he can begin to reconstruct his divided, desiring self. Like the other characters, he constantly muddles persons and commodities. He finally locates release through the most commonplace of consumer goods: a madeleine, dipped in tea, which releases a flood of involuntary memories. And that is where the conscious and deliberate stage of artistic reconstruction begins. The narrator must break free of self-absorption, connect with people who do not conform to his fantasies (such as his inamorata Albertine), in order to re-create the world in the light of art. Proust's great achievement was to devise an artistic life in the present that was rooted in the past. And the metaphorical collection of objects, from oil lamps and shirts with turned-down collars to a pastry dipped in tea, played a crucial role in that process.

However monumental Proust's accomplishment, his method was not unique. Between the wars, a number of artists and writers began to recognize the psychic importance of material artifacts for everyone, not just for the *rentier* class. They explored alternatives to the dominant "cult of the transitory," without retreating either into the temple of taste or the cork-lined room of the isolated artist. They embraced the humble articles of household use, or even, eventually, the discarded refuse of everyday industrial life. Thinking about things, playing with things, they deepened the discourse of objects.[26]

BETWEEN THE WARS: THE TRANSFIGURATION OF THE COMMONPLACE

The poet Rainer Maria Rilke thought about things a lot. There were times when he fell into the Jamesian and Whartonian opposition between Europe, the home of memorable artifacts, and America, the home of forgettable commodities. But his vision transcended that dualism. In 1925 he wrote to his Polish translator:

> Even for our grandparents a "house," a "well," a familiar tower, their very dress, their cloak, was infinitely more, infinitely more intimate: almost everything a vessel in which they found and stored humanity. Now there come crowding over from America empty, indifferent things, pseudo-things, DUMMY-LIFE. . . . A house, in the American understanding, an American apple or vine, has NOTHING in common with the house, the fruit, the grape into which the hope and meditation of our forefathers had entered . . . The animated, experienced things that SHARE OUR LIVES are coming to an end and cannot be replaced. WE ARE PERHAPS THE LAST TO HAVE STILL KNOWN SUCH THINGS. On us rests the responsibility of preserving, not merely their memory (that would be little and unreliable) but their human and laral worth. ("Laral" in the sense of household-gods.)[27]

This passage reveals more than a stereotyped antithesis between European and American things. It occurs in the course of Rilke's account of the philosophical meaning of the *Duino Elegies,* and it attains greater significance from that context. The elegies, Rilke claimed, were a plunge from

"Transitoriness" into "a profound Being," an attempt "to stamp this provisional, perishing earth into ourselves so deeply, so painfully and passionately, that its being may rise again, 'invisibly,' in us." Rilke said the elegies revealed "the continual conversion of the dear visible and intangible into the invisible vibration and agitation of our own nature, which introduces new vibration-numbers into the vibration-spheres."[28]

The critique of American "pseudo-things" brings this oracular pronouncement down to the level of everyday life. This is not merely the disgruntled European aristocrat railing against the fruits of democracy. Rilke melded the man-made and natural environments—"the house, the fruit, the grape"—and lamented the disenchantment of the whole. His complaint was not with vulgarity but with rationality in the Weberian sense, with the growing separation between human beings and the direct experience of the physical world. This was a nearly animistic worldview: "Nature, the things we move about among and use, are provisional and perishable; but so long as we are here, they are OUR profession and our friendship, sharers in our trouble and gladness, just as they have been the confidants of our ancestors."[29] Rilke's vision of cosmic wholeness encompassed paperweights and pianos as well as grape arbors—what held all these together (in addition to his idealist metaphysics) was their "laral worth." They were not priceless artifacts in ancestral dining halls but rather the "dear visible and tangible" things in everyday household use; they had, in fact, the character of "household-gods."

This was a key move, away from aristocratic preserves and toward the precincts of ordinary life. Rilke revealed some of its significance in a letter to Benvenuta (the concert pianist Magda von Hattingberg) where he described polishing his furniture.

> I was, as I said, magnificently alone . . . when suddenly I was seized by my old passion. I should say that this was undoubtedly my greatest passion, as well as my first contact with music, since our little piano fell under my jurisdiction as duster. It was, in fact, one of the few objects that lent itself willingly to the operation and gave no sign of boredom. On the contrary, under my zealous dustcloth, it suddenly started to purr mechanically . . . and its fine, deep black surface became more and more beautiful. . . . Politeness tinged with mischief was my response to the friendliness of these objects, which seemed happy to be well treated, so meticulously renovated. And even today, I must confess that, while everything about me grew brighter . . . the immense black surface of my work table, which dominated its surroundings . . . became newly aware, somehow, of the size of the room, reflecting it more and more clearly, pale gray and almost square . . . I felt moved, as

though something were happening, something, to tell the truth, which was not purely superficial but immense, and which touched my very soul: I was an emperor washing the feet of the poor, or St. Bonaventure, washing dishes in his convent.[30]

As Gaston Bachelard comments, this passage is "an accumulation of psychological documents from different mental ages." When Rilke was a child, one of his chores had been to dust the furniture; apparently, at least in his recollection of it, the task had become his "greatest passion" and his "first contact with music." Polishing his work table as an adult reconnected him with his childhood perceptions, reanimating the objects in the room and triggering Rilke's own imaginative identifications with saints and emperors. The performance of an ordinary household task links past and present, material and spiritual worlds; it is a case study in the transfiguration of the commonplace. Like Proust's experience with the madeleine, Rilke's epiphany suggests a relationship with the world of things that is more democratic, more available to ordinary people, than the connoisseurship examined by James and Wharton. Like Proust, Rilke provided a material embodiment of one abstract theme in the Frankfurt School's critique of commodity civilization: the argument that memories of wholeness were crucial to sustaining the solid sense of ego, without which individuals had little capacity to resist technocratic forms of social domination.

But Rilke's outlook was bounded by his elegiac despair; difficult as it was to imagine from his point of view, it might be possible as well to make artistic meaning even from those "empty, indifferent things" generated by commodity civilization. That was the agenda of Imagist poets like Ezra Pound and William Carlos Williams, who sought to rescue the thing itself, no matter how grimy or banal, from the vapors of Victorian ideality: "Say it, no ideas but in things," Williams insisted. It was also the path pursued by a number of idiosyncratic writers and artists on both sides of the Atlantic during the years between the wars—years when European culture itself seemed reduced to rubble, and about to be steamrollered by the American engines of progress. One rationale for this reclamation project was articulated by the French surrealist writer Louis Aragon. Recalling his outlook in his salad days, Aragon wrote in 1926 that "ordinary objects, no doubt steeped in mystery, could transport me beyond the everyday world." But this "sorcery" was not based on their capacity to evoke memory, as in Proust or Rilke—on the contrary, Aragon wrote, "I began to realize that their reign was predicated on their novelty, that its future lay under a mortal star. I therefore viewed them as so many transitory tyrants, the emissaries of chance, as it were, delegated to my sensibility. At last it dawned on me that I was enraptured with the modern." From this "modern" view the only value in the object was its capacity to call to mind (or eye) a hallucinatory image; Aragon, like other surrealists, enjoyed a "taste for confusion" that led his senses "to estrange every object from its use, to pervert it, as the saying goes." This surrealist view of objects was what allowed Aragon to make prehistoric monsters out of hair dryers and Egyptian divinities out of gas pumps: it subverted the utilitarian rationality underlying the construction of the consuming self, but it did not imply any alternative beyond the creation of confusion.[31]

Still, though Aragon claimed to be "enraptured with the modern," he felt the pull of the past—particularly when he wandered through the Paris Arcades. Those monuments to the variety and sensuality of nineteenth-century commerce were threatened by the drive toward the rationalization of everyday life.

> The great American instinct, imported to our capital by a Second Empire prefect, has ruled the map of Paris into rectangles, making it impossible to maintain these human aquaria which, though already gutted of their original life, deserve notice for the several modern myths they conceal—only now that the bulldozer threatens them they have become temples of a cult of the ephemeral, the ghostly landscape of forbidden pleasures and professions [the Arcades were a favorite haunt of prostitutes], incomprehensible yesterday and tomorrow gone.[32]

The desire to create "temples of a cult of the ephemeral" affected many surrealists, but it was especially pronounced in Aragon's contemporary André Breton. It led Walter Benjamin, another flaneur in the Arcades, to claim that Breton "was the first to perceive the revolutionary energies that appear in the 'outmoded,' in the first iron constructions, the first factory buildings, the earliest photos, the objects that have begun to be extinct, grand pianos, the dresses of five years ago, fashionable restaurants when the vogue has begun to ebb from them."[33] Yet in referring to "revolutionary energies," Benjamin may have implied something more complex than either Breton's band of surrealists or orthodox leftists envisioned.

In some ways, the aesthetic of the outmoded prefigured the later emergence of camp sensibility, without the camp devotee's insistent irony or flair for the outrageous.[34] A fascination with the recently outdated characterized the work of a number of literary as well as visual artists between the world wars, none of whom could be fit into textbook categories. In *Ulysses* (1922), for example, James Joyce evoked a fading commercial culture of charming soubrettes and drunken sandwich-board men; at the center stood Leopold Bloom, an advertising man but of a type already outmoded by the 1910s, a canvasser and space broker who called on local businesses and newspapers. For Bloom, scraps of commodity civilization, such as the torn piece of newspaper reading "What is home without Plumtree's Meat? Incomplete!" that recurrently pops into his field of vision, stir erotically charged memories of his wife Molly, his daughter Milly, and his dead son Rudy. These recollections are erotic in the strict etymological sense: they involve unfulfilled longings for people who are slipping away from him. But, like Proust's madeleine-induced reverie, they also depend on apparently insignificant fragments of commodity civilization to reawaken the dreamer to his place in a web of human connectedness joining past, present, and future.

By the 1930s, the aesthetic of the outmoded was most clearly on display in the visual realm, in the collages of Kurt Schwitters and Joseph Cornell. Their work demonstrated that it might be possible for the artist to reclaim the most forlorn, forgotten, and banal fragments of commodity civilization, the tram tickets and candy wrappers, ceramic collies and cinema posters, and resituate them in the architecture of the imagination, transforming them into numinous artifacts. Schwitters's whole career was dedicated to the elaborate collages and constructions he called *Merzbilder*. As the art critic Arthur Danto points out, *merz* is a fragment of an archaic German word whose closest English equivalent is "cull"—what has been culled or removed from the main batch as incomplete, inadequate, not up to standard. "*Merz* as practiced by Schwitters," Danto writes, "is . . . an act of including those things that have been excluded by culling: it is like a club made up of those who are not members of other clubs, a *salon des refusés*, or, paradoxically, a class whose members have no other class in common—a kind of classless society." Clockwork gears, used razor blades, glimpses of advertisements and promotionial leaflets—these and other bits of accumulated trivia in Schwitters's *Merzbilder* come to constitute what Danto calls "the inheriting meek," examples of an art that is not only democratic but Christian in some fundamental, forgotten sense. As Bachelard observed, to be moved by "the vast museum of insignificant things" that have accumulated in the contemporary world is to hear "a call to humility," for "worn objects deny splendor and luxury." Recontextualizing the detritus of industrial capitalism within the sacrosanct realm of Art, Schwitters accomplished a genuine transvaluation of value.[35]

Cornell (1903–1972) was an equally adept alchemist of the quotidian. With the Lithuanian poet O. V. de Milosz, he could have said that "motionless, mute things never forget: melancholy and despised as they are, we confide in them that which is humblest and least suspected in the depths of ourselves." For decades, beginning in the early 1930s, Cornell gathered discarded marbles, bits of broken toys, kitsch figurines, promotional brochures for defunct hotels and theater programs for passé ballerinas—anything that seemed to him to embody his obsession with "the pathos of the commonplace." He resituated these fragments in the boxes he called "pocket museums," and the fragments underwent "a sea change / into something rich and strange." They acquired a redemptive aura, as part of a storehouse of cultural memory in a society that systematically eroded it. By defamiliarizing once-familiar objects, Cornell's aesthetic of the outmoded provoked what Walter Benjamin called a "profane illumination": a moment that would call into question the given facticity of the existing social world and promote the hope of transcending it. For the dominant culture, "heaps of junk" were simply "the visible evidence of our willingness to shake off archaic traditions, methods, and equipment," as Julius Klein, a key official in Herbert Hoover's commerce department, wrote in 1930.[36] Like Rilke, Schwitters, and the surrealists, Cornell subtly undermined this progressive view. And unlike Andy Warhol, whose *Brillo Box* aimed to demystify the surrounding museum art by assimilating commodities to it, Cornell pushed his aesthetic in the opposite direction, toward the reanimation of the commodity world.

WELCOME TO JAMAICA:
THE WORLD OF JOSEPH CORNELL

In 1943, Joseph Cornell published a visual and verbal piece in *View* magazine called "The Crystal Cage (Portrait of Berenice)." It includes this story of a little girl:

> From newspaper clippings dated 1871 and printed as curiosa we learn of an American child becoming so attached to an abandoned chinoiserie while visiting France that her parents arranged for its removal and establishment in her native New England meadows. In the glistening sphere, the little proprietress, reared in a severe atmosphere of scien-

tific research, became enamored of the rarefied realms of constella-
tions, balloons, and distant panoramas, and drew upon her background
to perform her own experiments, miracles of ingenuity and poetry.[37]

Beginning with its dubious source, the anecdote is a canny self-revelation
of the artist, his obsessions and his methods. Cornell spent most of his
artistic life importing exotic artifacts to New England meadows, sorting
through the profusion of bibelots left by late-nineteenth-century bourgeois
culture in the "severe atmosphere" of an inherited Protestant cast of mind.
Protestant tradition had come to accept science but remained steeped in
the notion that the material world was merely a veil for the ineffable; its
embodiment, for Cornell, was Christian Science. Yet Cornell transcended
the endless dualisms that impaled so many of his American predecessors,
conflicts between surfaces and depths, profane and sacred illuminations.
Cornell sought the eternal harmonies of the sacred without abandoning
the sensuous surfaces of the profane; in his collages and boxes, he performed "miracles of ingenuity and poetry" by cultivating the childlike
capacity to see the most apparently ephemeral objects as parts of an animated universe. He wanted to devise a *lingua sacra* where literally everything could acquire a numinous significance.[38]

What is missing from the anecdote of the crystal cage, though, is some
sense of Cornell's connection to contemporary, urban mass culture. When
visitors came to Cornell's house on Utopia Parkway in Queens, the art historian Dore Ashton writes, they were

> surprised to find this thrall of the exquisite ensconced in a common-
> place house, crowded with too much furniture and too many traces of
> former family life, and with piles of books and papers everywhere.
> They noted shocking objects—shocking only in their humble and
> sometimes bad taste—such as plaster figures of animals, or a tablecloth
> with the garishly painted legend "Welcome to Jamaica" and a turbaned
> calypso singer beckoning. An anomaly—this man who could fashion
> exquisitely arcane images and who lived among the most ordinary of
> ordinary bric-a-brac.[39]

Cornell may have secretly relished the anomaly. He playfully resurrected
carnivalesque fragments, subverting cultural hierarchies, including the
elevation of the present and future over the past.

Cornell was anything but an ostentatiously rebellious bohemian; apart
from his shyness and social ineptitude, he seemed determined to lead an
extraordinarily ordinary life: caring for his invalid brother Robert, putter-
ing in the yard, taking out the ashes in the morning and greeting the milk-

man. To keep in mind his melding of mass and high cultures, it is worth noting an image from his diary of January 9, 1950. On that bitterly cold evening he was leaning against the stove, listening to Kitty Kallen sing "You Missed the Boat" while reading Rilke on Rodin. It was a typical moment for Cornell: he wanted to hear the music of the spheres, but he also liked the radio.[40]

In seeking to transfigure the banalities of everyday life, Cornell may in part have been making a virtue of necessity. Unlike James or Wharton, he had to earn his own livelihood. He was born to a prosperous, tight-knit family in Nyack, New York, in 1903, and he remembered his childhood as an idyll of fairy tales, amateur theatricals, and excursions to the Adirondacks and the Coney Island arcades. But in 1917 Cornell's father died of leukemia, leaving many debts and no will. Cornell attended Andover Academy, thanks to his mother's resourceful management of the family's dwindling finances, but in 1921 he was forced to take a job as a salesman with a wholesale textile company on Madison Square in Manhattan. He hated his dealings with customers but developed a growing sensitivity to the pleasures of street scenes and shop window displays. Laid off in 1931, he sold refrigerators door-to-door for a time, then took a job as a textile designer, which he found tedious and demanding. He was beginning to make boxes in earnest during this period, scouring the secondhand shops of lower Manhattan and cementing his relationship with Julien Levy, an innovative gallery owner with a fondness for surrealism. Cornell pursued his art on nights and weekends, later recalling that during the 1930s, his "things were done in a kind of Sunday spirit." Nevertheless, he managed, despite his reputation as a recluse, to cultivate enough contacts and receive enough notice that he felt able to quit his full-time job in 1940. He had been freelancing for *Harper's Bazaar, House and Garden,* and other glossy magazines since 1936, designing layouts for covers and advertisements (figure 12.1), and he kept at it faithfully (albeit sporadically) until the late 1950s, when his art was finally generating so much income that he could devote himself to it full time. His appointments at *Vogue* and *Good Housekeeping* were part of his regular routine on trips into Manhattan, an unfortunate interruption of curiosa hunts, perhaps, but far less oppressive than full-time work had been, and never a cause for anguish.[41]

There were, however, other causes for anguish. One was the gradual deterioration of his brother Robert, who had begun to show signs of a neurological disorder as a young child and who by the 1920s was confined to a wheelchair. Cornell took care of him for nearly forty years, encouraging

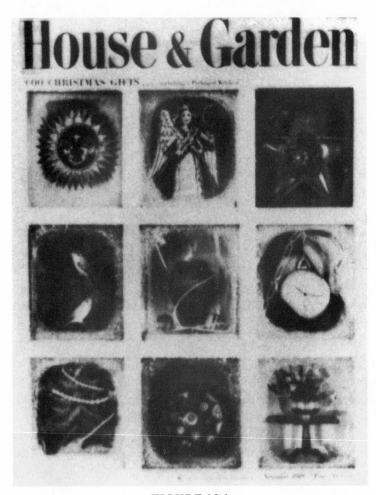

FIGURE 12.1

Joseph Cornell, cover design for *House and Garden,* November 1948. *Courtesy of the Joseph and Robert Cornell Memorial Foundation and* House and Garden. *Copyright © 1948, 1976 by The Condé Nast Publications Inc.*

him to draw, helping him assemble his model train sets, feeling inspired by his "heroic" smiles but also maddened by the trying task of caring for him. In a 1954 notebook entry, Cornell revealed a glimpse of the struggle involved when he referred to "typical feelings of unresolved menage condition (to avoid closing in or avoidance of state that brought on incident of gashed hand early this month)."[42]

But this obscure reference involved more than simply Cornell's suppression of rage against the helpless cause of his own frustration. Throughout his life Cornell was troubled by his sense that the atmosphere was "closing in" on him, creating the "feeling of pressure" that he often referred to in his journals. Cosmic despair haunted him from earliest Andover days. His sister Elizabeth recalled one night when he was home for Christmas vacation: "He woke me, shivering awfully, and asked to sit on my bed. He was in the grips of panic from the sense of infinitude and the vastness of space as he was becoming aware of it from studying astronomy."[43] Through the early 1920s he was tormented by nightmares and stomach pains with no organic cause. He would spend his lunch hours on a bench in Madison Square Park, moaning with anxiety. Then he discovered Christian Science. He was precisely the sort of person for whom Christian Science had most appeal: someone who distrusted the rationality of mainstream Protestant ethics, the preoccupation with willpower and control; someone who was yearning to reconnect body and soul in the stillness of Divine Mind.

Many art critics seem embarrassed or at best puzzled by Cornell's Christian Science, and it is admittedly difficult to sort out the meanings its doctrines might have held for his art. Nevertheless, the faith is central to understanding his life and work. It is not a matter of sorting through theological tenets (which in any case are minimal in Christian Science) but of breathing the atmosphere that enveloped Cornell's everyday life. His embrace of Christian Science not only brought him relief from his stomach disorders—apparently psychosomatic, though nonetheless "real"—but also helped him stabilize the mood swings that seemed to characterize his entire adult life, if only by providing him with a language of regeneration.

There were times when that language evoked the peculiarly ethereal doctrines of Christian Science. One morning in his cellar workroom in 1955, listening to the "Breakfast Symphony" program on the radio, he felt "one especially fine occasion of appreciation wherein externals are forgotten in favor of the 'other world' recreated by the music." His longing for release from the heavy weight of "externals" led him to describe "the healthy dream state" as "the sense of total freedom totally unfettered by the human body." But Cornell was far too sympathetically engaged with the material stuff of life to employ this idiom often.[44]

More commonly his jottings connected him not with his particular sect but with a broader, albeit still idiosyncratic, tradition in American Protestant culture. His diaries were filled with monitorings of his moods, searchings for signs of the "miracle of renewal" that could descend on him unawares. The surest sign seemed to be a sense of "clearing." The word is not the peculiar property of Christian Science; it resonates deeply with American Protestant tradition and romantic *Naturphilosophie,* with Jonathan Edwards and Walt Whitman. It evokes an open space on the forest floor, a break in the cloud cover, a freshening of the atmosphere. It strikes the note of cosmic correspondence heard by mystics from Edwards to Emily Dickinson: the discovery that "images or shadows of divine things" could be found in the common round of life. (Cornell felt a special kinship with Dickinson from 1952, when he discovered her poetry, until his death.) Like these spiritual ancestors, Cornell sought and occasionally found (as in this entry from 1948) "a world of complete happiness in which every triviality becomes imbued with a significance but difficult to communicate." The language was halting and ambiguous by comparison to his literary predecessors', but the lineage was plain.[45]

Still, the differences were important. Most of the figures in this American Protestant tradition had sought spiritual significance in the natural world. Cornell felt that same affinity—for silent seaside spaces, for rural rides on roads untouched by development—but nature for him was simply less available, except in more obviously mediated forms: his fascination with night skies was evoked in part by the "celestial ceiling" at Grand Central Station. For a few months in 1944, he worked at a garden center owned by a Christian Scientist in Flushing: the place acquired an arcadian atmosphere and a mysterious significance for him. Later he conceived "GC 44," a portfolio commemorating his experiences there, which he worked on for the rest of his life but never completed. In his diaries, the notation "GC 44" became a touchstone for evaluating all the other gusts of inspiration that sporadically blew through the architecture of his imagination. The feeling that everything around him possessed some ineffable significance, if he could only divine it, might overwhelm him in a variety of settings: sitting in an Automat at forty-second Street and third Avenue, drinking a glass of weak iced tea and eating a liverwurst sandwich and watching the "typical stream of motley N.Y. humanity"—this was one of those moments, one July afternoon in 1949, when "the minutiae of commonplace spectacle" led him to an " 'on-the-edgeness' of something apocalyptic, something really satisfying." After a day of depression, "thoughts lifted about things in general although not completely (pressure)." In other instances the experience could be equally fortuitous and fleeting, but more satisfying: "How marvelously does the decalc' [sic] sign on the little delivery truck become alive and germinal on such occasions," he wrote in 1954.

The real test of a "GC 44 type experience" was not its pastoral setting but its capacity to animate the actualities of everyday existence.[46]

When Cornell mentioned nature in his diaries he meant something different from what Emerson or Dickinson had had in mind. On an outing in November 1953, Dickinson's aphorism "These are signs to Nature's Inns / with invitation broad" popped into Cornell's head. But as he wrote in his diary, "Actually the humble nature of suburban shantytown bordering the el tracks is the scene 'with invitation broad.'" He was fascinated by that borderline where city turned into country—the Corona section of Queens, for example, where the facades of the old brownstone apartment buildings seemed to him like the faces of intimate friends, and where the natural surroundings had not been overwhelmed by the huge, impersonal artifacts of bureaucratic rationality: "Possibly the secret of the wild extravagant joy along these scenes is the warm appeal of nature," he wrote in 1954, "—simple direct, so often endlessly picturesque along this route, old houses, pigeon roosts, distant panorama."[47]

It was not the first time a passenger on the elevated had awakened to its aesthetic possibilities; the literature and art of urban realism was full of similar epiphanies. But Cornell's awakening was different. It belonged to a broader aesthetic of the outmoded. Part of the appeal of the old apartment buildings and the trademarks of small entrepreneurs was their human scale, which rendered them easier to animate. Downtown Flushing, which still had a village feel in the early 1950s, held a similar appeal; Cornell described an afternoon spent shopping there in September 1954: "not so much made of a borderline frame of mind as what may be salvaged from it—in the spirit of GC 44—this warmth and love for every least trifle of this village with its aspect of 'sanctuary' and the endless succession of remembered glints, crumbs of comfort, etc." Sauntering through Manhattan, he pondered "the abandoned, condemned boarded up facade of the buildings,—one area the grain showing through washed off green paint, windows with silver lettering 'Private Detective' all surmounted by the lettering 'Bach Building' vintage of about 1905." In this, as in nearly every other instance, his sudden bursts of "intense and sheer delight in the commonplace, the dingy, the banal, etc." was triggered by an encounter with artifacts that signified a vanished or vanishing era.[48]

To be sure, this nostalgia was not the only key to Cornell's creative process. He was capable of taking intense pleasure in the present, even occasionally in the commercial work he did to keep the macaroni and cheese on the table. He could describe a morning spent on sketches for *Good Housekeeping* as an "extraordinarily clear and vigorous burst of activity" and the completion of a *"perfume double spread for Vogue"* as a *"miraculous day of accomplishment"* (emphasis in original). His infatuation with movie actresses—Lauren Bacall, Jennifer Jones, Marilyn Monroe—is well known, and he could also rhapsodize over the counter girl at Bickford's as "Eurydice" in his diary. He was grateful for her smiles, as well as for the "beguiling smile" of the Rheingold Beer girl on the billboard in the Corona neighborhood. Glimpsing her face through the foliage, he was startled by the trompe l'oeil effect and dubbed her "a modern Daphne/Diana but with a Christian grace." This sentimental effusion was a far cry from the snarling hostility of most male seekers of authenticity when they confronted similar icons of advertising.[49]

Despite his capacity to derive pleasure from contemporary advertisements, Cornell's real creative home was in another country, the past. His first frisson at the sight of the Rheingold girl, in June 1947, came primarily because her image was linked to the Coney Island scenic railway, one of his childhood haunts. When he went to see the Christmas windows at Altman's, the three blind mice and Wee Willie Winkie evoked "the unutterable poignant poetry of childhood." When he meditated on a package of Adam's California Fruit Gum, it was not to celebrate its bold expression of modernity (as the painter Stuart Davis might have done), but to delight over discovering that it contained a biography of Adolphe Adam, the composer of the romantic ballet *Giselle* (1841). Trying in 1954 to reconstruct the process of assembling a series of boxes of twelve years before based on the nineteenth-century ballerina Fanny Cerrito, Cornell wrote: " 'the past' come to life via books, experience with browsing, etc. this very important factor in the Cerrito experiences but elusive, difficult to retain—yet it is really possibly THE only factor of significance in the exasperating task of putting the Cerrito into some kind of expression." When Cornell contemplated commercial artifacts, he contemplated his personal and cultural past.[50]

The two realms were interrelated. Cornell's browsings through second-hand book shops may have been at least in part an attempt to recapture the nineteenth-century European bourgeois culture that shaped his childhood as profoundly as the early-twentieth-century American culture of nickelodeons and slot machines. Nineteenth- and twentieth-century artifacts came together in his boxes (figure 12.2). This nineteenth-century culture was the world of Fanny Cerrito and Hans Christian Andersen, of romantic

FIGURE 12.2

Joseph Cornell, "Untitled" (Apollinaris), c. 1954, construction. *Courtesy of Mrs. E. A. Bergman, Chicago.*

reverie and sentimental paeans to childhood innocence. (And Andersen was a master at personifying objects.) To most modernists, except those attracted to the aesthetic of the outmoded, it was overripe and nauseating. Cornell expressed some of its appeal for him in his response to an exhibit of Italian poster reproductions:

> above all the utter delight in such things as certain of the Italian fin-de-siècle treatment of color, etc., particular pieces like children and bell-cons [balloons?], smalti [pieces of colored glass used in mosaics], touches of fantasy—remembering this as the background against which

the Futurist movement was soon to be staged (the essence of bourgeois is seen here, at least in its more charming aspects.)

In some ways, Cornell's collages and boxes took the most appealing part of
this "essence" and transformed it into art. The artifacts he assembled were
vestiges of the most fantastical, carnivalesque elements of an earlier commercial society—emblems of the sorcery of the marketplace before it was
stabilized by managerial rationality.[51]

They were also emblems of childhood, and evoked Cornell's own childhood memories. "On Thursday in cellar dismantling a Parmigliano box a
something came as in a far away distant childhood happening trees in sum-
mertime a street scene somewhere gone in a flash and leaving nothing but
surprise at its unexpectedness—for a moment I must have gone back to a
precious childhood moment not recalled since—remarkable if elusive
moment." Such moments could be "CREATIVE, RENEWING," Cornell
wrote—sometimes a melding of nineteenth-century bourgeois culture
with his own recollections of that culture in its afterglow.[52]

But those moments could pass quickly. After finding a collection of
cartes de visite and some old ballerina pictures in 1947, Cornell rhap-
sodized over their "never failing evocation of . . . another era so beautifully
recorded" and "enveloped in a nostalgic aura"; but then he acknowledged
that "at first these things are 'creative' but then the spark passes and they
become just a collection of 'old pix.' " Cornell could also associate nostalgic
moments with listlessness and indecision. For all his tendency toward mystical withdrawal from normal adult consciousness, there was also in Cornell the anxiety, so characteristic of Victorian Protestants, that one might
remain in such a mood too long: one had best be up and doing. "All the
things that give such an extravagance of happiness in the Indian Summer
mood now are enjoyed quietly but there is often the realization that this
enjoyment should transcend a mere 'poetic intoxication'—there is the dis-
quieting thought that too much time has been wasted already in this
mood," he wrote in 1948. The duty to produce paralleled the duty to
attend to the Christian Science sermons on the radio; Cornell frequently
hectored himself for "wandering" during the broadcasts. As in many other
American cultural figures, from Emerson to William James and Henry
Adams, the injunction to duty in the present pulled the dreamer out of the
pool of the past.[53]

Yet Cornell came to recognize that nostalgia—or at least the cultivation
of cultural and personal memory—was central to his own creativity. For a
long time he had dismissed Proust as a superficial novelist of manners;

then he read some of *Remembrance* and realized their commonalities of method. The trick, for both, was to emerge from the soupy haze of nostalgia with consciousness intact. On May 27, 1953, for example, Cornell heard Elizabeth Bowen, Frank Lloyd Wright, and Marianne Moore on the radio and received "real inspiration in the midst of preoccupation [with] PASTA [tiny boxes], lifting them into the present from nostalgia and futility." Perhaps a letter to a mysterious correspondent named Sonja Sheremietzew in 1949 best captured the state of Cornell's psychic weather on the subject of memory. The day, he wrote, was

> sunny and moderate. The kind of weather that brings back such a flood of memories from other years . . . that I almost drowned in nostalgia; so much seems to 'get away'—and yet the present with its invitation to adventure should rebuke all this. Perhaps this is not very well stated. The attempt to hold as much of the passing beauty as one is able to needs no apology.

Cornell's invocation of the present's "invitation to adventure" was unconvincing; like Faust, he wanted to say to the passing moment "stay," and unlike Faust, he realized that that impulse "needs no apology."[54]

The task, for Cornell as well as Proust, was not to wallow in regret over the passage of time but to recognize the living presence of the past in the present—to make of memory not a passive withdrawal into futility but a creative, shaping force. "Remembrance can never remain a passive attitude," Cornell quoted the philosopher Nikolas Berdyaev, "memory must needs be active; it is characterized by a creative, transfiguring power inherent in it." But it was not a simple matter to exercise that power, as Cornell noted in an unattributed quotation elsewhere in his diary (probably 1953): "To conjure, even for a moment, the wistfulness which is the past is like trying to gather in one's arms the hyacintine color of the distance. The past is only the present become invisible and mute, its memoried glances and its murmurs are infinitely precious." The task of conjuring the past was the task of a sorcerer, an alchemist of the quotidian, an artist like Cornell.[55]

If one thinks of Cornell's work as a kind of poetics of everyday life, then he had intellectual warrant for connecting it with childhood. Huizinga wrote that

> the function of the poet still remains in the play-sphere where it was born. *Poiesis,* in fact, is a play-function. It proceeds within the playground of the mind, in a world of its own which the mind creates for it. There things have a very different physiognomy from the one they

wear in "ordinary life," and are bound by ties other than those of logic and causality. . . . It lies . . . in the region of dream, enchantment, ecstasy, laughter. To understand poetry we must be capable of donning the child's soul like a magic cloak and of forsaking man's wisdom for the child's.[56]

The statement may not apply to all poets, and it may overestimate the adult's capacity for recovering childhood without ensconcing it in a carapace of self-consciousness. Nevertheless, the comments illuminate Cornell and his work with particular aptness. He was always something of a child himself, was always lunching on sticky buns and sweet desserts, and he always felt more comfortable in the company of children than with adults. The critics who referred to his constructions as "toys" in the 1930s may have unwittingly labeled his work more accurately than they have since been credited for doing—if one acknowledges that toys can be playthings in the largest sense, Huizinga's sense: aids for entering that realm of self-forgetfulness where work and play, subject and object are one. A clearing, if you want.

NOTES

INTRODUCTION

1. Anthony Forge, "Learning to See in New Guinea," in *Socialization: The Approach from Social Anthropology*, ed. Philip Mayer (London, 1970), p. 286.

2. The phrase "folklore of industrial society" is Marshall McLuhan's, in *The Mechanical Bride* (New York, 1951). As I hope this book will demonstrate, the equation of modern advertising with folklore ignores key historical distinctions between animistic and rationalistic modes of consciousness.

3. On this issue, I have been influenced by the pathbreaking essays of Hayden White, especially those collected in *Tropics of Discourse* (Baltimore, 1978).

4. See, for example, Roland Marchand, *Advertising the American Dream: Making Way for Modernity, 1920–1940* (Berkeley, Calif., 1985); Stephen Fox, *The Mirror Makers: A History of American Advertising and Its Creators* (New York, 1984); and for the retail side, William Leach, *Land of Desire: Merchants, Money, and the Rise of a New American Culture* (New York, 1993).

5. See, for example, Warren Susman, Introduction, *Culture as History* (New York, 1984); and William Leach, "Transformations in a Culture of Consumption: Women and Department Stores, 1890–1925," *Journal of American History* 71 (September 1984): 319–42.

6. Mary Douglas and Baron Isherwood, *The World of Goods* (New York, 1979); Michael Schudson, "Criticizing the Critics of Advertising: Towards a Sociological View of Marketing," *Media, Culture, and Society* 3 (January 1981): 3–12; and Schudson, *Advertising, The Uneasy Persuasion: Its*

Dubious Impact on American Society (New York, 1984), esp. chap. 4.

7. I have been influenced by Michael Taussig's lucid discussion of these matters in *The Devil and Commodity Fetishism in South America* (Chapel Hill, N.C., 1980), esp. p. 36. The *locus classicus* for any discussion of commodity fetishism is Karl Marx, *Capital,* 3 vols. [1867], trans. Samuel Moore and Edward Aveling, vol. 1 (New York, 1967), pp. 71–83. My discussion of fetishism in this introduction and in chap. 2 is dependent on my own reinterpretation of Marxian tradition.

8. Henry Adams, *The Education of Henry Adams* (Boston, 1918); Lewis Mumford, *Technics and Civilization* (New York, 1933) and *The Myth of the Machine,* vol. 2, *The Pentagon of Power* (New York, 1970); Max Horkheimer and Theodor W. Adorno, *Dialectic of Enlightenment* [1947] trans. John Cumming (New York, 1972); Herbert Marcuse, *Eros and Civilization* (Boston, 1955). For more recent arguments against the equation of consumption with hedonism, see William Leiss, *The Limits to Satisfaction* (Toronto, 1976), and Staffan Linder, *The Harried Leisure Class* (New York, 1970).

9. Igor Kopytoff, "The Cultural Biography of Things: Commoditization as Process," in *The Social Life of Things,* ed. Arjun Appadurai (Cambridge, England, 1986), pp. 64–91.

10. Georges Bataille, *Visions of Excess* (Minneapolis, 1985); Jean Baudrillard, "When Bataille Attacked the Metaphysical Principle of Economy," *Canadian Journal of Political and Social Theory* 11 (1987): 57–62; Lewis Hyde, *Imagination and the Erotic Life of Property* (New York, 1983). The classic text is Marcel Mauss, *The Gift: Forms and Functions of Exchange in Archaic Societies* [1924], trans. Ian Cunnison (New York, 1967). See also the exceptionally lucid Douglas Kellner, *Jean Baudrillard: From Marxism to Postmodernism and Beyond* (Stanford, 1989), pp. 42–45. For an important departure in the literature of gift exchange, which explores the role of things in orchestrating gender hierarchy and difference, see Annette B. Weiner, *Inalienable Possessions: The Paradox of Keeping-While-Giving* (Berkeley, Calif., 1993).

11. Hannah Arendt, *The Human Condition* (Chicago, 1958), pp. 126–28, 168, 176–78. For parallel distinctions, see William Morris, "Useful Work vs. Useless Toil," in *William Morris on Art and Socialism,* ed. Holbrook Jackson (London, 1947), pp. 175–87.

12. Jean Baudrillard, *Le System des objets* (Paris, 1968), p. 146; Susan Stewart, *On Longing: Narratives of the Miniature, the Gigantic, the Souvenir, the Collection* (Baltimore, 1984), pp. x, 1, 153–54; Kopytoff, "Cultural Biography of Things." Obviously, camp sensibility can be taken in a variety of cultural directions other than the one I mention here. See Susan Sontag, "Notes on 'Camp,'" in her *Against Interpretation* (New York, 1966), pp. 275–92, and Andrew Ross, "Uses of Camp," in his *No Respect* (London, 1989), pp. 135–70.

13. Arendt, *Human Condition,* p. 128. Huizinga's views on art and play are in his *Homo Ludens* [1938] (Boston, 1955), esp. pp. 119–45, 158–72. See

also Roger Caillois, *Man, Play, and Games*, trans. Meyer Barash (Glencoe, Ill., 1961), and Clifford Geertz, "Deep Play: Notes on the Balinese Cockfight," in his *The Interpretation of Cultures* (New York, 1973).

14. David Freedberg, *The Power of Images: Studies in the History and Theory of Response* (Chicago, 1989); Colleen McDannell, *The Christian Home in Victorian America* (Bloomington, 1988); David Harper, *Working Knowledge: Skill and Community in a Small Shop* (Chicago, 1987); Claude Lévi-Strauss, *The Savage Mind* (Chicago and London, 1966), esp. chap. 1.

15. Evelyn Fox Keller, *A Feeling for the Organism: The Life and Work of Barbara McClintock* (San Francisco, 1983), p. 200. For the ecological implications of this point of view, see Neil Eveinder, "Self, Place, and the Pathetic Fallacy," *North American Review,* December 1978, 16–20.

16. Henry Roth, *Call It Sleep* [1934] (New York, 1962), p. 132.

17. Octavio Paz, "Poetry and the Free Market," *New York Times Book Review,* 8 December 1991, 38.

18. See the sensitive and illuminating study by T. M. Luhrmann, *Persuasions of the Witch's Craft: A Study of Ritual Magic in Contemporary England* (Cambridge, Mass., 1989).

19. Lévi-Strauss, *The Savage Mind,* p. 17.

CHAPTER 1. THE LYRIC OF PLENTY

1. Robert Darnton, "Peasants Tell Tales: The Meaning of Mother Goose," in his *The Great Cat Massacre and Other Episodes in French Cultural History* (New York, 1985), p. 33. For another provocative treatment of this theme, see Piero Camporesi, *Bread of Dreams: Food and Fantasy in Early Modern Europe,* trans. David Gentilcore (Chicago, 1989).

2. David Potter, *People of Plenty: Economic Abundance and American National Character* (Chicago, 1954); Warren Susman, *Culture as History: The Transformation of American Society in the Twentieth Century* (New York, 1984), esp. the introduction. For more recent examples of this same framework in operation, see James D. Norris, *Advertising and the Transformation of American Society, 1865–1920* (Westport, Conn., 1990), and William Leach, "Transformations in a Culture of Consumption: Women and Department Stores, 1890–1925," *Journal of American History* 71 (September 1984): 319–42. A promising departure, which takes alternative cultural traditions seriously, is Andrew Heinze, *Adapting to Abundance: Jewish Immigrants, Mass Consumption, and the Search for American Identity* (New York, 1990), esp. pp. 42, 62–65, 84, 97.

3. Evelyn Fox Keller, *A Feeling for the Organism: The Life and Work of Barbara McClintock* (San Francisco, 1983), esp. chaps. 9, 12; Mihaly Csikszentmihalyi and David Rochberg-Halton, *The Meaning of Things: Domestic Symbols and the Self* (Chicago and London, 1981); David Harper, *Working Knowledge: Skill and Community in a Small Shop*

(Chicago and London, 1987); John Forrest, *Lord I'm Coming Home: Everyday Aesthetics in Tidewater North Carolina* (Ithaca, N.Y., and London, 1988); Claude Lévi-Strauss, *The Savage Mind* (Chicago and London, 1966), chap. 1.

4. The painting and the consciousness it embodies are brilliantly discussed in David Freedberg, *The Power of Images: Studies in the History and Theory of Response* (Chicago and London, 1989), pp. 283–91. See also Margaret R. Miles, "The Virgin's One Bare Breast: Nudity and Religious Meaning in Tuscan Early Renaissance Culture," in *The Female Body in Western Culture,* ed. Susan R. Suleiman (Cambridge, Mass., 1986), pp. 193–208.

5. Victor Turner, *The Forest of Symbols: Aspects of Ndembu Ritual* (Chicago and London, 1967), p. 44.

6. Irenaeus, *Against the Heresies,* book 3, chap. 33, in *The Ante-Nicene Fathers,* ed. Alexander Roberts and James Donaldson, 12 vols. (Buffalo, 1885), vol. 1, p. 563.

7. Ibid., p. 562.

8. Camporesi, *Bread of Dreams,* pp. 80, 109; Frank E. Manuel and Fritzi P. Manuel, *Utopian Thought in the Western World* (Cambridge, Mass. 1979), pp. 80–81; Katherine M. Briggs, *A Dictionary of British Folk Tales in the English Language,* 2 vols. (London, 1970), vol. 1, pp. 331–33; Darnton, "Peasants Tell Tales," p. 39; Peter Stallybrass and Allon White, *The Politics and Poetics of Transgression* (Ithaca, N.Y., 1986), p. 57.

9. Peter Burke, *Popular Culture in Early Modern Europe* (New York, 1978), pp. 189, 186; J. Taylor, "Jack a Lent," in his *Works* (London, 1630), p. 115.

10. M. M. Bakhtin, *Rabelais and His World,* trans. H. Iswolsky (Cambridge, Mass., 1968), p. 19. My understanding of Bakhtin has been influenced by the penetrating critique in Stallybrass and White, *Transgression,* esp. pp. 1–59, 171–202.

11. Camporesi, *Bread of Dreams,* p. 80; Burke, *Popular Culture,* p. 187; Stallybrass and White, *Transgression,* pp. 53–56.

12. Stallybrass and White, *Transgression,* pp. 35–43; Anon., "The Pedlar Opening His Pack," in *A Pepysian Garland,* ed. H. E. Rollins (Cambridge, Mass., 1922), pp. 116–20; Matthew Boulton to R. Chippendall, 9 August 1794, quoted in E. Robinson, "Eighteenth Century Commerce and Fashion: Matthew Boulton's Marketing Techniques," *Economic History Review,* 2nd series, 16 (1963): 59; N. M. Karamzin, *Letters of a Russian Traveller, 1789–1790,* trans. and abridged by Florence Jones (New York, 1957), p. 277, quoted in Neil McKendrick, John Brewer, and J. H. Plumb, *The Birth of a Consumer Society: The Commercialization of Eighteenth-Century England* (Bloomington, Ind., 1982), p. 79. The classic overview of these developments is Werner Sombart, *Luxury and Capitalism* [1913], trans. W. R. Dittmar (Ann Arbor, Mich., 1967). For a contemporary anthropological view, see

Chandra Mukerji, *From Graven Images: Patterns of Modern Material-ism* (Chicago, 1983).

13. Richard C. Trexler, "Florentine Religious Experience: The Sacred Image," *Studies in the Renaissance* 19 (1972): 31–33.

14. Arthur Barlow, report to Sir Walter Raleigh, 2 July 1584, in *Hakluyt's Voyages: A Selection,* ed. Richard David (Boston, 1981), pp. 445–50. See also Boies Penrose, *Travel and Discovery in the Renaissance, 1420–1620* (Cambridge, Mass., 1952), and Howard Mumford Jones, "The Colonial Impulse: An Analysis of the 'Promotion' Literature of Colonization," *Proceedings of the American Philosophical Society* 90 (May 1946), esp. 153–54.

15. John Speede, *Historie of Great Britain,* cited in Howard Mumford Jones, *O Strange New World* (New York, 1966), p. 123n. On More's belief in an earthly paradise, see Manuel and Manuel, *Utopian Thought,* p. 123. See also Howard Mumford Jones, "The Image of the New World," in *Elizabethan Studies and Other Essays in Honor of George F. Reynolds,* University of Colorado Studies, series B, Studies in the Humanities, vol. 2, no. 4 (October 1945), pp. 81–82; Louis B. Wright, *The Dream of Prosperity in Colonial America* (New York, 1965), pp. 42–43; and Charles Sanford, *The Quest for Paradise* (Urbana, Ill., 1961).

16. The fullest discussions of these themes are in Carolyn Merchant, *The Death of Nature* (New York, 1981); Annette Kolodny, *The Lay of the Land: Metaphor as Experience and History in American Life and Letters* (Chapel Hill, N.C., and London, 1975); and Louis Montrose, "The Work of Gender in the Discourse of Discovery," *Representations* 33 (1991): 1–41.

17. "Third Voyage of Columbus," in Christopher Columbus, *Four Voyages to the New World: Letters and Selected Documents,* bilingual ed., trans. and ed. R. H. Major (New York, 1961), pp. 130, 131, 135, 137.

18. Clare Le Corbeiller, "Miss America and Her Sisters: Personification of the Four Parts of the World," *Bulletin of the Metropolitan Museum of Art,* new series 19 (1961): 209–23; E. McClung Fleming, "The American Image as Indian Princess, 1765–1783," *Winterthur Portfolio* 2 (1965): 65–69.

19. George Alsop, *A Character of the Province of Maryland* [1666] (Cleveland, 1902), pp. 33–34; Kolodny, *Lay of the Land,* p. 67.

20. John Donne, "On Going to Bed," lines 25–30.

21. Pierre Grimal, "Greece: Myth and Logic," in *Larousse World Mythology,* ed. P. Grimal, trans. Patricia Beardsworth (London, 1965), p. 106; Seth Bernardete, ed., *Larousse Greek and Roman Mythology,* trans. Sheilah O'Halloran (London, 1980), p. 23.

22. Oxford English Dictionary, q.v. *matter.*

23. Stephen Toulmin, *Cosmopolis: The Hidden Agenda of Modernity* (Chicago, 1990), p. 75.

24. Merchant, *Death of Nature,* pp. 33, 169; Manuel and Manuel, *Utopian Thought,* p. 256.

25. This pattern is ably explored by Richard Slotkin, *Regeneration Through Violence: The Mythology of the American Frontier* (Middletown, Conn., 1973), esp. chaps. 2–6.

26. Sir Walter Raleigh, *The Discovery of Guiana* [1595], ed. W. H. Rouse (London and Glasgow, 1905), pp. 31, 81.

27. William Bradford, *Of Plymouth Plantation* [1651], ed. Harvey Wish (New York, 1962), p. 141; Thomas Morton, *New English Canaan* [1637], in *Tracts and Other Papers relating to the Origin, Settlement, and Progress of the Colonies in North America*, comp. Peter Force, 4 vols. (Washington, 1838), vol. 2, p. 92.

28. Morton, *New English Canaan*, p. 10.

29. John Sekora, *Luxury: The Concept in Western Thought, from Eden to Smollett* (Baltimore, 1978); John Bunyan, *The Pilgrim's Progress from This World to That Which Is to Come* [1684] (New York and Toronto, 1949), p. 318; McKendrick et al., *Birth of a Consumer Society*, pp. 27–28 and passim.

30. Max Weber, *The Protestant Ethic and the Spirit of Capitalism* [1904], trans. Talcott Parsons (New York, 1958).

31. For the early stages of this process, see E. McClung Fleming, "From Indian Princess to Greek Goddess: The American Image, 1783–1815," *Winterthur Portfolio* 3 (1967): 37–81. The enormous historiography on "republicanism" in early American political thought has established the centrality of this ambivalence toward economic abundance; even the advocates of the view that the American colonies constituted a "consumer society" have been forced to admit it. For a classic discussion of early American attitudes, see Edmund Morgan, "The Puritan Ethic and the American Revolution," in *The Reinterpretation of the American Revolution*, ed. Jack P. Greene (New York, 1968), pp. 235–250.

32. Benjamin Franklin, "Advice to a Young Tradesman, Written by an Old One," in *The American Instructor: or Young Man's Best Companion*, ed. George Fisher, (Philadelphia, 1748), pp. 375–77, reprinted in *The Papers of Benjamin Franklin*, ed. Leonard W. Labaree (New Haven, 1961), vol. 3, 306.

33. Crèvecoeur, *Letters from an American Farmer* [1782] (London and New York, 1912), p. 43. See the brilliant discussion of this passage (and the image accompanying it in an early French edition) in Werner Sollors, *Beyond Ethnicity: Consent and Descent in American Culture* (New York and Oxford, 1986), pp. 76–81.

34. James Fenimore Cooper, *The Pioneers* [1823] (Albany, 1980), pp. 243–47. For a similar description of passenger pigeons blotting out the sky (but without the denouement of destruction), see Washington Irving, *Astoria* [1839] (London and New York, 1987), p. 125. On the conjunction between "ecological abundance and economic prodigality," see William Cronon, *Changes in the Land: Indians, Colonists, and the Ecology of New England* (New York, 1983), and Stanley W. Trimble, "Perspectives

on the History of Soil Erosion Control in the United States," *Agricultural History* 59 (April 1985): 162–65.

35. D. H. Lawrence, *Studies in Classic American Literature* [1923] (New York, 1964), p. 32.

CHAPTER 2. THE MODERNIZATION OF MAGIC

1. Marcus Dickey, *The Youth of James Whitcomb Riley* (Indianapolis, 1919), pp. 105–10.
2. Ibid., pp. 110–31.
3. Ibid., pp. 193–211.
4. The best general survey of this tradition, especially with reference to the patent medicine show, is Brooks McNamara, *Step Right Up* (Garden City, N.Y., 1976).
5. On the carnivalizing impact of picaresque literature, see Mikhail Bakhtin, "Discourse in the Novel," in *The Dialogic Imagination: Four Essays by M. M. Bakhtin*, ed. Michael Holquist, trans Caryl Emerson and Michael Holquist (Austin, Texas, 1981), p. 408. For crucial cultural and economic background on the emergence of market society in the United States, see Lewis Perry, *Boats Against the Current: American Culture Between Revolution and Modernity, 1820–1860* (New York: 1993), esp. part 4; and Winifred Rothenberg, *From Market-places to Market Economy: The Transformation of Rural Massachusetts, 1750–1850* (Chicago, 1992).
6. Peter Benes, "Itinerant Entertainers in New England and New York, 1607–1830," in Benes, ed., *Itinerancy in New England and New York* (Boston, 1986), esp. p. 119; Richard W. Flint, "Entrepreneurial and Cultural Aspects of the Early Nineteenth Century Circus and Menagerie Business," in ibid., pp. 131–49. On peddlers in antebellum America, see Richardson Wright, *Hawkers and Walkers in Early America* (Philadelphia, 1927); J. R. Dolan, *The Yankee Peddlers of Early America* (New York, 1964); Lewis E. Atherton, "Itinerant Merchandising in the Antebellum South," *Bulletin of the Business Historical Society* 19, no. 2 (April 1945): 35–58.
7. Neil Harris, *Humbug: The Art of P. T. Barnum* (Chicago, 1973), esp. p. 25; James Harvey Young, *The Toadstool Millionaires: A Social History of Patent Medicines in America Before Federal Regulation* (Princeton, N.J., 1961), esp. chaps. 3, 6–9. The first Oxford English Dictionary entry using *magic* as a synonym for sleight of hand is dated 1831; I am indebted to Kenneth Cmiel for bringing this salient fact to my attention.
8. Jon Butler, "Magic, Astrology, and the Early American Religious Heritage, 1600–1760," *American Historical Review* 84 (June 1979): 317.
9. Alan Taylor, "The Early Republic's Supernatural Economy: Treasure Seeking in the American Northeast, 1780–1830," *American Quarterly* 38 (Spring 1986): 19.

10. James D. McCabe, *Lights and Shadows of New York Life* (Philadelphia, 1879), p. 729. See also the valuable study by Ann Fabian, *Card Sharps, Dream Books, and Bucket Shops: Gambling in Nineteenth-Century America* (Ithaca, N.Y., and London, 1990).

11. On female healers, see, for example, Laurel Thatcher Ulrich, *The Midwife's Tale: The Life of Martha Moore Ballard Based on Her Diary, 1785–1812* (New York, 1990), and for the exception (Lydia Pinkham) that proves the rule in the patent medicine business, see Sarah Stage, *Female Complaints: The Career of Lydia Pinkham* (New York, 1979).

12. Colin Campbell, *The Romantic Ethic and the Spirit of Modern Consumerism* (Oxford and London, 1987), esp. pp. 118–53. The classic discussion of "the Augustinian strain of piety" in Puritan thought is Perry Miller, *The New England Mind: The Seventeenth Century* (Cambridge, Mass., 1939), part I. Also see Patricia Caldwell, *The Puritan Conversion Narrative: The Beginnings of American Expression* (Cambridge, England, 1983), p. 195.

13. Quoted in Roger Shattuck, *Marcel Proust* (Princeton, N.J., 1982), p. 95.

14. Isaac Barrow, quoted by R. S. Crane, "Suggestions Toward a Genealogy of the 'Man of Feeling,'" in Crane, *The Idea of Humanities and Other Essays Critical and Historical* (Chicago, 1967), pp. 188–213.

15. Edward Payson on prayer (1830), quoted in Richard Rabinowitz, *The Spiritual Self in Everyday Life: The Transformation of Personal Religious Experience in Nineteenth-Century New England* (Boston, 1989), p. 161; *The Art and Mystery of Making a Fortune* (n.p., 1854) in Advertising box 5b, Warshaw Collecton of Business Americana, National Museum of American History, Smithsonian Institution, Washington, D.C.

16. John Keats, "Ode on a Grecian Urn," lines 11, 12.

17. Carole Shammas, *The Pre-Industrial Consumer in England in America* (Oxford, 1990), p. 299.

18. Karen Halttunen, "Early American Murder Narratives: The Birth of Horror," in *The Power of Culture,* ed. Richard Wightman Fox and T. J. Jackson Lears (Chicago and London, 1993), pp. 67–101. I am indebted to the pathbreaking discussion of American sensationalism in David Reynolds, *Beneath the American Renaissance: The Subversive Imagination in the Age of Emerson and Melville* (New York, 1988), esp. chap. 6.

19. Reynolds, *Renaissance,* p. 55; George G. Foster, *New York in Slices* (New York, 1848), p. 5.

20. Foster, *New York in Slices,* p. 94.

21. P. T. Barnum, *Struggles and Triumphs: or, Forty Years' Recollections of P. T. Barnum* (Buffalo, N.Y., 1872), p. 263; Henry P. Haynes, "The East," *Godey's Lady's Book* 47 (July 1853): 33; engraving, "The Circassian Beauty," in *Peterson's* 29 (September 1851): frontispiece; "Work Department: The Ottoman," *Godey's* 56 (June 1858): 555; advertisement for "The Castilian" in ibid. 58 (January 1859): 9; Emily May, "The Echarpe Orientale," *Peterson's* 27 (January 1855): 89–90; "Chitchat Upon Prevailing Fashions," *Godey's* 48 (May 1854): 479–80. See also Lois Banner,

American Beauty (New York, 1983). For more examples of soft-core pornographic exoticism in popular prints, see the lithographs in the Peters Collection, National Museum of American History, Smithsonian Institution: for example, "The Sea-Nymph's Cave" (#60.2268, c. 1840) and "Le Lever" (#60.2528, c. 1855). See also "The Indian Fruitseller," *Ladies World* 3 (March 1843): frontispiece.

22. "Thousand and One Nights," in *Encyclopedia Britannica,* 14th ed. (London, 1940), vol. 22, pp. 157–59; Alice B. Haven, "A Morning at Stewart's," *Godey's* 66 (May 1863): 429–33. See also Frazar Kirkland, *Cyclopedia of Commercial and Business Anecdotes,* 2 vols. (New York, 1864), vol. 2, p. 588.

23. Henry David Thoreau, *Walden* [1854] (Boston, 1957), p. 25; Peter Gay, *The Bourgeois Experience, Victoria to Freud: the Education of the Senses* (New York, 1984), p. 342.

24. See the review articles by Robert Shalhope: "Toward a Republican Synthesis: The Emergence of an Understanding of Republicanism in Early American Historiography," *William and Mary Quarterly,* 3rd ser., 29 (January 1972): 49–80, and "Republicanism and Early American History," ibid. 39 (April 1982): 334–56. For a sampling of the debate over the persistence of republicanism in nineteenth-century political culture, see John Diggins, "Comrades and Citizens: New Mythologies in American Historiography," *American Historical Review* 90 (June 1985): 614–38; Leon Fink, "The New Labor History and the Powers of Historical Pessimism," *Journal of American History* 75 (June 1988): 115–36; and Daniel T. Rodgers, "Republicanism: The Career of a Concept," ibid. 79 (June 1992): 11–38, which is the best available overview.

25. Gordon Wood, *The Creation of the American Republic, 1776–1812* (New York, 1969), pp. 179–83; Kenneth Cmiel, *Democratic Eloquence: The Fight over Popular Speech in Nineteenth-Century America* (New York, 1990).

26. Dekker and Webster quoted in Jean-Christophe Agnew, *Worlds Apart: Market and Theatre in Anglo-American Thought, 1550–1750* (New York and London, 1986), p. 57; Richard Campbell, *The London Tradesman* (London, 1947), pp. 191, 192. Here and elsewhere I am indebted to Agnew's penetrating analysis of early market culture.

27. Aleksandr Herzen, review of P. T. Barnum, *Struggles and Triumphs* [1855], quoted in *Struggles and Triumphs; or, The Life of P. T. Barnum, Written by Himself,* ed. George S. Bryan, 2 vols. (New York and London, 1927), vol. 1, p. xliv; Peter Marzio, *The Democratic Art: Chromolithography in Nineteenth-Century America* (Boston, 1978); Robert Jay, *The Trade Card in Nineteenth-Century America* (Columbia, Mo., 1987), pp. 28–29.

28. Walt Whitman, "The Terrible Doubt of Appearances" [1860], in *Leaves of Grass,* ed. Harold W. Blodgett and Sculley Bradley (New York, 1965), p. 120; George Lippard, *The Quaker City; or, The Monks of Monk Hall* [1844] (Philadelphia, 1849), p. 23.

29. Timothy Smith, *Revivalism and Social Reform: American Protestantism on the Eve of the Civil War* [1957] (New York, 1965), pp. 118, 143, 149, 160, 227; Edward Payson on prayer (1830), quoted in Rabinowitz, *The Spiritual Self in Everyday Life*, p. 161; Whitney R. Cross, *The Burned-over District: The Social and Intellectual History of Enthusiastic Religion in Western New York, 1800–1850* [1950] (New York, 1965), pp. 194–95.

30. Philip Schaff, *The Principle of Protestantism* (1844), quoted in Nathan O. Hatch, *The Democratization of American Christianity* (New Haven, 1989), frontispiece.

31. Butler, "Magic, Astrology, and the Early American Religious Heritage," 341.

32. Timothy Dwight, *Travels in New York and New England*, ed. Barbara Miller Solomon, 4 vols. (Cambridge, Mass., 1969), vol. 1, p. 158.

33. Mrs. C. M. Sedgwick, "Wilton Harvey," *Godey's* 24 (March 1842): 122.

34. *The Art and Mystery of Making a Fortune*, in Advertising box 5B, Warshaw Collection; Richard Hildreth, *Banks, Banking, and Paper Currencies, in Three Parts* (New York, 1840), p. 150; [Johnson Jones Hooper,] *Simon Suggs' Adventures and Travels* (Philadelphia, 1848), p. 12.

35. Benjamin Klebaner, *Commercial Banking in the United States: A History* (Hinsdale, Ill., 1974), pp. 17–18; Frazar Kirkland, *Cyclopedia of Commercial and Business Anecdotes*, 2 vols. (New York, 1864), vol. 1, p. 75; Daniel Sewall, *An Astronomical Diary or Almanack for the Year of Our Lord 1809* (Portsmouth, N.H.: by the author, 1809), in Almanacs box 63a, Warshaw Collection, contains a two-page description and warning of counterfeit bank bills. On the persistence of household production and suspicion of commercial activity, see James Henretta, "Families and Farms: *Mentalité* in Pre-industrial America," *William and Mary Quarterly* 35 (January 1978): 3–32; Michael Merrill, "Cash Is Good to Eat: Self-Sufficiency and Change in the Rural Economy of the United States," *Radical History Review* 3 (Winter 1977): 42–71; Christopher Clark, "The Household Economy, Market Exchange, and the Rise of Capitalism in the Connecticut River Valley, 1800–1860," *Journal of Social History* 13 (Winter 1979), 169–89; and Steven Hahn and Jonathan Prude, eds., *The Countryside in the Era of Capitalist Transformation* (Chapel Hill, N.C., 1985). Many historians of early America have challenged these views, arguing that yeoman farmers were enthusiastic agrarian capitalists: along with a mechanistic and one-dimensional psychology, this argument requires that its proponent attack the straw man of absolute self-sufficiency; once the historian shows that even a few items in a household were purchased rather than made, he believes he has uncovered full-blown participation in a market economy. See, for example, the claims in Timothy H. Breen, "An Empire of Goods: The Anglicization of Colonial America, 1690–1776," *Journal of British Studies* 25 (October 1986): 467–99.

36. For two of innumerable treatments of the problem of appearances, see William Cutter, "Introversion; or, Magical Readings of the Inner Man,"

Godey's 21 (July 1840): 10–12, and Harry Sunderland, "A Stage Coach Adventure, Or, Never Trust to Appearances," *Peterson's* 15 (August 1849): 54; for the reading of faces, see (again, two among many examples) Kirkland, *Cyclopedia*, vol. 1, p. 31, and "Kaladora Andros; or, the Advertisement," *Peterson's* 28 (August 1858): 167. The classic discussion of the problem of appearances in mid-nineteenth-century American culture is Karen Halttunen, *Confidence Men and Painted Women: A Study of Middle-Class Culture in Victorian America, 1830–1870* (New Haven, Conn., and London, 1982), esp. chaps. 1, 2. I am deeply indebted to Halttunen's analysis.

37. George Lippard, *The Empire City* (Philadelphia, 1864), p. 138.

38. Halttunen, *Confidence Men*, pp. 4–15.

39. John S. Haller, *American Medicine in Transition, 1840–1910* (Urbana, Ill., 1981), p. 105; *Confessions of a Magnetizer* (1845), quoted in Robert C. Fuller, *Mesmerism and the American Cure of Souls* (Philadelphia, 1982), pp. 87–88; Hawthorne cited in ibid., p. 35. For a brilliant manipulation of all the conventions surrounding mesmerism—exotic sensuality, twinning, loss of will, descent into a a psychic abyss—see Edgar A. Poe, "A Tale of the Ragged Mountains," *Godey's* 28 (April 1844): 177–81.

40. Emerson quoted in Fuller, *Mesmerism*, p. 34; [Sylvester Eaton,] *Burchardism vs. Christianity* (Poughkeepsie, N.Y.: by the author, 1837), p. 7, quoted in Cross, *Burned-over District*, p. 175. For advocacy of influence bent to moral ends, see "Editors' Table," *Godey's* 33 (December 1846): 284; Mrs. M. A. Denison, "No Influence," *Peterson's* 35 (June 1859): 423–24. The liberal Congregationalist Horace Bushnell used the idea of influence as a cornerstone for his career as a Christian educator; see his *Christian Nurture* (Boston, 1847).

41. Nathan G. Hale, *Freud and the Americans: The Beginnings of Psychoanalysis in the United States, 1890–1917* (New York, 1971); Donald Meyer, *The Positive Thinkers: Religion as Pop Psychology from Mary Baker Eddy to Norman Vincent Peale* (New York, 1980); Fuller, *Mesmerism*, pp. 94–102.

42. Edward Said, *Orientalism* (New York, 1979), esp. pp. 88, 167. The key text by Veblen on consumption is of course his *Theory of the Leisure Class* (New York, 1899); I began my critique of Veblen and his influence in "Beyond Veblen: Rethinking Consumer Culture in America," in *Consuming Visions: Accumulation and Display of Goods in America, 1880–1920*, ed. Simon J. Bronner (New York, 1989).

43. On glamour, see Banner, *American Beauty*, p. 24.

44. Stewart H. Holbrook, *The Golden Age of Quackery* (New York, 1959), pp. 38–40, 69–70.

45. William J. Gilmore, "Peddlers and the Dissemination of Printed Material in Northern New England, 1780–1840," in Benes, ed., *Itinerancy*, p. 89. The best overview of peddlers is David Jaffe, "Peddlers of Progress and the Transformation of the Rural North, 1760–1860," *Journal of American History* 78 (September 1991): 511–35.

46. On the mobility of Yankee peddlers, see B. A. Botkin, *A Treasury of New England Folklore,* rev. ed. (New York, 1964), part 1; Atherton, "Itinerant Merchandising"; Gilmore, "Peddlers and the Dissemination of Printed Material."

47. Entry dated 15 August 1838 in Nathaniel Hawthorne, *The American Notebooks,* ed. Claude M. Simpson (Columbus, Ohio, 1972), p. 110. Discussions of the confidence man as trickster can be found in Halttunen, *Confidence Men,* pp. 24–25; William E. Lenz, *Fast Talk and Flush Times: The Confidence Man as a Literary Convention* (Columbia, Mo., 1985); and Gary Lindberg, *The Confidence Man in American Literature* (New York, 1982).

48. Henry David Thoreau, "Walking" [1862], in *Walden and Other Writings,* ed. Brooks Atkinson (New York, 1950), p. 597; Clement Clarke Moore, "A Visit from St. Nicholas" [1823], reprinted as *The Night Before Christmas* (Philadelphia, 1954); Earl Wesley Fornell, *The Unhappy Medium: Spiritualism and the Life of Margaret Fox* (Austin, Texas, 1964), p. 13. On the link between ancient conjuring lore and dreams of fantastic abundance, see Paul Bouissac, *Circus and Culture: A Semiotic Approach* (Bloomington, Ind., 1975), p. 78. On itinerancy and exoticism, see Constance Rourke, *American Humor* (New York, 1931), pp. 108–109.

49. John Bernard, *Retrospections of America, 1797–1811* [1887] (New York and London, 1969), p. 43.

50. Fitz-Greene Halleck, "Connecticut" [1819], quoted in Odell Shepard, *Pedlar's Progress: The Life of Bronson Alcott* [1937] (New York, 1968), p. 51.

51. Kirkland, *Cyclopedia,* vol. 1, p. 80; John Beauchamp Jones, *The Western Merchant* (Philadelphia, 1849), p. 289; Joseph Holt Ingraham, *The Sunny South; Or, The Southerner at Home, Embracing Five Years' Experience of a Northern Governess in the Land of Sugar and Cotton* [1860] (New York, 1968), pp. 400–401; Edgar Rosenberg, *From Shylock to Svengali: Jewish Stereotypes in English Fiction* (Stanford, Calif., 1960), p. 206. See also Louis Harap, *The Image of the Jew in American Fiction, from the Early Republic to Mass Immigration* (Philadelphia, 1974); Rudolf Glanz, *The Jew in the Old American Folklore* (New York, privately printed, 1961), esp. pp. 2–8, 187 *n.* 21; and Mac E. Barrick, "The Image of the Jew in South-Central Pennsylvania," *Pennsylvania Folklife* 34, no. 3 (Spring 1985): 133–38.

52. Kirkland, *Cyclopedia,* vol. 2, p. 55; Harris, *Humbug,* esp. pp. 71–77; Botkin, *New England Folklore,* p. 460. For other examples of peddler humor, see Thomas Chandler Haliburton, *Sam Slick,* ed. Ray Palmer Baker (New York, 1923), pp. 35–39, 110–11, 244; Kirkland, *Cyclopedia,* vol. 1, pp. 277–78; vol. 2, pp. 413, 555; Francis Hodge, *Yankee Theater: The Image of America on the Stage, 1825–1850* (Austin, Texas, 1964), p. 194; "Roxy Croft," *Godey's* 66 (May 1863): 441; Richard Dorson, *Jonathan Draws the Long Bow* (Cambridge, Mass., 1946), pp. 20–21, 78–79, 88–91. The classic discussion of the relationship between humor

and aggression is Sigmund Freud, *Jokes and Their Relation to the Unconscious* [1905], trans. James Strachey, vol. 8 of the Standard Edition of Freud's *Complete Psychological Works* (London, 1960). For specific examples of aggression against peddlers, see Carroll Smith-Rosenberg, "Davy Crockett as Trickster: Pornography, Liminality, and Symbolic Inversion in Victorian America," in her *Disorderly Conduct* (New York, 1985), pp. 90–108; Dorson, *Jonathan Draws the Long Bow*, pp. 156–59, 180–81; and Glanz, *Jew in the Old American Folklore*, chap. 15.

53. Washington Irving, "Rip van Winkle and the Legend of Sleepy Hollow" [1820] (New York, 1893), p. 86; Wright, *Hawkers and Walkers*, p. 95.

54. Prof. W. J. Walter, "The Scotch Pedlar," *Godey's* 23 (December 1841): 241–42.

55. Ann E. Porter, "The Banishment of the Peddlers," *Godey's* 37 (October 1848): 227.

56. The consumption-as-liberation argument is implicit in Christine Stansell, *City of Women* (New York, 1986), and in Breen, "Empire of Goods," p. 75ff. For the independent minds of farm women, see, for example, Christiana Fischer, ed., *Let Them Speak for Themselves: Women in the American West, 1840–1900* (New York, 1978), and John Mack Faragher, *Women and Men on the Oregon Trail* (New Haven, Conn., and London, 1979). The anxiety about fashion is ably discussed by Halttunen, *Confidence Men*, chap. 3. The critique of fashion pervaded women's magazines such as *Peterson's* and *Godey's;* it was too widespread and too often articulated by women to be dismissed as merely a male ideology. Indeed, it often accompanied an attack on male extravagance in consumption or speculation.

57. T. S. Arthur, " 'Can't Afford It,' " *Godey's* 37 (October 1848): 209–11; Jane Weaver, "Gloves and Cigars," *Peterson's* 19 (April 1851): 193–94; Rodney Olsen, "The Sentimental Idiom in American Culture," paper presented at the National Museum of American History, Smithsonian Institution, Washington, D.C., 17 March 1987.

58. Sedgwick, "Wilton Harvey," 122; "Blanche Brandon," *Godey's* 56 (April 1858): 306; "Editor's Table," *Peterson's* 50 (September 1866): 210.

CHAPTER 3. THE STABILIZATION OF SORCERY

1. For a corrective to dismissive views of domesticity, see Glenna Matthews, *"Just a Housewife": The Rise and Fall of Domesticity in America* (New York and Oxford, 1987).

2. Ellen Ashton, "Never Contented Long," *Peterson's* 24 (July 1853): 65–66: E. A. Sandford, "Ambition," *Godey's Lady's Book* 56 (June 1858): 514–23; T. S. Arthur, "Three Scenes in the Life of a Worldling," ibid. 47 (August 1853): 146–48. For a comment that explicitly sets up the home as a counterweight to the centrifugal forces of "the world," see "Editor's Table," *Peterson's* 32 (August 1857).

3. Lydia Sigourney, "Horticulture," *Godey's* 21 (October 1840): 179; Annette Kolodny, *The Land Before Her* (Chapel Hill, N.C., 1984).

4. Rodney Olsen, "The Sentimental Idiom in American Culture"; Ann Douglas, *The Feminization of American Culture* (New York, 1977), esp. chaps. 2, 3; Mary Kelley, *Private Women, Public Stage* (New York, 1984).

5. Edgar Wayne, "Eleanor Hartley," *Ladies' National Magazine* 11 (June 1847): 201.

6. Thomas Haskell, "Capitalism and the Origins of the Humanitarian Sensibility, Part II," *American Historical Review* 90 (June 1985); 547–66.

7. Odell Shepard, *Pedlar's Progress: The Life of Bronson Alcott* [1937] (New York, 1968), pp. 41–74; "Annotation: Failure to Procure Occupational or Business License or Permit as Affecting Validity or Enforceability of Contracts," in 30 *American Law Reports* 834 (1924): 866–68. The classic study of these developments is Morton Horowitz, *The Transformation of American Law, 1780–1860* (Cambridge, Mass. 1978), but I have benefited most from my conversations with Robert Mensel about contract law and the stabilization of market relations.

8. *Merriam v. Langdon,* 10 Connecticut 1835; *Commonwealth v. Moses Stephens,* 31 Massachusetts 1833.

9. "Morals in Trade," *Hunt's Merchants' Magazine* 19 (October 1848): 454–55; "The Merchant Peddler, Or Buying Cheap," ibid. 26 (May 1852): 649. I am indebted to Scott Sandage for bringing these references to my attention.

10. *Commonwealth v. Dudley,* 3 Kentucky 1860; *Hirschfelder v. the State,* 18 Alabama 1850.

11. Lewis E. Atherton, "The Pioneer Merchant in Mid-America," *University of Missouri Studies* 14 no. 2 (April 1939): 26–42; Penrose Scull, *From Peddlers to Merchant Princes: A History of Selling in America* (Chicago and New York, 1967).

12. Contract, Cleveland Lightning Rod Company and John S. Porter, 29 September 1869, in Lightning Rods box 1, Warshaw Collection of Business Americana, National Museum of American History, Smithsonian Institution, Washington, D.C.

13. Guarantee, American Lighning Rod Company, Erie, Pa., 12 May 1865, in Lightning Rods box 1, Warshaw Collection; promotional pamphlet, Otis's Patent Lightning Conductor (New York: Lyon Manufacturing Co., 1858), in ibid. See also Earl W. Hayter, *The Troubled Farmer, 1850–1900: Rural Adjustment to Industrialism* (De Kalb, Ill., 1968), chap. 11.

14. James Guild, "Journal," *Proceedings of the Vermont Historical Society* 5 (1937): 249–313. David Jaffee has ably discussed Guild and other portraitists in "One of the Primitive Sort: Portrait Makers of the Rural North, 1790–1860," in *The Countryside in the Era of Capitalist Transformation,* ed. Jonathan Prude and Steven Hahn (Chapel Hill, N.C., 1986), pp. 103–38, and "Pedlars and Portraitists: Artisan Entrepreneurs and the Transformation of the Rural North, 1790–1860," paper presented at the American Studies Association Biennial Meeting, San Diego, 1985. On

professionalism as a control on the market, see Thomas Haskell, ed., *The Authority of Experts* (Bloomington, Ind., 1984).

15. George Orwell, "Why I Write" [1947], in *A Collection of Essays by George Orwell* (New York, 1954), p. 320.

16. Francis Hodge, *Yankee Theater: The Image of America on the Stage, 1825–1850* (Austin, Texas, 1964), pp. 50–51, 91; Rourke, *American Humor* (New York, 1931), pp. 20–21; Medical Society of the City of New York, *Nostrums, or Secret Medicines* (New York: privately printed, 1827).

17. "Editor's Table," *Peterson's* 39 (February 1861): 178; "How to Write Fashionably," ibid. 22 (November 1852): 230–31.

18. Roger Stein, *John Ruskin and Aesthetic Thought in America, 1840–1900* (Cambridge, Mass., 1967); "Adulteration of Coffee and Pepper," *Hunt's Merchants' Magazine* 24 (March 1851): 395.

19. Karen Halttunen, *Confidence Men and Painted Women A Study of Middle-Class Culture in Victorian America, 1830–1870* (New Haven, Conn., and London, 1982) chap.3; "Dress," *Godey's* 20 (April 1840): 187; "The Extremely Natural Young Lady," ibid. 22 (June 1841): 244.

20. Sam Slick is the yankee peddler hero of *The Clockmaker, or the Sayings and Doings of Samuel Slick of Slickville* (1837) and subsequent collections by the Canadian humorist Thomas Haliburton. On these issues, see the thoughtful discussion by Frank R. Kramer, *Voices in the Valley: Mythmaking and Folk Belief in the Shaping of the Middle West* (Madison, Wis., 1964), pp. 87–103.

21. "The Importance of Words," *Godey's* (July 1855): 81.

22. David A. Gerber, "Cutting Out Shylock: Elite Anti-Semitism and the Quest for Moral Order in the Nineteenth-Century Marketplace," in Gerber, ed., *Anti-Semitism in American History* (Urbana, Ill., 1986), esp. pp. 216–19.

23. "Lesser breeds without the law" is from Rudyard Kipling's poem "Recessional," line 22 (1897). Barnum, *Struggles and Triumphs,* pp. 577–78.

24. Miss Leslie, "The Rain King; or, a Glance at the Next Century," *Godey's* 25 (July 1842): 7–11.

25. George Presbury Rowell, *Forty Years an Advertising Agent, 1865–1905* (New York, 1906), pp. 5–32, 258–59, 443.

26. "The Philosophy of Advertising," in Volney B. Palmer, ed., *Business-men's Almanac* (1851), reprinted in *Hunt's Merchants' Magazine* 23 (November 1850): 582.

27. The most careful treatment of the nuts and bolts of early advertising agencies is Daniel Pope, *The Making of Modern Advertising* (New York, 1982), esp. chaps. 1 and 2.

28. Rowell, *Forty Years,* pp. 454, 310.

29. Ibid., pp. 311–12.

30. Ibid., pp. 192, 31–32.

31. Ibid., pp. 258–59; Ralph M. Hower, *The History of an Advertising Agency: N. W. Ayer & Son at Work, 1869–1939* (Cambridge, Mass., 1939), pp. 144–47.

32. Hower, *N. W. Ayer*, pp. 67–68, 70–77.

33. Ibid., pp. 94–118.

34. Ibid,, p. 134.

35. Walter Ong, *Orality and Literacy* (London and New York, 1982), p. 116; Mark Twain and Charles Dudley Warner, *The Gilded Age* [1873] (Hartford, Conn., 1888), p. 83.

36. Lucille Baldwin Van Slyke, "The Peddler," *American Magazine,* 74 August, 1912, 406. I am indebted to Miriam Formanek-Brunell for bringing this story to my attention.

37. Ibid., 410.

38. Ibid., 414.

39. Rowell, *Forty Years,* pp. 5–30, 163, 366, 401; Sarah Stage, *Female Complaints: The Career of Lydia Pinkham* (New York, 1979), pp. 112ff; Frazar Kirkland, *Cyclopedia of Commercial and Business Anecdotes* (New York, 1864), vol. 2, pp. 609–10. For the persistence of a comprehensive variety of rhetorical strategies in patent medicine advertising, see, for example, Patent Medicines box 2, Warshaw Collection, which contains the files of the J. C. Ayer Co. of Lowell, Mass., from the 1850s to the 1910s.

40. See, for example, "Advertising Agents and the Country Press," *Printers' Ink* 13 (21 August 1895): 44–45; "The Country Editor's Side," ibid. 19 (26 May 1897): 8.

41. Leon Howard, *Herman Melville: A Biography* (Berkeley, Calif., 1952), p. 216.

42. Herman Melville, "The Lightning-Rod Man" [1853], in *Herman Melville: Selected Tales and Poems,* ed. Richard Chase (New York, 1950), pp. 151–58. On the notion of liminality, see Victor Turner, "Liminal to Liminoid in Play, Flow, and Ritual," *Rice University Studies* 60 (Summer, 1974), 53–92. Johan Tetzel, a fifteenth-century Dominican preacher, was a notorious salesman of papal indulgences.

43. Herman Melville, *The Confidence Man: His Masquerade* [1857] (New York, 1964), p. 11.

44. Ibid., pp. 185, 119.

45. Ibid., p. 94.

CHAPTER 4. THE DISEMBODIMENT OF ABUNDANCE

1. On the origins of the word *nostalgia,* see Jean Starobinski, "The Idea of Nostalgia," *Diogenes* 54 (1966): 81–103. I have more fully discussed the issues raised in this paragraph in "Packaging the Folk: Tradition and Amnesia in American Advertising, 1880–1940," in *Folk Roots, New Roots: Folklore in American Life,* ed. Jane S. Becker and Barbara Franco (Lexington, Mass., 1988), pp. 103–40.

2. Edward Said, *Orientalism* (New York, 1979), pp. 88, 167. On the importance of home-leaving in nineteenth-century material culture, I am

indebted to Rodney Olsen, "The Sentimental Idiom in American Culture," paper presented at the National Museum of American History, Smithsonian Institution, Washington, D.C., 17 March 1987.

3. Mellin's Food trade card (1890), in Foods box 13, Warshaw Collection of Business Americana, National Museum of American History.

4. On the fascination with the devouring female among the fin-de-siècle intelligentsia, see Carl Schorske, *Fin-de-Siècle Vienna: Politics and Culture* (New York, 1979), and Brom Djikstra, *Idols of Perversity* (New York, 1987).

5. For several other among the many possible examples, see McCormick Reaper Company Catalogues 1885, 1894, 1901, in Agriculture box 4; Walter Wood Implements Company Catalogues 1874, 1889, in Agriculture box 6; and Allen & Co. Catalogues 1896, 1901, in Agriculture box 2, all in the Warshaw Collection.

6. On the persistence of magical thinking among farmers, see Earl W. Hayter, *The Troubled Farmer, 1850–1900: Rural Adjustment to Industrialism* (De Kalb, Ill., 1968), esp. pp. 6–10, and David Danbom, *The Resisted Revolution: Urban America and the Industrialization of Agriculture, 1900–1930* (Ames, Iowa, 1979). On the ambivalent and conflicted character of rural engagement with commercial agriculture, see Richard Wines, "The Nineteenth-Century Agricultural Transition in an Eastern Long Island Community," *Agricultural History* 55 (January 1981): 50–63; Jeremy Atack and Fred Bateman, "Self-Sufficiency and the Origins of the Marketable Surplus in the Rural North, 1860–1900," ibid. 58 (July 1984): 296–313; Peter H. Argersinger and Jo Ann E. Argersinger, "The Machine Breakers: Farmworkers and Social Change in the Rural Midwest of the 1870s," ibid., 393–410; Adam Ward Rome, "American Farmers as Entrepreneurs, 1870–1900," ibid. 59 (January 1985): 37–49; Jeffrey C. Williams, "The Origin of Futures Markets," ibid. (July 1985): 306–25.

7. The literature on the transformation of women's role is immense. See, for example, Nancy Cott, *The Bonds of Womanhood: "Woman's Sphere" in New England, 1780–1830* (New Haven, Conn., and London, 1977); Carroll Smith-Rosenberg, *Disorderly Conduct* (New York, 1984); Mary P. Ryan, *Cradle of the Middle Class: The Family in Oneida County, New York, 1780–1865* (New York, 1981); Suzanne Lebsock, *The Free Women of Petersburg: Status and Culture in a Southern Town, 1784–1860* (New York, 1984); and Laurel Thatcher Ulrich, *The Midwife's Tale: The Life of Martha Moore Ballard Based on Her Diary, 1785–1812* (New York, 1990). For evidence of the growing mobility and fungibility of capital, see Morton Horwitz, *The Transformation of American Law, 1780–1860* (Cambridge, Mass., 1977), and Steven Hahn and Jonathan Prude, eds., *The Countryside in the Era of Capitalist Transformation* (Chapel Hill, 1985). On corporations as persons, see Rowland Berthoff, "Conventional Mentality: Free Blacks, Women, and Business Corporations as Unequal Persons, 1820–1870," *Journal of American History* 76 (December 1989), 753–84; and Phillip K. Tompkins and George Cheney, "Communication

and Unobtrusive Control in Contemporary Organizations," in Tompkins and Robert D. McPhee, eds., *Organizational Communication: Traditional Themes and New Directions* (Beverly Hills, Calif., 1986).

8. Shredded Wheat advertisement, *Town and Country* magazine, 14 February 1903, 40, in Cereals box 41, Warshaw Collection.

9. United Fruit Company, *A Short History of the Banana and a Few Recipes for Its Use* (Boston, 1906), p. 11, in Foods box 45, Warshaw Collection. For more phallic eroticism, see American Cereal Company, *Cereal Foods and How to Cook Them* (Chicago, 1901), in Cereals box 41, Warshaw Collection.

10. Alan Trachtenberg, *The Incorporation of America* (New York, 1982).

11. Daniel M. Fox, *The Discovery of Abundance: Simon Nelson Patten and the Transformation of Social Theory* (Ithaca, N.Y., 1967), pp. 18, 25, 104–105.

12. Simon Nelson Patten, *The New Basis of Civilization* [1907] (Cambridge, Mass., 1968), pp. 15, 63, 123.

13. Ibid., pp. 137–39.

14. The most egregious example of this reductionist equation of consumption with status display was Thorstein Veblen, *The Theory of the Leisure Class* (New York, 1899). Veblen was hardly a managerial thinker in the sense that, say, Walter Lippmann was, but he shared the managerialists' preoccupation with efficiency and faith in pure technique.

15. Patten, *New Basis,* p. 141.

16. Ibid., pp. 19, 22.

17. The best overview of this process is Harry Braverman, *Labor and Monopoly Capital: The Degradation of Work in the Twentieth Century* (New York, 1977).

18. Charles Musser, "Archaeology of the Cinema: 8," *Framework* 22/23 (Autumn 1983): 4–11, argues that the shift from "dances, rodeo tricks, and peripheral incidents" toward a "seamless, self-sufficient narrative structure" in films reflected "a shift from an industrial (petit bourgeois) mode to one based on mass production." The change in the prevailing forms of advertising during this period, from surrealist pastiche to narrative transparency, marked a similar economic and social transformation. See below, pp. 466–70. On the persistence of working-class cultural forms, see Robert Allen, *Horrible Prettiness: Burlesque and American Culture* (Chapel Hill, N.C. 1990), and Robert Snyder, *The Voice of the City: Vaudeville and Popular Culture in New York* (New York, 1989).

19. Martha Banta, *Imaging American Women* (New York, 1987), pp. 532–33.

20. Advertising blotter, Kellogg Corn Flake Company, 1907, in Cereals box 41, Warshaw Collection; Christine Frederick, *Selling Mrs. Consumer* (New York, 1927).

21. Quinnipiac Fertilizer Company advertisement, *Farmers Journal*, 1897, in Fertilizer box 7; Provident Investment Bureau, *The Staff of Life* (Philadelphia, 1903), in Flour box n.n.; Dairy Association Company, *The Home Cow Care Doctor* (Lyndonville, Vt., 1924–25), in Dairy box 3, all in

the Warshaw Collection. For more evidence of the disenchantment of imagery, see the advertisements and other photographs in *Farm Mechanics* 8 (1923) in Agriculture box 4, and the catalog for Allen & Co., 1919, in Agriculture box 2, Warshaw Collection. On advertisers' appropriation of the cornucopia, see Leigh Eric Schmidt, "The Commercialization of the Calendar: American Holidays and the Culture of Consumption, 1870–1930," *Journal of American History* 78 (December 1991): 894.

22. With respect to the rationalization of the domestic interior, I have made a fuller argument in "Infinite Riches in a Little Room: The Interior Scenes of Modernist Culture," *Modulus* 18 (1987): 3–28. On masculine domesticity, see Margaret Marsh, "Suburban Men and Masculine Domesticity," *American Quarterly* 40 (June 1988): 165–86.

23. I have more fully discussed the issues raised in this paragraph in "Packaging the Folk." I am indebted to Warren Susman's brilliant reading of Depression-bred insecurity in his *Culture as History* (New York, 1984), pp. 150–210.

24. David S. Riesman, *Abundance for What? and Other Essays* (New York, 1964), esp. pp. 300–310; William F. Whyte, *The Organization Man* (New York, 1956).

25. Thomas C. Rainey, *Along the Old Trail: Pioneer Sketches of Arrow Rock and Vicinity* (Marshall, Mo., 1914), pp. 64–65, quoted in Lewis E. Atherton, "The Pioneer Merchant in Mid-America," *University of Missouri Studies* 14 no. 2 (April 1939): 17.

26. Gerald W. Johnson, "Greensboro, Or What You Will," in *The Reviewer* (Richmond) 4 (1923–24): 171–73, quoted in George B. Tindall, *The Emergence of the New South, 1912–1945* (Baton Rouge, La., 1967), p. 318.

27. Max Horkheimer to Leo Lowenthal, 2 June 1942, quoted in Martin Jay, *The Dialectical Imagination* (New York, 1973), p. 213; Theodor Adorno, "Veblen's Attack on Culture" [1941], in his *Prisms* (New York, 1986); Herbert Marcuse, *The Aesthetic Dimension* (Boston, 1978).

28. "The Big Rock Candy Mountain," in Alan Lomax, *The Folk Songs of North America* (London, 1960), pp. 410–11, 422–23. For an alternative to the productivist model of working-class consciousness, see Jacques Ranciere, *The Nights of Labor: The Workers' Dream in Nineteenth-Century France*, trans. Donald Reid (Philadelphia, 1988).

29. Jay, *Dialectical Imagination* , p. 96; Herbert Marcuse, *Eros and Civilization* (New York, 1955).

30. Bruno Schulz, *Sanatorium Under the Sign of the Hourglass* [1937], trans. Celina Wieniewska (New York, 1979), pp. 5–6.

31. Bruno Schulz, *The Street of Crocodiles* [1934], trans. Celina Wieniewska (New York, 1977), pp. 8–89.

32. Schulz, *Sanatorium*, p. 1.

33. Ibid., pp. 1–2.

34. Ibid., p. 5.

35. Ibid., pp. 8–9.

CHAPTER 5. THE MERGER OF
INTIMACY AND PUBLICITY

1. For examples of this tendency to conflate public and private, see Ronald Walters, "The Erotic South: Civilization and Sexuality in American Abolitionism," *American Quarterly* 25 (May 1973): 177–201; and Stephen Nissenbaum, *Sex, Diet and Debility in Jacksonian America: The Career of Sylvester Graham* (Westport, Conn., 1980).

2. In this and the following chapter, my argument is informed by Foucault's emphasis on the surveillance and control of personal life under the new and more diffuse systems of power that developed in the industrialized West during the nineteenth century, and by his stress on the capacity of particular hegemonic discourses to produce particular kinds of human subjectivity. See especially Foucault, "The Subject and Power," *Critical Inquiry* 8 (1982): 777–95; idem, *Power/Knowledge*, ed. Colin Gordon, trans. Colin Gordon, Leo Marshall, John Mepham, and Kate Sopher (New York, 1980), esp. pp. 55–62, 109–33, 183–92; idem, *The History of Sexuality*, vol. 1, trans. Robert Hurley (New York, 1980). Mary Douglas's *Purity and Danger* (London, 1966) is a pioneering effort to link concerns about bodily pollution with broader patterns of tension in the body politic.

3. Clifford Geertz, "Local Knowledge: Fact and Law in Comparative Perspective," in his *Local Knowledge: Further Essays in Interpretive Anthropology* (New York, 1983), pp. 167–234, is a useful introduction to the concept. Joanne Brown, *The Definition of a Profession* (Princeton, N.J., 1992), deftly uncovers the rhetorical strategies American professionals used to advance their interests in the early twentieth century. For an earlier effort to chart these changes, see Merle Curti, "The Changing Concept of Human Nature in the Literature of American Advertising," *Business History Review* 41 (Winter 1967): 335–57.

4. See, for example, David Harper, *Working Knowledge: Skill and Community in a Small Shop* (Chicago and London, 1983); John Forrest, *Lord I'm Coming Home: Everyday Aesthetics in Tidewater North Carolina* (Ithaca, N.Y., and London, 1988); Lizabeth Cohen, *Making a New Deal: Industrial Workers in Chicago, 1919–1939* (New York, 1990); idem, "Encountering Mass Culture at the Grassroots: The Experience of Chicago Workers in the 1920s," *American Quarterly* 41 (Spring 1989): 6–33.

5. On the physicality of the Puritan imagination, see David Hall, *Worlds of Wonder, Days of Judgment* (New York, 1989); Donald E. Stanford, ed., *The Poems of Edward Taylor* (New Haven, Conn., 1960), pp. 127, 129, 8, 64; John Owen King III, *The Iron of Melancholy* (Middletown, Conn., 1983), pp. 21, 57. For the secularization of concerns about self-pollution, see Anthony Comstock, *Traps for the Young* [1883] (New York, 1967), pp. xxviii, xxiv.

6. On the contested terrain of nineteenth-century medical practice, see Paul Starr, *The Social Transformation of American Medicine* (New York,

1983), chaps. 1–3; Charles Rosenberg, *The Care of Strangers: The Rise of America's Hospital System* (New York, 1987), pp. 36–59; James C. Whorton, *Crusaders for Fitness* (Princeton, N.J., 1982).

7. E. B. Rosa, "The Human Body as an Engine," *Popular Science Monthly* 57 (September 1900): 491–99. For other examples of mechanistic images of the body in nineteenth-century thought, see Cynthia Russett, *Sexual Science* (Cambridge, Mass., and London, 1990), chap. 5; Bruce Haley, *The Healthy Body and Victorian Culture* (Cambridge, Mass., and London, 1980), p. 33; J. W. Redfield, "Measures of Mental Capacity," *Popular Science Monthly* 5 (May 1874): 72–76.

8. Daniel Jay Sprague, "Guardian Angels," *Godey's Lady's Book* 57 (November 1858): 407; Robert C. Fuller, *Mesmerism and the American Cure of Souls* (New York, 1983), pp. 94–95, 102, 122. For more examples of the vitalist frame of mind, which fostered mesmerism, Christian Science, and a host of other soul-cures, see Haley, *Healthy Body*, p. 35; Charles F. Taylor, "Bodily Conditions as Related to Mental States," *Popular Science Monthly* 5 (May 1874): 40–56; Thomas Hitchcock, "Soul and Substance," *North American Review* 124 (May 1877): 404–16; Robert C. Fuller, *Americans and the Unconscious* (New York, 1986), chaps. 1, 2.

9. N. T. Oliver, as told to Wesley Stout, "Med Show," *Saturday Evening Post* 202 (14 September 1929): 12, 13.

10. The best general history of the patent medicine business is still James Harvey Young, *The Toadstool Millionaires* (Princeton, N. J., 1961).

11. Wright's Indian Vegetable Pills, Almanac (Philadelphia, 1844), in Patent Medicines box 33, Warshaw Collection of Business Americana, National Museum of America History, Smithsonian Institution, Washington, D.C.

12. *100 Special Receipts Selected from Dr. Chase's Receipt Book* (c. 1875), in Patent Medicines box 5, Warshaw Collection; T. P. Childs & Co., *Childs Catarrh Remedy* (Troy, Ohio, 1877), in ibid.

13. Shirley Dare, "The Arts of Beauty," *Standard Designer* 6 (October 1897): 56, in Ladies' Clothing box 1, Warshaw Collection; Pear's Soap advertisement, *Harper's Weekly*, 16 May, 1885, p. 631.

14. New York and London Electric Remedy Company trade card (1890), Patent Medicines box 24; Dr. Miles, *The Family Doctor* (1892), in Patent Medicines box 22a; pamphlet on Mosko silver pills, Drexel Drug Co., Chicago, Ill. (c. 1900), Patent Medicines box 7, all in the Warshaw Collection. See also "Triumphant Industries: The General Electric Company," *Forum* (18 February 1893), in Electricity box 15, Warshaw Collection; David Nye, *Electrifying America* (Cambridge, Mass., and London, 1990), esp. chap. 4.

15. Forepaugh Circus advertisement, (c. 1885), in Circus box 66; advertisements for "the celebrated and extraordinary exhibitions of the INDUSTRIOUS FLEAS" (British, 1840s) and Reynold's Marvelous Trained Dogs (1909), in Circus box 65; advertisements: for Brock's Cash Grocery (c. 1880), in Foods box 5; for James Wright and Co.'s Crown Brand Potted Meat, Anglo-American Provision Co. (c. 1890), in Meat box 1; for

Henry Mayo & Co., Boston, in Foods box 2; Quaker Oats trade cards (1894–95), in Cereals box 42, all in the Warshaw Collection; James Turner, *Reckoning with the Beast* (Baltimore and London, 1980), pp. 63–69. For animals as ethnic stereotypes, see Walter G. Wilson's Biscuit Co., Philadelphia, trade card, in Bakers and Baking box 3, and Dr. Thomas's Eclectric [sic] Oil trade card (c. 1885), in Patent Medicines box 10, Warshaw Collection. For references to Darwinism: Church & Co. Baking Soda trade card, in Baking Soda box 1, and Merchants Gargling Oil, *Romantic Life of Aggie Zolutie* (c. 1885), in Patent Medicines box 22, Warshaw Collection.

16. St. Jacob's Oil trade card, Landauer Collection, New-York Historical Society; Northrop's Botanic Compound and Medicated Appliance, *Truth, Reason, and Common Sense* (1880), in Patent Medicines box 24, Warshaw Collection. For the British background, see Harriet Ritvo, *The Animal Estate* (Cambridge, Mass., and London, 1987).

17. Kickapoo Medicine Company, Almanac (1893), in Patent Medicines box 18, Warshaw Collection; Church Kidney Cure Company, in ibid., box 5. For two among innumerable other examples of primitivism, see Lyon Mfg. Co., *Morning, Noon, and Night* (1872), in ibid., box 21; and Centaur Co., *Atlas, Almanac, and Receipt Book* (1884–85), in ibid., box 5.

18. Peruvian Catarrh Cure Co. pamphlet (c. 1890), in Patent Medicines box 25, Warshaw Collection; advertisement for Warner's Safe Remedies in *Warner's Artistic Album* (Rochester, N.Y., 1888), in ibid., box 34. For other examples of this pattern, see advertisements for Oregon Indian Medicine Co. (c. 1890), in ibid., box 24; and for Church Kidney Cure Company's Kava-Kava Compound (1896) in ibid., box 5.

19. Pamphlet for Dr. Wrightsman's Sovereign Balm of Life, Senger and Lipe Company, Franklin Grove, Ill. (1888), in Patent Medicines box n.n., Warshaw Collection. For correctives to the legend of monolithic repressiveness in Victorian culture, see David Kunzle, *Fashion and Fetishism: A Social History of the Corset* (Totowa, N.J., 1982); Karen Lystra, *Searching the Heart: Women, Men, and Romantic Love in Nineteenth-Century America* (New York, 1989); Peter Gay, *The Bourgeois Experience, Victoria to Freud: The Education of the Senses* (New York, 1984).

20. Bortree Manufacturing Company trade card (1875), in Corsets box 1; Holmes Company trade card (c. 1880), in Underwear box 1, Warshaw Collection; trade card with beach scene (c. 1880) in Scrapbook 1, Bella Landauer Collection, New-York Historical Society. There are a number of early examples of voyeuristic Victorian prints in the Peters Collection of American prints, National Museum of American History. See, for example, "Out for a Day's Shooting" (#60.2687), and "The Cool Retreat" (#60.2283).

21. Joseph Conrad, *Heart of Darkness* [1899] (Signet Classic ed; New York, 1950), p. 71.

22. For examples of erotic, voluptuous women, see Angostura Bitters adver-

tisement (1876), F. J. Taney Co., in Patent Medicines box 31a, Warshaw Collection; Taylor's Premium Cologne advertisement (1890), ibid.; London Toilet Bazaar advertisement (1886), ibid. On the voluptuous woman as beau ideal, see Lois Banner, *American Beauty* (New York, 1982), p. 111.

23. For fin-de-siècle images of the devouring woman, see the chamber of horrors assembled by Brom Djikstra in *Idols of Perversity* (New York, 1987). Pamphlet for Kawa, Darling Medical Company (c. 1890), in Patent Medicines box 7, Warshaw Collection.

24. On the erotic significance of the corset I follow the argument made by Kunzle, *Fashion and Fetishism.*

25. "The Passing of the 'Expert,'" *Printers' Ink* 41 (1 October 1903): 3.

26. The relevant data are summarized in Roland Marchand, *Advertising the American Dream: Making Way for Modernity, 1920–1940* (Berkeley, Calif., and London, 1985), pp. 130–38, and Daniel Pope, *The Making of Modern Advertising* (New York, 1982), pp. 177–80. Pope, drawing on survey samples from 1916 and 1931, shows that 97 percent of advertising people were men; not one in either sample came from Eastern or Southern Europe; in 1916 half had attended college and more than a fourth held bachelor's degrees; by 1931 more than two-thirds had gone to college and almost half had graduated. See also the revealing portraits in the J. Walter Thompson Newsletter for 1930, JWT Archives, Duke University.

27. "Profitable Stories," *Printers' Ink* 14 (5 February 1896): 17–25.

28. Starr, *Social Transformation* chaps. 3–5; Rosenberg, *Care of Strangers.*

29. Celerina pamphlet, Rio Chemical Company, St. Louis, Mo. (1890–95), in Patent Medicines box 28, Warshaw Collection; "The Conscience-Strain on the Medical Journals," *Printers' Ink* 23 (18 May 1898): 5. See also L. J. Vance, "To Secure the Physician's Influence," ibid. 18 (3 March 1897): 3–4.

30. Oscar Herzberg, "The Evolution of Patent Medicine Advertising," *Printers' Ink* 13 (25 December 1895); John Chester, "The 'Agony' Testimonial," ibid. 18 (27 June 1897); Edith Gerry, "Medical Advertising," ibid. 30 (14 November 1900); Henry M. Coburn, "Proprietary Advertising," ibid. 39 (28 May 1902). Emphasis mine.

31. Young, *Toadstool Millionaires,* chap. 13; Samuel Hopkins Adams, "The Great American Fraud," *Collier's* 36 (7 October 1905): 14–15, 29; Will Irwin, *The Making of a Reporter* (New York, 1942), p. 155.

32. "Healer of Men," *Printers' Ink* 59 (19 June 1907); Frank H. Holman, "Where Is the Medical Dividing Line in Advertising Copy?" ibid. 69 (6 October 1909): 43–44; Sarah Stage, *Female Complaints: The Career of Lydia Pinkham* (New York, 1979), pp. 253–54.

33. Quaker Oats advertisement (1903), book 50, N. W. Ayer Collection, National Museum of American History.

34. Shredded Wheat advertisement (1902), book 68, Ayer Collection; Quaker

Oats advertisement, *Good Housekeeping* 62 (June 1916): 109. For a similar example, see Welch's Grape Juice advertisement, *Saturday Evening Post* 177 (16 July 1904): 19.

35. Coca-Cola advertisement, *Harmsworth Self-Educator Magazine*, July 1907, n.p., in Beverages box 1, Warshaw Collection.

36. N. E. Ellison, "Progress of Advertising in 1911," *Judicious Advertising* 10 (February 1912): 52–54; N. W. Ayer & Co., *Forty Years of Advertising* (Philadelphia, 1909), p. 60, in Advertising box 2, Warshaw Collection. Also see E. E. Calkins, *The Business of Advertising* (New York and London, 1915), pp. 198–99.

37. *J. Walter Thompson Book* (New York, 1909), pp. 8–9, 22, in JWT Archives. The preoccupation with efficient control of the environment pervaded the literature generated by professionalizing elites around the turn of the century; for helpful introductions to the idiom, see Robert Wiebe, *The Search for Order, 1877–1920* (New York, 1967), and Samuel Haber, *Efficiency and Uplift: Scientific Management in the Progressive Era, 1890–1920* (Chicago, 1964).

38. Earnest Elmo Calkins, "The New Consumption Engineer and the Artist," in *A Philosophy of Production*, ed. J. George Frederick (New York, 1930), p. 114; L. B. Jones, "Advertising Men as the 'Cheer Leaders' of the Nation," *Printers' Ink* 102 (7 February 1918), 62–65; Leon Dabo, "Advertising Art's Influence on National Dress," ibid. 73 (27 October 1910): 92. On moralists' habit of seeking universalist justifications for changes in fashion, see Norbert Elias, *The Civilizing Process,* trans. Edmund Jephcott (New York, 1979).

39. Richard Surrey, "Advertising—Arch Enemy of Poverty and Disease," *Printers' Ink* 133 (10 December 1925): 49–52. For similar views, see J. George Frederick, ed., *Masters of Advertising* Copy (New York, 1925).

40. Helen Woodward, *Through Many Windows* (New York, 1926), pp. 242–43.

41. W. A. White, "The Ethics of Advertising," *Atlantic Monthly* 164 (November 1939): 665–71.

CHAPTER 6. THE PERFECTIONIST PROJECT

1. N. T. Oliver, as told to Wesley Stout, "Med Show," *Saturday Evening Post* 202 (14 September 1929): 12. On the persistence of sensuous imagery in retail commerce, see William Leach, *Land of Desire: Merchants, Money, and the Rise of a New American Culture, 1890–1930* (New York, 1993), esp. chaps. 2–5, 11.

2. James Turner, *Reckoning with the Beast* (Baltimore and London, 1980), p. 69.

3. Pamphlet for Ivory Soap, "What a Cake of Soap Will Do," in Soap box "Procter & Gamble" B. T. Babbitt's Best advertisement (c. 1885), in Soap

box A–B; Gillette Safety Razors advertisement (1910), in Barbering box 1, all in the Warshaw Collection of Business Americana, National Museum of American History, Smithsonian Institution, Washington, D.C.

4. Ruth Schwartz Cowan, *More Work for Mother: The Ironies of Household Technology from the Open Hearth to the Microwave* (New York, 1983), pp. 51–53; Claudia and Richard Bushman, "The Early History of Cleanliness in America," *Journal of American History* 75 (December 1988): 675–725; Richard L. Bushman, *The Refinement of America: Persons, Houses, Cities* (New York, 1992), chap. 3.

5. "The Philosophy of Modern Advertising," *Yale Review* 8 (November 1899): 229–32.

6. On the spreading preoccupation with efficiency, see Samuel Haber, *Efficiency and Uplift: Scientific Management in the Progressive Era, 1890–1920* (Chicago, 1964); Barbara Ehrenreich and Deirdre English, "The Manufacture of Housework," *Socialist Revolution* 5 (October–December 1975): 5–41; David Tyack, *The One Best System: A History of American Urban Education* (New York, 1974). For a witty analysis of the persistent preoccupation with personal efficiency in advertising, see Garry Wills, "Message in the Deodorant Bottle: Inventing Time," *Critical Inquiry* 15 (Spring 1989): 497–509.

7. Dr. Pierce, *A Badge of Sympathy* (Buffalo, N.Y., c. 1900), in Patent Medicines box 25a; Dr. Frank Crane, "The Colonic," *New York Globe*, 27 January 1916, in Baths and Bathing box 2, Warshaw Collection. For the earlier approach, see Benjamin Brandreth, *Purgation* (New York, 1840), and James Harvey Young, *The Toadstool Millionaires* (Princeton, N.J., 1961), chap. 6. Brandreth was a leading laxative manufacturer throughout the mid–nineteenth century.

8. W. H. Meadowcroft, "Interviews with Edison," *Ediphone Notes* (August 1928), in Edison Collection box 2, National Museum of American History, Smithsonian Institution, Washington, D.C.; Eno Effervescent Saline advertisement (1929), book 124, N. W. Ayer Collection, National Museum of American History; Nujol advertisement, *Saturday Evening Post* 203 (13 September 1930): 181.

9. John Stuart Mill, quoted in Turner, *Reckoning with the Beast*, p. 63. For excellent background, see Martin Pernick, *A Calculus of Suffering: Pain, Professionalism, and Amnesia in Nineteenth-Century America* (New York, 1985).

10. Edith Wharton, *Twilight Sleep* (New York, 1927), pp. 14–15.

11. Luther Gulick, *The Efficient Life* (New York, 1920), p. 157.

12. Russell H. Chittenden, "Physiological Economy in Nutrition," *Popular Science Monthly* 63 (June 1903): 123–31; Roger S. Tracy, M.D., "How to Live Long," *Century* 67 (February 1904): 616. For similar arguments, see E. B. Rosa, "The Human Body as an Engine," *Popular Science Monthly* 57 (September 1900): 491–99; Robert H. Thurston, "The Animal as a

Machine," *North American Review* 163 (November 1896): 607–19; Hillel
Schwartz, *Never Satisfied: A Cultural History of Diets, Fantasies, and Fat*
(New York, 1986), chaps. 4–6.

13. Brandreth M. Symonds, "The Mortality of Overweights and Under-
weights," *McClure's* 32 (March 1909), 319–20. See also James Allen
Young, "Height, Weight, and Health: Anthropometric Study of Human
Growth in Nineteenth-Century American Medicine," *Bulletin of the History of Medicine* 53 (1979): 218ff. For this entire paragraph I am
indebted to Lisa Norling, "The Origins of Popular Dieting in America,"
unpublished seminar paper, Cornell University, 1985, typescript in my
possession through the courtesy of the author. For a thorough overview,
see Harvey Levenstein, *Revolution at the Table: The Transformation of
the American Diet* (New York, 1988).

14. Dr. Charles Mercier, quoted in Howard P. Chudacoff, *How Old Are You?
Age Consciousness in American Culture* (Princeton, N.J., 1989), p. 57;
Grace Crawley Oakley in *Advertising Club News*, 14 June 1920, p. 1,
Advertising Women of New York scrapbooks, vol. 4, Wisconsin State His-
torical Society, Madison; A. H. Deute, "Is the Salesman Over Forty a
'Has Been'?", *Printers' Ink* 132 (27 August 1925): 41–48. An excellent
account of the devaluation of the old is Thomas Cole, *The Journey of
Life: A Cultural History of Aging in America* (New York and Cambridge,
England, 1992), esp. pp. 104–107, 139–58, 164–71, 210–11.

15. "Woodbury's Advertising," *Printers' Ink* 22 (23 February 1898), 24–26;
Wengarten Bros., *Beauty Book* (c. 1910), in Corsets box 4, Warshaw Collection; Palmer quoted in Michael Rogin, *Ronald Reagan, the Movie, and
Other Episodes in Political Demonology* (Berkeley, Calif., and London,
1987), pp. 238–39; Coca-Cola advertisement (1927), in Beverages box 1,
Warshaw Collection. On the growth of statistical definitions of normality,
see Chudacoff, *How Old Are You?* For one among many other examples
of efforts to define bodily perfection, see Luther Gulick, M.D., *Manual
for Physical Measurements* (New York, 1892), in Physical Culture box 1,
Warshaw Collection. This Luther Gulick was father to the founder of the
Camp Fire Girls.

16. On editorial advertising, see Roland Marchand, *Advertising the American
Dream: Making Way for Modernity, 1920–1940* (Berkeley, Calif., 1985),
pp. 103–106.

17. On the covert coercion involved in the emancipatory agendas of the
early twentieth century, see David Kunzle, *Fashion and Fetishism: A
Social History of the Corset* (Totowa, N.J., 1982), pp. 256–57; Carroll
Smith-Rosenberg, "The New Woman as Androgyne: Social Disorder and
Gender Crisis, 1870–1936, in her *Disorderly Conduct* (New York, 1985),
pp. 245–96; Margaret Jackson, "'Facts of Life' or the Eroticization of
Women's Oppression? Sexology and the Social Construction of Hetero-
sexuality," in *The Cultural Construction of Sexuality*, ed. Pat Caplan
(New York, 1988), pp. 52–81; Christina Simmons, "Modern Sexuality
and the Myth of Victorian Repression," in *Passion and Power: Sexuality*

in History, ed. Kathy Peiss and Christina Simmons pp. 157–77. Much of this literature is inspired by Foucault, especially his *History of Sexuality,* vol. 1.

18. Edward Atkinson, *The Science of Nutrition* (Boston, 1896), p. 35; Parksdale Butter (1909), book 127, N. W. Ayer Collection, National Museum of American History. An incisive and witty overview of the industrialization of eating is Laura Shapiro, *Perfection Salad: Women and Cooking at the Turn of the Century* (New York, 1986).

19. Lois Banner, *American Beauty* (New York, 1983), esp. pp. 39–47; Dewey's Dress and Coat Shields advertisement (1887), in Corsets box 2, Warshaw Collection; Hood Canvas Shoes advertisement, *Good Housekeeping,* May 1933, 175; Royal Gelatin advertisement, ibid., March 1934, 150–51; John B. Watson quoted in minutes of J. Walter Thompson Co. representatives meeting, 1 June 1928, in JWT Archives, Duke University; Odorono advertisement, *Good Housekeeping,* March 1930, 173.

20. Kleenex Tissues advertisement, *Good Housekeeping,* July 1932, 160.

21. Michael Williams, "Our Billions of Invisible Friends," *Success,* 1908, excerpted in brochure for Hood's Sarsaparilla, Patent Medicines box 14, Warshaw Collection; Watson quoted in minutes of J. Walter Thompson Co. representatives' meeting, 30 April 1930, pp. 7–8, JWT Archives.

22. Kleenex advertisement (see n. 20); Zonite advertisement, *Good Housekeeping,* April 1931, 126; Lysol advertisement, ibid., April 1930, 143; Guardian Memorials advertisement (1926), in book 134, Ayer Collection.

23. Hoover advertisement, *Saturday Evening Post* 203 (18 October 1930): 73; Lysol advertisement (see n. 22).

24. Advertisements: Martin Wagner Co., Baltimore (1910), in Foods box 14, Warshaw Collection; Burnham & Morrill Fish Flakes, *Saturday Evening Post* 183 (July 1910): 2; Squibb Cod Liver Oil, *Good Housekeeping,* February 1931, 187; Piggly Wiggly Stores, ibid., February 1930, 224; Eveready radios (1928), book 36, Ayer Collection. For the framework I am following in this paragraph, see Claude Lévi-Strauss, *The Raw and the Cooked* trans. John and Doreen Weightman (New York, 1969), and Judith Williamson, *Decoding Advertisements* (London, 1975).

25. Eveready Prestone Antifreeze advertisement (1927), book 39, Ayer Collection; W. Livingston Larned, "When the Appeal is Negative—Edit the Illustrations Wisely," *Printers' Ink* 152 (28 August 1930): 110–16.

26. The Bauer & Black advertisement, *Saturday Evening Post* 203 (6 September 1930): 120, presented the company as corner doctor; the Squibb Dental Cream advertisement, 1924–25, book 240, Ayer Collection, used expertise in scare tactics; and the minutes, J. Walter Thompson Co. representatives' meeting, 3 January 1934, JWT Archives, contain a discussion of the strategic appropriation of medical authority.

27. Richard Cabot, *Social Service and the Art of Healing* (New York, 1909), p. 33; Charlotte Tell, "The Neglected Psychology of Twilight Sleep," *Good Housekeeping,* July 1915, 17–24; Judith Walzer Leavitt, *Brought to Bed: Childbearing in America, 1750 to 1950* (New York, 1986), p. 140.

28. Rohe Walter, "Consumer Reactions at the World's Fair," minutes of the J. Walter Thompson Creative Staff meeting, 3 January 1934, JWT Archives.

29. Frances Williams Brown, "The Cult of Dirt," *Printers' Ink* 178 (4 February 1937): 16–24; Marsh K. Powers, "In Defense of Prudery," ibid., 11 March 1937, 15–17; Ervin M. Shafrin, "A Defense of Sex Appeal," ibid., 18 February 1937, 69–70.

30. Alice Katharine Fallows, "A Talk on Relaxation," *Good Housekeeping*, July 1908, 70–73; Raymond J. Cunningham, "The Emmanuel Movement: A Variety of American Religious Experience," *American Quarterly* 14 (Spring 1962): 48–63; H. Addington Bruce, "Religion and the Larger Self," *Good Housekeeping*, January 1916, 55–60. See also Nathan Hale, *Freud and the Americans: The Beginnings of Psychoanalysis in the United States* (New York, 1971), chap. 9.

31. Bruce Barton, "The Prodigal Son," *Good Housekeeping*, July 1928, 58, 192, 194; Harry Emerson Fosdick, *Twelve Tests of Character* (New York, 1923), p. 3.

32. Bruce Barton, "Does Anything Come After Death?" *American Magazine* 95 (March 1923): 5–7, 120, 122; G. Stanley Hall, *Morale* (New York, 1920), pp. 16–17.

33. Annie Payson Call, *Power Through Repose*, 2nd ed. (Boston, 1913), pp. 1, 60. For similar views see idem, *Everyday Living*, (New York, 1906), and David Starr Jordan, "The Evolution of the Mind," *Popular Science Monthly* 52 (February 1898): 441.

34. Hall, *Morale*, p. 208; Gulick, *Efficient Life*, p. 32.

35. Hall, *Morale*, p. 1; Gulick, *Efficient Life*, p. 18.

36. J. Walter Thompson Co., "From Bellman to Agency" (1901–1902), pamphlet in JWT Archives; Elizabeth Arden in *Good Housekeeping*, April 1930, 345; Hugh Baillie at J. Walter Thompson Company representatives' meeting, 9 April 1930, JWT Archives.

37. Advertisements: Eno Effervescent Saline, book 124, Ayer Collection; Hills Bros. Coffee, book 115, ibid. Sunkist California Orange Juice, *Saturday Evening Post* 203 (27 September 1930): 162.

38. Trine quoted in Robert C. Fuller, *Mesmerism and the American Cure of Souls* (Philadelphia, 1982), pp. 154–55.

39. *J. Walter Thompson Book* (1909), p. 5, in JWT Archives; Shredded Wheat pamphlet, *The Wonders of Niagara*, in Cereals box 41, Warshaw Collection; "Who's Who—and Why," *Saturday Evening Post* 183 (13 August 1910): 23.

40. American Tobacco Company advertisement, book 3, Ayer Collection; Batschari cigarette advertisements, *Town and Country* (1913), in "Tobacco Trade and Industry, A–G" box, Warshaw Collection.

41. Camel cigarette advertisements: 1927, book 89; 1929, book 92; Jordan Motor Car Company advertisement (1919), book 14, Ayer Collection.

42. For early examples of gender conflict over consumption, see Jane Weaver, "Gloves and Cigars," *Peterson's* 19 (April 1851): 193–94, and Mrs. J. E. M'Conaughey, "Saving Matches," ibid. 69 (February 1876):

109–10. On the shift from homosocial to heterosocial leisure, see, for example: Lewis Erenberg, *Steppin' Out: New York Nightlife and the Transformation of American Culture, 1890–1930* (Westport, Conn., 1979); Kathy Peiss, *Cheap Amusements: Women and Leisure at the Turn of the Century* (Philadelphia, 1986); Margaret Marsh, "Suburban Men and Masculine Domesticity, 1870–1915," *Americn Quarterly* 40 (June 1988): 165–86.

43. For two examples of this juvenilization process at work in widely diverse realms, see Alison Lurie, *The Language of Clothes* (New York, 1981), p. 74, and Carol Zisowitz Stearns and Peter N. Stearns, *Anger: The Struggle for Emotional Control in America's History* (Chicago and London, 1986), pp. 88–89.

44. Erving Goffman, *Gender Advertisements* (New York, 1979); Shapiro, *Perfection Salad*, p. 37.

45. Ibid, pp. 144, 196–200.

46. Quoted in Leavitt, *Brought to Bed*, p. 175.

47. Lysol advertisement, *Good Housekeeping*, March 1935, 117.

48. Blackwell's Durham Tobacco trade card (1878), in Tobacco Products box A–G; D. G. Yuengling Beer trade card (1896), in Beer box 57b, Warshaw Collection; Virgin Leaf Chew trade card (c. 1890), in scrapbook 17a, Landauer Collection, New-York Historical Society; Joseph J. Bukey, "Is All Feminine Advertising Bad?", *Printers' Ink* 67 (25 August 1909): 34; Helen Rosen Woodward, *Through Many Windows* (New York, 1926), p. 314.

49. Katharine Fisher, "Unfolding the Household Romance," *Good Housekeeping*, June 1931, 94–95; Margaret Sangster, "Other Woman," ibid., April 1935, 20–23, 150ff.

50. William Graebner, *The Engineering of Consent: Democracy and Authority in Twentieth-Century America* (Madison, Wis., 1987).

51. Advertisements in *Good Housekeeping* for Tangee Lipstick and Rouge, July 1932, 191; Lux Detergent, February 1934, 157; Palmolive Soap, April 1932, 109; Drano, January 1932, 135; Grape-Nuts, July 1931, 171. For a useful summary of the new, managerial version of domestic ideology, see the advertisement for *Ladies' Home Journal* in *Saturday Evening Post* 203 (20 September 1930): 139.

52. Crane Bathroom Fixtures advertisement, *Good Housekeeping*, February 1931, 215.

53. George Stevenson and Geddes Smith, *Child Guidance Clinics* (New York, 1934), p. 147; Warren Susman, *Culture as History* (New York, 1984), pp. 150–210; Marion Sturges-Jones, "Don't Be Afraid to Conform," *Good Housekeeping*, November 1936, 16, 24–25.

54. Advertisements in *Good Housekeeping* for Scott's Emulsion of Norwegian Cod Liver Oil, March 1932, 227; Cream of Wheat, July 1931, 153; Calvert School, September 1920, 213. M. K. Wisehart, "WHAT Is WRONG Between Us and Our Children?" ibid., March 1932, 28–29, 166ff; Frederick E. Stamm, "Don't Be Fool Parents," ibid., March 1935, 42–43.

55. William F. McDermott, "I Want My Daughters to Marry," *Good House-keeping*, December 1934, 30–31, 169, 170. Emphasis added.

56. Susman, *Culture as History*, pp. 150–210; Rita S. Halle, "Can They Pass in Emotion?" *Good Housekeeping*, September 1932, 26–27; Sturges-Jones, "Don't Be Afraid to Conform"; Vera Connolly, "Uncle Sam Wants Your Mark," *Good Housekeeping* December 1935, 24–25. On the link between private togetherness and public conformity in the postwar era, see Elaine Tyler May, *Homeward Bound* (New York, 1987).

57. Connolly, "Uncle Sam Wants Your Mark."

58. Betty Friedan, *The Feminine Mystique* (New York, 1963), chap. 4; Elizabeth Bennecke Peterson, "Wanted: Young American Couple," *Good Housekeeping*, May 1932, 30–33, 220, 222; Joanne Meyerowitz, "Beyond the Feminine Mystique: A Reassessment of Postwar Mass Culture, 1946–1958," *Journal of American History* 79 (March 1993): 1455–82; Kerry Buckley, *Mechanical Man: John Broadus Watson and the Beginnings of Behaviorism* (New York and London, 1989), p. 178.

59. Minutes, J. Walter Thompson Co. representatives meeting, 9 January 1929, JWT Archives.

60. Ibid., 13 February 1930, pp. 7–8.

61. General Electric Company advertisement, *Saturday Evening Post* 203 (6 September 1930): 62–65; *The General Electric "House of Magic"* (c. 1941), in Electricity box 14, Warshaw Collection.

62. Advertisements for Eveready Batteries (1927), book 35; Tuska Radios (1923), book 18, Ayer Collection.

63. "Disease Marches On," *Printers' Ink* 176 (13 August 1936): 12–14.

CHAPTER 7. THE NEW BASIS OF CIVILIZATION

1. "The Great White Way," *Printers' Ink* 64 (26 August 1908): 3, 8.

2. Helen Rosen Woodward, *Through Many Windows* (New York, 1926), p. 243. The point about the physical isolation of agency executives is made by Kerry Buckley, *Mechanical Man: John Broadus Watson and the Beginnings of Behaviorism* (New York and London, 1989), p. 143.

3. Wallace Boren, "Bad Taste in Advertising," J. Walter Thompson Forum, 7 January 1936, unpaginated, JWT Archives, Duke University.

4. Robert Rydell, *All the World's a Fair: Visions of Empire at American International Expositions, 1876–1916* (Chicago and London, 1984), pp. 34, 67, 119, 151. For an illuminating account of how public amusements in general grew more respectable and became an important site for assimilating diverse ethnic groups into a common (white) consumer culture, see David Nasaw, *Going Out: The Rise and Fall of Public Amusements* (New York, 1993).

5. Addison Archer, "Bates on Bates," *Printers' Ink* 13 (14 August 1895), 8; Helen Mar Shaw, "Original vs. the Conventional," *Judicious Advertising*

1 (July 1903): 16–17; "'Advertising Ideas,'" *Printers' Ink* 57 (5 December 1906): 11.

6. James Wood, *The Story of Advertising* (New York, 1958), pp. 285–95; Albert D. Lasker, *The Lasker Story as He Told It* (Chicago, 1963), pp. 53–58.

7. Truman A. De Weese, "With Brains Only" *Printers' Ink* 38 (12 February 1902): 46–47, reprinted from *Fame* magazine; John O. Powers, "Advertising," *Annals of the American Academy of Political and Social Science* 22 (November 1903): 470–74.

8. Charles R. Flint, "How Business Success Will Be Won in the Twentieth Century," *Printers' Ink* 35 (10 April 1901): 36–37, reprinted from *Saturday Evening Post;* Earnest Elmo Calkins, *The Business of Advertising* (New York, 1915), p. 57. See also Joseph R. Appel, *Growing Up with Advertising* (New York, 1940), pp. 23, 30.

9. "A New Profession," *Yale Daily News,* 26 May 1919, clipping from house ads file in JWT Archives. There is an enormous literature on the shift from entrepreneurial to corporate capitalism. Among the most useful studies are Alfred D. Chandler, *The Visible Hand: The Managerial Revolution in American Business* (Cambridge, Mass., 1977); Martin J. Sklar, *The Corporate Reconstruction of American Capitalism, 1890–1916: The Market, the Law, and Politics* (New York and Cambridge, England, 1988), esp. pp. 66–67, 70–71, 80–81, 154–55, 162–66, 354–61; Olivier Zunz, *Making America Corporate* (Chicago, 1990). Evidence for the incompleteness of the managerial "revolution" can be found in Robert Johnston, "The Persistence of Middle-Class Radicalism in Portland, Oregon, 1890–1925," Ph.D. dissertation, Rutgers University, 1993, and Michael McGerr, "Beyond Organizational History: Reinterpreting Modern America," paper presented at Organization of American Historians Annual Meeting, Chicago, April 1992.

10. James Collins, quoted in H. R. Document No. 608, 59th Congress, 2nd Session (1907), Penrose Overstreet Committee, xxxvii. I use the notion of a hegemonic historical bloc because I believe the Gramscian vocabulary is more flexible than the language of class, and therefore more appropriate for characterizing the shifting and unstable coalitions of managerial elites during the early twentieth century. See T. J. Jackson Lears, "The Concept of Cultural Hegemony: Problems and Possibilities," *American Historical Review* 90 (1985): 567–93. For the view that magazines' growing dependence on advertising democratized public access to information, see "Reaching the Millions," *Review of Reviews* 37 (May 1908): 608–9.

11. On the growth of "objectivity" as a journalistic ideal, see Michael Schudson, *Discovering the News: A Social History of American Newspapers* (New York, 1978), pp. 61–87, and Michael McGerr, *The Decline of Popular Politics: The American North, 1865–1928* (New York, 1986), chap. 5.

12. James Harvey Young, *The Toadstool Millionaires* (Princeton, N. J., 1961),

p. 211; Will Irwin, "American Newspapers: Our Kind of People," *Collier's* 47 (17 June 1911): 17–18.

13. The problem of losing sight of the big picture by focusing on specific instances afflicts the otherwise thoughtful work of Herbert Gans, *Deciding What's News* (New York, 1978).

14. Samuel Hopkins Adams, "Fair Trade and Foul," *Collier's* 43 (19 June 1909): 19–20. See also Adams, "The Art of Advertising," ibid., 22 May 1909, 13–15; idem, "Of Honesty in Advertising," *North American Review* 183 (5 October 1906): 693–95; Will Irwin, "American Newpapers: Advertising Influence," *Collier's* 47 (27 May 1911): 15–16; Richard Tedlow, *Keeping the Corporate Image* (Westport, Conn., 1974), pp. 32–33.

15. Clifton S. Wady, "Don't," *Fame* 3 (October 1894): 318; Your Uncle, "Maxims," *Art in Advertising* 6 (January 1893): 160; Tedlow, *Keeping the Corporate Image,* pp. 9, 12–13; Earnest Elmo Calkins, *The Advertising Man* (New York, 1915), pp. 34–35.

16. Harry Tipper, address to League of Advertising Women, 19 October 1915, quoted in *Newspaperdom,* 28 October 1915, clipping in Advertising Women of New York Papers, vol. 1, Wisconsin State Historical Society, Madison. On the growth of critical consumer consciousness during this period, see E. C. Billings, "Brains and Buying," *Atlantic Monthly,* June 1913, 768–70, and Agnes Athol, "The Housewives' League," *Advertising and Selling* 22 (March 1913): 58–64.

17. "The Campaign Against Fraudulent Advertising," *Printers' Ink* 90 (4 March 1915), 67–79; Appel, *Growing Up with Advertising,* pp. 123–136. See also Daniel Pope, *The Making of Modern Advertising* (New York, 1982), pp. 186–218.

18. New York organizer quoted in Pope, *Making of Modern Advertising,* p. 318*n*.

19. James B. Kirk, "Illiteracy and Advertising," *Printers' Ink* 12 (9 January 1895): 25; "Reaching the Rural Classes," *Judicious Advertising* 1 (March 1903): 27–29; "How Adler Proved that Farmers Want Snappy Clothes," *Printers' Ink* 72 (14 July 1910): 52–54; Richard Surrey, "Advertising—Archenemy of Poverty and Disease," ibid. 133 (10 December 1925): 49–52; Boris Emmet and John E. Jeuck, *Catalogues and Counters: A History of Sears, Roebuck, & Co.* (Chicago, 1950), esp. pp. 151–160. See also the long-running advertisement of L. N. Hammerling's American Association of Foreign Language Newspapers in *Printers' Ink,* 1900–1910, which emphasized the availability of translators and immigrants' eagerness for national brands.

20. James H. Collins, "A Socialistic Viewpoint," *Printers' Ink* 38 (1 January 1902), 14; George P. Sherman, "The Effect of Advertising on Our Internal Economy," ibid. 57 (31 October 1906); Waldo P. Warren, "By-Products of Advertising," *Collier's* 42 (6 February 1909): 34. On the tendency to equate consumption with the civilizing process among French intellectuals during this same period, see Rosalind Williams, *Dream Worlds: Mass*

Consumption in Late-Nineteenth-Century France (Berkeley and London, 1982), pp. 24, 222–23, 266.

21. *J. Walter Thompson Newsletter*, 27 June 1916, JWT Archives.

22. For a nuanced and illuminating account of the development of these beliefs in one discipline, see Robert C. Bannister, *Sociology and Scientism: The American Quest for Objectivity, 1880–1940* (Chapel Hill, N.C., and London, 1987). And for a superb overview, see Dorothy Ross, *The Origins of American Social Science* (New York, 1990).

23. The classic accounts are A. O. Lovejoy, *The Revolt Against Dualism* (Cambridge, Mass., 1930); Morton White, *Social Thought in America: The Revolt Against Formalism,* [1949] 2nd ed. (Boston, 1957); and Bruce Kuklick, *The Rise of American Philosophy: Cambridge, Massachusetts, 1880–1930* (Cambridge, Mass., 1980).

24. White, *Revolt Against Formalism* first recognized the antiformalist tendencies linking early-twentieth-century developments in psychology, sociology, law, and economics, but failed to see the conformist implications of a Darwinian emphasis on adaptation. For early recognition of this difficulty, see Randolph Bourne, "Twilight of Idols," *Seven Arts* 2 (October 1917), 688–702. For spirited defenses of Dewey, Cooley, and other antiformalists against charges of conformism, see Hans Joas, *Pragmatism and Social Theory* (Chicago, 1993), esp. pp. 23–25, 83; and James Livingston, *Pragmatism and the Political Economy of Cultural Revolution* (Chapel Hill, N.C., 1994).

25. Charles Horton Cooley, *Social Process* [1902] (Carbondale, Ill., 1966), p. 136. On the growing perception of interdependence, see Thomas Haskell, *The Emergence of Professional Social Science* (Urbana, Ill., 1977), esp. chaps. 1 and 2.

26. William Graebner, *The Engineering of Consent: Democracy and Authority in Twentieth-Century America* (Madison, Wis., 1987).

27. Walter Dill Scott, *The Psychology of Advertising* (Boston, 1908); Harry L. Hollingsworth, *Advertising and Selling: Principles of Appeal and Response* (New York, 1913); Bruce Bliven, "Can You Sell Goods to the Subconscious Mind?" *Printers' Ink* 102 (28 March 1918): 3–8, 92–97.

28. Will B. Wilder, "Hypnotism in Advertising," *Fame* 1 (September 1892): 196–97; Joel Benton, "Experiment in Advertising," ibid. 14 (April 1905): 81–82; John Lee Mahin, "Advertising—A Form of Organized Salesmanship," *Printers' Ink* 70 (30 March 1910): 5. On the popularization of psychoanalysis, see Nathan Hale, *Freud and the Americans: The Beginnings of Psychoanalysis in the United States, 1876–1917* (New York, 1971).

29. James H. Collins, "The Eternal Feminine," *Printers' Ink* 35 (26 June 1901): 3–5; "Pictures Catch Women," *Fame* 9 (April 1900): 168; Helen Mar Shaw, "The Ad for the Woman's Eye," *Advertising and Selling* 1 (November 1902): 27–28; Seymour Eaton, *Sermons on Advertising* (New York, 1908).

30. Martin quoted in *New York Tribune*, 2 June 1915, clipping in Advertising

Women of New York scrapbooks, vol. 1. See also "Advertising Big Field for Women, Says Mrs. Frederick," *Philadelphia Public Ledger,* 28 June 1916, in ibid., vol. 2, and "Ad Women: Kenneth Collins Sees Women Dominating Well-paid Advertising Field," *Literary Digest* 123 (13 March 1937): 42–43.

31. "Don't Tell Too Much," *Fame* 1 (October, 1892): 240–41; J. M. Campbell, "Some Reasons Why 'Reason Why' Copy Often Fails," *Printers' Ink* (9 March 1911): 25–27.

32. Charles Austin Bates, "Magazine Advertising," *Printers' Ink* 11 (8 August 1894): 187–88; James H. Collins, "Advertising and the Work Instinct," ibid. 70 (2 February 1910): 3–6.

33. "Interesting the Slapdash Hasty Newspaper Reader," *Printers' Ink* 72 (7 July 1910): 33–34; "A Typical Trade Mark," ibid. 3 (26 November 1890): 522; Frederick Flagler Helmer, "Advertisements of Double Value," *Profitable Advertising* 15 (May 1906): 142–43. On installment buying, see Free Lance, "The Rich or the Poor," *Printers' Ink* 15 (27 May 1896): 8, and "On Installment Plan," ibid. 35 (5 June 1901): 25.

34. Clowry Chapman, "Mental Images as Sales Factors," *Printers' Ink* 71 (6 April 1910), 92.

35. Charles Raymond, typescript memoir in J. Walter Thompson Archives. Susan Strasser, *Satisfaction Guaranteed: The Making of the American Mass Market* (New York, 1989), is a useful survey of the rise of market research.

36. Charles Mears, "Can 'Art' and Mere General Publicity Sell Autos?" *Printers' Ink* 69 (20 October 1909): 3–6; Lee Anderson, "How a Radical Departure in Automobile Advertising Came About," ibid. 73 (29 December 1910): 3–6; Calkins, *Business of Advertising,* 205–207.

37. "Barnum and Advertising," *Printers' Ink* 72 (14 July 1910): 193.

38. "The Practice of Advertising Baiting," ibid. 62 (29 January 1908): 32.

39. "Taking Advertising Seriously," ibid. 90 (9 March 1915): 87–88.

40. Jesse H. Neal, "Advertising the Spark to the Selling Engine," *Judicious Advertising* 10 (January 1912): 77–78.

41. Joel Benton, "The Persuasive Art," *Printers' Ink* 40 (16 July 1902): 12; "Too Much Professionalism," ibid. 67 (30 June 1909): 44; Elbert Hubbard, "Being Human in Writing Advertising," ibid. 71 (13 April 1910): 62–63; Woodward, *Through Many Windows,* p. 205. See also Claude Hopkins, "Sensational Advertising," *Printers' Ink* 13 (30 October 1895), and "Human Interest in Advertising," *Fame* 14 (November 1905), 254.

42. Milton J. Platt, "Ruts and Originalities," *Fame* 3 (November 1894): 345–46; "Confessions of an Advertising Solicitor," *Printers' Ink* 14 (22 January 1896): 70.

43. "Concentration, the Secret of Success," *Profitable Advertising* 3 (15 November 1893): 170–72.

44. Merrit O. Howard, "Successful Copywriters Are Self-Hypnotists," *Judicious Advertising* 10 (April 1912), 69–72; "Letter from an Advertising Manager," *Printers' Ink* 61 (30 October 1907): 12–13; J. Walter Thomp-

son Company, *The Thompson Blue Book on Advertising, 1906–1907*, pp. 52–53, in JWT Archives. Emphases in originals.

45. Eaton, *Sermons on Advertising* (1908) n.p., in JWT Archives.

46. L. F. Deland, "At the Sign of the Dollar," *Harper's Monthly* 134 (March 1917): 525–33.

47. For useful overviews of the wartime home front, and advertising's role in ideological mobilization, see David Kennedy, *Over Here* (New York, 1980), and Steven Vaughn, *Holding Fast the Inner Lines* (Chapel Hill, N. C., 1980). On the relation between the war and the rise of managerial policy, see Ellis Hawley, *The Great War and the Search for a Modern Order* (New York, 1979).

48. Lee Simonson, "Mobilizing the Billboards," *New Republic* 13 (10 November 1917): 41–43.

49. C. L. Benjamin and L. J. Vance, "Advertising a Presidential Candidate [McKinley]," *Printers' Ink* 17 (28 October 1896): 3–6; "Presbrey vs. Ayer," ibid. 65 (14 October 1908): 8–10. On Theodore Roosevelt's use of "sound bites" in press conferences, see Kenneth Cmiel, *Democratic Eloquence: The Debate over Popular Speech in Nineteenth-Century America* (New York, 1990), pp. 249–51. On the rise of "advertised politics," see McGerr, *Decline of Popular Politics*, chap. 6.

50. Charles Raymond memoir, n. p., JWT Archives.

51. "Advertising as a Weapon of War," *Printers' Ink* 105 (14 November 1918): 143–44; "Peace Treaty the World's Greatest Advertising Failure," *Literary Digest* 63 (20 December 1919): 130–36, reprinted from *Advertising and Selling*, November 1919. See also "Postering in the Third Liberty Loan," *Literary Digest* 56 (23 March 1918): 29–30.

52. Clarence S. Yoakum, *Army Mental Tests* (Washington, D.C., 1919), pp. 260–61.

53. For a succinct analysis of this project, see Christopher Lasch, "The Moral and Intellectual Rehabilitation of the Ruling Class," in his *The World of Nations* (New York, 1973). On the social meanings of intelligence testing, see Michael Sokal, ed., *Psychological Testing and American Society, 1890–1920* (New Brunswick, N.J., 1987), and Joanne Brown, *The Definition of a Profession* (Princeton, N.J., 1992).

54. Guy Emerson, "Publicity as a Recognized Business Force," *Nation* 106 (28 March 1918): 367–68.

55. Harry Emerson Fosdick, *The Challenge of the Present Crisis* (New York, 1917), p. v.

56. G. Stanley Hall, *Morale* (New York, 1920); Annie Payson Call, *Nerves and the War* (Boston, 1918); Luther H. Gulick, *A Philosophy of Play* (New York, 1920), p. 245.

57. Coca-Cola advertisement, *Cosmopolitan* (July 1918), in Beverages box 1, Warshaw Collection of Business Americana, National Museum of American History, Smithsonian Institution, Washington, D.C.; L. B. Jones, "Advertising Men as the 'Cheer Leaders' of the Nation," *Printers' Ink* 102 (7 February 1918): 62–65.

58. Clayton Hamilton, "Great Actors, as Other Great Men, Are More Alive Than the Herd," *Vogue,* 1 December 1917, 17, cited in Lewis Erenberg, *Steppin' Out: New York Night Life and the Transformation of American Culture, 1890–1930* (Greenwood, Conn., 1980), pp. 186–87. On the importance of testimonial advertising in the 1920s, see minutes of the J. Walter Thompson Co. representatives' meeting, 9 April 1928, JWT Archives.

59. Tedlow, *Keeping the Corporate Image,* p. 29; John Dewey, *Individualism Old and New* (New York, 1930), pp. 42–43; Sinclair Lewis, "Publicity Gone Mad," *Nation* 128 (6 March 1929): 278–79; Robert Wallace, "Lucky or a Sweet, or Both," Ibid., 13 March 1929, 305–7.

60. Edward L. Bernays, *Crystallizing Public Opinion* (New York, 1923), p. 150; idem, *Propaganda* (New York, 1928), pp. 156–57. See also H. F. Pringle, "Mass Psychologist," *American Mercury* 19 (February 1930): 155–62, and the classic works by Walter Lippmann, *Public Opinion* (New York, 1922) and *The Phantom Public* (New York, 1925).

61. Jesse Rainsford Sprague, "Patronize Your Own Church People," *New Republic* 37 (30 January 1924): 254–56; JWT Co. Newsletter, 11 June 1925, p. 6, JWT Archives; Stanley Resor, "Advertising as a Career," *Printers' Ink* 139 (12 May 1927): 65–80; Bruce Barton, "Changes and Trends in Advertising," speech to Boston Chamber of Commerce, 17 May 1927, in Bruce Barton papers, Wisconsin State Historical Society; "U.S.A. as an Advertising Achievement," *Literary Digest* 91 (13 November 1926): 15–16; James Wallen, "Emotion and Style in Copy," in *Masters of Advertising Copy,* ed. J. George Frederick (New York, 1925), pp. 110–11.

62. J. George Frederick, "The Story of Advertising Writing," in Frederick, ed., *Masters,* p. 27; Allen T. Moore, "I Prefer Knowing My Consumer to Knowing My Product," *Printer's Ink* 151 (17 April 1930): 57; George Raymond memoir; Strasser, *Satisfaction Guaranteed,* esp. chaps. 3, 4, 5.

63. R. M. Rhodes, "Has Advertising Reached the Dignity of Finance?" *Printers' Ink* 120 (27 July 1922): 54–56; Albert Haase, "A Professional Status for Advertising?" ibid. 139 (2 June 1927): 125–28; A Personnel Executive, "Do You Select Employees by a Bertillon System?" ibid., 7 April 1927, 49–50; Gordon Cooke, "What Is an Advertising Man, Mr. Buckley?" ibid., 14 April 1927, 57–60.

64. Orrick Johns, "American Portraits: The Advertising Agent," *American Mercury,* 2 (August 1924): 445–50.

65. Woodward, *Through Many Windows,* p. 289; W. Livingston, "Magical Effects with Pen and Ink," *Printers' Ink* 130 (26 March 1925): 33–36; Wallen, "Emotion and Style," pp. 93, 99.

66. Joseph H. Appel, "Axioms of Advertising," in Frederick, ed., *Masters,* p. 179; Frederick, "The Story of Advertising Writing," p. 25; Edith Lewis, "The Emotional Quality in Advertisements," *JWT News Bulletin,* April 1923, pp. 11–14, JWT Archives.

67. J. George Frederick, "Obsolescence, Free Spending, and Creative Waste," in his *A Philosophy of Production* (New York, 1930); Bruce Bar-

ton, "The New Business World: Number Five in a Series," transcript of radio talk dated 30 November 1929 in Bruce Barton Papers, Wisconsin State Historical Society; advertisement for *Life, Printers' Ink* 133 (5 November 1925): 94–95. Advertising executives communicated this sentiment privately as well: see S. L. Meulendyke, letter of 14 April 1926 to Earnest Elmo Calkins, box 1, Calkins Papers, Special Collections and Archives, Knox College Library, Galesburg, Ill. On the growing respectability of installment buying, see "New Wine in Old Bottles," *Printers' Ink* 39 (16 April 1902): 14.

68. "Messenger to the King," *Collier's* 85 (3 May 1930): 78.

69. Thompson Radio advertisement (1925), in N. W. Ayer Collection, book 19, National Museum of American History; José Ortega y Gasset, *The Revolt of the Masses* [1930] (New York, 1957), p. 82.

70. Arthur Holmes, "The Psychology of the Printed Word," in Frederick, ed., *Masters,* p. 344. See also Paul Sartorus, "Has Coué a Place in the Sales Programme?" (Émile Coué [1857–1926] was a French psychologist who introduced a system of autosuggestion based on chanting "Every day, and in every way, I am becoming better and better."), *Printers' Ink* 121 (14 December 1922): 33–36, and C. B. Larrabee, "What Place Has Psychology in Advertising?" ibid. 132 (24 September 1925): 81–84.

71. John Starr Hewitt, "The Copy Writer's Work Bench," in Frederick, ed., *Masters,* p. 323. For a few among many examples of similar views, see E. E. Calkins, "Gnats and Camels, the Newspaper's Dilemma," *Atlantic Monthly* 139 (January 1927): 1–14, and J. Walter Thompson house advertisements in *Printers' Ink,* 5 August, 9 December, and 23 December 1920, clippings in JWT Archives.

72. Paramount Pictures advertisement, *Saturday Evening Post* 203 (6 September 1930): 55.

73. Woodward, *Through Many Windows,* p. 345.

74. Paul H. Nystrom, *The Economics of Fashion* (New York, 1928), pp. 66–69; J. George Frederick, Preface to his *Philosophy of Production,* p. vi.

75. William Esty, comment at J. Walter Thompson representatives' meeting, 30 September 1930, in JWT Archives.

76. On the optimism of American theorists of mass society, see Gregory W. Bush, *Lord of Attention: Gerald Stanley Lee and the Crowd Metaphor in Industrializing America* (Amherst, Mass., 1991), pp. 90–172, and Eugene Leach, "Mastering the Crowd: Collective Behavior and Mass Society in American Social Thought, 1917–1939," *American Studies* 27 (Spring 1986): 105.

CHAPTER 8. TRAUMA, DENIAL, RECOVERY

1. Juliet B. Schor, *The Overworked American: The Unexpected Decline of Leisure* (New York, 1992), esp. chaps. 3, 5.

2. "Salute the Brave," *Good Housekeeping* 96 (June 1933): 8. See also "The Undeprest Advertising Mind," *Literary Digest* 113 (2 April 1932): 44.

3. Allen R. Dodd, "With Benefit of Budget," *Good Housekeeping* 94 (January 1932): 88–89, 174ff; Anne Sharon Monroe, "Lead from Strength," ibid., 93 (October 1931): 108–13; Bruce Barton, "Are You Happy in Your Work?" ibid. 90 (September 1930): 26–27, 248ff.

4. "The Grasshopper and the Ants," ibid. 98 (April 1934): 36–37.

5. G. A. Nichols, "Consumer Acceptance—What It Is and How It Works," *Printers' Ink* 154 (12 February 1931): 49–57; "Inflation and Advertising," *Literary Digest* 116 (29 July 1933): 34; F. J. Schlink, "Bear Oil," *New Republic* 64 (31 July 1929): 279; Roy Dickinson, "Stabilizing Employment," *Printers' Ink* 154 (1 January 1931): 49–52. For a good example of claims made to clients, see "Making Advertising Pay During the Depression," J. Walter Thompson new business presentation, c. 1933, JWT Archives, Duke University. For the scaling-down of claims, see "Deflating Advertising," *Printers' Ink* 154 (26 February 1931): 117–18.

6. James Rorty, "Advertising and the Depression," *Nation* 137 (20 December 1933): 703–4; "Whipcracking," *Printers' Ink* 155 (14 May 1931): 133; Walter A. Lowen, "You Can't Keep a Good Advertising Man Out of Work," ibid., 18 June 1931, 64. For more evidence of tension inside the agency, see William Day's lecture to the restless younger staff at J. Walter Thompson, minutes of the Creative Staff meeting, 5 March 1932, JWT Archives.

7. Aesop Glim, "Playboy or Business Man?" *Printers' Ink* 151 (17 April 1930): 93–94; "What Groucho Says," ibid. 154 (19 February 1931): 118.

8. "Fair Rivals of the Sandwich Man," *Literary Digest* 113 (23 April 1932): 41; "Cameron Raps Bad Reporting, Blatant Radio," *Advertising Age* 9 (21 February 1938): 24; One of the Twelve Million, "I've Got an Idea, But What Shall I Do With It?" *Printers' Ink* 171 (2 May 1935): 27–33.

9. "Advertising Analyzes Agents," *Business Week,* 24 May 1933, 7; Bernice Kenyon, "Housewife Looks at Advertising," *American Mercury* 29 (June 1933): 181–89; H. A. Batten, "Advertising Man Looks at Advertising," *Atlantic Monthly* 150 (July 1932): 53–57.

10. For early examples of the critical uses of consumer consciousness, see Dana Frank, "At the Point of Consumption: Seattle Labor and the Politics of Consumption, 1919–1927," Ph. D. dissertation, Yale University, 1988; Raymond Fuller, "Honesty in Advertising," *Nation* 125 (31 August 1927): 202–203; Stuart Chase, *The Tragedy of Waste* (New York, 1925); idem, "Blindfolded You Know the Difference," *New Republic* 55 (8 August 1928): 296–98. The locus classicus is John Ruskin, *Unto This Last* [1861] (London, 1907). Veblen's *Theory of the Leisure Class* (New York, 1899) cast a puritanical pall over much subsequent commentary on consumption. An exception is Hazel Kyrk, *A Theory of Consumption* (Boston and London, 1923), which emphasizes qualitative rather than quantitative aspects of consumption, and acknowledges that, under the right circumstances, consumption might have something to do with civilized leisure.

11. Stuart Chase, "Advertising: An Autopsy," *Nation* 138 (16 May 1934):

567–68; T. S. Harding, "Boondoggling in Private Enterprise," *Christian Century* 53 (25 March 1936): 460–62; "Consumer Movement; Report to Executives," *Business Week,* 22 April 1939, 39–52.

12. Stuart Chase, *The Nemesis of American Business* (New York, 1931), p. 95. On disaccumulation, see Martin Sklar, "Some Political and Cultural Consequences of the Disaccumulation of Capital: Origins of Post-Industrial Development in the 1920s," in his *The United States as a Developing Country* (Cambridge, England, 1992), pp. 143–96.

13. Robert Westbrook, "Tribune of the Technostructure," *American Quarterly* 32 (Fall 1980): 387–407; Theodor Adorno, "Veblen's Attack on Culture" [1941], in his *Prisms* (Cambridge, Mass., 1980).

14. Ralph Borsodi, *The Distribution Age* (New York, 1927); idem, *This Ugly Civilization* (New York, 1929).

15. Johnson quoted in Arthur Schlesinger, Jr., *The Coming of the New Deal* (New York, 1958), p. 130; Elizabeth Frazer, "King Cotton Heads the Big Parade," *Good Housekeeping* 97 (October 1933): 16–17, 116ff; "NRA's Big Drive to Start Consumer Buying," *Business Week,* 14 October 1933, 5–6; "Advertising As Usual," *Nation* 139 (4 July 1934): 5–6; "Advertising Boosted by New Tax on Undistributed Earnings," *Business Week,* 16 January 1937, 14–15; "FTC Tightening Rules, New Decisions Indicate," *Advertising Age* 9 (28 March 1938): 18; Thurman Arnold, "Mr. Arnold's Side of the Argument," *Printers' Ink* 197 (17 October 1941): 13–15, 62ff; Otis Pease, *Responsibilities of American Advertising: Private Control and Public Influence, 1920–1940* (New Haven, Conn., 1958), pp. 115–66. For more on consumer issues in the New Deal era, see Ronald Edsforth, *Class Conflict and Cultural Consensus: The Making of a Mass Consumer Society in Flint, Michigan* (New Brunswick, N.J., and London, 1987), esp. chap. 6, and Lizabeth Cohen, *Making a New Deal: Industrial Workers in Chicago, 1919–1939* (New York, 1991), esp. chaps. 3, 6–8.

16. Franklin Delano Roosevelt, "You Cannot Robotize Advertising," *Printers' Ink* 155 (18 July 1931): 44. On the struggles to define political culture within the New Deal coalition, see Nelson Lichtenstein, "From Corporatism to Collective Bargaining: Organized Labor and the Eclipse of Social Democracy in the Postwar Era," in *The Rise and Fall of the New Deal Order, 1930–1980,* ed. Steve Fraser and Gary Gerstle (Princeton, N.J., 1989), pp. 122–52. For a useful overview of political advertising, see Kathleen Hall Jamieson, *Packaging the Presidency: A History and Criticism of Presidential Campaign Advertising* (New York, 1984).

17. Colwell in minutes of J. Walter Thompson Company representatives meeting, 8 July 1930, JWT Archives; "Introducing PEOPLE," *People,* March 1937, JWT Archives.

18. "PEOPLE Like to Spend," *People,* October 1937, inside front cover, JWT Archives. For similar views of the mass audience, see "They Like It Simple," *Advertising Age* 9 (28 February 1938): 12; advertisement for *Liberty* magazine, *Printers' Ink* 178 (21 January 1937): 54–55; "Selling Discontent," *Saturday Review of Literature* 13 (28 December 1935): 8.

19. George Gallup and Saul Forbes Rae, *The Pulse of Democracy: The Public Opinion Poll and How It Works* (New York, 1940).

20. J. George Frederick, "The Research Basis of Copy," in Frederick, ed., *Masters of Advertising Copy* (New York, 1925), pp. 152–53; undated *New Yorker* cartoon in "The Largest Clinic of Advertising Experience in the World," JWT new business presentation, 1945, JWT Archives; information on Gallup in JWT Creative Staff meeting, 4 March 1932, JWT Archives, and "A New Technique in Journalism," *Fortune* 12 (July 1935): 65–68. See also Frederic Russell, "My Reply to Critics Who Say That Marketing Will Never Be a Science," *Printers' Ink* 131 (23 April 1925): 105–16.

21. For a fuller version of this argument, see Benjamin Ginsberg, *The Captive Public: How Mass Opinion Promotes State Power* (New York, 1986), and the perceptive review by Mark Crispin Miller, "Suckers for Elections," *New York Times Book Review*, 8 February 1987, 32. For a powerful conservative critique of opinion polling, see Robert Nisbet, "Public Opinion vs. Popular Opinion," *Public Interest* 41 (Fall 1975): 166–92.

22. R. Littell and J. J. McCarthy, "Whispers for Sale," *Harper's Monthly* 172 (February 1936): 364–72; J. Walter Thompson Company, *A Primer of Capitalism* (1937), JWT Archives; James Webb Young, "The Professor Looks at Advertising," *Good Housekeeping* 100 (June 1935): 86–87, 143ff.

23. Warren Susman, *Culture as History* (New York, 1984), pp. 150–210, brilliantly discusses the sources of the preoccupation with the American Way of Life. For the development of corporate interest in this idiom, see Lary May, "Making the American Way: Moderne Theatres, Audiences, and the Film Industry, 1929–1945," *Prospects* 12 (1987): 93–111, and Maren Stange, *Symbols of Ideal Life: Social Documentary Photography in America, 1890–1950* (Cambridge, England, and New York, 1989), pp. 94–101, 128–29, 142–43. Stange perceptively documents the convergence of New Deal and corporate image-making projects.

24. Donald Wilhelm, "Business Rushes to Government's Aid in Preparedness Crisis," *Printers' Ink* 192 (16 August 1940): 11–13.

25. Schor, *The Overworked American*, pp. 7, 75–77.

26. Frank W. Fox, *Madison Avenue Goes to War: The Strange Military Career of American Advertising, 1941–1945* (Provo, Utah, 1975), p. 92.

27. H. A. Batten, "This, or Silence," *Printers' Ink* 197 (14 November 1941): 11–13, 61–64. Emphasis in original.

28. "The Advertising Front," *Fortune* 26 (November 1942): 60, 64; "Advertising in Wartime," *New Republic* 110 (21 February 1944): 233–36; Fox, *Madison Avenue*, pp. 48–53; John Morton Blum, *V Was for Victory* (New York and London, 1976), pp. 38–43; Richard J. Barnet, *The Rockets' Red Glare: When America Goes to War* (New York, 1989), pp. 228–29. On the Ad Council, see Robert Griffith, "The Selling of America: The Advertising Council and American Politics, 1942–1960," *Business History Review* 57 (Autumn 1983): 388–412.

29. Curtis Nettels, "The Radio and the War," *New Republic* 106 (18 May

1942): 666–67; "Advertising and the War Effort," *Collier's* 114 (26 August 1944): 82. I discuss the appropriation of folk motifs by advertisers more fully in chapter 12 and in "Packaging the Folk: Tradition and Amnesia in American Advertising, 1880–1940," in *Folk Roots, New Roots: Folklore in American Life*, ed. Jane Becker and Barbara Franco (Lexington, Mass., 1988), pp. 103–40.

30. M. Losey, "More Seeing, Less Selling," *Saturday Review* 31 (9 October 1948): 61–63; Stange, *Symbols of Ideal Life*, pp. 142ff.

31. Edgar Kemler, "People's Capitalism," *Nation* 182 (25 February 1956): 151.

32. Paul Hollister, "Yes I'm Tired," *Atlantic Monthly* 177 (January 1946): 133–35; "Truth Makes Us Free," *Collier's* 119 (7 June 1947): 94; O. Kleppner, "Is There Too Much Advertising?" *Harper's* 202 (February 1957): 85–91. For more of the "advertising promotes pleasure" line, see David Ogilvy, *Confessions of an Advertising Man* (New York, 1963), p. 159.

33. Neil H. Borden, "Do Ads Pay?" *Business Week*, 3 November 1951, 26; "The Thrill of Advertising," *Nation* 186 (15 February 1958): 131–32.

34. "The Largest Clinic of Advertising in the World."

35. Northrop Frye, *The Modern Century* (New York, 1967), p. 45; Kenneth Jackson, *The Crabgrass Frontier* (New York, 1985), pp. 216–17. For powerful and influential evocations of this vision, see Aldous Huxley, *Brave New World* (New York, 1931), and *Brave New World Revisited* (New York, 1956).

36. Theodor Adorno et al., *The Authoritarian Personality* (New York, 1950); John Kenneth Galbraith, *The Affluent Society* (New York, 1958), p. 16; William H. Whyte, *The Organization Man* (New York, 1956), p. 310; Jackson Lears, "A Matter of Taste: Corporate Cultural Hegemony in a Mass Consumption Society," in *Recasting America*, ed. Lary May (Chicago and London, 1989), pp. 38–57.

37. Winston White, *Beyond Conformity* (New York, 1961), pp. 137–38. On this issue, see the discussion of consumption in Elaine Tyler May, *Homeward Bound: American Families in the Cold War Era* (New York, 1988), esp. chap. 7.

38. Huxley, *Brave New World Revisited*, chaps. 5, 6.

39. Joseph Seldin, "Selling to the Id," *Nation* 180 (21 May 1955): 442–43. For the business point of view, see "What Sways the Family Shopper," *Business Week*, 30 November 1957, 46–84. On the tendency of cultural critics to ignore the diversity of postwar American society, see Lears, "A Matter of Taste."

40. Joseph J. Seldin, "Selling the Kiddies," *Nation* 181 (8 October 1955): 305. For an updated version of this argument, see Tom Engelhardt, "Children's Television: The Shortcake Strategy," in *Watching Television*, ed. Todd Gitlin, (New York, 1987), pp. 68–110.

41. "Ads You'll Never See," *Business Week*, 21 September 1957, 30–31; "Diddling the Subconscious," *Nation* 185 (5 October 1957); "Invisible Mon-

ster," *Christian Century* 74 (2 October 1957): 1157; Vance Packard, *The Hidden Persuaders* (New York, 1957); idem, "Growing Powers of Admen," *Atlantic Monthly* 200 (September 1957): 55–59; Fairfax Cone, "Advertising Is Not a Plot," ibid. 201 (January 1958): 72–73.

42. J. K. Galbraith, "The Unseemly Economics of Opulence," *Harper's* 204 (January 1952): 58–63; Martin Sydell, "Galloping Consumption: *Fortune's* Way of Life," *Nation* 181 (30 July 1955): 91–92. For a critique of Galbraith's puritanism, see Michael Schudson, "Criticizing the Critics of Advertising: Towards a Sociological View of Marketing," *Media, Culture, and Society* 3 (January 1981): 3–12.

43. Rosser Reeves, *Reality in Advertising* (New York, 1961).

44. "The Mad Madison Avenue Primer," *Mad* no. 55, quoted in Maria Reidelbach, *Completely Mad: A History of the Comic Book and Magazine* (Boston and London, 1992), p. 47.

45. Reidelbach, *Completely Mad*, pp. 47, 105.

46. Robert Brustein, "Revolution as Theater," *New Republic* 162, 14 March, 1970, 13–17.

47. On the tightening of corporate control over the media, and the consequent need to distinguish between mass culture and popular culture, see Ben H. Bagdikian, *The Media Monopoly*, 3rd ed. (Boston, 1990); Herbert I. Schiller, *Culture, Inc.* (New York, 1989); and Edward S. Herman and Noam Chomsky, *Manufacturing Consent* (New York, 1988), esp. chap. 1.

CHAPTER 9. THE PROBLEM OF
COMMERCIAL ART IN A PROTESTANT CULTURE

1. This is not meant to imply that non-Protestant cultures ignored these issues; the art world of late-nineteenth-century France was characterized by protracted tension between the ideal and the real, as described, for example, by Richard Shiff, *Cézanne and the End of Impressionism* (Chicago, 1984). I am grateful to Michele Bogart for bringing this to my attention.

2. Neil Harris, *The Artist in American Society: The Formative Years, 1780–1860* (Chicago, 1966), p. 3.

3. Two efforts to grapple with some of these issues are Scott Casper, "Politics, Art, and the Contradictions of a Market Culture: George Caleb Bingham's *Stump Speaking*," *American Art* 5 (Summer 1991): 27–48, and Jackson Lears, "Beyond Veblen: Rethinking Consumer Culture in America," in *Consuming Visions: Accumulation and Display in America, 1880–1920*, ed. Simon Bronner (New York, 1989), pp. 73–97.

4. Miles Orvell, *The Real Thing: Imitation and Authenticity in American Culture, 1880–1940* (Chapel Hill, N.C., and London, 1989), pp. 40–72; Colleen MacDannell, *The Christian Home in Victorian America* (Bloomington, Ind., 1986), esp. chap. 2.

5. Ralph Waldo Emerson, "The American Scholar" [1837] in *Selections*

from Ralph Waldo Emerson, ed. Stephen E. Whicher (Boston, 1957), p. 78.

6. Joseph J. Ellis, *After the Revolution: Profiles of Early American Culture* (New York, 1979), p. 221.

7. A. M. F. Buchanan, "The Travelling Artist," *Godey's Lady's Book* 20, January 1840, 19–24. Also see David Jaffe, "One of the Primitive Sort: Portrait Makers in the Rural North, 1760–1860," in *The Countryside in the Era of Capitalist Transformation,* ed. Steven Hahn and Jonathan Prude (Chapel Hill, N.C., and London, 1985), pp. 103–38.

8. Camilla Toulmin, "The Peddler," reprinted in Anna Cora Mowatt, "An English Authoress," *Godey's* 46 (January 1853): 127; Charles Dickens, *American Notes* [1842] (London, 1972), p. 285.

9. P. T. Barnum, *Struggles and Triumphs* [1855, 1869, 1889], 2 vols. (New York, 1927), vol. 1, pp. 96, 103–18, 193–96; James Playsted Wood, *The Story of American Advertising* (New York, 1958), pp. 149–50.

10. Frederick Marryat, *A Diary in America with Remarks on Its Institutions* [1837], ed. Sydney Jackman (New York, 1962), p. 148; Barnum, *Struggles and Triumphs,* pp. 472–74. For one among many examples of the tendency to associate museums with humbug, see Virginia De Forrest, "Mrs. Daffodil at Barnum's Museum," *Godey's* 52, June 1856, 524–27. On the struggles of museums to achieve cultural legitimacy, see Neil Harris, "Museums, Merchandising, and Popular Taste," in his *Cultural Excursions* (Chicago and London, 1990), pp. 56–81.

11. Barnum, *Struggles and Triumphs,* vol. 1, pp. 317–42; vol. 2, pp. 463, 590; Neil Harris, *Humbug: The Art of P. T. Barnum* (Chicago, 1973), pp. 192–93, 209.

12. Barnum, *Struggles and Triumphs,* vol. 1, pp. 198–99, 129.

13. Orvell, *The Real Thing,* pp. 16–29; Laura Ingalls Wilder, *The Little House on the Prairie* [1935] (New York, 1953), pp. 117–18, and *On the Banks of Plum Creek* [1937] (New York, 1953), pp. 122–23.

14. Walt Whitman, "Song of the Exposition" [1871], lines 53–59, in *Leaves of Grass,* ed. Howard W. Blodgett and Sculley Bradley (New York, 1965), p. 198; Frazar Kirkland, *Cyclopedia of Commercial and Business Anecdotes,* 2 vols. (New York, 1864), vol. 1, p. 305; Whitman, "Of the Terrible Doubt of Appearances" [1860], in *Leaves of Grass,* p. 120. For more on Packwood, see Neil McKendrick, "George Packwood and the Commercialization of Shaving," in *The Birth of a Consumer Society,* ed. McKendrick, Brewer, and Plumb, pp. 145–94.

15. Elizabeth Robins Pennell and Joseph Pennell, *Lithography and Lithographers* (London, 1915), p. 221; Mark Twain, *A Connecticut Yankee in King Arthur's Court* [1889] (New York, 1963), pp. 46–47; Orvell, *The Real Thing,* p. 38. On the spread of chromolithography, see Richard W. Flint, "Circus Posters and Show Printers," M.A. thesis, State University of New York–Oneonta, 1979; Peter Marzio, *The Democratic Art: Pictures for a Nineteenth-Century America* (Boston, 1979); and Robert Jay, *The Trade Card in Nineteenth-Century America* (Columbia, Mo., 1985).

16. [E. L. Godkin,] "Chromo-civilization," *Nation* 24 (September 1874): 201–2. On Ruskin's influence, see Roger Stein, *John Ruskin and Aesthetic Thought in America, 1840–1900* (Cambridge, Mass., 1967). The phrase "landscape of fact" is from Kenneth Clark, *Landscape into Art* (New York, 1949), p. 59.

17. For Wilde's critique of dualism, see Richard Ellmann, *Oscar Wilde* (New York, 1988), pp. 199, 24, 285; Oscar Wilde, "The Truth of Masks" [1885] and "The Decay of Lying" [1889], in *The Complete Works of Oscar Wilde*, ed. Vyvyan Holland (London, 1966). For illuminating background, see Friedrich Nietzsche, *The Gay Science* [1882], trans. Walter Kaufmann (New York, 1974), p. 38; Jacques de Langlade, *Oscar Wilde, ou, La vérité des masques* (Paris, 1987). On the aesthetic movement's creation of an anti-utilitarian countercultural sphere, see Peter Burger, *Theory of the Avant-Garde,* trans. Michael Shaw (Minneapolis, 1984), chap. 1, and Regina Gagnier, *Idylls of the Marketplace: Oscar Wilde and the Victorian Public* (Stanford, Calif., 1986), p. 6. On Wilde's reception in the United States, see, for example, trade cards for Van Vranken's candies in Confectionaries box 96, Warshaw Collection of Business Americana, National Museum of American History, Smithsonian Institution, Washington, D.C.; Lloyd Lewis and Henry Justin Smith, *Oscar Wilde Discovers America, 1882* (New York, 1936), pp. 136, 237; and especially the superb study by Mary Blanchard, "Oscar Wilde's America: The Aesthetic Movement and the Hidden Life of the Gilded Age, 1876–1893," unpublished Ph. D. diss., Rutgers University, 1994. For later American outrage, after the exposure of Wilde's homosexuality, see Thomas Beer, *The Mauve Decade* [1926] (New York, 1960), p. 89.

18. Thomas H. Pauly, "American Art and Labor: The Case of Anshutz's *The Ironworkers' Noontime,*" *American Quarterly* 40 (September 1988): 333–58; Randall C. Griffin, "Thomas Anshutz's *The Ironworkers' Noontime:* Remythologizing the Industrial Worker," *Smithsonian Studies in American Art* 4 (Summer–Fall 1990): 129–43.

19. Thomas Haskell, "Capitalism and the Origins of the Humanitarian Sensibility," *American Historical Review* 90 (June 1985): 551; Wilde, "Decay," 980.

20. Northrop Frye, *The Modern Century* (Toronto, 1967), p. 26; Michael Schudson, *Advertising, The Uneasy Persuasion: Its Dubious Impact on American Society* (New York, 1984), chap. 7. On the connection between what Frye calls "stupid realist" art and advertising, see Ronald Berman, "Origins of the Art of Advertising," *Journal of Aesthetic Education* 17 (Fall 1983): 61–69.

21. On Taine, see Rachel Bowlby, *Just Looking: Consumer Culture in Dreiser, Gissing, and Zola* (New York and London, 1985), pp. 1–6; on James, see Jennifer Wicke, *Advertising Fictions: Literature, Advertisement, and Social Reading* (New York, 1988), pp. 113–19. John Kasson, *Amusing the Million: Coney Island at the Turn of the Century* (New York, 1979), discusses the containment of carnival at Coney.

22. [Rollo Ogden,] "The Itch for Publicity," *Nation* 56 (6 April 1893): 249–50. See also Sarah Burns, "Old Maverick to Old Master," *American Art Journal* 22 (1990): 129–43, which discusses the marketing of Whistler's image.

23. "Itch for Publicity," 250.

24. Richard Lingeman, *Theodore Dreiser: At the Gates of the City, 1871–1907* (New York, 1986), pp. 44–46; Dreiser, *Dawn* (New York, 1931), pp. 107–14, quotation at 113. Dreiser said that Paul sold Hamlin's Wizard Oil; Lingeman bases his more accurate account of Paul's early career on the biographical newspaper clippings in the Evansville Library. The best literary analyses of Dreiser's enthusiasm for consumer culture are Walter Benn Michaels, "*Sister Carrie's* Popular Economy," in his *The Gold Standard and the Logic of Naturalism* (Berkeley, Calif., 1987), pp. 29–58, and James Livingston, *Pragmatism and the Political Economy of Cultural Revolution* (Chapel Hill, N.C., 1994), chap. 6.

25. Lingeman, *Gates of the City*, pp. 403–12; W. A. Swanberg, *Dreiser* (New York, 1965), pp. 109–50.

26. I use the Meridian Classic edition of *The "Genius"* (New York, 1984). Subsequent page references are noted parenthetically in the text.

27. In pondering these questions, I am indebted to the sensitive account of Michele Bogart, "Artistic Ideals and Commercial Practices: The Problem of Status for American Illustrators," *Prospects* (1990): 225–81, and to her *Artists, Advertising, and the Borders of Art* (Chicago, 1995).

28. Uprez D'Buton, "The Art of Advertising," *Art in Advertising* 5 (June 1892): 126; George Henry Smith, "The Young Adwriter," *Printers' Ink* 29 (4 October 1899): 6. "Uprez D'Buton" was a play on the Kodak slogan "You press the button, we do the rest."

29. Edith R. Gerry, "Facts: A Protest," *Printers' Ink* 24 (10 August 1898): 37–38; "Don't Tell Too Much," *Fame* 1 (October 1892): 240–41; "The Use of Poetry in Advertising," *Art in Advertising* 9 (January 1895): 405.

30. Montgomery Ward & Co., *Here, I Want It!* (Chicago, 1895), in Dry Goods box 13, Warshaw Collection. For other examples of advertising appropriation of high culture, see I. L. Cragin & Co., Philadelphia, trade card for Dobbins' Electric Soap in Warshaw Collection, Soap box 1, which parodied Jaques's "Seven Ages of Man" speech from *As You Like It*, illustrating the final "mere oblivion" with a child disappearing amid soapsuds; and N. K. Fairbank & Co. trade card for potted meat that shows a pig posing as Falstaff in Shakespeare's *Henry IV* with the caption "He lards the lean earth as he walks along," in Warshaw Collection, Foods box 5.

31. Wolstan Dixey, "Advertising and Literature," *Printers' Ink* 24 (21 September 1898): 6.

32. Will B. Wilder, "Is Advertising an Art?" *Fame* 1 (October 1892): 228–30.

33. William Dean Howells, "Bates and His Book," *Harper's Weekly*, 9 May 1896, reprinted in *Printers' Ink* 15 (20 May 1896): 18–20. For another view of the interpenetration between advertising and fiction, see "The Literature of Business," *Nation* 83 (15 November 1906): 409–10.

34. Joel Benton, "Oversmartness," *Fame* 2 (May 1894): 116; Julius Fitzgerald, "The Art of Condensing," *Printers' Ink* 15 (29 April 1896): 10–11.

35. "The Professional Beauty," *Printers' Ink* 12 (20 February 1895): 13.

36. Howells, "Bates and His Book," 20; Frederick Flagler Helmer, "Too Many Talking at Once," *Profitable Advertising* 15 (December 1905): 840–44.

37. "Making the Truth 'Sound True,'" *Printers' Ink* 90 (1 January 1915): 82–85; Cabell Trueman, "The Sincere Trend," ibid. 34 (13 March 1901): 18; Joel Benton, "Vacuous Verbosity," *Fame* 13 (November 1904), 269–70; George Powell, *Advertising Writing Taught* (New York, 1903), p. 14, in Advertising box 3, Warshaw Collection.

38. L. DeLorme, "Force, Fitness, Tact, and Nicety in Business Words," *Judicious Advertising* 5 (January 1907): 73–75; Horace Towner, "The Uses of Understatement," ibid. 15 (June 1917), 81–85. For one of many similar arguments, see Percy Waxman, "The Sound Value of Words in Advertising," *Printers' Ink* 90 (6 May 1915):, 46–48.

39. Joseph Hamlin Phinney, "A 'Cut' Argument," *Printers' Ink* 23 (15 June 1898); "The 'Picture Habit,'" ibid. 17 (30 December 1896), reprinted from *Billboard Advertising* (Cincinnati, 1896).

40. Pierre N. Beeringer, "The Advertiser and the Poster," *Overland Monthly,* 2nd series, 28 (July 1896): 47; Harry Hollingsworth, *Advertising and Selling* (New York, 1913), p. 112; Charles Paddock, "Some Notable Posters," *Printers' Ink* 20 (7 July 1897): 8. Also see L. J. Rhead, "Moral Aspects of the Artistic Poster," *Bookman* 1 (June 1895): 312–14. Max Nordan's *Degeneration* (English trans. 1895) was a bitter polemic against the alleged decadence of modern culture.

41. T. O. Marten, "What Art Has Done," *Profitable Advertising* 15 (May 1906): 1452–53, emphasis in original; Oscar Meyer, "Co-operation Between Copy and Picture," *Judicious Advertising* 7 (May 1906): 41–43.

42. James H. Collins, "The Economy of Symbolism," *Printers' Ink* 34 (20 March 1901): 2–4; Walter Benjamin, "The Work of Art in the Age of Mechanical Reproduction" [1935], in his *Illuminations,* trans. Harry Zohn (New York, 1969), pp. 217–51.

43. McCormick Agricultural Implements Advertisement, reprinted in *Printers' Ink* 28 (5 July 1899): 37; James H. Collins, "The North German Lloyd," ibid. 37 (23 October 1901): 3–5.

44. A. L. Teele, "Sympathetic Advertising," *Fame* 1 (May 1892): 84–85; Clifton S. Wady, "Advertising and Design," ibid. 13 (January 1904): 20–21; "An Agency Booklet That Stands For Vitality in Advertising," *Printers' Ink* 53 (11 October 1905): 39.

45. W. R. Emery, "The Personality of a Product," *Printers' Ink* 72 (4 August 1910): 42.

46. Newton A. Fuessle, "What Copy-writers Can Learn From Story-writers," *Printers' Ink* 92 (12 August 1915): 33–36; An Agency Copy-writer, "The Story Form of Copy," ibid., 5 August 1915, 26.

47. Ibid., 27.

48. Emery, "Personality of a Product," 42.

49. W. L. Larned, "The Smile That Sells Goods," *Printers' Ink* 77 (30 November 1911): 3–8.

50. Rhead, "Moral Aspect," 312; John Brisbane Walker, "Beauty in Advertising Illustration," *Cosmopolitan* 33 (September 1902): 491–500; "Real People and Real Work," *Printers' Ink* 57 (3 October 1906): 10–13; F. R. Feland, "A Curious Place is Adland," ibid. 90 (28 January 1915): 88–89. For an example of American advertisers' admiration for European poster work, see "The Splendid Advertising Posters of Paris," ibid. 68 (22 September 1909): 32–34.

51. Samuel Hopkins Adams, "The New World of Trade. I. The Art of Advertising," *Collier's* 43 (22 May 1909): 13–15.

52. W. Livingston Larned, "The New Era of Advertising Art—Article #4—Fanny Munsell," *Judicious Advertising* 16 (November 1918): 37–42.

53. "American Advertising Through German Spectacles," *Review of Reviews* 6 (August 1892): 93; C. M. Robinson, "Artistic Possibilities of Advertising," *Atlantic Monthly* 94 (July 1904): 53–60.

54. C. M. Robinson, "Abuses of Public Advertising," *Atlantic Monthly* 93 (March 1904): 290.

55. F. L. Olmsted, Jr., "Reform in Public Advertising," *Brush and Pencil* 6 (September 1900): 247; Arthur Reed Kimball, "The Age of Disfigurement," *Outlook* 57 (30 October 1897): 521–24; Quentin J. Schultz, "Legislating Morality: The Progressive Response to American Outdoor Advertising, 1900–1917," *Journal of Popular Culture* 17 (Spring 1984): 37–43.

56. Robinson, "Artistic Possibilities."

57. "Father of Modern Advertising," *Literary Digest* 48 (30 May 1914): 13–23; Tim Shackleton, Introduction, in *Bubbles: Early Advertising Art from A. & F. Pears, Ltd.*, ed. Mike Dempsey (London, 1978); Hires Improved Root Beer advertisement (c. 1900) in Beverages box 1, Warshaw Collection; "Advertising Art," *Fame* 13 (January 1904): 17.

58. Waldo P. Warren, "Commercial Art Opportunities," *Collier's* 42 (13 February 1909): 29–30.

59. Coy Ludwig, *Maxfield Parrish* (New York, 1973), pp. 11–12

60. Grace Glueck, "Bit of a Comeback Puzzles Parrish," *New York Times*, 3 June 1964, section 2, p. 1; Ludwig, *Parrish*, pp. 13–18.

61. Letter, Maxfield Parrish to Rusling Wood, 30 September 1915, in Maxfield Parrish Papers, Dartmouth College Library, Hanover, N.H.

62. "Maxfield Parrish Will Discard 'Girl-on-Rock' Ideas in Art," Associated Press, 27 April 1931, quoted in Ludwig, *Parrish*, p. 129.

CHAPTER 10. THE COURTSHIP OF
AVANT-GARDE AND KITSCH

1. Stephen Spender, "Moderns and Contemporaries," in his *The Struggle of the Modern* (Berkeley, Calif, 1963), pp. 71–75.

2. Ibid., p. 76.

3. For one example of this link between form and the real, see Miles Orvell's discussion of Frank Lloyd Wright and Louis Sullivan in *The Real Thing* (Chapel Hill, N.C., and London, 1989), pp. 171–80.

4. See the provocative arguments made by Susan Sontag, *Against Interpretation* (New York, 1966), pp. 3–14, and George Steiner, *Real Presences* (Chicago and London, 1990).

5. Clement Greenberg, "*Avant-garde* and *Kitsch*," *Partisan Review* 6 (Fall 1939): 34–39; José Ortega y Gasset, *The Dehumanization of Art* [1925], trans. Helene Wehl (Princeton, 1948), esp. pp. 8–14. On the gendering of this process, see chapter 11, below, and Andreas Huyssen, "Mass Culture as Woman: Modernism's Other," in his *After the Great Divide* (Bloomington, Ind., 1987), pp. 47–57.

6. Greenberg, "*Avant-garde* and *Kitsch*," p. 39. For a thoughtful example of this argument, see Thomas Crow, "Modernism and Mass Culture in the Visual Arts," in *Modernism and Modernity*, ed. Benjamin H. D. Buchloh, Serge Guilbault, and David Solkin (Halifax, Nova Scotia, 1983), pp. 215–64.

7. W. L. Larned, "The Smile That Sells Goods," *Printers' Ink,* 30 November 1911, 8; John B. Watson, "Just a Piece of Key Copy," J. Walter Thompson new business presentation (external), 1925, p. 12, JWT Archives, Duke University.

8. Michel Foucault, *This Is Not a Pipe,* trans. and ed. James Harkness (Berkeley, Calif., and London, 1983).

9. Stuart Hall, "Notes on Deconstructing 'the Popular,'" in *People's History and Socialist Theory,* ed. Raphael Samuel (London, 1980), p. 233.

10. Harold Loeb, "Foreign Exchange," *Broom* 2 (May 1922): 178. The classic statement of European enthusiasm was F. T. Marinetti, "Futurist Manifesto" [1909], trans. and ed. Reyner Banham, *Architectural Review* 126 (August–September 1959): 80.

11. Stuart Davis, *Stuart Davis* (New York, 1945), n.p.; Rudi Blesh, *Stuart Davis* (New York, 1960), p. 11.

12. Stuart Davis, entries for May 1921, 11 March 1921, in *Notebooks 1920–1922,* reel 3842, Archives of American Art, National Museum of American Art, Smithsonian Institution, Washington, D.C. See also Earl Davis, *Stuart Davis: Scapes, 1910–1923* (New York, 1991), p. 12.

13. Stuart Davis, entries for May 1921, April 1921, in *Notebooks 1920–1922;* Andy Warhol quoted in Robert Hughes, *The Shock of the New* (New York, 1980), p. 348. Davis's self-description as "urban democrat" is quoted in John R. Lane, *Stuart Davis: Art and Art Theory* (Brooklyn, N.Y., 1978), p. 130.

14. Matthew Josephson, "Made in America," *Broom* 2 (June 1922): 266–70; idem, "The Great American Billposter," ibid., November 1922, 305. Also see David Shi, *Matthew Josephson* (New Haven, Conn., and London, 1981), pp. 62–66.

15. Josephson, "Great American Billposter," 309–10.

16. Ibid., 307. Emphasis in original.

17. Edna Ferber, *Personality Plus* (New York, 1914), and *Emma McChesney & Co.* (New York, 1915). Also see "The Ad Writer in Fiction," *Printers' Ink* 71 (13 April 1910): 58.

18. Brander Matthews, "The Advertiser's Artful Aid," *Printers' Ink* 119 (11 May 1922): 108–15; David Shi, "Advertising and the American Literary Imagination in the Jazz Age," *Journal of American Culture* 2 (Summer 1979): 167–75; George Seldes, "Note on Advertising," *New Republic* 43 (8 July 1925): 180.

19. On the subversiveness of early montage, see Arthur C. Danto, "John Heartfield," *Nation* 256 (28 July 1993): 918. On the beginnings of its transformation, see Sally Stein, ""The Composite Photographic Image and the Composition of Consumer Ideology," *Art Journal* 4 (Spring 1981): 39–45.

20. Millicent Bell, *Marquand: An American Life* (Boston and Toronto, 1979), pp. 112–13.

21. E. B. White, "Urgency of an Agency," *New Republic* 66 (1 April 1931): 180–81. For signs of the growing hospitality toward aesthetic aspirations, see, for example: J. Walter Thompson house advertisement, 17 October 1918, and John T. De Vries, "Eloquence in Advertising Illustration," *JWT News Bulletin*, no. 83, February 1922, JWT Archives; A Commercial Art Manager, "Commercial Illustrations with an Uncommercial Atmosphere," *Printers' Ink* 120 (17 August 1922): 49–52; "Art's Debt to Advertising," ibid. 132 (16 July 1925): 155–56.

22. Earnest Elmo Calkins, "The Natural History of a Soul," *Atlantic Monthly*, November 1925, 625–33; Calkins to Frederick Lewis Allen, 27 September 1938, box 13, Calkins Papers, Special Collections and Archives, Knox College Library, Galesburg, Ill.

23. Calkins, "Natural History," 631–33.

24. "Calkins on Calkins," *Printers' Ink*, 24 July 1953, 48, clipping in box 8, Calkins Papers; Calkins, *"And Hearing Not—," Annals of an Ad Man* (New York, 1946), pp. 144, 160–61.

25. Calkins to Wallace B. Donham, 26 March 1926, box 8, Calkins Papers; Calkins, *"And Hearing Not—,"* pp. 215–21; idem, "Phoebe Snow," *Saturday Review of Literature*, 16 September 1950, clipping in box 8, Calkins Papers.

26. Calkins, "Kicks and Halfpence," *Printers' Ink* 66 (27 January 1909): 22–24; F. N. Kimball, "Do We Want Art, and If So, How Much?" ibid., 10 February 1909, 22–24.

27. Calkins to Calkins & Holden staff, 21 May 1911, 14 June 1911, box 4, Calkins Papers.

28. Calkins to Calkins & Holden staff, 22 August 1924, 25 September 1924, 9 February 1922, 6 March 1922, 13 August 1924, 1 July 1924, 1 July 1925, ibid.

29. Calkins to C&H staff, 29 July 1924, ibid.

30. Calkins, "Beauty the New Business Tool," *Atlantic Monthly*, August 1927,

145–56; letter, Calkins to Welles Bosworth, 8 September 1925, box 8, Calkins Papers. Calkins's *Business the Civilizer* (Boston, 1928) contains the best summary of his views.

31. Calkins to C&H office, 29 July 1924, box 4, Calkins Papers.

32. Calkins, "Beauty the New Business Tool," 153; idem, *"And Hearing Not—,"* p. 239.

33. Calkins, "The New Consumption Engineer and the Artist," in *A Philosophy of Production,* ed. J. George Frederick (New York, 1930), pp. 126–27.

34. Calkins, "Beauty the New Business Tool," 153.

35. Calkins, *Business the Civilizer,* p. 21.

36. Calkins, "Artist into Advertising Man," in *Work for Artists: What? Where? How?* ed. Elizabeth McCausland, (New York, 1947), p. 149.

37. A Commercial Art Manager, "Pictorial Magnets Which Draw the Eye to the Product," *Printers' Ink* 131 (4 June 1925): 116–20; W. Livingston Larned, "Tricky Effects Obtained with Solid Black and White," ibid. 130 (8 January 1925): 114–20, 125.

38. A Commercial Art Manager, "Futuristic Monstrosities Are All the Rage," ibid. 133 (4 June 1925): 116–20; W. Livingston Larned, "Magical Effects with Pen and Ink," ibid. 130 (26 March 1925): 33–36. See also Larned, "Putting Futurism into the Border," ibid. 139 (7 April 1927): 185–91.

39. Manuel Rosenberg, *The Art of Advertising* (New York, 1930), p. 43. See also Theodore Menten, comp., *Advertising Art in the Art Deco Style* (New York, 1975). For a thoughtful account of advertising's appropriation of modernism during the 1920s, see Roland Marchand, *Advertising the American Dream: Making Way for Modernity, 1920–1940* (Berkeley, Calif., and London, 1985), pp. 140–47, 179–86.

40. Carl Sandburg, *Steichen the Photographer* (New York, 1929), p. 12.

41. Report, Ellwood Whitney to JWT reps' meeting, 23 December 1930, JWT Archives.

42. Bertram R. Brooker, "Business Man—1961 Model," *Printers' Ink* 154 (8 January 1931): 44–46.

43. Thomas L. Masson, "Of Such Stuff Are Dreams—and Businesses—Made," ibid. 156 (16 July 1931): 76, 81–83.

44. Amos Bradbury, "How Shall We Make the Words We Need?" ibid. 131 (16 April 1925): 69–72.

45. Richard Surrey, "Shunning Shakespeare!" ibid. 133 (12 November 1925): 17–20.

46. James Walton, "Emotion and Style in Copy," in *Masters of Advertising Copy,* ed. J. George Frederick (New York, 1925), p. 106; Arthur H. Little, "Whoa, Pegasus!" *Printers' Ink* 131 (23 April 1925): 25–28. For endorsement of high literary aspirations, see, for example, Aminta Casseres, "How Important Is the *Style* of the Copy?" JWT News Bulletin, 22 July 1923, 1–4, JWT Archives; Robert H. Isbell, "Tell Us Something! Hang the Length!" *Printers' Ink* 119 (4 May 1922): 73–76.

47. S.C.M., "Are You Crazy?" *JWT Jr. Newsletter,* 12 April 1935, JWT Archives; F. Irving Fletcher, "Advertising Copy and the Writer," in *Masters,* p. 123.

48. Edward Prager, "Millions for Artwork—But Not One Cent for Copy," *Printers' Ink* 151 (3 April 1930): 84, 89; Patricia Johnston, "Edward Steichen's Advertising Photography: The Strategies of Visual Persuasion," Ph.D. dissertation, Boston University, 1988, p. 125; Michele Bogart, *Artists, Advertising, and the Borders of Art, 1890–1960* (Chicago and London, 1995), chap . 4.

49. "Art Department Efficiency," *JWT Newsletter,* 4 July 1916, 1–2, JWT Archives; JWT News Bulletin, 12 February 1917, pp. 2–3, ibid. Calkins to F. K. W. Drury, 11 January 1929, box 8, Calkins Papers; "An Art Director Speaks a Few Words on Butchering," *Printers' Ink* 154, (1 January 1931): 90–96. Gordon C. Aymar, *An Introduction to Advertising Illustration* (New York, 1929), and Guy F. Cahoon, *Commercial Art* (Dallas, 1930), encouraged the artist to merge with the organizational agenda, but still maintained that his success depended on inner feeling or "spirit."

50. Roy W. Johnson, "The Receiver's Views on Be-driveled Copy," *Printers' Ink* 119 (20 April 1922): 41–44; Arthur H. Little, "Brevity—What For?" ibid. 132 (27 August 1925): 17–20; Lea & Perrins advertisement, book 149, N. W. Ayer Collection, National Museum of American History; F. R. Feland, "Who Orders Dull Copy?" *Printers' Ink* 139 (28 April 1927): 89–93. Feland was a vice-president at the George Batten agency. For the problems of getting copy approved at N. W. Ayer, see Ralph Hower, *The History of an Advertising Agency* (Cambridge, Mass., 1939), pp. 380–81.

51. Mac Artzt, "Should Copy Writers Sign Their Copy?" *Printers' Ink* 150 (23 January 1930): 61–64.

52. John F. Arndt, "Why *Should* a Copy Writer Sign His Work?" ibid., 6 February 1930; John Hall Woods, "Glorifying the American Copy Writer," ibid., 13 February 1930, 121–24; Jim Wood, "Copy Writers Need Their Cloak of Anonymity," ibid., 20 February 1930, 44; G. W. Freeman, "Let Copy Writers Sign Their Copy? I Should Say Not!" ibid., 27 February 1930, 84, 136.

53. "They Want Realism Today," *Advertising and Selling* 23 (January 1925): 14; C. W. Garrison, "Why Fear the Critics?" *Printers' Ink* 130 (12 February 1925): 162–65; "The Essence of Advertising Is—," *JWT Newsletter,* 15 October 1927, 436.

54. Mildred Holmes, *Bunk* (New York, 1929), p. 2; Richard Surrey, "Copy Writers with the Poet's Cast of Mind," *Printers' Ink* 131 (30 April 1925): 133–39; A Commercial Art Manager, "Putting the Human Back in 'Human Interest' Illustration," ibid. 120 (10 August 1922): 73–76.

55. John Starr Hewitt, "The Copy Writer's Workbench," in *Masters,* p. 324; W. H. Heath, "Giving the Consumer Booklet a Real Literary Flavor," *Printers' Ink* 120 (10 August 1922): 146–48. On eavesdropping in bourgeois realism, see John Vernon, *Money and Fiction* (Ithaca, N.Y., and London, 1984), pp. 87, 93–96.

56. "Sketches of Paris. The Daguerrotype," *Godey's Lady's Book* 27 (October 1843): 116–19; Vachel Lindsay, *The Art of the Moving Picture* [1915, 1922] (New York, 1970), pp. 21–22; Johnston, "Steichen's Advertising Photography," p. 129; "Photos Fail to Please," *JWT Newsletter*, 15 August 1927. For the literalist argument, see Richard S. Bond, "Proving Purity Pictorially," *Advertising and Selling* 32 (May 1922): 18.

57. W. Livingston Larned, "Pathfinders in Advertising Art," *Printers' Ink* 120 (24 August 1922): 53–56.

58. Preface, *Exhibit Catalogue* (Philadelphia, 1930), quoted in *Advertising and Selling* 14 (May 1930): 94; Edward Steichen, "Ye Fakers," *Camera Work* 1 (January 1903): 48; JWT News Bulletin, 21 May 1917, JWT Archives; minutes, JWT reps' meeting, 31 May 1927, ibid.; "Look Pleasant, Peas!" *Literary Digest* 113 (2 April 1932): 35–36.

59. Minutes, JWT reps' meeting, 21 June 1927, JWT Archives; Naomi Rosenblum, "Biographical Notes," in *America and Lewis Hine: Photographs 1904–1940* (New York, 1977), p. 21; Rosenberg, *Art of Advertising*, p. 54.

60. Edward Steichen, *A Life in Photography* (New York, 1963), n.p.; transcript of Steichen interview with Wayne Miller (1954), pp. 132–226, in Archives of American Art.

61. Walker Evans, "The Reappearance of Photography," *Hound and Horn* 5 (October–December, 1931): 126–27; Edward Steichen, presentation to JWT reps' meeting, Staff Meeting Minutes, 31 January 1928, JWT Archives.

62. Johnston, "Steichen's Advertising Photography," pp. 229, 315. On the formalist modernism of straight photography, see Allan Sekula, "The Instrumental Image: Steichen at War," *Artforum* 14 (December 1975): 34.

63. Steichen, Presentation to reps' meeting, Staff Meeting Minutes, 31 January 1928.

64. George Logan Price, "Over-Smartness in Advertising Copy Cuts Down Returns From Plain People," *Printers' Ink* 153 (11 December 1930): 17–19; minutes, JWT staff meeting, 1 February 1933, JWT Archives.

65. Johnston, "Steichen's Advertising Photography," pp. 229–46. Developments in advertising paralleled those in film. For some time, film historians have been studying the shift from the "cinema of attraction," which called attention to its own artifice, to the classical Hollywood film of the 1930s and 1940s, which sought to merge viewer and cinematic narrative in a seamless web of illusion. Miriam Hansen succinctly synthesizes this literature and brilliantly reinterprets the transformation in *Babel and Babylon: Spectatorship and American Silent Film* (Cambridge, Mass., and London, 1991).

66. W. Livingston Larned, "Injecting Motion Picture Drama into the Photographic Picture," *Printers' Ink* 154 (26 February 1931): 85–88; New York Illustrators, advertisement for "Dramatized Composite Photography," ibid., 19 February 1931, 121; James Yates, report to JWT staff meeting, 5

May 1931, JWT Archives. On the sharpening economic rivalry between artists and photographers, see "Camera Art, Threat to Artists," *Business Week,* 15 June 1935, 20–21.

67. Letter, Dan Danker to Stanley Resor, in minutes of JWT reps' meeting, 21 May 1930, p. 14, JWT Archives; "Agents a la Hollywood," *Printers' Ink* 187 (25 May 1939): 11; George Faulkner in minutes of JWT group meeting, 12 August 1930, JWT Archives. See also Charles Eckert, "The Carole Lombard in Macy's Window," *Quarterly Review of Film Studies* 3 (Winter 1978): 1–21.

68. Kirk Varnedoe and Adam Gopnik, *High and Low: Modern Art and Popular Culture* (New York, 1991), pp. 158–63; John Canemaker, *Winsor McCay: His Life and Art* (New York, 1987), esp. chaps. 4–9.

69. "'Funny Papers' Campaign for General Foods," *Printers' Ink* 155 (14 May 1931): 25–26; "Funny Paper Advertisements," *Fortune* 7 (April 1933): 98–101; Sylvia Stone, "Let's Look at the Funnies," *People* magazine, May 1937, JWT Archives; "Bissell Comic Copy Shows Fun in Some Chores," *Advertising Age* 9 (10 January 1938): 4.

70. Robert Jessup, report to JWT Creative Staff meeting, 12 March 1932, JWT Archives.

71. Quaker Oats, advertisement, *Good Housekeeping* 99 (July 1934): 155.

72. Mr. Gortakowsky, report to JWT Creative Staff meeting, 23 March 1933, JWT Archives; "Sir Veigh Rides Again," *Printers' Ink* 181 (21 October 1937): 15–18.

73. David Paul Nord, "An Economic Perspective on Formula in Popular Culture," *Journal of American Culture* 3 (Spring 1980): 25. Emphasis in original.

74. James True, "What the Public Thinks About Advertising Over the Radio," *Printers' Ink* 131 (2 April 1925): 113–21; "Radio Advertising," *Fortune* 1 (December 1930): 65–69, 113; "An Appraisal of Radio Advertising Today," ibid. 6 (September 1932): 37ff; minutes, JWT reps' meeting, 16 February 1928, JWT Archives; Robert Simon to JWT Creative Staff meeting, 22 June 1932, ibid. Cf. the comment by Calvin Kuhl in minutes, JWT Creative Staff meeting, 1 December 1931: "You cannot build a radio program without considering the personality of the client and his organization." For a useful overview of this period in the history of radio, see Robert W. McChesney, *Telecommunications, Mass Media, and Democracy: The Battle for the Control of U.S. Broadcasting, 1928–1935* (New York, 1993).

75. Undated letter, Irna Phillips to Young & Rubicam, box 5, Irna Phillips Papers, Mass Media Collection, Wisconsin State Historical Society, Madison.

76. Robert Colwell in minutes, JWT reps' meeting, 8 July 1930, JWT Archives.

77. "Eye vs. Ear: Radio's Battle with the Printed Word," *Literary Digest* 123 (22 May 1937): 40–41; E. P. H. James, transcript of speech dated 22 Janu-

ary 1940, box 7, E. P. H. James Papers, Mass Media Collection, Wisconsin State Historical Society.

78. Robert Colwell, report to JWT Creative Staff meeting, 26 March 1932, JWT Archives; G. A. Nichols, "Bar Carnival Spirit (and Spirits) from Radio Shows," *Printers' Ink* 153 (6 November 1930): 41–44; "Neither Sponsors Nor Stations Hear Radio Listeners' Grumblings," *Business Week*, 10 February 1932, 18–19. See also Susan Smulyan, "And Now a Word from Our Sponsors . . . : Commercialization of American Broadcast Radio," Ph.D. dissertation, Yale University, 1985.

79. Christian Brinton, Introduction, *New Poster* (Philadelphia, 1937), n.p.

80. Neil Harris, "Designs on Demand: Art and the Modern Corporation," in *Art, Design, and the Modern Corporation,* comp. Martina Roudabush Norelli (Washington, D.C., 1985), pp. 8–30; James Sloan Allen, *The Romance of Commerce and Culture* (Chicago and London, 1983), pp. 3–77; Hower, *History of an Advertising Agency,* pp. 336ff; "Surrealism Pays," *Newsweek,* 3 January 1944, 56–58; "Fine Art in Ads," *Business Week,* 20 May 1944, 76ff; Russell Lynes, "Suitable for Framing," *Harper's* 192 (February 1946): 162–69.

81. Coiner, quoted in Johnston, "Steichen's Advertising Photography," p. 125; Bogart, *Artists,* chap. 4; "Ayer Gets a Taste of O'Keeffe," *Advertising Age,* 7 April 1986, 60; Laurie Lisle, *Portrait of an Artist: A Biography of Georgia O'Keeffe* (New York, 1982), pp. 307–9; Hower, *History of an Advertising Agency,* p. 573.

82. All of the subsequent paragraphs on Lionni are based on my interview with him in New York City, 26 July 1990.

83. Rockwell Kent, "Dictators of Art," in *Work for Artists,* ed. McCausland, pp. 65–68.

84. W. P. Paepcke, "Great Ideas Campaign," undated clipping in scrapbook 10C, Bella C. Landauer Collection, New-York Historical Society; Allen, *Romance,* pp. 78–109.

85. Walter Paepcke, " 'Great Ideas' Recall Our Heritage, Help Build Container," *Industrial Marketing,* January 1955, 86.

86. Varnedoe and Gopnik, *High and Low,* pp. 314–25, 344.

87. Interviews with Hilary Lipsitz, Alan Pottasch, John Corbani, Ed Vorkapich, Pepsi Generation Oral History Project, National Museum of American History. The project was funded in part by Pepsico. Interviews were conducted by the historian Scott Ellsworth, who spoke to a variety of Pepsi and BBDO executives as well as independent artists involved with the campaign. Tapes are on file at the Archives Center, NMAH.

88. Interview, Ed Vorkapich, Pepsi Generation Oral History Project.

89. Interview with Hilary Lipsitz, Pepsi Generation Oral History Project.

90. Perhaps a parallel aesthetic legitimation of advertising was beginning in the world of literary criticism, with the publication of Leo Spitzer's "American Advertising Explained as Popular Art," in his *Essays on English and American Literature* (Princeton, N.J., 1962), pp. 248–77.

CHAPTER 11. THE PURSUIT OF THE REAL

1. Josephine Herbst, "A Year of Disgrace," *Noble Savage* 3 (Spring 1961): 150.
2. See John Murray Cuddihy, *The Ordeal of Civility* (New York, 1976); Daniel Bell, *The Cultural Contradictions of Capitalism* (New York, 1973), chap. 1.
3. Lionel Trilling, "On the Teaching of Modern Literature" [1962], in his *Beyond Culture* (New York, 1965), p. 30.
4. Theodor Adorno, "Gold Assay," in his *Minima Moralia: Reflections from Damaged Life* [1951], trans. E. P. H. Jephcott (London, 1974), pp. 152–55.
5. Sherwood Anderson, *Winesburg, Ohio* [1919] (New York, 1960), dedication page; Camel cigarettes advertisement (1919), book 83, N. W. Ayer Collection, National Museum of American History, Smithsonian Institution, Washington, D. C. The most effective example of this argument is Christopher Lasch, *The Culture of Narcissism* (New York, 1978).
6. Marianna Torgovnick, *Gone Primitive: Savage Intellects, Modern Lives* (Chicago, 1990); Michael Leja, *Reframing Abstract Expressionism: Subjectivity and Painting in the 1940s* (New Haven, Conn., 1993).
7. Andreas Huyssen, "Mass Culture as Woman: Modernism's Other," in his *After the Great Divide* (Bloomington, Ind., 1987), pp. 47, 52–53, 57.
8. Herbert Marcuse, *The Aesthetic Dimension* (Boston, 1978), pp. 9, 29, 65, 73; Peter Fuller, *Aesthetics After Modernism* (London, 1983), pp. 16–17.
9. David A. Hollinger, "The Knower and the Artificer," in *Modernist Culture in America,* ed. Daniel Singal (Belmont, Calif., 1991), pp. 50–51.
10. Norman Silber, *Test and Protest: A History of Consumer Research* (New York, 1983), esp. chap. 1; Lionel Trilling, "Sincerity and Authenticity: A Symposium," in *The Salmagundi Reader,* ed. Robert Boyers (Bloomington, Ind., 1981), pp. 48–50.
11. Trilling, "Sincerity," p. 50.
12. H. G. Wells, *Tono-Bungay* [1908], 2nd ed. (London, 1911); I use the Macmillan text. Page references cited parenthetically in text.
13. I have discussed these tendencies in *No Place of Grace: Antimodernism and the Transformation of American Culture, 1880–1920,* 2nd ed. (Chicago and London, 1994).
14. Walter Lippmann, *A Preface to Politics* [1913] (Ann Arbor, Mich., 1962), p. 13.
15. Mark Schorer, *Sinclair Lewis: An American Life* (New York, 1961), pp. 198–201.
16. I use the New American Library Signet Classic edition (New York, 1961). Page references in text.
17. Roger Burlingame, *I Have Known Many Worlds* (New York, 1959), pp. 87–88; "Roger Burlingame, Writer, Dies; a Biographer and Historian," *New York Times,* 20 March 1967, 31.

18. Roger Burlingame, *You Too* (New York, 1924). Subsequent page references in text.

19. For the creation of this child-world in the department stores, see William Leach, *Land of Desire: Merchants, Money, and the Rise of a New American Culture, 1890–1930* (New York, 1993) esp. pp. 95–101.

20. The classic discussion of inner- and other-direction is in David Riesman, with Nathan Glazer and Reuel Denney, *The Lonely Crowd* (New Haven, Conn., 1950). Jean-Christophe Agnew, *Worlds Apart: Market and Theater in Anglo-American Thought* (New York, 1986), explores the origins of the dialectic between theatrical and antitheatrical impulses in early market culture—which became, in my view, the dialectic between inner- and other-direction.

21. W. E. Woodward, *The Gift of Life: An Autobiography* (New York, 1947), pp. 172–75; "W. E. Woodward, Biographer, Dies," *New York Times*, 30 September 1947, 27.

22. Woodward, *Gift of Life*, p. 184.

23. Woodward, *Bunk* (New York, 1923), p. 158.

24. Woodward, *Bread and Circuses* (New York, 1925), p. 161 and unpaginated foreword.

25. Malcolm Cowley, "Portrait by Leyendecker," *Broom* 4 (March 1923): 240–47.

26. Hart Crane to Gorham Munson, 16 May 1922, in *The Letters of Hart Crane*, ed. Brom Weber (Berkeley, Calif., 1965), pp. 86–87.

27. Ray Lewis White, ed., *Sherwood Anderson's Memoirs: A Critical Edition* (Chapel Hill, N.C., 1969), p. 414. I have discussed Anderson more fully in "Sherwood Anderson: Looking for the White Spot," in *The Power of Culture*, ed. Richard Wightman Fox and T. J. Jackson Lears, pp. 13–37.

28. Sherwood Anderson, *A Story Teller's Story* [1924] (Cleveland, 1968), p. 236; *Memoirs*, p. 289.

29. Sherwood Anderson, *Beyond Desire* (New York, 1932), pp. 314, 164–65.

30. Matthew Josephson, "The Consumer Consumed," review of J. B. Matthews and R. E. Shallcross, *Partners in Plunder, New Masses* 14 (12 March 1935): 22–23.

31. Thomas Hart Benton, *An Artist in America*, 3rd ed. (Columbia, Mo., 1968), pp. 294–96.

32. "Business and Art, as Tom Benton Sees It," *New York PM*, 24 December 1945, reel D–255, Associated American Artists Papers, Archives of American Art, National Museum of American Art, Washington, D.C. See also Erika Doss, "The Art of Cultural Politics: From Regionalism to Abstract Expressionism," in *Recasting America*, ed. Lary May (Chicago, 1989), pp. 195–220.

33. Lionel Trilling, "Reality in America" [1940], in his *The Liberal Imagination* (New York, 1950), pp. 1–27. The most incisive account of the *Partisan Review* group remains James Gilbert, *Writers and Partisans*, 2nd ed. (New York, 1992).

34. D. H. Lawrence, *Studies in Classic American Literature* [1923] (New York, 1971), p. 67.

35. Robert Warshow, "The Gangster as a Tragic Hero," *Partisan Review* 15, February 1948, 240–44.

36. "Surrealism Pays," *Newsweek*, 3 January 1944, 57–58; David Sylvester, *Magritte: The Silence of the World* (New York, 1992); Suzi Gablik, *Magritte* (New York, 1985), esp. chaps. 1, 8, 9; Michel Foucault, *This Is Not a Pipe*, trans. and ed. James Harkness (Berkeley, Calif., 1983); Georges Roque, *Ceci n'est pas un Magritte: Essai sur Magritte et la publicité* (Paris, 1983). For the dependence of advertising strategies on dominant cultural conventions, see Judith Williamson, *Decoding Advertisements* (London, 1975).

37. Quoted in Irving Sandler, *The Triumph of American Painting* (New York, 1970), p. 185.

38. Adolph Gottlieb and Mark Rothko, letter, *New York Times*, 13 June 1943, sec. 2, p. 9; Tom Wolfe, *The Painted Word* (New York, 1975); Clement Greenberg, "Art," *Nation* 165 (6 December 1947): 630; Goldwater, "Art and Criticism," *Partisan Review* 28 (May–June 1961): 693–94.

39. Stuart Davis, "Arshile Gorky in the 1930s: A Personal Recollection," *Magazine of Art* 44 (February 1951): 58; Sandler, *Triumph*, p. 8; John R. Lane, *Stuart Davis: Art and Art Theory* (New York, 1968), p. 68. For more recent critiques that characterize Abstract Expressionism as a withdrawal from the social to the personal, see Serge Guilbault, *How New York Stole the Idea of Modern Art*, trans. Arthur Goldhammer (Chicago, 1983), and Leja, *Reframing Abstract Expressionism*.

40. Adolph Gottlieb, quoted in Sandler, *Triumph*, p. 64; Leja, *Reframing Abstract Expressionism*, chap. 4.

41. Meyer Schapiro, "Recent Abstract Painting" [1957], in *Modern Art, 19th and 20th Centuries: Selected Papers* (New York, 1978), 213–26.

42. Guilbault, *How New York Stole the Idea of Modern Art*.

43. Barnett Newman, "The Sublime Is Now" [1948], reprinted in *Barnett Newman: Selected Writings and Interviews*, ed. John P. O'Neill (New York, 1973), pp. 170–73; John Fischer, "Portrait of the Artist as an Angry Man," *Harper's* 241 (July 1970): 23.

44. I have discussed this transformation in "A Matter of Taste: Corporate Cultural Hegemony in a Mass Consumption Society," in *Recasting America*, ed. Lary May (Chicago, 1988), pp. 38–57.

45. Frederic Wakeman, *The Hucksters* (New York: 1946). Subsequent page references in text.

46. I use the Penguin Books edition (New York, 1985). Subsequent page references are in text. For invaluable background, see Steven Moore, *A Reader's Guide to William Gaddis's "The Recognitions"* (Lincoln, Nebr., 1982); for thoughtful interpretations, see John Kuehl and Steven Moore, eds., *In Recognition of William Gaddis* (Syracuse, N.Y., 1984), and Dominic LaCapra, "Singed Phoenix and Gift of Tongues," in his *History, Politics, and the Novel* (Ithaca, N.Y., 1987), pp. 175–202.

47. Kuehl and Moore, eds., *In Recognition*, pp. 5–7.
48. Hannah Arendt, *The Human Condition* (Chicago, 1958); I discuss this work in the Introduction.
49. William Gaddis, "Stop Player. Joke No. 4," *Harper's* [1950], reprinted in Moore, *A Reader's Guide*, p. 299.
50. I use the Vintage Contemporaries edition (New York, 1988). Subsequent page references in text.
51. William Butler Yeats, "The Circus Animals' Desertion" [1939], lines 39–40.

CHAPTER 12. THE THINGS THEMSELVES

1. On this point, see Lionel Trilling, "The Fate of Pleasure," in his *Beyond Culture* (New York, 1965), pp. 57–89.
2. For a sampling of this literature, see David Harper, *Working Knowledge: Skill and Community in a Small Shop* (Chicago, 1987); John Forrest, *Lord I'm Coming Home: Everyday Aesthetics in Tidewater North Carolina* (Ithaca, N.Y., 1988); Judith McWillie, "Writing in an Unknown Tongue," in *Cultural Perspectives on the American South*, ed. Charles Reagan Wilson, vol. 5 (New York, 1991), pp. 103–18; Mihaly Csikszentmihalyi and David Rochberg-Halton, *The Meaning of Things: Domestic Symbols and the Self* (Chicago, 1981); Victor Turner, *The Forest of Symbols* (Chicago, 1967); Claude Lévi-Strauss, *The Savage Mind* (Chicago, 1966); Evelyn Fox Keller, *A Feeling for the Organism: The Life and Work of Barbara McClintock* (San Francisco, 1983), esp. chaps. 9, 12; David Freedberg, *The Power of Images: Studies in the History and Theory of Response* (Chicago, 1989).
3. Richard Bowland Kimball, "Keeping the House Alive," *House Beautiful* 47 (May 1920): 404.
4. Esther Matson, "The Tyranny of Things," *House Beautiful* 36 (September 1914): 113; Oliver Coleman, "The Bric-a-Brac Habit," ibid. 16 (October 1904): 23; Katherine W. Hand, "Nerves and Decoration," ibid. 37 (May 1915); Russell Lynes, *The Tastemakers* (New York, 1972), pp. 242–53.
5. Clara H. Zilleson, "The Housewife—Purchasing Agent and Manager," *House Beautiful* 47 (May 1920): 422; National Home Furnishings Program advertisement, *Good Housekeeping* 89 (April 1930): 175; Sealex Linoleum Floors advertisement, *Saturday Evening Post* 203 (18 September 1930): 58.
6. A. Sandier, "The Dining-Room Silverware," *Decorator and Furnisher* 19 (October 1891): 22–25; Claude Bragdon, "The Architecture of the Home, Some Fundamental Principles," *House Beautiful* 16 (June 1904): 10; Edward Stratton Holloway, "Putting Individuality into the American Home," ibid. 47 (May 1920): 17.
7. Emily Post, *The Personality of a House* (New York, 1930), p. 4.
8. For illuminating background on this process, see *The Invention of Tradi-*

tion, ed. Eric Hobsbawm and Terence Ranger (Cambridge, England, 1982), esp. chaps. 1 and 7.

9. Kenneth Grosbeck, "When Advertising Returns to the Simple Life," *Printers' Ink* 158 (14 January 1932): 3–6, 112–13; G. B. Larrabee, "Grandma Jones, Buyer," ibid. 167 (3 May 1934): 29–36; Hurff's Soup advertisement, *Life,* 1936; John J. McCarthy, "Back to Homespun," *Printers' Ink* 158 (31 March 1932): 17–21; "Advertising Looks Backward," *Fortune* 13 (January 1936): 6.

10. I have discussed these developments more fully in "Packaging the Folk: Tradition and Amnesia in American Advertising, 1880–1940," in *Folk Roots, New Roots: Folklore in American Life,* ed. Jane Becker and Barbara Franco (Lexington, Mass., 1988), pp. 103–40.

11. Mennen Company advertisement, *Good Housekeeping* 71 (July–August, 1920): 114. On these trademarks and their history, see Hal Morgan, *Symbols of America* (New York, 1986), pp. 7, 55, 126.

12. For one such assertion, see "Memories" in May Hosiery Co., *The Story of Hosiery* (Burlington, N.C., 1932), n.p., in Warshaw Collection of Business Americana, National Museum of American History.

13. On Tench Coxe, see John Kasson, *Civilizing the Machine: Technology and Republican Values in America, 1776–1900* (New York, 1977), pp. 28–32. Paul Gaston discusses Henry Grady in *The New South Creed* (New York, 1970).

14. Henri Lefebvre, *Everyday Life in the Modern World* (New York, 1971), p. 82.

15. Johan Huizinga, *Homo Ludens: A Study of the Play Element in Culture* [1938] (New York, 1955), p. 141. For more finely calibrated uses of the play concept, see Roger Caillois, *Man, Play, and Games,* trans. Meyer Barash (Glencoe, Ill., 1961), esp. pp. 12–13, 32–41, 50–55, 74–77, 86–87, 96–97, 106–107, 129–47, and Clifford Geertz, "Deep Play: Notes on the Balinese Cockfight," in his *The Interpretation of Cultures* (New York, 1973).

16. I use the Houghton Mifflin Riverside Press edition (Boston, 1963). Page references are placed parenthetically in the text.

17. I use the Signet Classic edition (New York, 1960). Page references are placed parenthetically in the text.

18. See the probing discussion by Jean-Christophe Agnew, "The Consuming Vision of Henry James," in *The Culture of Consumption,* ed. Richard Wightman Fox and T. J. Jackson Lears (New York, 1983), esp. pp. 91–100.

19. Edith Wharton, *A Backward Glance* [1934] (New York, 1962), p. 57.

20. Edith Wharton, *The House of Mirth* (New York, 1905), pp. 14, 49, 77.

21. Wharton, *The Custom of the Country* (New York, 1913). Page references are placed parenthetically in the text.

22. Walter Benjamin, "Unpacking My Library" [1931], in his *Illuminations,* trans. Harry Zohn (New York, 1968), p. 60.

23. Marcel Proust, *Remembrance of Things Past* [1913–27], 3 vols., trans.

C. K. Scott-Moncrieff and Terence Kilmartin (New York, 1981), vol. 1, pp. 5–6. The original reads:

quand je m'éveillais au milieu de la nuit, comme j'ignorais où je me trouvais, je ne savais meme pas au premier instant qui j'etais; j'avais seulement dans sa simplicité première le sentiment d'existence comme il peut frémir au fond d'un animal; j'etais plus dénue que l'homme des cavernes; mais alors le souvenir–non encore du lieu où j'etais, mais de quelques-uns de ceux que j'avais habité et où j'aurais pu être—venait à moi comme un secours d'en haut pour me tirer du néant d'où je n'aurais pu sortir tout seul; je passais en une seconde par-dessus des siècles de civilisation, et l'image confusement entrevue de lampes à petrole, puis de chemises à col rabattu, recomposaient peu à peu les traits originaux de mon moi (A la recherche du temps perdu [Paris, 1954], pp. 5–6).

24. Ibid., pp. 6–9. A la recherche, pp. 6–8.
25. Gaston Bachelard, The Poetics of Space [1958], trans. Maria Jolas (Boston, 1964), p. 9; Roger Shattuck, Marcel Proust (Princeton, N.J., 1982), p. 111.
26. I draw the subhead of this next section from Arthur Danto, The Transfiguration of the Commonplace: A Philosophy of Art (Cambridge, Mass., 1969). Unfortunately, the book is too preoccupied with unpacking categories derived from analytical philosophy to be of much use to me, apart from its excellent title.
27. Rilke to Witold von Hulewicz, 13 November 1925, in Duino Elegies, trans. J. B. Leishman and Stephen Spender (New York, 1963), p. 129. The original reads as follows:

Noch für Grosseltern war ein "Haus," ein "Brunnen," ein ihnen vertrauter Turm, ja ihr eigenes Kleid, ihr Mantel: unendlich mehr, unendlich vertraulicher; fast jedes Ding ein Gefäss, in dem sie Menschliches vorfanden und Menschliches hinzusparten. Nun drängen, von Amerika her, leere gleichgültige Dinge herüber, Schein-Dinge, Lebens-Attrappen . . . Ein Haus, im amerikanischen Verstande, ein amerikanischer Apfel oder eine dortige Rebe, hat nichts gemeinsam mit dem Haus, der Frucht, der Traube, in die Hoffnung und Nachdenklichkleit unserer Vorväter eingegangen war . . . Die belebten, die erlebten, die uns mitwissenden Dinge gehen zur Neige und können nicht mehr ersetzt werden. Wir sind vielleicht die Letzten, die noch solche Dinge gekannt haben. Auf uns ruht die Verantwortung, nicht allein ihr Andenken zu erhalten (das wäre wenig und unzuverlässig), sondern ihren humanen und larischen Wert. ("Larisch," im Sinne der Haus Gottheiten.) (Briefe, 2 vols. [Wiesbaden, 1950], vol. 2, p. 483).

28. Ibid., p. 128.

Ja, denn unsere Aufgabe ist es, diese vorläufige, hinfällige Erde uns so tief, so leidend und leidenschaftlich einzupragen, dass ihr Wesen in uns "unsichtbar" wieder aufersteht. . . . Die "Elegien" zeigen uns an diesem Werke, am Werke

dieser fortwahrenden Umsetzungen des geliebten Sichtbaren und Greif-
baren in die unsichtbare Schwingung und Erregtheit unserer Natur, die neue
Schwingungszahlen einführt in die Schwingungs–Sphären des Universums
(*Briefe,* vol. 2, p. 482).

29. Ibid. "Die Natur, die Dinge unseres Umgangs und Gebrauchs, sind Vor-
läufigkeiten und Hinfälligkeiten; aber sie sind, solang wir hier sind, unser
Besitz und unsere Freundschaft, Mitwisser unserer Not und Froheit, wie
sie schon die Vertrauten unserer Vorfahren gewesen sind" (*Briefe,* ibid.).

30. Rilke to Benvenuta, 20 February 1914, quoted in Bachelard, *Poetics of
Space,* p. 70. The German original is in Rainer Maria Rilke, *Briefwechsel
mit Benvenuta* (Esslingen, 1954), pp. 136–37.

31. W. C. Williams, "Paterson" [1927], Book I, line 15, in *Collected Poems of
William Carlos Williams,* 2 vols. (New York, 1986), vol. 1, p. 263; Louis
Aragon, *Nightwalker* [1926], trans. Frederick Brown (Englewood Cliffs,
N.J., 1970), pp. 93–94, 41.

32. Aragon, *Nightwalker,* p. 10.

33. Walter Benjamin, "Surrealism," in his *Reflections,* trans. Edmund Jephcott (New York, 1979), pp. 179, 181–82.

34. Susan Sontag, "Notes on 'Camp,'" in her *Against Interpretation* (New
York, 1966), pp. 275–92.

35. Arthur Danto, "Kurt Schwitters," *Nation* 241 (3/10 August 1985): 89–91;
Bachelard, *Poetics of Space,* p. 142.

36. Dr. Julius Klein, "It's Great to Be a Young Man Today," *American* 109,
February 1930, 12–13.

37. Joseph Cornell, "The Crystal Cage (Portrait of Berenice)," *View,* series 2,
no. 4 (January 1943): 15–18.

38. Undated diary entry, reel 1059, Joseph Cornell Collection, Archives of
American Art, National Museum of American Art, Smithsonian Institution, Washington D.C..

39. Dore Ashton, "Joseph Cornell," in *A Joseph Cornell Album* (New York,
1974), p. 1.

40. Cornell diary, 9 January 1950, reel 1059.

41. Lynda Roscoe Hartigan, "Joseph Cornell: A Biography," in *Joseph Cornell,* ed. Kynaston McShine (New York, 1981), pp. 91–118.

42. Cornell diary, 26 January 1954, reel 1059.

43. Hartigan, "Biography," p. 95.

44. Cornell diary, 1 January 1955, reel 1059. One exception to the neglect of
Cornell's Christian Science is Sandra L. Starr, *Joseph Cornell: Art and
Metaphysics* (New York, 1982), but the interpretation tends to be more
systematically doctrinal than is warranted.

45. Cornell diary, 10 July 1948, reel 1059. For discussion of this romantic
Protestant tradition, see Sydney Ahlstrom, *A Religious History of the
American People* (New Haven, Conn., 1973), chaps. 19, 36, 37.

46. Hartigan, "Biography," p. 104; Cornell diary, 2 July 1949, 19 April 1954,
reel 1059; 1 October 1956, reel 1315.

47. Cornell diary, 7 November 1953, 28 November 1954, reel 1059. For a similar epiphany on the El, see William Dean Howells, *A Hazard of New Fortunes* (New York, 1890), chap. 2.

48. Cornell diary, 25 September 1954, 8 April 1953, reel 1059.

49. Ibid., late October 1948, 31 October 1947, 22 June 1954, 16 December 1954.

50. Ibid., 22 December 1954, 20 November 1953, 4 February 1954.

51. Ibid., 1 September 1953.

52. Ibid., 28 May 1955.

53. Ibid., 3 June 1947, 10 July 1948, 21 August 1953.

54. Ibid., 27 May 1953, 3 September 1949. Mysterious, at least, to researchers. Sheremietzew's identity remains unknown, even to such knowledgeable Cornell scholars as Lynda Hartigan, head of the Joseph Cornell Study Center at the National Museum of American Art. Hartigan speculates that Sheremietzew may have been one of the European correspondents Cornell discovered through relief agencies, and whom he helped during and after World War II with gifts of food and clothing.

55. Ibid., 28 October 1954, c. 17 February 1953.

56. Huizinga, *Homo Ludens,* p. 119.

INDEX

Abstract Expressionism, 362–67, 369, 371
Abundance theme: advertising in promotion of, 19; carnival and, 22–24; Cartesian dualism and imagery in, 19, 32; cultural traditions including imagery of, 17–19; dematerialization of desire and, 127–28; devaluation of female authority in, 118–20; female icons used in, 102–9, 111–13; ideology of national progress and, 109; Indian princess imagery in, 36, 104–5; Land of Cockaigne and, 22; managerial ideologies and idiom of, 113–26; market fairs and, 24–25; material progress and, 33–35; members of subordinate castes and imagery in, 123–24; New World and traditional language of, 36–37; Orientalism and, 63; Paradise theme and, 27–28; pastiche used to present, 104–7; Patten's vision of, 113–17; Protestant Ethic and, 48–51; psychic terms for, 49; rationalism of, 38–39; rationalization of symbols of, 109–13; recasting traditional symbols of, 102; sanitized images of, in twentieth century, 117–18; utopian fantasies of,

128–29; vision of preindustrial life used for, 102–3
Adam, Adolphe, 410
Adams, Henry, 6, 180, 412
Adams, Samuel Hopkins, 156–57, 203, 293
Addams, Jane, 114
Adler, Alfred, 189
Adler, Mortimer, 340
Adorno, Theodor, 6, 127, 242, 252, 347, 348
Advertising agencies: autonomy of artists and agenda of, 320–21; business relationships with, 91–92; contracts used by, 93–94; economic growth and moral progress and, 160–61, 205–6, 318–19; first appearance of, 88–89; language of professionalism and, 89, 113; magic in language used by, 97–99; patent medicine advertising and, 89–90, 139, 155–57, 161; Protestant culture common to, 111, 139–40, 154–55, 161, 329–30; quest for legitimacy by, 89, 155; rates charged by, 92; symbolism of abundance recast by, 110–13; talented people attracted to, 261–62

Advertising agents and executives: as agents of progress, 205–6; biographical notes on two early examples of, 90–94; control of consumer by, 206–7; distance between consumers and, 196–97, 209–10, 233; guessing what the consumer wants by, 211–12; as new-model professional, 89–90; privileged position of, 196–97; self-justification by, 197–98; social and personal conflicts experienced by, 139–40

Advertising Council, 248, 249, 251

Advertising Federation of America, 243

Aestheticism, 270–71, 280, 310–11

Aging, and preoccupation with youth, 168–69

Agnew, Jean-Christophe, 54

Agriculture: faith in technology and, 114; female icons of abundance based in, 102, 106–9; managerial approach to abundance and, 120–22

Alcohol, and patent medicines, 156–57, 181

Alsop, George, 29–30

Ambassadors, The (James), 387, 390–93

America, allegorical representations of, 28–29, 104–5

American Artists Congress, 305

American Lightning Rod Company, 81–82

American Magazine, The, 175, 207, 250

American Telephone & Telegraph (AT&T), 120, 338, 340

American Tobacco Company, 360

American Way of Life theme, 124, 125, 235, 246, 251

Andersen, Hans Christian, 410

Anderson, Sherwood, 346, 358–59, 371

Anglo-Saxon culture, 85–87, 111, 154, 163, 166, 169, 205, 221, 384

Animals, in advertisements, 145–46

Animism, 19, 20, 21–26; attitudes toward advertising and, 8–9; Christian tradition and, 21–22; market-place and, 24–25; symbolic consciousness of, 21

Anshutz, Thomas, 270–71

Antheil, George, 345

Anthropology, 1, 6

Anthropometry, 140

Anti-Semitism, 86, 205

Appel, Joseph, 205, 227

Aragon, Louis, 400–401

Arendt, Hannah, 7–8, 386

Armory Show, 336

Arnold, Thurman, 242

Art, 261–98; Abstract Expressionism and, 362–67; aesthetics and, 263–72; avant-garde movement and, 300–301, 302–303, 336–37, 345–46; Ayer's use of, 337, 338–339; Barnum and, 265–67; chromolithograhpic reproductions of, 268–69, 295; core of meaning in, 262; language related to, 287–88; machine civilization and, 303–8; marketplace and, 264, 265; modernism and, 312–22; organizational agenda of agency and autonomy in, 320–21; outdoor advertising and, 294–95; Parrish's influence on, 296–98; popular aesthetics and, 263–72; posters and, 292–93, 303; Protestant distrust of visual display and, 262, 269; realism during the period 1890–1915 in, 282–98; real life and, 272–82, 302, 322–36; scenes of everyday life in, 271–72; surrealism in, 363–64; vitalist cult of experience in, 272–73

Arthur, Timothy Shay, 76

Art in Advertising (magazine), 204, 283

Artistic creation, and play, 7–8

Arts and Crafts movement, 122

Artzt, Mac, 321, 322

Ashcan School, 272, 304

Ashton, Dore, 404

Associated Advertising Clubs of America, 204

Astrology, 45

Atkinson, Edward, 171, 172
Atlantic Monthly, 201, 255
Aunt Jemima (advertising character), 124, 384
Autointoxication, 166
Automobile advertising, 212–13, 214
Avant-garde art, 300–301, 302–303, 336–37, 345–46
Ayer & Sons. *See* N. W. Ayer & Sons
Ayers, Francis Wayland, 90, 93–94, 97, 154

Bachelard, Gaston, 397, 400
Bacon, Francis, 32–33, 114
Baillie, Hugh, 180
Bakhtin, Mikhail, 23–24, 39, 43
Ballyhoo (magazine), 194, 240
Banta, Martha, 120
Barlow, Arthur, 26
Barnes, William, 181
Barnum, P. T. (Phineas Taylor), 39, 54, 63, 263, 294; background and life of, 265–67; connection between advertising and, 213–15, 226–27; exotic estate of, 51, 52; stereotypes of Native Americans and, 86–87
Barnum & Bailey, 269, 273
Barrow, Isaac, 47
Barthes, Roland, 101
Barton, Bruce, 178, 224, 227–28, 237, 319
Bataille, Georges, 6
Bates, Charles Austin, 199, 210, 284, 285, 309
Batten, H. A., 240, 248
Batten, Barton, Durstine, and Osborn (BBDO), 342–43
Baudrillard, Jean, 6, 7
Bauhaus, 337
Beardsley, Aubrey, 281, 287, 295
Beauty, ideals of, 10, 285
Beecher, Henry Ward, 84–85, 143
Bellamy, Edward, 88, 197, 219
Benjamin, Walter, 128, 289, 395, 401

Bennett, Arnold, 299
Benton, Joel, 208, 216
Benton, Thomas Hart, 360–61
Berdyaev, Nikolas, 413
Bernard, John, 66–66
Bernays, Edward, 188, 224
Betty Crocker (advertising character), 384
Billboards, 294–95
Body: advertising references to, 176–77; cultural meaning of advertising's emphasis on, 152–53; emphasis on slimness of, 167–68; fascination with corsets and, 151–52; medicalization of, 173; revulsion against biological processes and, 171–73; scientific view of, 140
Bogart, Michele, 337
Bok, Edward, 156
Bonheur, Rosa, 271
Book-of-the-Month Club, 254
Borden, Neil, 251
Borsodi, Ralph, 242
Boulton, Matthew, 24
Bourgeois culture, 75–76, 83, 87, 100, 104, 113, 164, 246, 269, 285, 346
Bourke-White, Margaret, 327
Bradbury, Amos, 319
Bradford, William, 33–34, 36
Breton, André, 401
Brinton, Christian, 336
Broom (magazine), 357, 358
Brown, Charles Brockden, 332
Brustein, Robert, 258
Buckley, Kerry, 192
Bunyan, John, 35
Burke, Peter, 22
Burlingame, Roger, 353–55
Bushnell, Horace, 190
Butler, Jon, 57
Byrd, William, 37

Calkins, Earnest Elmo, 200, 204, 308–14, 316, 320, 326, 340

Calkins & Holden, 309, 312
Call, Annie Payson, 178–79, 183, 222
Calvinism, 46, 47, 50, 53, 99, 153, 262
Camel cigarettes, 182–83, 346
Cameron, William J., 238
Campbell, Colin, 46–47
Campbell, Richard, 54
Campbell's Soup, 173
Cano, Alonso, 21
Capitalism, 5, 6, 35–36, 128–29, 251,
    272, 298, 379–80
Capra, Frank, 383
Carnegie, Dale, 188
Carnival, 33, 50; imagery of abundance
    in, 17, 22–24, 37, 117–18; signifi-
    cance to advertising of, 10–11
Carnivalesque theme: advertisers and
    professionalism and, 197; Barnum's
    connection with advertising and,
    213–15; counterculture of 1960s
    and, 236, 258; Depression and
    revival of tactics with, 238–39; radio
    advertising and, 233; television
    advertising and, 256; tension
    between managerial professionalism
    and, 218
Cartesian dualism, 8, 19, 32, 81–82,
    153, 174, 177, 206–7, 263
Cartoons, 330–31
Cassandre, 337
Catalogs, 107, 108
Catholicism, 8, 24, 25
Cendrars, Blaise, 303–4
Cerrito, Fanny, 410
Chase, Stuart, 3, 240–42, 255, 256
Cherington, Paul, 324
Children: advice on rearing of, 189–91;
    television advertising and, 254, 256
Christian tradition: animistic tenden-
    cies in, 21–22; belief in Eden in,
    26–27; imagery of abundance in, 17,
    34–35; imperial primitivism theme
    and, 147; mind-body dualism in,
    177–78; modernism and, 347

Christmas, 22
Chromolithography, 54–55, 102–7, 154,
    263, 268–69, 295
Cigarette advertising, 181–83, 191, 346,
    347
Civil War, 55, 102, 107, 200
Clarke, René, 312
Cleanliness, 163–65, 173
Cleland, John, 65
Cleveland Lightning Rod Company, 81
Coca-Cola, 158, 159, 222, 248–49, 302,
    342
Cockaigne, Land of, 22, 26
Coiner, Charles, 243, 320, 325, 337,
    338, 339
Cold War, 251
Coleman, Glenn, 304
Coleridge, Samuel Taylor, 264
Collecting, 7
Collier's (magazine), 201, 202, 203,
    206, 228–29, 295
Collins, James, 201, 205, 209, 210, 289
Colonization, 26, 29–31
Columbus, Christopher, 27–28
Colwell, William, 243
Comic strips, 237, 330–32
Comic Weekly, 330, 333
Committee on Public Information, 219
Comstock, Anthony, 144
Cone, Fairfax, 255
Confidence man, 60–61, 67–68, 71–72,
    99–101, 264
Confidence-Man, The (Melville),
    100–101, 371
Connolly, Vera, 191
Conrad, Joseph, 149, 272, 346
Consumer culture, 246–47, 252–53;
    containment of carnivalesque and,
    198; creation of, after World War II,
    235–26, 246–47; criticism of adver-
    tising and, 251, 253; television
    advertising and, 256
Consumer education, 83–84
Consumerism and consumption:

assumptions and values of, 10–11; autonomy of, 229–31; control of, by advertisers, 206–7; craftsmanship and, 7; criticism of, 251, 253; dematerialization of desire and, 127–28; Depression and, 241–42; distance between advertisers and consumers in, 196–97, 209–10, 233; eroticism of, 47; ethos of personal efficiency in, 10, 11, 111–12, 138, 159; guessing wants in, 211–12; heterosocial styles of leisure and, 183–84; home and domesticity and, 76, 77, 78; household management and, 120, 121, 208; lack of self-control and temptations in, 73–74; mass society and, 198, 210–18; material progress and, 33–35; motivational research on, 253–54; peddlers and, 64–65; Protestant Ethic and, 48–49, 52–53; reformist movement in, 204–5; suburban affluence and, 126; truth-telling and lies regarding goods in, 84–85; women and, 120–21, 208; workers and, 114–16, 227–29

Consumer movement, 204–5, 239–42
Consumer Report, 349
Consumers Leagues, 204
Consumers Union, 240
Container Corporation of America (CCA), 337–38, 340
Contentment, and domesticity, 76–77
Contracts: advertising agencies and, 93–94; buyers and, 81–82; patent medicine advertising and, 201–2; speculation fueled by, 85
Control: advertising and idioms of, 87–88; mimesis and, 82–87; rationality and, 79–82; rhetoric of, 10; sincerity and domesticity and, 76–79
Conversion narratives, 43, 56–57

Cooley, Charles Horton, 207–8
Coolidge, Calvin, 224
Cooper, James Fenimore, 37, 38, 131
Copland, Aaron, 383
Cornell, Joseph, 8, 12, 317, 379, 402, 403–14
Cornell, Robert, 404, 405–6
Cornucopia, 31–32
Corporations: consumer culture after World War II and, 246–47; economic power of, 200–201; rise of, 88. *See also specific corporations*
Corsets, 151–52
Cosmetics, 143–44, 149, 171
Cosmopolitan (magazine), 222, 292–93
Counterculture (1960s movement), 236, 258
Cowley, Malcolm, 357–58
Coxe, Tench, 385
Crane, Frank, 165
Crane, Hart, 358
Cream of Wheat, 123–24, 293, 384
Creation: myths of, 29–31; play and, 7–8
Creativity, 216–17
Creel, George, 219, 220
Crèvecoeur, Michel Guillaume Jean de, 36–37, 38, 104
Crofutt, George, 109, 110
Cultural histories of advertising, 3–4
Cultural values: advertising and representations of, 1–2; American Way of Life theme and, 124, 125; Anglo-Saxon values in ethnocentrism and, 85–87; Barnum's impact on, 265–67; bourgeois ideal in, 75–76, 83; emphasis on body in advertising and, 152–53; imagery of abundance in, 17–19, 102, 106–9; language of advertising and, 97–98; muckrakers' critique of advertising in, 201–3, 255, 293; rise of urban market economy and, 109–10; vitalist cult of experience and, 272–73

Currier & Ives, 54, 103, 104–5, 109, 124, 343, 361

Curtis, Cyrus H. K., 156, 279

Custom of the Country, The (Wharton), 394–96

Dadaism, 306

Dali, Salvador, 363, 364

Danker, Dan, 329

Danto, Arthur, 402

Darnton, Robert, 17

Davis, Stuart, 304–5, 307, 312, 313, 317, 364, 410

Dekker, Thomas, 54

de Milosz, O. V., 403

Democratic social engineering, 188, 190

Depression, 124, 189, 190, 194, 233, 236–47, 254, 327, 329–30, 334

Dewey, John, 188, 207, 208, 223

Dichter, Ernest, 251, 254

Dickens, Charles, 76, 78, 265

Dickinson, Emily, 408, 409

Disney, Walt, 237, 318

Distribution system, 197, 199–200, 205–6, 239

Dixey, Wolstan, 283

Domesticity, 75–78; American Way of Life and, 124, 125; duties to husbands and, 187–89; as feminine sphere, 76–77, 122–23; technology and standards for, 173–74, 184–86, 189; vision of home in, 77–79

Donne, John, 30–31

Douglas, Mary, 4

Doyle Dane Bernbach, 342

Dreiser, Theodore, 274–81, 303

Dualism, 8, 19, 32, 81–82, 153, 174, 177, 206–7, 263

Dun & Bradstreet, 86

Dunton, John, 70

DuPont Chemicals, 125, 174

Dwight, Timothy, 57

Eaton, Cyrus, 217–18

Economic conditions: advertising agencies and contributions to, 160–61, 200–201; lack of standard currency and, 59–60; Stock market crash and, 229, 233, 235, 237, 240

Eddy, Mary Baker, 141

Eden theme, 26–27, 113

Edison, Thomas, 166, 193, 291

Edwards, Jonathan, 408

Eisenhower, Dwight, 251, 252

Eisenstein, Sergei, 343

Electricity, 180–81

Electroplating, 58–59

Eliot, T. S., 223, 231, 232, 233, 299

Ellis, Joseph, 264

Emergency Price Control Act, 247

Emerson, Guy, 221

Emerson, Ralph Waldo, 60, 62, 264, 267, 409, 412

Emery, W. R., 291, 292

Engels, Friedrich, 58

Enlightenment, 53

Erotic theme: colonization and, 29–31; consumption and, 47; gift exchange and, 6; medicalization of the body and, 173; peddlers and selling and, 70–72, 95, 96–97

Esty, William, 192–93, 233

Ethnocentrism, 85–87, 205; Anglo-Saxon ideal and, 85–86, 169, 170; language and, 87; rhetoric of nationality in, 112–13; stereotypes of Native Americans and, 86–87

Eugenics movement, 166

Euthenics, 381

Evangelical religion, 56–57, 67–68

Evans, Walker, 325–26

Exley, Frederick, 369, 374–78

Exoticism, 10, 51–52, 63, 103–4, 141–42, 149–51, 163, 272

Facts, in copywriting, 199

Fairs, 24–25

Fame (journal), 199, 208, 209, 216, 282, 283, 289, 295

Fan's Notes, A (Exley), 369, 374–78

Fantasy, 51–52, 148–49

Farmers. *See* Agriculture

Fashion: advertising and, 160, 231–32; peddlers and, 45, 63–64, 70

Faulkner, George, 329

Faulkner, William, 177, 359

Federal Trade Commission, 242

Ferber, Edna, 293, 306

Festivals, 22–23

Fetishism, 5, 64, 85, 292, 380–81

Fiction. *See* Literature

Films, 329, 342

Finney, Charles Grandison, 56, 62

First Law of Thermodynamics, 140

Flagg, James Montgomery, 310

Flaherty, Robert, 249

Fletcher, F. Irving, 320

Food industry: child-rearing advice and, 189–90; domestic science and, 184–86; emphasis on body slimness and, 167–68; processing in, 171; regeneration theme and, 157–59; scientific cookery and, 184–85

Ford Motor Company, 338

Forepaugh, Adam, 145, 269

Forge, Anthony, 1

Fortune (magazine), 244, 330, 339, 383

Fosdick, Harry Emerson, 221

Foster, George, 50–51

Foster, William Z., 246

Foucault, Michel, 137–38, 190, 191

Frankfurt School, 6, 127–29, 348

Franklin, Benjamin, 36

Franklin Mint, 336

Frauds, 203–4

Frazer, James, 272

Frederick, J. George, 225, 227, 232–33

Freeman, G. W., 321–22

Free market, 236

Freud, Sigmund, 27, 272, 346, 367

Fromm, Erich, 128

Frye, Northrop, 252, 271–72

Fuessle, Newton, 291

Full Employment Act, 247

Futurism, 312, 314–15, 337, 412

Gaddis, William, 369–74

Galbraith, John Kenneth, 3, 252, 255–56

Galen, 142

Galle, Philipp, 29

Galle, Theodore, 28

Gallup, George, 244

Gambling, 44–45, 60

Garciá Marquez, Gabriel, 359

Garden of Eden theme, 26–27, 113

Gast, John, 109, 110

Geertz, Clifford, 380

General Electric, 193, 298

General Foods, 331, 334

General Mills, 384

"Genius," The (Dreiser), 275–81

George, Henry, 45

Gerber, David, 86

Germ theory, 172

Gibbons, Floyd, 193

Gift exchange, 6

Gilbert, Price, 248–49

Gilbreth, Frank, 165

Godey's Lady's Book, 51, 60, 70, 72, 73, 76, 85, 86, 140, 183, 264, 265

Godkin, E. L., 269, 292

Goethe, Johann, 104

Goffman, Erving, 184

Goldwater, Robert, 364

Good Housekeeping, 174, 178, 179, 186, 188, 189, 190, 191, 207, 237, 239, 245, 330, 333, 405, 410

Gorky, Arshile, 364–65, 366

Gottlieb, Adolph, 364

Grady, Henry, 385

Graham, Martha, 383

Great Depression, 124, 189, 190, 194, 233, 236–47, 254, 327, 329–30, 334

"Great Ideas of Western Man" (ad campaign), 340–41
Greeley, Horace, 89
Greenberg, Clement, 300, 302, 343–44
Guild, James, 82
Gulick, Luther, Jr., 167, 179, 222

Hall, G. Stanley, 178, 179, 221, 222
Hall, Stuart, 302
Halleck, Fitz-Greene, 68
Halttunen, Karen, 50, 61
Hapgood, Norman, 156
Harding, T. Swann, 240
Harris, Neil, 43, 70, 262
Haskell, Thomas, 271
Hawthorne, Nathaniel, 61, 65
Hayek, F. A., 368
Health, 137–38, 143–44
Hearst, William Randolph, 330
Heartfield, John, 307, 343
Heath, W. H., 323
Hedonism, 11, 129, 231–32
Helmholtz, Hermann von, 140
Hemingway, Ernest, 177, 369
Henderson, Leon, 247
Henri, Robert, 304
Henry, Joseph, 82
Herbst, Josephine, 345–46, 348
Herriman, George, 330
Herzen, Aleksandr, 54
Hewitt, John Starr, 231, 323
Hildreth, Richard, 59
Hill, George Washington, 360
Hines, Lewis, 325
Hodgins, Eric, 369
Holden, Ralph, 309
Hollinger, David, 349
Hollingsworth, Harry, 288
Hollywood, 329
Holmes, Arthur, 230
Home: as corporation, 381–82; duties to husbands and, 187–89; as haven from marketplace, 76, 77; pastoral

vision of, 77–79; psychological fact of leaving from, 76–77; technology and standards for, 173–74, 184–86
Hooper, Johnson Jones, 59, 67
Hoover, Herbert, 403
Hoover, J. Edgar, 191
Hope, Clarence, 355
Horkheimer, Max, 6, 127
Household management, 120, 121
Howe, Irving, 252, 253
Howells, William Dean, 284, 285–86, 302
Hubbard, Elbert, 216
Huizinga, Johan, 7, 386, 413–14
Humor, 286; *Mad* magazine and, 256–57; parody in ads and, 283; peddlers and, 69–70
Hungerford, Edward, 220
Huyssen, Andreas, 348
Hyde, Lewis, 6

Ideals of beauty, 10, 285
Imperialism, 87, 163, 347
Imperial primitivism theme, 146–48, 163
Indian princess imagery in abundance theme, 36, 104–5
Industrial Workers of the World, 128
Influence, doctrine of, 60–62, 255
Ingraham, Joseph Holt, 69
Intelligence tests, 220–21
Internal Revenue Service (IRS), 242
Investment, and speculation, 57–59
Irenaeus (church father), 21–22
Irwin, Will, 157, 202–3
Itinerants, 42, 82. *See also* Peddlers

James, E. P. H., 335
James, Henry, 273, 274, 332, 379, 387–94, 397
James, William, 377, 412
Jazz, 303
Jesus, 178

Jews: anti-Semitic stereotypes of, 86, 205; lore of peddlers and, 68–69
Johnson, Gerald W., 127
Johnson, Hugh, 242
Johnston, Patricia, 328
Jones, John Beauchamp, 69
Josephson, Matthew, 305–6, 307, 312, 313, 357, 358, 359–60
Journalism, 282–83
Joyce, James, 8, 294, 299, 379, 402
J. Walter Thompson Company (JWT), 160, 169, 172, 173, 176, 179–80, 191, 192–93, 196–97, 206, 208, 217, 219, 224, 227, 233, 243, 245, 252, 301, 317, 320, 332, 339, 355, 384; market research by, 211; photography used by, 324, 325–26, 327, 329; radio advertising and, 334, 335; Watson at, 307

Kandinsky, Wassily, 122
Karp, Leon, 338
Keats, John, 48
Kelland, Clarence Budington, 383
Kellogg Cereal Company, 118, 119
Kennedy, John E., 199
Kent, Rockwell, 337, 340
Keynes, John Maynard, 246, 247
Kierkegaard, Søren, 346
Kipling, Rudyard 86
Klein, Julius, 403
Kolodny, Annette, 77

Ladies' Home Journal, 94, 156, 201, 279, 324, 338
Land of Cockaigne, 22, 26
Landseer, Edwin, 271
Language: art and, 287–88; deception of confidence man and, 100; ethnocentrism and, 87; marketplace and, 83–84; modernism and, 319; personal efficiency and, 183, 361–62; personality and, 291–92, 382; pro-fessionalism of advertising agencies and, 89; regeneration theme and, 141
Larned, William Livingston, 174, 292, 294, 315, 324
LaRoche, Chester J., 248
Lasker, Albert, 199
Lawrence, D. H., 37, 272, 299, 362
Laws: contracts with buyers and, 81–82, 85; patent medicine advertising and, 201–2; peddlers and, 79–81; reformist consumer movement and, 204–5; scientism and, 81–82
Leavitt, Judith Walzer, 176
Lefebvre, Henri, 385
Leja, Michael, 366
Lent, 22, 23
Lever Brothers, 331
Lévi-Strauss, Claude, 8, 13, 25, 380
Lewis, Edith, 227
Lewis, Monk, 69
Lewis, Sinclair, 223, 231, 352–53, 356
Leyendecker, J. C., 170, 306
Life (magazine), 125, 227–28, 384
Lightning rods, 81–82, 99–100
Lind, Jenny, 214, 266
Lindsay, Vachel, 324
Lindsley, A. B., 83
Lionni, Leo, 337–40
Lippard, George, 55, 60–61
Lippmann, Walter, 114, 188, 208, 223, 351, 352
Literature: criticism of advertising in, 353–62, 367–69; pastoral vision of home in, 77, 78; portrayal of peddlers in, 95–97; realism in, 83; similarities between advertising copy and, 201, 283–84, 293–94; vitalist cult of experience in, 272–73
Little Nemo (comic strip), 330, 331
Locke, David Ross, 89
Loeb, Harold, 304
London, Jack, 272
Lord & Taylor, 106

Lowell, James Russell, 83
Lowenthal, Leo, 127
Luce, Henry, 339
Luther, Martin, 46

McCabe, James D., 44
McCay, Winsor, 330
McClintock, Barbara, 8
McClintock, Mac, 128
McCormick Company, 108, 289, 290
McCrillus, S. B., 40–41, 42, 45
McDermott, William, 190
Macdonald, Dwight, 252, 253
McGuffey Readers, 58, 94
Machine civilization, 303–8, 345
MacLeish, Archibald, 246
McManus, George, 330
Macy, R. H., 81
Mad (magazine), 256–57
Magazines: domesticity and gospel of
    contentment in, 76; economic
    downturn and advice in, 237, 238,
    240; exotic versions of abundance
    appearing in, 63; faith in technology
    portrayed in, 87–88; language usage
    extolled in, 84; manufacturers and,
    280; mass society and, 210–11; por-
    trayal of peddlers in, 95–97, 264,
    265; power of national corporations
    and advertising in, 200–201; profes-
    sional woman in, 191; references to
    bodily functions in, 176–77; revenue
    from advertisements in, 273. *See
    also specific magazines*
Magic: copywriters and invocation of,
    216, 226–27; dream of metamor-
    phosis and, 43–46; fascination with
    exotica and, 51–52; imagery of abun-
    dance and, 19–20; language of
    advertising and, 97–99; oral perfor-
    mance and, 94–95; patent medicine
    vendors and other itinerants and,
    42–43; peddlers and, 67–68; popular
    acceptance of, 44–45; significance to

advertising of, 10–11; speculation
    and wealth and, 58
Magritte, René, 302, 363
Mahin, John Lee, 208
Mallory, M. H., 92
Management: commercialized forms of
    leisure and, 273; corporate advertis-
    ing's role in promoting, 138, 220–21;
    culture of consumption and, 10–11;
    idiom of abundance and, 113–26;
    marketing campaigns and, 261–62;
    political culture of, 242–44; scientific
    approach to, 165; standards for the
    sterile home and, 173–74; tension
    between carnivalesque and, 218;
    World War II and, 247–48
Mandeville, Bernard, 222
Mann, Horace, 82
Marchand, Roland, 3
Marcuse, Herbert, 6, 128, 129, 348–49
Marketplace: advertisements and, 9–10;
    aesthetic display and, 270–71; art
    and, 264, 265; confidence man and,
    99–101; fairs and, 24–25; faith in
    technology and, 87–88; home as
    haven from, 76, 77; lack of self-con-
    trol and temptations in, 73–74; lan-
    guage in, 83–84; laws governing ped-
    dlers in, 79–81; magic and imagery of
    abundance in, 19–20; professionalism
    and structure of, 82; selling as seduc-
    tion and, 70–72, 96–97
Market research, 138, 211, 225,
    244–45, 251, 333
Marquand, John P., 307, 318, 353
Marryat, Frederick, 266
Martin, Jane J., 209
Marx, Karl, 58, 241, 252, 341, 344
Marxism, 4–5, 129
Masson, Thomas, 318
Mass society, 210–18; advertising execu-
    tives and understanding of, 224; con-
    sumers and, 198, 210–18; magazines
    and, 210–11; modernism and, 348
Materialism, 140–41, 262

Matthews, Brander, 306
Medical Society of New York, 83–84
Medicine: regeneration theme and, 140–41, 142. *See also* Patent medicines
Medicine man, 45
Medicine show, 141–42, 163
Melville, Herman, 99–101, 362, 371
Mencken, H. L., 223, 231, 306
Mennen Company, 384
Mental hygiene, 179
Mercier, Charles, 168
Mesmer, Franz Anton, 61
Mesmerism, 61, 62, 71–72, 140, 177
Michelangelo, 340
Miles, Franklin, 144
Mill, John Stuart, 166
Millais, John Everett, 295
Mimesis, 82–87; ethnocentrism and, 85–87; invocation of natural in, 84–85; language use extolled in, 83–84; legal-rationality and sentimentalism combined in, 84–85
Mims, William, 192–93
Modernism, 299–300, 312–22, 329, 336, 343–44, 345–49
Moholy-Nagy, László, 337
Montaigne, 32, 47
Montgomery Ward & Co., 283
Moore, Clement Clarke, 66
More, Sir Thomas, 27
Morris, William, 268
Morton, Thomas, 33–34, 36
Motivation research, 251, 253–54
Movies, 329, 342
Mumford, Lewis, 6
Munsell, Fanny, 294
Mythology, 18, 29–31, 43, 65–67

Nation (magazine), 223, 269, 273, 292
National Recovery Administration (NRA), 242, 243
Native Americans: imperial primitivism theme for patent medicines and, 146–48; Indian princess imagery of abundance and, 36, 104–5; stereotypes in Barnum's representation of, 86–87
Nature, invocation of, 84–85, 142–43, 146, 163, 287
Nettels, Curtis, 249
Nevada Ned, 142, 163
New Deal, 233–34, 242, 245, 247
New Era, 240
Newman, Barnett, 364
New Republic (magazine), 219, 224, 249
Newspapers: advertising rates charged by, 92; manufacturers and, 280; muckrakers' critique of advertising in, 201–3, 255, 293; revenue from advertisements in. 203, 273
New World theme, 26–29, 33, 36–37, 104–5
New Yorker (magazine), 251, 340, 370
Nietzsche, Friedrich, 270, 273, 346
Nord, David Paul, 334
Norris, Frank, 272
Nostalgia, 382–83, 412–13
Novelists. *See* Literature
N. W. Ayer & Sons, 159, 181, 211, 243, 320, 321, 324, 325, 340, 360; artists working at, 337, 338–39; founding of, 90, 94
Nystrom, Paul H., 232

Oakley, Grace Crawley, 169
Office of War Information (OWI), 248–49
Ogden, Rollo, 273
Ogilvy & Mather, 342
Olmsted, Frederick Law, Jr., 294
Olsen, Rodney, 77
Opinion polling, 244–45, 258
Oriental themes, 18, 45, 51–52, 63, 64, 66, 96, 103–4
Ortega y Gasset, José, 230, 231, 232, 233, 300

Orvell, Miles, 267
Orwell, George, 83, 357, 369
Outdoor advertising, 294–95

Packard, Vance, 3, 255
Packwood, George, 268
Paepcke, Walter, 336–37, 340–41
Paine, Del, 339
Pain remedies, 166–67
Painting: portraiture and, 82–83, 264; realism in, 83. *See also* Art
Palmer, A. Mitchell, 169
Palmer, Volney B., 89
Paradise theme, 21–22, 26–39; allegorical representations of America and, 28–29; Christian tradition and belief in, 26–27; imagery of abundance in, 27–28, 36–37; material progress and, 33–35; religious idioms used for, 33; rhetorical representation of colonization in, 29–31
Parrington, Vernon, 362
Parrish, Maxfield, 296–98, 310, 311
Parsons, Talcott, 191, 253
Patent medicines, 41, 42–43, 45, 65, 69, 142–53; advertising agencies and, 89–90, 139, 155–57, 161; appeals to nature in, 142–43, 146; art in advertisements for, 269; confidence man and, 100–101; disclosure of contents of, 156–57, 181; early reports on, 83–84; female imagery of abundance and, 109; imagery of science used with, 120; imperial primitivism theme in, 146–48; magic in language used for, 97–99; medicine show and, 141–42, 163; mingling of spiritual and bodily health in advertisements for, 143–44; Orientalist exoticism and, 103–4; pain remedies with, 166–67; regeneration theme for, 141, 144; state laws and advertising contracts for, 201–2; testimonials for, 143

Patten, Simon Nelson, 113–17, 124, 129, 198, 227, 236, 252, 253, 318
Payson, Edward, 48
Paz, Octavio, 11
Peale, Charles Willson, 266
Peddlers, 25, 40–41, 42, 55, 63–74, 76, 102, 215; culture of consumption and, 64–65; evangelical ministry and, 67–68; fashion and, 45, 63–64, 70; German Jews and lore of, 68–69; humor of, 69–70; language of, 83; legal relationships governing, 79–81; magazine portrayal of, 95–97, 264, 265; mythic associations of, 65–67; selling as seduction and, 70–72, 95, 96–97; stereotypes of, 86
Penfield, Edward, 310
Pennell, Joseph, 269
Perfectionism: cleanliness and, 163–65, 173; emphasis on slimness in, 167–68; obsession with odor in, 171–72; personal efficiency and, 162; physiological, 162–177; preoccupation with youth in, 168–69; psychological, 177–83; standards for the home and, 173–74; women and, 183–92
Personal efficiency theme, 10, 11, 111–12, 138, 159; management and, 165, 183; perfectionism and, 162, 166, 167–68; psychological wholeness and, 178–79
Personal hygiene, 164
Personnel management, 225–26
Persuasion, 215–16
Peruvian Catarrh Cure, 146
Peterson's (magazine), 51, 60, 70, 74, 84, 183
Pharmaceutical companies, 174–75
Phillips, Irna, 334
Photography, 263, 323–29
Photo-Secession Group, 325
Phrenology, 60
Plain-speech tradition, 53, 75, 76, 83, 84. 203, 205, 212, 235, 242, 271,

330, 349–50, 352, 362

Play, and artistic creation, 7–8, 300

Politics, and marketing strategies, 219–20, 242–44

Pollock, Jackson, 367

Popular Front, 124, 249, 359, 362, 366

Populist movement, 121

Porter, Ann, 72

Portrait of a Lady, The (James), 387–90

Portraiture, 82–83, 264

Post, Emily, 382

Poster art, 292–93, 303

Potter, David, 19

Pound, Ezra, 301, 345, 400

Powell, George, 286

Powers, John O., 199–200

Prang, Louis, 55

Primitivism, 146–48

Printers' Ink (magazine), 169, 174, 177, 187, 196, 199, 204, 205, 209, 210, 213–14, 215, 216, 220, 225, 228, 238, 246, 271, 282, 283, 285, 286, 290, 293, 318, 319, 321, 323, 355; Calkins and, 309, 310, 314–15; founding of, 92–93; professionalization and, 154, 156, 157, 160

Proctor, Harvey, 270–71

Proctor & Gamble, 271

Professionalism: advertisers and other professionals and, 197; early impact of, 154–61; language of, 89, 113; marketplace structure and, 82; progress (1890–1917) in, 198–210; women and, 191

Progress, 382; abundance theme and, 33–35; advertisers as agents of, 205–6, 318–19

Progressive Era, 160, 165, 221, 223

Protestantism: advertising agencies and, 111, 139–40, 154–55, 161, 329–30; art and, 262, 268–69, 408; attitudes toward advertising in, 8; authenticity and selfhood in, 75, 224; consumption and, 48–49, 52–53, 114, 120, 139, 378; conver-

sion narratives in, 43, 56–57; distrust of visual display in, 262, 269; emphasis on authenticity in, 54, 56; imagery of abundance and, 17, 24, 48–51; medicine and, 140; mimesis and, 83; purification and, 165, 183; regeneration theme in, 10, 140–41, 142, 153, 179; speculation and wealth viewed in, 57–58; two Protestant Ethics rooted in, 46–53

Proust, Marcel, 379, 387, 396–98, 400, 412–13

Psychoanalysis, 208, 351, 362

Psychological perfection, 177–83

Psychotherapy, 178

Publicity, 203–4, 223

Public opinion: polling of, 244–45, 258; truth-in-advertising movement and, 205

Public relations, 223–24

Pure Food and Drug Acts, 97, 141, 157, 175, 181, 201, 202, 242

Purification theme, 165, 183

Puritan tradition, 33, 34, 44, 47, 55, 139–40

Quaker Oats, 158, 171, 293, 332

Quimby, Phineas Parkhurst, 141

Quinnipiac Fertilizer Company, 105, 121–22

Race and racism: abundance imagery and, 123–24; cleanliness obsession and, 164; ethnocentrism and, 86–87; science and, 140

Radio advertising, 194, 229, 233, 238–39, 335

Raleigh, Sir Walter, 26, 33

Rand, Ayn, 368

Raphael, William, 64

Rastus (Cream of Wheat advertisement), 123–24

Rationality, 79–82, 84, 86, 88

Realism, 83, 169, 269–72, 282–98, 311, 322–36, 345–78
Reason-why advertising, 199
Recognitions, The (Gaddis), 369–74
Regeneration theme, 140–41, 144, 157–59
Reeves, Rosser, 342
Reformist consumer movement, 204–5
Remembrance of Things Past (Proust), 396–98, 413
Renaissance, 32, 313
Repplier, Theodore S., 251
Resor, Helen, 327
Resor, Stanley, 169, 192–93, 196, 224, 355, 384
Reynolds, David, 50
Richards, Ellen, 165
Rickenbacker, Eddie, 249
Riefenstahl, Leni, 343
Riesman, David, 126, 236, 252, 395
Riley, James Whitcomb, 40–41, 42, 45, 66, 95
Rilke, Rainer Maria, 379, 398–400, 403
Rituals, and animism, 21–22
R. J. Reynolds Tobacco Company, 181
Roach, Hal, 329
Robinson, Charles Mulford, 294
Rockwell, Norman, 124
Romanticism, 75–76
Roosevelt, Franklin, 242–43, 247
Roosevelt, Theodore, 158, 219, 221
Rosenberg, Edgar, 69
Rosenberg, Manuel, 316, 325
Roth, Henry, 9–10
Rothko, Mark, 366, 367, 378
Rourke, Constance, 83
Rowell, George P., 90–93, 154, 271, 309, 310
Ruppert, Jacob, 355–56
Ruskin, John, 84, 240, 269

Said, Edward, 103
Sandburg, Carl, 317, 340

Sandler, Irving, 365
Sangster, Margaret, 188
Saturday Evening Post, 10, 94, 121, 124, 166, 170, 173, 174, 181, 200, 279, 318, 328
Schaff, Philip, 57
Schapiro, Meyer, 366
Schlink, Frederick J., 237–38, 239–40
Schudson, Michael, 4, 272
Schulz, Bruno, 12, 130–33
Schwitters, Kurt, 379, 402–3
Science, 92; domestic standards and, 174, 184–86; gendered metaphors in, 32; legal-rational idiom and, 81–82; magic of technology and, 193–94; patent medicines and imagery of, 120, 140
Scientific management, 165
Scott, Walter Dill, 208
Sedgwick, Catherine, 58, 59, 73
Seldin, Joseph, 254
Selfhood, 75, 76, 100, 137, 224
Sensationalism, 49–50
Sentimentalism, 76–79, 84, 272, 383–84
Shafrin, Ervin M., 177
Shahn, Ben, 339
Shakespeare, William, 42, 283
Shapiro, Laura, 184
Shattuck, Ross, 320
Shaw, George Bernard, 299
Shaw, Helen Mar, 199
Shepherd, George R., 168
Sherman, George, 206
Shinn, Everett, 226–27
Sigourney, Lydia, 76–77
Silent Majority, 236, 258
Simon, Robert, 334
Slogans, 94, 106, 309–10
Smith, Adam, 222
Social conditions: creation of consumer culture and, 235–26; morale during World War I and, 221–22
Socialism, 129
Soviet Union, 241, 252

Specialization, 200
Speculation, 57–58, 73–74, 78, 85
Speede, John, 27
Spender, Stephen, 299–300
Spiritualism, 62, 66
Squibb Pharmaceuticals, 177, 315
Standard Oil of New Jersey, 249–50
Statistics, 92, 138, 211, 225, 230, 244
Steichen, Edward, 317, 324, 325–27, 328
Stewart, A. T., 52, 81
Stieglitz, Alfred, 325
Stock market crash, 229, 233, 235, 237, 240
Stowe, Harriet Beecher, 77
Subliminal advertising, 255
Suburban living, 124, 236
Suggestion psychology, 208
Sunny Jim (advertising character), 309–10
Surrealism, 363–64
Surrey, Richard, 319, 322–23
Susman, Warren, 19, 189, 245
'Swheat Girl, 105–6, 123–24
Symonds, Brandreth, 168

Taft, William Howard, 93, 94
Taine, Hippolyte, 273
Taylor, Frederick Winslow, 165, 183
Tea Council, 254
Technology: advertising on magic of, 193–94; belief in, 87–88, 99, 114–15
Tedlow, Richard, 223
Television, 254, 256, 342–43
Tell, Charlotte, 176
Testimonials, 143
Theater, 83, 258
Thoreau, Henry David, 53, 374
Time-and-motion study, 165
Tipper, Harry, 204
Tobacco advertising, 181–83, 191, 346
Tono-Bungay (Wells), 350–51, 353
Toulmin, Stephen, 32
Townsend, C. M., 41, 42, 45

Trachtenberg, Alan, 113
Trade cards, 105–6, 111, 148, 150, 151, 152
Transcendentalists, 60
Transfiguration theme, 43–46
Transformation theme, 10, 56–57, 63, 67–68, 140–41, 144, 166
Trexler, Richard, 25
Trilling, Lionel, 346, 349–50, 362, 367
Trine, Ralph Waldo, 180
Truth-in-advertising campaigns, 161, 205
Tugwell, Rexford Guy, 242
Turner, Victor, 21, 380
Twain, Mark, 67, 95, 269

Uneeda Biscuits, 171
Unique Selling Proposition (USP), 256, 342
United Fruit Company, 112–13
United States Information Agency, 250–51
Utopia, and abundance imagery, 128–29

Van Slyke, Lucille Baldwin, 95–97
Veblen, Thorstein, 3, 63, 127–28, 240, 241, 255, 256, 350, 351
Victorian culture, 19, 41, 63, 75, 84, 98, 140, 144, 158, 177, 189, 264, 361; art and, 263, 264, 272; ethnocentrism in, 85–86; fascination with sexuality in, 149, 151; invocation of natural in, 84–85; reformers in, 137
Vidor, King, 223
Vietnam War, 258
Vogue (magazine), 222, 405
Vorkapich, Ed, 342–43

Wakeman, Frederic, 367–68, 369
Walker, John Brisbane, 292–93
Wallen, James, 225, 226

Wanamaker's department store, 200, 205

War Advertising Council, 248, 249

Warhol, Andy, 302, 305, 338, 403

Warner corsets, 151, 152

Warren, Waldo, 206, 295, 296, 298

Watson, John B., 171–72, 173, 191–92, 208, 301, 307

Warshow, Robert, 362–63

Weber, Max, 35, 46, 81

Webster, John, 54

Wedgwood, Josiah, 24

Weir, W. J., 332

Wells, H. G., 299, 350–51, 353

Westbrook, Robert, 241

Wharton, Edith, 166–67, 274, 332, 379, 387, 394–96, 397

White, E. B., 308

White, Hiller, 325

White, William Allen, 161

White, Winston, 253

Whitman, Walt, 55, 267–68, 304, 304, 408

Whitney, Elwood, 317

Wholeness theme, 178–79

Whyte, William H., 126, 252

Wilde, Oscar, 270, 271, 273, 281, 285, 298, 318

Wilder, Laura Ingalls, 268

Wilder, Will B., 283–84

Wiley, Harvey, 157

Williams, William Carlos, 317, 345, 400

Wilson, Woodrow, 220, 223

Wolfe, Thomas, 177

Women: devaluation in advertising of authority of, 118–20, 184; domesticity as sphere of, 76–77, 122–23; duties to husbands and, 187–89; ideology of national progress and, 109; imagery of abundance and, 19, 102–9, 111–13; medicalization of childbirth and, 196–87; mother theme and, 104, 118; patent medicine advertising and, 109; as primary audience of advertisers, 209; selling as seduction and, 70–72, 96–97; voyeuristic fantasies in advertisements and, 148–49

Women's magazines See Magazines

Wood, Rusling, 297

Woodward, Helen Rosen, 161, 187, 196, 216, 226, 231–32, 355

Woodward, William E., 355–58

Woolf, Virginia, 299

World's Fairs, 116, 198

World War I, 161, 198, 200, 208, 303, 218–25, 246

World War II, 87, 124, 246, 247–58

Yates, James, 329

Yeats, William Butler, 378

Young, James Harvey, 156

Young, James Webb, 245

Young & Rubicam, 334

Youth, preoccupation with, 168–69

You Too (Burlingame), 353–55